THE DIARIES OF
WILLIAM CHARLES MACREADY

WILLIAM CHARLES MACREADY

From the painting by Briggs, in the collection of E. Y. Lowne, Esq.

THE DIARIES

OF

WILLIAM CHARLES MACREADY

1833—1851

EDITED BY

WILLIAM TOYNBEE

WITH FORTY-NINE PORTRAITS

IN TWO VOLUMES

VOL. I.

BENJAMIN BLOM   New York/London

First Published 1912
Reissued 1969 by
Benjamin Blom, Inc., Bronx, New York 10452
and 56 Doughty Street, London, W.C. 1

Library of Congress Catalog Card Number 78-84519

Printed in U.S.A. by
NOBLE OFFSET PRINTERS, INC.
NEW YORK 3, N. Y.

PUBLISHER'S NOTE

Toynbee's two volume edition of *Macready's Diaries* is the most extensive selection ever made from the great actor's daily account of his professional and personal life. It contains almost five hundred more pages of entries than were printed in the first edition of the *Diaries*, prepared by Macready's intimate friend, Sir Frederick Pollock, in 1875, with the title Macready's *Reminiscences and Selections from his Diaries and Letters*.

The Pollock edition has been reprinted in the Benjamin Blom *Historia Histrionica* collection (1969) because it contains a considerable body of important material that Toynbee was not able to incorporate into his two volume edition. The most important of these omitted sections are described below.

Of first importance is the lengthy "Reminiscences," the two hundred and forty page account of his life until 1826 that Macready began to write in 1855. The "Reminiscences" are an essential source of information on the actor's early career. Toynbee also does not include the sixteen page section of diary jottings covering the years 1827-1832. In the Pollock edition, these entries provide a link between the "Reminiscences" and the longer, more formal diary which Macready began keeping on January 1, 1833. The Pollock edition also contains an invaluable selection of letters from Macready to Lady Julia and Sir Frederick Pollock, written after his retirement in 1851. These letters, together with Pollock's account of the farewell dinner tendered the retiring actor, a summary of the years in seclusion, and the brief but moving record of the last years, decline, and death are testimony to an intimate friendship of many years between the editor and the subject of his memoir.

For the most complete record of Macready's autobiographical writings, as well as for the insights of personal observation. Toynbee's volumes must be read in conjunction with Pollock.

PREFATORY NOTE

In 1875, two years after Macready's death, his *Reminiscences and Selections from his Diaries and Letters*, edited by the late Sir W. F. Pollock, Bart., were published by Messrs. Macmillan. At that time it was thought desirable to withhold a considerable portion of the diaries, but after the lapse of nearly forty years the reasons for this suppression no longer hold good, and the most important of the omitted passages are accordingly given, for the first time, in the present work. They are not only profoundly interesting, but constitute an invaluable addition to the literary and social history of the period. Besides shedding new light on Macready himself and his famous stage contemporaries, they abound in intimate glimpses of Dickens, Thackeray, Browning, Bulwer, Procter, Forster, Talfourd, and other Victorian celebrities; in fact, they present a series of character sketches unsurpassed even in the vivid pages of Greville and Creevey.

The editor's thanks are due to Messrs. Macmillan for kindly placing at his disposal the copyright portion of their volumes.

INTRODUCTION

In 1833—the starting-point of these diaries—Macready was, with one exception (Edmund Kean), foremost among English actors. His life, extending from 1793 to 1873, presents a remarkable span of years. He could recall Pitt's first premiership, and was still living when that of Gladstone was drawing to a close. He had trodden the boards with Mrs. Siddons, and survived to see the Bancrofts' successful management, and Irving rising into renown. At the age of twenty-three he was already a personage in his profession, and after the death of Kean his supremacy was undisputed. But although it was to the stage that he owed his fame, he would probably have won equal distinction in more than one other calling. He had, indeed, been destined for the Bar, but a calamitous stroke of fortune abruptly changed his career. While a sixth-form boy at Rugby, with the University and a learned profession in prospect, he was suddenly transported into the squalid atmosphere of a bankrupt provincial theatre which his father, hitherto prosperous, was precariously directing, shadowed by the sheriff's officer. To an aspiring and highly sensitive public-school boy such a transition must have been little less than torture. Worse, however, was to follow, for after a few months' hopeless struggle, the unfortunate manager disappeared behind the walls of Lancaster gaol, leaving his son to face the situation alone, a truly appalling plight for a lad of sixteen, with practically no experience and not a shilling in the treasury. But a great public school, if in some respects a defective training-ground, seldom fails to implant a certain degree of fortitude, and *Tu ne cede malis* was a maxim that the Rugby class-rooms had not inculcated in vain. Heroically mastering his distress, the friendless youngster took command of the stranded company, which, thanks to a dauntless spirit and no little resourcefulness, he contrived to hold together until his father regained his liberty, and was able to resume control.

The elder Macready's return to management was signalized by the inauguration of a season at Birmingham, a town in which he had long

INTRODUCTION

been a favourite, and there he wisely decided that his son should make his début. Although at Rugby a speech-day actor of conspicuous talent, the youth had necessarily received very little regular technical instruction, and in casting him on such an occasion for the part of Romeo his father must have formed the highest opinion of his powers. The event amply justified his decision. Modestly announced as "A Young Gentleman, being his first appearance on any Stage," on the evening of Thursday, June 7, 1810, the ex-boy-manager formally initiated his long and distinguished career. According to the portrait painted shortly afterwards by De Wilde, he cut a gallant and picturesque figure; and though the audience was prepossessed in his favour, and the local Press, perhaps, somewhat partial, the performance was evidently one of singular merit, revealing, if not exactly genius, artistic qualities of the highest order. So pronounced a success induced the manager to repeat the play two or three times, also to entrust his son with other rôles, in all of which he achieved fresh triumphs. The precaution of anonymity was now no longer necessary; thenceforward, the young actor was boldly "billed" under his own name, and for the next four years took the leading position in his father's company, playing a variety of parts with continuous success, to which his careful and unremitting study not a little contributed. During this period, while still in his teens, he was accorded an unexpected honour, being cast at Newcastle in two plays, *The Gamester* and *Douglas*, with no less a star than the illustrious Siddons. Naturally so august an associate inspired him with no little awe, and in the first few minutes he was on the point of breaking down; but she good-naturedly gave him the missing word, and, gaining courage, he acquitted himself so well as to evoke her hearty applause from the wings. From one celebrity he quickly passed to another, though of a very different type; for a few months afterwards he was cast at Leicester for Don Felix in *The Wonder* (by Mrs. Centlivre) to Mrs. Jordan's Violante. Her rare charm appears to have captivated him even more than her exquisite art, and it is not surprising that in after years he should have poured bitter contempt on the royal lover who, having profited for years by her splendid earnings, abruptly consigned her to poverty and neglect.

For the next six years Macready continued to act in the provinces, steadily adding to his reputation, which had now reached the metropolis, where, in 1816, he was definitely engaged for a five years' term at Covent Garden, making his first appearance there as Orestes in

WILLIAM CHARLES MACREADY

AS ROMEO

(1810)

From the painting by De Wilde, in the collection of Major-General C. F. N. Macready, C.B.

INTRODUCTION

The Distrest Mother. The result was a conspicuous success, the more gratifying since at that time he was almost a stranger in London. The severer test of Othello soon followed, and from that, too, he emerged with flying colours. Though he was not more than twenty-three, his position as an actor of the first rank was now assured; and at a banquet given to Talma in 1817 by the English actors, his status in the profession received public recognition from no less a celebrity than John Kemble, who singled him out for the compliment of drinking wine with him, a significant tribute from so illustrious a veteran to a new-comer on the London stage. A couple of years later the manager of Covent Garden theatre, the fortunes of which had sunk to a low ebb, resolved on the bold stroke of appointing him leading tragedian, and, with equal daring, chose for the inaugurating rôle Kean's most famous impersonation, Richard III. The experiment was one that Macready would gladly have escaped, for, apart from Kean's triumphant association with this character, neither his figure nor his features were in the least suggestive of Richard. But his apprehensions proved to be ill-founded. His performance captivated not only the public but the Press, and he had the special gratification of receiving a generous tribute to its excellence from Kean himself.

Macready's next great success was in the play of *Virginius*, by Sheridan Knowles. Though a striking drama, it was defaced by a good deal of turgidity, and would have little chance in the present day; but on reading it at the request of a friend of the author (then a stranger to him), Macready perceived that the name-part supplied many opportunities which he could turn to good account, and he promptly procured the play's acceptance. *Virginius* confronted the footlights with the advantage of distinguished literary sponsorship, two poets of repute, John Hamilton Reynolds and Barry Cornwall, respectively furnishing prologue and epilogue; the success, however, that ensued was attributable less to the author and his auxiliaries than to the actor, whose impersonation, powerful yet well-restrained, was pronounced on all sides to be a masterly performance. Such an achievement, following so closely on that of Richard III, set the seal on Macready's reputation. He was now not only in the first rank, but the acknowledged heir to the first place, an artist, moreover, who combined with professional dis-tinction an absolutely unblemished character, in those days a decidedly rare conjunction. But though a favourite with the public, he was, un-fortunately, far from popular with the members of his own vocation, a fact which at various times not a little prejudiced his career. The causes

INTRODUCTION

are not far to seek ; in addition to a naturally violent temper, he had a hearty and ill-concealed contempt for his calling. He loved his art, but he abhorred the atmosphere to which it subjected him. Haughty and inclined to be exclusive, he recoiled in disgust from the manners and customs of the green-room. His public-school education and his alienated prospects were constantly rising up in indignant protest against the associations, mostly vulgar and often sordid, among which he was doomed to pass his life. He was, in truth, " a cut above his calling," and was at no pains to disguise the fact that he felt it acutely. Moreover, for an Irishman, he had very little sense of humour, which furnished his fellow-actors with many tempting opportunities of " taking a rise out of him." Under such conditions it is hardly surprising that he had scarcely a friend in the profession, at any rate of the masculine gender. Coldly ceremonious when in a good temper, fiercely abusive when in a bad one, always on the watch for slights, and morbidly alert to conjure up affronts, his existence in the theatre was little better than a long-drawn ordeal to himself and a frequent source of exasperation to his associates. On this phase of his character the diaries are continually shedding a lurid light, and it amply accounts for many of the *contretemps* that chequered his distinguished and, on the whole, prosperous career.

An event now occurred that brought these unfortunate defects of temperament prominently into play. In 1822 the management of Covent Garden theatre passed into new hands, the principal control being assumed by Charles Kemble, the " first-rate actor of second-rate parts," as Macready, with envenomed accuracy, once described him. Hitherto Kemble had always been well-disposed towards Macready, who, however, very soon broke out into open revolt against him. He had various grievances, some well founded, but no doubt Kemble's main delinquency was an inadequate appreciation of his artistic merits and position. That Kemble was too prone to cast himself for parts to which he was little suited there can be no question, and he may have been at times somewhat autocratic ; but when it is considered that he was a man of nearly fifty, and not only manager but part proprietor of the theatre, while Macready was still under thirty, and, though an actor of established eminence, in point of actual status merely a salaried subordinate, it seems only too likely that the fault chiefly lay with the younger man. At all events, an incident soon occurred which revealed pretty clearly the extent of Macready's pretensions. Kemble had promised to play for some Benefit, but was prevented from doing so by the death of his brother John, whereupon the organizers approached Macready with a request for his services instead. "So, sir," was his preposterous reply to the emissary of the charity, "because the corporal refuses to do his duty you apply to the commander-in-chief." Such being his attitude, it is not surprising that his engagement at Covent Garden was but of short duration. After prolonged correspondence, squabbles, and attempts at arbitration, his relations with the management reached breaking-point, and in 1823 he crossed over to Drury Lane, to enlist under Elliston at the comfortable salary of £20 a night, though in reality it was less than it appears, as in those days an actor very seldom performed every night in the week.

The Drury Lane engagement did not add to Macready's laurels. In fact, his professional career, hitherto brilliantly progressive, now entered upon a comparatively uneventful period; though holding his own, he made no striking new successes, and certain acrimonious embroilments with the critics, whom, with exaggerated sensibility, he accused of a malignant attempt to belittle him, produced a condition of dissatisfaction and depression that contrasted painfully with the elation of previous years. But if he had his professional trials, he, at all events, found solace in the world outside. On the occasion of his youthful appearance with Mrs. Siddons, the great *tragédienne* had solemnly impressed upon him this excellent piece of advice: "Study, study, study, and do not marry till you are thirty." The counsel was faithfully observed, but the age limit had now been passed, and in June 1824 he embarked on marriage with a young lady some twelve years his junior, a Miss Catherine Frances Atkins, who had played Virginia to his Virginius in 1819, and whom he had first known as a child, when he took her to task for some shortcoming in a juvenile part. He had met her afterwards from time to time, and gradually assumed the relation of preceptor, an office that he seldom found uncongenial; but as the child grew into womanhood his attitude underwent a change, and adopting the rôle of suitor without altogether relinquishing that of mentor, he proposed and was—no doubt somewhat fearfully—accepted. The marriage proved on the whole a happy one, though Macready must have been in some respects a trying husband. With the tenderest affection he mingled a tendency to "preachiness" and to dogmatize on "rules of conduct" which can hardly have been palatable to so young a wife. "Improving the mind" was a process which he imported into his home life with an assiduity that would have inspired Mr. Barlow of *Sandford and Merton* renown with the liveliest envy. Nevertheless, in spite of his sermons and sententiousness, he was truly loved by his family, though not without a certain admixture of awe. But if he suggested in some features the "good husband and affectionate father" so frequently commemorated on eighteenth-century tombstones, it only needed a great sorrow to elicit the strong and poignant emotions that lay beneath the surface, and which he records in language of almost overpowering pathos. In his friendships, too, he often did himself scant justice, for, though generous and warm-hearted, he gave far too much rein to over-sensitiveness and a disposition to manufacture grievances. The diaries, indeed, teem with narrations of temporary estrangements due to these failings, Dickens being about the only member of his intimate circle who contrived to secure immunity.

During the two years that succeeded his marriage, Macready was seen comparatively little in London. For a time he was incapacitated by a serious illness, which necessitated a complete rest, and when restored to health he devoted himself to a series of provincial tours, re-appearing, however, at Drury Lane in the spring of 1826. This engagement, which was in no way noteworthy, was followed by a visit to America, where he first saw his future enemy, Forrest, then a youth of little more than twenty. The impression which Macready then formed of Forrest was that with diligent study he was likely to make a fine actor, though he anticipated (as it proved correctly), that the flattery with which the youth was constantly beset would lead him to rate himself as a finished artist before he had well mastered the rudiments of his craft. As a good deal will be heard of Forrest in the later portions of these diaries, it should be stated that Macready's attitude to him was from the first not only fair but generous, and that Forrest's savage and relentless hostility proceeded solely from insensate jealousy and baseless suspicions fomented by his admirers, in alliance with certain of Macready's enemies both on the stage and in the Press.

On his return to England, after a short and somewhat featureless interval at Drury Lane (where he came into contact with another individual also destined to become a formidable enemy, Alfred Bunn), Macready paid a visit to Paris, the *éclat* of which went far to compensate him for the uneventfulness of his recent appearances in London. The Parisian Press, in fact, acclaimed him with an almost universal chorus of praise, the culminating honour being paid by Jules Janin, who went so far as to pronounce him the equal of Talma.

The triumphs of Paris were succeeded by a series of rather humdrum

WILLIAM MACREADY

AS COLLOONY IN "THE IRISHMAN IN LONDON"

From a painting by De Wilde in the collection of E. Y. Lowne, Esq.

INTRODUCTION

provincial tours, which, however, were by no means unremunerative, their earnings representing an income of over £1800, a very considerable one for an actor in those days, unless he possessed the genius and magnetic qualities of an Edmund Kean.

In the autumn of 1830 Macready re-appeared at Drury Lane. With the exception of William Tell in Sheridan Knowles's drama of that name, his ventures in new characters, though always interesting, had for some time past made no particular impression; but in the name-part of Byron's *Werner* he now scored another notable achievement. In contrast to this sombre impersonation, he also enacted Joseph Surface and Mr. Oakley (in *The Jealous Wife*), the latter performance winning enthusiastic approval from the critics. This became his favourite part on the comparatively rare occasions when he appeared in comedy.

In 1831 a Captain Polhill (frequently mentioned in the diaries in far from complimentary terms) took over Drury Lane theatre, with Bunn as his stage-manager, and in the following year it was decided to run Kean and Macready as twin-stars. Hitherto Kean had firmly refused to act with Macready, in whom he recognized a dangerously formidable competitor; but he now, probably for monetary reasons, saw fit to withdraw his objection, and the two appeared in the same piece for the first time, Kean playing Othello to Macready's Iago. This combination was repeated on several occasions, but the amenities of former years had now been transformed into strained, if not hostile relations. Macready complained of Kean taking up unfair positions on the stage, while Kean, by this time sunk in degeneracy, with the brandy-bottle always at his elbow, treated Macready's rather pompous protests—conveyed through manager Bunn—with opprobrious insolence; recriminatory epithets—duly embroidered, no doubt, by Mr. Bunn—were, in fact, the order of the day between the eminent pair, and it was perhaps fortunate that Kean was soon removed from the scene, otherwise the warfare of words might have developed into physical reprisals, a species of *dénouement* with which Macready was destined to become disastrously familiar a year or two afterwards.

From this point the diaries will speak for themselves, and, as the reader will find, in no reticent fashion. The period at which they open is, socially and politically, one of the most interesting of the nineteenth century. The old order was beginning to pale before the new. Railroads were in their infancy, and the first Reform Bill had just passed into law. Gladstone, a ducal *protégé*, was " the hope of the stern,

INTRODUCTION

unbending Tories," while Disraeli, an embarrassed adventurer, was desperately coquetting with democracy. Dickens and Thackeray, Tennyson and Browning, had barely emerged into manhood, and formed a connecting link with Wordsworth, Coleridge, Lamb, and Southey, men who had made their mark well before the century began. Rogers was still distilling venom in St. James's Place, and Luttrell airing epigrams to the *élite* of Holland House; Croker was slashing in the *Quarterly*, Macaulay glittering in the *Edinburgh;* while Sydney Smith with every flash of his reckless wit was widening the distance between his motley and a mitre. In this brilliant world Macready had already won for himself a definite position, increasing in importance as years went on; and he appears before the reader a man in the prime of life, and prosperous, with a country home at Elstree and a *pied-à-terre* in London; a member, also, of the Garrick Club, then of recent origin, but steadily acquiring the prestige and popularity which it has so long enjoyed.

W. T.

30, South Eaton Place, S.W.
July 1912.

LIST OF PORTRAITS

LIST OF PORTRAITS

THE DIARIES OF
WILLIAM CHARLES MACREADY
1833

Elstree, January 1st.—With God's merciful help I trust to make my conduct and use of my time during this year more acceptable in His sight than that of my previous life has been; and I enter upon it with prayers for His blessings on my wife, friends and myself. Amen! Spent much of the day in purchasing necessaries; loitered away an hour, for rest, at the Garrick Club, where I read a violent letter of Bulwer [1] in reply to the impertinences of Lockhart. [2] How much precious tranquillity of heart and mind is lost by the inability of man, "weak man," to let these feeble injuries and perishable insults die of themselves. Our own self-love it is that blows the spark into a flame, which is fed by our own cares and pains! Short-sighted man! Looked idly through Napier's *Peninsular War;* an interesting account of senseless and wicked proceedings.

January 2nd.—My performance this evening of Macbeth afforded me a striking evidence of the necessity there is for thinking over my characters previous to playing, and establishing, by practice if necessary, the particular modes of each scene and important passage. I acted with much energy, but could not (as I sometimes can, when holding the audience in wrapt attention) listen to my own voice, and feel the truth of its tones. It was crude, and uncertain, though spirited and earnest; but much thought is yet required to give an even energy

---

[1] The author and politician (1803-1873); afterwards successively Sir E. Bulwer Lytton, Bart., and Lord Lytton. In 1833 his reputation as a novelist was already established; he had also sat for two years in Parliament as an advanced Liberal. In later years he joined the Conservatives, and became Colonial Secretary in Lord Derby's second Administration.

[2] John Gibson Lockhart (1794-1854); Sir Walter Scott's biographer, and for nearly thirty years editor of the *Quarterly Review.* His mordant pen and not too scrupulous tongue provoked many enmities, notably that of Harriet Martineau, who scathingly denounces him in her Autobiography.

and finished style to all the great scenes of the play, except perhaps the last, which is among the best things I am capable of. Knowles [1] is ravished with his own acting, and the supposed support it has met with. I wish I was with mine.

January 3rd.—Went home to breakfast. Spent an idle, but in all other respects a happy day. A well-spent day is pleasing while it lasts, and pleasant to remember when for ever gone; a day of mere pleasure is agreeable in its passage, but regret attends its close in the reflection that time which God has given for employment has been squandered, or lost in idleness. Compunction is injurious if unproductive of improvement; let my revision of this day enable me to be more resolute in my resistance of future temptations, and teach me for my own and my children's good the necessity of blending activity with enjoyment. In my absence from home I am sometimes inclined to question the prudence of living so far from town; but when, on reaching home, I taste the fresh air of the country, look over its extent of prospect, feel in a manner the free range of thought and sense through the expanse of earth and sky surrounding me, I confess to myself, in the delightful sensations I experience, that such enjoyment is worth some sacrifice.

January 4th.—I am again called upon to note down an instance of my indolence and weakness; the reflections of yesterday only expose me to further self-reproach to-day. I lay in bed until a very late hour. As some atonement I walked to town, redeeming part of the day from general censure by using it in the wholesome exercise of the body, which is the best use of time after employing it in strengthening and invigorating our minds. My acting to-night was coarse and crude—no

---

[1] James Sheridan Knowles (1784–1862); better known as a dramatist than as an actor, though he did not leave the stage till 1843. His principal plays were *Virginius*, produced in 1820; *The Hunchback*, produced in 1832; and *The Love Chase*, produced in 1832. Of these, *Virginius* was the most successful, and provided (in the name-part) one of Macready's favourite *rôles*, in which he, from time to time, continued to appear until his final retirement in 1851. To the present generation Knowles's plays are practically unknown; but in the early Victorian era he enjoyed a considerable reputation, according, at any rate, to Bulwer, who thus eulogizes him in a note in *The New Timon* (1847): " I have no blind enthusiasm for Mr. Knowles, and I allow both the grave faults of his diction, and the somewhat narrow limits within which is contracted his knowledge of character and life ; but no one can deny that he has nobly supported the British Drama—that he moved the laughter and tears of thousands ; that he forms an actual, living, and imperishable feature in the loftier literature of his time—that the History of the English Stage can never be rewritten hereafter without long and honorable mention of the Author of *Virginius* and *The Hunchback*." (The note concludes with a disparagement of Tennyson which, together with some bitingly contemptuous lines in the text, provoked the poet's celebrated retaliation in *Punch*, an episode that is fully dealt with later on.)

W. C. MACREADY'S FATHER

WILLIAM MACREADY

From the miniature by Halpin.

In the collection of Major-General C. F. N. Macready, C.B.

W. C. MACREADY'S MOTHER

née CHRISTINA ANN BIRCH

From the miniature by Cosway.

identification of myself with the scene; and what increased my chagrin on the subject, some persons in the pit gave frequent vent to indulgent and misplaced admiration. The consciousness of unmerited applause makes it quite painful and even humiliating to me. I thought this day of taking the Bath and Bristol theatres; it will probably go no further. After the play I read some chapters of Napier's *History of the Spanish War*. A book hard to lay down, sometimes ambitious in style, but full of philosophical observation and reflections, and containing most spirited and interesting narratives.[1]

January 5th.—I have made a proposal to take the Bath and Bristol theatres for a short season during Lent. I hope my vanity or sanguine desire of gain has not misled me in my anticipations and dependences. I wish to procure an independence for my dear children,[2] and I think this speculation likely to be productive of good in itself, and to offer me a certainty of remoter benefit. I have had some doubts as to the sum in which I should subscribe to Mrs. Jackson's[3] print; but I have decided upon the larger, which is still much less than I wish to give; I know that I expose myself to the charge of imprudence and extravagance, but am I to endeavour to feed the widow and the orphan literally with the crumbs that fall from my table? I cannot so interpret the text of that Teacher whose name be blessed by all who have hearts to feel the love He taught. Amen.

January 6th.—By an omission of my messenger I was not up before eight o'clock, which compelled me to undergo the expense of a chaise to Elstree. My thoughts, when led to more important things than the day before me, were divided between the character of Othello and my proposed speculation at Bath, etc. I saw my dear children quite well, and

---

[1] Macready's literary judgments are, for the most part, well worth quoting. Naturally endowed with much clearness of insight and correctness of taste, he never allowed himself to lose touch with the classical authors, of which he had acquired a sound knowledge when a sixth-form boy at Rugby. He thus attained a degree of scholarly culture that was wholly exceptional among the actors of that day, whose reading was mostly confined to the newspaper and the prompt-book. It is, accordingly, not surprising to find him the intimate associate of such men as Dickens, Thackeray, Browning, Carlyle, Bulwer, Henry Taylor, and other notable Victorian writers.

[2] The " wish " here expressed became, in fact, a cherished and paramount duty which Macready always kept steadfastly before him. To secure an adequate provision for his family was with him a far greater object than professional distinction, and one for which he made constant sacrifices of both health and comfort.

[3] The widow of John Jackson, R.A. (1778–1831), who had died recently leaving little provision for his family. He had painted a portrait of Macready, who had a warm regard for him.

3

observed with satisfaction improvement in my dear Christina.[1] I received some guests to-day to whom I have stood indebted in the dues of hospitable attention. So that some purpose was fulfilled to-day. The weather was beautiful, and made me enjoy the short walk I took, worshipping the God of Nature in grateful enjoyment of His blessings. A tranquil and comfortable day with my guests. My dear wife well and cheerful, and as I wish to see her.

January 7th.—A delightful morning, which made me still more reluctant to leave home. Acted pretty well this evening,[2] particularly in the dagger soliloquy, where I took time and felt what I did. The murder wants finish still, and the banquet scene revision and careful polishing. The manly colloquial tone that I often used to-night was earnest and good.

London, January 8th.—Paid some visits of ceremony—unmeaning, hollow practices, irksome and embarrassing in act and productive of no good results. I allude entirely to the G——s, who are incomprehensible to me; if they like me, why do they not cultivate my society? if they are indifferent, why not relinquish my acquaintance? [3] " What art thou, thou idol, ceremony? " Why is it that my spirits, rather depressed before, rose when I saw an expression of discontent on the face of Mrs. —— at the retired life she led? Is it an evil feeling? I think not—or that principle of our nature that makes all human happiness comparative?

---

[1] Macready's eldest child, generally referred to in the Diaries as Nina; her death in 1850, at the age of nineteen, was, perhaps, his greatest sorrow. His heart-broken account of it is one of the most touching passages in the Diaries. Though a strict, and not always judicious disciplinarian, he was tenderly devoted to his children, giving them every advantage within his power, and concerning himself unceasingly with their happiness and welfare. If at times too rigorous a taskmaster, he effectively supervised their education, and early familiarized them with sterling literature. There are almost daily references to them in the Diaries, but they are mainly of too intimate a character to admit of quotation. Their faults as well as their merits are impartially recorded, but even his severest displeasure was seldom untempered with evidences of deep and anxious affection.

[2] Macready's criticisms of his acting are always full of interest. His standard was of the highest, and it will be found that he was far more often dissatisfied than pleased with his performances.

[3] Macready was extremely sensitive as to his social status, and apt to suspect coldness and avoidance where they did not exist, but there is no doubt that at Elstree, as afterwards at Sherborne, he occasionally found himself looked upon askance by certain pompous nonentities simply on account of his calling. In London the honoured associate of nearly every literary and artistic genius, he was too often treated by " local gentility " with scant courtesy and consideration, an experience which had a decidedly embittering influence.

January 9th.—In attending the book-club last night I was furnished with another instance of that silly and unamiable ambition so common in men, particularly little men, of directing and legislating for others. Observation of the errors of others is wise or uncharitable according to its result—either as it affords us a practical lesson, or a subject to descant upon. This morning I rose betimes, and rode outside to Elstree. I felt pleasure in this little instance of economy both in time and money. A beautiful morning, and, though misty afterwards, giving me the opportunity of a delightful walk with my wife and sister. In the afternoon I read much of Frederick II's Life: an evidence of selfish vanity abusing great abilities, and brutal subserviency in the men who tolerated his dominion over them.

January 10th.—A letter from Mrs. Jackson accompanied the prints which she sent to my order; I found them on my return to town, and felt glad that I had not measured out more sparingly the amount of my contribution, when I ascertained from the expressions of her gratitude how much she and her children stood in need of assistance. This evening I was surprised with a billet-doux,[1] which ought to have found its way to the fire before me, instead of suggesting amusement to my vanity or curiosity. It is harder for a player to be a wise man than for most of his fellow creatures; he can never learn the lesson that time teaches when his own assumptions and the idle incense of those around him blind him to the fact of his growing old. "A fool at forty is a fool indeed" should be my text in future.

January 11th.—Little to comment on to-day, beyond my own loss of it. Rose late, and omitted dinner, in order to have my powers more at command during my performance, which was certainly better for my abstinence. I find the good effect of that natural manly tone of dialogue, with which I must endeavour to improve the colloquial groundwork of my acting. This evening I left at the theatre for the

---

[1] This species of attention was of frequent occurrence throughout Macready's career, though his powers of attraction hardly lay in his physiognomy. But, like Jack Wilkes, he was "only half-an-hour behind the handsomest," and, had he chosen, his conquests might have been numerous. But he resolutely held all fair besiegers at arm's length, though always with chivalrous courtesy. In one instance, however, the lady (a gifted and charming actress, nearly twenty years his junior) proved so persistent that, without any fault on his side, he found himself involved in a situation of the greatest embarrassment. To a man of less principle there could have been only one end to such an affair, but with every temptation to become her lover, Macready constituted himself her guardian, and, with inflexible honour, contrived to save her, in spite of herself.

managers a tragedy by a Mr. Heraud,[1] a dramatic poet in his own confident opinion, secure of success; perhaps misled by the injudicious recommendation of Mr. Southey which led him to experiment in tragic composition. Such advice leads me to a reluctant doubt of the Laureate's sincerity, for it is scarcely possible in this case to suppose defect of judgment. Can that be called good nature which shrinks from inflicting a slight pique to the *amour propre* of a friend with intent to cure his mind of a dangerous and still-strengthening delusion? It is selfishness, worldliness, anything, I think, but justice or kindness, yet how universally practised!

January 12th.—My thoughts wandering on idle, vain, unprofitable subjects, and only occasionally resting on the important consideration of economy in my expenditure for the sake of my dear children. Resumed my consideration of Othello, to which my mind must be given up. Visited by a lady, who mistook me for a relation of Mr. Macready, a writer of seven tragedies and various farces; this is one of the many who waste life and paper in their hopeless mockery of employment. Happy to return home; began with great delight Lardner's [2] volume on Mechanics.

January 13th.—Lost my morning in indolent and criminal slothfulness, when I should have been engaged in exercises for the purification of my mind and for invigorating my body, besides affording to my servants and poor neighbours an instructive example by my attendance at church. *Most blameable!* For my own part a much more devotional spirit is awakened in me by family prayers or lonely medita-

---

[1] John Abraham Heraud (1799–1887), critic and journalist; connected, at various times, with *Fraser's Magazine*, *The Illustrated London News* and *The Athenæum*; became a Charterhouse Brother in 1873; friend of the Carlyles and Lockhart, as well as of Southey, whose recommendation was certainly not justified by any dramatic success on the part of his *protégé*. The title of Mr. Heraud's tragedy is not given, but it appears that in 1830 he wrote a poem called *The Descent into Hell*, which may very well have appealed to Southey as the author of a kindred work, *The Vision of Judgment*. In point of fact, the Laureate, though an admirable biographer, was a very indifferent poet, and scarcely competent to pronounce on Mr. Heraud's qualifications in this particular instance.

[2] Dionysius Lardner (1793–1859), a scientific writer of considerable repute; in holy orders, but devoted himself entirely to literary and scientific work; editor of various useful compilations; at one time Professor of Natural Philosophy at London University (now University College). His career in London came to an ignominious end, owing to his elopement with the young wife of a Brighton magistrate, who pursued the pair to Paris and subjected the philosopher to a severe castigation, supplemented in the law courts with damages amounting to £8000. Macready, who had been on friendly terms with Lardner, though reprobating his conduct, characteristically declined to drop him in his disgrace, and visited him in America, during his tour there in 1843, when he describes the professor's fallen fortunes with quite a "Thackeray" touch.

tions than by the forms of church service, undevoutly listened to and often irreverently gone through, where charity is on the lip of the rich and learnt as a word difficult of comprehension by the poor. But for those who cannot profit by reflection, and in whom, for their own sakes, it is merciful to generate or induce, by the effect of repeated ordinances, respect for piety as a step towards its actual inculcation, it is charity to afford example and seriously remiss to neglect an occasion of impressing a notion of duty on their minds in their regular attendance at divine service.[1]

London, January 22nd.—I acted to-night with spirit and in a manly tone, better perhaps than ordinarily in the part Rob Roy.[2] A curious evidence of egotism and importunate demand of attention to business of no concern to me was afforded me to-night in Mr. Heraud's letter.[3] The universe is but an atom before the vastness of one's self!

January 23rd.—Although I cannot boast a victory over my lazy habits in the morning, the day has not been an idle one; indeed, too active in reference to its principal object—principal, as respects my means of life, of educating and providing for my children, viz. my performance, which I may here observe was "weary, stale, flat and unprofitable"—a lack of energy, of heartedness, with more than enough of muscular exertion, and all attempts at effect in expression overclouded by the perpetual scowl that contracted and darkened my countenance; a bad performance. Again I reproach myself with exhibiting that *odiosam et inutilem morositatem*, against which I am so anxious to guard myself, in the instances both of Mr. F.'s proposed election to the Garrick Club and of the performer's incorrectness in *William Tell.*[4] Could I sober or improve the latter?

---

[1] There was only one kind of religion that appealed to Macready: the practical carrying out of Christ's teaching. With mere forms and ceremonies he had no sympathy, while the narrowness and intolerance of the average clergyman of that day aroused his bitter indignation. But in the highest sense of the term he was essentially a religious man; a firm believer in the divine Spirit of Goodness, endeavouring his utmost to lead an upright, cleanly life, and ever ready to sympathize with and to help his suffering fellow-creatures. Highly strung, and with a naturally violent temper, he was occasionally betrayed into language and conduct that exposed him to grave misconstruction and caused him the keenest regret. But his fine qualities far outweighed his faults, and in scrupulous rectitude and true kindliness of heart he was surpassed by few of his generation, on or off the stage.

[2] The play had been revived in the previous October, followed by a Waverley Pageant, to commemorate Sir Walter Scott.

[3] In reference, presumably, to the drama submitted to the Drury Lane managers (see p. 6).

[4] By James Sheridan Knowles; first produced in May 1825, when Macready played the name-part and Mrs. Alfred Bunn (*née* Somerville) that of Tell's wife.

7

Whom but myself could I affect by such moroseness? Why cannot I act upon my "own gained knowledge"? In the other case both person and thing were equally beneath me; why should not a person like Mr. F—— belong to such a society? Why cannot I hold my peace and stay away? Such should be my course; I dread the effects of my own intolerant and impetuous temper. God be my friend, for I am too often an enemy to myself!

January 25th.—In discussing the propriety of Mr. F.'s admission to the Garrick Club this morning I so far improved upon my late violence of language as to refrain from any exhibition of temper: a very negative praise. Quite made up my mind to leave the managers to their own course in the particular of their pledge to me on the alternation of Othello and Iago.[1] Why did I feel excited and stung into a kind of nervous alacrity by Kean's[2] inability to act? Our interests in this profession come too frequently into collision to ensure, without steady vigilance, that magnanimity which makes the peace of conscience.

January 28th.—Found, on my arrival in town, the play of *Macbeth* substituted for that of *Othello*. In reply to ——'s invitation for to-morrow, preferred the society of my dear family to an evening spent with a relation who is humbled in his pride by the connection of a player, which I must, moreover, have purchased at the expense of a whole day passed in London. Acted parts of Macbeth well, but must be careful to preserve that *manly natural* tone, more especially in soliloquies.

January 29th.—In reading Scott's *Life of Fielding*, I fancy I

---

[1] The parts were to have been alternated, but owing, no doubt, to opposition from Kean, the stipulation was not carried out.

[2] Edmund Kean (1787–1833), the celebrated actor, now on the verge of his fatal illness. He died a few weeks later. Macready relates the circumstances under which he first saw him act in his *Reminiscences*. They were never on intimate terms, Macready being strongly repelled by Kean's dissolute habits, though he fully acknowledged his genius. Oxberry's *Dramatic Biography* gives the following account of Kean's career at Drury Lane: "Since Mr. Kean's first appearance at Drury Lane Theatre he has appeared in many characters, and though he has not in every instance gratified the unreasonable expectations of his admirers, yet he has always displayed considerable originality and unequalled talent. In portraying the emotions of the heart-sad Romeo and the whining Jaffier he has certainly not eclipsed his contemporaries, but in depicting the malignant revenge of Shylock, the bold villainy of Overreach, the soul-subduing agonies of the noble and unsuspecting Othello, and the vast phalanx of evil passions that swayed the daring, desperate and crafty Richard, Mr. Kean has not in our day been equalled, and perhaps will never be surpassed. In fact, every character which he has sustained has elicited some bright scintillation of his matchless genius."

8

perceive a restless discontent and something of an invidious depreciation of the dramatist's powers (when he makes the machinist and
scene-painter the sharers of his triumphs) in his estimate of the
difficulties of the novelist's and playwright's tasks.   In his *Essay on the
Drama* the same writer, unworthily I think, endeavours to degrade a
walk of genius which he could never reach, and affects a plea of disinclination to an art in which his repeated failures betray at once his
ambition and his incapacity to excel.[1]

January 30th.—Feel my mind fettered by the state of suspense in
which it is held in regard to Othello.[2]   Must give my attention to the
performance of it.

February 2nd.—The bad weather, considerations of expense, and
uncertainty of what was to be done, came to the aid of my inclination,
and kept me at home to-day.   My principal known business in town was
to oppose Mr. F—— at the Garrick Club ;[3] in practising Othello, and
acquiring the valuable and interesting truths in my perusal of Harris's
Hermes, which I have done to-day, I have been far better employed.

February 4th.—On my arrival in town I found the theatre closed
for this night ; the pretext is the preparation for the opera[4] to-morrow.
I believe it a piece of quackery of the manager, who did not anticipate
a good audience to *Othello* this evening.   The sort of showman's bill

[1] Scott himself places the subject in quite a different light, in a note on a passage in
Byron's *Detached Thoughts* relative to the large number of worthless plays submitted to the
Drury Lane Committee.   Byron had applied to him in the hope that he might write a play
for them himself, or at all events recommend some dramatist of promise.   In commenting
on this request, Scott says : "I remember declining to write for the stage, and alleging in
excuse not only the probability that I might not succeed, but the unpleasant yet necessary
and inevitable subjection in which I must as a dramatic writer be kept by the 'good folks
of the green-room.'"   This statement is hardly reconcilable with Macready's allegation of
Scott's "repeated failures" as a playwright.

[2] Since November 1832 Macready had played Iago to Kean's Othello ; they had never
played together previously.   Macready's "suspense" was apparently as to whether he would
have to play Othello during Kean's illness ; Cooper, however, replaced Kean at the only
performance given in his absence.

[3] Unsuccessfully ; Mr. F—— was elected.   Macready was never very happy in his relations
with the Club, from which he retired after a few years' membership, as a protest against the
election of certain intimate associates of his *bête noire,* Mr. Alfred Bunn.   But it is doubtful
whether in the Johnsonian sense he was "a clubbable man," at all events to the extent that
would have rendered the Garrick a favourite haunt.   There was a touch of rigidity about
him that was out of keeping with its spirit of *camaraderie.*   The atmosphere of the Athenæum
was more congenial, though his appearances there were by no means frequent.   He was,
in fact, too fond of his home to care much for Clubs.

[4] The management was running, as an additional attraction, a German Opera Company,
with Schröder-Devrient as its "star."

9

put forth to-day shocked my taste, but I am at the same time disposed to ascribe to offended vanity a small portion of the disgust I felt; I am uncertain on the point. Assuredly I was not pleased with the use of my name, but the general merits of the bill are enough to decide one's aversion to the mountebank who issued it, without having recourse to particulars.

February 6th.—A very restless night incapacitated me from the very early rising I had resolved on. Part of it I used in separating passion from my reflections on Mr. Bunn's [1] behaviour, regarding it with total indifference and determining to do all in my power for my family by perseverance and economy.

February 8th.—It is a strange weakness, whether imputable to some physical cause, or to an insuperable distrust of myself, I know not, that on arriving in town to play a part often done before, as Iago, I should feel a trepidation and sudden sinking of heart as I get sight of the bill announcing my performance.[2] But it is so, and, though my reason soon subdues the emotion, I go to the theatre with as much restlessness and more uncertainty than many untried and less favoured actors know. To-night, however, it did not affect my energy or skill; perhaps I have not played Iago with more entire self-possession, more spirit, and in a more manly unembarrassed tone.

February 9th.—I apprehend, though without temper or uneasiness, more baseness on the part of Polhill [3] and Bunn. The latter told me to-day that my Lent did not begin until Ash Wednesday. He is an unprincipled person. I saw Knowles, who told me his play would soon be finished—so will the season. Why am not I one of those " whose heart the holy forms of young imagination have kept *pure* "? Alas! my reason is too often my reproach.

---

[1] Alfred Bunn (1796–1860), manager of Drury Lane Theatre. Supposed to be the prototype of " Mr. Dolphin " in Thackeray's *Pendennis*. Ridiculed in *Punch* as the " Poet Bunn," in consequence of his not too felicitous ventures in verse. A vulgar and pretentious speculator in theatrical enterprises from which, oftener than not, he emerged in a state of insolvency with an unpaid salary-list. Between such a man and an artist of Macready's high quality and character sharp antagonism was inevitable. It culminated in an unfortunate *fracas*, which is fully described later on. In these days such managers as Bunn are fortunately rare, but it was otherwise in the Thirties.

[2] Macready remained liable to this feeling to the end of his career, even when on tour in small provincial towns.

[3] Captain Polhill, then largely interested in Drury Lane Theatre. His theatrical ventures nvolved him in enormous losses. He afterwards sat for some time in Parliament. He is requently bracketed with Bunn by Macready, though the manager was, in fact, mainly responsible for the " shiftiness " complained of.

February 10th.—The bad weather prevented me from going to morning church. Read over the debates of the last week. How disgusting it is to see men like Macaulay,[1] possessing a knowledge of truth, and gifted with the power of diffusing it widely, using those means of virtue in the base cause of a party for his own baser interests; trading in sentiments which are no longer held forth than they are marketable. What a theatre is the House of Commons; what wretched actors and what vile parts they play! Looking from my window over the clear landscape before, I feel how far beyond the vanities and cares of a town life are the pleasures of my country home. Thank God!

February 12th.—Fixed in my resolve to met the baseness of Messrs. Polhill and Bunn with the most perfect indifference, and to yield the night in question.[2] If I had always acted with so much foresight how different had been my lot!

London, February 14th.—A very busy day after a very disturbed night. My spirits became depressed after taking leave and losing sight of my dear wife and children, but the active employment of to-day, at chambers and abroad, has dissipated the gloom which hung upon me. I found myself announced for "the ensuing week" in the bills, but Mr. Bunn said it "meant nothing." My divinings were just! In writing to W—— I have adhered to my resolution of advancing nothing without security; I am right. His failings are not misfortunes, or I would distress myself (as I have done) to relieve him. I have practised a *finesse* in my negotiation for Glasgow, which may possibly lose the engagement; I surely ought not to do that from the want of money which I would not otherwise do. The highest principle is the best rule of conduct.

February 15th.—Divided between settling affairs, calling on persons, and packing. So much fatigued with the occupations of yesterday, that I lost two hours in bed to-day. Dr. Lardner proposed to me to advance with him £50 for W——; seemed quite agitated when I mentioned, on his inquiring, the amount with which I *had* furnished him. I agreed to his proposals only on conditions. I am not sure that I am right in doing so much. Saw Mrs. Watts and Mrs.

---

[1] Macaulay was at this time Secretary of the Board of Control and a member of the Whig Government, which was beginning to fall into discredit. Though a thorough-going supporter of his party, he had certainly no "base interests" in view. But Macready was a severe and not always a just critic of public men.

[2] See entry for February 9.

Talfourd,[1] and received a note from Sheil,[2] inquiring my address. This is different from his conduct last year, but we are all the creatures of circumstance in this world, and are only happy as we are above pride and pretence.

To Exeter, February 16th.—My morning was cut into as many portions as I had boxes, bags, notes, messages and hundreds of etceteras. I gave *too much* to the porter at the coach; this is a very *silly* fault, and a wrong to any poor creature that may need one's charity. There was nothing remarkable in the three passengers with whom I started; the woman was very vulgar, which was not her fault— her husband, an outside, was equally so and rather drunk, but redeemingly civil. I passed Edwardes Place, and marked the house where I left my dearest Catherine nine years ago; never shall I forget my feelings in quitting her. I looked with extreme interest too at the Inn at Hounslow where we breakfasted and changed our clothes on the morning of our marriage. Few have more cause to bless that important day than I.

February 17th.—I could see little of the beautiful country through which I passed to-day for the mist. Arrived at my lodgings, I entered immediately on business.

February 18th.—Greaves [3] called as I was on the point of going out to seek him. What long recollections he brings to me; he was what I may term the first cordial admirer in my art that I had; and he has been as unchanging as the laurel leaf. I acted pretty well this evening, but in the dagger scene wanted that fresh natural manner, so real and impressive on an audience. Thank God, was not angry or harsh.

February 19th.—The essay I read yesterday on the drama and its professors will, I hope, sustain me in my desire of upholding in myself

---

[1] Wife of Serjeant Talfourd ; he and Macready became lifelong friends in spite of periodical estrangements.

[2] Richard Lalor Sheil (1791–1851), author and politician ; Repealer, but accepted office from the Whig Government, 1837 ; was Master of the Mint, 1846–1850, and at the time of his death British Minister at Florence. A man of many gifts, but his transformation from an Irish " patriot " into a Whig placeman was ignominious, if not something more. He and Macaulay were sworn in together as Privy Councillors in 1839, an event which the *Times* recorded in the following passage : "These men Privy Councillors ! These men petted at Windsor Castle ! Faugh ! Why, they are hardly fitted to fill up the vacancies that have occurred by the lamented death of Her Majesty's two favourite monkeys !" A day or two later appeared the even grosser attack on "Mr. Babble-Tongue Macaulay," for having addressed a letter to his constituents from Windsor Castle. But at that period Mr. Barnes still wielded the bludgeon in Printing House Square.

[3] A retired solicitor ; an old friend of Macready.

and for my dear children a respectable as well as honourable character;
but an actor *has* more temptation than other men. I can scarcely enter
a theatre without seeing beauty that too often cares not to conceal a
flattering approval of one's talent, and that would not receive with
avidity a reciprocal homage. What other condition in life brings you
into personal contact with beauty under such dangerous circumstances?
It is my fortune, not my merit, God knows, to have escaped unscathed
in reputation.

February 21st.—My performance of Iago to-night was an example
of what I wrote this morning. There was a want of sustained earnestness and spirit—there was no proper direction of the sight, and in
consequence a scowl instead of clear expression, besides a want of
abstraction in the soliloquies.

Bristol, February 23rd.—Forgot, in stepping into the coach for
Bristol, my many expostulations with myself on the subject of temper,
and was guilty of a display of ill humour because a gentleman, a
Quaker, claimed, on the right of pre-occupation, the back seats! I
notice it to shame and condemn my absurdity! Last night I heard of
Kean's illness; a subject which has little interest for me, since his
ability to play or not will make no difference in the style of language—
qy. cant?—used on him and me.

February 25th.—Felt some ill effects of yesterday's indulgence.
In the Birmingham coach was accosted by Graham Clarke, whom I
remember a handsome, gay young man in Newcastle, and now see a
portly white-haired "country gentleman." Another of "the *bench*"
rode ten miles with us, and afforded me an amusing insight into the
quality of mind peculiar to this species—county magistrates. Turn-
pike roads, covers, poachers, rents, county politics, and important
county persons, never heard of beyond the boundaries of the shire,
give unwearied exercise to their tongues. Such men are not without
a certain interest to me in my cogitations on mankind and his purpose
here. Possessed of thousands per annum, this person G. C. gave a ready,
and seemingly an *habitual*, refusal to a beggar's request, and a most
imperious "good day to you" to the village inn-keeper on the road.
Is this superiority of sense, good breeding, or charity?

Liverpool, February 26th.—I had intended saving the price of
my dinner to-day, but the rain prevented me from walking, and
I felt some *mal à propos* pinches of hunger. Two poor creatures
came to the coach door to beg, one an Irishman with children and
no work, the other a child employed, as I suspect. Of the con-

13

dition of the Irish there can be little doubt, and is a Christian to deny
this poor fellow-creature? Too often hypocrisy assumes the mask of
religion; it is the almost universal face put on in this country by those
who call themselves Christians to hide their disgusting selfishness and
indifference to the privations of the poor. How men, with the divine,
the blessed precepts of our Saviour in their hands, can so blaspheme
His simple religion of meekness, love and charity as to turn from the
poor beggar and show reverence to the rich bishop, I cannot conceive.

Dublin, February 28th.—On my arrival this morning I was too
confused either to enjoy the beauty of the harbour, or to think much
upon the character presented to a stranger's contemplation in the
dilapidated, tumbling houses and cabins, made more painfully obvious
by the rotting verandas, or large shattered lamps that caricatured
instead of decorating them! My fellow-passengers I saw little of;
several were military who knew me; one claimed acquaintance with me.
The captain was very civil. Calcraft [1] sent me to my lodgings a letter
from Catherine—a very sweet letter—and one from Birch, declining
to be sponsor to my boy. I strive to reason myself into not feeling
this as a disappointment, but the consciousness I have of meaning it
only as the highest mark of respect I could offer makes it very difficult.
It is done, thank God!

March 1st.—Annoyed and displeased with Miss H.'s repetition of
the impudent falsehood, circulated, it seems, by Miss K——, now
Mrs. F——, of having received serious attentions from me. It is not
only a gross falsehood, but one unsupported by even the semblance
of foundation. How is it possible to guard against such calumniators?

March 2nd.—What an irascible disposition I must have *had*, when
even now I have such frequent occasions to rebuke my waspish impatience and pettishness at the various trifles that happen to cross my mood
as I sit here alone. I have attended rehearsal to-day, and received
calls from Sir C. Morgan [2] (whom I previously met in Calcraft's room),
Meldrum and Colonel D'Aguilar. Calcraft gave me *La vie de Faublas*,
but I neither wish to read nor retain a merely indelicate book; my own
thoughts are of themselves sufficiently disposed to evil. I wished and
intended to have played well this evening, but I was crossed by circum-

---

[1] Lessee of the Dublin theatre. His real name was Cole. He had been in the army,
and held some social position in Dublin. Subsequently he failed, not very creditably,
involving Macready, who had shown him much forbearance, in considerable loss.

[2] Sir Thomas Charles Morgan (1783–1843), physician and author; his wife (formerly
Sydney Owenson) was the well-known novelist.

stances in the piece, and did not satisfy myself, although the audience called for me. Since my return from the theatre I have read the debate on the Irish Coercion Bill, particularly Stanley's[1] and O'Connell's[2] speeches. The accounts of Irish atrocities are most disgusting and appalling; but where are efforts to prevent and ameliorate? The inequality of society arising from unequal laws is a human grievance, and ought to be corrected.

March 3rd.—I AM FORTY YEARS OF AGE! Need I add one word to the solemn reproof conveyed in these, when I reflect on what I am, and what I have done? What has my life been? a betrayal of a great trust, an abuse of great abilities! This morning, as I began to dress, I almost started when it occurred to me that it was my birthday.

Last night I began reading parts of *Faublas*, and, as is my custom with novels, sat up late and continued it in bed until half-past five this morning. I rose late, and was *shocked* and *ashamed* to think that I had wasted, or rather misused, so much precious time over such immoral, irrational and debasing stuff.

March 4th.—In my walk to-day with Calcraft I looked into the Adelphi theatre, and was introduced to Sir J. Kingsmill and several of the officers there. After dinner to-day I received a letter from my Catherine. I cannot call it unkind, because it was not intended to be so, but since she has been my wife I do not remember any pain or distress of heart to compare with the *dead pressure of misery* that she has laid upon my mind by that beautifully written letter. I cannot lift up my heart—I am unhappy—wretchedly unhappy; and shall not regain the quiet of my soul until I see her once again. I went to act Rob Roy before the Lord Lieutenant[3] in a very dejected state. The rabble tried to find applications in every speech to existing circumstances, but the house was decorous.

March 5th.—I rose earlier to attend rehearsal; the low spirits of yesterday still were upon me. Have determined on reconsidering that distressing letter, and answering it. Wrote to Gaspey[4] a hasty and

---

[1] Afterwards fourteenth Earl of Derby (1799–1869); twice Conservative Prime Minister. In 1833 he was Irish Secretary in Lord Grey's Administration. Left the Whig Party in 1835.

[2] Daniel O'Connell (1775–1847), the Liberator.

[3] Henry William, first Marquis of Anglesey, K.G.; soldier and politician; distinguished in the Peninsula and at Waterloo; "pro-Catholic" Viceroy in 1828; recalled by the Duke of Wellington in 1829; reappointed by Lord Grey in 1830; resigned in September 1833, and was succeeded by the Marquis Wellesley.

[4] Editor of the *Sunday Times*.

brief account of last night ; received and answered a very kind invitation from Mr. Colles, to whom I had shown some civility in London.

Acted Macbeth with spirit, earnestness, and self-possession ; carried into effect the corrections I had thought of in the morning ; was obliged to appear before the audience after the play. To what end is thought or care, when next morning we read notices of our labours by the ignorant and incompetent ?

March 6th.—Deliberated for some time on a very polite invitation to dinner this day from Sir Hussey Vivian [1] ; reflected that I must relinquish altogether, or imperfectly complete my letter of advice and consolation to my beloved wife ; and also distress myself in the accumulation of business that must result from this indulgence of my inclination and curiosity. The proper study of mankind is man ! and I like to contemplate him under his various phases. But I concluded, against the pressing entreaties of Calcraft, to remain at home. I neglected my calls to-day, but after a long walk wrote to my Catherine, and afterwards gave a reading which was much wanted to the *Merchant of London.*[2] I was right in remaining to attend to my duties.

Perceive that much improvement is to be obtained by attention at rehearsals ; and in my profession, as in my observation of Catherine's progress, discern the meaning, and admit the *truth*, of *the metaphysician* who defines genius to be patience.

March 7th.—My morning was spent in rehearsal and calls. I was right in desiring the repetition of the scenes at rehearsal, though by no means justified in betraying anger at the imbecility of the prompter. How much is to be gained at rehearsals ! I saw an old gentleman in the shop (who, Milliken told me, was Jno. Crampton) that had lost £10,000 in the theatre, and now called every day to read theological lectures to Mrs. M——! I saw him in 1815, a very fine, dashing man, with whom I made my first Dublin engagement. Being annoyed by some trifles in the early scenes of the play to-night, I was deficient in freshness and intensity of feeling, but I came out a different person in the third act, and maintained my power over the audience till I made my bow of acknowledgment after the play. I have not been idle to-day,

[1] Sir Richard Hussey Vivian (1775–1842) ; afterwards first Lord Vivian. A distinguished general officer, who in 1833 was commander of the forces in Ireland. Master-General of the Ordnance in 1835.

[2] A play by T. J. Serle, in which Macready took the part of Scroope ; it was produced at Drury Lane in the preceding year, but failed to attract, though well received on the first night.

16

but am checked in my desire of employment by the feeling of fatigue.

To Manchester, March 10*th.*—After completing my arrangements, leaving cards for Mrs. Hemans [1] and Mr. Colles, I set off in a carriage with Mr. Calcraft and Miss Huddart [2] to Kingstown. We dined at the Royal Hotel. How disenchanting in the female character is a manifestation of relish for the pleasures of the table!

Manchester, March 11*th.*—We landed after ten o'clock, and with some trouble got our luggage to the railway station, whence after waiting half an hour we rushed along to Manchester. I placed Miss H—— in a coach with her luggage, and saw her off, as I took my own course to my lodgings. With a handsome person, a good heart, and a fair average of understanding, she wants the charm of her sex, gentleness in manner, tact and delicacy. She gains respect for her good qualities, but neither admiration nor affection for the graces so fascinating in woman. I tried to play, but effort must have been too perceptible throughout the performance. The company is very indifferent—"two of the eleven" in a state of intoxication.

March 12*th.*—On returning home I sat down to read over Othello; the idea of which even here gave me a sensation of nervousness. I am inclined to reproach myself for my precipitation in declining the reduced terms offered me at Bath and Newcastle; perhaps, however, I was not wrong.

March 13*th.*—Have given up the entire day to the rehearsal, consideration, and preparation of *Othello.* The Iago of Cooper [3] was a very bad performance, neither distinctness of outline nor truth of colour. Of my own Othello I am inclined to speak in qualified terms. There was not exactly a lack of spirit in the early scenes, but a freshness and freedom in its flow must have been manifest. I was nervous, and under that oppression effort will show itself. The audience, as cold as the snow that was falling at the beginning, waxed warmer and warmer, and actually kindled into enthusiasm at the burst in the third act, which was good, but the part still requires much study.

---

[1] Presumably Felicia Dorothea Hemans (1793–1835), the well-known poetess.

[2] Mary Amelia Huddart, afterwards Mrs. Warner (1804–1854), an accomplished and popular actress, professionally associated with Macready for many years. She was strongly attracted by him and he had a true regard for her, which he proved by constant acts of generous friendship to the close of her life.

[3] John Cooper (1790–1870), an actor of some vogue, first in the provinces and afterwards in London. He made his first appearance in 1810.

The address to the Senate, the arrival at Cyprus, the second scene of the fourth act and the last act demand all my care and energy. The house was very thin, and I am yet irresolute as to my further course.

March 16th.—"It is in ourselves that we are thus or thus." The unhealthy condition of my mind, with which my body too closely sympathizes, is a comment on this text which I vainly strive to gainsay. I read nothing; I rise at the very latest moment, and have barely time through the day for the business demanded. I have cold on me, and my lodgings are uncomfortable; but still I ought to put myself above the influence of such petty matters. I should do so, were it not that I have suffered my mind to become the prey of unwholesome and enervating thoughts, that cling like disease about it, and which act in reciprocal support with my physical maladies. I have dispatched a large sum to my bankers to-day, for which I thank God. In the play I acted Iago pretty well, but was certainly disconcerted, if not annoyed, by the share of applause bestowed on Mr. Cooper. What little beings does selfishness make us! Where there is little time to think, how liable I am to fall into those vices and littlenesses which none more loudly condemn. In the farce I was mangled by the shameful idleness of the actors.

March 18th.—Read in last week's debate the Bishop of London's [1] vindication of the wealth of the clergy! Appeared before a wretched assemblage of devoted playgoers in the part of Virginius, which neither my health, spirits, nor interest could encourage me to act. I made some saving hits in passages, and tried experiments through it. Perceive that I have acted injudiciously, as respects profit, in not preferring Glasgow, but I feel that I must humiliate myself by going to that theatre.

March 19th.—For my health's sake took a walk of about three miles up and down Oxford Road. Thought on many things, my father's inconsiderate speculation here and consequent ruin—its effect on my destiny—the mystery of human nature; and the sweet musings on my darling children, on seeing a little girl about the age and form of dear Nina, came like delight upon my spirit. Read many pages of Racine's *History of Port Royal*. What fools and villains are the bishops, priests and particularly the Jesuits, of whom he speaks. My

---

[1] Charles James Blomfield (1786–1857). A vigorous champion of the privileges of his order, thereby incurring the trenchant denunciation of William Cobbett, whose views on the Church in general, and the bench of bishops in particular, were largely shared by Macready. Blomfield, however, was not of the perfunctory class of prelates, and did good work in his diocese, especially in the direction of church extension.

acting in Tell to-night was bad, but had the excuse of bad health and audience. I wish I could offer any excuse for my ill temper.

March 20th.—Acted Werner with unusual force, truth and collectedness; finished off each burst of passion, and in consequence entered on the following emotion with clearness and earnestness; the house was miserable. Came home and read the newspaper, until I became uncomfortable from the disgust I felt at the conduct of such men as Althorp,[1] Stanley,[2] Hobhouse,[3] in fact the base-minded clique of apostates that make up the present Ministry.

March 21st.—I have done nothing else to-day beyond rehearsing, taking a very short walk, and reading part of Oakley,[4] preparatory to my performance of it, which merits little commendation. It is a character, as being very easy, that I ought to play well; and merit censure for not doing it better than well. My opinion of Ministers does not improve. Who shall throw a stone at the guilty in this world? Yet political vice seems so poor in its gain, and so wide in its mischief, that the worst seem entitled to judgment.

March 22nd.—Went to rehearsal after a breakfast without appetite, where I was kept so long that I deferred till to-morrow my search for a surgeon. Oh! that to-morrow! that trap of fools, that cheat of idleness! When shall I learn to establish a principle of acting upon the demand that duty makes upon me? Read over Wolsey for to-morrow evening, and looked at my accounts, which, thank God, are more satisfactory than they have lately been. Read over again my Catherine's last letter, and let my thoughts loose on their ramble home. Read the part of Scroope, and acted it effectively, but not with the truth, reality and taste that would satisfy my own judgment. Acted the

---

[1] Viscount Althorp, afterwards Earl Spencer (1782–1845), Chancellor of the Exchequer and leader of the House of Commons in Lord Grey's Administration ; a statesman of absolute consistency and rectitude, in no way deserving this stigma of Macready, who was too prone, particularly in political matters, to pass ill-considered judgments. On Lord Grey's retirement Lord Althorp's position remained unchanged, but on succeeding to his father's earldom he necessarily resigned both the Chancellorship of the Exchequer and the Leadership of the House, a circumstance that was seized upon by William IV as a pretext for dismissing the Melbourne Ministry, the King insisting that there was no one in the Government capable of replacing Althorp as Leader of the House. There has been no juster appreciation of Lord Althorp than that of Macaulay, who described him as possessing " the principles of Romilly, with the temper of Lord North."

[2] See note, p. 15.

[3] Sir John Hobhouse, Bart., afterwards Lord Broughton (1786–1869). Best known as Byron's intimate friend; at this time Irish Secretary ; earlier in his career he advocated extreme Radical principles, and accordingly gave some colour to Macready's appellation.

[4] In *The Jealous Wife*, the most popular of Macready's comedy parts.

scene of J. Surface middlingly. The house was much better for the bill, and I am glad to have rendered Miss Huddart such a service. The play excited so much interest that Mr. Cooper was recommended to take it to-morrow night, but he preferred playing Henry VIII, which I do not envy him.

March 23rd.—I was wrong in suggesting *Henry VIII* for to-night, as I am not at home in Wolsey; after the rehearsal (during which Mr. Clarke paid me, and deducted the price of a pint of claret he had sent me—a silly economy) I called on Miss H—— and gave her some advice, for which I commend myself. My afternoon was passed in reading Wolsey (which I acted in a style not worthy of my reputation, though with effect) and getting calico, muslin, etc., and packing it for home. My landlady has given me the third dose to-day of "Tom and Jane"—an exercise of patience. Spoke to Mr. Cooper, in taking leave of him, on the state of the theatres; am hopeless of any good result from any combination of actors. This night finishes my Manchester engagement, and sets me free from a temptation, and my mind from a struggle, that has lost it much valuable time and cost me much self-reproach. I have no other person than myself to accuse.

March 24th. Read in the newspapers the announcement of Kean and son [1] in Othello; it is mere quackery. Wrote sundry letters on business. Feel in good spirits, and should be well, were I relieved from this disorder. I am grown much thinner.

March 25th.—After dinner I read, for idleness and digestion's sake, that offensive paper, the *Age*.[2] Went to the theatre to see *Victorine*, which increased the previous depression of my spirits. How very painful is the contemplation of a woman who has yielded up her virtue, and how miserable does the reflection on the brutal character of vice among the low thieves of a metropolis make the mind. It is hopeless

---

[1] Edmund Kean and his son Charles. Macready's admiration of the father as an actor did not extend to the son, whom he throughout regarded with exaggerated contempt. Though only a mediocre actor, Charles Kean certainly deserved a higher place in the profession than Macready chose to accord him. His name is of frequent occurrence in the Diaries, and seldom without the accompaniment of some strongly disparaging remarks.

[2] Probably the most scurrilous newspaper of the day, though the *Satirist* and *John Bull* ran it very hard. It was edited by one Westmacott, and was constantly the subject of proceedings for libel. The Duke of Wellington was among its many eminent victims, and it did not even spare the punctiliously decorous Fanny Kemble, who was, however, promptly avenged by a public horsewhipping administered to Westmacott by her father (Charles Kemble).

depravity. What are we here for? I was perhaps additionally moved by sitting in the box I used when a boy, before my prospects changed, seeing the very drop scene that my father placed there twenty-five years ago. Much of the past came back upon me.

March 26th.—Walked up (calling on Miss H——) to Ardwick Green, where I saw the house in which I lived, and cited up a thousand heavy times that at that miserable period had befallen me. Much to deplore, much to condemn. Returning to dinner I called at Mr. Clark's for the newspaper; the principal communications in which are, I think, the domestic occurrences of those little people who in their own eyes are great, such as dinners, dances, marriages and such trashery, as if the perpetuation of a race like our aristocrats were of the slightest moment.[1] The only importance in life is virtue, its exercise is the only honour, and love is the only happiness. Read some very good passages in Cowper's *Task*. He was clearly a republican in principle.

March 27th.—The *Herald* report of the quacking exhibition of Kean and his son is equal in style, judgment and impartiality. And *these* are the *conoscenti* and critics of our art! Heaven help me! for I have little chance here.

Carlisle, March 29th.—Woke before my appointed hour, but rose refreshed, and with a sensation of relief in quitting Manchester. My journey offered me little to remark upon; the sort of early loiterers in a manufacturing town made their wonted appearance about the coach, to make one question again the general influence of civilization. Lancaster Castle, from its soil, its present appropriation, and as having been the place of my poor father's confinement, arrested my attention, as did Garstang Castle from not having before noticed it, and Kendal Castle from its beautiful situation. I looked at a play bill on the walls at Lancaster; is it surprising that any one of common capacity should shrink from such a waste of time? A very heavy snowstorm on

---

[1] Macready was an uncompromising democrat, holding the monarchy in scant reverence, and attacking the aristocracy with persistent rancour. His attitude was, no doubt, in some measure attributable to his extreme sensitiveness regarding his social status. In those days knighthoods and other forms of royal recognition were hopelessly beyond the reach of the dramatic profession. Though occasionally " commanded " by the Sovereign and patronized by a great nobleman, an actor, however eminent, was seldom allowed to escape the consciousness that he was " outside the pale," an individual who, if by a fitful condescension addressed as " esquire," was in reality still under the ban of the unceremonious statute that defined him as " a rogue and vagabond." To a man of culture and refinement like Macready, this was inexpressibly galling and remained a rankling influence to the end of his life.

Shap Fells made that wild country more desolate and dreary than usual; I love the heath and the free breezes of the hills.

Passed by the theatre at Carlisle which my father built, in seeking my letters; thought of many days, acts and feelings for ever gone.

Edinburgh, March 30th.—A striking instance of the dangerous effects of precipitation showed itself to-day. A month ago I could not reason down the annoyance of wounded pride, arising from B.'s refusal to be my boy's godfather; this morning I took up his letter to answer it, and it seems to me most proper and affectionate. Pride and passion! where would ye have led me? Thank God! I have replied to it as I ought. My day has been an idle one, I have read some pages of Tasso, the combats between Ottone, Argante and Tancredi; some part of Terence's *Heautontimorumenos;* the excellent scene of Chremes rebuking Clitipho, and Syrus sending him away; two essays of Bacon on custom and nature; and Shakspeare's exquisite scenes between Angelo and Isabel. I walked upon the Calton Hill, after posting my letters. Disliking this city as much as I can suffer myself to dislike any place, I cannot be blind to its extraordinarily grand and beautiful appearance; it is more like a metropolis in the *coup d'œil* it offers than any British city. But I have been ill, and always disregarded here, and I am not patient of the unauthorized pretension of its inhabitants.

April 1st.—Rehearsal, and the business of preparing clothes, etc., occupied the day until the play hour. I think I acted Macbeth in a manner that would have gained me fame before any but an Edinburgh audience, which I look upon as one so like the vile pretender to superior wisdom described by Gratiano that I should as soon expect the standing pool to rise in waves, or become clear enough to reflect the images near it, as to observe one genuine display of sympathy from them. They seem to me grave coxcombs, presuming on the merit of individuals who have been born or lived among them to consider themselves as participating in their characters. I almost *quite* satisfied myself.

April 2nd.—Acted but in a mediocre style, my state of body having its influence, and deranged and cut up by the odd sort of Othello beside me; indeed I may say frequently disconcerted, several times annoyed, and once or twice irritated. Some of this person's eccentricities were, I think, intentional. He had his admirers, who were very liberal of their applause to him, nor is he devoid of talent; but I think it disfigured by imitation and affectation, and not of a very high class. Saw Allan [1] during the play, much older, but his mind seems still alive to its earlier delights.

April 3rd.—Still with a heavy sense of fatigue on me, which is aggravated by the distaste I have for my work here. I dislike the audience, and their wretched attendance leaves me no room to question any further their opinion of me. I must draw a scratch across the place. Mrs. W. Siddons called with a kind note of acknowledgment and invitation from Mrs. H. Siddons [2] which I answered, declining. I have only one feeling here, which I have never been in Edinburgh without : a desire to *get out* of the place.

Wrote to dearest Catherine. Received letter from her; and one from Mr. Farren [3] asking me to play Puff for his benefit ! ! Acted *well.* I perceive by my observation of last night that the great defect of my style is hurry and want of clear discrimination, I mean discrimination, not in one's own mind, but made palpable to and impressed on an audience. Let me not lose sight of this ! ! ! Particularly noted the superior effect, as well as the diminution of labour, in the marked discrimination with which I acted Virginius this evening, though unprepared and at first careless of my performance. This resulted from thinking on the too artificial style of the young gentleman who played Othello last night, and contrasting his and Kean's methods, though they are patches from one piece, with my own. I see *how much of my conception I lose by precipitancy :* it does not extract one spark of fire the less, but tempers energy so " as to give it smoothness." I hope I may now exclaim, εὕρηκα. To notice one among many instances of natural and powerful effect, I may record the embracing

---

[1] Sir William Allan (1782–1850), R.A., London, and P.R.S.A., Edinburgh ; originally a coachmaker's apprentice ; first became known as a painter of Russian life and scenery.

[2] Mrs. Harriet Siddons (1783–1844), widow of Henry Siddons, formerly manager of the Edinburgh theatre, and daughter-in-law of Sarah Siddons. An actress of some repute in Shaksperian parts. Her father, Charles Murray, a well-known actor in his day, was the son of Sir John Murray, Bart., of Broughton, Prince Charles Edward's secretary in 1745.

[3] William Farren (1786–1861), actor and manager ; chiefly impersonated old men, his Sir Peter Teazle being particularly successful ; he was the father of the late William Farren, who also excelled in Sir Peter. In private life he was, unfortunately, more identified with Joseph Surface, having allured a Mrs. Faucit, the wife of a brother-actor, from her marital allegiance. The dispossessed husband was apparently indisposed to console himself with his children, who followed their mother, thus acquiring a sort of " left-handed " step-father in the person of Mr. Farren. It was from this inauspicious *ménage* that Helen Faucit entered upon her distinguished career. These particulars will explain her connection with William Farren, who, it will be seen, represented her interests in her first engagement with Macready.

23

and rebuking Virginia, and committing her to Icilius just before hurrying away to the field, which I never did so well. Spoke very kindly to Mr. Ternan, last night's Othello, on some bad habits, and on his merits. Saw the announcement of *Macbeth* for Tuesday next!

April 4th.—Read a criticism in a newspaper which intends to be discerning, but which is a mere cold admission of power in myself, appended to the ordinary exceptions that the ferocity of the London Press used with so much bitterness to take against me; written by a person who evidently is ignorant of the characters he presumes to write on! Called on Allan, and saw his Orphan on the easel, his sketches of the rooms, etc., at Abbotsford, and the study of his picture of Rizzio's murder. He is a very interesting man; he promises to come and see me on his arrival in London. Called on Mrs. Spence and chatted. Received two petitions, but I unlearn my own precepts of generosity here. Answered Mr. Farren's letter, declining to act Puff. Played the Stranger pretty well, but had particular evidence of the comparatively phlegmatic temper of this audience in the applause to the burst in act sixth. Supped with Mr. Pritchard,[1] and met a party with whom I was amused, and who were too kind for Edinburgh. Why should one feel so uncontrollable a disposition to laugh at the torture of a man singing out of tune from fright? I do not know, but I incline to laugh at the mere recollection.

April 5th.—I see that I can improve myself in my profession considerably, and *I will do it.* Called about my trunks and letters on Mrs. Pritchard, was asked for autographs; saw an impromptu by a Mr. Power, headed " Du *mortuis nil nisi* JUSTEM "! And impudent ignorance like this has worshippers! Called on Mrs. H. Siddons; received a message from Miss Siddons. Struck with the surpassing beauty of this city, which I delight in getting free from. On my return home to fasten and send off my trunks (which I fear are sent by smack instead of steam) I received a letter from dearest Catherine telling of darling Willie's[2] head. The news quite struck me down, making me quite faint and sick. If it be the will of Almighty God to try my spirit by the illness of these dear babes, may He give me power of mind and body to support it; at present I am helpless under

---

[1] Probably John Langford Pritchard (1799–1850), then one of Murray's Edinburgh company.

[2] His eldest son, William Charles (1832–1871), educated at Westminster and Christ Church, Oxford; of the Ceylon Civil Service.

24

the idea. Obliged to dine with Mr. Bell,[1] where I met Allan and some agreeable legal men.

April 6th.—Inconvenienced by my late hours last night, I went to rehearsal, my mind continually recurring to my darling boy. Took a warm bath afterwards, and called on Mr. Coulson, who, I may say, has *beset* me with civilities. I escaped from him by a violent effort. On coming home I received a letter from my dear Catherine with better news of darling Willie, for which I thank God, while I pray for his complete restoration. Sent a verbal request to Mr. Murray[2] for an order for my hostess, which *I did not like to write;* he sent back : ' if I would write a note he would send one.' Upon this really impertinent piece of coxcombry I considered and *wrote* a note. I had, on a wrong belief of the terms we stood upon, placed myself in a bad position, and therefore recovered myself at once. What can a man say to himself on thus exposing his conceit and vanity? I acted as well as the bad support and imperfectness of the actors would let me. Much of Werner *well,* and J. Surface very well. Was called for by the audience, and instantly put on my cloak and left the theatre. Mr. Bell, a friend, called, told me there had been much noise and interruption, and that Mr. M—— told the audience that I had left the house. What could I have said to the Edinburgh audience?

April 7th.—I arose very early to be certain of my departure, which, after settling my various small accounts, I took by mail from that beautiful and queen-like city. I was angry—when shall I learn to abstain from such senseless intemperance?—with the coachman, and gave him nothing, wherein I was right, but justice should, to be justice, always be calm. It is impossible to imagine any objects more in harmony with the character of a city like Edinburgh than the hills and crags on and among which it stands. But my spirit felt lighter as I receded from it.

April 8th.—Reached York in a comparatively comfortable state. Left it with ruminations on its historical importance, and the waste

---

[1] Henry Glassford Bell (1803–1874), sheriff and author ; one of the founders of the Royal Scottish Academy.

[2] William Henry Murray (1790–1852), brother of Mrs. Henry Siddons (*q.v.*), manager of the Edinburgh theatre and an accomplished actor. Fanny Kemble describes him " as one of the most perfect actors I have ever known on any stage." Incidents of the sort here related were not infrequent with Macready, who while closely on the look-out for affronts from others was not always conciliatory in his own attitude and methods. He was not a man to " suffer fools gladly," or to treat with much ceremony fellow-members of a profession which, apart from its artistic element, he thoroughly disliked and despised.

of time and money in its twenty-four churches. Rode outside a few miles to enjoy the weather and the country. Amused with an inscription at Belford—the "Newcastle Arms and Conservative Hotel." Joined by some passengers, whose presence was anything but company. A son of Lord Grey's, about fourteen, got in at Stamford; a pair of unloaded pistols in his pockets, which he frequently presented. A perfect consciousness of the importance in some persons' minds to be attached to consanguinity with the Prime Minister made his exuberance of spirits very much resemble impertinent forwardness. But this was not so offensive as the obsequiously and adulating tone of approval and admiration that marked the discourse of my companions on the discovery of his claims to their homage. When he spoke of his brother, a post-captain at twenty-two, and another a colonel, my disgust at the rapacious patriotism of the Arch-Whig, Lord Grey, was centupled.[1]

London—Elstree, April 9th.—Had the comfort of reaching my chambers, stiff and wearied; disappointed in not finding Catherine and my baby there; dressed myself, and set out to catch the Crown Prince coach, which I missed, and came to the parting of the roads by a Hemel Hempstead one. Walked with a quick and light step towards Elstree, and reached my dear home about half-past ten. What can I record beyond this? As Francesca says: "Quel giorno più non vi leggemmo avanti." I found my darling boy much better than I could have expected; my dearest Nina in full health, and all well! I looked round the house, and about the ground, satisfying myself with reviewing what was pleasing for not being new. I only looked over my accounts, talking in idle gossip the rest of this happy day away. I can only thank God, as I humbly and fervently do, for so dear and precious a gift as the home with which he has blest me, and for the feeling to appreciate and enjoy it.

London, April 10th.—Immediately on coming down, which I did at a late hour, I lunched and set off in the carriage to town with Catherine and my boy. Called at the theatre, where I saw my name announced for Mr. Farren's farce; saw him, and observed to him how gross, impertinent, and ungentlemanly such an action was; he seemed ashamed of himself, and floundered about in some nonsensical

---

[1] For a " Friend of the People " Lord Grey was certainly rather a profuse benefactor of his family at the public expense. In nepotism, in fact, he was hard to beat, a failing which his numerous offspring rendered particularly formidable. It is not surprising that, in spite of his services to reform, he was regarded with disfavour by all thorough-going Radicals.

explanations or excuses.[1] Endeavoured at my chambers to prepare myself for night, but found a difficulty in settling and concentrating my thoughts. Endeavoured to act Macbeth well, but found myself strange to the stage, the size of the theatre, and the effect of my own voice. My earnestness must have been a redeeming quality in my acting, as the applause was frequent; as I advanced, I think I improved, and my death was very warmly applauded. I was called for at the fall of the curtain, and obliged to go forward.

April 19th.—Wallace [2] walked over from Mill Hill and staid dinner. He is grown lusty and florid, without the least shade of concern upon his brow, and speaking in high spirits of his *sanguine* expectations. He spoke of Wolfe's illness so as to recall Rochefoucauld's observation on our feelings of our friends' misfortunes, and also acquainted me with the stupid infatuation of O'Hanlon [3] in sending again for the vulgar little Frenchwoman from whom he had twice separated. The Haymarket theatre is closed until Wednesday next on account of the illness of the performers.

April 25th.—Saw by newspapers that Mr. Bunn is made lessee of Drury Lane Theatre; a more dishonest choice could not have been made, but I must " abide the change of time."

April 27th.—Called at the theatre, where I received several letters on various subjects; among them one from the Garrick Club, threatening me with " suspension as a defaulter " if my subscription be not paid. My disgust or indignation was a little excited by it. Saw Mr. Bunn, who is certainly the lessee of Drury Lane, under Polhill's security, and had some conversation with him; he seems inclined to be very civil, but it is only to try to make me useful to him. I know him to be destitute of honesty and honor, and from Mr. Reynolds's [4] communication to-day he is evidently doubletongued; my policy is *Silence and Vigilance;* I can do without him, and must not yield to his schemes. Learnt the success of Knowles' play, which will soon blow over. Saw Reynolds, and heard news of the Covent Garden Company at issue with M. Laporte; also some anecdotes,

[1] Farren's conduct was, of course, inexcusable; but such proceedings were apparently not uncommon at that time.

[2] A barrister and historical writer, with whom Macready was on intimate terms. His reputation has not survived, but he appears to have been considered noteworthy by his associates.

[3] Hugh Marmaduke O'Hanlon, counsel to the Irish Office; his friendship was occasionally somewhat embarrassing to Macready.

[4] Presumably Frederic Mansel Reynolds, editor of the *Keepsake*.

27

not very creditable, of the latter gentleman. Returned home; finished my race through *Woodstock*, which I altogether dislike. Tried to write a note to the Secretary of Garrick Club, but could not satisfy myself.

April 28th.—Received a letter from Birmingham, and read with much interest the history of the last week's politics, which do not improve my opinion of either the capacity or honesty of ministers. Am at a loss upon the proper course of proceeding with regard to the impertinent note of Mr. Winston; [1] am anxious to avoid acting from passion or with petulance, yet do not like to yield to such vulgar freedom. Answered Mr. Winston.

May 2nd.—After breakfast I read a few letters in Jefferson's correspondence. I assent to his declaration that it is " a charge of injustice on the Creator to say He made men incapable of governing themselves." I read as practice the chief part of *Hamlet's* second act; *must continue my professional studies.* Spent the evening in writing to John Twiss.[2] I may certainly note to-day as an improvement on yesterday, much of it, though not enough, being occupied in necessary or useful employment.

To London, May 3rd.—A messenger arrived with notes from Messrs. Bunn and Bartley,[3] asking me to act for benefit of latter, Monday, 20th inst. I assented, as I had no choice, though I have no motive for serving Mr. Bartley, whom I look upon as a false, base, treacherous hypocrite; but the impartial public are my judges, and " I must hold my tongue," with Hamlet, whatever vicious or bestial rulers usurp the influence that honest men should have.

May 4th.—Received letter from John Twiss, mentioning his purpose of appropriating funds here to our reimbursement. I never dreamt of such a thing, nor would accept one farthing for his boy, as our guest. Went to town on a morning so beautiful that it looked only to be enjoyed in the country. Called on Mr. Cooper and engaged him to go to Birmingham at Whitsuntide. Was surprised to hear him speak in what seemed to me a silly manner on the junction of the two

---

[1] Secretary of the Garrick Club, whose threat of suspension had so greatly incensed Macready.

[2] A member of the numerous Twiss Family, for whom Macready was a trustee.

[3] George Bartley (1762–1858), comedian; stage manager at Covent Garden in 1829. How Mr. Bartley incurred these opprobious adjectives there is no indication. Probably his offence consisted in being more or less allied with Mr. Alfred Bunn. Macready commanded an opulence of invective, which he too often discharged on insufficient provocation and in calmer moments sincerely regretted.

theatres, but he is to be manager of one, and is therefore salaried to approve. Called on Mr. Kenneth about Paris and on Mr. Spence; on Mr. Bunn about Birmingham, Benefit, W.'s melodrama, Raymond, etc. Met Captain Polhill, to whom eighteen of the actors or employés have given a dinner! For what? "Oh, father Abraham! what these actors are!" Returned home—after paying my subscription to the Garrick Club, and expressing my opinion, perhaps as well kept to myself, on the ungentlemanly tone of the note. Saw a quarrel on my return between a negro and a carter.—Who can say the negro is the inferior animal?

May 5th.—Knowles sent me his play of *The Wife, a Tale of Mantua.* The weather is really delicious, it is a luxury to breathe the air, to inhale the fragrance of the flowers, and listen to the music of the birds, watching the graceful motion of the gently-waving boughs. As a contrast I read the newspaper—the parliamentary debates, the actions and speeches of Lord Althorp, Hobhouse, Peel,[1] Spring Rice,[2] etc. Oh, Nature, let me find relief and comfort from the painful contemplation of so much baseness in the wisdom and benevolence observable throughout thy works!

May 6th.—I came to town with my family, principally that Mr. Earle might see Catherine and Nina. My morning was occupied in executing commissions for home, until I parted from my darlings to see Mr. Bunn at the theatre; my conversation with him was not satisfactory—my Benefit will probably be sacrificed, and I cannot see my way into next season. My conversations with Cooper and Reynolds, on the subject of Covent Garden being managed by myself, leave me still in doubt. I remained in town to see the German opera of *Fidelio,* which, though short, is to an English auditor rather heavy. The general acting also disappointed me; it was opera-acting—the same unnatural gesticulation and redundant holding up of arms and beating of breasts. Madame Schröder-Devrient [3] is a splendid exception to the

---

[1] The great statesman; at that time Leader of the Opposition. Macready, as a rule, had little liking either for Whigs or Tories, but in later years he was ready to acknowledge Peel's high-minded and enlightened statesmanship.

[2] Thomas Spring Rice (1790–1866), then Secretary to the Treasury; afterwards Chancellor of the Exchequer; retired with a peerage as Lord Monteagle in 1839. A colourless Minister whose one notable measure was the introduction of Rowland Hill's penny postage scheme.

[3] Wilhelmina Schröder-Devrient, whom Richard Wagner had seen at Leipzig for the first time four years before. The opera on that occasion was also *Fidelio,* and it is interesting to compare his impressions with Macready's. "The Italian Company (Wagner writes in his *Life*) "arrived from Dresden and fascinated the Leipzig audience with their consummate

commonplace of the rest: it was as tender, animated, passionate and enthusiastic as acting in an opera could be—she quite abandoned herself to her feelings; she was admirable. Next to her came the chorus. I am fatigued, and not very well. Have looked into the *Quarterly Review* and some dull books from the Club. I feel called upon so far to revise the opinions I may seem to hold of my conduct this day as to censure largely and unqualifiedly my imprudence in babbling or gabbling of plans, which might have found a prosperous issue had I played my cards with' discretion; but the fact is I had no clear resolve in my head, and wanted rather to drive others to decision than to rush into action myself.

May 7th.—*La Sonnambula.* The opera was the very excrement of trash! My morning, which began betimes, was occupied in the business of settling the disorder of my chambers, and attending to business of a domestic kind. I made several calls, O'Hanlon, Price, Mr. Dow,[1] with whom I began an acquaintance, H. Smith,[2] Birch. Looked into *Quarterly;* find in it opinions on the old dramatists and the blind worship of them by the Cockney school coinciding with my own; am obliged to assent to the justice of their satire on Alfred Tennyson.[3] Is this the writer from whom I read extracts in the *Tatler*? Went to Drury Lane, relinquishing my visit to the House, to see Malibran[4]—what an artiste! Whether it be that excellence gains an

---

mastery of their art. Even I was almost carried away by the enthusiasm with which the town was overwhelmed into forgetting the boyish impressions which Signor Sassarti had stamped upon my mind, when another miracle—which also came from Dresden—suddenly gave a new direction to my artistic feelings, and exercised a decisive influence over my whole life. This consisted of a special performance given by Wilhelmina Schröder-Devrient, who at that time was at the zenith of her artistic career, young, beautiful and ardent, and whose like I have never again seen on the stage. She made her appearance in *Fidelio.* If I look back on my life as a whole, I can find no event that produced so profound an impression on me. Any one who can remember that wonderful woman at this period of her life must to some extent have experienced the almost Satanic ardour which the intensely human art of this incomparable actress poured into his veins."

[1] A special pleader of the Temple with whom Macready for a time became very intimate; eventually, however, they drifted apart, though Macready always entertained a kindly feeling for him and visited him in his last illness.

[2] One of Macready's oldest friends. He was actuary of the Eagle Insurance Company, and Macready constantly sought his advice on financial matters.

[3] Though only 24, Tennyson had already produced some of his most notable poems. He was, however, regarded with little favour by the critics, certain of whom treated him with hardly more ceremony than that accorded by the *Quarterly Review* to Keats. It was not till the mid-Fifties that he became an established favourite with the public, though even then *Maud* (published in 1855) made very few friends.

[4] Maria Felicia Malibran (1808–1836), then at the height of her fame.

MADAME MALIBRAN

From a lithograph

advantage in competition by producing the last effect, and thereby leaving its impression strongest, I do not know; but perhaps it is to this cause I should attribute the superiority, as it seemed, of Malibran to-night over what appeared to me perfection in Schröder yesterday. It perplexes me to decide between these two gifted creatures—Schröder-Devrient absolutely thrilled me, made me start, and some time after the agitation into which she threw me had not subsided; Malibran delighted me—I think I may say there was greater *variety* of excellence in her performance, and I fancy, though loth to let it escape me, lest it should not be strictly just, that there is rather more finish in Malibran. I could not prevent the thought, as I sat in the theatre, of how much vice, frivolity, idleness and folly went to make up the world of mind enclosed within those walls. It is not my thought or wish to " throw a stone " at frailty; but I feel the slang of the Press on the unimportance of private character to a performer to be as false in fact as it is disgusting in principle. All are so far honest or hypocritical as to render virtue homage by applauding it in a theatre; and what mind of common decency but must feel pain at listening to asseverations of purity, sentiments of delicacy, and solemn protestations of truth and fidelity, which Heaven is called to witness and record, from a wanton's lips? It is a profanation of what should be held in reverence to make virtue a mere toy for our amusement, as this utter indifference to character actually does.

May 8th.—Rose early to meet the business before me; acknowledged to Knowles his play of *The Wife.* In his inscription upon it he terms himself " my attached," etc.; he does the same to Reynolds, of whom he knows nothing! Busied through the morning in domestic commissions and duties. Harley [1] called by appointment to talk over the state of the profession. Cooper came in to excuse himself, on account of a new farce, from his Elstree engagement. We had much conversation on the subject of the theatre; the opinion seemed to be that it would be much better for the profession that Covent Garden should be opened by others than by the Drury Lane manager; it was agreed to wait the event of Mr. Bunn's negotiation.

May 10th.—Heard from O'Hanlon that Hobhouse had lost his election; conceived that he had brought the disgrace needlessly upon himself, by first tampering with the integrity of his character, and then finessing too grossly for its reparation.

---

[1] John Pritt Harley (1786–1858), chiefly noted for his impersonations of Shaksperian clowns.

May 11th.—A letter from Harley asked to see me at the theatre between one and two o'clock. Though satisfied of the little importance of his information, I decided on going, in order to keep my promise with him, and to convince him that in business I was not disposed to trifle. Letitia at first determined to go with me to Cartwright,[1] but yielded her resolve to the hope of recovery. Received *Æthelgiva* from Serle; called at Reynolds's, and heard no more news, except that the decisive answer to Mr. Bunn's offer for Covent Garden theatre was deferred beyond to-day. Called at Morgan's.

May 12th.—Rose with the intention of going to morning service, and of devoting the after-part of the day to writing and reading. Unluckily a very short time after breakfast we were surprised by the arrival of Mr. Gaspey and his daughter, who came to breakfast, and to read a farce to me. There was a good deal of smartness in the piece, but it seemed overlaid with puns. After luncheon this good-natured, good-hearted little fellow left us to wish we had many friends as warm and faithful as himself. He spoke of Jerdan's[2] habit of laying his friends under contribution and cautioned me; it was kind, but needless.

May 15th.—Saw Reynolds, who had no other news for me than that the two negotiators for the union of the theatres, Moore and Robins,[3] came to words in their conferences, and could not talk without quarrelling. Returned with Dr. Lardner, invalided. My conversation with Dr. Lardner after dinner was very interesting, whether on politics, religion or science, in all of which one gains new or clearer views of a subject by its discussion with him. The facts he related in astronomy were to me new and most interesting. I have certainly been more industrious to-day; on my journey I thought on Macbeth.

May 16th.—Dr. Lardner was unwell, much, I conjecture, from his want of caution. The weather is perfectly Italian, and the indolence of basking in it too seductive. Took down my Shakspeare, and looked at *Macbeth*, but did little more. Endeavoured to render any assistance

---

[1] Samuel Cartwright (1789–1864), originally an ivory turner; the fashionable dentist of his day; famous also for his *recherché* dinners, at which he entertained many of his eminent patients, thus atoning for the tortures of the chair with the pleasures of the table.

[2] William Jerdan (1782–1869), editor and subsequently proprietor of the *Literary Gazette*, one of the most notable journalists of his day; his Autobiography contains much interesting matter, political as well as literary. Macready was on friendly terms with him, though at times sorely tried by his borrowing proclivities.

[3] George Henry Robins (1778–1847), the renowned auctioneer; a proficient alike in puffery and repartee.

to my guest, who continued very unwell. Spent much of the day in the garden. Dr. Lardner got up to tea, and afforded us by his communications a most interesting evening. The facts regarding the nebulæ of stars, the suggestions on the dis- and re-appearance of stars, the distance from the nearest fixed star conveyed in the supposed opacity of the earth's orbit only being a speck of light seen from it, Herschel not visible to the naked eye, the direction of the comets from the sun, were new truths to me. Campbell's, Knowles' and Moore's characters were interesting in their successive reviews.

May 17*th*.—In a letter from Reynolds I heard of Bunn's lease of Covent Garden, and of Kean's death. The chance of the first circumstance had already caused me to think over the probable conduct of Mr. B—— and its consequences. I therefore gave little consideration to it. Kean's death scarcely awoke a passing thought; he has lived his own choice of life; even his very indecencies have found eulogists, as the worst parts of (often admirable) acting have had loud-throated admirers.

May 18*th*.—Went to town for the rehearsal at Covent Garden of *Macbeth*; and having called on Calcraft, and read a short eulogium on Kean, passed on to the theatre. Everything seemed strange to me, and the affectation, pretension, hypocrisy and falsehood of Mrs. Bartley [1] were almost beyond the endurance of good manners. She is, I think, one of the very worst and most offensive women I ever saw or heard of. I recovered my self-possession as the rehearsal proceeded. Heard an absurd story of Kean's will, ascribing his death to the Jewess who lived with him! Saw Messrs. Bunn and Bartley at Drury Lane; appointed Tuesday with Bunn to settle my benefit. Made arrangements providing against the necessity of attending Kean's funeral, which I have no wish to do, as I entertain no feeling of respect for his character. Delighted to return home from the vulgarity, heartlessness and quackery of London. Spent a very pleasant evening with Dr. Lardner, etc., on their return from St. Albans.

May 19*th*.—Read the newspapers and suffered myself to descend to the feelings of impatience and annoyance at the lavish and indiscriminate panegyrics heaped on the memory of Kean. *This is unworthy of*

[1] Sarah Bartley (1783-1850), actress; wife of George Bartley (see note p. 28), identified with Lady Townley in *The Provoked Husband*, and Teresa in Coleridge's *Remorse*, a part which she created. It is difficult to realize how such a catalogue of faults and offences could be crowded into a single rehearsal, but Macready was apparently determined to make up for his self-possession at the theatre by "letting off steam" at home.

33

me. If they are just, I am guilty of envy in repining at them; if they are undeserved, of what importance are they? I believe that part of the world which is allowed an influence over my profession is invidiously unjust to me; but have I not consolation and compensation in that dearer part of it that affords me so much comfort and happiness? Passed again a very agreeable evening with Dr. Lardner, from whose conversation I derived much information; particularly got some new views on the subject of Political Economy.

May 20th.—Came to town with Dr. Lardner after writing a few lines and walking round the garden. Made some calls of business on my way from the coach, and at chambers read in the *Times* the intention of making a display at Kean's funeral. Privacy would become his memory better. The reflections raised by such a style of funeral do neither credit to the dead nor living. I have felt impatience at the adulatory effusions of his admirers and friends. I rebuke myself for a pettiness of feeling unworthy of me. Give him all; it does not detract from my share of comfort nor vitiate my title to respect, where it has existence. Let me speak what good I can of him, and be silent where I cannot praise. Devoted the whole day to preparation for *Macbeth;* Mr. Dow called. I acted, on the whole, I think, well; in several places I may *finish* more—much more—giving freedom to my deportment and manly freshness to my tones in many places. The audience seemed to go with me. Mrs. Bartley is a most inferior person —she is gone, unregretted and unrespected. She has no claim whatever to the character of an actress; her style is as false as her heart or tongue. She is a most unfair person.

May 21st.—Found it necessary to arrange the business of the day before me, and after reading the paper, in which I vainly looked for some notice of myself, set forward. Called to ask the meaning of the newspaper announcement of myself at Kean's funeral—found it true, but no more known. Met Young,[1] or rather spoke to him when he would not have met me—and perhaps some shame at seeing me is not

---

[1] Charles Mayne Young (1777–1856), comedian; but also successful as Hamlet; one of the few Etonians that have made a name on the stage. Macready thus commemorates him on his death in 1856: "The news of Young's death yesterday depressed me more than those who had witnessed our contention for the prize of public favour could have conceived. I had a very sincere respect for him. No two men could have differed more in the character of their minds, in their tastes, pursuits and dispositions; but his prudence, his consistency in his own peculiar views, and the uniform respectability of his conduct engaged and held fast my esteem for him from the time that the excitable feelings of immediate rivalry had passed away. I am thankful that I had the opportunity of proving that."

34

unbecoming to me; asked his intention respecting Kean's funeral, but he has no more to fear; papers have done their worst; nothing can touch him further; he will not go. I am under the thrall of opinion, and must. Saw Mr. Bunn, as bad as my worst thoughts of him. Called on Miss E. Tree,[1] who seemed pleased to play for me; on Reynolds, who, not very amusing, mentioned Mr. Harris's opinion that the united theatres would answer. I cannot see it. The *Post* has a panegyric on Mrs. Bartley, who bellowed most cow-like, never once looking in my face, nor ever producing the shadow of a change in her own—she was quizzed in the sleeping scene enough to awaken her—so much for papers.

May 24th.—I was in earnest beginning business, after my walk round the garden and playing with my children, when Sir Jno. Marshall arrived to interrupt me. He lunched, gave us a very warm invitation from Lady M—— and self; related anecdotes of Thurtell's[2] brother, and the early occupants of Mr. King's house, fate of the daughters, etc.—left us about three o'clock. Birch and self went down to the water and rowed till nearly five, when Messrs. D—— and S—— arrived and came to us. In conversing with them after dinner I allowed myself MOST IMPRUDENTLY to criticize the knowledge and impartiality of the public Press. Why cannot I be silent on what, if my opinions are promulgated, I only aggravate? This impotent display of contempt or anger is most unwise. Never betray hostility until you have the power to crush, and then use it only to prove a better nature than that of your paltry antagonist.

May 25th.—Came early to town. Got my clothes from Wilkins, and found a note from Miss E. Tree, expressing her regret at not being allowed to act for me. Saw Bunn at the theatre, where I took places for Lady Marshall. Packed up my trunk and wrote to Sir J. M——, with orders; saw the Covent Garden manifesto, which Bunn blackguarded in good set terms and I did not quite see the aim of; but counselled him to disarm and gain over the strong—he mentioned his wish to engage me. On my way to Richmond[3] with Harley, Birch,

---

[1] Ellen Tree, afterwards Mrs. Charles Kean (1805–1880); a capable actress of secondary rank; she was closely associated with her husband's enterprises, and on his death retired from the stage.

[2] John Thurtell, executed for the murder of William Weare, which created an immense sensation at the time (1823). He was the son of a Mayor of Norwich, and having failed as a manufacturer had taken to prize-fighting and gambling. He had lost money to Weare whom he murdered at a spot in the neighbourhood of Macready's residence.

[3] To attend Edmund Kean's funeral.

and Spence, met Jones who promised to do M. Perez for my night. Passed several pedestrian mourners on the road, and some carriages, Mr. Ducrow's.[1] On alighting among a vulgar crowd saw Mrs. and Miss Faucit.[2] Ushered into the room where Kean's remains lay—poor creature! Lee hoped that Mr. Harley approved what he had done. In the drawing-room shook hands with young Kean, Stanfield,[3] Knowles. Clint[4] introduced me to Mr. Forster.[5] After some delay furnishing mourners, etc., we were summoned, Braham[6] and self first, as supporters; we crossed the green and paced the crowding streets amid the loud remarks and repetition of names of the multitude. Kean's coffin, placed before our pew, led me into very sad ruminations—contrasting his moments of burning energy with the mass of cold corruption fronting me. The church was crowded by curious and gay visitors, and was distressingly hot—his son and Mr. Lee were much affected; the anthem was beautiful but long. The procession returned to the house in its original order. I could make little observation on anything around me, being under such a surveillance. Braham invited me to dine with him at the "Star and Garter," but I was obliged to decline. I shook hands very warmly with young Kean, who thanked me; and, with Harley, went in search of the carriage, which met us on the Green and very rapidly took us to town.

[1] Andrew Ducrow (1793–1842); the famous equestrian and pantomimist.

[2] Helen Faucit, afterwards Lady Martin (1817–1898); the leading mid-Victorian actress; married in 1851 Mr. (afterwards Sir Theodore) Martin. She was at various times associated with Macready, both in London and in the provinces, as well as in Paris. Her name frequently occurs in the Diaries, and, in spite of occasional misunderstandings, she entertained the highest regard for him to the last (see note on William Farren, p. 23).

[3] Clarkson Stanfield, R.A. (1793–1867); at one time scene-painter at Drury Lane; afterwards landscape and marine painter. Executed much scenic work for Macready, with whom he was on intimate terms.

[4] George Clint (1770–1854); portrait-painter, especially in theatrical circles.

[5] John Forster (1812–1876); journalist and biographer; eventually a Lunacy Commissioner. This introduction inaugurated a friendship that, with some vicissitudes, was destined to become an extremely intimate one to the end of Macready's life. Forster, in fact, became his trusted counsellor and referee on almost every subject, both private and professional, and, on the whole, he undoubtedly proved a good and faithful friend. But his egotism and aggressiveness (he was well described by an aggrieved cabman as a "harbitrary gent.") were faults which Macready, of all men, was little disposed to tolerate, and the Diaries contain many characteristic descriptions of various temporary interruptions in their intimacy.

[6] John Braham (1774–1856) the amous tenor; father of Frances, Countess Waldegrave. His real name was Abraham, his father being a German Jew in Whitechapel, where Braham as a child used to sing from shop to shop. At one time his voice brought him in £14,000 a year, but disastrous speculations reduced him to poverty.

To Birmingham, May 26th.—I kissed my darling babes in the nursery, and taking leave of Letitia, also of my wife, I went to the Plough to wait for the "Crown Prince" coach. My travelling companions, on getting into the coach, did not offer me the prospect of a very pleasant day; but the perusal of the translation of Goethe's *Faust* employed and amused my mind the greater part of the journey. A literal translation must leave much of the spirit behind, and in following, as I suppose, many of the inversions of the original adds to its obscurity. In the simple passages of Margaret's description of her little sister's life and death, and in the last scene her wish to have her own infant in her grave beside her, for "no other creature would be near her," I was much affected. On approaching Birmingham I saw the terrible *affiches* of Mr. Ducrow's, which with other ill-boding circumstances prepared me for a bad week. On arriving I inquired for my old admiring friend, and could not at first catch the low muttering tones in which the servant told me she was dead! I was quite shocked. I had known her since I could remember anything. Death has been very busy this year. Mr. Cooper called, and sat a short time.

May 27th.—I attended rehearsal, and the whole fate of the engagement was visible to me: a wretched company, and a mere wandering manager, who ventures because he has nothing to lose. It is quite unfortunate that I came; but it must be endured, and it is always wise to make the best even of the worst. Wrote to Bunn and Palmer, for I am in a terrible dilemma, my trunks not having arrived, in consequence of which we must change the play from *Macbeth* to-morrow. I acted in parts pretty well and seemed to carry the audience—they were not a heavy load to bear in any way—with the interest of the play. The house was *very* bad, but I have no right to complain of Birmingham; I noted several things in my acting which will lead to the correction, I think, of a faulty principle. Mr. Reynolds, who is a great bore, called. I tried to read *Hamlet*, but did little with it.

May 28th.—Went to the rehearsal of *Hamlet*, and convinced myself that by due care and attention, which means a *great deal*, I might act the part very well. On returning to dinner I skimmed through some of the nonsense of *Candide*, and looked with all the attention "my care-tired thoughts" were capable of at *Hamlet*. My trunks arrived before I went to the theatre. I acted Hamlet, although with much to censure, yet with a spirit, and feeling of words and situations,

37

that I think I have never done before. The first act was the best—still at the exit of the Ghost in both scenes, and afterwards, polish and self-possession are requisite. In the second act almost general revision; third act the soliloquy wants a more entire abandonment to thought—more abstraction. Ophelia's scene wants finish, as does the advice to the players. The play scene was very good, and most of the closet scene, but in parts my voice is apt to rise, and I become rather too vehement. Latter part wants smoothness. End of the play was good. Energy! Energy! Energy!

May 29th.—Letters from Mr. Bunn, deciding, by Madame Vestris's [1] performance of Estifania, my play, and from Catherine with bad accounts of my dear children. I could not write except to Bunn; the rehearsal was so late, and the play was so bad and so imperfect, that I was quite incapacitated from doing myself justice. I lost my temper. Shame!

May 30th.—Wrote very briefly to my wife, and also to my sister; went again to the torment of a rehearsal; tormenting in the anticipation it gives me of the night to come. At night the repetition of the same miserable exhibition behind the curtain, and equally poor assemblage before; I tried to keep my temper, but—— The thought of my intemperance quite distresses me. I cannot excuse myself, nor extenuate my folly—or rather madness! It is dreadful. On coming home I resolved, after some hesitation and disposition to relinquish it, to go on with Leon, and do my best in good earnest.

May 31st.—A letter from Bunn, in which he now mentions his uncertainty of getting Taglioni for my benefit, which before he taught me to rely on as sure! Wrote to him, but corrected my letter, and sent one solely on business. Went to rehearsal; made a trifling present to the little boy, who, in Albert [2] last night, so disconcerted and enraged me. *I deserved a severer penalty.* Walked with Mr. Cooper, discoursing on the chances of next season. Worn down with fatigue, slept the whole afternoon. Acted as well as I could under the circumstances of spirits, body quite oppressed with weariness—of course not

---

[1] Lucia Elizabeth Vestris, *née* Bartolozzi (1797–1856); being a granddaughter of the eminent engraver. Married first Armand Vestris, the dancer, at the age of 16; secondly, in 1835, Charles James Mathews, the actor. Except in certain comic parts a mediocre actress, but highly successful as a stage singer. Without any pretensions to beauty, she was singularly fascinating, and made numerous conquests, not always with credit to her reputation.

[2] In *William Tell.*

very well; the line " fled to England? " I discovered capable of more prominent effect. My dresser informed me of artizans, accustomed to receive 30s. and 40s. per week, rolling wheelbarrows of sand a given distance at 1d. a load, and only, if married, allowed to roll 18 per day. What a puzzle is this world! Is it not a *duty* to relieve such a distressed population by means of emigration or employment? The game of politics is a base one, I believe.

June 1st.—The newspaper this morning only confirmed my opinion of the base trade of those wretches who call themselves Whigs and Tories, and strive to engage the passions of men in a struggle of names, diverting their attention from their own best interests merely to get place and pension for themselves. I am sick of politics. I feel comfortable in the thought that my heavy work is over, though I am sorely pained and over-weighed by what I have done. After rehearsal, during which I finished the packing of my two trunks, I walked with Mr. Cooper to some of the manufactories, where I made some small purchases; but checked myself in the act of purchasing ornaments and trinkets for my wife, thinking that it is better to leave her the means of buying them, than perhaps the necessity of seeking means by selling them. A Mr. Perrin, an actor from a strolling company, applied to me. I refused him where I would not have refused an industrious tradesman. Let it not be thought that there is no value in recording maxims or precepts. I was deterred this day from sending a letter by glancing on my own quotation of " Conduct is Fate." This evening Mr. Cooper told me of Mr. Bunn's manifesto on the " maximum " of salary. After acting very ill, and being cut up in one scene and cut out of my death in another, I went home to read it. I was, as usual, irritated, disgusted and disquieted by Mr. Bunn's precious paper; I could not regain the tranquillity of mind necessary to reflection, and went to bed to compose myself. I tossed and turned in a feverish state for two or three hours. This is not the way to act wisely.

June 3rd.—Mr. Cooper called, and gave me an ill prospect of to-night, but—" tu ne cede malis." I sent him in pursuit of the manager to secure his money, of which, at least of my own, I do not feel quite secure. I only got into my dining-room about three hours before play time. I played only tolerably. I want to consider every line, and test each by a natural standard. The house was very bad, such as I never saw before to my benefit in Birmingham. I only made gratuities to my dresser and the doorkeeper; all else were so bad.

Mr. Fraser paid me punctually. I declined a purchase made, because the tradesman rose on the price agreed to.

London, June 4th.—At five o'clock left Birmingham in the " Red Rover," with a guard dressed for the part, in a red coat and red hat. Much of the way I slept, and was averse to produce my book of *Rule a Wife* on account of the fellow-passengers of my journey.   On arriving I found by a note from Bunn that Vestris declined Estifania, and I had a play to seek. After a few moments' talk *School for Scandal* was decided on, myself as Charles. Some time had elapsed before I had read the part, and saw my unfitness for it, I therefore took my name down and retained my former part of Joseph. This is not such a bill as the tragedian of the theatre should put out, and I feel it a sort of suicide, but look at the company, look at the time, and then what is to be decided on for Monday. I saw Malibran to-night in a state of ridiculous confusion, owing to a tumble she had had in a dance. She would have done better to have laughed.

June 5th.—Took up my pen to contradict a paragraph (" authorized ") stating my declaration of furthering the objects of the present lessee of the theatres. Think it better to reserve the *contradiction of the falsehood* until I can do it with more effect. Mr. Jones's [1] refusal of my request that he would act Sir B. Backbite gave me reason to congratulate myself on my prudence in not announcing him, as I had hastily thought of doing. Mr. J—— gave me several reasons for refusing what he was pledged to in a better character—Copper Captain. One good one would have been worth a thousand such. Harley made himself especially ridiculous in affecting a repugnance to the same, his own, part. What fools are actors!! Came home, found my dear family well. Delighted to look around me.

June 6th.—My cold kept me a prisoner in my bed the whole of the morning. I often wish for that energy with which I see some men under the pressure of heavy bodily ailment still continue the active exercise of their minds. No man is justified before experiment has been made in saying that he *cannot* do anything ; and I ought to have made proof of my inability to get through business and make use of time before I put forward this plea for inaction. Received a letter from Mrs. Gibbs,[2] accompanied by one from those jacks-in-office, the Covent Garden Committee at the Olympic, forbidding her (dogs in

---

[1] Presumably Richard Jones (1779–1851) ; a clever comedian, chiefly identified with "eccentric" parts.   Known as " Gentleman Jones."

[2] Formerly Susanna Graddon (1804–1854); actress and vocalist ; of no special reputation.

a manger) to play on my night. It was not of sufficient consequence
to disturb or harry myself about, and therefore I have deferred any
notice of it till to-morrow. Felt a strange disinclination to application
of any kind, and went to bed very early.

June 7th.—My day began earlier than yesterday, but still I felt
oppressed by slothfulness and inertness. I enclosed Mrs. Gibbs's
letters to Bunn, with one to Mrs. Orger,[1] requesting her, in my
dilemma, to resume on that occasion her part of Mrs. Candour. Went
again at an early hour to bed.

June 8th.—Obliged, through the forgetfulness of the carrier, who
omitted to bring my letters, to go to London; took Catherine and
Nina in the carriage with me; delighted with my little darling child's
remarks and playfulness. Found notes in chambers from Mr. Grainger,
importuning me about his play.

June 9th.—Went to church with Catherine. Mr. Chalk's baby
was to be christened; the entire duty was performed by a clergyman
whose vulgar appearance and pronunciation set me on conjecturing
who our curate's friend could be. After some reflection I thought
it probable he might be the son of a St. Albans tradesman, a boyish
companion of Mr. Chalk, who had subsequently been a sizar at college.
He, however, showed too little accuracy for such an education. He
gave out the wrong psalms, read the wrong lessons, made frequent
blunders, said "per*em*ptory "—" spir*i*tual," etc., and preached such
a sermon in such a manner as to offer the strongest arguments against
the genuineness of the Church of England's Christianity that a dissenter could wish. The reverend teacher proved to be Lord R——.
Shame on him, and the institution that tolerates his companionship.

London, June 10th.—Benefit. Amount of House with all the
foreign aid—£408 3s. 6d. Profit £116. Our hay began to be cut
under the hottest sun of the season; and I left it, with Catherine and
Letitia, to attend my *Benefit* in Town. Found several affairs connected with it demanding my attention. Arranged what was necessary for the night both at chambers and at the theatre. Mr. Dow
called. The Duchess of St. Albans[2] sent two guineas for two tickets,
which I did not think worth while otherwise to notice than by sending

---

[1] Mary Ann Orger, *née* Ivers (1788–1849) ; connected for many years with Drury Lane ;
was most successful in farcical pieces.

[2] Formerly Harriet Mellon (1777–1837) ; an actress of some attractiveness but moderate
capacity ; married in 1815 Thomas Coutts the banker ; and, secondly, the ninth Duke of
St. Albans. Her first husband bequeathed her an enormous fortune. A good-hearted

the messenger to the box office. The day was overpoweringly hot. I had some fuss about my dress, hat, etc. Acted as well as I could. Farren was very flat and coarse. Vestris pointless and vulgar. Miss Phillips [1] looked all that the author would have imagined of the beauty and modesty of Maria. Mr. Bunn mentioned to me the base conduct of Mr. Farren, who, it seems, in aggravation of his impertinence in advertising my name for his benefit without my leave, contrived to have me paragraphed in the newspapers. Qn. What shall I do with the contemptible blackguard? I am almost ashamed to be angry with such a reptile. In order to avoid the Cav: Servent: of the prima donnas, I hurried to Catherine's private box; I fancied Malibran took umbrage at it, but was perhaps mistaken. She sang the "Deep Sea" in quite a poetical manner. She is a creature of genius. And what is Taglioni? A realization of some young poet's dream whose amorous fancy offered to his slumbers beside some stream or fountain the nymph whose divine being consecrated the natural beauty of the scene. She presents to me an idea of the soul of the Peri tenanting a woman's form. She looks wholly *la Bayadère*—and her graceful pensiveness is only equalled by Flaxman's *Pandora*. Our hired carriage was not to be found, and we were obliged to send for our own from Lincoln's Inn Fields. It was two o'clock—a beautiful twilight of summer morning—when we reached Elstree. The moon was in beauty in the eastern sky—the birds singing around us. Quite indisposed to bed, we retired at three o'clock.

June 11th.—My indisposition, or feeling of inability to rise this morning was at least equal to my reluctance to go to bed. The wind was high, even to tempest, occasionally; the hay cut yesterday looked very well, but the rain has come to place all our hopes in jeopardy. Walked in the fields and garden—is not this better than to have been one of the rout whose carriages and servants filled Portland Place last night? Thought and talked upon Mr. Bunn's declaration that his manifesto "*did not apply to me.*" Looked over my accounts. All of us weary and languid and sleepy after yesterday's gaiety. The straps of our carriage were stolen! The tempest to-day has been almost alarming; the weariness and oppression among us all extreme. This

---

vulgar woman, who, notwithstanding her lavish entertainments and high rank, was not generally accepted in society.

[1] Louisa Anne Phillips, a pleasing young actress who had made some success as Julia and as the original Ida Stratenheim in *Werner*. She joined Macready's company at Covent Garden in 1839.

morning I thought how comfortable my wife, children, house and comforts ought to make me. I shall think still further on that vile thing, Mr. Farren.

June 12th.—Answered Farren's application in the negative. Vining's [1] doubtfully. "Yes" to old Angelo. [2] Thanks to Honble. Misses Hill. Came to town, leaving my hay to the mercy of the elements, for the rehearsal and performance of the *Exile* this evening, the closing night of the season. I took no notice of Mr. Farren, the chances are that every one would say : "How could you notice such as ass?" In a conversation with Mr. Bunn, he seemed anxious to accede to all my proposals; how these preliminaries will end is a separate question. A delightful rebuke to the self-importance of myself and Madame Vestris on Monday night! I imagined, as did Catherine and Letitia, that Malibran was angry because I did not lead her on. It appears there was a dispute for precedence between her and Vestris, who, on Malibran's slipping on before her, declared she would not sing at all —about which the audience was quite indifferent, never noticing the omission.

June 14th.—Thomas Dibdin [3] sent me a letter, *too humble to be pleasant*, of acknowledgment for my subscription to his work. Dined with H. Smith, and in consequence of Mr. Knowles not sending him orders (*proh pudor !*—the man to whom he has owed the bread he ate), went with him to the House of Commons. Was much amused. Gisburne and, I think, Aglionby spoke well. E. Ruthven cut a most ludicrous figure. Littleton [4] spoke with confidence, but not like a Secretary for Ireland! Altogether it is a great farce. How long will the country consent to be amused with it?

June 15th.—Received Mr. Bunn's written proposals; if this were my first transaction with the man, I should set him down as a shuffling fellow. As it is, he only confirms my confirmed opinion of him. Saw Farren at the theatre, who wanted to be very friendly, and was evidently very uneasy; Cooper, who seemed very anxious that I should not break

---

[1] James Vining (1795–1870); an actor of no particular note; his son, George J. Vining, was a well-known Victorian actor, connected at one time with the Princess's theatre.

[2] Henry Angelo (1760–1839); the famous fencing-master.

[3] Thomas John Dibdin (1771–1841); dramatist, song-writer and actor; wrote nearly 2,000 songs and about 200 operas and plays.

[4] Edward John Littleton, afterwards first Lord Hatherton (1791–1863). As J. Walhouse, he was a school-friend of Macready at Rugby. His unauthorized communications with O'Connell in 1834 led to his resignation of the Irish Secretaryship. His wife, a natural daughter of Lord Wellesley, was one of the most beautiful women of that day.

off with Bunn, and P. Farren, who seemed to have an itching to bring me some overture from Morris.   Arrived at home to see the men carting the last load of hay.   All well.

June 17th.—Came up to London in company with a very gentlemanly, and a very vulgar man, both of whom I often meet; in waiting at Brewster's [1] the *Age* was put into my hand, in which I read some low abuse of myself, probably suggested by Mr. Bunn; it did not long annoy me.   At my chambers after rehearsal I read Wolsey, and endeavoured to satisfy myself in my answer to Mr. Bunn's proposal. I could not do it.   My performance of Wolsey was, on the whole, the best I have ever given of the part; there is care and concentration of feeling and energy upon some of the striking points particularly needed; but in the general portraiture there was more freedom, a more natural and yet more earnest delivery, a less stern and ascetic demeanour and appearance than I ever before gave to it; above all I was *in possession of myself*, and paused with meaning, and therefore with confidence. The applause was great at my entrance and final exit.   I gave my usual gratuities to the servants.   Received notes of thanks from Messrs. Gurney and Hussey about their plays, which are rejected. [2]   Talfourd [3] came to my room, highly pleased with the performance, and after going to the Temple, returned to sup with me.

June 18th.—Began the day in bed by reflecting on my last night's performance, and cogitating on the best mode of proceeding with Mr. Bunn.   In calling at Drury Lane for my account, saw Serle, with whom I had much talk on the memorial for a third theatre, which he had just signed.   His arguments on the reduction of rent were quite just, but did not seem to me to justify the measure they are pursuing. Appointed a meeting with Dunn for to-morrow.   Mr. Bunn not in the theatre.   Wrote to Mason and to Walker on the subject of the latter's visit.   Went to the Temple, and embarked with Dow in a fast sailing-gig on a very intricate navigation—arrived at Camberwell.   Made myself quite comfortable and at home in my new friend Dow's house. Spent a quiet, pleasant day—the good of human nature is always agreeable.

[1] Macready's hairdresser and wigmaker.

[2] Macready was always studiously considerate and polite to playwrights, however unknown and insignificant, though at times he was sorely tried by them.

[3] Thomas Noon Talfourd (1795–1854); lawyer and man of letters, attaining considerable reputation in both capacities.   Serjeant-at-Law in 1833.   Judge in 1849.   Died suddenly while charging the Grand Jury at Stafford.   Author of *Ion*, produced by Macready with marked success.

44

June 19th.—After a disturbed night in my strange bed I was shown something of the locale and live stock of my kind host, and driven by him to town, with the promise of a pair of laying fowls. Arrived tired and lanquid! Set out shopping with Letty, who was waiting for me. Returning, I first sought vainly for Mr. Dunn and then successfully for Mr. Bunn. I found him installed at C. G. He seemed confused when told I did not understand his note. He talked much, but "not to the purpose." I conceded the point of benefit, but remained inflexible on payment while in town, *play or no play.* After a long and interrupted conference he agreed to all—£30 per week for 200 consecutive nights at D. L.—the option resting with me to play or not at C. G. Saw *The Wife;* disappointed in E. Tree; much to praise, but much exception to make; her voice, sometimes unpleasant, not always distinct, is subject to abrupt, artificial transition; but she has the *matériel* of the best actress on the stage. E. Tree has seen Miss Kemble [1] to her own disadvantage. Ward was very bad. Bennett but middling. Abbott bad. C. Kean, with the promise of something good, often came near to pleasing me much. Knowles—was *Knowles;* raw, energetic, harsh, but with mind and purpose, badly and bluntly expressed, that gave interest to his performance; but he is no artist, nor, in my opinion, can he ever be such.

June 21st.—The day was beautiful, the garden and lawn were delightful to me, and the presence of my wife and children made me feel that there are moments and hours of bliss even here. "What is the world to us, Its pomps, its pleasures, and its nonsense all?" Contrasting the sky above me, "the glory of the grass, the splendour of the flower," with the recollection of the gilt-bedaubed guards, the plumed women, the tumult of spectators, I could not help feeling the difference of the joys that belong to a town and country life. Catherine and I took down the dogs to the reservoir, found the boat injured by some blackguard boys from Stanmore, but enjoyed a delightful row upon the water.

June 22nd.—Went to town in the carriage, called on Lord Lyttleton [2]

---

[1] Frances Anne Kemble, afterwards Mrs. Butler (1809–1893); daughter of Charles Kemble, generally known as "Fanny Kemble"; a gifted but somewhat unequal actress; also wrote dramas and poems. She and her sister Adelaide (Mrs. Sartoris) were much sought after in cultured society.

[2] William Henry, third Baron Lyttelton of the second creation (1782–1837); Whig politician and eloquent speaker. Macready's animus against the aristocracy, which constantly asserts itself throughout the Diaries, appears in this instance to have rather sought for a cause of complaint.

45

at Lord Spencer's. Shown into the small library, where were many editions of the classics. Lord L—— came down, apologizing for his delay; I asked of him the favour of presenting W. Birch at court previous to his going abroad; after answering his various inquiries respecting the condition, residence, etc., of W. B., he assented, and engaged to accompany him on third July. Lord L—— is really a good-natured man; *but* although he apologized for delaying me, invited me to Hagley, and consented to introduce my kinsman, yet from his allowing me, who had been his guest more than once, to be shown into a *lower* room, from which he, after some conversation, asked me to walk into the drawing-room—from the business that he appeared to make of the affair, and some etceteras observable *even in him*, one of the *very best* of "his order," I am inclined to think aristocratic titles incompatible with that lowliness of heart which man, to be just to his fellow-creatures and himself, must preserve.

June 27th.—Received a letter from Mr. Cooper calling on me to play to-morrow night at D. L. This is another instance of the roguery of Captain P——, alias Mr. Bunn; also one from Miss Strickland,[1] wishing to have assistance in reading Shakspeare. Continued to make up arrears. Walked to Edgeware, and took Doug's coach to Duke Street. Met at dinner with Mason a Mr. Gretton, and a Dr. Elwin and son; the doctor seemed to me a person of more pretension than actual title to respect—coxcombical and superficial. Mason and I had some conversation on religion, when left alone, which much interested me. The more I hear or see of sects, *i. e.* the endeavour of individuals to flatter their own opinions by gaining assent to them among men, instead of attempting to reconcile them to God—the more I see the prudence of placing morality before religion.

June 28th.—My first visit to-day was to the British Gallery, where I had the pleasure of looking at some of the masterpieces of Sir Joshua, his own portrait in spectacles (equal to any in my opinion), the marvellous expression of the *Ugolino, Dido, Iphigenia, Infant Samuel, Fortune-teller*, Dr. Johnson, Rodney, Keppel, Dyer, Nelly O'Brien, Chancellor Lifford, and several other pictures, gave me great pleasure. My judgment would point out few of Lawrence's, besides the heads of young Napoleon and himself, Lady Blessington and Kemble. West [2] I cannot like; to great painters he stands among the mediocre;

---

[1] Agnes Strickland (1796–1874); the well-known historian.

[2] Benjamin West, R.A. (1738–1820); much patronized by George III. Best known by the picture of the Death of Wolfe, now in the National Collection.

his *Mentor* and *Telemachus* pleased me as much as any of his selection.

June 29th.—At the Exhibition this morning (my first business) saw a person who appeared to know me; I neglected to ascertain whether he did or did not—a neglect that was not courteous, and might make an enemy of one who was inclined friendlily. Bad! Much to please me. Wilkie's *Confessional*, Collins's *Stray Kitten*, Landseer's *Jack-in-office*, Mulready's *First Voyage*, all good. Etty, Callcott, Turner and others have beautiful specimens of the high state of English art. The newspapers instruct us farther in the indecorous and indecent conduct of the House of Commons, disgusting us with the ignorant impatience they exhibit as reasoners upon a nation's welfare. Pleased with the Water-colour Exhibition, the most equal collection among the London galleries. Suffolk Street shows great improvement, and gives promise of much more. The *Panorama of Antwerp* interested me as the representation of a siege; but Niagara is a failure. There is no distance, vastness, effect of colour—nothing. I almost felt indignant at the artist's presumption. It confirms my opinion of the impossibility to paint or describe this sublimest phenomenon of nature. Met Knowles at the Garrick Club; his son is not going on well; do I notice this from Rochefoucauld's motive of satisfaction at our acquaintance's mishaps? I fear, if I search, I shall find it so. 'Tis unworthy a thinking man. I paid Knowles some comparative compliments on his acting; he pleased himself with the unascertained quantity of praise contained in my words. Met Vining, with whom I settled the terms of a Brighton engagement. Called at the theatre, and am to see Dunn next week. Dined with Talfourd, where Catherine and Letty met me. We spent a very cheerful day; in the evening Leigh Hunt [1] came in, whom I was curious to see, and gratified in meeting. Our conversation was chiefly theatrical; we seemed to part mutually good friends. I returned with Catherine and Letitia in the carriage to Elstree.

July 2nd.—I read Coleridge's *Christabel*, which, though rich in the dress of poetical language, and stirring the heart with the thrill of expectation, yet leaves little impression on the mind. Read some passages from Milton aloud as a double exercise; also four acts of Serle's tragedy of *Æthelgiva*, which is beneath every other attempt he has made. Dunstan in love is too patent an improbability for the historical reader.

---

[1] James Henry Leigh Hunt (1784–1859); the well-known author and poet of the "Cockney" school.

July 3rd.—Began my day, after a very disturbed night, with the discovery of a sore throat and lounging about the garden with my children. Received letters from Talfourd declining invitation, and George. Wrote to Gaspey. Read the last act of *Æthelgiva*, and wrote to Serle upon it, declaring my opinion of its feebleness; wrote to Mr. Grainger for instructions on his play. Looked through a guide to Padua for materials for a *Keepsake* article : am apprehensive that I shall not be able to satisfy myself with it; looked into Duppa's [1] *Travels*, and *Landscape Annual*, for the same purpose. Walked in the garden, and watched the bees.

July 6th.—Began to read in bed Voltaire's *Adelaide du Guesclin.* Wrote a letter in reply to Mr. Bunn, which I am now doubtful of sending. The less a man writes the better. The old Irish saying has much truth—" When the devil has a spite against a man, he sticks a pen in his hand.'' Wrote to Fanny Twiss a brief answer to her selfish letter, in which she declines not only seeing, but even inquiring about a school for her nephew Arthur. I noticed in it the rude and ungentlemanly conduct of her brother Horace. [2]

July 7th.—In the newspaper was much struck with the grand appropriation of Lord Grey's expression of "standing by his order,'' which Mr. Brotherton [3] made in the debate on the Factory Bill, declaring himself to have been employed in the factories till sixteen—pitying the children, and resolving to "stand by his order.''

July 8th.—Called at Covent Garden theatre on Bunn—saw Mr. Cooper, who goes to Liverpool, where therefore I shall not go this season. Bunn agreed to every clause I mentioned of my engagement, exemption from fine, etc. He told me much of Farren's and Knowles's absurdity. I promised to send him *Antony and Cleopatra* and *Maid's Tragedy.*

July 9th.—Began with alacrity to make the most of what would be allowed me of the day. In reading the *Examiner* was struck with a quotation from Bentham ; speaking of the people he says : " They have not *that pride which keeps men from getting better.*'' I attentively

---

[1] Richard Duppa (1770–1831); artist and miscellaneous writer.

[2] Horace Twiss (1787–1849) ; lawyer, politician and journalist, K.C., M.P. ; held minor offices in the Administrations of Lord Liverpool and the Duke of Wellington. Nephew of Mrs. Siddons and John and Charles Kemble. A good though somewhat dogmatic talker, and one of the recognized wits of the day. His dinners to celebrities are frequently mentioned in contemporary Diaries and Reminiscences.

[3] Joseph Brotherton, M.P. (1783–1857) ; manufacturer and social reformer.

48

revised and corrected two acts of the *Bridal*,[1] and finished the perusal of a tragedy called the *Countess of Provence*, sent to me yesterday by a Mr. Sulivan, whom I had known some eight or nine years ago in London. There is much merit in it, and I should recommend its trial, but am not confident of its success. How events seem to arise in this world to deride our foresight and expedients!

July 10th.—My mind feels fatigued after suffering the society of men whose tastes and ideas differ so widely from my own as those of my guests. I was relieved by the departure of Mr. Gaspey—a man whose kindliness of heart I really esteem, and whose other good qualities have my respect, but whose manners and conversation shock me. Wrote a laudatory note to Mr. Sulivan on his play. Resumed the revision and correction of the *Bridal*, which occupied me, as far as I was employed, during the remainder of the day. Enjoyed the beauty of the day, and the sight and society of my dear wife and children. I feel that there is a want of completeness in the *Bridal*, which shakes my confidence in its success. Many of the scenes are excellent, but there is not that singleness of interest throughout so necessary to great triumphs.

July 12th.—After looking at the workmen about the house and in the field, resumed my study of Lear, the difficulty of which does not yet diminish before my attempts; studied in practice parts of Hamlet and Antony in the drawing-room. I ought to have begun this as the season closed, while my mind was active in thinking upon different characters—from disuse and relaxation labour becomes harder and the faculties duller. To stop is to lose ground—most men in this world have to pull against a stream; at some period of their lives, all— I must work hard; in an interval of study I was playing with my little Willie, and the sight of him gave a spur to my work.

July 17th.—Saw Reynolds, as usual humorous, shrewd and indecent. After further business, snatched an uncomfortable dinner at the Garrick Club. Went to Drury Lane to see Paganini[2]; foolishly allowed myself to be angry at the door-keeper's obstinacy, refusing me passage. Dignity is only truly displayed in coolness. Passion is the snare of reason. Saw Paganini; his power over his instrument is surprising; the tones he draws from it might be thought those of the sweetest flageolet and hautboy, and sometimes of the human voice; the expression he gives to a common air is quite charming. His playing

---

[1] Adapted by Macready, Knowles adding three scenes, from Beaumont and Fletcher's *Maid's Tragedy*, produced at Dublin in the following year.

[2] Nicolo Paganini (1784–1840). He was then visiting England for the first time.

of *Patrick's Day* was the sweetest piece of instrumental music I ever heard, but he is a quack.

July 18th.—Got a seat to Edgware, and on my way read the debate in the Lords on the Irish Church Bill. It is irritating, as a degradation to human nature, to see the weal of millions subjected to the nod of the imbecile wretches who inherit the office of law-givers in that House. Who would not, that could, be the Samson to crush them at one effort once and for ever? Delighted to feel myself at home once more, to look upon my wife and children. After looking over the premises, and settling some affairs, I resumed my reading and practice of Lear, in which I begin to think I feel myself advancing. I saw in Paganini last night a striking illustration of Locke's arguments on the effect of perseverance, and I will try to force myself to work.

July 20th.—Much better to-day; received a letter from Reynolds on the subject of my two alterations of *Antony and Cleopatra* and *Maid's Tragedy.* Our tastes in the construction of plays so differ, that it is not a surprise to me to learn his disapproval of them—nor is it in the smallest degree an annoyance; he looks at them with an eye to their chance of profit, and in that regard his judgment is probably correct.

July 21st.—Was delighted to hear in bed the little improvised song of my Nina, mentioning her fault of yesterday, and promising to love her little brother. God bless the darling! After dinner had an argument with Mr. Dow, in which I took exception to the unqualified eulogy he passed on Buchanan's character. This is an unamiable part to take, and likely to bring in question my sense of justice. I fear it originates in an impatience of others' praise, which annoys me to believe existent in myself. I fear I am envious; and although I could not be led thereby to any offence against justice, yet the vice is wearing, degrading, and disturbing to the mind. I must endeavour to eradicate it.

July 22nd.—Heard news of the Theatre Bill [1] to be passed—the conceited ignorant fools! Was glad of a motive to get me earlier than usual out of bed; saw my wife, sister and party of visitors off to town; like Dow very much; he is downright and hearty. Heard the children their lessons. Gave my morning to the study of Lear, and practised a little of Othello. When I look at my children I think how little I

---

[1] Presumably Bulwer's Bill, which was afterwards thrown out of the House of Lords. In principle it was against the "monopoly" theatres, and should therefore have met with Macready's approval, but as he was contemplating management at Covent Garden (one of those theatres), the Bill would f course have seriously affected his interests.

have deserved the blessings that are heaped upon me—I *wish* to deserve them. In looking again to-night at the comforts around me, house, garden, country, etc., I cannot repress my gratitude for the bounty that out of nothing has given me so much.

July 23rd.—Received letter from Serle, written on the fly-sheet of a circular from the Society of Dramatic Authors; how easy it is to legislate for one side of a question, and how weak and ineffectual is such legislation! This Bill in my opinion will be as impotent in its operation as it is unjust and partial in principle. Serle seems to have lost his head in the success of these his schemes; he is a most amiable man and a very pretty poet, but Acts of Parliament will neither make him a more powerful writer nor more skilful actor; his profit therefore will be much what it now is, or would have been. Gave several hours to Lear. Wrote to Reynolds, maintaining my opinion on *Antony and Cleopatra.*

July 24th.—Last night I finished Voltaire's Play of *Adelaide du Guesclin*, which has little ingenuity of plot, no extraordinary power or beauty of language, and not much felicity in its situations. The fulsome compliments to the Bourbons have made more impression on my memory than any other passages. On rising this morning I looked after some matters in the fields and about the premises, and afterwards took up my usual study of Lear and Hamlet's soliloquy. Finished the perusal of *Sardanapalus*, which for the fourth time, I think, I have examined on its capabilities for undergoing adaptation. It *might have been* an acting play, but it is too monotonous, passionless and devoid of action, I fear, to satisfy an English audience. My whole evening has been spent in revolving the possibility of turning it to a representable form, and of considering the effect of his other plays. I reluctantly conclude upon abandoning the hope of them. We purchased a new cow to-day, a very interesting event in our farmyard.

July 25th.—Last night I began in bed the *Mariamne* of Voltaire. Suffered myself to lose two hours this morning, which I cannot now afford. After my customary walk in the garden, sat down to the consideration of the mad scenes of *Lear;* I have much to do with it yet; was not so persevering to-day as I should have been. Went with my servant, Green, to the reservoir to clean my boat; had much trouble in getting to her; afterwards rowed for a short time with Catherine and Letitia; the day was most beautiful; if I can enjoy the beauty of this country and the comforts of this residence, putting by a property for my dear children, I shall have reason to be most grateful to Almighty God.   After walking about the premises I turned over the leaves of Massinger's plays, in the faint hope of finding some convertible material, " but I find none, sir." Must make more use of my time, as my classical reading is fading from me.

July 26th.—Called on Reynolds ; from thence to Jonathan Birch's, where I saw Mrs. Walter, and invited her here. Jonathan met me in Russell Square, and, taking me back, detained me an hour with letters and relations about William. On leaving me he presented me with a finger ; this is either unintentional ill-breeding or gross impertinence. I shall return the compliment—— No ; another's rudeness or insolence is no warrant for my adoption of the same offensive practices. Dined with Reynolds ; heard that Lord Castlereagh,[1] on being asked by Bunn to oppose Bulwer's theatrical Bill, asked : " Bulwer ! oh ! he's a low fellow, is he not ? "

July 27th.—Read *Lear*, with scarcely any practice (the weather was so hot) for two hours ; made the alteration, judiciously suggested by Reynolds, in *Antony and Cleopatra*, and wrote a note enclosing it to him ; wrote to Dr. Woodroffe and to George.

July 28th.—I have begun more seriously this month to apply to the study of my profession, impelled by the necessity which the present state of the drama creates. I do not feel that I have the talent to recall attention to an art from which amusement cannot be drawn but by an exertion of the intellect. The age is too indolent in part, and in part too highly cultivated. But while I see the desperate condition to which, at this late period of my life, my profession is reduced, I am not thereby inclined to let my spirits sink under the disheartening prospect. To do my best is still my duty to myself and to my children, and *I will do it.* I will contend while there is ground to stand on— even with neglect, the bitterest antagonist, and I will try to merit honours, if I cannot obtain them. I have resumed my classics, to keep myself prepared for the education of my boy.

July 31st.—Wrote to make an appointment with Bunn, walked in the garden and gave orders to the workmen. Resumed the counsel of Artabanus to Xerxes in Herodotus, the simplicity of whose style

---

[1] Eldest son of the third Marquis of Londonderry and nephew of the statesman, the second Marquis. He dabbled in music and was a conspicuous admirer of Grisi, which involved him in a duel with her first husband, M. de Melcy. His contemptuous comments on Bulwer proved him to be a true son of his father, probably the most preposterously arrogant peer of the day. In point of fact, Bulwer was of quite as good family as Lord Castlereagh, whose grandfather but little more than forty years before was an Irish Commoner who owed nearly every one of his many steps in the peerage to his son's political influence.

delights me; returned to Cicero, *De Oratore*, which I take up chiefly as an exercise. Gave three hours of attentive practice and reading to Lear—touching on Antony, Hamlet and Othello. I fancy, and hope I do not deceive myself, that I perceive improvement in my manner. Walked with Lydia and dear Catherine to Lechmere Heath, and afterwards to the reservoir. Who ought to be contented, if I, with so much to enjoy, and so great a spirit of enjoyment, cannot make myself so? How much have I to be grateful for!

August 1st.—Before setting off for town to meet Mr. Bunn on business I read some lines of Herodotus, and tried to think of Lear as we drove along. Found, on reaching my chambers, that there had been some omission of duty in the care of my note to Mr. B——, and that I could not expect to see him. Gave Brewster directions about Lear's coiffure; and, waiting for Bunn's note, read a little of the *De Officiis*. From my chambers went to the Garrick Club, met Fladgate,[1] who showed me Bulwer's retaliation on Mr. Westmacott,[2] which immediately recalled to me some excellent remarks on anger, which I found in Cicero this morning; met Abbott, J. H. Reynolds,[3] Barham[4]; looked in Hamilton Smith's[5] *Costume* for a dress for Lear; found what I wished. Called on Reynolds, met Bunn and Dunn, who had been beating up for Lords' votes against the Theatres' Bill.

August 3rd.—After my garden walk (in which I felt the comfort of my health, and the pleasure of feeling " the chartered wind to be free to blow against me ") I betook myself to Herodotus, whose manner and matter delight me in their simplicity and wisdom. Read a little Homer, and pursued my study of Cicero, who tells us how very rare in his day were even tolerable actors; it seems that the scarcity has been of all time.

August 4th.—In looking steadfastly at the comforts I possess, I am convicted of equal folly and ingratitude when occasionally I permit reflections on particular advantages possessed by others or on the imagined slights cast upon myself, to assume the appearance of discontent, or to cast a shade across the sunshine which the bounty of the Almighty has shed upon my heart. I am led to this observation by some extracts from Bulwer's book, which I read in the *Spectator* this

---

[1] An eminent solicitor much interested in theatrical matters.

[2] The editor of the *Age* (see note, p. 20).

[3] John Hamilton Reynolds (1796–1852); poet and friend of Keats.

[4] The Revd. Richard Harris Barham (1788–1845); author of *The Ingoldsby Legends*.

[5] Colonel Hamilton Smith, an authority on historical costumes. Macready frequently enlisted his aid and entertained a great regard for him.

morning. Letters from Best on business, and Reynolds announcing the defeat of the Dramatic Performances Bill.[1]

August 6th.—Received a notification this day from Reynolds of Bunn's intention to act my version of *Antony and Cleopatra;* heard also of Bunn's hostile correspondence with Bulwer, and reflected on Bulwer's recommendation of kicking as a cure for calumny. I look calmly and dispassionately on the irrationality of such reprisals. The character for manly spirit is not wanted where the virtue exists; it is like the loaded gun, if touched in the right place you will soon be made sensible of the danger you incur. Where you can disprove a falsehood, do it as placidly as if in the cause of abstract truth—your end is obtained. Where an insult is offered you by an unworthy person, your best triumph is in an exhibition of utter indifference; the sting is harmless, if the flesh it wounds is not in an inflammatory state.[2] My professional practice of Antony and Lear was very loose and unsatisfactory. Worked in garden till dinner : walked there afterwards. Read some pages of Cicero—read *Examiner.* Read the character of Antony through : it is not very powerful.

August 12th.—I finished the chapter of Thucydides' account of the ancient Greeks, and read in Homer the battle array of the Myrmidons, and Achilles' exhortation, which is abrupt and stirring. Practised Lear, which I feel to be a benefit. After tea, went over the words of Lear, Catherine holding the book, whereby I discovered how much I have yet to think of in the part, and how much to practise of that already thought upon, to arrive at any moderate degree of confidence; remained thinking on the part afterwards. Must give more attention still, and with it all, I fear, I never can produce a finished performance.[3]

London, August 15th.—Arranged my stage clothes, and packed up what was ready for my tour. Saw J. Palmer, and gave orders for beard and Lear's dress. Met Jerdan, and agreed to stay and dine

---

[1] In 1832 Bulwer had, in the House of Commons, attacked the monopolies of the patent theatres, Drury Lane and Covent Garden. On his motion a Select Committee was appointed to investigate the subject, and the Committee reported that the monopolies of Drury Lane and Covent Garden had "neither preserved the dignity of the drama," nor "been of direct advantage to the monopolists themselves." It considered that the number of theatres should be determined by the demand for theatrical performances, and that the Lord Chamberlain should cease to administer a system of monopoly. Bulwer introduced a Bill to give effect to the Committee's report, but it was thrown out by the House of Lords in 1833 and again in 1834.

[2] Excellent precepts, which unfortunately Macready failed to put into practice on a memorable occasion a little later in his career.

[3] Lear was considered in after years to be on the whole Macready's greatest performance.

54

with him at the Garrick and go to the Victoria. This day I wrote a short statement of my wish as to the disposal of my property after my death, which will serve for my will until I can have a better made out. Dined with Jerdan and Captain Williams, whom I invited on Wednesday next to Elstree. Went with them to the Victoria theatre —a very pretty *salle*, and well appointed—but Warde's [1] acting was the most elaborate defiance of nature and taste I ever witnessed. At the Victoria theatre I saw Mr. Keeley [2] and Miss Garrick : why did I not speak to them? it was not pride, but a false shame which is always taken for it, and does the exhibitor equal injury.

August 18th.—Have received answers to my invitations from Dunn, Cooper and Planché ; [3] the two first not coming, the latter doubtful.

August 20th.—Went to the drawing-room, resolute to give the whole morning—or what remained of it—to Lear. Practised the first act, and, desponding and dissatisfied, was told Mr. Best had arrived with bed for the west room. This settled my study, and with Catherine and Lydia I went into the fields to shoot with the bow. Mr. Best finished the room, and we returned to approve of his work. After dinner turned over the *Elegant Extracts*, and was much gratified by a song of Shirley's on death ; it is worth remembering. Read the last act of *Antony and Cleopatra*, and Hazlitt's [4] observations on that play and *Lear*. What conceited trash that man has thought to pass upon the public, and how willingly many of them received the counterfeit as sterling.

Bristol, August 24th.—It is nearly twenty years since, with a heart palpitating between hope and fear, I first entered Bath. What changes since ! What revolutions in the world around me, and the world within me ! Is life worth possessing? I, who have so many blessings in it, cannot decide the question at once. On reaching Bristol, was

---

[1] James Prescott Warde (1792–1840) ; his real name was Prescott ; first appeared at Bath ; was not a success in London, and died in poverty.

[2] Robert Keeley (1793–1869), the well-known comedian ; was associated with Macready at Drury Lane in 1841–1842.

[3] James Robinson Planché (1796–1880) ; dramatist, theatrical manager, and authority on heraldry. His career was a varied one, as he was at different times manager of Vauxhall Gardens and of the Adelphi theatre, ending as Somerset Herald and member of missions for the investiture of foreign sovereigns with the Garter. He was a prolific writer for the London theatres, but his plays have made no permanent reputation.

[4] William Hazlitt (1778–1830) ; journalist and critic, especially on the drama. He had certainly plenty of vanity, but though many of his criticisms provoked a good deal of dissent, he can hardly be accused of writing "trash." His pen, however, could be exceedingly rancorous, and when dramatic critic to the *Morning Chronicle* he may possibly have given Macready just cause for resentment, but he was on the whole an able and accomplished writer.

55

most civilly received by Mrs. Niblett; read newspapers, and went to bed.

Swansea, August 25th.—Rose in good time, and went to pay my fare at the Bush; remarkably civil people. Wrote to my dearest Catherine. After leaving the White Lion inn, found myself too soon for the mail, and walked about the streets; interested by looking into a sort of crypt underneath one of the churches. Started with a full coach, and proceeded in "dumb amazement all" to Passage. The view of the Severn, and the splendid prospects presented by the road through Wales, made me wish for the presence of my dear Catherine. Colonel Cameron of the 79th was one of our passengers. The ice was broke, and conversation became general from Passage. In the course of the day he mentioned the behaviour of Lord Hill,[1] first promising to present his petition for his father's regiment and then refusing, on which he retired. There is much upon the road to interest and delight a traveller. On arriving at Swansea I had to stand the brunt of much curiosity. At length I was set free, and went to take tea with Mr. and Mrs. Woulds, who have very sweet children.

August 26th.—Mr. Woulds[2] called before I had left my bedroom; until the hour of rehearsal I employed myself in making up my accounts. Rehearsed Iago with a very loud and bold Othello. Afterwards walked by the road to the shore and along the beach to my lodgings with Mr. Woulds. After dinner read over Iago and slept—laid out my clothes and wrote to my dear wife. Acted Iago pretty well to an indifferent house—drank rather more sherry than was good for me, and in consequence returned to my lodgings fevered, and incapable of business or reflection. I fell on the stage, from treading on a purse, as I rushed off in the assassination scene—it was, however, before I had drunk wine. Mr. Woulds showed me a letter from Knowles, which, from its hilarious condescension, seemed to me the strongest evidence I have yet seen of the idea he entertains of himself. Could not help wishing for the quiet of a country life, as I passed a very neat villa here, that I might dedicate my remaining years to the culture of my own mind and the careful education of my children's.

---

[1] Rowland Hill, first Viscount Hill (1772-1842); Commander-in-Chief of the Army. Made his reputation in the Peninsula. As Commander-in-Chief he was opposed to innovation and reform; accordingly many of the old abuses still flourished under his administration, creating much dissatisfaction among officers who had only their merits to look to for advancement.

[2] Manager of the Swansea theatre.

August 27th.—Mr. Woulds again surprised me in my bedroom, not much refreshed from a feverish night. Continued my arrears of accounting until ten, when I went to my first rehearsal of *Lear*, with which I was much dissatisfied : I am not yet at ease in the character. I have much labour yet to bestow upon it before I can hope to make it such a representation as I am ambitious of. Spent five hours in rehearsing, and left the theatre jaded and worn out. Lay down after dinner, and with pain in my limbs, and "between sleep and wake," made myself perfect in the last scene of *Lear*. A poor player called Dunn, whom I remember in a dirty old coat as D. Dashall at Wexford calling *rouleaux* "*roorloors*," sent in a petition to me to buy some fishing-flies from him. Acted particularly well William Tell, with collectedness, energy and truth ; the audience felt it. I spoke in my own manly voice, and took time to discriminate. I was much pleased. Received letters from Calcraft and from dear Catherine. Learnt from the last Dr. Dibdin's call at Elm P., which gratified me very much ; but am not satisfied with her state of health. What would life be to me under the load of regret that I should bear to my grave if I were to lose that dear woman? Went to bed very much fatigued.

August 28th.—Rose very reluctantly to attend an early rehearsal of *Hamlet;* I am better to-day, but feel my labour heavy on me. Wrote an answer to Calcraft's letter, and went to rehearsal, at which I paid much attention to my business. Took the opportunity of writing to my dear Catherine, chiefly on the subject of her health, about which I am very anxious. Talked with Woulds about the Bristol theatre ; if let on reasonable terms it might be a fair speculation, at least for one year. Went to his lodgings to hear his little girls play and sing, which they do very charmingly. Heard much of Malibran's extravagances while visiting at Loder's ; what a wonderful creature she is! Found cards of Dr. Howel and Mr. Thomas, the port-reeve, on my return home. Acted Hamlet very unsatisfactorily ; having rehearsed it very well, I anticipated a good performance, but I did not begin *well*, and Horatio quite threw me off my balance. I did the best I could, but I had not my audience in my grasp. Returning home, I sat down on the loose stones to gaze at the moon and listen to the silence, recalling scenes of bitter anguish endured under the same bright, clear, and tranquil light.

August 29th.—Endeavoured to make the most of the day by beginning to pack up my clothes before rehearsal. At the rehearsal of *Lear* I found myself very deficient, undecided, uncollected ; in short,

57

unprepared for the attempt.   After rehearsal took a walk of two miles and more to return the port-reeve's call—the way along the hills about Swansea afforded beautiful views of the bay.   Reposed, and tried to think of Lear, during the afternoon, but vainly ; my thoughts gain an evil mastery over me—a great misfortune, or a great crime ; *the latter.*   Acted Lear ; how ?   I scarcely know.   Certainly not well—not so well as I rehearsed it ; crude, fictitious voice, no point ; in short, a failure !   To succeed in it I must strain every nerve of thought, or triumph is hopeless.   Woulds called and paid me ; not a very profitable engagement, but I am seldom discontented.   Letter from dearest Catherine ; thank God, she is better.   Packed up the remainder of my things.   Paid servants of the theatre.

Gloucester, August 30th.—As I walked along the street to the coach office this morning a little before four, I perceived clearly my want of directness, reality, and truth in Lear.   Will not give it up.   My failure last night, like Peter's overthrow at Narva, may be a step to final success.

Birmingham, August 31st.—Balanced my wakefulness of the previous night by my sleep last night.   A crowd passed along the street, but my curiosity did not induce me to mingle in it.   I afterwards learned it was eager to see two ignorant creatures (a young man, whose angry feelings were excited by bad cider, or short measure, and violent expulsion, consequent upon his dissatisfaction with it—and a passionate woman) executed for arson.   A cavalry regiment, 8th, passed along the street.   Is not a man an ass or a monkey in mind for condescending to put on a fool's jacket, and sell his time and opinions, at least the power of uttering them, for the return of soldier's pay and rations ?   When will the soul of man walk abroad in its own majesty ?

Harrogate, September 2nd.—Shall I ever be able to obtain a perfect control of my thoughts ?   And, until I do so, of what use are my purposes and aspirations ?   This morning I called on McGill in reply to his letter, but he was from home.   Walked to Harrogate, thinking of Lear, and saw Benn at the Granby ; [1] he gave me no assistance in furthering my wish to dispose of the property, but promised his rent.   Went along the beautiful wood on the river's side to the Dropping Well, which is both beautiful and curious ; found some specimens of petrifaction ; continued my walk along the opposite bank (and the walk is so varied and pleasing it needs no object beyond itself) to the cave

[1] A hotel in which Macready had rather incautiously invested.

58

where Eugene Aram and Houseman deposited the bones of Dan Clarke. It had been a Hermitage, but nearly choked up with earth; it is now cleared away, and exhibits in its regular floors and steps its original purpose. Called on Mr. Powell, absent, and enjoyed the lovely and extensive view through the dingle and over the distant country from the castle grounds. Called again on Mr. Powell (again was gratified with the splendid view from the castle), and deputed him to advertise and try to find a purchaser for the Granby. Mr. Gill called, and I gave him my name to oppose the public-house licence opposite the Granby. Read the newspaper and *Eugene Aram*. Have been more interested this evening with the very ingenious and staggering defence of Eugene Aram than by all the external beauty of the woods and waters, the overhanging cliffs and distant hills, the bright green slopes and shadowy outlines that have held me in rapturous gaze this morning. I am even now almost inclined to doubt his guilt; my difficulty is in reconciling the cold-blooded meanness of the transaction with his clearly discriminating perception of right and wrong, his habits, his wants, and his pursuits. I would rather have hung Houseman and Terry—but perhaps this, like many anomalies in the physical world, is placed before us to teach us the impotency of our own reasoning. God and His works are inscrutable.

September 3rd.—My self-broken rest, or rather entire absence of it last night, made me only wake to-day each time to sleep again. I have observed nothing, and have been able to think on little. Lear has been the only subject on which my mind has been employed with any advantage, and I think my reflection on my late experiment has furnished me with the key to the truth of the character. My obstinate impatience of imposition cost me my breakfast this morning at Sheffield, and instead of the filthy smoking-room into which we were shown, I went in search of my razors, which Barber had done for me and is to send to town. My companions were nothings, and one a little below that harmless character inflated by ideal importance into something disagreeable. I really slept through the entire day, which was rainy and dull. I was asked at Sheffield, after some impertinence and much incivility, if I would go outside to " accommodate "; this modest request, instead of either not answering or slightly refusing, I so far forgot myself as to rudely repel, which was forgetting my own pretension to the character of a gentleman, and which I regard as highly censurable. At Birmingham I read an extract from Grattan's reminiscences of Kean, which offended my stomach; but am I capable of

59

judging that man? If others see his merits with the magnifying-glass of the telescope, perhaps I turn it to examine them!

Elstree, September 4th.—At intervals of sleep or conversation read various *Essays* of Bacon; they made me think, and, as they always do, gratified me extremely. That on envy led me to question and condemn myself for the occasional " discontentment " in which I sometimes indulge, which I can find no reason to call by any other name than envy. It is as unjust to my condition in life as it is mean and debasing in itself. I never suffer it to have a place in my mind, when perceived, and I pray to God I may be able to eradicate it. Reached home, and had the comfort of finding my family well, for which I truly thank God. Listened to all the news, and noted down my accounts.

Brighton, September 7th.—Set off with Catherine, Nina and Hales to London. Our journey offered little to remark upon; we were rather inconvenienced by the heat and dust; my little Nina was a very good child, and I felt the pleasure at my heart of looking upon such dear treasures as the wife and child beside me. The country about Cuckfield is very beautiful. We drove, unluckily, to the Clarence Hotel, which is now become, from a private hotel, a commercial and coach house. Glad to escape from it. W—— and myself went in search of lodgings, which through the kindness of a house-agent, who knew me, we found after some perambulation. My dislike to Brighton was mitigated by the clean lodgings into which we got. I took a room for Wallace over the way.

September 8th.—Walked out to post office and round the Steyne as far as Kemp Town in company with Wallace; met Mr. Broadwood; saw Mr. C——, a man to make men think—selfish, sensual, obdurate, vindictive to the last and vilest degree, injuring any one in his way to wound the object of his hate! And this man is extolled by the Bar and Press for his amiable and honourable character! He sold up poor old Boaden for inability to pay his rent. In the evening read some of Wallace's History, which I thought, with some exception, good. Passed the evening in conversation, not very amusing, but affording one further insight into the vanity of human nature, in showing how we colour to ourselves the motives of our conduct. Am already wearied with Brighton, a place to which my aversion increases with my experience of its monotony.

September 9th.—After a little writing, went to rehearsal, where I received my luggage and settled the business of the week. Discovered that I had been announced by mistake for the previous Monday, and that the play of *Macbeth* had been acted with an apology for a substitute, owing to an error of Mr. Vining's. Rehearsed tolerably well, and afterwards took a warm bath. Received an invitation to Worthing from Mr. Stanley, the manager, which I answered doubtfully. After dinner I lay down from fatigue, and endeavoured ineffectually to recover my spirits, while Catherine, Nina and Wallace went out to drive about the cliff. Acted Macbeth to a very fair house, but indifferently; there was a want of self-possession in the performance that caused an exuberance of physical effort which never can have a proper effect when perceptible to an audience. There were precipitation and stress throughout, which often cost me the applause I ought to have gained; my best attempt was the "to-morrow and to-morrow." Was very much fatigued and went beaten to bed.

September 10th.—The rehearsal of to-day gave little hope of our passing muster at night; no one perfect, and every one indifferent even where the words were spoken. Endeavoured to rehearse naturally and gain my self-possession; abandoned the idea of acting Lear here from the confused manner in which it must be done. Scarcely able to conceal my disgust at the conceit of a very bad actor, called Haynes. Lay down in the afternoon, while Catherine, Nina and Wallace drove about the cliff. Met them on my way to the theatre, but shrank from a parley, owing to the manner in which W—— tried to stop the coachman. Acted Werner, for the most part very well; although the characters were imperfect and ill acted, the play was received with interest and enthusiasm. I was master of myself, and felt what I was doing, and how to do it. Mr. Stanley came from Worthing, and settled an engagement with me for Saturday next. He brought me a very kind message from Dr. Wooll,[1] inviting me to his house. Came home in a fly, and thought much upon Sir H. B. Dudley's [2] objection to my acting, that I "was too lavish *of physical effort.*" He was right.

September 11th.—At rehearsal bore in mind Sir H. B. D.'s criticism, and endeavoured to act from the mind direct, and not lash myself

---

[1] The Rev. John Wooll, D.D. (1767–1833); Headmaster of Rugby for over twenty years. Macready was under him for a short time before he left; he gives an interesting account of him in his *Reminiscences.*

[2] Presumably Sir Henry Bate Dudley, Bart. (1745–1824); clergyman, journalist, and newspaper editor. Nicknamed the "Fighting Parson." Edited the *Morning Post,* and originated the *Morning Herald.* Having been imprisoned for libel and practised simony, he eventually settled down as prebendary of Ely. His baronetcy was the reward of "delicate services" rendered to the Regent. He assumed the name of Dudley, his rightful surname being Bate.

into excitement by physical exertion. Wished to act well, and to bear in mind the principle inculcated in Sir H. B.'s objection. Proceeded with tolerable success to the third act, but, owing to the inattention of the Lucius, my scene at the camp was utterly destroyed, and I incapable of recovering my self-possession through the night. I must not omit to notice the temper I displayed on the occasion, which calls up my bitter regret, as it merits the heaviest censure. What would I not do, or give, to cure myself of this unjustifiable, dangerous, and unhappy disposition? Regret is no expiation of a vice that injures others and degrades myself.

September 12th.—At rehearsal I again took the same precaution as yesterday, and hoped to have given a fresh and earnest representation of Hamlet this evening. Returning from the theatre, I called at the agency office to show all the sense I could of the attention I had received there. On the parade met Liston,[1] looking pretty well, but older and much graver—the flexibility of that humorous visage seems to stiffen under the chill of age. Wrote a letter of acknowledgment to Dr. Wooll. Lay down, while Catherine, etc., took their daily drive. Procured her a private box at the theatre; was anxious to play well, but felt myself ineffective, and was told by her of my hurry and want of deliberate method. In comparing my performances with my rehearsals, when I frequently speak and act with an abandonment and a reality that surprises me, I feel the great advantage which Kean, Miss O'Neill, and Mrs. Siddons enjoyed in passing their earliest years upon the stage, and thereby obtaining a power of identification only to be so acquired.

September 13th.—Finding scarcely any one at the rehearsal, I went into my dressing-room, and began the packing of my clothes. I might have done this without an angry comment or sarcasm. Took a warm bath, and walked on the chain pier, where I met Mrs. Liston, who accosted me, and chatted for some time. Going home, I met and returned with Catherine and Nina, whom we accompanied in her little goat-carriage; again met Mrs. Liston, and was too proud of introducing my little girl to her. Saw a steam-carriage pass and repass us. Catherine made some purchases. Acted Werner pretty well, but not as on Tuesday night. The audience were cold and very difficult to excite. Gave an explanation, as some atonement, to Lucius, with whom I had been so angry on Wednesday. Made

---

[1] John Liston (1776–1846), the famous comedian; began life as a schoolmaster; retired from the stage in 1837.

largesses to the servants. Settled with manager, and received his compliments.

Worthing, September 14th.—After settling all my accounts, and waiting some time for Wallace, we set off for Worthing. Most journeys are interesting to me, if merely from the change of object. On this road there is the western end of Brighton, the church of Shoreham, the Duke of Norfolk's suspension bridge, and "the sea, the sea," to keep attention awake. The last time I travelled on this road my feelings and my situation were as wretched as man's could well be. How grateful ought I not to be for the blessed contrast which this day affords! We reached a very pleasant hotel at Worthing, on the beach, and from rehearsal, which offered me a doubtful prospect, I called on Dr. Wooll. Poor Dr. Wooll! "Heu! quantum mutatus!" I dressed as well as I could without dresser, and acted as well as I could, earnestly wishing to please my poor old master. Much I did well—in the betrothment of Virginia the thought of my own beloved wife and child flashed across me, and I spoke from my soul—the tears came from my heart.

September 15th.—I saw in the *Globe* an announcement of my name for Prospero in the *Tempest* on the opening night of D. L. theatre. I felt very indignant at such an opening part, which Mr. Bunn knows very well I except to. I settled my bill, and set off on a very pleasant road towards London, through Horsham, Dorking and Leatherhead. At Kingston we lunched, and turned off through Twickenham, Isleworth, and Ealing, crossed the Uxbridge and Harrow roads, and reached Elstree by the Bushey road. Was soured and annoyed (without any due cause) by the occurrence of the morning, and suffered myself to break into passion upon the slightest provocation, or, to speak truly, without any provocation at all. Spoke in an overbearing and impetuous manner to Wallace, who endured my insolence with most friendly forbearance. How bitterly I reproach myself! On my arrival at home found my dear boy and sister quite well, for which, as for His other mercies, I thank God.

September 16th.—Wallace returned to London; our manners and habits of thought and action grow so diversely, that it is not to be wondered at if friendships cool. Was vexed at the loss of my bloodhound bitch Luath, but amused with Letty's Irish handbill—"Deaf, and answers occasionally to the name of Luath." Went over the garden, etc. Considered Mr. Bunn's letter, which I thought rude and imperious; returned the part of Prospero, as not being yet engaged

63

in the theatre. Wrote to Pritchard, inviting him here to-morrow. Made arrangements for the current fortnight—which occupied in canvassing them much time. Wrote to Mr. Kenneth about Richmond, but on a change of plan held back the letter. Have felt very languid and ailing through the day, rheumatic and cold. Much vexed by having to deal with such an unprincipled person as this Mr. Bunn, but hope I have acted rightly by him. Read some of Voltaire's *Candide*.

September 17th.—News was brought me in my dressing-room of Luath's return, having been brought back by the men-servants. Mr. Pritchard arrived to dinner. He informed me of his discharge from Edinburgh and his engagement at Dublin. I also learnt from him the confirmation of what I had long suspected, an envious dislike on the part of the manager at Edinburgh—Murray—to me. It is no discredit to me.

September 18th.—Was met at rising by a letter, in an altered tone, from Bunn; resolved on going to town. Met Letitia in chambers, and after looking over papers went to Mr. Bunn's appointment at Drury Lane; he was absent, and after some delay I crossed to Covent Garden. He "could not understand" me, nor "I him." He was ready to agree to everything in my "Algerine" engagement, as he called it; but when we came to the stipulation for "collateral security," he demurred, and, reference to the motive becoming necessary, I was obliged to ask Dunn to withdraw. I then observed upon the debt of £200 due to me on my Dublin engagement, and that we did not meet on equal footing; he talked and evaded, said "my father had also been unfortunate," and much that had no relation to the case, and ultimately I altered my security to a stipulation that "upon infringement I should be free to leave the theatre," and so agreed on the engagement. Afterwards walked out with Letitia pricing barouches. Looked at some books while waiting for Billing's coach, and returned together to Elstree, bringing with me the *Yeoman's Daughter*, which Serle very kindly sent me. Talked over the day's events and read *Prospero*.

September 19th.—Began the morning with reading the dull, ungrammatical version of *Prospero* by Dryden and Reynolds—oh, the genius! Walked in the garden and yard, and spent the whole of the day in altering and writing out copies of my engagement, an accompanying letter, making part of the agreement, with a letter to Mr. Bunn, intended only to put on record, *litera scripta*, the position in which we stand towards each other. Mr. Tomlins called, and offered

ALFRED BUNN

From a lithograph

me £35 for my largest rick, and left me requesting I would not part with it for a pound more. I read Serle's *petit* drama in the evening and was very much pleased with its humour, character and pathos; the keeping of the piece is excellent. Before I went to bed I read *Prospero*, and as long as my eyes would keep open to it, in bed too. I am indolent, and my mind is in an unsettled state. I have no good augury, in my feelings, of the engagement I have made. Mr. B—— is destitute alike of honour and common honesty, and my trust is in Providence only.

September 21st.—Was led, by paying the week's charge, to a consideration of the cost of maintaining this house, which, at its present rate, is far more than I can afford, and more than I *will* afford. The subject would not depart from my thoughts the whole day; the reflection that I might leave my beloved wife and children with bare support quite distressed me. I spoke to Catherine and my sister upon it.

London, September 25th.—Went to rehearsal of the *Tempest*, and, to my astonishment, no less than that of the acting-manager and prompter to see me, found there was none. This is an omen to draw prediction from. Went to the Garrick Club; read the papers, and was directed to the *Age*, where I read, evidently on the dictation of Bunn, some abuse of myself—a good beginning! Saw Bartley there, who observed that Westmacott[1] was always in his room, and that he did not yet know the Covent Garden opening play! Returned to chambers, and wrote to Letty, invitations to Wallace and F. Reynolds. On my way to Bricklayers' Arms overtook Price, who told me Talfourd had bought in £1500, 3 per cents., since Xmas. *Non equidem invideo*—but it is hard that I should be the subject of envy. Returned by a flying van to dinner, and passed a pleasant afternoon, playing at whist.

September 30th.—Went by Billings's coach, outside with Dr. Lardner, to town; on our way he made me acquainted with the French and Prussian systems of education, of which I was wholly ignorant; they are admirable—the beginning with natural history is excellently conceived to awaken interest and exercise the memory in an agreeable manner. In London, after executing several domestic commissions, and calling at my banker's, I went to the rehearsal of the *Tempest* at Drury Lane. Here I found that the opening was postponed to Saturday, and received fresh evidence of the ignorance and utter

---

[1] The editor of the *Age*.

incompetency of Bunn in his treatment of poor King, a new actor from Dublin. The prospect of the theatrical season scarcely presents a hope of its continuance, but fortune is oft pleased to baffle judgment and calculation.

October 1st.—After dinner I received a parcel, containing a note and the part of Ford from Cooper; I was quite angry at this seeming succession of bad parts, and felt really exasperated. I wrote an angry note through Cooper, but had the sense to destroy it, and sent another to say I had never done it. Afterwards I read it, and did not dislike it.

October 2nd.—Walked in the garden; and sent, by Crown Prince, D'Aguilar's *Fiesco* and Sulivan's *Countess of Provence* to Bunn, with strong recommendation. Began to read Prospero : looked through some parts of Bulwer's *England*, etc. Dressed and walked to Dr. Dibdin's. The party consisted of Dr. Fitton, Mr. Newcome, Jenkins, Phillimore, two Howarths. The day was not disagreeable, and to me amusing in giving me the power of estimating the value of that society which has set itself so much above me. I owe them no resentment. I expected from Dr. D.'s language to meet only a gentleman's party, and was astonished as well as hurt in going in to coffee to see the room half filled with women—Phillimores, Haworths, Boltons, Jerkins, and unknown etcs. This slight on my dearest relations was inexcusable either in regard to my feelings or my position in this neighbourhood. He detained me to talk to Miss Haworth, and I " marched out by moonlight wearily."

October 3rd.—The thought occurs to me as I begin this day, dejected but grateful to God for the undeserved blessings I enjoy, " what is ever gained by resentment? " What benefit do we meet from exasperating men? We sink ourselves to the level of those who have injured us; and we justify the fate that oppresses us. These reflections arose as I ruminated on the strange behaviour of Dr. Dibdin yesterday, and its effect upon my wife and sister. I was detained in bed by a very bad headache, and on rising walked with Catherine round the garden. The chief occupation of the day has been to perfect myself in Prospero, which has no charm or recompense to allure me. I am more indolent than I wish to be; my pursuit is so distasteful to me. I read the lives of Blake and Sir Francis Drake by Johnson, very much praised (I think, over-praised) by Dr. Dibdin. Received a note from Dr. Dibdin, extremely free and cordial in its tone, which therefore I had much rather he had not sent, as it will

66

tax my art of contrivance to answer it without betraying some symptom of my real feeling.

October 5th.—To-day being the opening of Drury Lane theatre, I went to town by Billings, and, executing some domestic commissions previously, attended the rehearsal of the *Tempest* at half-past eleven. There was nothing to notice but its tedium, and the offer made me of a night's performance at Richmond, which I declined on the double reason of interference with my attention to business and anticipation of a longer and more lucrative engagement. Received two letters about new plays. Dined on a chop at the Garrick Club (really a blackguard place), where I saw G. Robins, Winston, T. P. Cooke, Raymond and Collier [1]—the two last are worthy of better society. Mr. King, the débutant of Monday next, came to request my advice as to his best course under the fearful responsibility forced on him by Bunn. As he thought he could get through it with some effort, I recommended him to set to work manfully: though I fear he miscalculates his powers. Was obliged to force the locks of my trunks for my dress of Prospero, acted the part unequally, but maintained myself in the only great passage retained in the characterless, stupid old proses of commonplace which the acted piece calls Prospero. The house was good, and the play went off well.

October 6th.—After a night that only afforded me two hours' sleep, I rose to catch the Crown Prince, and walked above four miles before it overtook me. The guard informed me that Knowles was one of the passengers on the day the coach was detained 2½ hours at Elstree by the breaking of the axle tree, and with another passenger took a chaise on after waiting 1¾ hours at this place. Am I to wonder that he did not call to inquire after my family? After the benefits he has received from me, I think I am justified in classing it with other evidences of unthankful conduct noticed in him. Found all well (L. D.) at home; wrote two civil notes to authors (G. Pattison and Phillips) who had applied to me. Enjoyed the mild beauty of the day in the garden; went to afternoon service; a gentleman here, who has not called on me, seemed anxious to get an opportunity of speaking, which I manœuvred to avoid. Looked into Bulwer's book, which has this advantage, at least, that it may lead others to right conclusions,

[1] Probably John Payne Collier (1789–1883), Shaksperean critic and essayist; forged marginal corrections in first and second folios of Shakspeare, on the basis of which he brought out annotated editions and a new text. His forgeries were afterwards exposed. He also forged ballads, and falsified various documents and public records.

even where he is wrong. Thought on my arrogance to men when I was but a boy, and lament the want of proper discipline in my youth. Read through the part of Ford.

October 8th.—Did not feel well at rehearsal, but tried to take pains. Went to dine at the Garrick Club, where I saw Savory and Raymond, who described Miss Placide as a "Rule Britannia kind of woman." Was very glad to hear that Mr. King had made so favourable an impression in Rollo. Acted partially well, my voice was not in complete management. Some things I did well—particularly last act. I was very low-spirited to-day, and in my view of my profession I see little ground for hope; the Press will not accept me as a *first actor*, and my genius and talent, whatever it may be, has not its free scope with a public whom I fear (on account of my family), and have little occasion to love for all they have done for me.

October 9th.—To my great surprise saw the cards of Messrs. Haworth, and learnt that the ladies of the family, with Dr. Dibdin, had paid a morning visit yesterday. It became a question, in the event of their proceeding further in the acquaintance by sending invitations, what course was best to adopt, as the choice was in our own power. For the mere convenience of making up parties to meet our London friends I would willingly overlook their slighting behaviour to us before, and consult my own convenience; but the consideration of the expense it might induce, the distraction of time and thought, when time and thought should be applied to the care of and provision for my children, made me decide against accepting more than a mere calling acquaintance from them.

October 10th.—At theatre received an anonymous note on the subject of Lear, which came like a friendly breath upon my dying enthusiasm—a very kind note also from Gaspey, with extract from the *Observer's* critique on Prospero and his own remarks on Macbeth. Acted Prospero but indifferently; there is little to sustain one's spirits, and mine could not bear up against the weight of the part (Dryden's Davenant!) and the oppression of my cold. Came back not well, and read the part of Oakley, before I went to bed, and, in order to get the start of the study on my mind, read Biron again in bed. I wish to play what I have to do in an artist-like manner, but I feel I shall never receive the recompense which comparatively my attention and care might claim.

October 11th.—Read Ford in bed, which I am very anxious to act well. In reflecting on Lear I begin to apprehend that I *cannot*

68

make an effective character of it.   I am oppressed with the magnitude of the thoughts he has to utter, and shrink before the pictures of the character which my imagination presents to me.   Did not intend to go to rehearsal, but reflecting it was for a novice, I thought it my duty to go.   I saw Miss Phillips and talked to her (perhaps more kindly than wisely) on the subject of the business cast to her.   My own concerns are enough for me; at the Garrick Club, where I dined, I also allowed my opinions to be suspected, if not known, which I might as well have kept to myself.   Nature has given us two ears, but only one mouth—why do we not take the hint?

October 12th.—Went to the rehearsal of Oakley.   Many jests in the green-room, one of Fawcett [1] falling through a trap on a man and thrashing him for it.   Went to Garrick Club.   Read papers, *Lit. Gazette* and scrutiny on Bunn.   Dined and saw Raymond, Williams, Fladgate, Blood, T. P. Cooke, Duruset—looked through magazines.   Saw Grattan's memorandum of his own play under the hand of Edmund Kean—looked into some of the vulgar abuse of Fraser.[2]   Read Oakley.   Acted with more self-possession and nature than formerly, and should have done much better but for Miss P.'s interruption.   Talfourd called in room; supped with him at Garrick Club.   Saw that reptile Westmacott behind scenes; he betrays his consciousness of having injured me.   Talfourd—*friend*—told me of the general denial of my ability to act Shakspeare!!

October 13th.—Late in bed made late rising.   Gave about five hours to the study of Pierre.[3]   It has occurred to me to write a current review of this season and endeavour to show the incompetency of Mr. Bunn from his ignorance of the art he has to deal with.   "Send them on" is his plan of tactics; like old Thornton's, "they must go forward!"   Thinking over Grattan's Kean made me consider what was Kean's generosity—his Irish benefit was a *trick*—his drunken prodigality and his distressed family make up a bad account of generosity.   It is not worth undeceiving the world, which is willingly deceived; but it is well to know the world and see the hollowness of its judgment in the value of its opinion.   *Our own* good opinion is all we ought to care for, but our title to that ought to be severely questioned.   At dinner with Talfourd (Price, Serle and afterwards Forster) I indulged my besetting *vice*—for it is more than weakness

---

[1] John Fawcett (1768-1837), playwright and comedian; he and his contemporary, T. P. Cooke, were reputed to be the best Falstaffs of their day.

[2] *Fraser's Magazine.*   [3] In *Venice Preserved.*

69

—in speaking on Knowles, when I might better have kept silence. The world is to me a lesson which I am ever learning, but I should die without being perfect in it. May my example and experience teach my children—and I am content to bear.

October 14th.—Went to the rehearsal of *Venice Preserved*, curious to see the bepuffed Mrs. Sloman,[1] who was standing on the stage as I entered. I listened with interest to her opening speech, but the first five lines spoke disappointment to me. I soon, as the play proceeded, became convinced that no permanent success could follow so artificial and vulgar a manner. At the Garrick Club, where I dined, saw some rather favourable criticisms on Oakley, which gratified me in making me feel that I was not now so much the object of personal dislike. My acting of Pierre did not satisfy me, though I felt it to be better than my former efforts in the part. Mrs. Sloman more than realized my anticipations; it was the worst kind of rant that pervaded her performance. Wrote a note of excuse to Talfourd for next Sunday's dinner, in consequence of being announced every night this week.

October 16th.—Seeing immense placards of Mrs. Sloman's success, I called at the Garrick to see yesterday's papers, all of which, except the *Post*, let her down gently. What an injudicious ass Mr. Bunn is! Saw Knowles at Garrick. Nothing could be *cooler* than his greeting, as mine, I daresay, to him. If ever a man was at heart ungrateful, it is this man—I would not have his genius for his heart. At rehearsal Cooper spoke to me about Antony, and tried to cast it. Oh! what these managers are! Bunn also talked to me; it is evident he already begins to feel himself *enscraped.*

October 17th.—Lay late in bed, thinking over characters; and busied myself in chambers during the short interval before rehearsal. Attended a very tedious rehearsal of *Cymbeline*, in the course of which I went over to the Garrick Club to dine and read the papers. Mrs. Sloman seems a complete failure, and certainly she communicates no pleasure to me in her acting—not one tone or look of truth have I yet witnessed from her. Our rehearsals are more like country ones than those of a patent theatre. Acted part of Posthumus with freedom, energy and truth, but there must have been observable an absence of all finish. To-night there was a delay of nearly half an hour and consequent clamour at Covent Garden, the singers having

---

[1] A tragic actress who had made some reputation at Norwich, which she failed to maintain in London.

been unable to go through their songs.   The play of *Antony and Cleopatra* was called for to-morrow as a *new play*, but I induced Mr. Cooper to alter it to Saturday.   On coming home read part of Antony.   The more I see of the management of Mr. Bunn, the more I find cause to blame the proprietors who gave the theatre to him!

October 18th.—Read over *Antony and Cleopatra* in preparation for the next day's repetition of the task to the performers.   Continued my attention to Antony through the evening.   My long absences from home make my visits there so many holidays; I ought not to indulge in the delicious idleness into which I fall, but there is so much to say and to enjoy in the society of my dear wife and children, that I am unable to resist its influence.

October 19th.—Rehearsed the *Stranger*.   Mrs. Sloman thanked me for *my support* in Isabella; I do not know whether this was conceit or humility.   I am inclined to believe the former.   Afterwards I read the play of *Antony and Cleopatra* in the green-room, with which, to my surprise, the performers expressed themselves much pleased.   I acted but indifferently—may claim some right to excuse myself in part from the noise made by the irruption of the half-price.   My first suspicion of Mrs. Sloman is fully confirmed; she has neither imagination, feeling nor grace—of course, cannot have expression.

October 20th.—Lay in bed meditating on the characters now on my mind for study, and occasionally thinking on the information, foolishly given me by Gaspey last night, of the *Satirist's* abuse of me; he told me that it dismissed my Macbeth with the simple epithet "execrable," which gave me very little concern.   It seems strange to me how men can cherish malignant feelings, and how they can seek to gratify them at the expense of truth; there is much baseness certainly in human nature.   Wrote two notes, one to Mrs. Hatton declining to subscribe for her book, another to Mrs. Lewis, enclosing £1 for a poor sick actor; I do not like to expend my money, but the really wretched have a claim which duty bids me not evade.   Read over my part of Antony, and afterwards that of Cardinal Wolsey. Went to dine at Talfourd's chambers, where I met Price, Serle, Knowles, Abbott, Forster and two Reading gentlemen.[1]   Spent a very agreeable evening, but drank rather more wine than was good for me, though begging for coffee.   Knowles was very dejected, perhaps it is not charitable to think that his oddity looked like acting occasionally; still he was very odd—to me as cordial as he was cold some days

---

[1] Talfourd was a native of Reading, for which borough he afterwards sat in Parliament.

ago. Forster walked home with me at a very late hour; he appears quite an enthusiast; I like him.

October 21st.—Headache and nausea were this morning the penalty incurred for last night's enjoyment; I overcame them just in time to reach rehearsal at the moment I was wanted. All was confusion; so much tumult and noise, that it quite made me nervous. Went to the Garrick Club, where I dined. Met T. Hill,[1] Bartley and Robinson; read the papers., Bartley told me that the management was three hours (!) in settling to-night's play. Read in a sleepy manner Wolsey. Acted it not quite to my own satisfaction, for I did not feel collected, nor always identified with the part, but Talfourd, who came into my room, praised it very much (still, he is so good-natured), and Cooper observed how well the last scene went. I might have done it better. Read Hotspur, on which character I received some hints from Talfourd, which, if I had time to polish my examination of, would greatly improve my performance.

October 22nd.—Rehearsed well, but still all was uncertain and unsettled in my mind. Dowton[2] recommended me to try Benedict. I must pause before I decide on it; I stated positively my inability to act Osmond (!) on Monday. Notes from Captain Medwin,[3] whom I do not like, and a Mr. Carroll, wanting an engagement; answered both. Lay down to recruit my spirits and read Hotspur. Acted Hotspur—I scarcely know how. I could and should have done it well if I had had rehearsal to prove myself, and a few days to think upon it. Received a severe blow on the eye and cheek in falling, which I apprehend will be a large black eye. Cooper thinks I am so furious and so strong! Felt tired and dissatisfied with myself.

October 24th.—On arriving in town hurried to rehearsal, where I saw Mr. King, congratulating him on his success; he did not appear quite so modest as before, but how very excusable under the applause he has received! He afterwards told me he felt himself in a " false position " and that he " was in a fever." Received a book of *Castle*

---

[1] Thomas Hill (1760–1840), a familiar figure in journalistic and theatrical circles; depicted as " Hull " in Theodore Hook's *Gilbert Gurney;* a liberal entertainer and discriminating book-collector; mentioned as "a character" in many contemporary Journals and Reminiscences.

[2] William Dowton (1764–1851), an actor of note; his principal parts were Dr. Cantwell, Falstaff, Sir Anthony Absolute, Sir Christopher Curry.

[3] Thomas Medwin (1788–1869), cousin of Shelley, through whom he made the acquaintance of Byron; wrote a *Life of Shelley* and *Conversations of Lord Byron*, neither of which is regarded as trustworthy.

Spectre—a fit play for Mr. Bunn's management. In my chambers found a parcel containing notes and a play from Mr. Hiscox, a very dull bore, who wanted me to read and champion his rejected play. Answered Mr. Hiscox. Lay down and tried to read Werner, but was too tired for anything but sleep. Took especial pains in acting Werner, made due pause, so as to discriminate clearly, and subdued all tendency to exaggeration. Satisfied myself. Read *Osmond*—ugh! trash!

October 25th.—Before I went out a note arrived from Captain Medwin, requesting an order, which I sent—"I do not like thee, Dr. Fell." At rehearsal, where I went for Mrs. Sloman's scenes, Mr. Cooper informed me of the favourable newspaper reports, which I went to read at the Garrick Club; was truly sorry to see Mr. King so severely handled, much, I believe, resulting from Mr. Bunn's injudicious puffery.

October 27th.—Read the *Spectator*, a paper that extols Mr. Knowles as an artist above myself, and thought upon and read part of the character of Antony. Spent some time in my dressing-room, and on coming down settled my accounts; read Leontes, and endeavoured to methodize and temper with more skill my delivery of the passionate part. Read some judicious remarks on the evils of English society, particularly in the point of pride of caste, extracted in the *Spectator*. After dinner I bestowed some attention on the reading of Ford, and listened to Captain Ross's narrative; after which I read Hotspur through, and then read family prayers. The demand of the theatre upon my time leaves me none for attention to my mind's improvement.

October 28th.—Arrived in town, found myself late for the rehearsal, which was called at ten. Went to the theatre, and under the sensation of wearied body and mind proceeded with the play. In the wardrobe found no dress for me, and lost my temper at the *black-guard* (I have no other word descriptive of the man) Bunn for his behaviour. Reflection, however, convinced, and convinces me, that if I want to yield him occasion of success, I shall do so by *passion*. Read some very warm panegyrics on Wolsey and Werner by Forster —dined at the Garrick. Medwin sent for an order, which I refused, having none to give. Read a little of Leontes, oppressed with weariness. Acted very ill, being literally imperfect—this disgusting management! Notes from Mr. Atherstone, an ass! Mr. Crooke, a knave! Mr. Hiscox, a bore; Mr. Young, I know not who; worried and kept up to a late hour in answering them.   Sent a note to Cooper stating my inability to play Ford on Tuesday.

October 29th.—Awoke with uncomfortable thoughts upon the conduct of the theatre; distressed by the exacting ignorant management.   Soothed down my angry musings into a resolution to be quiet and to receive annoyances quietly, but to stand firmly upon strong grounds of resistance.   Answered several notes, and proceeded to read Ford, which I did with much attention.   Sent a poor fellow with his drama, at his request, to Abbott.   Answered very kindly Serle's request to read again his play, as upon my decision is to rest the performance of it.   Took the note to Miller's, where I saw Serle and explained to him how much I was oppressed by the management. Dined at the Garrick Club, found very pleasant mention of my Leontes in the papers, and held a cheerful conversation with some whom once I thought my enemies.   I read through Hotspur, but failed in giving the effect of the previous evening to it, it was not collected, nor artist-like, an absence of finish and point throughout.   Is this my fault, or to be attributed to the hurried state of mind in which the manager keeps me?   If it be the last, I ought to combat and overcome its evil influence.

October 30th.—Acted Werner fairly, not so well in some parts, but better in others than the previous evening.   *Time, time, and discrimination; but time ensures discrimination.*   Poor King was hardly used by the audience; he came to speak to me, and I gave him the best comfort I could.

October 31st.—At Garrick Club saw the papers, laudatory of myself in *Werner*, and announcing the damnation of melodrama.   Met Mr. Bernard, the author, very dejected, poor fellow!   What a change from the smile of hope that lit up his countenance a day or two ago! Mr. Bunn has announced the *Merry Wives*—if for me, *I will be quiet.* Gave a good reading to Ford, and sent notes to some advertising servants and to Wallace.   Received three plays, *Countess of Provence, Adorno* and *The Bridal*, from a Mr. Girard by order of Mr. Bunn without word of comment or explanation; this so far from vexes me that it really amuses me; I like to see such a person show himself out in things that are innoxious.   I also received a call for Ford, on which I sent a note to Mr. Cooper explaining my inability to play the part on Tuesday.   Mr. Bunn appears to me in a Malay humour, ready to run amok—pitiful wretch!   Read Macbeth over to correct some faults in my last performance.

74

November 1st.—Rose late and did little before rehearsal (Ford). At the theatre I heard Dowton speaking to Duruset on the subject of Kemble's erudition, which I have always believed to have been falsely attributed to him, and quoting Cumberland,[1] Sheridan,[2] and G. Colman,[3] as persons who had a most contemptuous opinion of his classical acquirements. Cumberland, a ripe scholar, said that he scarcely knew anything of Latin and no Greek at all. A man, called Jones, said he was only *a year* at Douay!! In a conference with Bunn it was decided that Ford should be laid aside, and that *Antony and Cleopatra* should be done (sacrificed) on Monday sennight. Mr. Bunn is such a blackguard, and so out of the pale of respectability, that I have resolved to have no more dealings with him, but transact all my business with Mr. Cooper. Acted Macbeth passably, held in check by Mrs. Sloman, who I think derived her fire from what would have quenched many others.

November 4th.—Came to town. Ran directly to rehearsal and very attentively went through *Henry V*. My dress was *beggarly* as usual from the theatre, and inappropriate from my own wardrobe. Dined at the Garrick, where I saw Yates,[4] from whom I got an order for Colonel Birch. Went home; lay down in bed and read Henry very attentively. Acted it with more self-possession than I have felt before a London audience for years. Three accidents, however, occurred (on such trifles does an actor's success depend!) that damped the *general effect* of the play which, I incline to think, I acted well: my truncheon broke in my hand during the great speech to Westmoreland, which for a moment disconcerted me—Mr. Russell was not called to his time and cut out his part—and Miss Phillips bewildered me in the last scene by forgetting her speech to me. I never, in my own mind, acted the part so well. After the play I marked two acts of *Antony and Cleopatra*, and at a very late hour went to bed and thought upon Othello.

November 5th.—Was up in good time and out to the theatre with

---

[1] Richard Cumberland (1732–1811), Fellow of Trinity College, Cambridge ; Secretary to the Board of Trade ; wrote various plays.

[2] In point of classical attainments it is questionable whether Sheridan was much better off than Kemble.

[3] George Colman the younger (1762–1836), dramatist and examiner of plays (1824–1836) ; educated at Westminster, Christchurch, Oxford, and Aberdeen University.

[4] Frederick Henry Yates (1797–1842), actor and theatrical manager ; possessed considerable talent and versatility, but never attained the front rank. He was the father of Edmund Yates, the novelist and journalist, and the husband of Mrs. Elizabeth Yates, an accomplished actress.

the book of *Antony*. Rehearsed part of Antony and noted the sulkiness of Miss Kenneth—a person surely not at all fit to be in a London theatre. Offered some advice to Miss Phillips, to whom Bartley behaved very ill about the Queen in *Richard*. Mr. Cooper showed me my name in the bills for *Othello* on Friday next, which I said I would not do. Why should I be thrust before my audience in an unprepared state, because Mr. Bunn's incapacity involves him in a dilemma?

November 6th.—Rehearsed *Antony*; inclined, from aversion to *row*, to yield on the question of *Othello*; dined at Garrick Club. I gave Cooper notice that on the terms of my engagement I claimed, in right of choice, Iago—which induced a correspondence that I retain as evidences of Mr. Bunn's character. I received his note to Cooper after twelve o'clock, and did not see the simple grounds on which the question rested, viz. *I could*, or *I could not*. Sat up until four o'clock, writing answers and copying notes. More annoyed than I ought to have been by a mere question of law. Acted Werner very well, and to a fair house, though Mr. Bunn said it was £62 ! ! !

November 7th.—Rose very early from anxiety to settle this unpleasant business ; " in nocte consilium " the view I now took of it was totally different from that of last night. I looked with perfect indifference on any possible attempt of Mr. Bunn's to embroil me with the public, regarding the matter as merely a difference of opinion, on which I must be the best judge ; saw that I had written too much, and set off to ask counsel of Wallace. He at once decided so, and agreeing together on what should be said, he wrote a note of about ten lines, with which, after just shaking hands with Lardner, I omnibused down to Drury Lane. Thence I returned to the Garrick Club, where I looked at the papers and talked for two hours with Mills, then went and presented myself to rehearse Iago to Mr. Cooper. All was right, and Iago it was to be. Cooper sent me afterwards the second epistle of Mr. Bunn on the subject, which I copied. Most thankful to God for the relief I felt in disengaging myself from that ruffian, Mr. Bunn. Read first act of *Hamlet*.

November 8th.—Began my day with the rehearsal of Iago, in which I had to encounter and try to fortify myself against the prospect of an imperfect Roderigo, the gentleman only having received the part the morning before, or late the previous evening. This is most shameful. Dined at the Garrick Club, where I saw Fladgate and Harley ; returning, met Knowles and Mr. Weekes, an actor whom I did not at all recollect. Wrote to Catherine and had a visit from

Ellen and one from Dow, who sat long, too long for the necessary self-possession and nerve of Iago. I must be resolute when I have important characters on my mind, and must refuse to expend either spirits, thought, or voice in idle conversation. Of course I acted indifferently, and I think I may ascribe much of my deficiency to the miserable support. Wallace came round to my room. I was satisfied that I acted ill. Mr. Perkins lent me a volume of plays, containing one of *Antony and Cleopatra*, by Sir Charles Sedley, in rhyme—mere trash. Forgot to notice that in going to the theatre this morning I saw my name in the bills for Hastings, in which Mr. King had been announced the whole week at Covent Garden for to-morrow!

November 9th.—Saw a nursemaid for Catherine, who looked more like a producer than a rearer of children; dismissed her. Rehearsed *Jane Shore* without Dumont or Ratcliffe in order to regenerate the drama. Dined at Garrick Club, saw the papers, which gave me certainly not less commendation than I merited in Iago, if indeed they did not give me more; but I was knocked up. Oh, Mr. Warde's " mi-i-i-ser-r-ry ! " Sent Colonel Birch orders, and wrote to dear Catherine. Forster called, whom I have real pleasure in seeing. I returned Mr. Grainger's play of *Adorno* with a note of self-exculpation. I acted Lord Hastings well—really well; I almost satisfied myself; a little more truth in part of the last scene would have made it a very commendable performance.

November 10th.—Dined at the Garrick Club, and looked at all the papers except the *Age*, which I expected would abuse me. I certainly acted Iago inefficiently, but for it must throw *much* of the blame on Roderigo and Othello. Looked through Fraser's disgusting magazine. Came home after coffee to resume my reading of Hamlet, about which I am most anxious and anticipate disappointment.

November 11th.—Birthday of my beloved, my adored Catherine; God for ever and for ever bless her! Amen. This day I devote to Hamlet, for which I post to rehearsal at ten, though feeling the pains and languor of fatigue before entering on my day's work. Rehearsed Hamlet so well, that could I act it in the same manner I should not fear criticism—but diffidence and nervousness have to come with night. Mr. Baker (Guildenstern) was ordered to leave the rehearsal, but I said if he left I would. Dined, seeing newspapers, which praised my Lord Hastings, at Garrick Club. Found notes at home, which I could not read, but betook myself to bed, where I endeavoured to impress my purpose in Hamlet on my mind, and to gain some refreshment to my body and spirits. Letters from Mr. Close and Butler about a play, which I could not read. I acted Hamlet—how? Not so well as I rehearsed it, but still I think *well*. I can infuse more effect, and spread more finish over it, if the newspapers will only give me the confidence in the audience necessary to effect so much. A Mr. Hiscox followed me out of the theatre and very ludicrously badgered me about his play.

November 12*th*.—Have not yet seen the papers, but can scarcely expect them to gainsay their former opinions on my Hamlet. I must endeavour to "unassuming win my way." Rehearsed Antony, and was gratified in reading a good report of my Hamlet in the *Herald* and *Post*. Acted Prospero merely in reference to general *style*. Notes from Mr. Lough on my Hamlet, from Mills on the *Bridal*. Set off after the play for Elstree through a fog so dense that I thought at Kilburn I must turn back : we ran on the bank, against a gig, a post, and at last to my great comfort arrived safely.

November 14*th*.—Went to rehearse *William Tell;* was much concerned to hear and read of the success of the gewgaw opera at Covent Garden, as likely to protract the period of this wretched fellow's management, and to confirm the ignorant in the belief of the extinction of dramatic art. Acted William Tell middlingly. The glee and chorus and all the female peasants were omitted, because the chorus were at Covent Garden.

November 15*th*.—Read a little of Plutarch's *Cato;* how he brings you into the chambers, nay, into the very hearts of men! I began Hamlet very languidly, my spirits were low, and my mind not in the part. I felt the absence of what the French justly term, inspiration ; but in the middle of the second act I rallied, and asserted myself through the remainder of the play, acting the advice to players and some passages better than on Monday.

November 16*th*.—Went to the theatre about my dress for Antony, which I persisted, after evasion and delay, in seeing. Was disgusted with the ignorant impertinence of Mr. Cooper informing me, that because he studied his parts at so short a notice, I might also do the same. Called at hairdresser's, and at the Garrick Club, where I saw the papers, and railed (qu. wisely?) at the state of things. Jerdan hoped I would keep account of the various absurdities in the management, which I will do. Read Plutarch's life of Antony, and then gave a careful reading to the part itself, which is long, and I fear not effective.

November 18*th*.—Acted Werner as well as I could against my

78

illness. Made several strong effects by management and taking time—
the great secret. My indisposition was so manifest that Mr. Cooper
sent over for Mr. Bunn, counselling him not to keep me in the bills
for the morrow. Mr. B—— seemed not to think me ill or hoarse, but
offered to "shut the theatre if I wished." I peremptorily declined,
and said I was ready to act, if able. He decided, it seems, on closing
to-morrow. Settled dresses for Antony, of which nothing was allowed
to be new but a cloak.

November 19th.—On walking through the streets from the
Hummum's to my chambers the inhalation of the air was like breathing
prickles. I met Mr. Lee, who noticed my illness the previous evening.
Found dear Catherine weak, but better. I felt very unwell myself,
cold, hoarse, and with a catch on my breath. Went to rehearsal of
Antony, which was in a very backward state, and mounted with very
inappropriate scenery, though beautifully painted by Stanfield. Earle
called to see me, said I ought to lay by for several days, and forbade
me to play on the morrow. I reported his words to Cooper and left
the rehearsal at a quarter before five! Wallace called and Cooper sent
a note from Bunn requiring, "for the satisfaction of the public,"
Earle's certificate. On Henley's return from Savoy and Moore's I sent
him to H. Earle; he kept me in a state of some anxiety, not returning
till nearly ten—with a certificate, ordering me not to play for "several
days," which I instantly sent "to Mr. Bunn's satisfaction."

November 20th.—Forster called, and had a long theatrical gossip;
Catherine and Letitia liked him very much. Cooper called, and on his
promise that I should have Friday and Saturday for rest, obtained
my consent to play the following day. Bunn had intended publishing
my certificate, but on perusal withheld it. Earle called, desired me not
to play on the morrow, if not feeling perfectly well. Sent note to
the theatre to that effect, notwithstanding which Mr. B—— persisted in
announcing me. Read Antony through the whole evening and discovering many things to improve and bring out the effect of the part,
though unable from a pain at my heart, impeding my respiration, to
practise it. I found that I had just got an insight into the general
effect, but had no power of furnishing a correct picture or of making
any strong hits.

November 21st.—Went to rehearsal, certainly with amended health,
but still rather hoarse, not quite free from the pain at the heart, and
generally depressed and weak. I remained there until four o'clock,
and protested to Messrs. Wilmott and Cooper against the hurried

manner in which I was thrust before the public. Mr. Bunn came for
a short time, and spoke to me about *Lear*, to which I returned a
vague answer, and about "a great go," on which he wished to speak
with Stanfield and myself. Felt quite knocked up and very unwell.
I was so wretchedly low, fretted and exhausted, that I could not speak
to him. I nursed the minutes on the sofa until five, when I went to the
theatre. I acted—what shall I say? As well as I could under the
circumstances; was raw, efforty and uncertain in the scenes of passion,
but had just taken precaution enough to make my pauses, although not
to make use of them—it was not a performance to class with what I
have lately done. Wallace and Dow came into my room. Wallace
congratulated me! *Beaten.*

November 22nd.—Went to the theatre to speak to Cooper about
my exhausted state of body and mind. From him I learned that I
was announced for William Tell to-morrow; he quite sympathized with
me, and took from me a proposal to Mr. Bunn, to the effect that "if
he would for the next fortnight limit my performances to three nights
per week I would try to go on without impeding the business—if
not, I would be guided by Mr. Earle." Cooper went with me to see
some very beautiful gold coins, among which were several of Antony.
At G. Club saw Fladgate, and spoke to him on the subject of a bust
to Mrs. Siddons. Read the newspapers, which were, I thought, very
liberal in their strictures on Antony. Acted Antony better to-night
than last night, but it is an hasty, unprepared, unfinished performance.
Mr. Cooper's report of Mr. Bunn's reply to my proposal was that he
asked, "Is Mr. Macready disposed to give up half his salary for that
fortnight?"

November 23rd.—H. Earle's answer, desiring me to rest from
acting, was brought. I acted languidly, but not very badly, William
Tell; I did not wish to possess the actors with an idea of good
health by any desperate efforts to act well. Received note from Mr.
Bunn, humble and *false*, stating that Cooper said I "*demanded*"
what I proposed, which Cooper directly denied. I learned also that
he had stopped my salary for the Wednesday night!! At Cooper's
request I left a note intimating that I should not play next week.
On reaching chambers I wrote to H. Earle.

November 24th.—Began a letter to Cooper, which I found too
long. Read prayers to my family. Wrote a letter to Cooper, tendering through him the resignation of my engagement, and offering a
premium for it.

November 27th.—I was awoke in the morning by letters from Messrs. Bunn and Cooper. Mr. Cooper's informing me that Mr. B—— would reply to my proposal, and Mr. Bunn taking up a very friendly tone to say nothing in extenuation of his annoyance to me, but promising that in future my wishes should be consulted, at the same time refusing to relinquish my engagement. All this is mere froth, and the froth of a venomed dog, too; he has been mighty in his promises before, and they have only become means of alluring me to cajolement. Henceforth I *put no trust in him whatever.* On getting up, I applied myself to answer him, which I did—not very satisfactorily to myself, but mildly and in a temper rather inclining to smooth asperities.

December 1st.—The news which letters conveyed to me this morning from the papers was the death of my old master Dr. Wooll. I really regret him, he was kind, most hospitable, ready to enjoy and delighted to look upon enjoyment, in short of a most benevolent disposition; this made the weaknesses of his character, his vanity and French abbé-like manner less unamiable. He had little or no pretensions to profound learning, but he was a thoroughly good-natured, kind-hearted man. After giving up some time to my darling children, sat down to read through the character of Antony, which I can see how imperfectly I have played, yet have not time nor motive to re-study. Dow called just in time to intercept me going to church; he sat and chatted some time; I was glad to hear *him* (with his idolatry of Kean) say that he liked my Hamlet. He stayed some time and accepted an invitation for Miss D—— and self for Christmas Eve and day. Dow asked me to-day about *Sardanapalus;* I will look once more at it, but I have no hopes of it.

December 2nd.—At the theatre I began Antony very feebly, but rallied and acted parts of it better than I had yet done. I learned from Cooper that *Sardanapalus* was to be done with a grand scene, the proposal I made in the beginning of the season to Reynolds! This, I take it, is the "*great go* "! I was *very indiscreet* in speaking to that sottish man, Mr. ——, about the acting of the last scene. I cannot sufficiently blame myself. I was quite foolish.

December 3rd.—Walked with Harley to Garrick Club, saw Raymond, etc.; they said Sheil was suspected to be the *traitor* spoken of by Hill.[1]

[1] Mr. Matthew Davenport Hill, M.P. for Hull, in a speech to his constituents made at this time stated that an Irish member who spoke violently against the Coercion Bill had in private advised members not to relax any of its provisions, and that he had asked, "Who is the traitor?" On the 5th February, 1834, Mr. O'Connell called the

December 4th.—Dear Letitia's birthday : may God bless her and send her many happy ones! At Garrick Club, where I dined, I chatted with Collier on the drama, and with Bartley on the subject of my late correspondence with Mr. Bunn—he saw my first letter, and thought it a most temperate and straightforward one. I sent Smith orders in answer to his note, and went to bed, so very tired and weak was I. Looked at the part of Sardanapalus, which Mr. Cooper had given me with "Mr. Bunn's best compliments." Acted Virginius not to my satisfaction, was tame and inefficient in the early part, but warmed with the progress of the play, and was myself in the two last acts.

December 5th.—Read through the part of Sardanapalus, which I think (but had better not say) is injudiciously cut. Dined at Garrick Club, and looked at some of the magazines; a criticism in the *New Monthly*, finding fault with a passage in my Jaques, pleased me much from its truth and good taste. Came home, and read *King John*, after looking over the parts of Shakspeare for one to excite attention in. I fear it is not to be done, but by slow degrees, and "while the grass grows," etc. Looked at parts of *Coriolanus*. I should have been taught to think and look through the subjects of my consideration.

December 6th.—Only rose to attend the rehearsal of *King John*, which, if I wish to act well, I must give much of to-morrow to, for I am not master in execution of my own wishes and exceptions in the part, which I ought to act grandly. I looked after my John's dress, and received a letter of thanks for Virginius. Brewster called, ordered wig for Coriolanus; if the public choose to be pleased, I will spare no pains nor expense to please them. Sheil is in a predicament, I would counsel him to fight, but that I do not like to incur the possible consequences of reflection. Acted leisurely, without inspiration or perspiration, still I seemed to produce an effect upon the audience, but I was not identified with Werner. "Je n'étais pas le personnage." Lost my temper (*oh! fool*) about an interference with my order for King John's dress.

December 7th.—Rose at a very early hour with perfect pleasure to return home by the Crown Prince coach; endeavoured on my way to keep my thoughts on King John, but they ludicrously mixed them-

---

attention of the House of Commons to this subject, and on behalf of the Irish members asked for an explanation. Lord Althorp, then leading the House of Commons, declined to assure Mr. Sheil that he was not the member intended. A duel seemed impending, and they were both put in the custody of the Sergeant-at-Arms. Mr. Sheil was afterwards cleared of the suspicions raised against him by a Select Committee (*note by Sir F. Pollock*).

selves with other subjects and lulled me into invincible slumbers. Arriving on a very rainy and tempestuous day, I found my darling Nina better, but very thin, and dearest Willie better, but fretful and not quite well. After breakfast, I read with a desire of improvement *King John,* and remained in the drawing-room (coming down only twice for short periods) until past four o'clock. I then took up *Sardanapalus,* which I read, comparing it with the original and marking my book by it. I do not think, with whatever adjuncts, that it can do; it seems to me very undramatically prepared; and most injudiciously have the selections of its poetry been made. After dinner (what with a yule log, and good port wine, I enjoyed my fireside) I returned to my tiresome task of collating *Sardanapalus.*

December 9th.—Came to town by Billings, and went to rehearsal, at which there was no Hubert; an unusual and not very pleasant occurrence. From the theatre went to dine and see the papers at the Garrick Club. Returning to chambers, wrote notes and was a good deal disturbed, by loss of temper as well as time (a loss attributable only to my own folly), on the subject of my armour for King John. Captain de Visme called about Mr. Sulivan's play; I have to charge myself with some deficiencies in good breeding during his stay. I told him of the manager's answer, and parted from him with at least civility; but I was careless in my interview with him of the "fashion and ceremony" due to a gentleman. I went to the theatre, thinking first of my dress and secondly of King John! I am ashamed, grieved and distressed to acknowledge the truth: I *acted* disgracefully, worse than I have done for years; I shall shrink from looking into a newspaper to-morrow, for I deserve all that can be said in censure of me. I did what I feared I should do, sacrificed my character to my dress!! Wallace and Talfourd came into my room, and I felt what they thought of my performance; it has made me very unhappy.

December 10th.—I could neither go to bed last night from self-dissatisfaction, for I sat up reading Luke and *Sardanapalus* till past one, nor could I get up this morning from the same depressing cause. Sat a long time in conversation with Forster, who called. I feared to look into the papers, but found them, on going to meet Fladgate by appointment at the Garrick Club, very indulgent indeed. The *Herald* remarked, in objection, upon my dress; so that I suffered as I ought, but not in the degree I merited. Went with Fladgate to call on Chantrey [1] who received us very kindly, and with whom we had a most

---

[1] Sir Francis Legatt Chantrey, R.A. (1781–1842), the famous sculptor.

interesting conversation. Our purpose was to ascertain his price for a bust of Mrs. Siddons, to be placed in Westminster Abbey by the Garrick Club. He told us 200 guineas, but that the price should be no obstacle; he spoke most pleasingly and liberally. Fladgate was delighted with him. On leaving him to inquire at his request of Deville if he had a cast of Mrs. Siddons, we arranged our plan of operations, viz. to learn all, ask the practicability of the plan, and then at a "house dinner" engage members of the Club to support it. We went to Deville's, saw the cast of Siddons, Miss O'Neill, etc. Looked through the illustrations of Byron's works, in which are some very beautiful and some very indifferent engravings. I think I should be ashamed to see a portrait of myself with the expression of coxcombical pertness that marks that of Moore.[1] I was very much gratified with Chantrey's conversation. He observed that to satisfy relations or friends it was desirable that the likeness of a bust should be as exact as possible, but that in the case of a person of genius we must have something to engage the attention and respect of those who could never be able to judge of a likeness. His remarks on the necessity of supplying the want of colours by shadows pleased me much; that if he copied exactly a face, as it actually was, it would neither have effect nor resemblance, but that he was obliged to vary, always with due caution and care, the exact surface, giving prominence where shadows might be needful to give the corresponding effect to colour.

December 12th.—How strange it is that our experience of the pain as well as unprofitableness of passion should not teach us the lesson of subduing it! How many times this morning had I to accuse myself, and reason myself out of my wrath and impatience, as I drove along, because Healey had brought me a *slow coach* instead of a fast cab? If there be one folly more injurious to man than another it is the senseless fury of anger. Read the heavy part of Sardanapalus. Turned the leaves of Byron's *Don Juan*, a wanton display of thought, wit and brilliancy. Thought of going by a late coach to-morrow, but the recollection of poor Billings's empty vehicle this morning determined me to rise and go by him.

December 13th.—Came to town by Billings, and found a call for rehearsal. Paid Healey, and went to rehearse *Coriolanus*. At the theatre found a pamphlet enclosed from Mr. G. Farren on the char-

---

[1] Thomas Moore (1779–1852), the poet. He and Macready were acquaintances, but there are many strictures on him in the Diaries. It would certainly be difficult to find two Irishmen more unlike in character and temperament.

acter of Shylock, which I felt as rather an impertinence. I acted Hotspur in a way that showed me my ability to play it much better, and indeed very well. I took more time over the opening speech, but found, as I proceeded, the want of study, and how very little pains would make it good. I also found in the progress of the scene the *vast benefit* derived from keeping vehemence and effort out of passion. It is everything for nature. The reading the letter was not bad, chiefly on that account. The other scenes would have been better had I taken less wine, but it made me dry and hurried. At home I looked through the leaves of V. Hugo's play.

December 14th.—Awoke late, and got up in great haste to dress for rehearsal; was there in time, saw the play, *Coriolanus*, in so disgraceful a state that it was useless to bestow a word upon the *mise en scène*: had not even the power to try myself in the feeling of the part. After rehearsal went to pay in some money at Ransom's, and called at the Garrick Club, where I found Robins,[1] Reynolds, Fladgate, etc. Our conversation was on the state of the theatres; Robins denied being the cause of their present state, and mentioned that it had been reported: "Polhill had said at the Blackguard, *alias* Beefsteak Club, that he was the manager, and Bunn merely put in by him." This was contradicted, as was said, by Dunn. Mention was made of Mr. Bunn's letter stating, in obscene and disgusting language, his design to produce a licentious spectacle! A worthy caterer for English taste! At dinner indulged too much in the luxuries of home, and found the evening gone when I wished to begin my work.

December 15th.—Rose late, and, on coming down, looked through the *Spectator*, which grows more and more dull. Dow called while I was looking through Shakspeare's *Julius Cæsar*, with an eye to its *mise en scène*.

December 16th.—Acted languidly and ineffectively most of the two first acts of *Coriolanus*, but in the third act I assumed the character, and in the last blazed out; the audience were much excited. Wallace came into my room, and said it was splendid.

December 18th.—At the theatre I found a note from Kenneth, overtures from Bath. I acted William Tell tolerably well. Forster called for me in a coach with Talfourd and Procter.[2] I met at his

---

[1] George Robins, the auctioneer (see note, p. 32); he was connected with various theatrical enterprises.

[2] Bryan Waller Procter (1787–1874); poet, conveyancer and Lunacy Commissioner. Wrote under the name of "Barry Cornwall"; a school-fellow of Byron at Harrow, and on

lodgings Blanchard,[1] a pleasing man, Abbot, Knowles and others. A pleasant but too indulging evening. Toasts and commendations flying about. A great deal of heart, and when that is uppermost the head is generally subjected. Procter is to send his play.

December 19th.—Quite unable to get up, or to hold up my head from the effects of my facile temper last night. I lay in bed from hour to hour expecting an amelioration of my condition. Ruminated on the bygone evening; the facility in summoning and uttering their ideas so conspicuous in Talfourd, Blanchard, and even Abbott, contrasted with the difficulty I have in arranging and expressing my thoughts. Forster called to bring my cloak, which I had left last night, and my pocket-handkerchief, which Knowles in jest had taken from me unperceived. Read through Coriolanus, which I am very anxious to make a part of, but fear the uninteresting nature of the story and the recollection of Kemble are objections too strong to overcome. Made calculations on the various proposals from Dublin, in reference also to my future country excursions and my general income, which occupied me some time, and wrote thereon a long letter to Calcraft. Felt much better. In future I will not be betrayed into such weaknesses.

December 20th.—Called at the theatre and spoke to Mr. Cooper about Colonel D'Aguilar's *Fiesco* and my own absence. Spoke to Kenneth about Bath and Newcastle. Dined at the Garrick and read the article on Sheil. I looked upon him as lost,[2] for want of discretion in involving himself, and want of firmness to extricate himself. Wrote invitations to Stanfield and Abbott. Wallace called. Note of excuse from Stanfield. Acted Coriolanus, not so well as on Monday, the scene with Volumnia *much better*, but gave too much voice to some speeches in the last scene, chiefly through that pleasant actor, Aufidius, purposely disconcerting me.

December 21st.—Had a long conversation with Mr. Meadows on the subject of the theatres; spoke to him about a dinner to Dowton, which I requested him to speak to the actors about; told him that

---

intimate terms with Charles Lamb, Dickens, Leigh Hunt and most of the eminent literary men of his day. He was the father of the poetess, Adelaide Anne Procter.

[1] Samuel Laman Blanchard (1804–1845); by turns proctor's clerk, itinerant actor, secretary to the Zoological Society, and, latterly, editor, author and journalist.

[2] Macready's pessimism regarding Sheil proved to be at fault, for in 1837 his "lost" friend became a member of the Whig Government and thenceforward was uniformly prosperous, ending his career as British Minister at Florence.

B. W. PROCTER

From an engraving

I should be glad to see him at Elstree. Read over the two first acts of *Sardanapalus* in the carriage, which does not improve upon me. Must employ the few days of leisure before me in getting ahead of business and digesting some plan towards the re-establishment of my profession. How much might be done if opportunity were only in my power.

December 22nd.—Went to morning service and gave Mr. Chalk £20 to be distributed in coals among the poor. I do not perceive why, with the sentiments I entertain of this as a religious and moral duty, I should mix myself with persons who have nothing else in common with me. " My order " is an extensive one—that of humanity, and " homo sum " is my motto, a truly Christian sentiment uttered by a heathen poet.

December 23rd.—Read through attentively an adaptation of Goethe's play of *Egmont;* unacquainted as I am with the language, and knowing by translation but a very few of Goethe's works, it would be impertinent to hint an opinion on them; all I may say is that I do not feel the power of those I have read.

December 24th.—Received a letter from Mr. Cooper (which, from the utter want of sense displayed in it, I do not like to dwell on), asking me from Mr. Bunn to resume the part of Joseph Surface, especially excluded in my engagement, " out of kindness "! I read the *Examiner*, and answered this silly application, desiring to retain the terms of my engagement. Walk to Mr. Fowler's. As I walked I went over several scenes of *Richard III*, which, Mr. Cooper's note announced to me, I am to play on Monday. Shortly after my return home, Mr. and Miss Dow arrived; we did not wait for Wallace, as his former visits warranted us in not doing. About eight o'clock he came, whitened by his contact with sacks of flour, having travelled to Edgware in a wagon, and thence walked here. I felt unwell in the evening from imprudence, which I must be careful in future to avoid.

December 25th.—Wrote an answer to Serle on his application respecting the theatrical monopoly, suggesting, as some security to actors, authors and the public, a price graduated according to the quality of the dramatic exhibitions, to be set upon the licence granted. Wallace came in while I was speaking on it to Dow, and opened a furious invective against the plan, contending for universal and unrestricted licence to act the drama in every street.

December 26th.—On this day three years my beloved Christina was given to me. I bless the day, the name of the Almighty Giver, and the darling child, whose life, I pray God, may be one of virtuous happiness. Received a letter from Mr. Willmott, prompter, informing me that *Richard* should not be acted on Monday, in order to give me leisure for the study of *Sardanapalus*. This makes me believe what I before suspected, that the announcement of *Richard* was an artifice of Mr. Bunn's! Did very little through the day. The presence of people is always a hindrance to me, and I found it particularly so to-day.

December 28th.—Our friends, Messrs. Forster and Price, also Mr. and Mrs. Smith arrived in the afternoon; Dr. Lardner just before we sat down to dinner. We spent a very pleasant evening, and in the drawing-room sat down to whist. After the retirement of the rest, which did not happen until very late, Forster acquainted me with the strange fact of Knowles having written a letter to him, repudiating his friendship on the plea of F—— having done him an injury by his, F.'s, criticism on Knowles's performance of Macbeth!

December 29th.—Again an idle day! Up late, and losing the morning in idle chat and skimming over the papers. Sent to every probable possessor in the village for a newspaper containing the theatrical advertisements to know whether or not I was to play to-morrow; after much search learned that I was announced for Werner. After dinner Wallace got into a high tone of invective against what he termed the "impertinence" of Lough,[1] for making Milo's hand, and not his "hands," caught in the tree. I hope the ardour of my defence did not provoke—I am sure it did not justify—the rudeness of his tone and manner to me. After dinner Forster showed me in the drawing-room Knowles's letter and his own criticism—the gentlest and kindest, nay, most flattering apology that one friend could have made for the deficiency of another. But Knowles will have defenders.

December 30th.—Forster called, whom I advised to let Talfourd arrange a reconciliation with him and Knowles. Acted Werner very well in some parts, and not so well in the third and fourth acts. Found a number of Fox's paper on my return (Dow walked with me) containing an enthusiastic eulogium on *Coriolanus*.

December 31st.—The last day of the year! I sit down to take my everlasting farewell of it; to write my adieux to a period of time on which I look back with many pleasing recollections to soothe me in the thought that I have approached so much nearer to my grave, with some melancholy ones, and with some compunctious ones. I sent a note to a Miss Cope, who I fancy must be crazy, poor creature! as

---

[1] John Graham Lough (1806–1876), a sculptor of no special note.

she informed me that the fate of Lucretia bore so close a resemblance to her own! Serle called, and I had a very long conference with him, as adjourned from yesterday. I could not, on reconsideration, be a party to throwing open the drama indiscriminately, so ruinous did it appear to me to the general interests of the profession. We at last concurred in the expediency of confining the right of acting the classic drama to the four large theatres of Westminster, restricting its performance elsewhere to a great distance, not including therein the Garrick and Pavilion; I agreed to see Arnold on the subject, and Morris; and if the former entered into our views, to endeavour to move the actors to join in a petition to Parliament.

And now having reached this point of time, the verge of another year, which warns me how rapidly I am nearing the brink of eternity, I turn my thoughts to my God, the giver of all the good I enjoy, either in external things, or in the feelings with which I appreciate them. I bless and praise His sacred name for the undeserved mercies He has showered upon me, and I close this year's record with my humble and fervent prayers for the continuance of His mercy and many blessings on my dear wife and children and myself, beseeching Him to instil wisdom, virtue and love into our hearts, and make us merit as well as enjoy His divine blessings. Amen.

1834

London, January 1st.—Forster related to me an anecdote of much
interest—that Hazlitt in his emergency had applied to Kean [1] for
the loan of £50, which K——, on the pretence of inability, refused! I
called in at Miller's to look for Serle; not finding him went on to the
Garrick Club, where I dined, and heard, among other observations on
Messrs. Bunn and Ducrow from Mr. Meadows, that the language of
the former to the women was so horridly revolting that had a relative
of his been there he must have knocked him down.

January 4th.—Rose very late after a night through which I
scarcely slept, but occupied myself with thinking on my present condition in the theatrical profession, and attending to my darling child,
as she turned in her bed. The necessity of rising still in my profession, and of gaining suffrages to my reputation, presented itself
so strongly to my mind, that I determined, contrary to my original
intention, of offering such benefit as my advice could yield towards the
play of *Sardanapalus,* and of doing my best to make the play successful,
which notwithstanding I have no hope of effecting. Coming home I
sat down to read with attention the play of *Sardanapalus,* which I did,
and confirmed myself in my opinion of the expediency of cutting much
and restoring some passages to give any chance (and even then a faint
one) of the play's success.

January 5th.—Mr. Monro followed me and asked me to sign a
petition to the Chancellor in behalf of Mr. Chalk, who, it appears, is
about to leave this cure in consequence of Dr. Morris coming to reside.
As curates go he is, I should say, of average respectability; but
measuring him by the standard I set up for a minister of that beautiful
and philosophic system of charity and universal love which our
Redeemer set up, I think him wanting in the essentials of talent, zeal,
and independence : the worshipper of any golden calf that may be the
neighbourhood's god, and without reach of thought or comprehension
to adore the Creator and Sustainer of the Universe. I wish him well,
but am indifferent about his going or staying.

[1] Edmund Kean.

January 6th.—Read and marked for curtailment the play of *Sardanapalus*, anticipating the freedom to do so; it occupied me the greatest part of the morning. After luncheon Catherine walked with me to call on Mr. Chalk, which I thought necessary as he was said to be leaving Elstree. We found upon our visit that it was at present doubtful. We heard too, for the first time, that Lady Pole had been resident in the parish above three weeks, and of a marriage in the Monro's family; facts to us of less interest than the arrival or increase of so many rats in our stable. Dear Nina fell asleep in my arms in the dining-room, and kept me some time from my employment. These blessed children, even when I am most busy, allure me from my resolves of diligence for a time; I cannot speak the overflowing love with which I look at them. After dinner we received the Twelfth-cake from London, which as a household superstition I had ordered. In the evening I read four acts of Serle's play of the *Spanish Maid*, which I think a pretty, pleasing comedy or play, but do not regard the part of the Duke as beyond that of—if indeed equal to—Sir William Dorrillon; still, I think the play too good to be rejected.

January 7th.—Rehearsed part of *Sardanapalus*, which was stopped by a conversation on some suggestions of mine. Mr. Cooper is a person as capable of directing the *mise en scène* of a play as a man devoid of information, industry, genius or talent may be supposed to be. He could not understand the object of what I pointed out as necessary, but wished me to correct the various errors, grammatical as well as dramatic, that fell in my way, which I declined doing, and at length Mr. Bunn ordered the MS. to be sent to my chambers to be cut. Mr. Cooper, Mr. Willmot [1] and Mr. Bunn—to arrange the characters and body out the imaginations of Shakespeare! . . . and in England!!! Saw Dowton, and Bartley, and Dunn. Called at Miller's for Serle, who caught me going away, and went home with me. To my surprise and regret he told me that his opinions had changed, and that he found he could not consistently abandon a principle he had advocated before. We went into the question [2] and handled most of its bearings, in all of which, except upon the one great principle of universal licence (which may also be met by its consequence, universal annoyance), Serle was manifestly a weak, interested and sophistical arguer. Forster called in during the discussion, and quite concurred in my opinion on the shallow and self-delusive reasoning of Serle. Mr. Hollingsworth called, and reflecting that I

---

[1] The prompter.   [2] That of the monopoly theatres.

too might have been no richer than the " poor player " who applied to me, I gave him seven shillings. Forster drove with me to the coach office to wait for Bryant's last coach. On our road he told me of a most extraordinary letter from Knowles to Abbott, insisting on " open- ing " in *Macbeth*, asking if he was to be " slain by a cold," and speaking of the cruellest and weightiest blow that had ever been dealt upon him, as that inflicted by Forster's kind notice of him—writing Macbeth on the outside of the letter, and not subscribing his name. Forster promised me that L. Hunt would do what I asked for Reynolds. While waiting, my old school-fellow and master, Lateward, passed me, and turning to recognize me, introduced his daughter (*labuntur anni!*) to me, and asked me to procure a private box for his children, which I promised to try to do. Coming home I thought on *Sardanapalus*, and arriving set to work upon reducing my own part to form.

January 9th.—Went to rehearsal of *Sardanapalus*, saw Bunn, who asked me if I would speak Mr. Moore's prologue, which I declined, having enough to speak. Miss Phillips observed to me what a " wooden-headed " man Mr. Cooper was, and so he appears to the people on the stage. Dined at the Garrick Club, saw among others Linley,[1] and *very foolishly* allowed myself to get into a silly discussion with him on Bunn's management ; a club-room was not a place for such an argument. Saw Bartley also, and told him of the chance lost to the profession in Serle's opposition to his former agreement. Bartley professed himself charmed with the plan, and ready to go all lengths with such a one. He told me of Polhill's purchase of half the *Age* newspaper from Westmacott for £5000. Went to Talfourd's (from whom I had received a note of invitation to supper in the morning) to meet Charles Lamb ; met there Price, Forster, Mr. and Mrs. Field (I fancy a Gibraltar judge), Charles Lamb, Moxon the publisher, and *not* Mrs. Moxon,[2] whose absence was noted by those present as a most ungrateful omission of respect and duty, as he (Lamb) had literally brought her up, and wanted her attention and assistance. I noted one odd saying of Lamb's, that " the last breath he drew in he wished might be through a pipe and exhaled in a pun." Spent a pleasant evening and walked home under a " pitiless storm " with Price. Talfourd apologized to me for the critique, for which I

---

[1] Probably George Linley (1798–1865), playwright and verse-writer.

[2] Lamb's adopted daughter, Emma Isola, who had married Moxon in the preceding year. Lamb died a few months later.

thanked him, as he avowed he felt he had not done me justice and had been seduced by his imagination.

January 10th.—At rehearsal (*Sardanapalus*) I heard of the great expectations formed of the new play, read yesterday, and in the regret I acknowledge to have felt at the intelligence I afford an evidence of the selfishness which must accompany an actor's professional career. If he is idle, he feels he is or fears to be lost sight of, and his income suffers in the exaltation of those who "push him from his stool." "The present eye praises the present object." I say this without any spleen, merely wishing it were otherwise, which perhaps ere long it may be. Miss Phillips again railed at Cooper's dogmatic and dull correction of errors, which, she said, she threw in his way on purpose. He sent for a family box for me, of which I sent the card to Lateward. Returning to chambers I met George Robins, and walked with him to his door, mentioning the necessity there was for moving some interest towards opening the monopoly of the drama; he wished me to call on Lord Glengall,[1] and ask him what he had in project on the subject. I agreed to do so. Looked for Serle at Miller's, and left my name for him, being desirous of trying to persuade him out of his resolve on the dramatic Bill. Called at the Garrick, had a little conversation with Bartley, and settled with T. Cooke the outline of plan of our dinner to Dowton.[2] Made some purchases, posted letters to Mrs. Twiss and Ellen McCready, and called on Horace Twiss. Waited long at the door, and met with a wavering answer to the question if at home, not in keeping with the situation, and suggesting uncomfortable and doubtful thoughts. In the drawing-room, to my surprise, saw Fanny Twiss! the so-called pretty Mrs. T——, and the daughter, whom I had last seen almost an infant! "Oh! world, thy slippery turns," etc. Horace Twiss soon appeared, "white his head as mountain snow" (!), as if to greet the friend he parted from yesterday! He gave me some advice on Mrs. J. Twiss's trust,[3] which may prove serviceable, and in some general conversation Fanny stated her intention of paying Catherine a visit. I neither saw the excelling beauty nor surpassing grace of Mrs. H. Twiss. I paid my visit as easily as I could, and came away.

January 11th.—At Dr. Spurgin's met a party of seventeen, and spent a very pleasant day; the only name I caught was Mr. Warren,

---

[1] One of the Drury Lane Committee.   [2] See note p. 72.

[3] Macready was one of her trustees, and in that capacity had for a time taken charge of her child Arthur.

the author,[1]—he is agreeable but too conscious of being somebody, and I write this observation reluctantly, because he seemed desirous of being pleased with me. Why is it that in society I so often have the pleasure of receiving marked attention and *particular* courtesy, and that my acquaintance is so little sought?—so little, as to make me think myself either disagreeable in manner or dull in conversation. Mr. Warren followed me and requested my acquaintance.

January 13th.—Went into the drawing-room to try *Sardanapalus*, and received quite a disgust at the want of directness, truth and passion in the language. It is out of my way, and I can make nothing of it. I went through much of it.

January 14th.—Before setting out for town received a card of invitation to supper from Mr. Bunn, to "celebrate the fiftieth night of *Gustavus* III." The least that decency could have suggested would have been to have enclosed the amount of his debt to me with the card. Went to rehearse *Sardanapalus*, requested Mr. Cooper to acknowledge Mr. Bunn's invitation, and say that I should not be in town. Bartley spoke to me about a letter from C. Kemble, but I did not well understand him. Inquired of Miss Phillips if she intended going to the supper; she said: ' yes; she was given to understand that she was *expected* to go, and that she *must*.' I am sorry she did not feel her own value more correctly. She makes me suspect that she was not much grieved to be "forced" to go. Went to Garrick Club, where I saw papers and dined—heard of Miss Kemble's great houses in New York; on reflection this is not to be wondered at, the circumstances of her marriage to an American [2] and her approaching retirement sufficiently explain it. After vainly seeking a coach at the Golden Cross, got a place in the mail to Canterbury. Is it possible for a mind of any reflection to see the departure or return of the mails at the Post Office without emotions of delight and wonder at the progress which the human intellect has made? I was highly gratified. There was little to note on my journey; I tried to think over Macbeth. My companions were a conceited officer-sort of person, of whom I thought very little, and two foreigners; one was the third of a party who were outside, and but lightly clad against the intense cold of the wind over the river. But they were young, looked like soldiers, and perhaps cheered themselves onward in life by the hope

[1] Samuel Warren (1807–1877), the author of *Ten Thousand a Year;* Q.C., M.P., and eventually a Master in Lunacy; a constant subject of ridicule by reason of his egregious egotism, which exceeded even that of Lord Erskine.

[2] Pierce Butler, whom she married in 1834 and divorced in 1847.

of a marshal's baton, or some such toy! Poor fellows—I felt for them. Arrived at Canterbury ten minutes past three and got a comfortable bed.

Canterbury, January 15th.—Rehearsed *Macbeth*, and resolved not to mind the absurdity, incorrectness or inattention of the other performers, but to think of how I could best act my own character. Short-sighted mortal! After rehearsal walked up to the Cathedral to learn my way there, and was taken by Mr. Dowton[1] to the Philosophic Institution, where he had been giving a short course of lectures on Phrenology. The building is very neat; the museum a very pretty beginning, and its purpose most pleasing to those who wish well to human nature. Came to my hotel (the Lion) and wrote to Catherine. Acted Macbeth in a very inferior manner; there was scarcely even *reality*, and very often positive affectation. A total absence of that directness of look, voice and attitude that tells to the actor far more truly than the thunders of an audience that he is possessed with his part and *must* bear his hearers with him. It is certain (I do not write it in extenuation of my own faults) that some of the actors were so attired, and others so inaccurate, that my morning's resolution was blown to Heaven, or worse. When the murderers came on one was dressed up in an old tattered cloak wrapt round him, no bad garb for Edgar as Mad Tom. I could not look at the audience, and was obliged to slur the scene—at any rate my nerves quite failed me. I feel ashamed of the professional relationship between us. I cannot subdue it, and money is bought dearly by the pain I suffer under operations of this sort. Mr. Dowton so pressed me to play another night, and gave me to understand how very much it would benefit him, that chiefly on his account I suffered myself to be overruled and consented to play to-morrow.

January 16th.—Hurried my toilet to keep my appointment with Mr. Dowton, who accompanied me to call on Mr. Austin, surveyor, architect, etc., to the Cathedral. I was struck with the acquired knowledge and unlettered lore of my friend Mr. Austin; his observation of " Oliver Cromwell at the Reformation " and Queen Elizabeth granting the crypt to the French emigrants at the revocation of the Edict of Nantes made me smile, but his conversation was not therefore less interesting. Austin's anecdote of the late Lord Tenterden[2] was

---

[1] William Dowton, junior, manager of the Kent Circuit from 1815 to 1835. He became a Charterhouse Brother in 1846, and remained so till his death in 1883.

[2] Charles Abbott, first Lord Tenterden (1762–1832), Lord Chief Justice of England; son of a Canterbury barber; one of the most distinguished judges of the nineteenth century. In

worth recording. Acted Iago very indifferently, indeed the habit of scowling or looking from under my brows, especially when an audience is close upon me, as in a small theatre, is a direct prevention to good acting. I wanted reality and directness, indeed a revision of the execution of the character, and strict attention to my general style. The anecdote told by Mr. Austin of Lord Tenterden, which, he said, " so warmed his heart to the old man, he could have given him a cheer," was on the occasion of his revisiting Canterbury, where he had been born and educated in the Grammar School. Mr. Austin was attending him about the place, when he came opposite to the west entrance. He turned to his son, who was with him, and said, " Charles, on this very spot your grandfather shaved for a penny ; never forget it, it is the proudest reflection of my life, do you never forget it." My cicerone's indignation at the intrusion of two bodies within the burying ground of the cloisters was very droll. " You see, sir, those two gravestones covered with ivy ? " " Yes." " They were two excisemen ; fellows like those, sir, sneaked into a burial-ground like this was too much, so I just put a slip or two of ivy under the stones—it looks quite picturesque, don't it, sir?—the rascals! I've settled their immortality ! "

London, January 18th.—Forster called and made some report of what he had heard of Mr. Bunn's supper—his own and Mr. Westmacott's women seated with His Majesty's Reverendships! What can be more truly disgusting ?

Elstree, January 19th.—I returned to my copying work (alterations of *Riches*), which detained me in my study until the time to expect O'Hanlon and Brydone. The accounts he gave us of the society of the Castle and Phœnix Park were as interesting as those of his own love affairs were amusing. Sheil seems quite to have played a false game, letting his private opinions, in opposition to his public assertions and acts, be as carelessly reported as if they were harmless or even beneficial to him. Littleton's [1] is a life, with all his proud advantages of place and wealth, that I do not envy. I am an actor

---

his last years of office his infirmities necessitated his being carried on to the Bench ; his abilities were, however, unclouded to the end. Before being appointed Chief Justice he had served for two years as a puisne judge, to which post he was promoted from the outer Bar. He is the only instance, at any rate during the nineteenth century, of the Head of the Common Law attaining that position without having sat in Parliament and served as Attorney-General. Like Lord Penzance, Lord Blackburn and Lord Bowen, he won judicial eminence unaided by political status or the adjunct of a silk gown.

[1] Then Chief Secretary for Ireland (see note p. 43).

for a few hours, his is a life of acting. His children's minds are not the objects of his concern and anxiety. His existence, like all fashionable ones, seems selfish and unreflecting, and affords one illustration of Bacon's essay on, I think, "Great Place." Our discussion on *Hamlet* only served to show how little the judges of the drama in England understand what they presume to criticize. Our guests stayed late, but the subjects of our discourse were to me the contrary of tiresome.

January 26th.—Read the *Examiner* and *W. True Sun* newspapers, in the latter of which was some news of the Kembles which I was not displeased to see. This is an unworthy kind of satisfaction. It is the business of a man to steadily and vigorously strive for his own advancement by his own desert, and not measure it by the retrogression or demerits of others. In the same paper was a criticism on *Lear* by Forster, which was well worth the perusal, and made me regret the mistake he committed in his oversight of the great line "if yourselves are old." It has had the effect on me of making me revolve the prudence and practicability of acting the original *Lear*, which I shall not abandon without serious reflection.

London, January 29th.—Dined at the Garrick Club with Forster, and made an appointment with Fladgate; had much theatrical conversation, and went out with my friend, who indeed reeled after me,[1] to Covent Garden theatre, where the box-keeper, rudely as I think, knowing who I was, refused me admission. We then went to the Olympic, but finding no room returned to my chambers, and took tea. Forster showed me some criticisms, one on *Macbeth*, which I could not clearly comprehend, requiring "imagination in lieu of feeling." He told me in confidence of the *affaire de cœur* between Ellen Tree and Mr. C. Kean, with the proceedings of the family. Forster kept me up until half-past two—sobered himself and bade me good-night at an advanced hour of the morning.

February 4th.—As I lay in bed this morning longer than I should have done, reflecting on my own precarious condition, and the anxiety almost painful which I sometimes feel to leave some provision for my

---

[1] It is difficult to associate this post-prandial episode with the verge of the Victorian era. The tipsy critic lurching through Covent Garden, preceded by the sober and somewhat scandalized actor ; their repulse by the surly box-keeper ; the return of the baffled pair to chambers ; the critic, still unsteady in spite of the tea, roaring out dicta and sputtering scandal till the small hours, while his sleepy host sits inwardly chafing, yet not daring to cut short so potent a pressman—the whole scene suggests the era of coffee-houses and sedan chairs rather than the third decade of the nineteenth century.

97

blessed wife and children, the inutility, often experienced, of striving to fashion circumstance or induce events was forced strongly on my reflection, and gave birth to the resolution to endeavour steadily in the labour of self-improvement, and leave results to that Providence whose benignity I feel within me and around me. I could not forbear measuring out half an hour's reading of the sweet book I began last night, and which indeed I persisted in devouring till my dying candle robbed me of my enjoyment: it was Mrs. Brunton's [1] *Self-Control*. I did not close the book until I reached the last page exactly as the fingers of my watch pointed twelve. It is one of the most delightful books I ever read—the only exception I should make is to that gratuitous piece of romance and "hair-breadth escape" at the conclusion, which is not in keeping with what reads like the sober and instructive truth of the rest of the work. It has touched my heart and temporarily, at least, improved my mind. I know no book in which religion wears a more alluring form. I ought not, however, to have sacrificed my study of *Macbeth* to this delightful indulgence. Received a pettish and offended note from Mr. Holme about his play, which I answered.

February 5th.—Was at least busy during the early part of the morning, though only in domestic duties of arrangement, payment, etc. Read two or three stanzas of Tasso, and did little more than open Cicero, and proceeded to read through *Macbeth*, in which I have much to improve and polish. After a thorough perusal of it I sallied forth to the theatre first, where I got an order from Cooper, and told him of the Dowton dinner, which he heard of with anything but a resemblance of satisfaction. This person could give a dinner to Captain Polhill—to Mr. Wallack, etc., but talent and integrity are not the objects of his admiration or hospitality. He *sickened* me, but I had the sense not to show it. At Garrick Club, dined; saw Taylor, Duruset, Price, Villiers,[2] Collier, etc. Heard of Mr. Westmacott's speech at Mr. Ducrow's dinner—that his "unspotted character had raised him to his present eminence"!!! Oh! Virtue! Forster called. I laughed at him about his notice of the Garrick anniversary dinner, and he seemed annoyed at his own defect of judgment. Acted Macbeth

[1] Mary Brunton (1778–1818), a novelist whose works have apparently passed completely out of notice.

[2] Presumably the Right Hon. Charles Pelham Villiers (1802–1878), afterwards for sixty-three years M.P. for Wolverhampton. He was a prominent opponent of the Corn Laws. President of the Poor Law Board from 1859 to 1866, when he retired from public life ; drew an ex-Minister's pension for the unexampled period of thirty-two years.

JOHN M. KEMBLE

From an engraving by G. Adcock of a painting by Sir Thomas Lawrence, P.R.A.

not, I think, altogether badly; I was distressed by that worst substitute for an actress that I ever saw in London, Mrs. Sloman,[1] but I exerted myself where I could. In striving at too much in the last act I injured my effects in some measure, but taken altogether it was not a bad performance, though much attention and pains are yet required to make it a finished picture. I hope it may yet be thought so. Forster came into my room, and gave me an account of the ballet at Covent Garden, which he reluctantly admitted had succeeded; he walked home with me.

February 6th.—Letty arrived before I had finished my toilette, and a newspaper was sent for. To me it contained inexpressibly painful matter in its report of the hostile conference between Sheil and Lord Althorp.[2] I actually suffered *intense pain of mind* in feeling the triumphant position in which Sheil's conduct had placed his antagonist, and my anxiety that his fame should stand clear made me regard his credit more depressed than I subsequently found it. Lord Althorp beyond all question acted his part like a man and gentleman; but I was distressed to see him reaping credit at Sheil's expense. I could not avoid asking myself the question " should I have acted so well, if similarly circumstanced ? " I do not know; but indiscreet and thoughtless as I sometimes am, I think I never should have placed myself so gratuitously in such a predicament, or that I should have preferred an early and private settlement of the affair, with all its danger, to the test I should have to encounter before such an assembly. Called on Chantrey, and after a long and very pleasant conversation left him to proceed on his recommendation to endeavour to influence individually the Dean and Chapter of Westminster to remit the fees for a monument to Mrs. Siddons. My visit to Chantrey was equally interesting with my former one. We were shown into his studio, where a bust was in a state of working, and several marble pieces were placed around. He soon informed us that his conversation with the Dean [3]

---

[1] See note p. 70.

[2] Lord Althorp had declared in the House of Commons that more than one Irish member while publicly opposing the Coercion Bill had in private approved it. When pressed for names, he mentioned Sheil, who immediately declared in impassioned tones that the charge was a gross and scandalous calumny. This produced a " scene," and eventually both Althorp and Sheil were taken into custody by the Sergeant-at-Arms, but were liberated on agreeing to submit to the authority of the House. A committee was then appointed to inquire into the affair, with the result that Althorp's information was found to have been derived from a reported conversation at the Athenæum Club, the truth of which there was no evidence to support. Sheil was, accordingly, exonerated, receiving an apology from Althorp.

[3] John Ireland (1761–1842), Dean of Westminster from 1816 to 1842; founder of the

on the subject of remitting the fees for Mrs. Siddons's monument in Westminster Abbey had produced merely a vague and doubtful answer. He questioned us on our views of the description of monument, in which we were disposed to defer to his judgment. He observed that such a record of a great and interesting person should afford posterity the means of knowing and feeling something of the character of the individual through a portrait, which would impart some sentiment in its elevated expression ; and that could only be done by a high relief —a bust, or a statue. As to any allegorical device he was *toto cœlo* opposed to it. He referred to his communication with the committee for Wilberforce's monument, who had voted £500 for that purpose, quite forgetting the fees, nearly half that sum, to the Dean and Chapter. Chantrey read his letter to Gally Knight, in which he recommended upon the hospital, college or whatever the subscription should be appropriated to, a slab inscribed with Wilberforce's name, and claims to the honour of giving a title to such an institution ; but deprecating any paltry record in Westminster Abbey, where it would teach no lesson and attract no attention ; or if any monument were placed there he advised a statue, concealing his deformity, but bearing in its expression indications of those great qualities which had distinguished him—if desirable let there be a bas-relief upon his pedestal representing his giving freedom to the negroes. He denounced allegory without reservation—take the wings from victory and what is she? In young Bacon's [1] monument of Sir J. Moore, he told us, a stout fellow, representing Valour, was lowering the feet of the dead hero, and a winged Victory letting down by a wreath under the arms the body into the grave, *i. e.* Valour and Victory burying Sir John Moore. When Valour is represented digging a grave, put him on a soldier's jacket and he becomes a pioneer. His account of his employment by the Committee of Taste showed what such committees are ; yet Sir George Beaumont [2] was on this referred to, but had honesty enough eventually to confess himself in error. Chantrey never would send in a sketch, or submit to their criticism. He would not

Ireland Scholarships at Oxford ; son of an Ashburton butcher ; his intimate friend, William Gifford, the famous critic and editor of the *Quarterly Review*, was the son of an Ashburton glazier.

[1] John Bacon (1777–1859), son of John Bacon, R.A. ; both father and son executed monuments for Westminster Abbey and St. Paul's.

[2] Sir George Howland Beaumount, Bart. (1753–1827), country gentleman and amateur painter ; best known as the friend of Wordsworth ; one of the originators of the National Gallery.

allegorize, and therefore he was vulgar and unpoetical. Once, for a freak, he sent in a sketch of a relievo for Lord ——'s monument, who recovered the day, almost lost, by a desperate charge, in which he was killed and twenty-two bullets were picked from his coat and waistcoat. He portrayed the event in relief—the hero in the act of charging with his troops: he copied the same, only substituting a figure of Victory for the General; sent both. The Committee chose the Victory! Chantrey pointed out the folly and bad taste they had been guilty of, and, when too late to rectify, they began to know their mistake. Chantrey has not received £8000 of the money voted for public monuments, while others have taken above £40,000. I asked him if he did not value highly, in comparison with himself, his statue of Washington; he said he did; and I observed to him how strongly the simple dignity of the figure, and the happy union of the military and civil characters, had impressed themselves on my memory. He said that he had been most anxious about it, and as the order had been transmitted to him through Mr. West [1] he thought it only a due compliment to him, as an American and President of our Academy, to consult him upon it. In consequence he called on him and requested that he would sketch a design for the statue. West promised that he would. Six years elapsed, during which Chantrey had often urged and as often been answered by the old man, that "he was thinking of it, that it was a difficult subject." At last, having heard that he was ill, Chantrey went determined to press him upon the subject. He found him so much weakened that he evidently had not a fortnight to live, and yet the old man was indulging in dreamy hopes and intentions of completing pictures on a scale far beyond anything he had ever yet attempted. Chantrey pressed him on the design for Washington's statue. "Why, sir, I am thinking of it; I have thought a great deal about it, but it is very difficult." Chantrey, clearly perceiving this to be the last opportunity he should ever have of learning his views, requested some intimation of the idea that had presented itself to him. "Why, sir," said West, "I intend representing him with one hand laying down the sword and with the other taking up the plough-share." "This satisfied me," said Chantrey, "as to my hopes of assistance from him, and six days after I left him I heard of his death."

The impossibility of distinguishing which hand was in the act

---

[1] Benjamin West (1738–1820); succeeded Sir Joshua Reynolds as P.R.A.

of laying down and which of taking up was directly apparent; but Chantrey gave an instance of it, which I do not wish to forget. Horne Took, with whom he was on terms of intimacy, told him that when his book, the *Diversions of Purley*, was coming out, Cipriani offered to make the design for a frontispiece, and Bartolozzi to engrave it; Horne Took accepting the offers, mentioned the subject he wished: Mercury putting off his winged sandals. The piece was completed and sent to Horne Took, who could not distinguish the precise action of the figure, who, instead of taking off, seemed to him to be putting his sandals on. I questioned him on the applicability of sculpture to subjects of such extent as precluded the power of taking in the whole at a *coup d'œil*, in reference to Lough's group of the Centaurs and Lapithæ. He at once pronounced against it, or against more than one figure, except where combination is necessary to explain and strengthen the sentiment of part. He instanced the Niobe, and our conversation rambling to the Laocoon, an exception to the general rule against action in statues laid down by Chantrey, he called on us to note that the attitude of the Laocoon, though one of active and agonizing pain, was still one of ease, and sitting down he threw himself into the attitude of a man yawning, which exactly corresponded with the figure of the Laocoon before us.

Returned home much fatigued, which I ascribed to my unrecruited expenditure of strength last night. Went to Mr. Warren's[1]—met two or three pretty, agreeable women. Mr. Holt,[2] Bencher, Mr. Malins,[3] Perry,[4] Smith, who had just published a tragedy, Dr. Spurgin and others, not omitting a very interesting man, Mr. Walpole,[5] who came in after dinner. I enjoyed a pleasant day, except that Mr. Holt introduced a discussion of Homer and Greek during dinner, which

[1] See note p. 94.

[2] Francis Ludlow Holt, of the Northern Circuit, and Vice-Chancellor of the Duchy of Lancaster.

[3] Richard Malins (1805-1882), Q.C., M.P., and eventually one of the Vice-Chancellors, in which capacity, nearly forty years later, he tried a case which must have greatly interested Macready, namely, that in which Dr. Hayman sought redress against Dr. Temple and others in connection with his Headmastership of Rugby School.

[4] Fellow of Jesus College, Cambridge, and for some time principal secretary to Lord Lyndhurst when Chancellor.

[5] Spencer Horatio Walpole (1806-1898), Q.C., M.P. Home Secretary in three Conservative Administrations. Proved unequal to his responsibilities during the Hyde Park " Reform " riots in 1866, when he retired from official life. His lachrymose interview with the Reform League leaders, at which he concluded an ignominious peace, was much derided at the time.

drew a common line of Homer from me, and gained me very undeserved credit for my general knowledge of the poet. A long discussion on religion, in which I was opposed by all the remaining party, kept me there till half-past one, as I did not chose to leave my character behind me. I walked home with Mr. Walpole, whom I liked much.

February 7th.—Called on Wallace to learn his feeling on Sheil's affair; he was in the House on Wednesday night, and told me that Sheil behaved well, that he had seen him on the previous day, dissuaded him from allowing O'Connell to interfere, and gained his assurance that he would stand forward and vindicate himself; at the same time Wallace dissuaded him from his first intention of speaking on the address. All this good counsel was neutralized by Sheil's want of firmness and judgment to resist the offer of O'Connell's interference; and Wallace's plan was abandoned for the less direct one of O'Connell's leading. Nothing could be more frank than the testimony Wallace bore to the unaffected cheerfulness with which Sheil consented to place himself in his hands and go to any necessary extremities. I was greatly relieved by this, and in hearing Wallace's confident expectation that he would come triumphantly out of the inquiry. At Warren's yesterday he was spoken of more respectfully than I had anticipated, but my own anxiety for him blinded me to his actual position. Wallace said that the two men who showed the most generous and friendly spirit to Sheil were Sir H. Hardinge[1] and Sir Robert Peel. Read Pemberton's review of my King John, which is too eulogistic. His imagination lends me attributes not my own.

February 9th.—Read eight chapters of Leviticus. In reading these chapters of the Bible, it occurred to me as a question why the present Churchmen hold us partially and not generally to the Jewish law; why we are called on for a literal belief of everything asserted, yet exempted from obedience to many things commanded—especially as Christ came not to destroy the law, but to confirm the law; and especially as we find by St. Paul that circumcision was practised among the Christians after the death of our Saviour. It is merely an additional instance of how much the intermeddling hand of *man* has

---

[1] Henry Hardinge (1785–1856), afterwards first Viscount Hardinge; on Sir John Moore's staff at Corunna and present at his death; served with distinction throughout the Peninsular campaign; entered Parliament 1820; member of Wellington's and Peel's Administrations; Governor-General of India 1844-7; Commander-in-Chief in England 1852-5; Field Marshal 1855. He imported into politics the chivalry that distinguished him in the field.

103

perverted for his own convenience the divine religion which Jesus Christ taught.

February 10*th.*—Could not get up when called this morning, so overcome did I feel from want of sleep; all the coaches had passed, and left me to make a virtue of necessity, which I did by sending my cloak, etc., to town, and setting off in the sharp air of the morning upon a most delightful walk. It thawed as the sun shone out, but not enough to lessen the pleasure of my exercise and the enjoyment of my respiration in the fresh pure air. I quite luxuriated in the exhilarating sensations I experienced. As I came in sight of the fourth milestone a gentleman in a very neat gig reined up and inquired : "Mr. Macready, would you like to ride?" I thanked him with all the courtesy I could summon, but told him I was walking for exercise, and very thankfully declined his offer. This circumstance, and having met several of our villagers wheeling home the coal I had given them, united to increase the cheerful spirits which enlivened my walk. The coach passed me, but I would not use it. Took an omnibus as I approached the New Road; coming home found notes from Smith, Fred. Reynolds and Atherstone. Went to the Garrick Club and saw newspapers—the *Times* basely endeavouring to prejudice Sheil. The translation of Scribe's comedy has succeeded, but is said by those who saw it to be overpraised in the papers. Wallace called for me, wishing me to call with him on Sheil at the Athenæum, which we did, but in vain; he was absent. Returning Wallace asked me to lend him £16 and accept his note at three months. I received the application very ungraciously, for it is unfeeling, indelicate, and scarcely honest to importune me who have a family to provide for, whose expectations are seriously injured by what I have already done for Wallace and some others. I know not what to think of it, but I feel it is *too bad!* Returning to Club, saw Abbott, Fladgate, etc. Wallace came in from the House, and represented Sheil's position as greatly improved by the debate of the night.

February 12*th.*—I took up Mr. Atherstone's tragedy of *Philip,* and with the single intervention of one quarter of an hour to the newspaper, persevered even to its complete perusal. I wrote a note to Mr. Atherstone expressive of my opinion of its very great merit, and recommending him to send it to the manager with a reference to me, if he thought such a testimony of any value. There is much to praise in it—some very sweet poetical passages, and a very good attempt at character in Philip; but a want of acquaintance with effect, and dramatic tact is too frequently manifested to leave hope of its success in representation. Wrote also to Mr. Condy, Manchester, and Rev. Mr. Butler, Nottingham (who sends his hero into a dog-kennel with the exception of one leg, by which the heroine discovers him, imagining that it is all that is left of him, the dog having eaten the rest!), and returned them their plays from the theatre. Read the review (*Edinburgh*) of Wiffen's *House of Russell*, which was lively, and gave a confirmation of all that one had heard disgusting in that disgusting man George III; represented Lord Chatham much less amiable than I had believed him; and accused Burke of wilful defamation in his character of the first Earl of Bedford, under Henry VII and VIII. Wiffen traces the family to a Norman descent, du Rozel.[1] As a family they do not appear conspicuous for talent. Lord William Russell [2] is the most interesting name in the whole line. Read a review on the Law of Libels against Christianity, in which an acute and sensible work, by a writer under the name of Edward Search, is cleverly and liberally examined. Coming home found my dear family all well, thank God! Read the review of Thackeray's [3] *Lord Chatham,* which gives amusing sketches of himself and his contemporaries and some entertaining anecdotes: Temple's parallel of Byng at Minorca and the King at Oudenarde, etc.

February 13th.—On going to my study I looked over the towns that seemed likely to afford me employment in the summer, and thought over some plans for profit, which do not promise much—one was the Birmingham theatre, but the recollection of this being the Oratorio year and the opening of the new Town Hall obliges me to lay aside any further thought on the subject. In looking at the *Edinburgh Review* the name of Stanley [4] arrested me, and I was led into an inquisition on the cause of my dislike to that man. It is very much owing to his pertness and petulance, something to the quality which is the theme of praise in the review, his skill in debate, which argues subtlety and disingenuousness such as I have more than once noted in him. It also occurred to me to ask how far it may be referable

---

[1] A myth; see " The Origin of the Russells " in *Studies in Peerage and Family History* by H. Round.

[2] William, Lord Russell (1639–1683), the Patriot.

[3] Not the novelist, but his relative, a clergyman, whose *Life of Chatham* was very contemptuously treated by Macaulay, though he used it as a peg on which to hang his two famous essays on the great statesman.

[4] Afterwards Earl of Derby, the Prime Minister. Macready's comments on his character were not unjustified.

to that envious impatience of others' progress in life, when we feel ourselves stationary; I would not deny the existence of such an unbecoming motive, lest I should deprive myself by such confidence of the power of eradicating what I utterly condemn. Read review (*Edinburgh*) of Miss Aikin's memoirs of Charles I. We may be mistaken in our ideas of that man's belief of his prerogative's extent; we can have no doubt of his barbarity, injustice, and treachery. What horrid blasphemy is the form of prayer on his martyrdom! Read two party reviews against the Tories, which were too manifestly Whiggish to interest one who would despise any distinctions but those of right and wrong.

February 14th.—My valentine was Mr. Bartley, whose letter communicated to me the reluctance of the actors to join in giving a dinner and testimonial to poor old Dowton. For myself this resolution takes much care from me, and renders to me time which I want. It liberates me, moreover, from any notion of interest or concern as due from me to my "professional brethren." There is no single feeling or idea of duty common to us. "Down to the dust with them, slaves as they are." They are low men, of low extraction, uneducated, and unrestrained in their naked baseness by any moral or gentlemanly feeling. So be it![1] Answered Mr. Bartley's note in a civil and regretful strain, and really I felt regret at the loss of an occasion to gladden the declining years of a meritorious actor by an acknowledgment from his profession of his worth and talent, and at the obligation pressed upon me of thinking less kindly of the members of my unfortunate profession. I took up Miss Austen's novel of *Emma*, which engrossed my attention the whole evening.

Elstree, February 15th.—Finished Miss Austen's *Emma*, which amused me very much, impressing me with a high opinion of her powers of drawing and sustaining character, though not satisfying me always with the end and aim of her labours. She is successful in painting the ridiculous to the life, and while she makes demands on our patience for the almost intolerable absurdities and tediousness of her well-meaning gossips, she does not recompense us for what we suffer from her conceited and arrogant nuisances by making their vices their punishments. We are not much better, but perhaps a little more prudent

---

[1] Macready's kindly interest in Dowton somewhat moderated when that veteran not long afterwards joined his company at Bath. The profession probably had good reason for not considering him at that time an appropriate subject for a complimentary dinner; moreover, it is likely that, with the best intentions, Macready was not an ingratiatory advocate. His demeanour to his "professional brethren" was somewhat reserved and haughty, making them feel that though of them he was not with them.

for her writings. She does not probe the vices; but lays bare the weaknesses of character : the blemish on the skin, and not the corruption at the heart is what she examines. Mrs. Brunton's books have a far higher aim; they try to make us better, and it is an addition to our previous faults if they do not. The necessity, the comfort and the elevating influence of piety is continually inculcated throughout her works—which never appear in Miss Austen's.[1]

London, February 17th.—Went to Garrick Club, lunched, and read the *Times*—the honourable *Times* of Saturday—on Sheil's acquittal. How difficult to repress the murmurs of discontent, beholding success attendant on such base persons as the writers of this paper,[2] the *Age*, *Satirist*, etc., but it is our duty to think to our own good, and as little as possible to others' evil. Came home very uncomfortable in mind. Reynolds's information of the money Bunn had last year received— £25 per week, and an immense benefit, was an added proof (even let the man hereafter do what he may, for he could not then know, nor guess at subsequent events) how vile a being he is. My own condition, and the fate of my blessed children, which only makes it fearful, looked most uncheerily to me. I could not rally my spirits to go to the theatre or the House of Commons, but sat for a time in unhappy and sickly musing. I then began to think on what was necessary to be done, and on one point am satisfied : that I must shake off my indolence for my children's sake. Thought on the necessity of cultivating my profession *daily*—of rising early—using industry and energy. Let me hope these will not turn out mere resolutions, but have the seeds of good within them.

February 18th.—Went to Drury Lane to see the *Minister and Mercer;* felt it heavy, and was disappointed in the acting. Farren, who is highly praised, was as hard and harsh as a crabstick and artificial to the last degree; a man speaking points *at* an audience all through the play. Dowton was better than my fears, often very humorous. Miss E. Tree is not *the* actress; she is good, but not more; in embracing Mrs. Glover [3] her heart should have been in her arms, but there

---

[1] Macready may have been right, but at the present day Miss Austen ranks among the most honoured of English novelists, while probably Mrs. Brunton cannot be credited with a single reader.

[2] As may be gathered from quotations given elsewhere, the style and tone of the *Times* were then very different to those which, inaugurated by Delane, invariably distinguish it at the present day.

[3] Julia Glover, *née* Betterton (1779–1850) ; a brilliant *comédienne*, but at her zenith in the second decade of the nineteenth century.

was no *élancement*, no forgetfulness of self; it was pretty and moderately interesting; it might have been much more. Cooper was a very dull middle-aged man acting the part of an ardent boy; Webster was as coarse and unreal as the clown of an amphitheatre; a most unartistlike performance. Read Livy in bed, and was impressed with the graphic power of the historian. Read *Childe Harold* aloud for practice and amusement. I have reflected much of late on my condition; my mind, that emanation from and best gift of the Divinity, has elevated me to the mere rank of a player, whose merit, as such, is admitted by few, or when admitted in a degree, grudgingly and with indifference by the many. And it is this for which I have lived! to be classed in common repute with things like Mr. H . . l . y [1] and Mr. Farren, or sunk beneath the ungenerous, vulgar nature of Kean! And in the future no prospect, no hope of redemption; my energies must be, ought to be, and I trust will be, bent to improve myself in my profession, in the dear hope of my heart—its dearest—to leave my children at least independent of a world that, with much of individual good, is a mere material for a higher mind to use in compassing the object of its ambition. Perhaps I might have been far happier had my education been level with my situation; let it be a lesson to me in the formation of my dear children's minds.

February 19th.—Felt disgusted and ashamed of the prostitution of the word honour, when I hear it assigned to men like Althorp and Stanley, who would gloze over such baseness as appears in the pension list,[2] and denounce men, as in Sheil's supposed case, for mere levity of conversation. Went out, as soon as I could despatch my business within, and called at the theatre for Mr. Bunn, then at his house; was denied, afterwards admitted into a richly, not tastefully furnished dining-room. Turkey carpet, damask curtains, liqueurs and cake on the sideboard, easy chairs—which my unpaid £200 and gift of £100 would have more than paid for. He acknowledged Dunn's mistake, and said it was rectified. Talked much ridiculous slang about the theatres—"Knowles's Blind B . . . r of Bethnal Green," and such like ribaldry; pretended that he merely wished to get afloat, and then give the drama its chance. *Yes!!!*

Elstree, February 24th.—Rose again in good time, and immediately proceeded to the business before me; wrote to Mr. Mackie about my

---

[1] Presumably Harley.

[2] The Whig Government's pension list was hardly in accord with their gospel of retrenchment, but Macready's invective was (as too often) greatly exaggerated.

books, and read nearly a hundred lines of Virgil, continuing the sixth book, *Æneid*, from where I had left off : the interview between the shade of Deiphobus and Æneas ; there seems little judgment in making the ghosts of the victor Greeks fly in terror from the sight of a leader who had so frequently been discomfited by them ; it is unworthy of the poet, and does not tend to elevate his hero. There were several lines which impressed me strongly. A letter from Kenney,[1] stating his having heard of my wish to belong to the Athenæum,[2] and that if it were so, he thought it might be accomplished, requesting me at the same time to keep his communication a secret. I answered it, thankfully accepting his good offices, if they could procure me admission without a ballot. The whole of the afternoon was occupied without intermission in replacing my books in the study. After dinner I began Pope's preface to his *Homer*, but desisted from it to read Fox's speech on the law of libel, which is clear reasoning, and I think demonstrative in its effect.

February 26th.—Read the last acts of Luke,[3] which, though possessing a considerable share of truth and much originality, is still little more than a sketch : the result is not enough ; there are no struggles of the heart, no gradual revolutions of man's nature—it is a brief dramatic tale. Walked in the garden, enjoying the beauty of the day, the fond rough salutations of my dogs, the peeping flowers, and, most of all, my darling Christina's playfulness. A note from Forster about Knowles's play, Talfourd's speech, Bulwer's bill and other miscellanies, which I answered in equal variety. A note also from Kenney, explanatory of the mode of getting me into the Athenæum, by naming me as a candidate for a yearly nomination : I answered it.

Dublin, March 4th.—Miss Huddart was saying at rehearsal that I was the only person she had known who had not forfeited their title to reputation, or rather to personal consideration. If she could lay bare my heart and mind, and see the inclination of the one and

---

[1] James Kenney (1780-1849), author of *Raising the Wind* and other successful pieces ; a friend of Charles Lamb, who was godfather of his son, C. L. Kenney, also an author of some repute.

[2] The name appears in the Candidates' Book of the Athenæum Club, under date of Feb. 28th, 1834. No. 1029. W. C. Macready, proposed by James Kenney, seconded by Charles Mayne Young, and afterwards as elected by the Committee on June 21st, 1838, when forty members, to be so elected, were added to the Club by a vote of the annual meeting held in May of that year (*note by Sir F. Pollock*).

[3] Macready's part in *Riches.*

weakness of the other, she would see that I owe my good fortune, if indeed I possess it, to the goodness of my destiny rather than my own virtue. Looked at my dress: Colonel D'Aguilar called, and said he would return at four. In the meantime I looked at the paper, and read and thought on Tell. Colonel D'Aguilar called again, and sat nearly an hour. I went to the theatre, and acted *remarkably well*—in a sustained, impressive, *measured* style of enthusiasm and nobleness. I *felt my improvement.* My foolish friend, Pritchard, was the means of sending me on to the call of some silly roarers in the gallery before an audience that really did not want to see me. It almost put me into low spirits. I forgot to notice my want of presence of mind in suffering myself to be *angry* with the little boy that acted Albert in *William Tell;* he forgot all his principal directions, and disconcerted me; but had he been ten times more negligent, I could not find a justification for my behaviour in his inattention. Mr. Mercer, who was so rude in this very play in London, was Melchthal—poverty-stricken and spiritless, from intemperance and cares. Mr. Arden, who was such a vulgar and insolent person that I would not have engaged to act with him, sent to Cooper requesting a *subscription* from the Drury Lane Company, before I left London. "Oh world! thy slippery turns."

March 5th.—The information of the wretched profligates at Elstree throwing down our rick in wantonness disgusted and annoyed me. Went to see a piece which has been very attractive here, *Life in Dublin*—a piece neither calculated to raise the genius, nor to mend the heart, and only fit for a minor theatre; but the indifference of the public to more intellectual amusements is some justification to a needy manager for any attempt he may make to sustain himself even at the expense of taste. Have been in low spirits throughout the day, which may be attributable to my health, but which I am inclined to ascribe rather to my frequent ruminations, and generally sad ones, upon the gloomy complexion of theatrical affairs. *En Dieu mon espérance!*

March 7th.—Called on Miss Huddart, with whom I sat the whole evening. Nor have I the least cause to reproach myself for so doing. I was so low-spirited that nothing but the presence of female society could soothe my fretful state of mind; and spending the evening in tranquil and rational conversation gave ease to my spirits. I came home to write, but the apprehension of an intruder from the next room made me hurry off to bed.

March 8th.—Rose late again, but with a feeling of improved health, and indeed remained thinking in bed from mistaking the hour on the watch. Before I went to rehearsal I wrote a copy of my answer to Mr. Cooper, in which I shall not let Mr. Bunn have an opportunity of saying I thwart him ; if he wishes to ruin the little chance belonging to *Sardanapalus*, I do not feel that I have the right to stop him ; at any rate it is not worth a contest. Went to rehearsal. I do not like Mr. Ternan's mode of behaviour : it is difficult to say who will or will not be an actor, but I do not think this person in his private capacity will ever shed lustre on the theatrical profession. He seems to me opinionated, jealous, and of course little-minded. Walked out with Calcraft afterwards for a short distance ; returning, sent for the *Freeman's Journal*, which was not worth its cost ; rested myself, and read a little of Werner, which for my own particular sake, and to bear down the nasty little attempts to detract from my effect in Mr. Ternan, I wished to act well. I think I did play the greater part of it *very well*. I was collected, and had my energies at my command. Mr. Ternan, without the shade of an excuse, tried to disconcert me, but I punished him by playing my best, and was satisfied with the effect produced. I do not like him—he should associate with Mr. Vandenhoff,[1] a man who merits, what only baseness can deserve—contempt.

March 9th.—Walked out to the Military Hospital, where on leaving our cards the servant told us that Mrs. D'Aguilar was at home, and my odious *mauvaise honte* made me commit the inexcusable fault of refusing, on an idle pretence, to go in ! No words can sufficiently condemn this puerile and shameful folly. I do not like Madame, but in common courtesy I ought to have gone in. I have nothing to offer in extenuation of my absurd conduct. It quite annoys me to think of it. Called on Miss Huddart, and sat with her for three hours, talking chiefly on acting ; I have nothing to reproach myself with, except indolence in this indulgence, and it is a sort of repose to my mind and spirits to lounge away a few hours in the society of an agreeable and handsome woman.

March 10th.—I took some pains with the rehearsal of *Macbeth*, and gave myself a good lesson. It was with much concern I observed the exceeding folly of Mr. Pritchard, who exposes himself on every possible occasion ; he almost seemed desirous of doing mischief in rehearsing the fight, and I was obliged to speak to him on his conduct. Calcraft was annoyed by a demand of £5 per night from Mr. Knowles for the *Wife*, whose performance has not averaged the nightly

[1] John M. Vandenhoff (1790-1861), an actor of the second rank, better known in the provinces than in London.

expenses of the theatre. Went to the theatre, hoping and expecting to act well, but the lightest breath will blow down the airy fabric of an actor's hopes. Some irregularities in the early scenes, and the crying of a child through the greater part of the play "overturned my patience," and though I wished to act well to Colonel D'Aguilar, and he seemed bent on being amused, I could not produce before him the Macbeth of my full conception. I laboured, and when labour is requisite, the inspiration is not present. I was called for by the audience, and obliged to go on.

March 11th.—I had taken a newspaper from Calcraft's table that gave me very moderate praise for Macbeth, observing that though good, it was not so good as Kean's, which was a total failure; and I sent for another, in hopes it might afford me an opportunity of sending to Gaspey, but it was no jot better—*par nobile*. I read after dinner part of Hamlet, and took a quarter of an hour's rest. Went to act Virginius, trying to think of Hamlet, but observing some persons in the theatre, who seemed to have come for the play, I buckled to my task, and played a great deal of it very well. Was *obliged* to go on afterwards at the call of the audience. Calcraft wished me to go to tea with him, but I declined. I sent for Pritchard, and in the utmost kindness remonstrated with him on his behaviour, and, I fear, ineffectively. He had shown me very kind attentions in Scotland, and I did not wish him to suppose that I could forget, or think lightly of them.

March 14th.—Went to rehearsal of Wolsey, where I saw a newspaper expressing an opinion that Mr. C. Kean's Hamlet was beyond all comparison with mine, and that the Horatio was excellent. I could not be offended with it, especially after having seen the editor. Called on Lady Morgan,[1] was graciously received and made a visitation. She is clever, and perfectly self-possessed, but rather affected in manner and in phrase; she seems, however, good-natured and is agreeable. I was pleased with my visit. Went with Calcraft to Colonel D'Aguilar's. Disposed to *frissonner* at meeting Mrs. D'Aguilar after my cavalier behaviour on Sunday, but was *most graciously* received; met Captain du Plat, Boyle, A.D.C. to the Lord-Lieutenant, Colonel Drummond (Guards), Mr. and Mrs. Kane, a family of the Arnotts, army agents. Among strangers, and not being exactly *fêté* I did not anticipate a very agreeable day, but it turned out *assez agréable*. What is the most sensitive point of our nature? Is it not our vanity?

[1] See note, p. 14.

I believe so, and wish it were not so. My complacency was restored by hearing, after a cessation on my part from conversation, an undertone of Mrs. Kane's to Colonel D'Aguilar, "I wish you would make your neighbour talk." From that moment I was myself, perfectly comfortable. I found Colonel Drummond a *gasconading dust.*[1] Mrs. D'A—— and Madlle. were unusually agreeable, and we parted *la meilleure société.*

Manchester, March 18*th.*—Arriving there, received a paper, the *Age*—to me the most disgusting and odious publication that has yet profited by outraging decency—it was sent to me by Forster, with whom I was not pleased for the present. I acted Werner languidly. I was put into ill temper by the newspaper, and could not shake off the weight it laid upon me. I played parts tolerably well, and tried to make it a lesson throughout, but I was not satisfied with myself. A circumstance in the play amused me a good deal and at my own expense. I was inconvenienced and rather annoyed by Ulric looking on the ground, or anywhere but in my face, as he should have done ; my displeasure, however, vanished on seeing the tears fast trickling down his cheek, and forgiving his inaccuracy on the score of his sensibility, I continued the scene with augmented energy and feeling, and left it with a very favourable impression of the young man's judgment and warm-heartedness. In the course of the play he accosted me, begging my pardon for his apparent inattention to me, and explaining the cause, viz. that he had painted his face so high on the cheek that the colour had got into his eyes, and kept them running during the whole act. What an unfortunate disclosure !

March 20*th.*—Used my morning in thinking over Richard III, which I shall play in a much more lively vein than I have hitherto done ; it is an absence of all feeling that forms the basis of his character, and he would necessarily be vivacious from the difficulty of disturbing his purposes. I was not sufficiently imbued with the feeling of Macbeth to do complete justice to myself, but I tried much to throw myself into the part, and should have been much better than I was but for the offensive woman, Mrs. Brooks, *alias* Miss Morton, who played, in ignorance of text and meaning, Lady Macbeth. This is the woman who wrote to a poor mad actor, Mr. Salter, an account of her having borne a child to him and of its death, when nothing of the sort had happened. And Mr. Mathews, brother-in-law of Miss Kelly, declaims upon the respectability of the profession ! Mrs. Wood, now,

---

[1] A term often used by Macready, signifying, apparently, a pompous bore.

I believe, in her eightieth year, came into my room to shake hands with me, and lament over the decay of the drama—poor old lady.

March 21st.—Read the *Manchester Chronicle*, which Clarke gave me, containing the account of the theatrical dinner. How truly disgusting to hear men like Mr. Mathews and Mr. Harley requiring respect for a profession which they in their speeches as leading members prove to be stored with ignorance, vulgarity and charlatanism. Mr. Cooper also, returning thanks for Mr. Bunn (!) and Mr. Bunn, an insolvent debtor, giving £5 to the charity, complete the farce. Oh, England! thou art a beastly country in every respect of credulity and gullibility.

March 22nd.—When dressed I scarcely knew how I should get through the work before me, and thought of the peculiarity of this profession, which obliges the sickly frame to dilate itself with heroic energy, and the man of sorrows to affect an immoderate buoyancy of spirits, whilst perhaps his heart is breaking. I was most attentive to the necessity of subduing my voice, and letting the passion rather than the lungs awaken the audience. In consequence I acted well. I fail, when I allow my tongue and action to anticipate my thought. I cannot bear this too strongly in mind—Puff I managed with tolerable vivacity and earnestness, and the audience were evidently disposed to be pleased with me. Clarke paid me £91 odd for the week, which made me think most gratefully of the good I receive.

To Elstree, March 27th.—Paid my bill, made gratuities to my kind attendants, and was at last seated in the coach. It felt a relief to me, even to be on my way home. I was disappointed in my hopes of being alone by the entry of a middle-aged plain woman on the road, who seemed to me too proud to mount in an inn-yard. I gave her *au diable*, and endeavoured to reconcile myself to my obnoxious companion and an open window the best I could. The sight of Nottingham Castle from the plain it overlooks, recalled to me the days of Edward II, the first raising of the tyrant Charles's standard, and the more recent destruction of the building, with the consequent perquisite of that precious sample of an aristocrat with the title of Newcastle.[1] Another and another filled the coach. I caught a glimpse of the

---

[1] The fifth Duke (1785-1851); a bigoted opponent of Reform, in consequence of which Nottingham Castle, his property, was burned by a mob in 1831. Mr. Gladstone obtained his first seat in Parliament (for Newark) by the Duke's interest, being then "the rising hope of the stern unbending Tories." Lord Lincoln, the Duke's eldest son and college friend of Gladstone, became the Duke of Newcastle who had the misfortune to be War Minister during the most critical part of the Crimean campaign.

Roman milestone at Leicester and Eleanor's Cross at Northampton, where we dined. I thought little on my journey, except on reaching home. My disagreeable companion became more civil as our day closed in, and more disposed to converse; the others were merely animal. At St. Albans I ordered a chaise to Elstree, and anticipated every part of the well-known road. At last I saw the line of London light behind the Elstree hill, and soon was at home. *Thank God! thank God!!* After which Mr. Cooper called, and gave me to understand that *Richard III* would be again announced for Monday next—observing that he "thought it quite as easy as *Werner*." I called at O'Hanlon's chambers, but not a mouse was stirring in them. We returned home, I sleepy and tired; found Catherine not very well, and my darling children going to their suppers. Wrote a note to Mr. Forster, and then sat down to a dinner *gras*, as ordered by Earle.

April 1st.—Wallace told us of Sheil's affected manner of speaking, and of the denunciations of his book (the continuation of Mackintosh's History with his memoir and character) at Holland House—of Brougham's letter to the Longmans on the hostile tone of the strictures, and of his answer, as also of the letters and notices in the *Globe*, with his reply. I was this morning compelled to do a violence to my feelings in punishing my beloved Nina—it agitated me very much, but, thank God, my doting affection for these dear children does not, nor ever shall, make me guilty of such injustice to them as to spare my own feelings at the expense of their future, perhaps their eternal welfare.

April 2nd.—Before I came down my tenderness was put to a severe trial by my dear child repeating the offence for which I had punished her yesterday. I felt there was no alternative, and I punished her with increased severity. It *cut my heart* to look upon the darling little creature's *agony*, as she promised to be good. I ordered her to be put to bed, and came downstairs in low spirits. God bless the dear child—my heart dotes on her, and I could weep with her, while I make her suffer; but I love her too well to bring her up with false indulgence. God grant that my desire to make her wise and virtuous may answer all my hopes. Amen! I wrote to Calcraft, sending him the proofs of *Virginius* and *Henry IV* promised to him, and requesting him to expedite the *opinion* on Mr. Bunn's liability. Read the account of an ascent by some English officers up the mountain of Peter Botte in the Mauritius, an undertaking so perilous, that it affected my stomach in the perusal. Wrote to Mr. Cooper, expressing my hope, that I should not be announced for Richard on Monday next.   Walked round the garden, examining the lately planted trees.   Was very much pleased with the behaviour of my dear little girl, so good and amiable.

April 3rd.—Did not rise so early as yesterday, and received in bed letters from Dr. Spurgin, accepting Catherine's invitation, and from Mr. Cooper, announcing *Sardanapalus* for Thursday next with Mrs. Mardyn [1] for Myrrha, "who received the part *vivâ voce* from the lips of Lord Byron."   The nasty motives which actuate Mr. Bunn in thus presenting to the public a woman, who with youth and beauty to arrest attention was never able to retain it, merely because some suspicion may be circulated of her connexion with Lord Byron, only confirm the disgusting character of the man.   His ignorance of the drama, his utter disregard of its interests and respectability, his wish to attract a house by any empirical advertisement, however disgraceful, are so undeniable, that one passes by him and his actions, as we would the most offensive nuisance which the negligence of the police has over-looked.   Finished reading an article in the *Quarterly Review* on Guizot's edition of Gibbon's *Decline and Fall*, which for the *Quarterly* seems written in a tolerably fair spirit.   Altered the arrangement of my books, and then went out to plant some flowers in the garden, and to have the walnut tree moved.   Whilst there received a note from O'Hanlon, communicating the sad intelligence of Wallace having broken his leg a little above the ankle by falling with or from his horse near Kingsbury.   After lying a day at Hendon, where he was removed by a farmer in his cart, he was conveyed to town by Brydon and placed under Davies's care.   It is very dreadful to contemplate such an accident to such a man; what will become of him!   What is to be his end!   We are all too prone, perhaps, in the vain confidence of our own superior wisdom, to arraign the want of prudence in those who are the victims of their own wilfulness, but perhaps all we have any right to do is to pity and to deplore.   Answered O'Hanlon's note. After tea read the three last acts of *Sardanapalus*, which would have been safe with Miss Tree, but cannot, I think, pass with this quad-ragenarian Myrrha.

[1] A *comédienne* with some talent and many personal attractions, who was falsely credited by the scandal-mongers of the day with having caused the rupture between Lord and Lady Byron.   In point of fact, Byron had only seen the lady for a few minutes, when she called upon him in reference to a part for which she was anxious to be cast.   On the occasion men-tioned by Macready, Mr. Bunn's announcement proved abortive, for Mrs. Mardyn never appeared, and it was generally supposed that the manager had been made the victim of a hoax.

April 4th.—Set myself to *Sardanapalus*, and went entirely through it with all that want of alacrity that want of love occasions, and an anticipation of the utter unprofitableness of my labour. At luncheon I received a letter from Forster, enclosing paragraphs, which *I knew* were going the round of the papers, and declaiming against the profligate and shameless indecency of this Bunn, and engaging to come home with me on Monday night; also one from Mrs. Fosbrooke, applying for orders which I shall not give. This woman applied to me seven weeks ago in a state of destitution, and having then procured her an engagement beyond my hopes, I still find her here. She is not better than she should be! In my study I read the principal part of a new weekly paper started by Leigh Hunt, which breathes that gentle spirit of humanity which flows from a kindly heart tempered and improved by the experience of misfortune.[1]

April 6th.—On coming down I read the newspapers, and was very much pleased with some extracts from a book of Essays by " Conversation Sharp,"[2] which is a testimony to the reputation of his conversational powers beyond all that mere listeners could bear. It is a valuable book, if only for the small portion of it that I have seen. I have decided on giving up the *True Sun*, it is vulgar and stupid, and now that L. Hunt and Forster are leaving it, there is little worth looking at. Received a call to *Sardanapalus* for to-morrow. Was forcibly struck by the admonition conveyed in the extracts from Sharp's book, on the abuse or waste of time, and immediately applied myself to *Macbeth*, which I read through, but felt very languid and unwell, which deterred me from going to church, as I had intended doing. Walked in the garden with Catherine and Christina, and in the farmyard. Amused by an anecdote of Miss E. H.'s—the Bishop of St. Asaph commending the exemplary punctuality of an old woman there in her attendance at every church service, it was such an excellent example: " Dear, my lord," was her answer, " I've nothing else to do "—which might explain the piety of many regular churchgoers.

April 7th.—Shakspeare's birthday. Called on Wallace, whom I found much reduced and suffering, his leg still unset, and himself unable to satisfy me on any points respecting his accident or his present condition. He seemed impatient, I thought, and so much exhausted by

---

[1] This was somewhat too optimistic a view of Leigh Hunt, who was certainly very far from being improved by misfortune.

[2] Richard Sharp (1759-1835), F.S.A., F.R.S., for many years in Parliament as an advanced Whig; a well-known figure in the political and literary circles of his day.

conversation that it lessened my regret to leave him. Went on to Ransom's, and on my way met Hastings Robinson,[1] now grown a large lump of a man, with all the look of a Calvinistic preacher. Went on to chambers, where I found a note from a Mr. Creswell, inquiring the right pronunciation of Sardanapalus, and asking me for three admissions— modest in a man, of whom I know nothing! Went to rehearse *Sardanapalus;* was detained a long while by the prompter; went over three acts of it. Bunn told me of Mrs. Mardyn's letters, and said he began to suspect that it was a humbug of Dimond's.[2] I asked him what he would do, if on rehearsal he found her unpresentable. His answer was: "Kick her—and send her back again! " So much for the caterer to English taste! Made some purchases in Covent Garden for the house and dined at the Garrick Club, where I saw Fladgate, Raymond, etc. Forster called and stayed some little time with me. I wished him gone. I wrote him an order. Palmer came for my trunks. I went to the theatre, and acted better than I could have expected, sustaining myself on biscuit and wine; the last act I played *well, taking my time.* Talfourd, Dow and Forster came to my room. Subscribed a pound to Alfred, the call man, ill and his father just dead. Returned with Forster in carriage to Elstree.

April 8th.—Mr., Mrs. and Miss Haworth came to dinner, and O'Hanlon. Mr. H—— is a sportsman—"then let him pass," etc. Mrs. H—— was thought to have exerted herself, but the more you move an empty vessel, the more certain evidence you obtain that there is nothing in it. Miss H—— seems a person that has the power of being agreeable. We passed a cheerful day, but one that I was not sorry to see gone, in the discharge of this necessary matter of form to our country neighbours.

London, April 9th.—Went to rehearsal, where I learned that Mrs. Mardyn had not arrived, and had sent a letter declaring herself to be "too ill to undertake the journey, and begging Mr. Bunn not to delay the performance of the play any longer on her account." I was only confirmed in my former belief, that the whole business was a hoax. We began the rehearsal of the play without any Myrrha, Miss E. Tree having declared, in answer to Mr. Cooper's message, that she would not act it. Mr. Bunn assumed a dictatorial tone,

---

[1] Rev. Hastings Robinson (1792–1866), Master of the Temple and Honorary Canon of Rochester. He figures as Robinson Major in the Rugby speech-bill of 1808, which is reproduced in Macready's *Reminiscences.*

[2] Author of the *Royal Oak* and other plays ; also manager of the Bath and Bristol theatres.

and after outraging her feelings by taking the character from her, now offered a reparation worthy of himself by endeavouring to compel her to act it at this sudden notice; his observation to Mr. Cooper was that " Punch has no feelings." Shakspeare alludes to the quotation of Scripture by that imaginary being whose fabled blackness would well typify this unprincipled scoundrel, but who is deficient in the filthy and dastardly vices of his substantial likeness. Why may not Mr. Bunn then gabble the trash of Johnson? Miss E. Tree at last *came*, induced or seduced by the cant of the high-souled and upright Bartley. She spoke to me, and I recommended her to stay and rehearse the remainder of the play, which she concurred in thinking most advisable. Mr. and Mrs. Warren made their appearance, bringing an apology for Dr. Spurgin, who was detained by patients. We spent a very cheerful afternoon, though I am not an admirer of Mr. W.'s effort at effect. He overrates himself and his powers of amusing, and is very often in extremely bad taste; but he seems good-natured, and his seeming desire of showing civility to me engages a reciprocal wish on my part. I had the good sense to be carefully abstemious, thinking upon the morrow's demands upon me.

April 10*th.*—We talked a little on Mr. Warren's relation of his brother's death the previous evening, who, dying, observed : " Sam, you have a brilliant career before you, but brilliant as it may be, never forget your brother." This was all in *mauvais goût* and the details of his stories still more so. I could not defend him, but endeavoured to mitigate the censure on him. Read *Sardanapalus* through. Went to the theatre, and rehearsed it. Came to my chambers very much fatigued, and ordered a mutton-chop there. After dining I lay down on bed for an hour. Very reluctantly I rose to go to the theatre feeling my spirits and strength much exhausted. The play began— and I acted much better than from my over-laboured spirits and strength I could have expected. I was self-possessed, and often very *real;* the audience were quite prepared to applaud whatever could be interpreted as deserving notice, and my spirits rose to meet their indulgence. In the fifth act I cut a small artery in my thumb against Mr. Cooper's dress, which bedabbled my whole dress as well as Mr. Cooper's and E. Tree's, flowing profusely at times, and then spurting out like a spring of water. Was called for by the audience, but was ignorant that no one had been sent on, or I would not have gone forward; in the erroneous belief that Mr. King had been on, whom I heard desired to give out, I led Ellen Tree forward amid much applause.

Elstree, April 11th.—Took a chaise to town, for I felt quite unequal to walk to Edgware; on the road went over Sardanapalus. Arriving at my chambers, which I did in very good time, I found a letter without signature, the seal was the head of Byron, and in the envelope was a folded sheet with merely the words: " Werner, November 1830; Byron, Ravenna, 1821; and Sardanapalus, April 10th, 1834." Encircling the name of Byron, etc, was a lock of grey hair fastened by a gold thread, which I am sure was Byron's, and which I have no doubt was sent to me by his sister, Mrs. Leigh.[1] It surprised and pleased me. At one o'clock I went to the theatre to cut the play— but who was to cut it? Half an hour at least should have been taken from it, and Mr. Cooper, an incompetent booby, was the stage-manager, whose business it was to have arranged its cutting. From thence I went to the Garrick Club to read the newspapers, which were all very favourable to me, and to dine—saw Collier, Taylor, Bartley and several others. I fear I carried the effort at modesty, which the pride of success puts on, upon my deportment, but it was against my will if it was so. On my way there Kenney called to me, congratulated me on Werner, and acquainted me with the circumstances of the introduction of my name at the Athenæum—that if not elected this year I should be next, or if driven to a ballot (to which I would not consent to go) I should be sure of success. Came home very much tired. Tried to read *Sardanapalus*. Went to the theatre and acted very feebly—every one seemed unstrung and languid from the effects of the preceding evening. Mr. Cooper seemed anxious to prevent the notice of the audience in any effects I tried to make. This is base in Kean—ridiculous in a man like Cooper.

April 12th.—Went out to dine at Garrick Club, where I saw the papers; looked again at the *Times* of yesterday, which is, as usual, the coldest of all the notices on the play. Came home very tired, and turned over the leaves of *Rowland Hill's Life*, when Forster came in bringing for Catherine extracts, cut out by him from the papers, on *Sardanapalus*. He spoke with asperity on the *Times* criticism, which he thought most illiberal. When he had left me, I read over Sar-

---

[1] The Hon. Augusta Leigh, Byron's half-sister, and the subject of Mrs. Beecher Stowe's atrocious imputations which, although revived by the late Lord Lovelace in *Astarte*, are now regarded by those best competent to judge as completely discredited (see *Lord Byron and His Detractors*, by John Murray and others; also *The Love Affairs of Lord Byron*, by Francis Gribble, and the *Diary of Frances Lady Shelley*).

danapalus, and went to the theatre, having sent Healy to inquire after Wallace, who was going on pretty well. I acted with considerable spirit, and much more effectively than last night—still, I think the play will not be attractive. On coming home I read the *Literary Gazette*, and went very much tired to bed.

April 13th.—Went to afternoon service—was struck with the 2nd lesson, the 2nd chapter of the general Epistle of James. How clergymen can read that chapter from the pulpit and pay the homage they do to wealth and power, and call themselves ministers of Christ's religion, they best know;—to me their conduct is a reason for their unpopularity. Walked round the garden, which is always a pleasure to me. Played with my darling children, while dressing for dinner. Spent an idle day—tired and languid with the past week. Made up my accounts. Read prayers to the family, and felt truly grateful to God for his great and many blessings. May I merit them, and estimate them, and teach my dear children to seek for, and obtain, and appreciate similar ones! Amen!

April 14th.—Acted very indifferently—even I felt the effort I made to be gay and animated, and the consciousness that the audience could not be insensible to it increased the weight upon my spirits. The house was indifferent, and though Mr. Cooper gave the play another chance to Wednesday, I felt its fate is decided. Came to chambers, and amused my idleness and fatigue with the newspaper. In the fourth act I was at fault for the words, which after some hesitation and substitution I recovered.

April 15th.—After dinner in a note from O'Hanlon, I had the pain to hear that Mr. Davis expressed himself in the most melancholy way upon Wallace's state, and that he even entertained doubts of his life. This is very unexpected, and very sad news to me. Poor Wallace has long since destroyed that high, that exalted opinion, which I once held of him; and subsequently has done much to sap and shake the esteem and regard which I have wished to bear him; but the habits of attachment, long acquaintance and confidence are not broken; as the root is plucked from the earth it carries some of the soil, however hard, with it. I hope sincerely and devoutly, for his own sake, that he may be spared.

April 16th.—Deferred getting up to the last moment, but rose in very good time for Billings's coach, in which I came to town, employing myself on the road with thinking over Sardanapalus. Was set down at Cambridge Terrace, and called on Wallace, whom I found, I thought, better; stayed with him until he seemed to wish me gone. Was glad to find he had so relished the rusks. Went on to Mackie's, bookseller, and spoke about the shameful binding of my books. He is a tradesman who would sell a customer like myself, ready to buy from him, for a few shillings—a fool! At the Garrick Club saw papers—among others the *Age*—speaking of ' Mr. Reynolds's clever adaptation of *Sardanapalus*, which I had merely cut a little.' There is not an effect of any import in the part that is not a restoration or introduction! I looked into Crabbe's life; lay down for about half an hour, and read part of *Sardanapalus*. I acted—I know not how; I went prepared and anxious to play well, but I cannot work myself into reality in this part—I have not freedom enough to satisfy myself. Miss Tree and self nearly singed in the last scene. Mr. F. Vining called, and spoke to me about going to Brighton. My dresser told me of Mr. Farren's acting in the farce to-morrow night, and of his intention to dress in my room, which I am not disposed to permit. It is idle, but I despise the wretched fellow.

April 17*th.*—In bed this morning I read over Sir Edward Mortimer,[1] which I feel difficult, and do not think a natural character, but I will do my best. *I have no time to lose.* Mr. Fox[2] called; a gentleman of peculiar appearance, a good physiognomy, and bland and gentle manners. The object of his call was to bespeak my interest in the case of a fair aspirant to theatrical success. I was as courteous and candid as I could be, and made an appointment with him and her for Monday morning next. With an ill feeling towards that nasty person, Mr. Farren, yet condemning and ashamed of myself for retaining it, yet not liking to retract, I put the copy of my engagement in my pocket, and resolved on settling it easily if I could by seeing Cooper. Read *Sardanapalus*. Acted with much more spirit in the first four acts than heretofore, but did not satisfy myself in many things in Act V; my manner was too constrained—I wanted reality. Mr. Bunn asked me if I would act Joseph Surface on the King's command. I declined; I am out of the character, and it is tempting further solicitation to voluntarily commit myself to it again. The King cares for neither the play, nor the actors, nor their art, and I see no reason why I should inconvenience myself for him.

April 18*th.*—Forster called, and talked much; I begin to see (for

[1] In Colman's play of *The Iron Chest*.

[2] William Johnson Fox (1786–1864), preacher and journalist; prominent member of the Anti-Corn Law League. M.P. for Oldham 1847–1863. This interview inaugurated an intimate friendship much valued by Macready.

scrutiny of character is a part of life's business, if done in a gentle and indulgent spirit) that he talks much, and that his imagination anticipates facts. I do not say this derogatorily of him nor unkindly, but it is so. We walked together to Wallace's, whom I saw. He seems ill, but I am no judge. He told me Davis wished to see me : I do not think that looks well, though he said that it was merely " in kindness." With Forster took an omnibus down Oxford Street, and walked to the Garrick Club, where I dined : was introduced by Forster to Villiers; saw Mr. Barham; asked T. Cooke [1] to the Shakspeare supper on Wednesday, and to dinner on Tuesday, to which last he could not come. Saw Mr. Charles Kean and shook hands very cordially with him, but I thought he seemed cold. Came home. Acted Sardanapalus with more spirit than on any previous night. Still it is improvable.

April 19th.—Went to the theatre. Found a card from Gillett (!) and a note at the theatre from Mr. Telbin,[2] requesting a recommendation. Acted Sardanapalus indifferently, harassed and worn down. Invited Stanfield to dinner on Tuesday; he accepted the invite. Note from Price that Talfourd would come. Forster called; he is in a scrape—what sort I know not. Jones brought me my salary £5 short, which I refused to take.

April 20th.—Disgusted with the shameful behaviour of Mr. Mackie in again sending my books so very badly bound. I shall never buy a book from him again; but I will not, as in my younger and sillier days I should have done, tell him of this intention, and *make* an enemy when I can avoid it. Had I always shown like consideration and self-government, how much I should have profited by it. Went to afternoon service, when young Mr. Phillimore did duty. What a waste of time to listen to the utter nothingness of those congregated words that he has ranged together in the form of a sermon. It is a mockery. I must think of other and deeper things, or sleep.

April 22nd.—Talfourd, Price, Stanfield, and Forster arrived to dinner. We had a cheerful day—rather more excited than usual; our conversation in the drawing-room was in a somewhat livelier and more boyish vein. Our guests left us a little before twelve.

April 23rd.—Shakspeare's birthday. Looked at an article in *Blackwood* in defence of Sheil, and heaping sufficient opprobrium on the head of Lord Althorp! He deserved it and more, in my mind, for his weakness and injustice. Acted Sardanapalus in an indifferent style;

---

[1] Presumably Thomas Simpson Cooke (1782–1848), composer and vocalist.
[2] The scene-painter.

felt, while uttering it, the unreal tones in which the dream was delivered, and wondered at the applause which continued so long after. I did not deserve it. 'After the play, dressed and went to the Garrick Club, where I took coffee, and was looking at the *Quarterly Review* of the modern French drama when I was joined by Talfourd, Forster, White and others. I found our private supper, which was to have consisted of eight or ten, swelled into a greater number, and many of the guests strangers to me. Jerdan was amongst us! and I thought (not, I hope, uncharitably) that it would have been more graceful to have absented himself from a festive meeting under his peculiar circumstances,[1] which he evidently cannot feel very strongly. Talfourd was placed in the chair, and in the course of the evening made some very good speeches. My health was the third toast from the chair—and toasting, as applied to me, such a compliment may well be called; for I curl and shrink under the operation as much as if I underwent literally the process of being brought to the stake. Under the fervency of Talfourd's panegyric I might employ Shakspeare's words: "Beneath this fire do I shrink up." I met Mr. Hayward,[2] to whom I was introduced, and who gave me his card, promising to send me his translation of *Faust*. It was to me a very pleasant evening. Reached home at a quarter past three.

April 24th.—Looked into the *Foscari* of Byron. I am of opinion that it is not dramatic—the slow, almost imperceptible progress of the action, and the strain required from our belief to sympathize with the love of home in Jacopo will prevent, I think, its success in representation. I was interested by the coincidence of two men's fortunes depending on a casualty, to which they voluntarily submitted the course of their destinies. Robert Bruce hung the determination of his future course upon the strength of a spider's web, and Francisco Sforza threw the future chances of his life with his mattock upon an oak; when asked to enlist he said: "Let me throw my mattock upon that oak; if it remains there, I will." It remained, and he enlisted; from a peasant becoming soldier, general, prince.

April 25th.—Read with much delight, and not without emotion,

---

[1] Probably of a financial nature.

[2] Abraham Hayward (1801–1884), the well-known essayist and *causeur;* Q.C., but relinquished practice on not being elected a Bencher of his Inn (Inner Temple), owing to the hostility of John Arthur Roebuck; a "political henchman" to various statesmen of the day, notably to the Duke of Newcastle and Lord Clarendon; friend and adviser of Mrs. Norton. A talented writer and accomplished talker of the "Croker" school, who, though made much of in his day, has, like most of his type, left little permanent mark.

several poems by Mrs. Hemans: *Arabella Stuart*, in which is much
that is beautiful, particularly her notice of the year's progress and the
unchanging stillness of her own misery, as well as the blessings she
pours upon her lover. *Korner's Sword*, or—I forget the title—his
" death-day," I think—and *Korner's Sister* are both charming. I did
not before know the sad tale of this young, gifted enthusiast—" he
should have died hereafter." *The Maid of Scio* is another of this
extraordinary woman's poems that I read with deep interest, and even
wonder at the depth of thought and feeling that mark all her writings—
one on the love of life, and the losses of our heart's loves that make
it wax cold and weak—I forget the title. Called on Wallace, whom
I found not so well. Brodie[1] had seen him, and spoke to him most
encouragingly. Dr. Lardner was at home; we talked together. I
saw he was not satisfied with Wallace, who has certainly done enough
to weary out his patience. He has already had in advance the *price of
another volume !*[2] This I do not think he knows—that is, he *will not*
know it. He spoke to me about the £16 he last borrowed from me, but
I desired him not to think of it—*it is the last*. Both he and Lardner
talked of that silly fellow Mackintosh, who in a letter to the *Globe*
spoke of his friend as " a man incapable of anything but being misled,"
etc. Wallace intends to demand an explanation of the note. Query:
is it worth while? Came home: found the *Faust* of Mr. Hayward, sent
by him. Wrote note to Dow with *Blackwood*, which I looked over for
Sheil's defence, which would have been very strong, had the writer
confined himself to the reason of the case. Calling names is a sign
of anger, wishing to hurt beyond its power of harm—consequently
undignified. Went to Garrick Club, dined, saw Collier, Reynolds, etc.
Our supper seemed to have pleased. Looked at the debates on the
Repeal. I suspect O'Hanlon helped Littleton in his speech.

April 26th.—I feel, or fancy so, such a heavy sensation of fatigue
after *Sardanapalus* that I am by no means so disposed as I would wish
to rise in the morning. I particularly feel the effect of being so long
upon my feet, and in an erect, sometimes almost strained, posture; my
loins ache with this. I cut the leaves of *Faust* this morning and read
some of it, but it is not to be read with common care. An author
called with a version of *Pericles*, which I very courteously persuaded
him I could not assist by my influence. A man called, who, as I
thought, set his head at work with a palsied motion as he came in;

---

[1] Sir Benjamin Brodie (1783-1862), first Baronet; the distinguished surgeon.
[2] Wallace was contributing to a *History of England* in Lardner's *Cyclopedia*.

he has been before, and I relieved him; I dismissed him now. Posted
Catherine's letter, and bought eau de cologne for Wallace. Went to
Garrick Club, read the Repeal debate, Lambert's, Sheil's, Peel's
speeches; struck by the unfairness of the *Times* report. Dined; saw
Captain Williams, who told me of a rupture between Bunn and Polhill
—too good to be true—Duruset, etc. Met Procter, wrote him an
order for to-night. Spoke to Kenneth about acting all the summer.
Procter walked with me nearly to the Temple. Called on Hayward;
like him very much; engaged to dine with him on Sunday week. Called
on Price; he talked of Forster, of whom Procter had also been speaking,
stating that Mrs. P—— and Forster had quarrelled on the merits of
Knowles's acting from the obstinacy of F.'s persisting in asserting him
to be a fine actor. This is strange! I talked of Dowton's dinner
to Price, and he agreed to forward it. Coming home, found notes
from Reynolds about Wallace, and Burrowes Kelly about a play of
his; also Mason's card. Answered Reynolds and wrote to Wallace,
sending eau de cologne and for Mrs. Hemans' books. Lay down *very
tired*. Acted Sardanapalus with much animation, and the dream particularly with a good deal of reality; the audience felt it. Talked with
Stanfield. Dr. Lardner came to my room.

April 28th.—Called at Reynolds', and learnt from him that the
quarrel between Bunn and Polhill ended in a *partnership* between them.
The enormous folly of this unfortunate man, Polhill, is scarcely
credible. Went to Garrick Club, dined with Fladgate, Mathews,[1] who
was annoyed at not being of the Shakspeare Supper; I do not regret
it. I mentioned to him Dowton's dinner, to which he was as cold as
decency would let him be; it was *premature*, etc. He is a quack, a
coxcomb and a humbug. It occurred to me that I could gain no
reputation by acting Sir E. Mortimer. It was Kean's masterpiece; it
is a feeble play in the country, and could not serve me there nor in
town. I turned over many things, and rested in the conclusion that
it behoved me to make a vigorous effort and endeavour to strike a
blow in Lear. Why should I not make the effort? I have " cause,
and will, and means, and might," and I will make the essay, trusting
in the Power that has guided and protected me for the result. Received
a note, very civil, from Mr. Burrowes Kelly about his play, which I

[1] Charles Mathews (1775–1835), the famous comedian. Macready has seldom a good
word for him, but in this instance, as in many others, his dislike was largely founded on prejudice. Oxberry, whose biographies are seldom over complimentary, describes Mathews as
"generous and humane; a good husband; a kind father; and an honourable man;" while
in his art he pronounces him to be unique.

in consequence folded up *for Mr. Cooper* to be transmitted to Bunn. Acted Sardanapalus; not, I really think, badly, but I could not rouse the audience, which still makes me doubt myself; but I certainly tried to act. Mr. Cooper sent me the opera box for Madame. Speaking of the new *partners*, Messrs. Bunn and Polhill, he observed, "One was a fool, the other a blackguard." Considerable tired—my back! my back!

April 29th.—Letitia and Miss E. Hughes left me for town, Miss H—— putting into my hand a letter in which was an extract from one of Blanco White's [1] worth preserving. Walked in garden, and felt as a luxury the beauty and comfort around me; my enjoyment, if not actual gratitude, is very like it. Took down *Lear*, but was interrupted by my precious children; heard darling Nina her lesson, and soon afterwards gave her and Willie their dinner. Was so languid after that I could screw myself up to nothing; I was quite inert—painfully conscious of it, annoyed and helpless under it. I wished to walk, but had not the energy. Took down Rousseau's *Confessions*. What a book! How could a man record the bestialities it contains? Of what benefit to mankind are such revolting disclosures? How childishly he seems to endeavour to delude himself in his own and others' motives! What was he? A scoundrel of genius; was he more or less? There is, however—and this aggravates its offensiveness—much in the book worth reading. Looked at Byron's notes. Query: what in his heart was he?—Rogers—Hobhouse—was he very much better? Thought on my own abuse of time and sensations of indisposition, the consequence of my own indiscreet indulgence. *I must reform this*, if I wish to see my children what I pray to live to see them.

April 30th.—Dow called, bringing me a number of the *Sporting Magazine*, which contains a portrait and notice of his dog Rapp, and a brief memoir of a man named Mytton,[2] who spent an immense fortune in—I do not well know how to name it—*sporting*, or folly of all sorts. He told me of the *Age* containing some comments on my not acting Joseph Surface. Oh, how sickening it is to be mixed up with such a blackguard as this Bunn! Lay down, intending to read, but the

---

[1] Joseph Blanco White (1775–1841), theological writer; successively priest, agnostic, Church of England clergyman and Unitarian. Author of a sonnet entitled *Night and Death*, which Coleridge pronounced to be the finest in the English language.

[2] Macready was apparently as little familiar with sporting celebrities as are certain judicial magnates with the cynosures of the stage. Poor Jack Mytton hardly deserved to be snuffed out with the indefinite article. He was indubitably a great sportsman, whose fame in Leicestershire is little less than Macready's in Drury Lane.

return of the party prevented me. I slept a little. On reaching the theatre I found myself announced for every night this week! Sent dear Catherine word of it, which reached her as she was setting off for home. Acted Sardanapalus is a passable manner, many parts of it with more spirit than usual; but Miss E. Tree destroyed me in the dream by looking at some persons in the boxes instead of myself. Forster called at chambers to ask me to accompany him to-morrow to the Court of King's Bench to hear Talfourd's speech for the *True Sun's* editors. Looked at a notice of Kean in the *New Monthly*, and cut its leaves.

London, May 1st.—Forster called as I was at breakfast, wishing me to accompany him to hear Talfourd's speech. It was important to me to give my attention to Lear, and I declined a pleasure I wished to enjoy. When he left me, I began reading and thinking upon Lear, which I am most anxious to succeed in, but in which I fear no man can who appreciates the character. Saw the *Age* newspaper, with its attack on me for not playing Joseph Surface before the King, "by whom I breathe, who is the breath of my nostrils." To be mixed up with a blackguard like Mr. Bunn is an annoyance; to be in the mouth of a reptile like Westmacott is annoyance; filth is an annoyance; they are all one and the same. Planché took me from the club to Miller's to present me with his play of *Reputation*, which seems to have much merit; saw C. Dance,[1] on whom I promised to call. Looked over *Sardanapalus*. Went to the theatre, took pains, and acted it well; so well, that I could think with indifference, or indeed amusement, on Messrs. Bunn and Westmacott's overflowing loyalty and gratuitous baseness. Was *earnest* and impassioned. Went into a private box to see the farce of *Secret Service*, which was well acted generally, but particularly well in Farren's character: as much superior to the *Minister and Mercer* as reality is to bad copying. Much pleased with it; what a pity that so good a player should be such a wretched ass!

May 2nd.—Began a late morning with a little of the sixth book of Virgil's *Æneid*, wherein we find the purgatory and the punishments of the Romish Church. It is curious how much of that religion is made up from the paganism it supplanted. Hurried out to my appointment at Canning's statue with Fladgate at twelve; met him there, and with him called on Dr. Ireland, the Dean of Westminster, on the subject of the fees for Mrs. Siddons's monument; found him a very

---

[1] Charles Dance (1794–1863), playwright and official of the Insolvent Debtors' Court.

gentlemanly and pleasant person; he promised to send me an account of the expense, which should be as low as he could make it.   On leaving him, we went over Westminster Abbey, and I saw the sorry affair they have placed to Kemble; in my opinion quite good enough, but in itself a wretched thing.   What a contrast to that living piece of marble that keeps for ever alive the person and personal character of Horner [1] by Chantrey.   Roubiliac's [2] I now thought little of; the dying woman is well done, and there is expression in the man, but I quite feel the unreality of mingling allegory with fact.   Was prevented by fatigue from reading *Sardanapalus*.   Acted the first part very well—better than I have yet done it, but I am tired with it; still, I did much well, though I did not finish off the dream so earnestly and really as last night.   Mr. Cooper gave me notice of my benefit, on which I shall see him to-morrow.   Price and Fladgate to-day both agreed with me on the badness of Farren's Bertrand and on the excellence of his last night's performance.   What a wretched blockhead is that Cooper!—to be an actor! and to be a manager!

May 3rd.—Some doubts which rose in my mind on the propriety of trying Lear were overruled by the seeming necessity of making some effort, and also of not leaving a character, now not performed for three or four seasons, to the chance of an actor like Mr. V——.[3]   This weighed strongly with me.   Cooper called twice about my Benefit night, which, in consequence of Mr. Bunn's irregularity, I am compelled to take on a diminished notice.   What a very obtuse man is Mr. Cooper! the most impenetrable head I ever met with.   Called on Reynolds, who thought Wednesday 21st not objectionable, and who approved of *Lear* with Shakespeare's text.   Saw Frederic, and chatted with him for a few minutes.   Went to the theatre, saw Cooper, and accepted the night; was guilty of an *unpardonable folly* in condescending to prate to him of Mr. Young's unworthy behaviour on his retirement.[4]   "Oh! I could divide myself and go to buffets " for my absurd thoughtlessness. Went to theatre and acted Sardanapalus as if a milestone were about

---

[1] Francis Horner (1778-1817); Whig statesman and political writer, whose premature death cut short a career of the highest promise.

[2] Louis François Roubiliac (1695-1762); of French origin; settled in England and obtained considerable vogue as a monumental sculptor.

[3] Presumably Vandenhoff.

[4] This aspersion is hardly reconcilable with Macready's statement on Young's death, over twenty years afterwards, when he records his esteem for his former colleague's "uniform respectability of conduct." Possibly Young's "unworthy behaviour" consisted in his making a temporary return to the stage after pronouncing a "final farewell," whereby he would certainly have incurred Macready's disapprobation, having been one of his most formidable rivals.

my neck—I could not divest myself of the weary sensations I felt. Read an anonymous letter about my shabby dress—well deserved. A puppy came into the green-room, who sat down, and with perfect familiarity entered into conversation with others in the room and myself, though I believe known to none there. The vulgar coxcomb! Came home, headache and fatigue. Sat down to proceed with Lear, of which I marked a great deal.

May 4th.—Lay in bed to rest, and at the same time to concentrate my thoughts more closely upon Lear, which I read through with great attention. Thoughts and vain imaginations will intrude, but had I earlier learnt to subdue my mind, or rather my passions, of how much greater length would the useful part of my life have been, and how much more I should have done for myself and others. I settled my accounts, and set at once to work on the cutting, and then marking fairly the copy of *Lear*—a task to which I assigned about two hours, which has cost me seven or eight. I have finished it, and I humbly hope for a blessing on my work. Amen! Made it in a parcel for Cooper and sent it to, him. Dressed and went out to dine with Hayward.

May 5th.—I awoke very early this morning with the heat of the atmosphere, and my own excited system; was kept awake by a sort of horror that possessed me on thinking that " tapis " was a Latin word, and that I had used it as a French one. It is ludicrous to remember how much I suffered from this fancy, and how my silly pride attempted to set me at ease. I could not sleep, so read over some observations I had written for Catherine on Burke's *Sublime,* and some of the thirteenth book of the *Iliad.* To Garrick Club, where I dined, and wrote a hurried letter to Bourne ; looked at newspapers ; amused with R. Linley's dislike of the "early purly " reading in *Macbeth.* Found a note from Dow in chambers, acknowledging the amount of bills, and reclaiming, to my great relief, Pollok's *Course of Time.* Answered Dow, and wrote note to Brewster about Lear's wig. Wilkin called, and told me that the answer to his mission at Mathews' was that Mr. M—— had no intention of disposing of his pictures. Acted Sardanapalus unequally; my first scene I can scarcely ever test, for Mr. Cooper (*risum teneatis ?*) is so very unfair that he really neither allows the audience nor myself a chance. I thought I did the first act and the dream very well. Miss E. Tree asked me to act Lord Townley [1] for her ; I gave a conditional promise.

[1] In *The Provoked Husband.*

Elstree, May 6th.—Awoke by Healey in time to be ready for the Crown Prince, but with no chance of such a walk as I had contemplated last night. Thought on Lear as I waited for the coach, and came pleasantly on the outside to Elstree, where I found the trees in full leaf, as if magic had been at work on our little domain. My beloved family all well. Walked round the garden with a feeling of its quiet and comfort that will not bear translation. After breakfast resumed my promenade, and afterwards noted down some memoranda, and decided on Lear's dress, etc. Looked through prints for a head, but found none affording more information than I already possessed. The day has been lovely, and closed in with a most beautiful evening, and this place appears to me almost lovely in itself, although it owes its charms to the lights and colours of universal nature, always adorable, and to the moral atmosphere that breathes about me here.

London, May 7th.—Found notes from Wallace and Hayward, the latter mentioning Mrs. Jameson's [1] wish to "make my acquaintance" and to see *Sardanapalus.* Went to the theatre, desperate as to my prospect of getting through the play, but by acting with collectedness and presence of mind and imposing earnestness through the perform- ance, I made a much better Macbeth than I could have calculated upon. I was more than ordinarily fortunate in the soliloquy upon the com- mission of the murder, and upon the death of the queen; also with the murderess. My reception of the news of Birnam Wood was correct, but my last scene was marred by my antagonist. Altogether I got through well enough to have satisfied myself, and so well that I do not conceive I have any excuse left for the ill-temper I manifested towards two persons, Mrs. Sloman and Mr. Cooper, whom I ought not to have noticed except in a kindly spirit. I hope to amend this foolish and unamiable fault.

May 8th.—Anxious to act Sardanapalus well to-night on account of the Birches, but more particularly for Mrs. Jameson, I took all pains, and I thought was in a good vein of acting, ever combating the stupid malice (for I am sure he nightly tries to cut me from applause) of that unfair actor, Mr. Cooper; but as I did not move my audience to my own satisfaction, I am obliged to believe that I did not represent the character to theirs. Still, I thought myself better in many things than I had yet been.

May 9th.—Had some little conversation with Dowton about *Lear,*

---

[1] Anna Brownell Jameson (1794–1860); best known as the authoress of *Sacred and Legendary Art.*

which did not tend to strengthen my confidence. Very much disgusted with the impudent conceit of that miserable coxcomb, Farren, but I believe I am more impatient of it than usual from the success which at present seems to increase it. I ought to be above such things; but we get angry, and see its folly afterwards.

May 10th.—Wrote a French note (which tasked my memory) to Grisi, inquiring her charge for a song, and went to rehearsal of *Lear.* Returning to chambers, wrote another French note to Paganini on the same subject as to Grisi. Wrote a note on Benefit matters to Madame Vestris, who, unluckily, is on the Continent. Answered others, from Hayward, Pemberton, and Captain Medwin, who dates South Molton Street, and is represented by his messenger " as the gentleman living at Mr. Tibbs's, Dean Street." He seems a complete shuffler; his request was for an order to *Sardanapalus.* Acted Sardanapalus pretty well to a miserable house—two persons in the second gallery at the opening! From the frequent and almost uninterrupted repetition of this play, I feel myself relapsing into my old habitual sin of striving for effect by dint of muscular exertion, and not restraining my body, while my face and voice alone are allowed to act. It is of the utmost importance to be on my guard against this vicious habit. Came home under a beautiful starlight night, which reminded me of the sweet nights I have travelled in Italy—came home in an hour and a half, and found Letitia sitting up for me.

Elstree, May 11th.—The morning was so beautiful, the leaves and flowers so fresh and sweet, and the singing of the birds so charming that I could not go in to breakfast until I had walked round the garden with my darling Christina. I felt the sweetness of all bounteous Nature, and my heart acknowledged, and acknowledges the many blessings which in this life my Gracious God has heaped upon me. My children are looking rich in health, and growing good little creatures. Ought I not to be grateful? Looked over the newspaper, and settled my accounts; then turned my thoughts to Lear, but did not give the practice to it which I had intended; thought over and looked over much of it, but desultorily, and testing few of my thoughts by experiment, for which I must blame myself; but this place, with all its endearments of wife, and children, and animate beauty is my Capua. I cannot labour well in it until familiarized with its enchantments. It has never looked so sweetly to my eyes, and both Catherine and Letitia think it delightful. To-day it has proved too much so for me, winning me from severe labour, to which I am bound, and lapping me in enjoyment.   Was again with my children in the garden, and then retired to the drawing-room to think over Lear, but made little progress with it, and am obliged to condemn in strong terms the surrender of so much valuable time to such dear indulgence.   Read a very touching extract of a story from the *Examiner*, and made up some arrears.   Read prayers to the family.   Let me hope that by my future diligence I may repair the fault of this day's indolence, and make out a better title by my conduct to the blessings I enjoy than I can now pretend to.   Amen!   The blessing of God I pray for on me and mine!   Amen!   Amen!

London, May 12th.—Came to town by Billings, and was luckily enabled by what I conceived a supercilious glance of one of my fellow travellers to give the whole of the journey to rumination upon Lear. Called on Wallace, whom I found with his work before him, and extremely cheerful; saw Dr. Lardner, who appears in unusually good health and spirits.   Rehearsed *King Henry IV* and saw the play-bill with the lithographed plan of the orchestra and the assurance that *" there would be no advance of prices."*   How long is this fellow to parade his Warren and Dr. Eady stuff before the public!   Saw him on the subject of my Benefit, and now the knave refuses the written conditions of my engagement!   The dancers at Covent Garden, all of whom I can claim by my agreement, he refuses!—but it is useless to speak or think of such a published *cheat*.   I trust to see his disgrace —if such a wretch can be more disgraced than by being what he is. Met Dow, and was strongly dissuaded by him from giving up my night, and recommended, as he said it was impossible two opinions could exist on my engagement, to send Mr. Bunn legal notice of my claims. I wrote the letters to him and Cooper, also to Paganini, and to Catherine; informed her that I could not come home to-morrow. Looked at the box sheet of my Benefit and saw Talfourd's, Forster's and Davis's name down!   no more!!   Sheil called and sat a short time, asked me to dine on Sunday, but I declined on account of Lear. He told me of his making a fool of himself in his last speech.   Wrote to Braham.

May 13th.—Sent back the volume of *Shirley* to Mr. Mackie, and despatched Healey to Mr. Braham to purchase his unprofitable though indispensable aid for my night.   Received an acquiescing note on his *" usual terms "* from Braham.   This was too bad—an attempt to get 5 guineas more from me than Bunn gives him.   At the theatre, how- ever, he consented to the 20—enough.   Wrote to Paganini for an answer, which I received, to the effect that he had a concert on the 23rd which would prevent him engaging with me. The note was written by Mr. Watson. At the Garrick Club dined and heard them talking of the last night's dinner, which seemed to sit heavy on the souls of the diners, for they seemed miserably dull. Put down my name to Pierce Mahoney's proposed election. Dow called, and seemed so anxious about Grisi, that I began a note to Laporte, but on looking at hers found she could only come between half-past 7 and three-quarters past 8—which if she brought me £500 I would not accept.

May 14th.—Went to the theatre about my dress and then walked up to Wallace's. I found him in excellent spirits, and Dr. Lardner well. Wallace quite approved of my passing Bunn's behaviour without notice. But what a scandal, that the accursed law of this country only allows me to eat my bread and to provide it for my children through connection with this wretch! My temper yields in spite of my judgment. Miserable as my profession is, its wretchedness is aggravated by the persons allowed to degrade it. Felt unsettled in my part of to-night—read it, and went over it, but the mind was not there. I had neglected it; an act of folly with the lightest as with the heaviest character. I ought to have acted Henry IV very well; it is short, easy, and the public prepared to expect something from me in it. I acted it *very badly* : I should say, the worst part I have played in London this season. An utter want of reality and truth—in fact very bad. Went with the orchestra to hear Grisi, Tamburini, Rubini and Ivanhoff singing in coats and waistcoats; and the band similarly clad, only with bits of cloth round their necks to distinguish them, playing before Henry V, libelled in his representative, Mr. Cooper—oh! Coming out I was told that Mr. Bunn had said the dancers could only dance between the acts of my play—this was quite intelligible—Mr. Bunn knew I *could not* have them there —and this is my engagement! Is it easy to be patient or temperate with a destiny that links one to such?

May 15th.—Vexed and dispirited; not yet subdued to the reason of my predicament; chafed and depressed by angry and desponding thoughts, which only consume at once the time, the energies, and heart of him who submits himself to them. If the mind were as earnest in revolving the proper subjects of our study and pursuit as it is in the indulgence of its own sad or splenetic fancies, how secure we should be of success in our undertakings and how healthful a state of body and mind would be likely to result from such a cheerful exercise. I dismiss Mr. Bunn to his deserts or destiny. For my own part I will do my best for my family—(oh, how truly has Bacon said that a married man gives hostages to fortune)—and trust in God for the event. Almost directly after writing this, while talking with a servant, Catherine and the children came in—the darlings! My playbills were brought, too, and I was in a very equable state of mind, prepared to take the worst of the Benefit with complacency. Forster called, whom I soon took away; called at the theatre to leave my tickets at the box office; returning, met Mr. H. Phillips,[1] who informed me he could not play on my night, being engaged at the Ancient Concerts. This drove me into a corner, for Braham would be worse than useless without him. *Quoi faire?* Went to Garrick Club and read the newspapers high in praise of my last night's performance, which was not what it should have been. The *Times* was, as usual, insidious and malignant under a seemingly candid and liberal admission. I am not mistaken in that paper—it is my *enemy*. Went to Drury Lane where I saw Bunn, and very temperately pointed out the utter variance of the circumstances of my night with the terms of the engagement; he cannot speak like a gentleman, and was inclining to talk rudely and wide from the point, which I gave him to understand could not avail at all, and abruptly left him. At chambers I drew out a sketch of notice to serve on him, and drove up to Wallace with it. Our mutual view of the case left me only the choice of taking the night with all its drawbacks, or declining it. Decided on the latter and left Wallace, taking an omnibus to chambers; found Dow and the children with Catherine. Dow was sadly averse to my relinquishment of the night, but I thought it the best course. Wrote notice to Bunn, sending it through Cooper; wrote note to Braham and advertisements for newspapers. Note from the Dean of Westminster respecting Mrs. Siddons's bust.

May 16th.—Began the day with serious and sad reflections on the small account of money I had realized, and the unpromising condition of the profession; my own experience of the painfulness of struggling without assistance through life makes me nervously anxious to afford my dear children some little support in their journey through life, which I wish to be an active and industrious one. I must put *a padlock on my purse*, and relinquish all right to spend my money. Dismissed a petition from a swindler, whom I had subscribed to before,

---

[1] Henry Phillips (1801–1876), well known as a bass singer.

of the name of Lacy. Went to the rehearsal of *Lear*, which I feel myself *capable* of acting, if I used—perhaps I ought to say—*had used* the necessary diligence; I almost fear there is not time left to mellow myself in my own conceptions. Rehearsed three acts of the play. Mr. Cooper came to me from Mr. Bunn to express his regret (!) at my resigning my night, and his readiness to do everything in his power to meet my views, if I would take it! I declined, observing, "If Mr. Bunn had used this language yesterday, I should not have thought of taking such a step, but that his behaviour drove me to the alternative." Mr. Cooper was anxious that the night should be taken, or another in its place; I said distinctly I would run no farther risk; content to pay what I had incurred, I would not engage myself for one farthing more; if Mr. Bunn thought my name of any value, he might put it up, and take the full charges, £210, if in the theatre; if not, the amount whatever it might be, but that I was not liable for one shilling. If there should be a surplus, beyond the £210, it should be paid to me; adding, unless you think this a very liberal and gentlemanly offer, you are not at liberty to make it. He did, and hurried away with it, so that my name goes up for this day week. I did not act well, and should have been better pleased and more convinced, had my good-natured friend's, Forster's, praise been more moderate. I could not yield him credit for his sincerity in his extravagant delight. I felt it as a reproach to me. I have seldom acted Henry IV worse. Satisfied by this additional experience that a man is a fool who yields to passion.

Elstree, May 17th.—Rose at an early hour, and learnt at the coach office that the Crown Prince was full, but that I had better wait for a chance, which I did. A chance presented itself in the seat of a person to be taken up at St. Albans. After passing half an hour in the coach, during which I read the paper, I was dislodged to make room for longer passengers. Took a cab, and came in tolerable time to the 8 mile stone, where I dismissed my vehicle; the fellow demanded back fare, which I would not give; he was inclined to be insolent, which I would not submit to, and believing that he had no claim for backfare I refused to pay it; I find on examining the regulations that I was wrong. Walked to Elstree, meeting a wretched old dumb beggar, and an Irishwoman, of course, pregnant. Found my dear children in good health, but dearest Catherine not so well. After breakfast walked round the garden, and was delighted to see everything so flourishing. On coming in I found myself so heavy and worn down with

WILLIAM CHARLES MACREADY

AS RICHARD III

From the painting by De Wilde, in the collection of E. Y. Lowne, Esq.

sleep, that the book of *Lear* was useless before me; I fell asleep, and remained inactive for some time. On recovering myself I began to think of, and read over Lear. I fear I have little chance of executing my conceptions. Dined at luncheon hour in order to accommodate the servants, and thereby still more cut up my day; but application is so difficult here, especially with a guest in the house, that I may almost declare it impossible. Was in the garden again in the afternoon with dear Catherine, and at tea read the abridgment with extracts from Mrs. Gore's [1] novel of *The Hamiltons*, which has great merit, also extracts from one called *Trevelyan*. After tea I returned to Lear, giving my attention particularly to the last scene, which I find much more difficult than I had supposed. I ought not to know home while such a work is on my mind—I shall not succeed in it!

May 18th.—Before coming downstairs I received a letter from Mr. Cooper, requiring me to act Richard III at Covent Garden Theatre on Monday week; I am quite disposed to put up with an inconvenience for the sake of quietly terminating this engagement, and think I will do it—though it is both a sacrifice and a serious inconvenience. Had some doubtings on the point, but I will do it, because in doing it, I have done with Mr. Bunn as far as his power of annoying me goes. Walked out in the garden with my sweet children—regulated my accounts, and began the practice of Lear; gained some confidence in it by studying before Catherine; went through the two first acts—and thought of it onwards. Went to afternoon church with Letitia and Miss E. Hughes—read in Greek Testament 19th chapter of Acts, and 14th of St. Luke on that beautiful principle of our religion, self-humiliation. After dinner walked round the garden, while " the clear cold eve " was declining. Read prayers to the family, and afterwards read over the latter part of Lear, which requires both more practice and thought than I shall have time to give. I must husband what is left to me, and trust to the Goodness which has hitherto befriended me to strengthen and assist me in this important trial.

London, May 19th.—Took leave of my dear wife and children at the gate and watched them looking after me. Saw Mr. Phillimore at the coach, and had some short converse with him, in which I heard of the reconciliation of Brougham and Sugden,[2] Brougham making

---

[1] Catherine Grace Frances Gore (1799–1861), novelist, dramatist. and musical composer.

[2] Edward Burtenshaw Sugden (1781–1875), son of a London hairdresser; twice Irish Lord Chancellor and eventually Lord Chancellor of England. A great real property lawyer, and consequently indignant at Brougham's promotion to the Chancellorship, which in those

the advance, because it is thought Sugden must be brought in! Came to town outside Billings's coach, and tried to keep Lear in my mind. Called on Wallace, whom I found much better, and highly satisfied with the result of my notice to Mr. Bunn. Saw Dr. Lardner, who informed me of Campbell's *gaucherie* and McKinnon's *poltronnerie* in the affair of the Clarence Club. Took a cab to the theatre and rehearsed *Lear*, also tried my dress. At Garrick Club read newspapers and dined. Miss Phillips informed me that she had engaged to go to America, which I was sorry to hear; her good conduct and lady-like deportment will cause her to be missed in a green-room where she leaves so little like herself. I promised her letters to the States and will do all I can for her. Went to theatre, did not satisfy myself by my acting Henry IV, nor can I give my mind to it, until I have decided the fate of myself in Lear. My mind has room for nothing else. Gave Cooper Mr. H. Phillips's (the ill-bred coxcomb!) note, and inquired after Mr. Kelly's play, about which he is to ask. Talfourd came into my room, and sat a short time. I told him I had tried, but vainly, to purchase Mathews' picture. Dow called, and walked home with me, taking tea; when he had left me, I gave my attention to the last scenes of Lear.

May 20th.—Before rising thought over the madness of Lear, which now begins to obtain something resembling that possession of my mind which is necessary to success in whatever we desire to reach excellence. Messrs. Twinings, the most gentlemanly merchants in London, sent to me for tickets, as did Mr. Gass, receiving the order for the alteration of the zone for Lear. In looking over a book observed the narration of a circumstance that is only credible from our experience of the folly and ignorance of human nature. A woman in the boxes of a theatre or concert-room, exclaimed, "One God, one Farinelli!" Would not a mad-house have been a light punishment for such an idiot? After tea, took up Lear, which I read through, and very much fear my success in it, the nearer I approach to the trial.

May 21st.—Mr. Brewster came to cut my hair, and to arrange my Lear's coiffure: he also asked me for tickets. Mr. Warren called on

---

days involved the functions of principal equity judge, for which Brougham was notoriously unfit. Sugden was leader in Brougham's court, and openly displayed his contempt for him. Though more fortunate than Brougham, who was destined in a few months' time to leave the Woolsack never to return to it, Sugden was forced to content himself until 1852 with an occasional tenure of the Irish Chancellorship. In that year, when past seventy, he at last obtained the Great Seal, but he had to relinquish it in less than a twelvemonth, owing to the fall of Lord Derby's Government; and never held office again.

the latter part of his errand, and sat with me while I despatched my breakfast. In the course of my conversation with Mr. Warren, I was much struck with his indiscreet divulging of things which one ought to weigh well over before confiding to a friend. When not called on in our own justification to disclose such things, respect for others and for ourselves should make us endure the burthen of the secret. He told me that he had an interview with Lord Lyndhurst on Sunday, who I scarcely think would lay much upon him, however *he* might lay on Lord Brougham. He mentioned that he had spoken of me to Lyndhurst,[1] who observed I was a man of genius. Why mention me?—and why mention it to me? A sad want of tact. Rehearsed *Lear* very unsatisfactorily—several important persons not being there, and I at intervals tormented with a toothache. Went to the theatre, and acted Henry IV very indifferently indeed : the truth is I can give my mind to nothing until the fate of this Lear, which indeed is my fate, be decided. I have not satisfied myself any night in the part, and, least of all, this evening. It may be some extenuation that during part of it the couch I lay on was one of torture from a racking toothache, but this is not an excuse. Finished the article in *Foreign Monthly* upon Turkey and Egypt, which is able and interesting. Received a pamphlet from Mr. Warren, the purpose of which I do not clearly see. A paroxysm of pain with this treacherous tooth —an old ally turned corrupt and traitorous.

May 22nd.—An invitation, which is very complimentarily worded, but which I do not quite understand, from the Literary Fund Society. Was in considerable perplexity what course to pursue in regard to the newspapers ; decided at length on sending *tickets* to the morning and evening ones. Wrote notes with orders to Pemberton and Leigh Hunt, enclosed to Forster. Went to the Garrick Club, where in the newspapers I read the account of Lafayette's death. I feel this dropping off of those who knew and regarded me ; the good of my acquaintance are fast diminishing : he was a good, not what is usually admitted to be a great man—or perhaps to speak of him truly, great only in his

---

[1] It was at Lord Lyndhurst's that Warren once exposed himself to the quaint sarcasm of Charles Lamb. They met there at a breakfast-party, and Warren rashly ventured on telling some anecdote in French, a language of which he knew very little ; consequently the anecdote fell flat. Thereupon, by way of covering his discomfiture, he turned to Lamb with the characteristic remark : "Not that I know much French—*for a gentleman*." To which Lamb rejoined with a stutter : "Nor I—*for a bl- bl- blackguard*." Not the least amusing part of the incident was Warren's inability to perceive the rebuke. He used to quote the retort as an instance of Lamb's occasional commonplaceness.

goodness. My dress for Lear not nearly ready, and what done, done *very badly*. I was too much concerned and distressed to be in a passion; if we allow the importance of the occasion to measure out our quantity of wrath, we should lose very soon all self-commend. I did bridle myself, though I was made very nervous by this worthless fellow's conduct; it is not easy. Received a very comfortable letter from dearest Catherine, and read over with attention the whole of Lear. I have now only to keep myself collected, exert myself to the utmost, and put my hope and confidence in God to prosper my desires of providing for, and well educating my dear children. May it be so! Amen!

May 23rd.—Benefit. *King Lear*—first time—and *Lord of the Manor*. Rose in good time, with the impression that the day was one of serious results to me. Sent tickets to the *Literary Gazette, Athenæum* and *Sunday Times*. I justified myself in my experiment in the reflection that otherwise I should leave unbroken ground to an adventurer who might work it to my disadvantage. Rehearsed—I should say—exceedingly well, giving great promise for the night, Miss Kenneth's wish to see the play, and Cooper's confidence in its going well were all the indications of approval I could pick out from the company. Arranged my dresses, and kept a strong check upon myself, not permitting anything like an ebullition of discontent or violence. Returned to my chambers, settled all that was necessary for the night, dined, and went to bed at ten minutes past two, giving orders not to be disturbed—I could not sleep for the state of my mind and the heat—I thought over some of the play. Went to the theatre—dressed—became excessively nervous—took wine—went on the stage—as nervous as the first night I acted in London, without the overbearing ardour that could free me from the thraldom of my fears. My performance in the two first acts was so unlike my rehearsal, that, although I goaded myself to resistance by suggestions of my own reputation, of my wife and children's claims upon me—still I sunk under the idea that it was a *failure*. In the third act, the audience struck me as being interested and attentive, and in the fourth and fifth they broke out into loud applauses; the last scene went tamely, but I was called for by my friends, and went on—was much applauded, and said that " gratified as I was by their approbation, I hoped when relieved from the nervousness of a first appearance to offer them a representation more worthy their applause." Dow, Talfourd and his little boy, Bourne and Forster came into my room—they were all much pleased. Cooper came afterwards and told me the play was to be repeated on Monday at Covent Garden. I told him to say to Bunn that I was gratified with this act of justice, for had I *failed*, it ought to have been repeated. Came to chambers, and lay upon the sofa to collect and ascertain my tumultuous, mingled, and quickly-passing thoughts. I felt the excitement of wine, and of what seems success, but I must wait until to-morrow to know with certainty the impression I have produced. This is the last of the great characters of Shakspeare that I have left unattempted, and the tone which the Press takes up on it will materially influence my after life. I can put no reliance on the partial feelings of friends. I do not feel that I have *yet* succeeded, but it is consoling to me to believe that I have not failed. Persons think that we carry the applauses of the audience to our pillows, and that the sound still rings as a delightful lullaby in our ears. I have no such pleasure; I wish the night past, that I may make up my mind to the impression diffused through the public mind. My old friend, the *Times*, will not forget me, but either treat me with contempt, or damn with faint praise, and I wish to *know* the worst that he may choose to say. I must admit that there is an immense deal to except at in the performance, but there is a spirit of persecution as well as of taste and sensibility. *Attendez; nous verrons.*

May 24th.—The worst is known, and varies little from my expectations. The *Times* does "damn with faint praise," but the *Herald* writes in a tone of gentlemanly liberality, and the *Post* is not less courteous. I could not sleep; at half-past three I was wide awake, and at a quarter-past four I read *Lear* through and then got up to bring the *Foreign Quarterly* into bed. I looked through an article on home colonization, and then slept till nearly eight. Sent for the newspapers, and read them with extreme anxiety. Is the *Times* justified in the partial view it takes of the characters which Mr. Kean had acted? I wish I could think the writer less base than I believe him. Lardner was very warm about the play and wondering at the *Times*. Before leaving chambers, I sent for a cab to take me to Elstree this evening; wrote a note to Mr. Fox to one received last night, and one of enquiry to H. Smith. My mind was in the state of a sea after a storm—still tossed and agitated as if from the upturnings of its deepest feelings. I *want a sedative.* Called at Covent Garden, and saw Bunn—told him I was gratified by his announcement of *Lear* in place of *Richard*, and that as I expressed my discontents, I thought it only fair to acknowledge acts of justice. He stated his continual wish to serve my interests, and that he had made it a point with Westmacott to be civil to Lear. Saw Liston on the stage and talked to him, C. Dance, G. Dance, etc. Went to Garrick Club, where I dined and read a *very* kind notice on Henry IV in *Athenæum;* saw Forster—I did not comprehend him; but kindness is valuable with whatever peculiarities. Saw Jerdan, Price, Bartley (who *praised*), Meadows, Douglas, etc. Found at home notes from Pemberton—he is a partizan; 'twere well for me, if I had many such. Made up my bag for home, and went to theatre, where I received a note from Mr. Benson Hill—unworthy of an " officer and gentleman " to write, in my opinion—and one from Misses Hill, enclosing five guineas for their box. Acted Henry IV pretty well. Forster came into my room and told me Fonblanque [1] had been looking at the play and expressing himself in the highest terms of praise on the improvement of my style. Came home by 11 to Elstree. Forster brought me *Globe*.

Elstree, May 25th.—I slept well, not awaking until 8 o'clock ; and recruiting my nerves and spirits from the demand made on both, yesterday and the day before. I had much to tell to very anxious inquirers ; I had brought the newspapers, not forgetting the extract from the *Globe*, which appears to me equally liberal and discriminating. I shall bear in mind the caution it suggests. On coming down I could not resist walking out upon the lawn before I sat down to breakfast, and never did I feel the charm of " rural worth " more deeply. The garden was quite delicious to my senses, and I could not but think it was an enjoyment that deserved my pains and labour, and the resolution followed the thought to labour in gratitude and hope for my dear wife and children, for whom my heart constantly sends up its prayers to God to bless and to protect them. Amen! Hastily summed up my accounts, and wrote notes enclosing orders to Dow and Pemberton, from both of whom I had received applications. Irksome as is the study of my profession to me, I set to work at Lear, to correct the errors of my performance, and to give myself confidence and finish. My intention of going to afternoon service (which was sincere) was frustrated by the state of mind I found myself in with this difficult character, and I thought on reflection that my duty was not compromised by remaining at home and steadily pursuing my practice and study. I did so ; Catherine listening to me, in order to overcome

---

[1] Albany Fonblanque (1793-1872) ; journalist, newspaper editor and proprietor ; also, later in life, Board of Trade official. He was at this time editor of the *Examiner*, and a staunch supporter of Macready.

my nervousness. I found much to correct, and much to confirm myself in. At half-past four I had finished, and ran down into the garden to enjoy a romping play with my dear children; dressed for dinner and walked in the garden with dear Catherine. After dinner read the *Examiner*, that excellent paper, and paid some attention to the trees I had planted. Read prayers to the family.

London, May 26th.—At my chambers found a note of excuse from Lord Belfast or Duke of Bedford, I know not nor care which, about a private box, and one from the treasurer of that disgusting ugly pauper, the ——;[1] I know no better—*i. e.* no truer designation for her. Rehearsed *Lear* at Covent Garden. Went to Drury Lane about my dress. Came home and answered a note from that everlasting indefatigable bore, Mr. Atherstone, sending him orders. Went to bed, and thought over some of the work before me. Was a little flurried in dressing, but soon collected myself, and acted to prove the baseness and the falsehood of the *Times :* an avowed enemy—Bacon.[2] I acted really well—and felt that my audience were under my sway— I threw away nothing—took time and yet gave force to all I had to do—above all, my tears were not those of a woman or a driveller, they really stained a "*man's* cheeks." In the storm, as indeed throughout, I *greatly* improved upon the preceding night, I was frantic with passion, and brought up expectation to the dreadful issue of such a conflict. I lost the great effect of "every inch a king," but will be more careful in future. The scene with Cordelia and the death were both better than the first night. Dow came into my room, and thought me greatly improved throughout.

Elstree, May 27th.—Applied myself to business in my chambers, which occupied time, and then sallied forth. In the hall I saw two persons at Mr. Dyne's door, and had gone but a few steps when I heard a strange sort of hailing, that I never guessed was for myself, and passed on; it followed me into the Square, and a gentleman accosted me in French, observing that he had known me in Paris and mentioning the name of De Fresne. I inquired of him whom I had the pleasure of addressing—he told me "Monsieur de Fresne."[3] I was delighted to meet him, but grieved to see what I recollected as a handsome young man so much altered. I asked his address, which he promised to leave with me, and invited him to our house. He told me he had lost his wife, and that he had one child. I felt deeply the joy of seeing him,

---

[1] A certain economical "Royalty."   [2] One of the *Times'* staff.
[3] A Parisian friend to whom Macready was much attached.

but it was sorrow to my heart to see a man of such a prepossessing exterior, such cheerful manners, and such elegant tastes, so changed. Took a cab to Reynolds's, where the foolish servant paid the driver 1s. 8d. instead of 8d., and where I learned that Bunn drove a carriage with a liveried attendance. This will follow his former carriage—knavery is not of durability enough to do this long. Called on Wallace, whom I found in excellent spirits, and on Lardner, who showed me a very interesting map of the London and Birmingham Railway. Came home by Bryant's coach, and found my darling children and wife quite well.

London, May 28th.—Came to town by Reeves's coach; found a note from Dr. Spurgin about a young lady *aspiring* to be an actress—"God help thee, silly one!" Paid the furrier's bill for Lear, and wrote an answer to Mr. Gandy's [1] critical letter on my performance and costume of Lear, by which I had been gratified, and for which I felt obliged. Went with some anxiety to the Garrick Club to see the result of last night's debate, and found, after the Irish Church had been brought on, that Lord Althorp had moved an adjournment to Monday. I am glad to hear that Stanley is out. [2] Called on Hayward, who proposed an immediate visit to Mrs. Jameson, to which I assented, and we started on a short cut by Carlton Place to Margaret Street, Cavendish Square. He is agreeable, with a little of the—what we all have. I left a card at the lady's, and then, after struggling through the crowd at St. James's—a horrid annoyance—parted from Hayward, and went on my way to call at Sheil's, where I left my card. Returning, I inquired at Robins's, and learned he had sent a note to me which, a very kind one, I found at my chambers, with Mr. Warren's book and a very warm presentation of it. Heard from Hayward by mistake on his part that it was the intention of some members of the Garrick Club to invite me to dinner on my performance of Lear. This is really a great and flattering compliment. Acted Henry IV pretty well; was requested by Mr. Cooper to study "either Sir Edward Mortimer or Shylock" by Monday week for his Benefit. I should not hazard—certainly shall not injure advisedly—my reputation for him; I could not justify myself in committing so gross a folly.

May 29th.—Received a very kind and gentlemanlike letter of apology from Leigh Hunt, in answer to my note. Wrote to Cooper an explanation of the impossibility of my acceding to his request of my

[1] Probably a member of the well-known family of architects.
[2] Lord Stanley shortly afterwards joined the Conservative party.

WILLIAM CHARLES MACREADY

AS KING LEAR

From an engraving

studying Mortimer or Shylock without doing myself a serious injury; this dull-brained clod has no idea beyond his own £ s. d. Forster called and staid only a few minutes. Sent £2, which I grudged, to the prompter, Willmott, and wrote to Calcraft on the subject of Dublin for November; to Messrs. Penley and Anderson, agreeing to visit Leicester, but leaving the time open. Went to Garrick Club, where I saw the papers and dined; returning to chambers, I crossed O'Hanlon, who walked with me here, and sat some few minutes. He acknowledged that he supplied Littleton with the most of his speech on the Repeal question, and observed that he got it off admirably. He thought Lear was a failure from the report of the *Times*, and this impression upon him sank my spirits very low. Acted Virginius *infamously*, with the exception of the beginning of the Forum scene, into which I rushed with resistless earnestness. I was out of temper with myself, which did me no good, and with everybody else, which was impertinent and unjustifiable. Talfourd came into my room to invite me to dine with a party of the Garrick Club members, which, of course, I gratefully accepted, but could not fix a day. Forster came in, and I learned that he was excluded, as the committee would not sit down with him. It seems they sent him a letter of which he took no notice. He is very indiscreet.

May 30th.—Miss Rudall arrived with Miss Tucker, a very pretty, interesting girl of fourteen, with all the enthusiasm of a novice, and all the fearlessness of inexperience. She has an insight into the art of playing that gives promise of great success—she may be a great actress—she has most of the requisites to make her so, but promise has been so delusive in this particular that it is unsafe to trust it. She rehearsed some scenes of *Juliet*, and recited a poem called *The Captive*, with very considerable effect. I promised to endeavour to procure her an engagement with Calcraft of Dublin, and to hear her rehearse occasionally. Called at theatres in search of Bunn; found Cooper and Bartley *locked up* together—two knaves in manifest collusion; but the theatre is a chaos, and knaves and fools the jarring atoms that compose it. Saw Bunn, who talked about the Kembles, Power, Wallack, etc. Called at the Literary Fund Office, and saw Mr. Snow the secretary, who explained, in answer to my inquiries, that nothing but a compliment was intended by the invitation to me, and that they would not even drink my health if it was objectionable to me. I accepted the invitation.

May 31st.—Received a note from a Mr. Jackson, requesting an interview about his play and a book on Shakspeare—evidently an unfortunate believer in his possession of talent which no one else would give him credit for. Called at Drury Lane and Covent Garden in search of Bunn, to ascertain from him my nights of performance next week; could not see him, but met Mr. Bartley, who is brimful of discontent, and evidently looking towards the Kembles with some hope of help; he told me, privately, that Mr. Cooper had sent in his resignation. Now, as Mr. Cooper exultingly told me the other day that he was engaged for three years, I think his thought of resigning must have grown out of his *conference with closed doors* yesterday. Bartley spoke of the attack upon him in the *Age*, and that he was sure he should not be there next season. I did not feel pity for this man, but listened with complacency to his grumblings, for he is deep-dyed in treachery—a hollow, Fawcett-like kind of fellow, *i. e.* a traitor. At Garrick Club I dined, and saw the *Athenæum* and *Literary Gazette* on my Lear, both complimentary. Forster's criticism in the *New Monthly* was lengthy and over-done; he directly attacked the *Times* for its article on me, which will assuredly provoke the dirty scribblers of that profligate paper to revenge themselves upon me the very first opportunity. One must feel grateful for his intention, but at the same time it is not easy to suppress the sigh that rises with the wish of " Save me from my friends! "

Elstree, June 1st.—Woke with a feeling of great fatigue, but rose in tolerably good time, intending to give a reading to Lear. On coming downstairs I could not resist the beauty of the morning, and walked round the garden with my precious children, enjoying the bounty and blessings of nature. How much have I to be grateful for! And how strange it is that, surrounded by so much of real pleasure, I should sometimes wish to mingle in the less pure and unalloyed ones of the world! After breakfast went down to see my dogs, and then went into the drawing-room, where I read aloud two acts of *Lear*, and finished the remainder to the reconciliation-scene in my study. The ringing of the bell announced arrivals and Messrs. Phipson and King came, with whom I chatted and lounged round the garden; we afterwards walked down to the reservoir. Returning, I observed that the Dows had arrived, and after a little further lounge in the garden I went to my study and settled my accounts. Attended to the concerns of the house, and sat down to dinner with my guests. Our day was spent cheerfully enough, but I began to look with apprehension on the wine Mr. King drank, fearing, from the gradual alteration of his manner, lest he might fall into excess. Fortunately he did not. Mr. Dow, against all declaration and evidence, maintained that T. Moore finished Mackintosh's *History of England*, and offered to cut off his finger if it were not so—which it is not; but, notwithstanding, he will not hurt his finger. King became very theatrical and affected; but told me very truly and discriminately of the failure of the exit in the fourth act, which I must try to amend. The Dows left us at ten o'clock.

London, June 2nd.—Rehearsed Kent's scenes. Here is one among the many instances afforded by Mr. Bunn to prove his utter disregard of the interests of the drama. Kent is to *Lear* the most important personage in the play, requires powers for comedy and tragedy, and should be entirely at his ease in the business of the play. Mr. Bartley was removed from it to take a very insignificant old man in the opera of the *Cabinet* at Drury Lane, and Mr. Mathews (Mr. Mathews!), without time to learn the words and with one rehearsal, was to be the Kent of Covent Garden. And thus are directed the rational amusements of the English public! Posted Calcraft's letter on my way to the Garrick Club, where I read the papers; returned to chambers and saw Ellen, who repeated to me the impertinence of her landlady, which amused me a little; her assertion that she knew many persons who would not sit down to table with an actor of any kind diverted me a good deal. Ellen's vindication of my respectability was equally ridiculous; once perhaps, however, I might have been annoyed by such nonsense! Went to bed after dinner, slept and read a little of *Lear*, but could not bring my mind to that feeling of *possessing* all my purposes of manner and degree which is indispensable to success. In the performance of Lear, thanks to my audience, I was better than my fears. I was not good in the early scenes of passion, not real, not clearly possessed of my intentions, and therefore effort took the place of wit and inspiration. I was not *le personnage*. In the madness and latter scenes I reasserted myself. Mr. Cooper (it is scarcely worth noting), upon Miss Phillips declining his request to act Y. Ly. Lambert for him, thanked her ironically in the green-room, told her he was the less obliged to her, and that she must have done it if he had sent it in his official capacity. The impertinence of a second- or third-rate actor,[1] not good as such, speaking thus to a young lady holding first rank, is really difficult to hear with patience.

[1] According to Oxberry, "Just as good an actor as art without one spark of genius or any effort of the mind could make, has been made in the person of Mr. Cooper. Coldly correct, scrupulously exact, minutely perfect, are his qualifications; he is about as much like a real first-rate actor as a fine statue is to a living being."

June 3rd.—Went to Garrick Club, on my way posting a *True Sun* newspaper, and read last night's debate, with which, as far as ministers, Tories, and trimming Whigs are concerned, I was sufficiently disgusted. The ministers are base, dishonourable, place-loving men; to —— with them as soon as possible, Grey, Althorp, Brougham, Russell, etc.! Called to pay bill at Colnaghi's; saw the engraving of the cast of Napoleon's face—very striking, but scarcely retaining a resemblance to the portraits of him in life; if the nose were more curved it might pass for a head of Julius Cæsar. Colnaghi related a curious fact of the Countess de Grey, who when stone-blind used to take him to a picture which she had bought at a great price as an *original*, and would feel different parts with her hands, pointing out to him its beauties. She would make him put her hand on the different parts of prints which he would bring her, telling her the subject and the parts of it she touched; and on observing once there was a little cat in the corner of one, she immediately exclaimed, "Oh, I'll have that." With only the power of imagining what was before her, which on blank paper she would have done as satisfactorily to herself, it is curious that she should be content to pay money for enjoyment beyond her reach.

June 4th.—Acted pretty well, to a very bad house, *King Henry IV.* Talfourd came to my room, and mentioned to me that from the Oxford Commemoration and Ascot Races they could not muster on Tuesday next such a party as they had expected, but that if I would meet "the few," their pleasure would be the same. I expressed my deep sense of obligation, and left it to his own judgment to decide as he, on deliberation, might think best.

June 5th.—Having the appointment with Mr. Fox before me, which I knew would engross much of my morning, I took the opportunity of visiting the Exhibition at nine o'clock. I saw much to delight me, particularly Hilton's, Landseer's, Wilkie's, Etty's, and Eastlake's pictures. Returning, I found Mr. Fox and his friends had anticipated our appointment nearly half-an-hour. I thought Miss S. Flower intelligent and clever, but I fear that she is too conscious of it, and am almost certain she is too old ever to make much proficiency in the dramatic art. I heard her rehearse in Lady Macbeth and Ophelia, and recommended her to study Constance and let me see her in a week, when I would give her a more decisive opinion. Went to the Garrick Club, where I saw the newspapers, dined, and had some conversation with Price about the Kembles; by his account they must have realized

£15,000. I felt vexed and chagrined to hear it, for the man, Kemble,[1] is—no matter; but it is my business to dismiss any concern about the matter, for perhaps I should not have felt much less if he had been as unstained as Bayard himself.

June 6th.—With a good deal of business before me, I was somewhat annoyed by my messenger's late arrival, but employed the interval in thinking of my speech to-morrow at the Literary Fund Dinner. At eleven o'clock Miss Allison (*alias* Tucker) called with her aunt, Mrs. Tucker, a very fine-looking woman, and went over some scenes of Virginia and Juliet before me, and also read a page of Milton, of which I perceived she understood little or nothing. This *ought* to be a reason on which one might augur ill success, but it is not. There is much in Milton and Shakspeare which I am sure Kean could not understand, nor Miss O'Neil, nor, I am confident, Mr. C. Kemble, nor Mr. Young. From the appreciators, therefore, of her efforts she need not fear on the score of her own ignorance, as acquirement and information are certainly of little value. Is it the critic of a newspaper, or, still less, those who take their judgments from him, that are to set me right on the question of taste, erudition or metaphysical truth? Of course, among that audience are a few—but, alas, how few!—whose highly cultivated minds enable them to judge an actor by the standard of his poet, to detect his errors, and to confirm his researches by their acquaintance with his authorities. But these are very, very rare instances, and generally their sentiments extend no further than their most intimate circle. A Mr. Zach. Jackson, with a play and a book on Shakspeare, called—one of those "fools who rush in" to criticize, where modest knowledge shrinks from the sacredness of the temple. Called to see O'Hanlon's house, which is really beautiful in its carvings, but for him quite out of keeping. To the Athenæum, which I liked exceedingly. To Garrick Club, which looked unusually vulgar, where I dined and saw papers. Met Hayward, who inquired of me about the dinner to myself, on which I could not satisfy him. Received a note from R. Price with intimation of the dinner having been fixed for Tuesday next. Returned to the subject of to-morrow's dinner, and endeavoured to collect the substance of what I ought to say in answer to the proposal of my health, which I think, as a person before the public, I ought not to shrink from, although I feel myself so uncertain upon the mode in which I may acquit myself. I could not satisfy myself with sentence after sentence, nor was it until three o'clock that

---

[1] Charles Kemble, for whose character Macready had very little respect.

I wrote down, without hiatus, what I thought might do, and went to rest, jaded and spirit-tired.

June 7th.—Again returned to this annoying and perplexing speech, which would have been most annoying to a looker-on ; but which, like the frog in the fable, I could truly say was " death to me." My whole day was the speech—not always the whole speech, but certainly nothing but the speech. Took a cab to reach my place of appointment with Fladgate, whom I saw at the fixed place to the moment. It should be the very first principle of a gentleman, among the lesser obligations of society, *never to break an appointment.* A man who is guilty of such a dereliction of good manners cannot justify his title to the rank of gentleman ; his rudeness exposes another to real inconvenience, and he himself has pledged his word to a falsehood. Waited some time at Chantrey's and at last saw him ; he mentioned the Duke of Welling-ton's expectation of seeing him at Oxford—that he was therefore obliged to go. Settled to apprise Fladgate, who was to notify the same to me, of his interview with the Dean, etc. Read papers at the Garrick Club, having walked there with Fladgate, and discussed the mode of laying the proposal for Mrs. Siddons's monument before the Club ; also having related to him some very creditable anecdotes of her. Returned to my chambers, and my eternal and infernal speech, at which I laboured, but so unsuccessfully that as I was leaving the room to go out I found on trial every word gone from my mind ; an effort at recollection called back to me its substance, and I went along, conning it over, uncertain whether or no to request my health to be omitted. I saw T. Hook [1] in the reception-room, and Jerdan, by whom I was presented—a mere matter of form—to the Duke of Somerset ; [2] Lord Mulgrave,[3] who chatted a little, as did Villiers, who seemed very ill. Lucien Bonaparte and Tricoupi, the Greek Minister, were also there, and Holman, the blind traveller. At dinner I was placed next to Murray, opposite to Captain Marryat, Theodore Hook—to my great surprise, Dick,[4] and, near me, Gleig, Lockhart, and, also to my great surprise, Christie, who reintroduced himself to me. I spent rather a

---

[1] Theodore Edward Hook (1788–1841), the notorious practical joker and improviser ; at that time editor of *John Bull*, the scurrilous Tory and " Society " newspaper.

[2] Edward Adolphus, 12th Duke of Somerset (1775–1855), K.G. ; president of various scientific and literary societies, including the Royal Literary Fund.

[3] Second Earl and first Marquis of Normanby (1797–1863) ; then Lord Privy Seal in Lord Melbourne's Administration.

[4] Probably Quintin Dick, a wealthy Tory M.P. whose name was prominently before the public earlier in the century in connection with a borough-mongering transaction with Lord Castlereagh, then leader of the House of Commons.

pleasant day, only overshadowed by anticipations of my speech, which, like many good and evil anticipations of our life, never came. The Duke left the chair—I followed. *Parturiunt montes, nascitur—nihil.*

Elstree, June 8th.—It is ludicrous to think on the annoyance I suffered myself to feel from the care and thought I had given to the consideration of what I should say in answer to the compliment, of which I had been officially notified, and the disappointment I endured in the ridiculous sacrifice of so much valuable time and thought.   Still I had scarcely an alternative between looking as miserable as poor Pickersgill, whom I pitied from my soul, or making some preparation for what I unfortunately have so much neglected in my general self-instruction.   No man should speak without clear thought—without a perfect arrangement of his ideas; if he has these, words are as certain to follow them as—what?   Here is the very error of my life, continually beginning a half-arranged sentence, and then reduced to a perplexity, of which my habitual hesitation is the offspring, to find words and exact ideas to conclude it.   It is one of the *most important* principles in forming the manners of man or woman to check in them that tendency to precipitancy which commits the speaker to the utterance of words before his mind has clear and full possession of what ought to be said.   Foolish persons will flatter you (they have done so by me, and I believed them) by saying this hesitation and confusion of sentences arises from a too rapid flow of ideas.   " 'Tis a foolish saying ; " it arises from a total want of ideas, or such a huddled mixture of them as makes them inapplicable to use.   At breakfast read the *Examiner;* was surprised, and not pleased with its criticisms on my Lear, which the writer *could not* have seen.   He accuses me of too great a show of senility, when the general exception, where any is made, is upon the opposite side.   Walked much in the garden, and submitted myself to the hands of Catherine and Letitia to take out the footmarks of time upon my head.

June 9th.—Walked down to the lower field with my little Nina and Willie to look at the mowers, who had begun to cut.   What delight it is to see these little creatures running about one, and how thankful ought I not to be to the Giver of so many blessings, which my life has so ill deserved !   Blessed be His name ! and may I show myself in their education at least sensible, though not worthy, of His divine goodness. Amen.   After breakfast walked with my dear Catherine in the garden. Gave up the entire day to think on what I ought to say to-morrow at the Garrick Club, where, of course, the very compliment of the invitation, and the certainty that my health will be proposed as the leading toast, make it incumbent on me to endeavour to express my sense and appreciation of the kindness of my friends. The difficulty I had in retaining, as it was written, a prepared speech on Saturday, induced me to try if I could from my own feelings utter in order and proper arrangement such an answer as might suit the occasion. I thought on the matter, walking on the lawn, and at last fixed something in my mind, which I thought would sufficiently translate the warm emotions of my gratitude; I repeated it to Catherine and my sisters, who thought it sufficient. Looked at the flowers, the shrubs, and grass, the beauty of the day, with inexpressible delight—nor was the night less lovely than the day. It is not hard to be happy, if we will but look for wisdom; if we will open our eyes to the beneficence of our Creator and the benevolence of His laws; if we will but put that restraint upon our evil passions which repays us in its very act. Returned to the subject of to-morrow, and was preparing to go to bed satisfied with the preparation I had made, when Catherine same into my study to inform me that she thought what I purposed saying would make me enemies. This was ill-timed, at least. The lateness of the hour made it a nervous as well as difficult task to alter it, and the uncertainty of retaining clear possession of what I might substitute harassed and perplexed me. I altered it and went to bed.

London, June 10th.—I was dressing to go to town by Bryant, when a note came from Alger, at Bartley's order, informing me that I was announced for *Hamlet* this evening at Covent Garden, and that the rehearsal was at eleven! I as usual *felt, before I thought,* and imputing this step of the manager to malice prepense, went downstairs to make Catherine write a note by Billings, saying that I was not at home, and I was to go out to give the semblance of fact to the equivocation. A very little reflection showed me the unworthiness and imprudence of such a course, and, muttering indignant reproaches on Messrs. Bunn and Bartley, I returned to my dressing-room and continued my toilet to be ready for the coach, that I might not lose the rehearsal. I consoled myself in the thought that it would be practice, and tend to help me on, but of all characters I am most disconcerted by being called on suddenly for Hamlet. I came up and was first at rehearsal; from the prompter's table I wrote a hasty note to R. Price, requesting him to intimate my inability to dine at the Garrick to Talfourd, and sent it by Healey. Rehearsed with much care—I cannot entirely dismiss the suspicion that this play has been announced partly to cross me; but perhaps I do Bunn an injustice. Dined and looked at papers at the Garrick Club. Wrote orders for Pemberton and Dow; lay down in bed, where I had some matters to *raccommoder* about my dress which only I could do. Acted very well, considering the circumstance of my surprise and little preparation, very well indeed. With due pause and care, and real, not vocal, energy. I was, however, foolish enough to lose my temper in two instances : once at the gross buffoonery of that drunken old man, Blanchard [1]—a sad instance of abused talent—and again at Mr. Warde,[2] who distressed me by his incorrectness, which was occasioned by his absenting himself from rehearsal; he was very inexcusable, but I was more so, for I ought to have known better. Talfourd came from the dinner, which took place without me, to tell me the party had resolved on carrying their purpose into effect at the close of the season.

June 11th.—Mr. Fox and Miss Flower called; heard her rehearse part of Constance; confirmed in my opinion that, with a mind quite equal to the first place in the profession of a player, she has applied herself too late in life to its practice to give her a hope of success. This I endeavoured, as delicately as possible, to suggest to her; but as she did not scorn to take my view of the subject, I recommended to her the experiment of a short engagement at Liverpool, if it could be obtained, and promised to write to the managers there on the subject.

June 13th.—Hayward called for me; I got into his coach, and went with him to Mrs. Jameson's.[2] She was not present; on her coming down, I was introduced by Hayward in a low tone, and conversation began. Hayward mentioned my name, saying he had detained Macready. "Oh," said she, "why did you not bring Macready?" "This is Mr. Macready," he said. I bowed and smiled, she apologized, curtsied and blushed. After a little conversation, she introduced me to Mrs. Austin,[3] who seemed to me grave-minded, austere, if not haughty; she was looking at some German outline engravings of illustrations; we talked a little. Hayward took me away to introduce me to Miss Martineau,[4] with whom I talked a little on America, where she is going

---

[1] William Blanchard (1769–1835), actor of broad comedy ; performed chiefly at Covent Garden.

[2] See note, p. 131.

[3] Sarah Austin (1793–1867), translator and editor of various well-known historical works. Wife of John Austin, the Professor of Jurisprudence.

[4] Harriet Martineau (1802–1876), the well-known writer, then at the height of her reputation.

this summer. Talked with Mrs. Buller,[1] a very handsome, intelligent woman; asked to be introduced to Eastlake, and conversed with him for some time; fell into conversation about Miss Wright. Mrs. Opie [2] objected to her. I liked very much the benevolent, cheerful countenance of Mrs. Opie; she looked what I should have expected. Mrs. Jameson talked about the stage and Miss Kemble,[3] whom she affected not to have considered a great actress. I heard nothing particular. The people were agreeable and well-bred. Walked home.

June 15th.—While dressing, received a note from Sheil, accepting my invitation for Tuesday; I was pleased with the hope of seeing him. The *Examiner*, which last Sunday contained so unfriendly and, I may truly say, so unjust a remark upon my Lear, has to-day a sort of note of preparation to Mr. Vandenhoff's appearance to-morrow night—unusual in any paper, and most particularly so in the *Examiner*. If the sequel does not prove this preparatory to puffing and indicative of factious intrigue, I do the writer great injustice. For my defence against the treachery and business of newspapers I have no reliance but on my God's bounty to me, and my own industry. Walked round the garden before breakfast and was charmed with the deliciousness of the air, the trees and flowers; I have never remembered so delightful a spring. Coming in, I referred to my past accounts, and ascertained that the expense of carriage to and from town, not including goods, nor hackney coaches, had exceeded, since last October, £52 10s., which makes me think of using horses of my own, if I am still stationary in London. After dinner the children came down, and I took a walk round the garden and in the field, to examine the hay, with Catherine. Read the newspaper and listened to arrangements for our party on Tuesday. The situation in which I stand, dependent as I am for my own means of subsistence and for my hopes of making provision for my

---

[1] The mother of Charles Buller, the brilliant Whig statesman, alluded to by Thackeray in his touching lines on Buller's death—

> "Who knows the inevitable design?
> Blest be He who took and gave!
> Why should your mother, Charles, not mine,
> Be weeping at her darling's grave?
> We bow to Heaven that willed it so,
> That darkly rules the fate of all,
> That sends the respite or the blow,
> That's free to give or to recall."

[2] Amelia Opie (1769–1853), the second wife of John Opie, the well-known R.A.; an accomplished writer; also devoted to philanthropy.

[3] Fanny Kemble, about whose acting opinions appeared to have been greatly divided.

154

children, accounts for the kind of uncertainty, or perhaps anxiety, with which I regard every effort to displace me or share with me the leading station of my profession; and as the conduct of the newspapers towards me renders this particularly easy to any new aspirant, it can scarcely be called weakness if I look forward with uneasiness till the result determines for me.   May the blessing of God be with me and mine! Amen!

June 16th.—A note from Pemberton for orders, and one from Mr. Cooper, requesting me " to meet him in Mr. Bunn's room at twelve on the subject of the Theatrical Bill in the House of Lords."   I answered him that my brother's promotion took me into the City, and that I could not go.   This is an attempt to curry favour with Mr. Bunn, on his and Mr. Bartley's part, at the expense of the interests of all the actors—these are " basest of the basest," these ignorant, servile stage-managers; but " fit body to fit head."   Went to the Garrick Club, where I met Forster, who accepted our invite for Sunday.   Bartley came in, who, very reserved upon the subject, told me that nothing was done in Bunn's room, the intention having been given up of petitioning. Dined, and, returning to chambers, received notes from Dance, declining, Miss P—— accepting invitations for Sunday.   Lay down. Letitia returned and dined.   A Mr. Bromley wrote a note to Catherine, which was a very great impertinence, asking assistance on the plea of having seen her as a child; I tore it.   Acting Macbeth with much earnestness and freedom; was good in the soliloquy on the murder— very good; in the murderers', murder, banquet scenes, also good; and before the battle, though my effects were injured by Messrs. Warde and Mathews being strange in their respective parts.   Dowton spoke to me about the requisition of the morning, and was, of course, opposed to it.   I was *angry* (which I had *no right* to be—in consideration of *him and myself*) with Mr. Warde.

Elstree, June 17th.—Received note from Mason, intimating his intention of dining with us to-day.   Walked in garden and gathered some fruit; went into the field and looked at the hay; the wind was high, and, though occasionally showery, the men were carrying. Looked out wine for our dinner, as I knew no time would be left me if our guests should have anticipated me.   At about two o'clock Captain Thruston arrived, and after sauntering in the field and road, I proposed our entering upon the business of his early visit; he read to me his play called the *Sister's Tragedy,* with several scenes of which I was much pleased, and also with the individuality of character sustained through the piece; it appeared to me to possess much merit. I recommended him to leave it with me in the hope I might be able to suggest some more effective termination, which is strained, without either terror or pathos. Before five o'clock Dr. Lardner and the Chevalier De Fresne arrived, and for an hour we held a discussion— to me very interesting—on *les beaux arts* and the drama, particularly on the play of *Macbeth*, Mrs. Siddons and Talma. In the drawing-room we found my family, my sweet children with their dear mother, looking like two little cherubs, or emblems of innocence. A servant in livery brought a note from Sheil, regretting that the continuation of the Coercion Bill by Ministers obliged him to press a motion, which he had purposed to suspend (in order not to embarrass ministers), but which he was urged by the Irish Members to press this evening, and that, in consequence, he " could not come." It was a disappointment, but I believe it was undesired on his part. Hayward and Mason arrived, and we sat down to dinner. *Le Chevalier* was particularly interesting, his account of some letters in his own or his friend's posses-sion engaged our deepest attention : one was from Herault de Sechelles to the Librarian of the Bibliothèque du Roi for a copy of the laws of Minos to frame a code from. The sudden demand upon my French gave me less trouble than I expected, and I contrived to convey my meaning in my translated English thoughts. All our guests left us except Dr. Lardner; Captain Thruston taking away with him, to my great regret, M. De Fresne. We had an hour of most interesting con-versation, or rather information, from Dr. Lardner before retiring. Of Newton he observed he made about a dozen discoveries, any one of which would have immortalized any other man.

June 18th.—Battle of Waterloo—1815. Woke with oppressive headache, and unable to talk or play with my little darling Nina, who was awake in her crib beside me, and who lay in patient silence not to disturb her mother till the servant came for her—the sweet child ! On rising, I walked round the garden, drawing refreshment and pleasure from the freshness of the air. Dr. Lardner was at breakfast, which was prolonged to an unusual hour by the cheerful and interesting con-versation. Found no opportunity of sitting down to business of any kind. Dr. Lardner fixed on going to town by the Bedford coach, and seemed resolute to be idle until his departure. Mentioned his intended tour to Paris, etc., and wished me to accompany him, which dear Catherine's situation, independent of the expense, would not permit. We walked for some time in the garden, and then, on his proposal, to the reservoir, taking Luath with us; we found the water so low that I countermanded my boat, when we returned, which in the early morning I had ordered down to be floated. We discussed the subject of keeping horses and carriage, which he computed would amount to £70 per annum. This is so much more than I had thought, although only £10—or little more—(perhaps not so much) above my present annual amount of carriage expense, that I am disposed to pause upon it. The advantages would certainly be great, but I must be sure that I do not purchase them at too dear a rate. Walked up with Dr. Lardner to the coach, and saw him off. Met our old servant, Green; again out of place, I fear. Felt very much fatigued; more, I apprehend, from indulgence of appetite and stretch of attention, than from absolute exertion. Read some notices on the poet Gower, Henry IV, and their tombs, in Blore's *Monumental Remains.* Was sorry to hear from Lardner to-day the weakness of Babbage [1] in his childish—query base?—anxiety for the notice of titled persons. In Moore such meanness is notorious, and in a mere song-writer may not so much surprise one; but in a man of science we are obliged to blush for the character of philosophy.

London, June 21st.—Dined with Talfourd, where I met Hayward, Whitmore, Baines, Price, Forster and several others of legal note— a very pleasant afternoon.

Elstree, June 22nd.—Talfourd and Forster arrived, and we sat down to a very pleasant dinner. We were certainly a very merry set of people, with much to enjoy, and with a spirit of enjoyment amongst us. We carried our last bottle of claret into the summer-house, where we found a "locus desipere." We rambled about the garden in the beautiful summer twilight, and at last went into the drawing-room, where Mr. Lough was so engrossing in his attentions to that very sweet girl, Miss P——, that parties were detached to her rescue. I felt I had taken too much wine, and could not trust myself; so went into my study, where I sat in the dark in my easy-chair, endeavouring to steady my head and tranquillize my nerves. They left us at a late hour, Mrs. Sloman lowing good-night to them, and we soon retired, I most gladly, to bed.

June 23rd.—Went to the Garrick Club, where I dined, read the newspapers, and looking through *Quarterly Review* was, of course, offended and disgusted with that puppy Lockhart's notice of *great*

---

[1] Charles Babbage (1792–1871), the eminent mathematician and inventor of the calculating machine.

tragedians. Went to Mrs. Jameson's at eight—for whom I waited till half-past, and with whom I had to endure a tête-à-tête—"too much Mr. Merriman" of two hours. Phillips—of musical-lecturing celebrity —called, I knew his voice, and heard her dismiss him as if she feared to let me know of her acquaintance. She told me much of Fanny Kemble, and her father's making a trade of her. I waited impatiently for the announcement of the carriage, and when it came got very thankfully into it to return to Elstree—to my home—my dear home.

June 24th.—On this day ten years ago I was married to my beloved Catherine, whose affection, mildness, and sweet disposition have made the greater part of my life since that dear event most truly happy. The cares and concerns which have taken up my thoughts for the last few days have made me unobservant of the approach of this blessed anniversary, and it was not until the morning had nearly passed away that I remembered it, and insisted upon its being kept as well as our brief notice and domestic party could mark and do it honour. I bless the day and bless the dear woman whose love and virtues consecrate it in my thoughts, and I humbly and devoutly thank my God for the bounties He has vouchsafed me, and fervently implore a continuance of His divine blessings on my wife, my children and myself. Amen!

June 26th.—Began my work of preparation for Dublin by marking the first act of the *Bridal*, which I almost fear rushes too abruptly *in medias res.*

June 27th.—Mr. Lee arrived with a letter from Mr. Kenneth, informing me that a committee had been appointed to set on foot a monument to Mr. Kean, and wishing to know if I would act at Richmond next Thursday for him; also sending a list of the committee, of which I, *uninvited*, was set down as one! I talked to Mr. Lee much more than I ought—how sadly am I deficient in discretion and self-government!—and wrote a cool, stiff note back, stating that I was engaged on Thursday, and being engaged at Richmond could not act there until such engagement was over, when I would do it or give my name to a subscription—which I feel *ashamed* of doing.

London, June 28th.—Went to town by Billings, endeavouring to arrange in my mind what I should say at the Garrick Club dinner, but distracted by the intervening thoughts of this disgusting piece of quackery, the monument to Mr. Kean. Went to the Garrick Club and ate a sandwich, which gave me a headache; read the papers—think that the tone is lowering on Mr. Vandenhoff's merits; was vexed and surprised to hear that I was expected to subscribe £10 to Kean's monument—the greatest disgrace to the art of all the disgraceful members that ever practised it! . . . Met Stanfield, to whom I mentioned Mrs. Siddons's affair; he asked me if I would sit to Mr. Simpson, who wished to present my portrait to the Garrick Club. Of course I acknowledged the compliment.

July 3rd.—Mr. Z. Jackson called; one of the most adhesive and troublesome of all burrs or bores. I promised to look over his stuff— which he calls a play—and had the pleasure of restoring to him an octavo volume of nonsense, which he calls corrections of Shakspeare's text. Paid Freeman and Healey, and still repeated and repeated what I had to say. Between my speech, the heat, want of exercise and luncheon I was quite oppressed, and lay down in the hopes that a little sleep would tranquillize my nerves, which were much and painfully excited. To the very last moment I persisted in thinking over and repeating my speech—oh! this annoying compliment!—and went at last to the dinner. Saw Fladgate in the drawing-room, who agreed to bring forward the business of Mrs. Siddons's monument, and I engaged that Talfourd should press it forward. Introduced to Messrs. Thackeray,[1] Graves, Bredel, Maynard, Maitland, Brown, Murphy, Palmer, besides met Talfourd, Price, Forster, J. Smith, White, Simpson, Blood, Willett and three or four more gentlemen, whose names I cannot remember. There was venison, etc., and excellent wines. Talfourd proposed my health, with a speech as eloquent as it was kind—which says all for it that truth and admiration can wish to say. I answered it as well as I could with self-possession, but under strong nervous excitement. We had some very good songs from James Smith[2] and Blood, and the evening was very pleasant. Talfourd left us on business with a promise to return. Shortly after Thackeray and one or two others dropped away, and I intimated to Fladgate the necessity of proceeding with our purpose, lest our audience should become too diminished. He accordingly broached the subject, which he very shortly transferred to me, and I had to lay before the party my views as to the desire of myself and others that the Club exclusively should have the honour of erecting a monument to that great actress, alluded to the generosity of her character in encouraging merit in obscurity, relating an anecdote of Kean's appearance before her, and of her kind predictions, which I hinted at, of my own success.

---

[1] Thackeray, then only twenty-three, had just embarked on miscellaneous journalism, and, as yet, made no literary reputation.

[2] Joint author of the famous *Rejected Addresses*.

I mentioned what Fladgate and myself had done in the interviews we had had with Chantrey and the Dean of Westminster, and concluded by hoping that they would not think I wished to dictate to them, but that they would concur with me in thinking that it would confer honour on our Society to carry this object into effect. It was very cordially received, resolutions were passed, and upwards of £50 was voted instantly. Talfourd returned, and was informed of it—he rose to return thanks for his health being drunk, and spoke on the subject of the monument, again adverted to the occasion of the meeting, and pronounced a most brilliant panegyric upon me. The day passed off most happily, and at twelve, or nearly so, we went into the drawing-room, where I introduced myself to Simpson, and where Bredel introduced himself to me. We talked on the merits of Mrs. Siddons, Kemble, Miss O'Neil and Kean very agreeably until one o'clock, when I went to my chambers, leaving the few behind to broiled bones and iced champagne. In bed I read short memoirs of Vauzan and William III, and went to sleep in great dread of to-morrow's headache.

July 4th.—Turned over in my mind the events of yesterday—what had been said to me, and what I had replied, and resolved to act up to the pledge I had given in my speech, and to endeavour to merit the character Talfourd had drawn of me. Read newspapers—the quarrel between Littleton and O'Connell,[1] weakness in the one and total disregard of punctilio in the other. Read the *Observer* respecting myself in the matter of Kean's monument. It was very absurd—extremely ridiculous, but not mischievous. Saw Captain Williams, who told me that it was certain Polhill had applied to Bunn for the lease of Covent Garden, which he refused to surrender. At Kenneth's, where I went to order a book of *Sardanapalus*, I met Meadows and Cooper—suffering from the effects of the brandy and water they had drunk on their way home from Richmond, where they played last night for Kean's monument—the house was £44. These are the men who do honour to Mr. Kean—*laudari a laudatis!!!* I was so disgusted with them

---

[1] Littleton, without the authority of the Cabinet, had, as Chief Secretary, intimated to O'Connell that certain clauses in the Coercion Bill would be dropped. A majority of the Cabinet, however, decided to bring in the Bill in its integrity. Consequently, O'Connell considered that he had been duped, and disclosed his interview with Littleton to the House. Littleton resigned, and Althorp, who was personally opposed to Coercion, followed his example. Thereupon Lord Grey, feeling that he could not go on without Althorp, also resigned. Althorp was induced to reconsider his resignation, which he reluctantly did, and at his instance Littleton was reinstated. Lord Grey, however, finally retired from official life, and was succeeded in the Premiership by Lord Melbourne, whose administration was ignominiously dismissed by William IV in the following November.

EDMUND KEAN

From an engraving

that I fear I showed them great coolness, if not incivility. I could not command myself. This was very wrong. One ought to receive b—g—ds, with whom necessity compels one to act, as b—g—ds of course. Called on R. Price and settled with him a meeting at two o'clock on Tuesday next on Mrs. Siddons's monument. He told me that he had acquainted Forster with all his extravagances, and certainly had been of service to him. Called on Hayward and got Miss Martineau's address, who wished, he said, to see me. He told me that C. Kemble [1] had shown himself the greatest scoundrel in his behaviour to his daughter Fanny, which did not surprise me.

Elstree, July 5th.—Enjoyed the beauty of the morning and the sweetness of the air on coming down into the garden before breakfast. The country was delicious from its contrast with the few days of town life I have lately had. Answered Mr. Vining's letter, received yesterday. I was amused with his passing from " My dear Sir " to " Dear Sir," which shows me he has taken offence at something. The style of Fugglestone is that of all players—we are a vile set. I answered him as before. After tea I read through the whole of the *Maid's Tragedy* once more, and was highly gratified with much of its excelling beauty and occasional truth to nature ; how much to be lamented that it should be disfigured by so much absurdity, coarseness and extravagance !

July 6th.—Walked in the garden before breakfast, enjoying the freshness of the flowers and foliage after the rain. Read the *Examiner*, which as usual contains more clear and honest reasoning than all the rest of the periodical Press together. Sat down to arrears of my record of which I finished one page when Dow arrived, and made me gossip in the garden and my study until the time for afternoon church. He told me he had seen Vandenhoff in *Hamlet*, and that he could not sit the performance through—that he was coarse, ill-bred and vehement. He also mentioned that a friend of his had questioned Barnes [2] as to the depreciating tone of the *Times* about me, and that he had disavowed any unkind feeling towards me, adding on the contrary that he entertained a high opinion of me. When Dow had left us I went to afternoon church, where I read a little Greek Testament ; saw Miss

---

[1] Hayward was an inveterate scandal-monger, and his statements must always be received with a considerable amount of caution. Kemble's " scoundrelly " treatment of his daughter consisted in his making the most of her earning power on the stage, his financial affairs being in a critical condition. He was warmly attached to her, as she was to him, if we are to judge by her *Records of a Girlhood*.

[2] Editor of the *Times* from 1817 to 1841.

Munro, and chatted with Mr. Chalk.   Returning I spent an idle but very pleasant evening, enjoying the delicious temperature and looking through Nattali's catalogue, while Catherine was the Minerva of my Ulyssean locks, and my darling little children were rolling about me. Must not let another day thus escape me.   Read prayers to the servants and family, and went betimes to bed.

July 8th.—Called on Warren; how very much possessed with himself he is!   He gave me a pamphlet he had written, an attack on Brougham, which he says has infuriated the Chancellor—like Cleveland, he might be induced to hang himself if he discovered that it was not so.   He told me a very shocking story of a baronet and his wife, and talked much on his own kind and a little on mine.

July 10th.—Read the account of the Ministerial resignations. Waited some time sauntering by the river's side, and at last got a sight of the *Times*.   The deportment and tone of Lord Grey I thought feeble, and unbecoming a proud character—let men at least be so far consistent as, if unwise enough to show pride in prosperous circumstances, not descend to betray humiliation in adversity.   Lord Brougham, I think, must have been drunk [1]—it is scarcely possible to imagine anything more undignified.   Returned, and wrote a short letter to dear Catherine.   Dressed for the archery meeting, and went with B. and Mrs. B. in the pony chaise to Danson; met Miss Johnson in their carriage at the gate, and proceeded in it to North Cray.   We were received by a knot of servants in a very handsome hall that ran the length of the house, and presented in the drawing-room to a pretty-looking, waning woman; one side of the room was occupied by gaily dressed women, and I got into a window looking out upon the lawn with its tents and archery preparations, and chatted with Bourne. Mrs. Wilkinson, the lady of the house, merely received me, did not speak to me, and I wished that my kind friends had taken me to a hovel that would have welcomed me rather than to this heartless scene of vanity and gaiety.   Without Bourne I should have felt the solitude,

---

[1] Brougham was undoubtedly given to "deep potations," under the influence of which he frequently spoke and acted.   On one occasion, during the Reform Bill debates, mulled port led him to indulge in some amazing antics while speaking from the Woolsack.   This habit, and his wild eccentricities, gave rise to all sorts of rumours as to his mental condition, and at one time it was actually reported that he was passing the long vacation in the seclusion of a private lunatic asylum.   Lord Broughton, in his *Reminiscences*, records an extraordinary incident of Brougham's circuit days, when his friends found it necessary to seclude the future Chancellor for several weeks.   His conduct at times certainly suggested, if not insanity, an unregulated intellect, and savoured more of a political Suwarrow than of the Head of the Law and Keeper of the King's conscience.

the terrible solitude, of finding myself alone in this throng of strangers. We soon escaped to the lawn, and after an introduction to Mr. Wilkinson, began to shoot for exercise or trial. The scene was very animated : three stands of targets were fixed on an elevated turf terrace of the lawn, behind which were two tents, and hidden among the gardens and shrubberies beyond was a band playing occasional airs through the day. The rain interrupted our shooting and drove us to the tents. Whilst here Lord Bexley[1] arrived, looking good-natured and as shallow as he is thought to be. There were many members of the Toxophilite Club in their uniform—among them Dan. Finch, as slovenly and vulgarly looking as when a boy at Rugby ; Sir Henry Martin, a wizened old admiral, with three Toxophilite badges on his breast—one medal would have been more in character with his profession. He shot left-handed. Young Mr. Haworth also was there, with whom I chatted a little while, and two or three whom I remembered at Gillett's party five years ago. After a little more shooting we were summoned to dinner and sat down to a cold repast with various wines but little enough of everything from want of attendance, and the attention which so many paid exclusively to themselves. The ladies soon left the room in which we were, and the men were soon following, when called back by some one telling Sir H. Martin the health of the Toxophilite Society had been drunk, which was not the case, but nevertheless the old man returned thanks. The match came on, and the prize was won by a Mr. Bernard, the ladies' by Miss Johnson and Mrs. Bourne. We walked about the grounds with the Johnsons, who were all there. Got some tea in the drawing-room, where I saw and chatted with young Palmer of the Garrick Club ; looked at the dancing, which was very bad, promenaded the hall and a tent fixed outside of it ; longed for ten, and at last got home, sickened and tired.

July 11th.—Rose with a slight cold and sensations of general uncomfortableness ; packed up my clothes and came down, having forgotten my prayers, which I remembered as I knelt down with the family in the dining-room. In our conversation after breakfast Mrs. Bourne mentioned some anecdotes of our host and hostess of yesterday. She is a silly woman, in the real acceptation of the term ; he, Mr. Wilkinson[2] (who obtained his fortune by opening his pew-door in

[1] The *ci-devant* Vansittart, Lord Liverpool's puzzle-headed Chancellor of the Exchequer and Cobbett's favourite butt.

[2] Originally a Mr. Green, his " pew-door " acquaintance being a Mr. Wilkinson, who endowed him in the manner described. He then became Mr. Green-Wilkinson, and the

church to an elderly gentleman; from chance an acquaintance sprang, which ended with the death of the old man, and the bequest of his whole fortune to Mr. W——) seems a good-natured, thoughtless person; his first morning's employment is to feed his canaries, of which he keeps a great number; he then shoots with the bow till one, rides over to Crayford and plays at chess with a gentleman there till five; rides home, dresses, goes out to dinner, talks till twelve, and has not time even to read the newspaper. Walked in the garden, and having given a gratuity to the servant, took leave of Mrs. B——, who gave me a note for Catherine, and went down the village with B——. While waiting for the coach we read the paper—no Ministry yet settled and Brougham still drunk; looked at the trout; at length I came away, and arrived in town about two o'clock. Took a cab for John Birch's. Met John Morice, Dr. Moore and, I suppose, his curate. Saw a letter from William Birch—was not favourably impressed by Dr. Moore; he seems to me consequential, shallow and unprincipled. I call every churchman unprincipled who advocates pluralities, defends or palliates non-residence, and asks from a bishop only courteous manners and good address—" to be known by his works " is avowed by him as unnecessary to the calling. He asserts much, which politeness declines contradicting, but which is not only dogmatism, but falsehood to boot, and he is a popular preacher—" Milton, thou shouldst be living at this hour; England has need of thee."

London, July 12th.—To Garrick Club, where I met S. Price, Loudham, Wallack, Fladgate, Harley, Meadows, etc. Harley expressed himself much disappointed in having been unable to attend my dinner, and equally so at the proceedings upon Kean's monument; to which, Meadows observed, he had given his services, but certainly should not subscribe. Called at Miller's to inquire about the expense of publishing *Lear;* learnt that it would cost about £20, which is more than I can afford; at the same time I denied the title of the Drury Lane managers to *Werner* as acted; the alterations are my property. Called on Miss Martineau and sat with her about twenty minutes, talking of America and Miss Wright, whom she thought very shallow and illogical. She wished to have letters with the power of delivering them as she might feel convenient, which I promised to send her. Went to R. Price's chambers, where I met Willett and White at dinner. We passed a pleasant day, and proceeded to the Victoria Theatre, to see

founder of a family that by dint of ample means and auspicious matches won a considerable position for itself in the social world.

Charles I. The play is wretchedly constructed, with some powerful scenes, many passages of power and considerable effect in the sketch of Cromwell's character, which, deserving first-rate support, was consigned to the murderous hands of Mr. Cathcart—a very poor pretender indeed. There was so little plot in it that I could not remember the order of the scenes. Some German musicians afterwards were very fair, and some Spanish dancers *excellent.*

Elstree, July 13th.—Sent Healey with the bottle of Natchitocha snuff to Fladgate at the Garrick Club to be prepared for Chantrey. Was only just in time for Billings's coach. On my study table stood Mr. Lough's Horses of Duncan in plaster, with a note from him requesting my acceptance of them. I was pleased with the gift itself and the estimation in which the giver appeared to hold me.

July 14th.—To my great surprise, while writing in my study, Bales announced Mr. Mathews, and ushered in Mathews and his son;[1] I should as soon have expected the Bishop of London. He told me he was at Cannons Lodge, and had come over to see me—admired the prints, apologized for his absence from my dinner, explaining it, etc. (but he would not have been there had all been otherwise than he says it was)—there were ladies in the carriage at the door, whom I invited in, but Catherine's indisposition caused him to decline; going he told me he should sail for America next month, and take Mrs. Mathews with him—there must be a dire necessity to cause this. They left me perfectly surprised and very much amused by so unexpected a visit; I am suspicious enough to think it has a motive which I shall know before the end of next month.

July 18th.—In the afternoon I received a parcel, containing a note from Mr. Bunn, wishing me to open the theatre and perform *Manfred,* postponing for that purpose my Dublin engagement. I do not like the thought of this, as I see no chance for the success of *Manfred*— it is, as I observed, not a monodrame, but a monologue; splendid as the poetry is, it is not at all dramatic.

July 19th.—Received a letter from Sheil enclosing franks and the expression of his regret at not having seen me, and one from Knowles, asking me to act Alfred for his benefit on Monday 28th at the Victoria Theatre. Came downstairs, and answered Mr. Bunn's letter, exposing the impracticability of my studying Manfred before my visit to Dublin. After breakfast sat down to answer Knowles; I confess, though it is

---

[1] The two gifted actors; the elder Mathews died in the following year.

a great inconvenience and I feel it rather a descent to play at the Victoria, yet I am gratified in receiving this application from him; it is the best rebuke I can give to his avoidance of me, his coldness to me, and his omission to do me the common justice of contradicting the paragraph in the *Morning Chronicle*, as also the behaviour of his wife and daughter to me. I answered him in the kindest tone, assenting to his wish. Finished completely the arrangement of the *Maid's Tragedy*, which I think is improved. Began to put *Sardanapalus* in acting form. While waiting for Calcraft took up Feilding's *Amelia*, and was pleased with much of the story, but more with the happy maxims and excellent counsel with which it abounds.

July 21st.—My dear Daughter Catherine Frances Birch born.[1] Thanks and blessings on the name of God!

July 24th.—For exercise walked down to the reservoir with Willie and the dogs; am much concerned to observe my dear boy's timidity, so different from the spirit he used to show. I must set myself to cure it, for his own happiness' sake. He continued his morning walk with Nina and the servant, whilst I returned home, and entered yesterday's record. Found letters from Jonathan Birch, congratulating me, and from Calcraft, informing me that his brother-in-law, but married on Sunday last, had died in thirteen hours of cholera, and that he had his funeral expenses to defray—requesting the loan of £25. Read the newspaper, and think Lord Brougham cannot long continue Chancellor.[2]

July 25th.—Coming down I heard dear Nina her lesson, in which, though with many attempts to control myself, I grew impatient and spoke with temper. This is without qualification *wrong;* it is the business of parents to endure the levity and inattention of these dear creatures, and be contented to assure themselves that a patient repetition of the often forgotten or unheeded precept insures for it a permanent place in the memory at last. Children should be

---

[1] Died and was buried at sea on her voyage from Madeira, March 24, 1869. She was the author of some very tender and beautiful poems published under the title of *Leaves from the Olive Mount* (1860), *Cowl and Cap* (1865), and *Devotional Lays* (1868). Enjoying a large share of imaginative capacity, she was a person of warm and enthusiastic affection which was amply returned by those who knew her; and she inherited much of her father's artistic temperament. Her devoted ministrations among the poor during the time of Macready's residence at Cheltenham will be long remembered there (*note by Sir F. Pollock*).

[2] He was turned out with the rest of the Ministry by William IV four months later, and never held office of any description again for the remaining thirty-four years of his life, during which (to borrow Canning's expressive phrase) he "pounded and mashed" both friend and foe with impartial savagery.

lured to knowledge, until its acquisition, like that of meaner gain, creates a passion for its increase. I hope to be more circumspect. Read through Major Crosse's play of the *Cid*—a translation, I believe, from Lope de Vega—if so, I have no great opinion of the dramatic literature of Spain; the original, I doubt not, contains poetry, high sentiment and some passion, but is utterly deficient in construction and situation—the climax of action.   Gave the rest of my day to the wearying, slow and unimproving task of preparing my acting copy of *King Lear* even to the last hour of evening.

July 26th.—Rose somewhat earlier this morning, and on coming down walked through the fields to the back of the village with my darling children, taking the dogs with us.   The feeling of health, resulting from the temperance of my life for the last week, uniting with the beauty of the scenery, the freshness of the morning, and above all the sight of my precious children made me think myself peculiarly blessed—not so much in those dear gifts of God which are common to our nature, as in the power of appreciating them, and in the tranquillizing turn of mind that referred them to an indulgent and merciful Creator.   We returned home very wet; and I received a letter from Calcraft, enclosing the opinions of Pennefather [1] and Creighton on the case of Bunn's liability for his Irish debts; they are too vague for me to trust, but they may be of use to me. Read the newspaper, in which, bating the violence, I was not sorry to read the reception of the apostate Hobhouse [2] at Nottingham, where, however, the Whig purity will return him; nor gratified in seeing a man like Brougham precipitating himself so rapidly and disgracefully to the ruin of his reputation. Heard my Nina part of her lesson, and with great cheerfulness and kindness; she did very well.   Read and practised, not indolently, Milton—King Lear—Melantius—and Virginius for about three hours and a quarter—and truly gratified did I feel in the consciousness of having discharged a duty.

July 27th.—Went to afternoon service, where I was made impatient of the unprofitable stuff that is served out to hungry minds from the pulpit—citing the book of Revelation, and declaring that the commandments were "written on tables of stone by the *finger* of the Almighty." Letitia made a very good observation on this, viz. that churchmen who used such language were not justified in abusing the

---

[1] Edward Pennefather (1774–1847), afterwards Irish Lord Chief Justice.

[2] John Cam Hobhouse, afterwards Lord Broughton (see note, p. 19). In his *Recollections of a Long Life* he clearly indicates a candidate's indispensable *modus operandi* at Nottingham.

Roman Catholic artists for introducing as a person that Incomprehensible Spirit of Life and Virtue, since their conception of his
attributes were equally limited.

July 28th.—Knowles's benefit at the Victoria. On my way to the
Victoria Theatre called at Drury Lane and sent for Palmer about my
clothes. At the Victoria Theatre, saw Broad, Knowles, Liston,
Abbott, Miss Jarman, etc., applied to by Abbott to engage. On the
way there called on Forster, who told me that the idea of the application to me originated with himself—explained to me how very gratefully
Knowles expressed himself. Returned (in company with Forster over
the bridge) to chambers to dine, and lay out my clothes, which I gave
to Palmer, who called just in time to take them. My dressing-room
was more inconvenient and ill-appointed than many provincial ones,
and when I went on the stage I found the wings literally choked up
with people. I was rather inclined to be out of temper with this, but
soon recollected myself, and acted as well as I could—much of the
character, Virginius, very well—really and with heart. My reception
was *most enthusiastic*—certainly the most of any that appeared. At
the end I was called for, but declined going on and went to undress.
In consequence of the continued clamour Abbott promised that I should
appear at the end of the farce. Saw Sarah Garrick, and begged her
to remember me to her mother—" Eheu! fugaces, Postume." Captain
Williams, Dance, Price, Forster, Jerdan, Egerton and Mr. E—— came
into my room, and generally expressed their feeling of my coming
forward on this occasion of Knowles's farewell benefit. Abbot *distressed* me with importunities, on personal grounds particularly, to
engage for a few nights. I good-naturedly but firmly resisted, and
I *was right in doing so*—how satisfactory it is to be able to say that to
oneself on any occasion! Went on the stage, or was rather pulled
on by Knowles—the applause was tumultuous—I bowed and retired.
Knowles made his speech, in some instances ludicrously familiar, but
from its earnestness and from the occasion deeply interesting the
audience. He pronounced an enthusiastic eulogium on me, and denied
the assertion that I had instigated him to write or heighten characters
for myself. This was but an act of justice—tardy, perhaps, but still
justice, and therefore obliterates offence.

July 29th.—Mr. Palmer, a sculptor—*soi-disant*—called, requesting
I would submit to having a cast taken for him to make a marble bust,
which he hoped would bring him business—I could not refuse, though
detesting the idea of the operation. Called at Garrick Club, where I

saw the ghost of C. Kemble under a dark peruke. I did not envy him
his gains, character or feelings—he is sordidly base. Saw the papers,
of which the *Times* was, of course, the coolest, or perhaps more
correctly studiously cold to me, directly contrary to the others. Went
to Cartwright,[1] who was glad to see me, and whose reputation alone
supported my trembling confidence that he would not pull the teeth
out of my head. I engaged to revisit his terrible room on this day
fortnight, and after another operation to dine with him. He has some
beautiful specimens of art and interesting curiosities. I forced him
to take £5, but he made me promise not to repeat the infliction.
To the Garrick Club. Dined; Thackeray, Fladgate, Price, Keene came
in for a short time. Knowles made his appearance as I was taking my
wine. I asked for a pint of claret, which we drank together and came
to a mutual explanation—his motive for not doing me the justice of
contradicting the falsehood in the *M. Chronicle* was that I was high
upon it—this is not an excuse, but I believe he feels that he has not
done me justice, and I cancel all. I took leave of him, and sat with James
Smith nearly an hour and a half in the drawing-room very agreeably.

July 30*th*.—Before I rose I read the first part of *Philip Van Artevelde*, which I had begun last night, and laid down a little before those
kind of southern rains came pouring out of the heavens like thunder on
the deep rush of the wind—it was indeed " densissimus imber." This
dramatic poem, *Van Artevelde*, pleased me very much : profound thought
displayed in the happiest adornings of fancy, and excellent ideas of
discriminated character, if the persons are not sufficiently individualized
by their language. The description of Ukenheim and his dead children
affected me very much—I am greatly pleased with what I have read.

July 31*st*.—At about half-past five I took up the second volume of
Philip Van Artevelde, in which I had made little progress last night,
and read until past seven ; I was, and am possessed with the book—I
think there is affectation in the unrequired coinage of words which
distinguishes the poem, and occasional obscurity, but there is so much
truth, philosophy, poetry and beauty, combined with passion and
descriptive power of no ordinary character, that I was obliged to force

---

[1] See note, p. 32. Even Cartwright was not infallible. On one occasion he proceeded
to extract a tooth which the patient declared was the wrong one. Cartwright insisted to the
contrary, and applied the fatal forceps ; the patient, in a frenzy of desperation, sprang from
the chair, but the dentist still maintained his grip ; a struggle ensued in which they both fell
on the floor ; finally the dentist proved victorious, and exultingly flourished "the bone of
contention." His triumph, however, was short-lived ; the hapless patient was right ; a good
sound molar had disappeared, but the aching one remained !

myself to lay the book down. On coming down I heard dear Nina
her lesson, and gave her some toys, which quite charmed her. Resumed
my slowly advancing work upon the prompt-book of *King Lear*, and
am more reconciled to expending my time on these or any other of
Shakspeare's works than on all the Sardanapaluses that ever were
written. In the course of the morning some ideas on the part of
Melantius entered my head, which led me to think farther on it, and
to encourage a more sanguine expectation on the success of the
character than I have yet ventured to entertain. Sainton[1] arrived,
and after resting and repairing himself, accompanied me to the
drawing-room, where I beguiled the tediousness of the operation of
sitting for a portrait with the remainder of the volume of *Van Artevelde*, which I think the work of a master spirit, whose politics I fear
are strictly Tory.[2]

August 3rd.—My vanity, or avidity for notice or praise, which I
see is a weakness, or more properly a folly, entailing uneasy hopes and
doubtings, and perhaps occasionally mortification, received a check this
morning which I hope will prove a wholesome one. In the expectation
(for so it must have been, though I never whispered it to myself) of
reading enconiums on my acting and my friendly conduct to Knowles,
I sent for the *Spectator* and the *Athenæum;* they arrived this morning,
with not one word of the Victoria Theatre, and in the *Examiner*, which
gave a short article to Knowles, my name was not mentioned. I was
really not at all displeased at this, for I thought it a very mild and
good lesson.

August 4th.—In bed I finished the first part of Wallenstein, and
rising in good time, walked round the garden to enjoy the freshness of
the morning. Heard Nina the chief part of her lesson before breakfast, and immediately after, having seen and inquired after Catherine,
began my morning's study of *King Lear*. I was interrupted by the
arrival of a Mr. Palmer (whom I had entirely forgotten) come to take
a plaster cast of my face; I lost as little time as I could help, and
found the operation not so formidably uncomfortable as I had been
led to expect. The *artists*, whom Catherine declares to be image-men,

---

[1] A portrait-painter who had asked Macready to sit to him.

[2] The author was Henry, afterwards Sir Henry Taylor (1800–1886); a Colonial Office
official, to whom the poem brought well-merited fame, though it failed as a play when adapted
and produced by Macready in 1847. Sir Henry Taylor was "strictly Tory" to the extent
of opposing the abolition of the Slave Trade and of supporting Governor Eyre, but he was
an official of marked ability and statesmanlike views, and one of the most cultured and
accomplished men of letters of his day.

were dismissed with a good luncheon, and I was left to Shakspeare and Fletcher again. I pursued my practice and reading until dinner. I was obliged to punish my dear Willie for obstinacy and ill-temper. I love these children so fondly that I must be cautious lest my affection lead me into extreme indulgence which can only terminate in their unhappiness and my own bitter self-reproach.

August 8th.—Received letters from T. Arnold, inquiring after his play; from Abbott, asking me to act Virginius at the Opera House on Monday, 18th inst.; from Edmund Elliston, asking the same favour from me at the Surrey Theatre. I replied to Arnold that I had sent in his play, to Abbott that I would play, though it is very inconvenient, to Elliston that I could not. I do not know him, and only knew his father as a foolish and unprincipled man, who cheated me where he could.[1]

August 10th.—In the *Examiner* read a long extract from a tale of Crabbe's—which was of power to draw the waters from my eyes, though I do not like his style; it is to my sense hard and laboured. Thought upon Winkelman's life, and the value of such biographies to give us experience, and turn our eyes in upon ourselves. How many, unconsciously, believe the world to be interested in their proceedings, and chafed about circumstances, which are scarcely known, perhaps, beyond our own acquaintance, and never thought of even by them. Self is such an immense object in every man's eye, and such a little dim shadow to his neighbour's, that it is surprising there are not more instances of human vanity on record than there are—but there are enough, and we all swell the list. Resumed the *ennuyant* employment of marking book of *King Lear*, and by dint of perseverance finished the third act.

August 11th.—Rose in good time this morning, in the hope that I might get the start of the troublesome task of making up my prompt-book of *Lear*, and immediately sat down to my desk on my coming downstairs. In musing on various things, and forcing my thoughts on my profession, the account of Mrs. Siddons's nervousness on first appearing before Queen Charlotte recurred to me; and in the confidence she endeavoured to regain by the thought that she had often acted Queens I thought she gave an unconscious testimony to her identification of herself with the characters she represented.

August 12th.—Read Corneille's *Cinna*, or part of it, on my way

---

[1] The well-known actor and manager (1774–1831); if Oxberry is to be credited, he certainly deserved Macready's severe reprobation.

to town—in which I saw many lines worth extracting. I was not in a mood to do anything, and felt that Forster's call would be a relief to me; he did call, and told me that Mr. Bunn had engaged Mr. C. Kemble and Mr. Vandenhoff. This was not news to exhilarate me; and, indeed, it sunk deeply upon my mind. I did what I thought to be the best, and if I could not see what would be the best, it was not my fault. How uncertain are the issues of our own precaution!

August 15th.—Laboured at Hamlet, in which I found great difficulty in coming *within sight of* my own meaning; touched one short scene of Lear and worked unavailingly at Melantius, which grows harder as I grapple more closely with it; but this will grow easier. Read a letter from Angelo, the fencing master, applying for my subscription—poor fellow! he has wrung my wrists and I have d——d him for an old rascal, little dreaming of our reversed situations. After dinner went into the garden and gave a bone to old Tip, which choked him; the poor old dog lay down and foamed; I did not know whether he was going mad or dying; I patted him and smoothed his throat and called Phillips, hurrying away the children. Phillips very cleverly poked a rope down his throat, and the old dog stood up, looking very uncomfortable, but relieved from his misery.

August 17th.—Went to afternoon church, and slept through Dr. Morris's sermon. He, too, left out the second collect!—he did not know what he was about. To my horror, returning home with Mr. C. Monro, the figure of Gaspey stood like the dreadful reality of vulgarity before me, and I had to summon all my presence of mind to stand the encounter. I cannot do these things well; I seized the occasion to persevere in my resolve of visiting Arnold, and after making my salaam to Miss G——, had the dog loosed, and, when I could get Luath to follow, set off with my little vulgar friend across the fields. Arnold received us very cordially, and I made a slight second dinner with him. His daughter and son-in-law were there; we were very good-humoured, and he seemed pleased that I had come. Returning, we went out of his back door for a short cut, and, losing our way, rambled over deep grass fields till we got close to Elstree, Gaspey frightened at the trees, mistaking them for men, and persuading himself that there was no cause for fear.

August 18th.—Came to town by Billings', endeavouring to think over Virginius for the evening. Went to theatre; incommoded by the size of the house (the Opera House). In the second scene, as I stood at the wing, I saw Grisi in the opposite box; rallied, and played very fairly. The house was much moved, and called for me. After a time I went on, and was greatly received. When dressed, I asked Abbott to say to Grisi that I wished to be presented to her (she had expressed herself delighted with the play), and on her saying she should be delighted to make my acquaintance I went into her room and sat with her some time. Lord Worcester came in, and after a time I went to go with Forster to see Miss Landon,[1] who had been in the boxes. I sat with her and two other nice girls till past twelve—Jerdan was in the box. Saw Grisi's last scene of Anna Bolena, which was very fine. Went home and got some tea as I looked over my bound book of *Lear*, which pleased me very much.

August 23rd.—Turned over the leaves of the *Connection of the Sciences*, by that wonderful woman, Mrs. Somerville,[2] which she has dedicated to that wretched piece of hired inanity, ——. Why did she not honour the honourable by inscribing such a work to them—to the good—the learned or the wise—the only truly great? It is sickening to see real greatness grovelling before a gilded puppet, tricked out in tinsel and feathers for a stupid blow; it is really disgusting.

August 24th.—The servant had told me that poor old Tip would not touch any food this afternoon, that he had drunk a little milk in the morning, but was now much worse. The rain was over, and I went down to look at him, thinking to myself it would be probably for the last time I should see him alive. Phillips was looking over the palings of the first yard (why, I do not know), and, seeing me, came forward to tell me that he thought Tip was dead; I was quite grieved; went to see the poor old dog, who lay stretched out. It is very mournful to think I shall never see the fine creature rolling about and coming to be caressed again. He makes a gap in my affections, for I was fond of the creature, and associate his idea with many scenes of pleasure and of happiness. He is in every way a loss to me. I can fully sympathize with the poor old man in Sterne's pathetic scene of the dead ass.

August 25th.—Went in the carriage, which is now very shabby, to Richmond; saw no scenery more beautiful there than the views I left behind, particularly in the neighbourhood of Harrow Weald. On my way, went over fourth part of fifth act of *Melantius*. Arrived before eleven, and was obliged to wait in the theatre and on the green,

---

[1] Letitia Elizabeth Landon (1802-1838), the poetess, who wrote under the initials "L. E. L."

[2] Mary Somerville (1780-1872), the distinguished scientist.

173

to catch a little sunshine until twelve o'clock. Saw Farren, Mrs.
Faucit, and two children of theirs—emblazoned in the most unblushing
manner.[1] The effrontery of this connection makes it extraordinarily
disgusting. My rehearsal let me into a dreadful catalogue of woes to
come—the company was fearful, and Thompson shone among them
like a protecting angel. He walked with me along the river's banks
to show me the way to Kew, which I found a tough walk; the scenery
pretty, but luckily I prefer the character of our own. Captain
Williams came out to meet me, and with his wife, a nice little woman,
gave me a very hospitable reception, a very good dinner and excellent
wine, in company with Jerdan and Mr. Barham. I waited till the last
moment for a fly, that had been sent for to take Mrs. Williams, party
and self to Richmond, and was obliged to take a boat, which Captain
W—— engaged for me at the Bridge, and away I went with a bad
headache, the fear of cold, and anticipation of being late. We passed
three steamboats, on one of which a party was dancing. Old Thames
must have been astonished! I arrived and dressed in time, and played
as well as I could (*not well*) with such a company, and in so small a
theatre. Took Jerdan, Captain and Mrs. W—— back to Kew,
resisted their entreaties to take supper, slept along the road, and
reached home in good time.

August 26th.—Walked in the garden, and brought Luath out of
the yard, where she seemed quite lonely and out of spirits, I suppose
from the loss of her poor old companion. After dinner I took the
children (the dear children!) with me to the farmyard to feed Luath,
and afterwards walked down with them and Catherine to the reservoir.
Before I went I had marked out the place for poor Tip's grave, and
saw him laid in it and covered over. His loss is quite felt by us all,
and it will be long before I shall forget him in the pleasure I have in
looking around my home. On coming to it, I read Coleridge's beautiful
poem of *Christabel*, and really was annoyed at finding it only a frag-
ment—the lines on the ancient quarrel between Sir Leoline and Sir
Vaux, which Talfourd is so fond of, are perfectly beautiful.

August 27th.—Rose with the feeling that this is the last day for
many to come that I shall have the happiness of being with my beloved
wife and children. On coming down, went into the garden, and looked
at Luath; after breakfast, read over the whole of the character of Lear,
occasionally attending to dear Nina and Willie in their lessons. After
dinner, read Mrs. Austin's [2] translation of the *Story without an End*,

[1] See note, p. 23.   [3] See note, p. 153.

which, in defiance of the numerous puffs I have read upon the book, I think a most unmeaning piece of mystification, and wonder at a sensible woman thinking it worth transplanting from Germany. As Coleridge said of Klopstock, when some one spoke of him as a German Milton, " Yes, a very German Milton." One might call this book a tale of " very German " simplicity; the embellishments are beautiful.

August 29th.—Went in a chaise to Richmond, reading as I could the play of the night, *King Lear*, on my way; I did not feel well, nor was I in the best spirits; the ride was very beautiful in village scenes over the Hammersmith Suspension Bridge. The rehearsal was most disgraceful; the persons put into the characters below contempt. Mr. Thompson no jot exalted above the rest, and all imperfect—Messrs. Thompson and Lee restoring the beautiful diction of Tate! I saw Montague, once a very decent actor in the Bath Theatre; now a cripple, hobbling on crutches, but in excellent spirits! The person that played Gloster—one of those idle men who give a character of baseness to an art by attaching themselves to those who cultivate it—would have been rude if I had furnished him with opportunity. He was quite disposed to resent my desire that he would use " no action " in my most particular speech to him. These are the tools I have to work with; how can clean hands escape soil by contact with such? The rain would not allow me to walk to the bottom of the lane. A chop was sent from a tavern to the room I occupied in the theatre, where I slept out the afternoon. I had a silly sort of note from old Angelo, who appears to me a model of a " dust." Acted but tolerably King Lear, being distressed and harassed beyond measure by the imperfect state of the actors. Mr. Twining came into my room afterwards, lamenting the want of support under which I laboured. I was glad to see him.

Bristol, September 2nd.—Went to the theatre. Was disposed to do my best, but acted indifferently. I will not say that it was not my own fault, but Mr. Mude, a miserable bawler, who exactly answers Hamlet's description of a " robustious periwig-pated fellow," distressed me in the outset of the play, sticking out his arm to me like a ramrod, and I could not recover my temper again, which was often tried through the night, particularly by Lucius and Virginia. And here one of those curious things occurred that show how much we are the victims of our own fears. I thought that Mrs. D. Lee did not appear well pleased with my indifference to her, and the distance at which I kept her, and in the fourth act her writhings and gaspings made me think she was going to make a display by a *faint* to excite interest;

when I came to stab her, I took most especial precaution not to let the knife touch her: she fell, and, as I thought, in a mock faint—nay, I even fancied I heard her hysterics from my room and from the stage, and expected she would impute it all to my violence. I expected her husband every moment to come into my room. I went through the remaining scenes with the ideas of paragraphs—pictures of ruin before my mind that were absolute agonies. I dressed, spoke for some time to Mr. Mude on business—nothing was said or hinted, but I went home in a state of mental torture, which was only partially subdued by my reason before bed.

September 3rd.—Awoke more tranquil from sleep, and having considered how utterly groundless were my sickly apprehensions; still, I could not quite reassure myself until I had seen the lady, which I resolved to take occasion to do. The vision, for such it almost may be called, that had haunted me had a manifest effect upon my state of body. I was really unwell from it alone. A woman called with a letter, describing herself as the daughter of Edmund Kean's mother, unpaid by her manager, etc. I felt no compassion even if her tale were true, there is something to me so unredeemably disgusting in the life and character of that man that I feel a sort of sickening to all that belonged to or allied itself to him—Messrs. Lee, R. Phillips, J. Hughes, and the whole train of parasitical bl—g—ds. Went to rehearsal in a very low state of mind; rehearsed only the scenes where others were concerned particularly with me. Seized the occasion of sending for Mrs. D. Lee on the plea of speaking to her about her dress for Myrrha. When I saw her all smiles and curtseys—oh, what a relief! It is difficult to describe the lightened feeling of my heart, the pleasure which the return of complacency afforded me. I spoke very kindly to her on her dress, and also on some points of her acting, by which she seemed much obliged. At my lodgings I looked over what I could of Hamlet, and, going to the theatre, acted it really well —the advice to the players particularly so; and, indeed, the whole performance was good. Came home with a body very much fatigued, but with my mind greatly relieved.

September 5th.—Went early to rehearsal upon the promise, though not with the expectation of seeing it realized, of having the last scene of *Sardanapalus* tried. On reaching the theatre I found nothing ready, all things in confusion. The general inactivity, from the sleepiness of the manager to the sulkiness of the property man, was remarkably conspicuous. There was no head to give impulse and energy to the

176

limbs of the concern, and I felt annoyed to see this woman's [1] money thrown away by the supineness and apathy of those whom she was paying. I therefore gave my assistance and saw much done, and ordered more, that contributed to put the play forward. Acted the character of Sardanapalus very fairly, and the audience gave it their fullest sympathy. By dint of urging on the people and giving them proper directions all went smoothly, and the curtain fell amid loud plaudits. I was lustily called for, and went on to make a very cheerful bow to my kind Bristol friends. Went to bed and read the preface to *Esther,* by Racine, and some chapters of *Tom Jones.*

September 6th.—On coming from my room, I immediately set myself to an examination of my affairs, and a consideration of the offered terms from Liverpool; I did not hastily relinquish the certainty of gaining money, but if I am at any sacrifice to seize upon every offer of direct emolument without respect to its influence on future experiments and on other engagements, I may as well play *right ahead* as I used to do, and relinquish my increasing hope and strengthening trust of attaining real eminence in my art. I decided not to go there, and wrote to Clarke to that effect.

September 8th.—Settled accounts, paying my board and lodging, and learned that Mr. Mude would not play Ulric—even on Friday. I have never entertained a high opinion of this person; now I hold him at his worth—he is a low-minded person. The box with the dress of Sardanapalus arrived, and a note of the repairs, with a very cool demand for a cheque to the amount—which, of course, I shall not send. Went to rehearsal, annoyed by a wearing toothache and cold in my head, and endeavoured to prevail on Mathews to undertake Ulric, but he excused himself on the score of illness and depression. I could not urge it. Rehearsed the few scenes required of *Sardanapalus,* and came home much worse with this odious toothache—the very tooth with which, a few weeks since, Cartwright had put me to torture for its preservation. On going to the theatre, I apprehended that I should be put *hors de moi* by the new dress, and I was so, more particularly that in two important points it did not fit. I did not act well, except the conclusion of the dream, and, in conformity with the usual accident of a second night, the whole piece went flatly.

September 9th.—Mr. Mude, with nothing to do and doing nothing, came late to the rehearsal and thus threw away a night and morning, while pretending he *could* not study Ulric. He is a very shameful

---

[1] Mrs. Macready, his father's second wife, the lessee of the Bristol theatre.

fellow. Coming home, arranged my money and wrote to dear Catherine. After dinner lay down on the sofa, well wrapped up, and slept some time in hopes of lulling the pain in my face. Went to the theatre very much disinclined to act—was disappointed in seeing a very indifferent house, but it seems the play has been "hacked" on every occasion. A note was brought to me in a vulgar rhodomontade style from a Mr. Dickson, calling himself an American, requesting an *interview or an order for two*. I returned for answer I was merely a visitor, and as such had not the power of giving orders. Acted very indifferently the part of William Tell, which I now thoroughly dislike; I was in low spirits, in pain, and disturbed in my best effects by the carelessness of the performers. How much it is to be lamented that there is no probation for players to pass!

September 10th.—Looked over Sardanapalus and went to the theatre. *Invitâ Minervâ*, I had to force my spirits, which were depressed by languor and uncomfortable sensations, but I did the best in my power with Sardanapalus, though I was not very good. I was cross and morose, which was as bad as it was unnecessary. After the play, on coming home very tired, I wrote a letter to Woulds, entreating him to let me off from my next week's engagement, as I risk in health so much more than it is worth, even if it were reasonable to expect a good result, which it is not.

September 12th.—Entered some arrears previous to going to rehearsal, where I was disappointed in seeing Mr. Ross so imperfect that it was evident he could do nothing with the part of Idenstein. Here is another instance of the utter want of respect to the art and occupation in which these impostors (for so the present race of actors may be rightly termed) are engaged, which is observable through every branch of the drama. I requested this man to take pains with the character, which seemed in every respect adapted to him, in order that I might have an opportunity of recommending him for the second old man—and the man with three times the necessary time was not perfect in three consecutive lines! Acted some of the character of Werner extremely well; was much distressed by the imperfectness and unfitness of Mr. Carroll as Ulric, but was not displeased with him; on the contrary, obliged by his good-natured attempts. Was, however, very angry about some trifles in other parts of the play, for which I condemn myself, and suffer deep pain in reflecting on my folly. I do not mean to extenuate the general idleness and inattention of manager, prompter, servants, actors, etc., which are deplorable. Mr. Mude, the manager, is the very first and very worst; he is really disgusting in his indifference to everything going forward. Two letters from Woulds, refusing to remit my engagement, and trying to make out a case, but this is a very poor one.

September 13th.—In dressing, I reasoned with myself upon my petulant and morose behaviour, and brought before my eyes the little, and to other persons the imperceptible, defects, which the negligence of these idle and unskilful men cause in my theatrical portraits; besides, in what do I amend them or improve myself by abandoning myself to temporary fury? It grieves me, and shames me to think of it. Went to rehearsal, settled William Tell, and rehearsed *King Lear*—without ill-humour. A letter from Mrs. Glover, asking me to go to her son at Aberystwith for a few nights, and to play for her benefit at the Haymarket. Mude told me that Madame Vestris's shoe bill *averaged*, for the time it was made out, eleven shillings per diem!

September 16th.—My night's rest, short as it must have been, was still further diminished by my own restless and ill-imagining mind; I rose, however, at an early hour, and finished everything that I had to do in the way of packing. I started with a tolerably agreeable and intelligent man, whom I suspected to be Mr. Adam, but who was not, and others—*fruges consumere*. This person wrote with great ease as the mail proceeded, and on my asking, he showed me how it was managed: simply by holding the right hand firmly and immovably down upon the book on which you write. I tried it. We had rather a long passage over the Severn, during which my right-hand neighbour asked the guard if that—pointing to one of the passengers—was not Macready. The guard gave him a good nudge, and, to his repetition of the question, slyly pointed to me. Heard of the wreck of the *Osborne*, 300 tons, higher up the river, laden with salt; the strength of the tide broke her up directly. A very agreeable man—as I surmised, a solicitor, and, from his own account, a Catholic, educated at Stonyhurst—came in at Newport. I liked him very much. As we entered Neath, where I expected a chaise to be waiting for me, I perceived two or three young men running and looking into the coach, and the sympathy with their curiosity spread as we went along. I knew I was known—at the inn there was a crowd. On inquiring for my chaise: "Yes, sir, Mr. Macready; which is your luggage?" There was Woulds, looking as if just clutched by a bailiff; every one was in motion, some staring into my face, others getting down and running with the luggage, and in the course of five minutes we cantered off.

It seems Woulds had walked over and spread the alarm, which was certainly very widely diffused, and which served to amuse me very much. We went merrily along, leaving the excited inhabitants of Neath to talk of the event, and reached Swansea—the stage door of the theatre—at about four minutes past seven. Here, again, was a crowd at the door, and so much chattering and hurry and confusion that after Woulds had given the postilion seven shillings and sixpence for his fee, the fellow returned and asked, with great anxiety: " Who the devil have I been driving? " I dressed, having my flesh-coloured stockings on under my trousers, in about twenty minutes, and, going on, played Macbeth, considering all things, not discreditably. But how truly did I feel in this instance the *proof* of what I had so often advanced about actors injuring themselves by playing upon worn-out frames and jaded spirits! It would have ruined Miss O'Neil very soon, and did almost ruin me.

Swansea, September 17th.—Took a warm bath, and walked on the pier, and along the sands, enjoying the beauty of the bay—really beautiful—and listening to the music of the waves gently breaking upon the shore—feeling within myself a relish of the air, the sea, the sky—of nature and of life, that was most delicious. Came home, and before and after dinner read in Homer the pathetic death of Patroclus.

September 18th.—Before going to rehearsal entered some arrears due. Was very courteous and well conducted at the theatre, though disgusted with the impertinence of a man called Edmonds, who refused to speak what the prompter told him. Mr. Adderley, about whom Calcraft had written to me, was very civil, but indifferent. Mr. Mason told me of the character Mrs. H. Siddons gave of her brother Mr. Murray,[1] which confirms what I have unwillingly but unremittingly thought of him, that he was a selfish, cold-blooded, designing schemer. She has certainly been a good sister to him, and her evidence is of great weight. Went advisedly to sleep after dinner, and, having despatched my clothes to the theatre, packed up what remained, and prepared myself for my night's work. The house was very good, and taking considerable pains I acted Werner really well—almost too well for some part of the house, to which I make no doubt the grinding and roaring and grimacing of my hard-working colleague Stuart in Ulric must have seemed much more like acting than my more quiet mode of speaking. My friend Herod is a worthy painstaking man, but one with whom a cat would have no more chance than Lictors with

---

[1] See note, p. 25.

ELIZABETH O'NEILL

From a lithograph of a painting by W. Davis

Hercules. I acted with general taste, and have little exception to take, except where my intentions were interfered with by the imperfectness or maladroitness of my coadjutors.

September 19th.—Was called, to my great annoyance, at twenty minutes before three, and obliged to get up to speak to the porter, with whom I had bargained for this call last night. On opening the window I perceived it was raining—settled for the man to return for my luggage, and, having made most of my toilet before going to bed, was not long in putting my bags, etc., ready for his call; delivered them to him, and after getting a little tea walked up to the coach office; took my seat in company with another man, a woman and infant, for whom I felt much interest. My own babes came across my mind, and how I should like them to be exposed to the raw fogs and vapours of such a morning made me anxious to see her comfortable. We started at four. We had other occasional passengers, there being a great demand for places. As we left Cowbridge I was interested by this woman, herself rather interesting, showing much knowledge of the localities, and dwelling on the beauty of certain places with a sort of fond recollection. On inquiry I found her youth had been passed here, and she was now, with her husband and large young family, revisiting her early home. Here had been the scenes of her early love, and many a dell and many a hill-top with its lovely views preserved associations of painful and pleasing memory, perhaps, both dear to thought. As we set down this little colony another family, following us in a chaise, took up their places—rather pretty women; but the day was Indian in its sultriness, I had no book, no power of going outside, no capability of thought—patient perspiration was my business through the day, and I went through it like St. Lawrence on his gridiron. At Cardiff we took up Miss Callcott, a daughter of Dr. C., who is handsome, though not young, and, as I heard, a very fine singer. Dined — if dining it could be called—at Chepstow, where the coach for Gloster was again inhumanly loaded, and I resumed my sort of catacomb position. "The longest day will have an end "; we reached Gloster safely, and after giving some advice about her baby to the lady, my companion, I left them, sought out my luggage from Bristol, took my place for Birmingham, read an old newspaper on sorry Lord Brougham, entered arrears of record and was glad to go to bed.

Gloucester, September 20th.—Bought a small volume of Gifford's [1] *Baviad* and *Mæviad* to read on my journey. Looked at the news-

---

[1] See note, p. 99.

paper, paid my bill, and came away. Read Gifford's life—with the direct simplicity of its narration I was pleased, and affected by the touching enumeration of his sufferings; his answer to Lord Grosvenor's inquiry—that he "had no friends, and no prospects of any kind "— moved me very much. What a lesson is such a life! but what a lesson is every man's life, if we would only use our own minds in their examination! Read the *Baviad* and *Mæviad*; preferred the former; the subject was too much exhausted for a new satire, at least, to equal in pungent effect the former one. They are, however, both extremely good, and must have fallen like a giant's arm upon the insect-like flutterings of the half-formed witlings whom they aimed to crush. But to imagine that Burns lived in comparative neglect while these apes were attracting notice by their absurdities! I should like to read these satires to dear Catherine. At Worcester I saw a face which I thought I knew. I could not recollect until I went into the inn, and then it occurred to me as that of William James, Dr. James' son, who was the head boy at Rugby soon after I first went there: it must be very nearly thirty years since I have seen him. Heard a good deal of Birmingham news from a Birmingham man in the coach; arrived, took my place to Chesterfield, saw and chatted with old Waddell, read hastily the account of the Edinburgh dinner [1]—I question the extent of service of Lord Grey.

September 21st.—Rose early to set out by the Sheffield coach for Chesterfield: was so extremely drowsy during the two first stages that I neither read nor looked at the country: slept continually. Read over the Latin citations in the *Baviad* and *Mæviad;* then read both poems over again, having gone through the trial of John Williams, *alias* Anthony Pasquin *v.* Faulder: there are observations in the speech of Erskine that will well apply to many of the scoundrels, viz. Fraser, Westmacott, Gregory, etc., of the present day. —— is dead, and though as base a libeller as ever blackened his own soul, or tried to do so by another man's character, he is spoken of by some of the Press as respected and lamented! Arrived at Chesterfield in the usual *agony*

---

[1] The complimentary banquet to Lord Grey, memorable for the altercation between Brougham and Lord Durham, which led to their long and bitter quarrel. Brougham was at that time making a sort of triumphal progress through Scotland, posing as a Conservative in one town and as a Radical in another! In addition to these political pranks, he brought his office into discredit by the "high jinks" in which he indulged at the country houses where he was a guest, on one occasion actually permitting the Great Seal to be taken possession of by a bevy of mad-cap young ladies for a game of "hide-and-seek," in which the Chancellor groped about the room blind-folded to the rising and falling notes of a piano!

of anticipated playing, had my luggage carried to the Angel Inn, where the rooms offered me were tobacco-perfumed and dirty. I was at last driven to take refuge in the ball-room. Sent for my letters, and received one, worth all, from my Catherine; answered it before dinner; after dinner received a note from a Mr. Mason, asking me to sit for my portrait. Wrote an answer, declining his invitation.

Chesterfield, September 22nd.—I saw an *affiche* of Mr. Cathcart's running away £9 in the manager's debt stuck up in the green-room!! This man seems utterly despicable! Walked round the market-place, and so home by the church—examining the wooden spire, curious and unsightly, observed the date 1003 upon a porch. Laid out my clothes, sent for a play-bill and a History of Chesterfield—not very interesting. Wish to see Hardwick and Chatsworth, if practicable. Read a little of *Hamlet*, which I acted to the dullest, most insensible audience, and among the most brutish I ever yet had to endure. I did my best, but occasionally felt the lethargy of the audience steal over me. My friend Horatio did everything at night contrary to what I had requested in the morning, but I think I never either looked or offered an ill-natured thing. Was tired, and beginning to grow *home-sick*.

September 23rd.—Went to rehearsal, where I preserved the same affable and gentlemanly demeanour that I had done yesterday. I was once near lapsing into impatience, but it passed over. How desirable would it be for me if I could but maintain this deportment! I can at least try. Began Virginius very well, with considerable earnestness, and learning to relax my stiffness; but in the third act was seized with a return of the toothache, only more violent than I had at Bristol, which affected my head and nerves generally. I combated it as well as I could, but was acting under a heavy load during the remainder of the day. Forgot to notice, for I must not omit to record my reprobation of my own indiscretion, that I was angry with both Lucius and Appius, but merely said to the latter: "Oh, sir! you have distressed me exceedingly," which he did by his imperfectness; the other was nearly as bad. Still, it would have been more sensible to have passed over what could not be amended.

September 25th.—Between Loughborough and Leicester the remembrance both of my journey, its minutest details, my being alone, passing (as I thought) "Boots'" (one of our boys) house, dining at Nottingham alone on a leg of mutton and tart, the feeling of melancholy that was on me, though going home for my first holiday from Rugby —all the sensations attending a journey taken thirty-one years ago which led me unconsciously to the last sight of my blessed mother's remains—came back upon me this afternoon with a sort of vividness that the events of his past life are said to present themselves with to the mind of a drowning man. The sight of her corpse was the first deep impression I remember to have received—I can see her now so placid in her sleep-like death—as I kissed her marble-cold forehead. I well remember too how she used to caress and weep over me when I returned to see her, though I fear, indeed I know, though deeply attached to her, my violent passions made me often undutiful and disobedient to her—God bless her and forgive me! He has been much, much more merciful and bountiful to me than I have merited.

September 26th.—On coming downstairs saw the yeomanry trotting to their several muster-places; while standing at the window, and smiling at the awkward figures before me, to my great surprise Arnold, my old school-fellow, entered in yeomanry costume with a helmet like Goose Gibbie's, and seemed quite pleased to see me; wished me to dine with him, and see what he could of me. My employment was my excuse.

London, September 30th.—Forster came in again, and told all he had to tell, which was not much; at his request I read him an act and half of the *Bridal*, which he seemed to like, but—who can tell? Whilst he was with me a note came from Bunn (I had sent back to Willmott the books of *Sardanapalus* and *King Lear* by which, I suppose, he learned that I was in town), he said he would endeavour to run over to my chambers, but if he could not would I write down my demands for his consideration—and the matter might soon be settled; he mentioned also a "glorious part" he had for me, etc.

Elstree, October 1st.—Looked at newspapers and wrote to Bunn, taking copy of the same, asking my former terms, varied only by the division of the Benefit, and the erasure of about half-a-dozen characters from my list.

Leicester, October 3rd.—Saw Braham's carriage start for Birmingham; I can look without the least envy on his great wealth. I have too much to thank God for to covet anything of his.

Nottingham, October 4th.—At the theatre Mr. Manby informed me of the "extravagant praise" bestowed by the papers on Mr. Vandenhoff at Covent Garden; this was not very agreeable or encouraging just going on for *Hamlet*; it annoyed me, but I soon overcame it, and acted the part well—very well; but I was tetchy and angry—I suppose from the news reported to me!

Liverpool, October 6th.—I rehearsed Macbeth with particular care,

184

and with a freedom of deportment and freshness of manner that gratified me in causing me to believe in the perception of my improvement. Miss Huddart was the Lady Macbeth, and seemed to me both nervous and falling into another vice of pronunciation, against which I shall caution her. Laid out my dress, giving parts of it to Marshall to mend, and after dinner went to bed, being anxious to play well; slept soundly and went to the theatre much refreshed. Dressed in good time, was cool and self-possessed, and played with a truth, grace and energy that, I think, should place this as the best representation I have yet given of Macbeth. The audience, proverbially the most insensible and apathetic of any, seemed to feel it, for they went with the stream that bore me on, and became so much excited that after much applause they became tumultuous for my reappearance—a very unusual practice here—and at Clarke's request I went on to make my bow before them. I was angry with a well-meaning but most inaccurate man, Mr. Vining, and (so blind is anger) made my complaint of him directly before his wife, whom I did not see. From abstinence in diet and taking but a very little wine I did not feel much distressed by fatigue.

October 7th.—Dr. Lardner came into my room, and chatted with me for some time; among other things, in speaking of the tour he had made through Scotland and by the lakes, he mentioned his visit to Southey at Keswick. On passing the drawing-room he noticed several ladies apparently in a very cheerful mood; on giving his name, after waiting about five minutes, Southey came to him, the very image of distraction, took his hand and led him into his study. For a long time he remained silent—at length told him he believed he must dismiss him; in fine he disclosed to him that within the last five minutes, since he rang the bell at the lawn gate, Mrs. Southey had, without previous indication or symptom, gone raving mad, and to that hopeless degree that within an hour he must take her to an asylum. These are the cruel liabilities of our nature, which no human power can cure, but which only resignation and the hope that religion offers can alleviate and soothe.

October 8th.—Felt considerably tired from the exertion of last night, and was confirmed in my opinion of the necessity of intervals of rest in a week's labours. Gave Marshall my dress for Sardanapalus to alter, and went to rehearsal, where I took pains with my character, and hoped to satisfy myself as well at night. Was talking with Clarke about the opinion of persons in this place upon myself; we agreed that much pains had been taken by the ignorant Press here to root deeply a prejudice against me. He was very sanguine about the house to-night and quite raised my expectations. Went to the theatre, where I found a most wretched house—this was a sad surprise and damp to my hopes, as I regard my engagement's success as depending on this night. It staggered me, but I did not permit it to hang upon my spirits, but went through the part of Sardanapalus with as much spirit as the wet blanket of Mr. Weldron, a miserable pretender to his art, would allow to burst forth—and indeed the performance was a very fair one. But the house! the house!—I was almost vexed. Dr. Lardner came into my room, and interested me with an account of the hospitable arrangements of Edinburgh, upon the meeting of the *savans* there. Returning home, half fretful (which I had no right to be, for I have made a speculation which has failed, whilst others have succeeded) I read the *Examiner*, and on going to bed a scene from Racine's *Iphigénie*.

October 9th.—Rose with sore and almost fretful feelings on the utter neglect I experience in this place, but a little reflection—looking to the bottom of the page—soon righted my mind, and with the quotation : *Tu ne cede malis, sed contra audentior ito, qua*, etc., I went cheerfully to the work of my toilet. The falling off in the week's revenue made me think of relinquishing the plan I had formed of spending Saturday and Sunday at some bathing-place in the neighbourhood, but my state of body seems to require some such restorative. Wrote a little and went to rehearsal, where I took pains and pleased myself with my manner of going through Virginius. Applied to Clarke and Lewis to let me off from Tuesday, but I learn the danger of ever yielding a straw to these managers; they never will relinquish what they once obtain.

October 10th.—Went to the rehearsal of Wolsey, and felt my cold very bad. Whilst at the theatre Clarke told me of the *Liverpool Mercury*, my systematic defamer, having turned round, and spoken of me as the best actor of the day—this was wonderful. Miss Huddart was offended at my speaking to her on the stage, which I should not have done, but she so exceedingly distressed me that I quite forgot myself. Came home, took some tea, medicine and went to bed, forgetting my prayers and thanksgivings to God—an ungrateful fault.

October 11th.—Dressed myself, and went into the drawing-room to see Miss Huddart who had called about the reading of the *Bridal*. I apologized to her, and told her (what she could plainly see) that I was not equal to the undertaking but hoped to be so to-morrow. She sat a little while, imparting some theatrical gossip which she had just heard, and left me to call to-morrow for the same purpose, when I hoped to find myself able to do justice to the play.

October 12th.—Miss Huddart called on the same errand as yesterday—to hear the *Bridal* read. I did not feel equal to the task. After some time Clarke left us, and on Miss Huddart rising to go I thought, as it was so late and the day nearly gone, it was better to despatch this affair now rather than break up another day with it. I read it as cautiously as I could—Miss Huddart dining here—and finished the three last acts after dinner, on the very point of which Clarke returned. Mentioned the *Examiner's* criticism on Mr. Denvil,[1] from which, his repetition of Shylock and his announcement to-morrow for Richard III, I apprehend he has something in him beyond the common run. It is, of course, the interest of the managers to make it appear so, if they can. For my own fortune, which is dependent on these sort of casualties, I can only say : *In Deo spes mea.*

October 13th.—At the theatre, where I went to rehearse Wolsey and William Tell, I received letters from Mr. Bunn, Calcraft and Forster. Bunn refuses on the grounds of "impossibility" to accede to my demand of half a Benefit; I shall pause before I answer him, which I shall deliberate on and I hope in God I may decide with proper judgment. Calcraft tells me of my lodgings, and the failure of his Italian speculation. Forster writes a long letter, chiefly on Mr. Denvil, of whose exact place in the scale of actors he seems unable to determine. It appears to me that he has, from what I read of him, a mind above the common theatrical level and the intellectual material to furnish forth an artist. What will come of it is in the will of other powers. By the negligence of Mr. Clarke or Mr. Lloyd, I am fixed with the whole play of *William Tell* to-night, instead of three acts, which is in every respect, as regards time, effect and labour, an annoyance. I at last yielded to Mr. Clarke's request, which was a most unjust one, on every principle of reciprocity—he having refused to remit me my promise for to-morrow night; *mais il faut cultiver*, etc. Went to the theatre; cannot sufficiently condemn my want of thought, discretion, and relaxation of principle in the carelessness with which I had awaited the arrival of this evening. I was guilty of the greatest injustice to myself, my family and my reputation, in omitting to prepare myself as I should have done for Wolsey; the consequence was that my performance, though it passed with some applause, was far beneath myself

[1] H. G. Denvil, whom Bunn had experimentally engaged; he was, on the whole, not a success.

and not equal to my reputation. If I am to excel, it must be by consistent labour, not by capricious efforts; I hope I shall never have such cause so to reproach myself again. The real cause was (which is no excuse) that I expected an indifferent house. Thank God there was a very good one! I acted William Tell (as a second piece) as well as Wolsey was badly performed. Thought of something to say in case of accident, but, like most of my speeches, it was not required. Was very tired, but not ill.

October 14th.—Marshall brought me a letter by the penny post. It is from a woman who acted one season—I think not more—in London —Covent Garden—her name was Ogilvie. She appeared in Queen Katherine, played Constance, Lady Macbeth, and I forget what besides. She was taught, I believe, by C. Kemble, and was recommended by a Mr. Foote, of private theatrical notoriety. She was an indifferent actress, but a striking appearance. After playing as the leading actress in several country theatres, a young man—almost a boy, whom I remember an interesting child at his father's funeral —named McNamara, was base enough to marry this creature. She now writes to me from the Liverpool workhouse, describing herself as destitute of the necessaries of life, afflicted with paralysis, and almost starved. What a picture! What a lesson! Decency of conduct might have saved this miserable wretch from the state she now endures. How thankful ought they to be who, having escaped the snares of dissipation and the impulses of headstrong will, can safely look upon and compassionate the faults and frailties of their less happy fellow-creatures! I cannot think of what ill-conduct might have made me without really shuddering. Blessed be the name of God for all His goodness to me! Sent for the newspapers, in which was nothing worth notice. Acted Werner as well as I could (which was not very well) with an overstrained throat and exhausted system. It has made me resolve not again to do courtesies in the shape of business. I will give my money, but, according to Dr. Johnson's advice to Thrale, "I will not give my beer—I will sell that." Received a very sweet letter from dear Catherine—how much have I to be grateful for in that amiable and excellent woman! Made some small presents to the servants of the theatre, and after an effort (oh, *mauvaise honte !*) bade the gentlemen of the green-room good-night. Dr. Lardner came into my room and sat with me.

To Dublin, October 15th.—Enclosed bill for £170 to Ransoms, and ten shillings to Mrs. Ogilvie. I believe she is not deserving; but

188

I fear to judge too rigidly, and, under the penance she is now suffering for her faults, it cannot be wrong to temper it with so slight an alleviation.   God help us all!   There is much more atrocious villainy in this world that passes unpunished, and sometimes remunerated (look at the *Age* and *Satirist* newspapers), while this unhappy wretch, uneducated, and perhaps reared to dissipation, is beggared and abandoned for her frailties!   The landlady, when I was paying my enormous bill, offered to take off what I objected to, but as the only mode of taking off would be to remodel the bill, I declined doing so, paid her, and there's an end.   I asked for some luncheon; and after taking some cold beef and writing to Catherine, the little girl answered me rather pertly that they "never charged for cold meat."   I wish I had known that.

Kingstown, October 16th.—After a very coarse passage, the wind nearly ahead the whole way, and increasing in violence toward morning, we arrived at Kingstown about half-past eleven.   The captain recognized me, and came up very cordially to address me.   I saw, as I think, Mrs. Littleton [1]—if it was she, Sir Thomas Lawrence's picture is a gross flattery.   Gave my luggage in charge to the true Peter, and made directly for the Kingstown Hotel, where I got rooms, took a bath, breakfasted, wrote to Catherine, and after walking nearly three miles was taken up by a car and went into Dublin.   How beautiful is all about this city!—how very fine are some of the streets, and yet what paltry little shops we see in some of them, and what dirty, almost ragged servant boys one sees opening the doors of splendid-looking mansions!   Dined, and read the *Times* newspaper criticizing Messrs. Denvil and Vandenhoff; both of which, by the efforts of that base and profligate paper to uphold them at my expense, I clearly see are failures—the latter a complete one.   Mr. Vandenhoff is "the best representative of Macbeth that has been seen since Mr. Kean "—who *failed* in the part, and was admitted by his admirers to be *very bad* in it!   The Richards of Messrs. Young and Kemble, both of which were *notorious failures*, are spoken of with high esteem; whilst I, whose fortune was made by Richard, am not noticed as even existing!   It is not easy to see such dirty malignity and (as I try to teach myself) "suffer and be still "—but can I wrestle with a scavenger?   Filth is the commodity in which men like these—Messrs. Westmacott, Nugent, Gregory, Barnes,[2] Bacon, Thompson, Sterling, Keene, etc.—deal, and what has a gentleman and man of honour to do with such vermin?

---

[1] See note, p. 43.

[2] Barnes was editor of the *Times*, and Bacon and Sterling were two prominent members

October 17th.—Wrote a little, and then began to consider on the best mode of arranging the plays for this engagement; am apprehensive of it from the want of that particular talent in several instances which is so important, if not indispensable to success. Attracted by the vessels under the heavy breeze, or rather gale, that has been blowing all the morning; how much we find to interest in everything around us! How beautiful—too beautiful—would life be if mankind were less the wretched and vile animal, taken in the mass, that he is!

October 18th.—Got tea and read the *Times*, in which was ample satisfaction for the slight thrown on me in the paper of the day before, as Mr. Vandenhoff's performances are here pointed out, and cannot be mistaken, as "most cruel butcheries," etc. It appears as if the writer had felt the injustice and folly of the yesterday's criticism. It is of so much consequence to me that my engagement may depend on the tone the newspapers hold upon the present performances.

Dublin, October 20th.—I did not feel satisfied with my rehearsal of Macbeth. There was great confusion and much delay, which took me from the concentred thought upon my own character which I so much wish to give. Mr. Collins, the prompter, an unfortunate victim of dissipation, was unable to attend, being in a state of raging madness in a straight waistcoat. My dresser did not call for my things at the appointed hour, and I, with some struggles against it, was certainly angry. Whether this tended to detract from my performance, or whether the interruption given at particular points by a few ruffians in the gallery, or whether (which I always most incline to conclude on) I did not surrender my whole mind and heart to the performance, I cannot say; but, though desirous to do well, I did not satisfy myself in Macbeth as I did on this day fortnight. The very best passage of the night was the soliloquy in the first act. The dagger soliloquy was not bad, although twice accompanied by the blackguard noises of these worst specimens of human nature, the Dublin ruffians; the murder was mostly good; but I want my natural key. Saw Creighton behind the scenes, who was very cordial—was this because I had an opinion from him? Was called for by the audience, and went on very reluctantly; was very much fatigued, and sat up thinking upon the money I received and the sums I had expended. *Eheu !*

---

of its staff. Though of the "slashing" school of writers, they hardly deserved to be catalogued with such journalists as Westmacott and Gregory, who were bywords in the profession. Sterling was the father of the more famous John Sterling, whose biography was written by Carlyle.

October 21st.—Went to the theatre, calling in Calcraft's room
to settle some business with him of the *Bridal* and respecting other
casts. Calcraft does not raise himself in my opinion by his mode of
transacting business. He quite sacrifices his interest to his vanity in
his mode of putting his plays on the stage, and does not meet the
emergencies of business with that clear, searching view and decision in
applying remedies or expedients which make the wise and worldly man
successful. He trifles with time, and I do not think him, therefore,
safe to join with in any speculation requiring personal exertion.
Rehearsed four acts of the *Bridal*. I am quite in the dark as to its
effects. Went to see Miss Allison's attempt in Juliet, and saw a very
deplorable exhibition—the whole play was bad ; I saw Calcraft afterwards to talk with him on a substitute for this young lady in the event
of her failure, and my interview with him quite confirmed my late
opinion. When business of a particularly dangerous and important
character is coming towards him he wishes to blink the contemplation
of it. Bad ! Read the *Bridal*, and cut several of the speeches of the
young lady's.

October 22nd.—Went to the rehearsal of the *Bridal*, where again
I thought Calcraft very unlike a man of business. I cease to wonder
at this theatre not paying ; he is not an active and observant man :
his eye is rarely on his workmen. Drilled Miss Allison a little, who is
quite unfit for Aspatia—utterly below it ; but Mr. Calcraft satisfies
himself by saying to himself (of what use to say so to the public ?) that
she is the best he has ! If a commodity is not good enough, although
the best in the shop, the customer does not purchase. He, C——,
wants stern and steady principle. Found letters from Catherine,
urging me to succumb to Mr. Bunn (certes, a desperate policy !), and
from Dow, who is most kind.

October 23rd.—Hurried to rehearsal of Werner, after which the
Bridal was begun ; poor little Miss Allison was so bad that I could not
remain at the prompt table ; in my despair I sent for Miss Hyland and
asked her if she had any objection to rehearse a little of Belvedera to
me. She went through the first scene in Calcraft's room so decently
that I asked her to call on me with her mother and hear me read
Aspatia, if she were disposed to make an experiment in it. She very
gladly assented. I was quite in a nervous state from the rehearsal ;
when shall I learn philosophy ? Whatever the effect of this may be,
it will be, like all others good or bad, so effaceable that it is folly to
add to its own disaster the pain of grieving for it. Miss Hyland and

her mother came, and I read the first act of *Aspatia* to them; she promised to come to me and try it over before rehearsal to-morrow. Went to the theatre, very much displeased with Calcraft for his unfriendly behaviour respecting this unhappy play, and not satisfied with his fair dealing in it. Tried to act with care and force, and thought I did much of the character, Werner, in my best manner, but the audience were not enthusiastic, which I wanted them to be, and I was dissatisfied with them, and inquired if the fault lay with me, but I think it did not. A note from Mr. Dillon McNamara, inviting me to dinner; and a letter from Jacob Harvey, with a pleasing account of Miss Phillips's success; on which dear Catherine had written comfortable news, for which I thank God.

October 24th.—Answered Mr. McNamara's invitation, engaging myself to dinner for Wednesday next. Miss Hyland called, and repeated what she had learnt—only two or three speeches—of Aspatia, adding her inability to become perfect in the part by to-morrow evening, which was, of course, conclusive on the subject. Went to theatre to rehearse the *Bridal*, which detained me till four o'clock. I think, with justice done to it, it ought to succeed; but there are strong objections here, and I have neither time nor tranquillity to satisfy myself in my own character. Dr. Lardner came in to rehearsal, and went into a box to look at a little of it. I was often very angry and much excited during the rehearsal, which is inexcusable; because the only palliative that offers itself is in the very little time afforded and the ill-disciplined actors employed to produce the play. " We are in Heaven's hand! " Thought over the two last acts of Melantius before dinner, and tried to make a characteristic conclusion—the experiment only can decide on that. After dinner sent a note to Calcraft about the daggers required, which I did not think he would otherwise remember, and also for the book of the play to make some further excisions. Went over the whole part of Melantius with much care, and now I have only to do my best and to hope in God for success. Whatever He sends in this world I ought to have learnt to trust in as best for me.

October 25th.—Went direct to rehearsal, where (an ill omen!) I found a scene put on for the first act by Mr. Calcraft's directions which he had settled for the second with me; this was the beginning of the " arrangement." Nothing was in place of " everything " that had been promised, and the scenes that were given were shabby and of all dates and orders. Mr. C——, who had never yet been present during a rehearsal, was, as usual, a mere casual visitor during this. I was hurt by the utter indifference and the selfish unconcern this gentleman showed, as well as by two or three light and pleasant remarks upon the situation in which we stood. I have done him some kindness, some service, and had a right to expect a little more consideration. I kept my spirits even, like a man who wishes to " die with decency " ; but before the end of the rehearsal—three o'clock—I was beaten in heart and hope. Laid out my clothes and went to the theatre. Low and distressed ; forgot the beginning of my first speech to Amintor ; acted as I used to act three or four years ago, not like myself now. Could not do what I proposed at rehearsal. The scene with Amintor and Evadne went very well, that between Amintor and myself very well, also that with Evadne ; the scene with the King and the last with Evadne fairly ; Evadne's murder scene very fairly, but no enthusiasm throughout ; the poor little girl, Miss Allison, was quite a *dépaysagement*. The audience called for me and I was obliged to go on. What I said " I had better have kept to myself." I talked of the pleasure I had in announcing, with their permission, the work of those bright names which illuminated the brilliant atmosphere of our poetical region (qn.: what does this mean?), "those twin stars," etc., touched by the hand of our highly-gifted countrymen, Knowles, etc. I hesitated so much as to be quite unhappy. Mr. Calcraft came into my room and talked for a long time, " but not to the purpose," feeling I was dissatisfied, and trying to find causes in the play for the moderate success it experienced, and declaring his opinion that Miss Allison had no material whatever, etc., asking me to dine with him to-morrow, which I declined.

October 26th.—The thoughts of yesterday haunted me. I strove to avoid them, and rushed to any other ideas, good or bad, to fill my imagination and exclude the painful recollections of yesterday. I could not get up, and was wasting time and thought in bed. Relief came to me in the words of a sweet letter from my beloved wife, with accounts of herself and my blessed children. My God! how constant should be my thoughts of thankfulness and praise towards Thee for the precious blessings I enjoy in my dear home! Rose, and just as I finished dressing was visited by Dr. Lardner, who was going to the Provost's to breakfast. He told me of the engine on the Liverpool railway going from Newton to Manchester at the rate of sixty miles an hour. I promised to procure him orders. Wrote, which was to me a comforting occupation, to dear Catherine. I wrote to Bunn a

193

letter adhering to my terms, but on reflection thought that nothing could be lost by waiting, as such a letter could be written at any time; and in taking *a decisive step*, it is well to be certain, if it is possible, of the consequences. Approve the revokement of my purpose. Went out to drink tea with Miss Huddart. Spent the evening with her, talking much on the event of last night, she feeling and perceiving Mr. ·Calcraft's neglectful and heartless behaviour; conversing, too, on poetry and literature. She showed me what I had not noted, Sir W. Raleigh's Poem to his Soul—a charming *morceau*. Spent a tranquil, rational, and irreproachable evening.

October 27th.—Before going to the theatre, I was anxious, very anxious, to see the newspapers on my poor ill- or hardly-treated play. I could not bear to go to rehearsal until I knew the extent of what I had to bear. My relief was great, and my satisfaction amounted to positive pleasure on reading the highest praise of the adaptation in *all of them.* My quotation of the " twin stars " redeemed the bungling of my speech and was noticed with commendation. I could not have desired more eulogistic comments, and went to the theatre in a very comfortable state of mind. Calcraft met me, evidently with an uneasy sense of his unjust behaviour; he told Miss Huddart afterwards that I was " sulky," but she answered that she thought me in a very good temper. I only rehearsed my own scenes of the play, going off the stage when not wanted. C—— asked me about the scenes of *Sardana-palus*, which I explained to him, the painter, and carpenter. He *importuned* me to give an opinion on the comparative want of capacity in his ladies to play Zarina, which I steadily refused to do. Miss Huddart called to see the papers, and I asked her to direct one set of them to Bunn, which she did. A letter from Forster gave me some theatrical gossip, and made me rejoice at the arrest of my purpose to write yesterday. Was over-excited; could only think of the *Bridal*, and the effect of the tidings on Bunn, etc. Acted Virginius to an excellent house in a manner *very unworthy of* myself. The only part I did at all well was the beginning of the fourth act. I must *resume* my *study*, or I shall retrograde. Dr. Lardner came into my room. Invited me to the railway on Wednesday—promised to come to Elstree at Christmas.

October 28th.—Stayed at home all day, and became listless, weary and drowsy; this day to me has been in the most exact sense " weary, flat and unprofitable," but my own want of energy has been the cause. I must rouse myself, or I perceive consequences which are painful to contemplate. This *Bridal* has thrown me off my centre. I find Sheil was in Dublin, and in the theatre during the representation on Saturday, but he did not show himself to me. The time has been he would have been too glad to have done so, but, according to the old example in the Latin grammar, *tempora mutantur*, etc. My own shyness, perhaps, or neglect justifies him; I have no angry thought about it. Acted Melantius to an indifferent house indifferently. I must *study the character*, if I ever act it in London.

October 29th.—Received a note from Sheil informing me of his being in town and wishing me to dine with him to-day. Read a little of *King Lear*. Sent a newspaper to Dow and answered Sheil's note. Looked over the remaining nights of my engagement, and endeavoured to make some arrangement of my plays for them, but the desperate state of *Sardanapalus* as to any promise of attraction leaves me quite at a loss. Miss Huddart going through the shop, stopped and told me that there had been a rehearsal of *Sardanapalus* and that Mr. Calcraft almost seemed disposed to quarrel with her. Walked out to the Military Hospital; the day was beautiful, and the view up the river of the gate at the bridge, the obelisk and park very striking. Met Colonel and Miss D'Aguilar at the gate of the Hospital. Bulwer came up, to whom he introduced me; he invited me to dine on Friday, and, as I would not hear of his returning, they pursued their ride, and I called on Mrs. D'Aguilar, with whom I found Lady Vivian, whom I did not admire nor like, and some other women, equally unnoticeable. Learnt from Mrs. D'Aguilar that Mrs. Leigh had sent me the lock of Lord Byron's hair.[1] Returning, I called on Sheil, who was absent, and on William McCready, whom I found at dinner with his family— three very fine children; it pained me to see them, for I fear his imprudence has very much straitened their means. At my lodgings I got a note from McNamara, and, while dressing for dinner, Sheil came in and, inviting me to supper, stayed with me till dressed, and then I walked with him to Morrison's, thence to McNamara. Was agreeably disappointed in the party, among whom were some very pleasant men: old Mr. Burroughs, the advocate of Emmet[2] and one of the opposers of the Union, Mr. Tench, etc., the Lord Mayor—really I spent a pleasant evening. Supped with Sheil, which I liked much better, and came home very late. He gave me a good hint on Lear.

---

[1] See p. 120, and note.

[2] Robert Emmet (1778–1803), the Irish rebel executed in 1803; the "young hero" alluded to in Moore's famous lyric "She is far from the land," etc.

October 30th.—Heard Calcraft enter the drawing-room, before I had left my bed.   I rose and spoke to him on the subject of his visit, which was the arrangement of the plays.   Again I perceived not only a want of that steady industry and vigilant circumspection necessary in such an undertaking as this, but also a want of capacity. The engagement he has made with me, unless he intended to make a serious and vigorous effort towards ensuring the attraction of *Sardanapalus*, was ill-judged in every way—too quick upon the heels of the last, and too long in itself.   Had I not put faith in his assurance that he would "get up" *Sardanapalus*, I should never have given my time in making a prompt-book, have reduced my insurance to such a sum, nor have gone to the heavy expense I have done for my dress—useless to me on any other occasion; I am minus a very considerable sum by this understanding.   I rehearsed Tell, and, at Mr. Calcraft's request, went into his room, where I was disgusted with hearing him talk to his painter and carpenter on the subject of the scenery, which evidently not one of them understood—and the play to be done on Saturday! He asked me what dresses the characters were to wear ! ! !   The great scene of the Hall of Nimrod the painter knew nothing about, and was sent away to look for something ! ! !   I was wearied and disgusted, and glad to come away.   Called on Miss Huddart and spoke to her about Myrrha.   I find a sympathy in her friendship, a strong, good sense in her observations, and an acuteness of penetration that makes her society soothing and pleasing to me—it is, in fact, *relief*.   Dined and read the *Examiner;* became drowsy as I was going to the theatre, where, however, I acted much of William Tell in very good style, chastely and powerfully.   In the second act I *was not called*, and the stage waited; the whole play was so shamefully managed that Mr. Calcraft came and, *more suo*, scolded.   What that is to do of good I have yet to learn.   Was called for by the audience, to whom I made my bow.

October 31st.—Was not up so soon as I should have been, and went directly to rehearsal, where I had to lament neglected opportunity. The play of *Sardanapalus* might have been done to draw money; I fear it cannot now.   The more I see and hear of Mr. Calcraft, the more he shows me his uneasy consciousness of having done an injustice by me; he would not be at such pains to reason and endeavour to persuade upon the subject if he were satisfied with himself.   Rehearsed *Sardanapalus* without a scene or property.   Returning to my lodgings, I read over the third act scene of Myrrha to Miss Huddart; received a

196

dear and blessed letter from my own Catherine, also a note from Mr. Colles inviting me to dinner. Met, at Colonel D'Aguilar's, Bulwer, whom I liked very much; Sir Hussey Vivian, whom I thought very amiable and agreeable; Major Forster and Mrs. Forster, whom I was struck with for her animation and smartness—whom I should like very much as any other man's wife, though not so well as my own. I passed a very pleasant day. Bulwer was quite what Sheil described him, very good-natured and, of course, intelligent. I was amused by an anecdote he reported of Hume,[1] accosting Lord Hill at the Fire of Westminster Hall : " My lord! my lord!—there are but eight pioneers here, and the country pays for ten." Sir H. Vivian spoke with great confidence on the probable collision of the two Houses before two years had passed. I urged Bulwer to write a play; he told me he had written one, great part of which was lost, on the death of Cromwell. In the drawing-room I found Colonel Mitchell, with whom I got into a long conversation, and from whom I heard first of the basaltic columns in Auvergne. Saw Lady Vivian, but came not near her. Got into an *amusing* discussion with a very intelligent and naïve young lady, Colonels D'Aguilar and Mitchell, on moral philosophy, in which I was greatly entertained by the young lady's pertinent observations and acuteness. Bulwer offered to set me down, and hoped to meet me in London.

November 1st.—Again late in bed, which makes my rehearsal the beginning of the day. Previous to its commencement an aide-de-camp of Sir Hussey Vivian brought Calcraft and myself invitations to dinner from him for to-morrow. I was perplexed as the bearer was urgent, and on the spot I said I would endeavour to come. Rehearsed without properties and with partial scenery—*l'affaire était assez mauvaise !* Leaving, I went up with Calcraft to the railway office to endeavour to see Lardner and sound him on to-morrow; I did not in my heart wish to be released from his engagement, but I thought it as well to make so much outward demonstration of not being backward to make the experiment. We could not gain admittance. Returning, I found a note at the theatre from him, L——, which put it out of my power to make any alteration; showed the note to Calcraft, who acknowledged the impossibility of making an excuse. At my lodgings I found Sheil and a letter from Bunn, requiring an answer to his former; also one from Mrs. McC—— for orders. Sheil stayed and

---

[1] Joseph Hume (1777–1855), the well-known advocate of economy and retrenchment; entered Parliament as a Tory, but subsequently sat as an advanced Radical.

chatted long; he is extremely agreeable.   Had scarcely more than time
to dine and lay out my clothes, before I was obliged to return to the
theatre.   I was *again*, as on last Saturday, worn out and dispirited
by the long and unsatisfactory rehearsal—properties not forthcoming;
acted, as might be expected, very coldly and very unlike my former
representations of the part.   In the very first scene the ottoman which
I had to use through the play had cushions stuffed *with straw*, and
covered on all sides but one!   It was quite discomposing to any purpose
of playing.   I was miserable; played without spirits, flatly, heavily,
badly.   I could not help myself.   Letter from H. Smith offering me
the Bath theatre.

November 2nd.—Rose very late, and before I had sat down to
breakfast Dr. Lardner called, with whom I made an appointment to
walk to Monkstown at two.   Received a dear letter from my beloved
wife, and immediately wrote out the letter to Mr. Bunn of which I
had made the draft last night.   I adhered to my point, in which I
hope and believe I am right.   God grant it!   Wrote a note to
Calcraft, withdrawing *Othello* from my list, in which I am not easy,
and which I have no motive for acting with the very inefficient cast
of the theatre; to Woulds, putting the direct question to him for
yes or *no* on his desire to have a share in the Bath theatre; to H.
Smith, stating the only terms on which I would be concerned in it; to
my dearest Catherine, wishing her to invite her sister to stay with
her.   Called on Dr. Lardner, and set out with him through the railway office, where I saw the model, the carriages, etc., along the railway
to Monkstown.   The view in many parts is very beautiful, and I
enjoyed the scene, the exercise and my company.   Met Tom McC——
near Monkstown, and chatted with him a short time.   Reached Mr.
Busby's (having met and been introduced to Messrs. Pym, who
regretted my exclusion on Saturday from the experimental runs) where
our dinner party was made up of Mr. Oldham,[1] a man of scientific
acquirements and much humour, a Mr. and Mrs. Kinahan, and
Mr. ——.   The dinner equipage was very handsome, and I spent a
very pleasant day—more interesting and more agreeable than I should
have done, I think, at Sir H. Vivian's.   Heard anecdotes and account
of Leslie, which interested me.   Mrs. Busby sang very pleasingly, and
the landscape illustrations of the Bible kept my thoughts agreeably,
delightfully occupied.   Mr. Oldham invited me to see the Bank at a

---

[1] John Oldham (1779–1840) invented machinery for printing and numbering of bank-
notes; also paddle-wheels for steamers.

quarter before one on Tuesday and to dine with him on Wednesday; to both I said *yes*. Mr. Kinahan brought us home in a sort of "sociable," through one of the loveliest nights that ever blessed the earth—Mr. Oldham giving us imitations of the old Dublin actors on the way—and I delighting in the sea and stars so beautifully bright. Could not get to sleep till past four o'clock.

November 3rd.—Thought over the first scene of the play, and went to the theatre. The house was very bad, which will induce Mr. Calcraft to say that "nothing will draw." Do men of such a degree of understanding deserve the opportunities with which they are favoured? Acted Sardanapalus extremely well, even to a dull, bad, dispirited house; the dream was particularly in earnest, and the performance was sustained throughout. Dr. Lardner came into my room, and sat for some little time. He mentioned to me that Oldham at one time was *starving* at Kilkenny, when after long neglect a letter reached him from the Bank, the postage of which he had not money to pay! He pawned his furniture to get to Dublin, where on the production of his plan the Bank of Ireland settled £200 per annum on him, which they increased to £500, and on Vansittart's [1] noticing him to £1000. Saw nothing of Calcraft.

November 4th.—Again! and again! I shall really sink into indolence and sensuality altogether if I do not make some permanent reform in my habits. I rose at a shamefully late hour this morning. Received a note from Calcraft with a play to read, which I could have well dispensed with; I think he has had enough of my time and I grudge any more to him. Note from Mr. Oldham, reminding me of my appointment, and my invitation to dinner. Made up a parcel of the *Bridal* for Forster, and sent a letter to him by the post. Mrs. Fosbrooke called to ask for my intercession with Mr. Calcraft for better business, which I explained to her was useless, and sent her to him. Went to my appointment with Oldham at the Bank; was surprised and delighted at the beautiful contrivances to economize labour and prevent fraud; to ensure the safety of the building from fire, and the health of the workmen; the mode of damping the paper was simple and beautiful and the check upon deception equally so—the telegraphic communication by numbers, and the mode of keeping accounts all in the most certain and simple manner. His improvement on the lithotritical instrument showed great ingenuity. I was very much gratified, though my nerves *twisted* under the description of lithotrity. Dr. Lardner

---

[1] The Chancellor of the Exchequer; afterwards Lord Bexley.

called to invite me to dine at Busby's on Friday, which I could not do. Forgot to notice a great rudeness I was guilty of, through forgetfulness or absence—leaving the gentlemen to whom I had been introduced without notice—I felt ashamed and uncomfortable in thinking of it. Took up the play sent by Calcraft, and read it through with interest, emotion, and pleasure; if I could—which I cannot—trust my first impression, it would be most favourable. Began the part of Virginius, with my mind upon the *Provost of Bruges*, the MS. just read, and was very flat; still, wishing to act well, I rallied in the third act, which I acted really well—with energy and taste—and finished the part in corresponding spirit. Colonel D'Aguilar was there. Spoke to Calcraft about the play, repressing the expression of the high opinion I had of it which it had been well I had always done; it is well, however, to be discreet at last. Began a letter to Mr. Lovell.[1] Read the *Provost of Bruges* again in bed.

November 5th.—Was really delighted to find myself in my bath at 7 this morning. Went to the railway office, where I found Mr. Pym, Colonel Burgoyne and one of the steam-engine constructors, but no Dr. Lardner! After waiting some time we sat down to coffee—the conversation entirely scientific—to which I was, of course, a listener. We went out, and after due preparation started in an open carriage with the *Vauxhall* Engine for Kingstown; the wind was in our faces, but it was very pleasant; returning, the view was beautiful; quite charming. A serious accident had nearly occurred: a man opened one of the gates; an old policeman ran across the road to stop him and shut it—the engine was close, he had only time to throw himself down, the carriage struck the gate and carried off one of its steps: the old man cut his hand and bruised his knee, and no doubt was *seriously* frightened, but he bore it well; we went back, but he was put upon another engine and carried to a house to lie at rest for a day or two. The party were going to Monkstown to breakfast, but on arriving at the station I made my bow and came to my lodgings, where I wrote to Mr. Lovell on his play; received a note from Colles, deferring his party; wrote a note of inquiry to Miss Huddart; received a letter from Mrs. McC—— wishing me to go to Cardiff, which I answered in the negative, it being impossible. Miss Allison called and gossiped; Mr. B. Kelly, author, the same. Miss Huddart answered my note. I wrote to my dearest Catherine. Began once more the *Provost of Bruges*; whilst reading Sheil called, condemned

[1] Author of the *Provost of Bruges*.

Sardanapalus and objected to the coarseness of Miss Huddart's voice and manner—a general and true objection. Pursued my task of reading the *Provost of Bruges*, and made several remarks tending to remove the defects in the conduct of the story. Dr. Lardner and Mr. Busby called and took me to Mr. Oldham's; I met Dr. Butler, who sang a song in praise of water, because it gave and brought us " Wine, Rosy Wine," very well—Dr. Smith—a charming singer. His duet, " Could Man be secure that his Life would endure," his song of " Why Soldiers " of General Wolfe, were really masterpieces. Hay, who played a piece of his in such a style that the vocal was lost in the instrumental music—Robinson—Pym—Dr. Okie—Surgeon Crampton [1] came in in the course of the evening. Oldham's story of the Fogerty was admirable—his best.

November 6th.—Rose late, and while at my toilet gave my thought to Othello and Hamlet. While making memoranda Miss Allison called to ask me to hear her in Amanthis: I deferred it, and she remained, amusing me by her innocent and playful conversation, ending with a request for a lock of my hair; I sent her away with a note to Calcraft about Dr. Lardner's box. Went out, and called on Miss Huddart to ask Mrs. Donnelly's good offices in the purchase of my linen; Mr. Brown called and I left him there. Purchased the poplins which Catherine requested, and an additional one for her: also liqueurs and anchovies, another commission; pencils; left a card at Colonel King's, and returning, Calcraft called to ask me about the play for Tuesday next, the Marchioness's visit: [2] I approved of Werner, and he wrote the note to the Park, deciding on it. Letters from dearest Catherine; Mr. Knowles, offering the Bath Theatre to me for £700; rent and taxes; and from Bunn, resisting my demand. Went to the theatre, where I wished to act Werner in my best style, but wanted preparation and singleness of purpose for it, was angry, and strove to tranquillize myself; seeing Calcraft much dispirited, all my displeased thoughts left me. I am certainly very irascible, but not slow to be appeased. Lord Glengall met me in Westmoreland Street this morning, and held me nearly a quarter of an hour, discussing the state of the London theatres. After the play Dr. Lardner came into my room and sat some time, as did Calcraft; they both seemed of opinion that I might safely withstand Bunn's attempts to bring me down. I feel in a certain degree independent of him; but chiefly think I ought not to let him

---

[1] Philip Crampton (1777–1858), F.R.S., an eminent Dublin surgeon ; created a baronet.
[2] The Marchioness Wellesley, wife of the Lord-Lieutenant.

201

think I want him. Spent two hours in thinking on this subject, and making rough calculations on Bath.

November 7th.—Was called in good time, but lay in bed ruminating and casting up figures upon this Bath speculation, which assumes a very probable aspect of success. The more I look at Mr. Bunn's situation, and search for the likely results of this season, the less cause I see for anxiety to be in his power; and to go to him on *his estimate* of my worth with the means of insulting me, which he thinks he has in the persons who now fill my characters, would be unavailing for any good purpose; I am disposed to dismiss the negotiation at once, but that I am reluctant to charge myself with the consequences, should they be untoward; I therefore make what preparation I can against my absence, and commit the event to Providence, resolving not to give way to Mr. Bunn. Sent note to Calcraft—wishing to see him; he came, and I inquired of him the expense of his company, was amazed to hear him state it at £120—it is not worth more than half that sum. I talked about Bath, which he seemed to think very safe. He appears greatly dispirited—still looking forward to future nights in which there is no hope beyond a decent average. The truth is, had he not deceived me and himself by throwing the engagement on *Sardanapalus* and then bringing it out in this trashy manner, I should have come for a fortnight, which would have given me and him within £60 as much as *the month* will do; it is too bad.

November 8th.—Still not improved in my hours of rising, which is very bad. Mr. Patrick O'Reilly sent for an answer to his application, and another petition came, from an *old offender* also, both of which I resolutely denied. Thought—why do I not do more than think?—on my profession—the necessity that there is, if I wish to steadily persevere, for applying myself to study. I must do so, or meet the inevitable consequences: *no man can excel without labour;* or rather I should say without exercise, it is disinclination that makes it *labour.* Wrote and returned poor Mr. Bigeri's play; he states that he is a poor man, though of a properly independent spirit, which I greatly respect—*homo sum;* he has a feeling for poetry, but not the faculty to write it, and so I told him. Wrote a few more lines, and sealed my letter to dear Catherine. Practised professionally a little Othello. Miss Allison called and told me of last night's house, which I heard was £14!!! Went to theatre, where I saw a Dublin paper, in which was a letter from Sheil to Lord Wellesley; and a correspondence on Littleton's behalf, calling on Lord Londonderry for explanation; he thought—so the papers had reported—that Londonderry had implied he was a knave—he had only insinuated that he was a fool; which was, of course, satisfactory, and there the matter rests.[1] Went into Calcraft's room, who wished to consult me on a complaint he had received from Mrs. Hamilton of Mr. Pritchard engaging her daughter's affections, and declining to state his intentions; the girl is not more than seventeen; this is very bad. I advised him to point out to him *as a friend* the danger he, Pritchard, was incurring by his conduct, if the Dublin gallery should get wind of the fact—and went into particulars. Calcraft decided on adopting the method, complimenting me as a Machiavel.

November 11th.—The *Age* newspaper from Calcraft with impertinent notice of myself; what a filthy wretch is that Mr. Westmacott, but not more so than Mr. Bunn! Wished to act Werner well, as the Marchioness Wellesley was to be at the theatre, but she did not come (*ill*), and it was an audience attracted chiefly by her and not myself, which makes it very hard to kindle them to enthusiasm. I acted unequally—striving against my own feeling of *hors de moi*, and many annoyances, particularly Mr. Pritchard's imperfectness, and a drunken man talking loud. Some things I did very well. Miss Huddart held me to my promise to visit her on Sunday, as she said it was her last chance. The house was very good. Calcraft came into my room to abuse Pritchard.

November 12th.—Refreshed and strengthened by my sleep last night, I went to rehearsal of Hamlet, with which I took much pains, but did not feel myself, as I like to do, free from effort, prompt and spontaneous in my passion, with complete absence of all muscular exertion. Went to the theatre collected and at ease, but not with that *certainty* of preserving the *tout ensemble* that in the characters of Shakspeare I am ambitious of doing. I felt confident of being very fair, but not entirely Hamlet. My performance seemed to give great satisfaction, and there were a great many things that I did really well—scenes that I played well. Some of the first act was good— particularly the concluding soliloquy, from time and self-possession; the third act had much to praise, the soliloquy, scene with Ophelia, part of advice, part of closet scene—the rest was to me unsatisfactory, the grave-scene was not good till Laertes's entrance—the death was very well, and the whole of last scene. Calcraft came into my room

---

[1] The third marquis, a vituperative Tory of the most bigoted type. Littleton's indiscretion (see note, p. 160) was, of course, a capital asset for the Opposition.

and seemed quite satisfied in thinking this will be one of my Dublin plays—it ought to be, for there is more thought in it than in all I do. Supped on oysters.

November 13th.—Received a newspaper from home, but no letter; I thought Mr. Bunn would have written, but I have perhaps imagined myself of more consequence to him than he considers me; I am not sorry that affairs stand as they do so long as I have reason to believe that they are not prosperous to the management at London. Went to the theatre to rehearse *Lear*, which I did very badly, and what is worse in very bad temper. Ridiculous as it is, I really believe the cause of it—at least principally—was the sight of my neat book in the dirty prompter's hands, suffering with every turning of the leaves. Received a note for tickets from Mr. McNamara and also from Lady C. Whiteford. Notes from James about freedom of the City and coat-of-arms, and from a young ass called Maxwell, wishing to play Edgar for my night. Read the newspapers, in which to my disappointment there was no notice of Hamlet. Acted Sardanapalus—during the three last acts very indifferently—annoyed very much in the last by the vulgar and malicious noises of some fellows in the gallery. Calcraft came into my room, and talked about the Woods, etc. Miss Allison kept me in the passage, playing with me. Miss Huddart asked me to see her home, as her servant had not arrived, but I showed so much reluctance that she relinquished it. I did not like persons to see me walking out of the theatre with her or any young woman at that late hour.

November 15th.—Went to rehearsal, with which I took pains, and I find from experience that care and attention is all in all. *I cannot be just to myself without.* Sheil called; expressed himself greatly pleased with Werner and recommended me to think of *Philip Van Artevelde*, promising that he would think of it for me. *Quite tired*—dozed on my chair for about a quarter of an hour, and then looked out my clothes. Tried to act, but could not satisfy myself—all was effort, which in William Tell gives a vulgar and melodramatic character to the part, that I dislike and feel ashamed of. Also I ought to—and I do—feel ashamed and deeply sorry for my morose and petulant behaviour to *everybody;* it is really *outrageous.* I must curb this hateful and most distressing infirmity of temper.

November 17th.—Dressed and went on the stage prepared to act my best, and resolute to do so, but such a Babel of a house was scarcely ever heard—from the beginning to the end of *King Lear*—and through the interlude of the screen scene of *School for Scandal*, almost all was dumb show. Colonel D'Aguilar came round in despair. I had to go on to address them. I told them I had the greatest pleasure in playing before them when they chose to be an *audience*, and how ambitious I was to uphold myself in their opinion. It must have been the only entertainment of the evening. I made gratuities to the servants—shook hands with those actors I saw—came home. Woulds called and supped, and we signed the agreement of partnership. *Quod felix sit.*

November 19th.—Got on shore about 9 o'clock, took a car up to the Angel Inn, where I breakfasted, and read the newspaper account of the discharge of the Ministry. The question that rises to me on this is simply—how long will men permit such an impious and inequitable arrangement as the possession of power by any one man, or set of men, without the severest responsibility?[1] Dined and went to the theatre, to see if there was anything decent there. The play was *Brutus* and a brute part of him that played it—Tarquinia—all very miserable. A Miss Leclerq, a dancer, and a Mr. Simpson, in an old man, were the sole exceptions to the general badness of the company. Hammond, who was a good actor, has *spoiled* himself by managing; let me not forget that!!

Lincoln, November 23rd.—At 10 Mr. Robertson called, and having paid my bill and posted my letters, I got a sight of the gorgeous front of the Cathedral, and the Heaven's Gate, as I passed down to the river. This canal-like stream, the Witham, embanked on both sides, offers no variety of prospect; the cattle in the water, or grazing along its sides, a horseman on the bank, recall Cuyp and Wouverman to one's recollection, and afford us a guess at what Holland must be. We walked six miles, sometimes turning to look upon the regally-sited Cathedral, which alone is worth a visit to this city—and constantly enjoying the freshness of the brisk cool air, the beauty of the morning, and our exhilarating exercise.

---

[1] William IV had for some time past been greatly dissatisfied with the Whig Ministry, and, on Lord Althorp (who had succeeded to his father's earldom) vacating the Leadership of the House of Commons, he (the King) dismissed the Ministry on the pretext that there was no one qualified to replace Althorp. This *coup-de-main* was generally regarded as an abuse of prerogative, and naturally created bitter resentment in Whig circles, Brougham signalizing his indignation by despatching a communication the same night to the *Times* (concluding with the words, "The Queen has done it all"), which appeared in that newspaper on the following morning. Brougham's conduct was the more discreditable in that Lord Melbourne had imparted to him the news under a pledge of secrecy; he subsequently aggravated the affront by sending the Great Seal back to the King in a bag instead of returning it in person.

Boston, November 26th.—Read the *Examiner*, and felt my blood boil at the disgusting conduct of the senseless, heartless old wretch whom we call a King. " Is there no hidden thunder in the stones of Heaven, red with uncommon wrath to blast that man? " How shocking that the well-being of millions of reasoning beings is at the mercy of him or any man irresponsible for his conduct! [1] Acted indifferently —the accompaniments are so bad I cannot sustain the feeling, or persevere against so much that annoys me.

November 27th.—Arrived at Louth, which seems a miserable little place. After dinner (too good a one!) lounged away some time over old magazines—accounts of young Betty's [2] first appearance—much violent abuse of Napoleon as the " Corsican assassin," and of Josephine as the most notorious strumpet. Things have mended, judging both from the prose and poetry, which is horrid stuff.

Louth, November 29th.—Read an ode and part of an epistle in Horace; found on examining the current in which my thoughts set, that management would never answer for me; I have not that management of my mind that would enable me to dismiss one subject, and substitute another; I should lose my profession by it, and already I am alarmed at its effects in the possession it takes of my thoughts. Walked with Mr. Robertson to the post office and to the theatre, which answers also the double purpose of a Sessions House; it is not the worst I have seen. Went to the theatre—dressed in the magistrates' room—" quite convenient." When ready to go on the stage, Mr. Robertson appeared with a face full of dismay; he began to apologize, and I guessed the remainder. " Bad house? "   " Bad? Sir, there's no one! "   " What? nobody at all? "   " Not a soul, sir—except the Warden's party in the boxes."   " What the d—l! not one person in the pit or gallery? "   " Oh, yes, there are one or two."   " Are there five? "   " Oh, yes, five."   " Then go on; we have no right to give ourselves airs, if the people do not choose to come and see us; go on at once!! "   Mr. Robertson was astonished at what he thought my philosophy, being accustomed, as he said, to be " blown up " by his *Stars*, when the houses were bad. I never acted

[1] This fierce outburst was prompted by the King's dismissal of the Melbourne Ministry, which Macready had denounced in terms almost as scathing. William IV had certainly stretched his powers, but it must be borne in mind that the Whig Government had outlived its usefulness, while the antics of Brougham, personal and political, were daily discrediting both the Crown and the nation. The King was wrong in principle, but there was much to extenuate his action.

[2] The Infant Roscius, with whom Macready had performed in former years.

Virginius better in all my life—good taste and earnestness. Smyth, who was contemporary with me at Rugby and has a living in this neighbourhood, came in and sat with me, and saw the play, with which he was greatly pleased.

November 30th.—Read the newspaper, in which my abhorrence of that wretch Cobbett [1] and his beastly faction was kindled anew. Note came from Mrs. Robertson, inviting me to tea, which I accepted. Went there, and was much amused by Mr. W. Robertson's account of the extremities of ludicrous distress—though sometimes it was no laughing matter—to which he was reduced in his vagabondizing tours in Scotland and Cumberland.

December 1st.—Walked out with Mr. Robertson; posted my letters, and then walked two miles on the Horncastle road. He related to me two anecdotes of Kean, to which he was witness: once of his having, on coming off the stage in Othello, thrashed a man of the name of Williams, whom I remember well, for distressing him by being imperfect in Iago! and another—a pure specimen of his char- latanry. A vagabond who lived upon petitioning companies and drank their charity, applied for the third or fourth time while Kean was with Mr. Robertson. Mr. Robertson represented to Mr. Kean that he was a worthless drunken man, and lived upon this practice. Mr. K—— (there were several present) said : " You dined very well yester- day, sir, and you will have a good dinner to-day; why should you wish to prevent this poor man from doing the same ? " And this Kean left his wife without one shilling for herself and son; the woman that lived with him having taken the comparatively small residue left of his disgusting and reckless dissoluteness ! ! Enjoyed my walk very much; wrote directions for my luggage. Dozed from fatigue after dinner; wrote a letter to Kenneth, made my toilet, and went to theatre. Felt that the house was not very good; but determined to make a study of the night, which I did, and certainly acted great part of Hamlet in a very true and impressive manner. I hit upon the exact feeling in the passage which I have often thought on : " He was a man," etc. ; my intercourse with Horatio, Rosencrantz, Guildenstens, etc., was earnest and real—*ad homines.* Indeed, it was a good performance. Smyth came into my room after the play, and talked of my speaking

---

[1] William Cobbett (1762–1835); the famous Radical journalist, whose political views were calculated to enlist Macready's sympathy rather than his "abhorrence," for both were good haters of peers temporal and spiritual, besides entertaining scant respect for the Crown.

the closet scene at Rugby. He also told me of endeavouring to commit a poacher. He is a clergyman! Thought and calculated for Bath. Read in Racine's *Esther.*

Sheffield, December 10th.—Went to the theatre, where I acted William Tell only tolerably; was a good deal distressed by the actors, imperfect and inattentive, and once or twice rather angry with them, but very kind to the poor little child who acted with me, though several times disconcerted by her, but this is from having children of my own, the dear ones. My dresser is a Benedictine monk on leave from the convent in Ireland on account of derangement; his trade is a tailor.

December 11th.—Went to theatre, where I acted very ill, but should not have been so bad but for the shamefully neglectful and imperfect state of the play. Idenstein, Josephine and Guba were all more or less imperfect; Ulric did not know two consecutive lines of the three last acts. I sat down at last attempting nothing. I never was so completely *terrassé* in my life. But I was rude and uncivil to no one.

Nottingham, December 12th.—Went to theatre, and found a horrid fellow in the part of Gesler, whom I had met at Richmond—it was enough! Rehearsed, dressed and acted William Tell to a very good house in a creditable manner; but was very cross with the little dull boy whom they had placed in Albert, and fined myself half-a-crown, which I paid him for my ill-behaviour.

Brighton, December 18th.—Read the newspapers. Sir R. Peel's address to his Tamworth constituents—and Sir J. Graham's to his. Little opinion have I of the honesty of either, but the first I think a cold, heartless man.[1] Went to the theatre, where in the play of *Sardanapalus* not one person was perfect, and whenever I attempted effect I was foiled; still, I did not play well, and want study. Heard the news of Mr. J. Webster taking fright at Ulric, and in consequence the play of *Werner* cannot be done to-morrow—pleasant! Was told of Polhill having retired from Drury Lane on paying £2000—this, I suppose, is not the exact truth—or all of it, but there is some truth in it. He takes with him the execration and contempt of every real actor.

December 19th.—Ellen called; she told me of *John Bull* having said that "I had been playing in a conventicle at Louth." I was not at all angry—how mad it would once have made me!

Elstree, December 26th.—Dearest Christina's birthday.

---

[1] Macready, like many others, changed his opinion of Peel in later years.

December 28th.—Mr. Lovell [1] arrived before I had finished my toilet; after detaining him some time I went down and found him in the study. I explained to him the necessity under which I lay of inviting him so abruptly, and hurried forward breakfast, that I might complete my critical task before Forster's arrival. When we had breakfasted we adjourned to the drawing-room, and I went scene by scene through his play, suggesting remedies to what seemed faults to me and giving him my candid opinion on the merits of his play. He received it with earnest expressions of gratitude and confidence, and assented to every proposal of correction. On coming downstairs, and after introducing him to Dr. Lardner, with whom it appeared he had previously been slightly acquainted, Forster arrived; and while the morning was whiled away in conversation by them, I cut the leaves and arranged the pages of the three-act arrangement of *King Henry V.* A letter from Mr. Lovell, accepting my invitation, had arrived in the course of the morning. Went to afternoon church, accompanied by Mr. Lovell, where I read two chapters of Greek Testament, and was struck by the Samaritans appropriating the well to Jacob—the wells in Arabia and Syria being believed to have been the work of the Patriarchs—see Dyer. Returning I read the *Examiner*, and afterwards gave myself to my domestic duties of preparing for and entertaining my guests, with whom I passed a very pleasant afternoon. Mr. Lovell I was disappointed in—I had expected a very modest, very intelligent, very gentlemanly man; I did not think him on general matters a very modest man, and only of an average character as to intelligence and address. Read prayers to the family in the study—thanking God Almighty for the blessings of the expiring year, and praying for a continuance of them to me and mine for those to come. Amen!

To Bristol, December 31st.—Sent a note to Miss E. Tree, questioning her upon an engagement at Bath. Left Catherine to go out and buy her presents for herself and sisters whilst I sought and found Mr. Bunn. He was extremely civil about the Overtures, for which I asked him, and professed himself anxious to give me every accommodation. Sent for the musical copyist, and settled the mode of sending the Overtures to Bath. About Farren and Miss E. Tree he was to give me an answer in a fortnight. Miss E. Romer was out of the question. [2] Wrote to Wallace requesting him to contradict the *Morning*

---

[1] Author of the *Provost of Bruges*, performed in the following year.

[2] Emma Romer (1814-1868), afterwards Mrs. Almond, a singer of considerable reputation; made her chief success at Covent Garden; manageress of Surrey Theatre in 1852.

Chronicle's assertion that I was the Bath manager. Paid Healey and went to Gloster Coffee House, where I took tea, and got into the Bristol mail, after waiting some time to see my luggage put into the coach. My companions were very great asses, talking much nonsense about politics, and vehement Tories. I said my prayers and endeavoured to compose myself to sleep. In closing this year, which has been a prosperous and a happy one, I turn to the Cause of my felicity and success, and humbly and devoutly bless the name of Almighty God, and offer up to Him my earnest thanks for all the good bestowed on me and mine; grateful for what is given, and humbly imploring a continuance of His mercies. Amen! Amen! Amen!

Bath, January 2nd.—Sat down to read with deliberate care the piece of *Beau Nash;* I read and reconsidered it. With one or two smart sayings there is nothing to do in it; it leads to nothing. The "tendency" of which the author speaks I looked in vain for—except it be to puzzle his readers. Tried to find some means of making it convertible, but relinquished it as hopeless.

January 3rd.—Went to the theatre, and was satisfied with the performance of the *Rivals,* but *distressed* by the very discreditable manner in which *Lodoiska* was played, and got up. I feel at this early stage that I am not fit for a managerial speculation. No more spectacles!

January 4th.—Thought over the third act of *Othello,* which ought to be one of my best characters if I could realize my own conceptions. Read over *Macbeth.* In bed read an essay in Locke on despondency which did me good.

January 5th.—Went to theatre and fell into ill-humour with the old and incapable hairdresser; dismissed him, but sent for him again, not wishing to distress or offend him. He made a figure of me! I acted, as I thought, the first scene of *Macbeth* well, but the audience were perfectly apathetic, and in the second became vulgarly unquiet. This unhinged me, and I did not recover myself the whole night. I am ready to ascribe the greater share of blame to myself, but the audience were like no other I ever saw; they did not notice me on my first entrance—on the bridge—and very indifferently afterwards. I acted very ill, but better than such an audience deserved, which is not saying much. The play was excellently done.

January 7th.—Wrote to Catherine, whose presence, and my children's, I feel necessary to me now, for I become irritated at the mistake—blunder—folly I have committed in coming here. Went to the theatre and acted Werner as well as the imperfectness of Mr. Thompson and the vulgar rant of Mr. Saville, which often interfered with me, would let me. But this—with the face-making mysteries of

Mr. Stuart—the enlightened audience applauded as much as myself, who was using the utmost care to act in the best taste. I feel as if I could willingly give £300 to be released from this unfortunate engagement. I scarcely know what I should do—I cannot attend to my profession if this continues, and I see no prospect of change. It is a bitter passion when we are angry with ourselves! Oh, God, assist me! I dread to look forward.

January 8th.—Acted Othello with a feeling of having no sympathy from my audience; thought myself deficient in earnestness and spirit, but do not regret having done it, as it was a useful rehearsal to me. I never saw the Senate put so well upon the stage. I think I may play Othello well, but the prescriptive criticism of this country, in looking for particular points instead of contemplating one entire character, abates my confidence in myself. Mr. Woulds told me that he had heard from Mr. Field of general discontent at the prices being restored. The house to-night was wretched, but what could be expected at such a time?

January 9th.—My landlady brought me up her bill, and began some inquiries about my stay—the number of my family and some etcs., which showed a disposition to impose; she added that Mrs. Woulds had not mentioned my *profession.* My blood rose at this impertinence, and I was foolish enough to be so angry as to observe that there was no person in Bath, whether titled or not, that could claim a higher character and that I would relieve her of the inconvenience of such an inmate. She attempted to excuse herself, but I cut the matter short. Heard from Mr. Woulds the account of the first week's balance, which was very satisfactory. Read the newspaper, and to my astonishment and satisfaction saw Talfourd member for Reading!

January 10th.—Expedited the rehearsal as much as possible, but it proceeded slowly owing to the inattention of the actors. What a calling this is! How deeply I feel the degradation of belonging to it, which yet for my dear children's sake I will endeavour cheerfully to pursue. One of the actors (whom Mr. Woulds boasted he could do anything with) refused to act a part he had agreed to play; he is a fool, and nearly crazy. Laid out my clothes; saw old Mr. Taylor, who talked about "next season" recovering *this.* If they catch me in this hateful occupation again may all its worst consequences fall on me! Acted William Tell to an improved house very fairly—parts of it very well, and should have done so throughout, had the actors been perfect with me. I was very angry, and wish I could avoid showing temper as I do, but I fear this is a vice which will accompany me to my grave.

January 13th.—Went to the rehearsal of *King Henry V.* Mr. Thompson proposed to me a play by Lord Byron's natural daughter [1] —he supposes me very simple. Read the newspaper in which I see Captain Polhill is made a legislator. Shame!

January 14th.—Rehearsed *King Lear*—not well, for I do not feel quite prepared for the character—and settled the outline of the business of *King Henry IV.* Found a letter from Mr. Wood written in rather an impertinent strain; these are the *fellows* that make up the *profession* of a player! I answered it in a mild and gentlemanly tone. My dear Catherine and my babes arrived—God bless them!

January 17th.—In going through the box-office heard a woman inquiring for something entertaining for children. Brownell mentioned that Mr. Macready and Dowton would play on Monday. "Oh no," she replied, "they are very good actors, but I want something entertaining for children; when will *Aladdin* be done?" So much for Bath taste! Acted King Lear unequally—wanted the sustaining stimulant of an enthusiastic audience—wanted in them the sensibility to feel quickly what I did, and the ready manifestation of their sympathy; some parts I did tolerably well; acted with some degree of vivacity and nature in Puff.

To Bristol, January 26th.—Went to the theatre, and acted Macbeth extremely well, with earnestness, care and feeling : never before spoke the "To-morrow and to-morrow" with such truth. Dowton (!) made a complaint that his name was in smaller letters than mine, and wrote the same to the prompter.

January 30th.—Going out of the theatre Mr. Mude addressed me, having heard that I had said "It was very beastly in him as acting manager not to be at rehearsal in time." I distinctly told him that "it was wholly untrue, that I had been very angry at the person who had to begin the play not being there and had given his words to another; the expression I used was in reference to the general mode of doing the business—that I knew he was not the manager." Acted Lord Townley effectively, but not with the ease to please myself.

---

[1] In all probability an apocryphal author. Byron was still a name to conjure with ; accordingly, *liaisons* and illegitimate offspring were fastened on him as occasion required. The only natural daughter with whom he was and is publicly identified was Allegra, who died when little more than an infant.

February 6th.—Mr. Moutrie, our landlord, knocked, and entering told me a lady like a dissenter wished to see me—that she had a message to deliver to me in person. I begged him to excuse me to her, being too harassed to see any one—that she could write, or see me a fortnight hence in Bath. She went away, saying she would write, for that it would not suit to see me in Bath. In less than a minute she returned with a letter which he brought up; to my great surprise it was anonymous and contained a £5 note. How very strange! how very kindly intended!

To London, February 7th.—Travelled through the night from Bristol—not so rapidly as I expected, but very comfortably, thanks to dear Catherine for suggesting the carriage! Breakfasted, etc., at Salt Hill, saw the *Times*, that disgustingly profligate newspaper. Was extremely disgusted with the pert, flippant and vulgar tone of some extracts from Miss Kemble's Journal. I had given her credit for rather a superior understanding; I think her a shallow instead of a clever impostor.[1]

To Manchester, February 8th.—Rose at half-past four for my day's journey to Manchester, which, though the manner in which it is performed calls forth my admiration, is very fatiguing. The coach was full, outside and in, of very uninteresting people. Read the newspapers I borrowed from my fellow travellers. *Bell's Weekly Messenger*, and that most disgusting of the base and rascally tribe the *Satirist*, in which scandal and obscenity were the only remarkably prominent qualities.

February 10th.—At the theatre received letter from Mr. Gould, wishing, I suppose, to exculpate himself, but I do not clearly see the drift of his vulgar letter. When a person alters his superscription from " Esqre." to " Mr." he only makes one laugh at the impotence of his spleen.

February 11th.—Sent a note to Clarke for a newspaper: he sent me three *Heralds*, and I was disgusted beyond patience; one piece of intelligence was satisfactory, viz. that that odious pauper, ——, is not likely to transmit her principles in her race to curse this country. What rank villains politicians are! What signifies the name?

February 15th.—Rose late, and spent much time in my bedroom before I came down. Applied myself to my accounts, and to the

---

[1] Fanny Kemble's Journal is occasionally affected, but Macready's epithets are as usual exaggerated. Whatever her shortcomings, she was undoubtedly remarkably clever, and in no sense an impostor.

consideration of the best mode to improve their condition; am perhaps too impatient to increase my store; I think it is as much for my
dear children's sake as my own; I hope more. Mr. Clarke called, and
made a very long visit. I made up the cast of next week's business at
Bath, settled all and wrote the heading of the bill, which I inclosed
to Mr. Woulds. Received letters with receipts and balance up to
Friday at Bath; from Mr. Fox, respecting the MS. play sent to me,
in whose letter Catherine wrote a hasty greeting.

February 16th.—Began to read the MS. tragedy of *Cosmo*, and
after an interruption of a long visit by Clarke, finished it. It is a
bold, irregular attempt to give the workings of various minds, and
display their effects upon the outward forms of men. I cannot say
it will be successful, but there is more than sufficient talent in it to
deserve and make me anxious for its success. Went to theatre, acted
Werner very well to a good house; but was *very cross* with one of the
actors—which was very reprehensible in me.

February 17th.—Wrote to Jeston about the money paid by mistake into Drummond's bank for me. Am forced into reflection upon
the system of delusion which the world subscribes to, when I address
this good-natured, thick-headed old fellow. This man, according
to churchmen, is gifted with the Holy Ghost, and qualified to take
care of the *souls* of men! Mighty God! when will this blasphemous
abuse of Thy Holy name, this infamous traffic in the beautiful
religion of Christ become a crime before men, as it must be before
Thee?

February 18th.—Arrived at Halifax. Went to rehearsal; poor
Guildenstern had only one eye. From rehearsal one of the actors,
Mr. Nantz, went with me to show me the Gibbet Hill, where the stone
on which the criminals laid their heads is still visible, though deeply
embedded in earth; from thence he accompanied me to a public-house,
formerly the gaol, and now called the Jail Inn, where the blade of
the axe, called the Maiden, was shown to me; it is very like the
blade of a spade with two holes in it. Not so weighty as I should
suppose its office would require. Some of the actors, the principal
with his family, lived in the public-house, seemingly domesticated,
and mixing in all the business of the place! Such a residence would
have suited in every way Mr. Kean, and no doubt he often took up his
abode contentedly in worse—and I am abused, libelled and an object of
persecution because I do not make companions of actors! Oh, world,
what a scene of quackery thou art!

February 20th.—Heard the cheering news of Sir R. Peel's defeat

in Abercromby's election (as Speaker).[1]   Went to the theatre, where
I found letters from Letty in a frank from Forster inclosing a request
from Mr. W——, formerly 30th Foot, to procure him any, the
humblest situation in some theatre, so dreadfully was he reduced by
his extravagance and thoughtlessness.

February 27th.—Again greeted by a letter of ill news.   Our house
at Elstree has, it seems from dear Letitia's letter, been entered by
robbers, whom an early alarm obliged to escape before further mischief was done than the breaking our windows.   A letter also from
Mr. Fox, franked by Roebuck.[2]   Received a *very vulgar* note from
that *very vulgar, vain* and *foolish old man* Mr. Dowton,[3] which I
answered very mildly.   Oh, what a curse it is to connect oneself with
ignorant, conceited and obstinate people—these fools !

February 28th.—Went to the theatre, and acted Rob Roy languidly.
Felt provoked to think that I was paying everybody concerned, even to
that *sot*, Mr. Woulds, by my own unrequited labour.   Saw Mr. Perkins,
who told me that the business at Edinburgh was great—*his* second
night £187.   Nothing under £80 or £90.   I felt envious and angry
—to my shame I note it.   Oh God, exalt me above this demoralizing
atmosphere !

Bristol, March 2nd.—My mind is still returning to the subject of
reduced expenditure, but often interrupted by the savage wishes of
revenge and passionate desires that agitate, disturb and distress me ; I
feel ashamed of them and grieved at them.   I school them down, but
they return in a variety of forms.   The connection with this theatre
at Bath seems to have brought back my mind to its former littleness ;
I feel disgusted with the beings in connection with me and ashamed
of myself.   Acted Hamlet in my very best manner to a very good
house, and in my own voice.   Saw Mr. Lovell ; talked with him about his

---

[1] This was the first of several defeats sustained by Sir Robert Peel during his short-lived
Administration, 1834–1835.   Manners-Sutton, who had been Speaker for nearly twenty years
and had remained at his post at the urgent request of the Whig Government, was now opposed
by Abercromby, a Whig nominee, who was elected by a majority of ten.   He proved an
indifferent Speaker and resigned four years later.

[2] John Arthur Roebuck (1801–1879) the well-known politician, then Radical M.P. for
Bath.   Promoted the inquiry into conduct of the Crimean War which resulted in the overthrow of Lord Aberdeen's Ministry.   In his later years he relinquished his extreme views and
became a supporter of Lord Beaconsfield's policy, receiving in recognition a Privy Coun-
cillorship.   In 1835 he attained prominence by representing in England the Lower Canada
House of Assembly.

[3] Mr. Dowton must have sadly deteriorated since the preceding year when, it will be
remembered, Macready considered him worthy of a complimentary dinner.

play. Received my coats of arms from Mrs. McC——, enormously dear! May they be useful to my boy when my name is past away!

March 3rd.—My birthday! Awoke unrefreshed from a night made restless by the storm to a sense of great unhappiness; said my prayers, imploring Almighty God (as I fervently do) to enable me to bring up my children in a course of virtue and in the paths of peace. The summer of my life is gone, and what has it left me? My domestic blessings, which indeed are great, are all; and these from their very dearness are made aggravations of every disappointment I encounter in my endeavour to raise them above the world's pity or scorn. The embarrassment of my little property through by own imprudence and my lawyer's incorrectness make this day, which ought to be cheerful, a very wretched one. I do not recollect a more unhappy anniversary of my birth than this—my forty-second. Went to rehearsal—or rather to my morning's annoyance—striving and wishing to master my fretful, impatient temper, but in vain. Letter from dear Catherine, giving the news of the house, and acquainting me with my being *blackballed* at the Athenæum. I do not wish to disguise truth; it was a bitter annoyance to me. I had objected to undergoing the trial of the ballot, knowing the dirty tricks practised at this and other clubs, and only consented to the insertion of my name upon the assurance that it was decided on I should be admitted this year.[1] The advantages of the club are not equivalent to the subjection to any blackguard's caprice. I use a strong term, but Mr. Croker,[2] having been my excluder, justifies it. It shall not occur again. My pride has been destined to a series of mortifications this day; perhaps it is wholesome that it should be, for I discover by what I suffer that I have "much too much." I hope and trust I may be able so to educate my darling children as to save them much of the smart that I have borne—I will not say undeservedly. I feel the present rebuke is an insult; I cannot qualify it to myself; holding the rank I do in my art and with no aspersion on my good name, it is nothing less. The conviction of my own sensitiveness to

[1] Macready had evidently hoped to be elected under the special rule, but he was, apparently, "put up" in the ordinary way. Thackeray experienced a similar repulse, but both were elected, under the special rule, on a second attempt.

[2] Croker (the Wenham of *Vanity Fair* and the Rigby of *Coningsby*), though an "excluder" at the Athenæum had himself been "excluded" at White's. The Candidates' Books at Clubs supply curious reading, men of the highest rank and distinction figuring among the rejected while the "colourless obscure" have often secured unanimous acceptance. In fact, at certain clubs "nobody" has a far better chance of election than "somebody," even Earldoms and Garters proving powerless, at times, to avert disaster.

such an affront prevented me from having my name inserted, nor would I ever have consented to it, but under the assurances of the secretary through Mr. Kenney.[1] It teaches, as all things do, its own lesson. A principle once established by reason in the mind should be held with the same temerity as virtue. I have suffered keenly—for to hide is not to diminish pain; how forcibly has Peel's quotation from Dryden been brought to my mind—

'Tis easy said :—but oh ! how hardly tried
By human hearts to human honor tied !
Oh, sharp conclusive pangs of agonizing *pride!*

March 5th.—Low-spirited from the ascendency my temper gains over me; and not much cheered by the universal dirt of my lodgings. Played much of Rob Roy very well, and should have been uniformly good if the very bad company would have permitted it. Oh, my temper! my temper! how truly unhappy—even to sometimes growing indifferent about existence—does this morose and impatient temper make me! These theatres have brought it on in its early offensiveness.

March 6th.—Received a very sensible and affectionate letter from dear Catherine. Reasoning has power over grief, but pride is a fool that stops its ears. I can put aside the thought of the insult offered me at the Athenæum, but have not that enviable self-command to reflect on it and the names connected with it indifferently; it chiefly annoys me because it was in the bargain of my consent that I was secure of admission. When men like Messrs. Mathews, C. Kemble, Young,[2] Hook, Croker, etc., are eligible it is difficult to flatter oneself into the belief that there is no indignity in being rejected. To forget it is my wish, for the recollection is not pleasing to me. Went to theatre, and should have acted Oakley well, but that in the only scene in which the performers were not *very imperfect* with me, the prompter in every pause I made in a scene where the pauses are *effects* kept shouting "the word " to me till I was ready to go and knock him down. I was cut up, right and left, root and branch and—as usual—I grieve and shame to say it—was very angry.

Bath, March 7th.—Spoke to Mr. Thompson, assuming all the

---

[1] See entries under February 24 and 26, 1834.

[2] If Macready considered Young ill-qualified for the Athenæum it is strange that he should have chosen him as his seconder. Hook, with all his brilliant gifts, was certainly a questionable acquisition, but the other names cited were at least without reproach, though possibly Mathews found admission easier than he would have done now-a-days, when comedians, however eminent, would hardly be regarded as eligible.

load of accusation made upon his being cast for the actor in *Hamlet*. Mr. Woulds had told me of letters having been sent to the newspapers abusing me, stating that I was only here because I could not get engaged in London!—that I sent puffs of myself to the papers, etc.—this he more than suspected to be the work of that scoundrel Thompson! Acted Sardanapalus indifferently; the whole appointment of the play was *wretched*—Myrrha execrable! I as morose and foolishly passionate as hate could wish me! Oh! why cannot I cure myself of this odious vice which seems growing on me?

Elstree, March 13th.—Began Bulwer's *Pelham*.

London, March 15th.—Forster told me of Talfourd having completed a tragedy called *Ion*. What an extraordinary, what an indefatigable man!

Salisbury, March 16th.—Reached Salisbury at five o'clock, where I went to bed at the Black Horse and was called at ten; rose, breakfasted and went to my lodgings; after some search found the theatre, and went through the rehearsal. My Lady Macbeth was a relic of a style gone by, the veritable "ti-tum-to" "jerk and duck and twist" in a most engaging manner. Tried to act Macbeth, but, "confusion to my Lady!" it was too farcical, and would have been good as Dollalolla, but quite a travesty in the part she played. Nearly betrayed on one occasion my anger at one of the performers, but was very thankful that I subdued it before an opportunity for explosion was given; most happily I did not expose myself. The end of the play found me very much exhausted. My spirits have been much depressed; the heavy labour of my onward life, indispensable to secure my blessed children's independence, makes more uncertain the fulfilment of my desire to watch over and direct their education; but the consideration of the truth condensed in the precept, "To thine own self be true, and it must follow as the night the day, thou canst not then be false to any man," has comforted and reassured me. After rehearsal I walked to Brodie's shop, the bookseller, printer, banker, member of parliament, etc., of this city. I like to see such a choice. Bought guide and history of Salisbury, and experienced great attention from the gentleman in the shop; read the papers there. Went to the next door to see a Gothic banqueting-hall, which had been many years built up, but was now restored to its original form and decoration; it was very interesting as the hall of a merchant and shows the wealth of this city in earlier times.

March 18th.—Letter from dear Catherine, and the *M. Post* newspaper sent by Mr. Gould (I think he is not hard to fathom!) containing a criticism of Mr. Vandenhoff's Werner, and speaking of it as the last and most signal of a long list of failures. I would not wish to disguise my feelings and thoughts; it gave me satisfaction to see even this vindication of myself and my claims on popular favour; this man is no artist; he is a very vile imitator, a servile slave of the Press, and I believe an utterly low and worthless character. The article upon him was like justice to myself, and it really cheered me. Acted Hamlet *remarkably* well, and made some manifest improvements in the first scene, third scene and second act.

March 19th.—Began my packing before I came downstairs; received letters from Mrs. Bennett conceding the alteration of the time of my engagement, and from Mr. Beetham, stating his opinion that Mr. Bunn meant to defend an action for the £30 due. What will not such a miscreant do! Acted Werner but middlingly; was harassed and disconcerted occasionally by the performers, and disturbed by various riotous spirits in the course of the performance. The door-keeper asked me for something, and I rebuked him for *asking*. The check-taker (who next?) put in a claim which I with much reserve and cold civility said I would speak to the manager about, and, if usual, would satisfy him—the impudent fellow! I perceive Sir Edward Sugden has thrown up the Chancellorship of Ireland. This very intemperate man's behaviour is a lesson to any observer; his precipitation constantly places him in dilemmas which his want of temper and of judgment make real evils to him. His wife, *ci-devant* mistress, wished to go to the Irish Court. The Lady-Lieutenant would not receive her, and the Lord Chancellor gave up the Seals! [1]

Elstree, March 23rd.—I took up the novel of *Pelham* again, which interested me less from its story than from the maxims and deductions which the reader is enabled to draw from it, among these, not among the least profitable, if well weighed and duly acted on, is that wise remark: "Common sense never quarrels with any one." Oh, that I had early received the benefit of such wise inculcations. Let me hope that my children may learn to be wise from their father's errors. Catherine, Letty and children returned, bringing with them medicine, etc., and a Salisbury paper for me with a criticism of the most detracting character. I thought the incivility of the sender, the superintendent of Mr. Brodie's shop, quite

---

[1] This was, apparently, a *canard*; Sugden may have contemplated resignation but he did not relinquish the Irish Chancellorship till a week or two later when Sir Robert Peel's Government quitted office.

inexcusable; I was annoyed by it and by the article. Ought I to look at newspapers? they irritate and pain me, as affecting in a degree my income. Should I not, with "my wing on the wind and my eye on the sun," go onward, right on, without looking for or heeding aught save what I feel affects my interest. I very soon dismissed it. Finished *Pelham*, which I think a very useful book.

London, March 26th.—Calling at Forster's, Procter came in, haggard, old and miserable with grief and care; he very soon told his story—nine of his family sick at once with the scarlet fever!—in one month 100 visits from a physician to his boy, his hope and delight, whom he had buried, only six years old, ten days since; my heart turned to my own blessed children and my prayer now lifts itself to God for His mercy upon them. How light are the causes of my complaining when weighed in the balance with poor Procter's ills!

To Bath, March 27th.—Towards the latter part of my journey fell into a musing on the questionable profit of indulging the imagination by the study of poetry and history, or even by the glance upon the surface of truth which the limited advance of science can give us. It seemed to me, whose remaining years on earth are so few, as merely "vanity, vanity." Virtue is the only real good—love the only real enjoyment in this world. Moral philosophy, which is the practice of religion, is the only study about which man needs to busy himself, yet surely it is that which last and least seems to concern him. My life seems to have gone from me, and what have I made of it, either for myself or others? The care (and an anxious, almost a fretting care it is) which now agitates my heart is the provision for and education of my beloved children. My life to come, whatever it may be, is theirs. May God of His infinite mercy grant that it may be spent in effectual endeavour to confirm them in virtue and to secure to them in every respect the means of happiness! Amen!

March 28th.—Went to the theatre, and acted both Cardinal Wolsey and Sir C. Rackett very indifferently; in the latter I was made much worse than I should have been by the gross imperfectness of Mrs. Lovell, but I *did not scold*.

Exeter, March 30th.—Saw Hayward on the box of a britzska, and recognizing him followed him to the inn—saw Douglas, and was introduced to Mr. H. Williams, Vinerian Professor at Oxford. Walked out with Hayward, who gave me the history of my rejection through Croker at the Athenæum. He talks of "bringing people over to me"; but I do not wish to enter that or any society on such grounds, and I say *cheerfully* with Coriolanus: "Why, let it go!" Met Greaves, who had been to call upon me; settled that he should call on me to-morrow at ten; walked with Hayward and half promised to breakfast with him. Coming to lodgings, laid out my clothes for night—dined cautiously—rested—and looked over part of Macbeth: acted it unequally, but of the entire personation I must speak in censure; want of tone, want of collectedness, time, countenance, and many important items; among the most important, *temper!*

March 31st.—Greaves called at ten o'clock, and after sitting a short time, during which he alluded to his loss, I accompanied him to his house over the bridge; he told me that in forty years' practice a Leicester lawyer could not say he had seen five Chancery suits fairly carried through, nor could he acknowledge more than one; he spoke of the premises he intended taking when first setting up in Leicester, but hearing they were the subject of a Chancery suit "to be finished next term" he declined them; they stood to become a ruin, past which he used to walk, as if accidentally, his clients whenever they wished him to *file a bill*. It saved many suits.[1]

April 2nd.—Kept awake by a long train of angry and vindictive thought upon Mr. Croker's hostile interposition at the Athenæum upon my election. So much for the desirability of our mental conquests! Pride is the most deaf of all the follies that buzz their falsehoods into the ears of men. An anecdote in *Chambers' Journal* exposing the weakness and littleness of revenge restored me to complacency. How strong my passions must have been! and how unfit to cope with the world! How grateful ought I to feel, ill-regulated as they have been, for the comparatively little mischief they have drawn upon me when I reflect on what they might have led me to!

April 3rd.—Went to rehearsal, and on my return took a warm bath; learnt that the baths are very little used, and that throughout England the same observation is to be made; this does not say much for our cleanliness. I acted Werner indifferently—(*Quâ fugere vires?*), was very much distressed; played Delaval a little better, but not buoyantly. I am a middle-aged man, and not beseeming a juvenile levity.

To London, April 4th.—Paid all dues on self and luggage, and took my seat. Slept to Ilminster, where I was astonished to see Hayward again. He told me he was going to town by the coach— asked me of the Ministerial minority on which I could say little. We

---

[1] The term "in Chancery" had still the dread significance revealed by Dickens in his famous description of *Jarndyce* v. *Jarndyce*.

talked away much of the journey and some of the skin of my throat. He is very intelligent, good-natured, and, if a little vain, may find an ample set-off in his deservings. He reasoned very clearly, I thought, against the Local Courts Bill, observing, if it were passed, it should presume the existence of a Code of Laws to make the law certain and equal. He produced some—several—extracts from Whittle Harvey's [1] own defence, which utterly condemned him. How necessary it is to receive with caution *ex parte* statements, or evidence of any kind! Gave me a little of the scandal of *high* (!) life, which only shows its lowness more disgustingly. Saw in the newspaper the death of Dr. Maton,[2] a loss to his country, and individually to me a great one from the confidence I had in his skill, and the gratitude with which I have ever remembered him. He saved my life, I firmly believe, in my very serious illness.

April 6th.—Wrote to old Mr. Knowles,[3] who had, I think, importunately and indelicately applied for my subscription to his dictionary. He has been, I believe, instrumental in exciting ill-will against me in the Press, and has been the disseminator of much falsehood and misrepresentation respecting me. I told him that I should not object to purchase his completed work, but that I disliked subscribing.

April 9th.—Letter from H. Smith, informing me of the rejection of Ministers ; [4] I felt little exultation at their disgrace, as their acceptance of office appeared to be more disgraceful to them than their dismissal ; nor do I concern myself much about their successors ; they are all selfish knaves—I know little difference among them.

London, April 10th.—Called on Forster, who said that it had

---

[1] Daniel Whittle Harvey (1786–1863) solicitor and M.P.; an eloquent speaker and thus of service to the Whig Government who, however, hesitated to give him a place owing to his doubtful reputation. Having been frequently passed over, he at last sought an interview with Lord Melbourne, to whom he complained of the neglect with which he had been treated, citing as an instance a small Commissionership which had not even been offered to him. "My dear sir," replied Melbourne, "there you do me an injustice. I wanted to give you that post, but took the precaution of first sounding your future colleagues and, would you believe it, the d——d fellows flatly refused to sit with you!" Eventually, in 1840, Harvey obtained a Commissionership of Police which he held for over twenty years. An old Parliamentarian of that day who entered the House in 1826 informed the Editor that he considered Harvey the most eloquent speaker he had heard in the House of Commons since Canning.

[2] William George Maton (1774–1835) an eminent physician ; M.D. Oxford and F.L.S.; physician-extraordinary to Queen Charlotte and the Duchess of Kent, also to the Princess, afterwards, Queen Victoria.

[3] James Knowles (1759–1840) author of *A Pronouncing and Explanatory Dictionary of the English Language.*

[4] Sir Robert Peel's Government ; it had been outvoted six times in six weeks.

been proposed to Fonblanque [1] to go into Parliament and take office; I question it, not his ability or desert, but the ripeness of time is not yet come when a man will be judged by his merit alone. In the coach to Crayford. Walked with Bourne through Bexley to North Cray; went over the villa where Lord Londonderry lived and died—into the room where he destroyed himself. Men more different in temperament, intellect and disposition could scarcely be found than Whitbread, Romilly and Londonderry, yet the same fate attended all. [2] An enigma! The grounds are pretty.

April 11th.—Dined at Garrick Club, saw Captain Williams, heard that news of Mathews's death is daily expected. Is it as we near the verge of life we mark more attentively the departure of our fellow-men? Or is there an unusual hard run on life at the present period? Went to Drury Lane, saw Poole's [3] new comedy: old jests, not good, and the old style of jest—a violent and vulgar caricature, with no pretensions to the title of comedy; void of all semblance of character, wit or situation, its humour (if it be allowed to possess any) of the most exaggerated kind. How remote in appearance, dress, manners and deportment from well-bred persons were the "ladies and gentlemen" of the play! how destitute of grace, freedom and address! Messrs. Cooper and Vining and Miss Taylor [4]—how can a comedy be acted with such persons to represent educated or fashionable people? Much is not needed to give a *beau ideal* of the class that affects the latter designation.

Elstree, April 14th.—Read in a paper of Mr. Kean's [5] continued success. Here is an evidence of the evil tendency of our profession— there is so little room for talent, and degrees of success are so unimportant below the first (for scarcely any below the very head can reckon upon an income to give a surplus) that we look with apprehension upon every aspirant to a first rank and feel our own means of subsistence

---

[1] Albany Fonblanque (see note, p. 142).

[2] Whitbread was suffering from a specific disorder of the brain, and Romilly's mind, or rather his mental control, gave way under his overwhelming grief at the loss of his wife. Lord Londonderry (better known as Lord Castlereagh) had long been the victim of an infamous gang of blackmailers, who, plying their persecutions when his nervous system became unstrung from overwork, drove him, in a paroxysm of apprehension, to destroy himself. Ordinarily both he and Romilly were characterized by imperturbable courage and fortitude.

[3] John Poole (1786–1872) a comedy and farce-writer of some popularity in his earlier days.

[4] Harriette Deborah Taylor (1807–1874) married Walter Lacy, otherwise Williams. In spite of his depreciation Macready enlisted her in his company later on.

[5] Charles Kean.

trenched upon by the progress of youthful genius. Hence that selfish feeling of fear and in too many that desire of detracting from contemporary merit that too frequently disgraces us. God grant that I may neither manifest nor entertain such unworthy sentiments!

April 16th.—Received letter from Mr. Bunn, offering me £30 per week to act four nights in the week and half a clear Benefit. Considered all the motives that my desire to form a right judgment could suggest, and thought it unadvisable to appear in London under the circumstances of the present season. I have endeavoured to see the path most likely to lead to good for my own and my dear family's sake; I hope in God that I have chosen it. I wrote to decline the offer.

Norwich, April 21st.—Saw some letters of a vulgar, *troublesome* player who would demonstrate to any one needing it the paltriness and uselessness of striving to say bitter and insulting things. *What is ever obtained by an insult?* Nothing but an enemy.

April 22nd.—With an earnest desire of acting Hamlet well, lay down on the bed after dinner striving to keep it in my mind. Went refreshed and rather confident to the theatre, but very much disappointed in my own performance. I might find an excuse for my inability to excite the audience in the difficulty of ascertaining where the audience was, but I allow no plea or reservation in the question of playing as I ought or not. I did not satisfy myself. My only consolation was that, though provoked once or twice, I manifested not the slightest appearance of anger. How is it that, with the pains and precaution I take, I should thus disappoint myself? Am I too fastidious and too careful? Were I less so, what would become of me? In the opening speeches to the king and queen I was better than usual— more direct, and with more meaning and true feeling. My soliloquy was, at least the latter part of it, flurried, not well discriminated, not well given in regard to action—it wants finish and study. The scene with Horatio, etc., still requires study and earnestness; the interview with and address to the Ghost, re-arrangement, except the latter part, which I did well to-night. The last scene of the first act was amended to-night, but needs study, finish, clear discrimination. Act second— scene with Polonius—more ease, abstraction, and point; with Rosencrantz and Guildenstern, more ease and dignity and purpose; with the players, more point and discrimination. The soliloquy also requires a little finish. Act third—soliloquy requires, and always will require, study and practice. I was pretty well to-night; with Ophelia, a little softening and practice; with the players, throughout, rearrangement and study; the scene with Horatio, a little more melancholy and tender-

225

ness. The music beginning *piano* is very good, the play scene is good, and the remainder of the act. The closet scene requires a little revision and correcting. Act fourth—try over that scene often. Act fifth—requires much earnestness and much study; it was, as a whole, the best part of the play to-night.

April 23rd.—I must not forget an anecdote Mr. Simpson told me of Madame Schröder [1] which evinces clearly the love of their art with which the German actors are inspired. He asked her, after the play of *Romeo and Juliet,* how she, who could so delineate the sublime character of Lady Macbeth, could condescend to represent one so inferior as Lady Capulet? "Condescend," she replied, "is it not Shakspeare I acted?"

To Elstree, April 29th.—Read the *Times,* being curious to see their reasonings and their tone of politics; was shocked and disgusted at the *insidious* attempt to make their deluded readers believe that the safety of their religion was endangered by the Catholic leaders. If ever there was venal turpitude in a larger amount to one man's share than to another, Mr. Barnes or Mr. Walter,[2] or both, are covered with sin and infamy.

London, May 1st.—From chambers took cab to St. James's Square. Dined at the Windham (the best club in London) with Lardner, and went with him to the Royal Institution. Saw in the theatre [3] Mr. Willett, Faraday,[4] Hume, Brown, General Peachy, Tomlinson, and George Ward. Was very much interested by the lecture on Halley's comet and pleased with Lardner's delivery.

May 6th.—Came to town by Bryant, reading the pleasing poem of *Van Artevelde* on the road. Found at chambers Talfourd's play of *Ion,* in the preface to which is a most kind mention of myself. Called on Forster, whom I found in a mysterious sort of uneasiness —he talked of having expected to "go out" with some one,[5] and

[1] Schröder-Devrient (see note, p. 29).

[2] John Walter (1776–1847) the second of that name. Proprietor and joint editor of the *Times,* and that time M.P. for Berkshire. Originator of the foreign "Special Correspondent."

[3] Of the Royal Institution.

[4] Michael Faraday (1791–1867) then at the height of his fame as a scientific discoverer.

[5] This duel did not take place ; Forster's pugnacity had an admixture of prudence which always contrived to obviate the ordeal of pistols. Once, however, he narrowly escaped coming to a violent end by the hand of the usually amiable Robert Browning, who, stung beyond endurance by his offensiveness at a friend's house after dinner, seized a heavy cut-glass decanter with murderous intent, and was only prevented from hurling it across the table by the nimble intervention of his host.

of his possible journey into Devonshire. All that I could collect to the purpose was that he could not see me at dinner to-morrow. Lunched, and came home by Billings, continuing the perusal of *Van Artevelde*, and admiring the clear and pearly beauty of the sky and the extent of prospect it afforded. Pleased with the extracts of Bulwer's book.

Elstree, May 7th.—Read Talfourd's tragedy of *Ion;* pleased with the opening scenes and, as I proceeded, arrested and held by the interest of the story and the characters, as well as by the very beautiful thoughts, and the very noble ones, with which the play is interspersed. How delightful to read his dedication to his master and benefactor, Dr. Valpy,[1] and the gentle outpourings of his affectionate heart towards his friends and associates; if one did not love, one would envy such a use of such abilities. Letter from Forster mysteriously repeating his answer of yesterday. Wrote to Talfourd on his tragedy, and inviting him to dinner. After dinner I watered some of the plants in the garden and enjoyed the freshness of the air, the verdure and the flowers, and the lightly clouded sky that was soon naked and bare, one placid depth for the moon's brightness to sail through. It was enjoyment.

May 8th.—A note from Bunn, inquiring if I would play in conjunction with Malibran in *La Juive,* to which I answered *no.* Read three acts of Miss Agnes Strickland's[2] play; how much time I am forced to expend in this kind of unprofitable labour!

To London, May 10th.—A letter from Dr. Lardner, accepting our invitation and sending us two—one to dine on Thursday, the other to an evening party on Tuesday week; read *Examiner.* Wrote notes to Messrs. Warren, O'Hanlon, Walker, inviting them; to Dr. Lardner accepting invitations, and to Fred Reynolds on Miss Strickland's play. Came to town by Billings's afternoon coach, and read some cantos in Cary's *Dante,* much of which I found difficult, and to some of which I could make out no meaning. Arrived in town; my spirits were particularly low, and the *mauvaise honte,* which makes me uncomfortable in being *seen*—for my reason contradicts the notion of being *looked at*—quite annoyed and distressed me.

To Bath, May 11th.—A woman in the coach to-day was very anxious in her inquiries after "the lord," a young lad on the top of the coach—whether he *dined,* etc. It seems Mary Bucknill stared at

[1] Richard Valpy (1754-1836), D.D.; headmaster of Reading School, over which he presided for nearly fifty years with great distinction and success.

[2] Agnes Strickland (1796-1874) the historian, best known by her *Lives of the Queens of England.*

the dull face of Lord Northland all church time—to satiate her gaze on a lord, I suppose. When are these people *lords*, except when they are called so? If a few men would refuse to call them so, what are they?

May 12th.—Ruminated on the sore subject of my expenses, and certainly were I not hampered with the lease of my house I would leave it; as it is, I do not well know what to do. A case of self-interest brought to my mind the counterpart of the case of a graduated property-tax, and feeling in my own person the injustice of such a scale I am obliged to apply it where the argument makes for me. A graduated property-tax is an injustice. Fonblanque is right.

Worcester, May 13th.—Arrived about five; and, after looking at my rooms, proceeded to the theatre; could not gain admission, and had to wait about a quarter of an hour in a public-house for the arrival of the housekeeper. Unpacked and dressed; though the rain poured down the house was very good, and I acted Virginius very well, and without any anger at all. It was very decently done; only Dentatus had put a surplice over his street clothes and put part of a sheep's fleece on his chin for a beard. Mr. Bennett paid me, and I came to the Star, where I read the paper.

Elstree, May 17th.—Talfourd, White, Price and Mrs. Talfourd arrived. Talfourd brought me four books of *Ion*. An agreeable day, except that the argument on Malthus between ourselves and Dr. Lardner became loud and earnest.

London, May 21st.—Called at Forster's chambers to arrange with him a visit to Mr. Maclise.[1] Accompanied Forster to Mr. Maclise's lodgings—found him a young, prepossessing, intelligent man, anxious to paint my picture. Saw his large one of Captain Rock, and several smaller of great merit. Agreed to sit to him.

May 22nd.—Read newspaper, in which was an account of a dinner to Mr. C. Kean by the inhabitants of Waterford. It is not pleasant to me to see these frequent demonstrations of partiality to him, as they naturally excite the apprehension that he must merit them.

May 23rd.—Proceeded to Warren Street, and called on old Reynolds,[2] whom I found the same in inveteracy, obscenity, and only changed in politics. Note from H. Smith, acquainting me with a message from M. Cloup, the director of the French company, regretting he had not known of my visit that he might have offered me a box, and wishing to know if the speculation would answer at Bath; a note

[1] Daniel Maclise (1806–1870) the eminent painter. R.A. 1840.
[2] Frederic Reynolds (1764–1841) the dramatist.

228

from Bunn, stating that he had called yesterday. Dined with Mr. Warren, where I met Mr. Brockedon,[1] whose acquaintance I desired to make. Passed a very cheerful afternoon.

May 24th.—Dined with Catherine at Talfourd's, where we met Sheil, Procter, Douglas, Whitton, Chilton, who seemed quite glad to renew our acquaintance, Messrs. Healey and Northcott; after dinner Mrs. Talfourd's sisters came with their father, a most intelligent, interesting old gentleman. Returned to Elstree, where we arrived at half-past one, and I found notes from Dr. Lardner, pressing me to dine on Tuesday with him to meet Mrs. Stanhope, Mrs. Norton,[2] Jenny Vertpré, Fonblanque, etc., inviting Catherine to join the party, and asking me for an introduction to Malibran.

May 26th.—Went to read the papers at the Garrick Club, where I saw Talfourd, Fladgate, Raymond; went upstairs and read Miss F. Kemble's Journal—a confirmation of my original opinion of her presumption, conceit, vulgarity of mind and quackery—a correction of the idea I had entertained of her literary talent. It was evidently written for publication, and the papers are not the actual thoughts and feelings which a person notes down for the purposes of reference and self-correction, but what a person besotted with the flattery of the ignorant and undiscriminating elaborates for effect, and to support the reputation she arrogates as belonging to her! Coming downstairs, saw Price, Forster, Stanhope, Villiers. Went to Dr. Lardner's; met Mrs. Shelley, Miss Sheridan, Lord Adare, Colonel[3] and Mrs. Stanhope, Mr. and Mrs. Norton, Fonblanque and Miss Keene. I could not look at Mrs. Norton without looking long—her face is one to think of. Mrs. Stanhope is lively, but trifling. She spoke of the "vulgarity" of a blue coat, not perceiving that I wore one. She endeavoured to amend it, but patching such a thing only makes the place more remarkable. I liked Fonblanque very much and Colonel Stanhope—Lord Adare was very quick. Mr. Norton[4] is a coxcomb—I *think*. Saw the Sheils, Hayward, O'Hanlon (who told me that the French of my note to Vertpré was much better than the English), Martin, to whom

---

[1] William Brockedon (1787–1854), F.R.S., one of the founders of the Royal Geographical Society; a well-known painter and illustrator.

[2] The Hon. Mrs. Norton (1808–1877); the famous "society beauty" and authoress.

[3] Colonel the Hon. Leicester Stanhope (1784–1862) afterwards fifth earl of Harrington. Well known as Byron's friend and colleague in Greece.

[4] The Hon. George Chapple Norton; Mrs. Norton's husband, who in the following year brought an abortive action for crim. con. against Lord Melbourne. He was a moody, pragmatical man, but Mrs. Norton with her Sheridan temperament and troops of admirers was in many respects a trying wife.

I was introduced, Lady Seymour and I think Mrs. Blackwood [1] Babbage. Mrs. Norton, on going away, returned to find me, and expressed her wish to see me at her house. I do *not* understand this; I cannot feel that I contribute to the pleasure of society, and must suppose that the policy of persons "in the world" suggests the expediency of having, when mere civility can purchase it, the good word of every one. It is wise, but hollow. I was distressed in fearing I had used a wrong expression in French to Mrs. Shelley.[2] What satisfaction I had in finding at home that I was correct!

May 27th.—Lay very late, though early awake, but I continued *Van Artevelde* from where I left off last night until my headache warned me to sleep again. I am not formed for the world's vain pleasures—they must be substantial ones of feeling, thought or sense to hold me captive. Sent Healey upon errands, and made *Van Artevelde* my breakfast companion. Talfourd objects to the second volume, and seems almost to feel his—Artevelde's—love for Elena a pollution of his own heart and a wrong to the memory of Adriana. I do not feel it so. We are human beings; the heart of man cannot endure a state of solitude and bereavement; it is not that alone which is lovable that induces us to love, the disposition to love is part of our being, we lean towards something with a natural yearning, and if we find it not we weaken or grow hard in selfish purpose. To live alone a man must be either brutal or divine, as Bacon tells us, and what loneliness is like that of a desolated heart? I feel, in Artevelde's love for Elena, that it is a pillow on which he rests his heart, bruised and somewhat weakened by its affliction and desert state, and wearied with the cares, from which hope slowly is detaching itself, that have no other solace. What a charming book it is! Forster called in, and wished me to write a review of Miss F. Kemble's book; but I cannot conceal the fact from myself that I cannot write now for the public. I have been left behind in the world's march. It is not vanity that makes me case myself in pride, but a consciousness of not having won a secure title to distinction, and the nervous and unquiet apprehension of its being questioned. Called on Pickersgill,[3] who introduced me

---

[1] Mrs. Norton's sister, afterwards respectively the Duchess of Somerset and Lady Dufferin.

[2] The widow of Shelley the poet, who was now "cultivating society" for the sake of her son (the late Sir Percy Shelley), much to the indignation of her rejected suitor, Edward Trelawney.

[3] Henry William Pickersgill (1782–1875), R.A., a portrait-painter greatly in request during this and the earlier Victorian period; his reputation, however, has not survived, and, to judge by the existing examples of his work, with good reason.

to his wife and daughter and showed me his pictures—one very good of Wordsworth, and one that interested me much, of H. Taylor— P. Van Artevelde.   Bought gloves, and, to escape the threatening storm, took cab and drove to the Garrick Club.   Read the papers, dined, and proceeded in Mrs. Butler's Journal—what affected, vulgar, stilted trash! Yet despite the general disgusting character of her book you see evidences of thought and a superior intellect.   To my deep sorrow I committed myself most rashly, most foolishly, in speaking before a stranger, Mr. McMahon, of the *Quarterly Review*, which on account of the ill-blood it stirred between America and this country I stigmatized as that " accursed book."

May 28th.—Called on Bunn in Prince's Place; talked long on other matters, and at length came to the point of our meeting, and agreed on next season's engagement: £30 unsubtracted; four nights per week; half a Benefit; *Bridal* [1] on usual terms; three weeks' vacation, last of Lent.   Which I pray to God may be fortunate and prosperous. Sent to order carriage for the evening.   Dined at Garrick Club, where I was much amused by a quiz—put upon a Middlesex magistrate there —of giving power of expelling five members annually to the Com- mittee.   Went to Horace Twiss's.   Saw Hook, Dance, Hayward, Mrs. Whitlock [2]—quite *old*—Mrs. Arkwright,[3] Twisses, Lockharts and Lord and Lady Courtenay.   Was very much delighted with the singing of Mrs. Arkwright, whose powers of expression, with but little voice, proves the truth of the theory I have always held with regard to music. Her style is what we would suppose the troubadours or bards to have been.   Heard Hook improvise a song on " The Child's Christening." I was disappointed in this exhibition—it seems more a knack to me than a talent; as for himself, I think him a very vulgar buffoon— wonder at his admission and still more at his retention of place in society.[4]   Planché's imitation of James Smith [5] was admirable.

---

[1] The dramatic copyright of the *Bridal* belonged to Macready   (*note by Sir F. Pollock*).

[2] Elizabeth Whitlock (1761–1836) *née* Kemble, sister of Mrs. Siddons, but very inferior to her as an actress.

[3] One of the Twiss family, a charming singer, made much of by the fashionable world ; the Duke of Devonshire had a great regard for her.

[4] Macready undoubtedly underrated Hook's improvising powers, which according to con- temporary accounts and quotations amounted to a good deal more than " a knack," though the gift was not, of course, of an exalted order.   That he was " vulgar " and a " buffoon" is, however, undeniable, but in order to be well amused " Society " was as tolerant of vulgarity in those days as it is at present.

[5] The joint author of *Rejected Addresses*.

231

May 30th.—Took cab to St. James's Square and called on Lardner at Windham Club; found Mr. Donovan with him, a chemist; accompanied them to a lamp shop in Regent Street, where I saw a curious French lamp and heard of one by Donovan to burn naptha. Went in the coach to call on Mrs. Norton; found Lord Castlereagh [1] in the drawing-room, who stared, as I, entrenching myself in my democratic pride, did again. We waited some little time, when Mrs. Norton appeared, dressed for a walk; she introduced us, and, after a little chat wherein we heard of the duel between Lord Seymour and Sir Colquhoun Grant,[2] we ended our short visit, and took the way to Malibran, on whom we left cards. I had written to Bunn for opera-box, and wished to go home to hear of my success. Called at the Garrick Club, and read in papers the account of the duel. Saw Price, H. Reynolds, with whom I shook hands, etc. Coming home, made out parties for Sunday and Monday next, and sent out notes. Dressed and went to Fonblanque's. Saw there Lucien Bonaparte, Maclise, Colonel Alexander (who recognized me), Cattermole,[3] O'Hanlon, who is offensively coarse: saying Mrs. M—— danced too well, and appealing to Mrs. Norton, who, with Mr. Norton, was there, to explain his meaning—the brute! I was at one time much overcome by the heat—Countess Winterton, Colonel Evans, Lardner, were there. I did not enjoy it. My hat was lost, as I left it on a bench to hand Mrs. Norton into the refreshment-room. Set off Catherine and Lydia, and obliged to wait till the last for the *left hat.* Fonblanque's son at half-past two set the curtain on fire and crept under the sofa. Mr. and Mrs. Norton took me home—at least part of the way—and were at infinite pains by the way to explain their freedom from blame in the late elopement. Sir C. Grant had very absurdly, I think, insulted Norton upon it, who had replied very properly that he was not present. They are too anxious to exculpate and justify themselves to be wholly free from censure. Mrs. Norton is most beautiful, witty, clever, but not elegant; she is affected and an intriguer. I suspect *purpose* in all she says. Went to bed sick and wearied at daylight, to rise again in three hours' time. Oh, pleasure! what a fatiguing, unwholesome business art thou!

May 31st.—Went to Forster's to dine. Met Stanfield, Bulwer, Fonblanque, Blanchard, Talfourd, Howard, Maclise, Cattermole,

---

[1] See note, p. 52.

[2] Relative to the elopement of Sir C. Grant's daughter with Mr. Sheridan, Lady Seymour's brother, which Sir C. Grant alleged had been encouraged, or, at any rate, countenanced by Lady Seymour and Mrs. Norton.

[3] George Cattermole (1800-1868), the well-known artist and illustrator.

THE HON. MRS. NORTON

From an engraving by Thomson of a painting by Sir George Hayter, Kt.

Procter, Leigh Hunt, T. Fonblanque, Price. Pleasant day. Howard wanted me to go to Lady Blessington's, but was not dressed.

Elstree, June 3rd.—Received notes from Talfourd and Maywood accepting their several invitations, and another from Gaspey, declining, and at some length observing upon the Chancery Bill. He intends me kindness, and I can only feel kindly the manifestation of his good-will. His manners are unpolished, even to disagreeableness, but through evil report and good report, known and unknown, he has been uniformly consistent in advocating my claims to public favour, and now that he has relinquished the situation which enabled him to serve me I will not let him suppose me quite undeserving the opinion he has held of me. He is kind-hearted and true.

June 6th.—Read the remainder of first book of *Paradise Lost*; with the exception of Addison, Milton seems almost as unfortunate in his commentators as Shakspeare. How shallow and coxcombical are the remarks and exceptions of the sparrow-like flock that try to pursue his eagle-flight! He actually makes us believe in his Satanic host, and they live in our minds, armed and endowed and created after his mighty will.

June 7th.—Messrs. Forster and Maclise arrived, literally drenched with rain, having been caught in the thunderstorm which had fallen during the afternoon. Gave them entire changes of garment and made them very comfortable. Fonblanque, Miss Keene and Dr. Lardner arrived, Mrs. Fonblanque being too unwell to come. Passed a very pleasant day. Liked Fonblanque the more I saw of him. Got into a very long conversation with him and Smith, with which Lardner did not seem pleased. They left us late; and, against our remonstrances, Messrs. Forster and Maclise rode home.

June 8th.—Received the *Spectator*, which contained a reference to myself of the most ill-natured and injurious tendency; a statement made on no grounds, for I am certain the person who wrote it has not seen me act Shakspeare for years. It annoyed me and disgusted me; I sicken at the subjection to which I am doomed, and these base assaults make my thoughts turn mournfully and forebodingly to my beloved children. I was in very low spirits, but soon recovered myself.

June 9th.—Letter from Bulwer at some length, excusing himself from dining here on Sunday. One expression in his letter I disliked—the "honour of my acquaintance." My acquaintance can be no honour to such a man as Bulwer, and it almost seems like irony.

June 11th.—Read over Lord Byron's *Foscari*, which does not seem

233

to me to contain the power, or rather the variety and intensity of passion which many of his other plays do.

June 12th.—Received notes from Frederick Reynolds, regretting his inability to visit us on Sunday, which I believe he would desire; from Lardner, informing me that his editors' party was to take place *this* (last) evening; I would have gone had I been sure of it, as I would not willingly leave a means untried to aggrandize myself for my dear children's sake. With the exception of those few and high-souled spirits such as Fonblanque, Wallace, Forster, Dance, and some kind ones as Jerdan, Threlford, Gaspey, etc., I may say of them, "I do despise them, for they do prank them in authority beyond all noble sufferance." Began to read *Marino Faliero*, but read it drowsily. I wish I could think it dramatic, at present I do not.

June 13th.—Note from Procter, excusing himself on the plea of illness from dining with us to-morrow. Came to town in carriage with Christina and Letitia, reading by the way *Marino Faliero*, which contains much beautiful poetry, lofty sentiment, but little action, and, consequently, little dramatic situation. Called at Garrick Club. Planché proposed to me the half of the Adelphi theatre. I could not give up my whole self to the employment of conducting it, and if I did not, it would not answer.

June 14th.—Omitted going to church. The Talfourds came. Walked with Talfourd and Chilton and Willie some time in the garden, awaiting the Sheils' arrival; they at length appeared, not, however, to remain the night, and we sat down to an excellently-served dinner. O'Hanlon was evidently conscious of his past rudeness, the sense of which seemed to sit heavy on him the whole day; which was, generally speaking, spent cheerfully and pleasantly. Sheil invited us to dine on Thursday and accompany them to Dr. Lardner's; we accepted his invitation. No prayers!

June 15th.—The newspapers arrived; in one, the *Spectator*, I again read a pert and vulgar tirade against the actor's art, which this refined critic asserts must still be considered the "vagabond's trade." Wrote to Bunn for boxes at the theatre and opera, and to sound him on the subject of *the drama*. Played—idled away the day with my children; going into the hayfield, was discontented with the appearance of the crops, from which I thought O'Mery, my harvest-man, had been filching for his own fields. If I do him wrong I shall be sincerely sorry, but it looks very ill.

June 16th.—Went into the garden and hayfield with my children, and played with them before and after dinner. In the evening sat in my study ruminating upon the possible consequence of my dining to-morrow with the Literary Fund—viz. that I *may* have to make a speech—and meditating on my own inability to collect, arrange, and give utterance to my ideas. I ought to cure this very bad habit of hesitation, and for my children's sake apply myself to a more rapid and precise delivery of my thoughts.

London, June 17*th.*—Thought upon what I ought to say at the dinner—and dressed for it—Dr. Lardner called for me, and we went. I saw Wyse,[1] whom I liked much, Christie, French, Emerson Tennent.[2] The whole proceedings of the day were dull and wearisome with the exception of Wilkie's[3] speech, in which he noticed the connection of literature and art; and the Turkish Attaché, who in acknowledgment of the compliment paid to him in drinking his health, rose and gulped down a bumper of wine, then sat down. Urquhart,[4] his cicerone, spoke very well, but in a low tone of voice. Lord Teignmouth spoke pretty well, and Murchison[5] fairly. On paying my subscription, Mr. Snow told me that my name was in the list of toasts. This decided me. I feel unequal from the want of habit, and the uncertainty of my position. I read in every newspaper of this week that my art is a very humble one—if indeed it be an art at all—and that its professors are entitled to little respect; and here, when in courtesy I am admitted as *Mr. Macready* among the esquires of the Royal Academy, the King's Printing Office, the *Quarterly Review*, etc., I am to speak without the possibility of knowing what place is allowed me as an artist, or what degree of particular consideration may be extended to me as a man consistent in his private conduct.

June 18*th.*—Is it twenty years since, in Greenock, I waited with anxiety the particular return of the dead and wounded from the Battle of Waterloo—wishing to be certified of dear Edward's safety? Went

---

[1] Thomas Wyse (1791–1862), afterwards British Minister at Athens, K.C.B.; a successful diplomatist in various affairs connected with Greece, especially the famous Don Pacifico incident.

[2] James Emerson Tennent (1804–1869), author and politician; M.P. 1832; supporter of Lord Grey, afterwards of Peel, in whose second Administration he was for a time Secretary to the Indian Board: created a baronet 1867.

[3] David Wilkie (1785–1841), the famous painter; he was knighted in the following year.

[4] David Urquhart (1805–1877), diplomatist and political writer; notable when in Parliament as a bitter opponent of Lord Palmerston, who had recalled him from Constantinople (where he was Secretary of Embassy) in 1836, owing to his hostile attitude to Russia.

[5] Roderick Impey Murchison (1792–1871), the distinguished geologist; afterwards K.C.B. and baronet.

to Sheil's. Wallace dined there. Catherine and Lydia arrived from Elstree. The Sheils *are* good-natured, but there is pride somewhere among them. Catherine and Lydia do not perceive it, but there is an instinctive quickness of feeling this myself that, like a torn skin, quivers at the slightest touch of what offends it. Had I married (as I might) a fortune, should *I* have yielded to this weakness of an *ambitieux*? I think it is more than probable; men are to all appearance as happy with much substantial good to hug themselves in. I have my disappointments, but resulting from my own temperament. Went on the box of Sheil's carriage to Dr. Lardner's, where I saw and was introduced to the Guiccioli [1]—saw Mrs. Norton, Mrs. L. Stanhope, etc. Was surprised to see Mr. Cooper, Miss Betts, and Miss —— enter the room. Oh, Dr. Lardner! Is this society for a philosopher?

June 19th.—Saw Malibran in *Fidelio;* the dulness of the opera was really wearisome; it was, with the exception of this gifted creature's performance, miserably done; and even she was not in her own element —the part seemed a weight upon her that she energetically but vainly struggled with. The scena at the end of the second act was superior to Schröder-Devrient's, but in all besides she was inferior—straining at effect, melodramatic, elaborate, but not abandoned; her resolution was strong, but her identity never seemed for a moment lost. Her costume was admirable—will our actors never learn?—*Never.* I went into her room after the opera—there were several persons, Mr. Cooper among them. She saluted me most affectionately, and, perhaps, to her I was what she was to me—a memorial of years of careless, joyous hope and excitement; she said I was not altered; I could not say what I did not think of her. I could have loved—once almost did love her, and I believe she was not indifferent to me. It often occurs to me on such recollections : how would my destiny have been altered! I should have possibly been an *ambitieux*—should I have been happier?—should I have had my Nina, my Willie and little Catherine? Left Malibran with a very great depression of spirits.

June 21st.—Read *Examiner*, pleased with the clear views taken by Fonblanque, and disgusted with the paltering conduct of these Whigs —can there be a baser political character than an aristocrat timidly

---

[1] The comtessa of that name, who had become a celebrity owing to her much-discussed relations with Lord Byron, of which her second husband was so proud that he used to introduce her as "Madame la Marquise de Boissy, autrefois la maîtresse de Milord Byron."

professing just and liberal principles of government for the sake of place? Such is a Whig!

June 30th.—Cut the leaves of Procter's *Life of Kean*, and consigned the volumes to the store-room shelves. I have made some remarks which savour of anger; on reviewing them, and comparing them with his conduct, there appears to me no reason for qualifying them. My first acquaintance with him was of his own seeking—he sent me his Dramatic Scenes, which I greatly liked, and like; and thence grew acquaintance, which soon ripened into intimacy. We were very much together, and as I believed—a belief that it *was pain to me to part with*—we were really friends. He brought his poetry to me as he wrote it, and fancied it more as I read it; he wrote sonnets on my performances of Rob Roy and Coriolanus, and held me (it is long since) only not before the best. I felt towards him fervidly and affectionately. He was the person to whom I rushed in a state of excitement that approached to intoxication with the news of *Virginius*, after I first read it. He was ambitious of writing a play. He chose for his *subject* Don Carlos—or Parisina—began a scene at random in the second act—it was very good; there he stuck. He wrote another —the opening scene; he then began to consult me; he wrote the second scene of the first act: he stood still—the second act was neaily completed, and he could not move—"I must write him down a plot." I did, and consulted Sheil, who had been staying with me many weeks on a visit, upon its fitness; he said he could not mend it, hedged in, as the fabricator must be, between the beginning already made and the necessary catastrophe. Procter did not altogether like it, nor did I, but gave it as the best his predicament admitted. He wished Sheil to be again consulted, who very peremptorily returned as his opinion that under the peculiar circumstances no better plan could be suggested. He went to work again, and brought the scenes piecemeal to me—altering them, three or four times *individually* to the passion I acted over before him—I may really aver he almost wrote the play of *Mirandola* under my inspection; he has been with me from ten till five o'clock, when I have sent him away, having to dress for dinner. It was I who urged Warren to give him £300 for the copyright. Unusual pains were taken with it, and it was bolstered by the zeal of his friends into a sudden, temporary reputation. His preface spoke in a very cool manner of my performance, and acknowledged an obligation to me for *suggesting a curtailment in one of the acts!* He came, manifestly afraid and ashamed to see me; he "hoped I was satisfied."

I said "I was not—that I could have been well satisfied had he given me credit for sufficient high-mindedness to have rested content in the satisfaction of serving him, but to acquit himself of my services in such a manner was anything but satisfactory." He said that this was "a greater annoyance to him than anything that had happened—that he had been told he ought to dedicate the play to an old friend of his, but that he had said, 'If I inscribe it to any one, it must be to Macready.'" I explained to him that such a compliment at that time, so far from being desirable, would have been injurious to me. Well, time rolled on and took Procter with it. I did not alter my demeanour to him, for I do not easily wrench kindly feelings from my heart. He sat silent and heard my character attacked, till a friend of mine in indignation said to him, "Have you not a word to speak for your friend?" He was silent. I believe the Rev. Mr. Harness[1] was among my slanderers at the time. Procter was so full of spleen against J. H. Reynolds for not quoting passages from a book of his (P.'s) which he reviewed, that he declared, with the most energetic malevolence, that he would take an opportunity of punishing Reynolds when any book of his came out. Forster showed me a note, wherein Procter manifestly ascribes (disclaiming all the time any such intention) the authorship of a hostile critique on *Kean's Life* in the *Observer* to him, Forster! His flippant and contemptuous toleration of players in his book is in keeping with his indifference to those he has made all possible use of.[2]

July 1st.—Called on Forster, who told a lamentable tale of Procter's littleness and excessive soreness, which made me feel less sorrow for the violence of Blackwood's review of his book.

July 5th.—Went to the Garrick Club, where I dined, saw the newspapers, and looked into some books. Forster and Price came in. Forster asked me to accompany him to Talfourd's, to which I agreed. We spent the evening there. Talfourd took me into the other drawing-room, and, talking over *Ion*, expressed his firm resolve that no one

---

[1] The Rev. William Harness (1790–1869), well known as a friend of Byron, whose school-fellow he was at Harrow. He attained some eminence as a preacher and was the author of various works, including an edition and "Life" of Shakspeare, and the *Life of Mary Russell Mitford*, published after his death. Macready, who had had a difference with Miss Mitford relative to a play of hers, suspected Harness of having attacked him in her interests by means of an anonymous article in *Blackwood*. The matter is gone into more fully in a later portion of the Diaries.

[2] Over the foregoing entry Macready wrote the following comment presumably, at a later period; " TRUE ; I cannot in justice cancel this—though I really love Procter."

should act the character but myself. I shall therefore address myself to it. Talfourd walked home part of the way with Forster and myself.

Elstree, July 6th.—Read the *Examiner.* Every newspaper now gives its record of Mathews's [1] death, and all write in celebrating his powers of entertainment and his private virtues. I may seem envious in noting down my own exceptions to this cant of praise; the papers certainly do not speak from knowledge—"I am to speak what I do know." His talents for mimicry were most extraordinary, and, though a very indifferent actor of the comic drama, his personations of the characters imagined for and by himself were admirable and inimitable. He was amusing for a short time as a companion, few persons more so, but as he merely unpacked his memory of his anecdotes and imitations, when the best samples were delivered he grew tiresome in offering the same goods and requiring, not always agreeably, the same price of attention and applause. Of his "high and honourable character," he was, generally speaking, respectable in life—he was not so dishonourable as C. Kemble, nor so penurious as Liston, but he was not a high-souled man, nor what I distinguish as a gentleman.

July 12th.—Letters from Morris, wishing to negotiate for the Haymarket, and from W. Birch. The latter imparts to me the significant tidings that the reviews in the *Quarterly* on Procter's book and Miss Kemble's are written by an "*enemy* of mine." It is sufficiently intelligible that I am abused. This is not agreeable—simply, *as I believe from the bottom of my heart,* because it may by possibility bear upon my income. Whether it be written by Mr. Harness, Mr. Lockhart or Mr. Croker, Maginn [2] or T. Hook, in point of *feeling* it does not reach me—it is the apprehension I endure for my power of educating and providing for my children that makes me at all attach importance to it. I feel myself in intention and duty to my fellow-men far above such persons, who gain their livelihood and draw their gratifications from the imagined triumphs of their envious and malignant nature; the contest, if such it can be called where the attack is all on one side and from ambuscade, too, is not a very chivalrous one. But I can truly say, "I am richer than my base accusers" in all that man is justified in valuing. The yearning of my heart is for tranquil independence, to form the minds of my beloved children, and learn the lesson to die well in teaching them to live so. Did the fiendish host whose name was legion, not being destined to drown, survive their leap

---

[1] The elder Mathews.

[2] William Maginn (1793-1842), the well-known journalist, founder of *Fraser's Magazine.*

and transmigrate through the bodies of certain reviewers, Antoine Pasquin, Dr. Wolcot,[1] J. W. Croker, J. G. Lockhart, W. Harness, etc., etc., etc., in after ages, that spirits so out of harmony with the beauty and benevolence of the Creator's works should be *of those?* Walked with Dow down to the reservoir : he spoke of the hostility of the Press to me. My children are the stimulants I bring to my mind to counteract my despondency.

July 14th.—Looked at the *Quarterly Review* and found that the passages from which W. Birch inferred hostility to myself were two separate declarations that Mr. C. Kemble was the best actor now living. As this only proves the ignorance of Messrs. Croker and Lockhart, the profound Aristarchi of the *Quarterly*, it in no manner annoyed me.

London, July 15th.—Went to Mrs. C. Buller's, where I saw Mrs. Austin, who does not like me—I *feel* it—*tant pis pour moi*—talked a little with her, a good deal with M. C. Buller,[2] saw O'Connell; talked the remainder of the night with Fonblanque—the rooms are exceedingly pretty, but the attendance was thin : H. Bulwer,[3] Lord Devon, Elphinstone, Count Morel. Fonblanque came away with me. Count Morel and his friend had taken my coach and were for retaining it, but I very good-naturedly made them understand their mistake and offered to set them down, which offer they accepted. Fonblanque told me of the King's rudeness to Lord Durham ; he seems a very disgusting old man. Instead of returning home after parting with Fonblanque (who wished to see me when I came again to town), I drove to the Garrick Club. On entering, Talfourd and Price uttered joyous exclamations, and I shook them both cordially by the hand ; a person with his back to the room at their table, turning round, displayed the face of Mr. C. Kemble, and, to my great surprise, said, "*Come !*" and took hold of my hand, which I instantly withdrew ; he said, "What, you won't shake hands with me ? "—which I believe he repeated. He was drunk, or nearly so. I am not quite clear how I should have behaved. I do not mean as to whether I should have

---

[1] John Wolcot (1738–1819), the notorious satirist who wrote under the pseudonym of "Peter Pindar."

[2] Charles Buller (1806–1848), M.P. for Liskeard ; best known as secretary to Lord Durham, when Governor-General of Canada, in which capacity he displayed statesmanlike qualities of a high order. He and his brother Arthur (afterwards a Ceylon Judge) were pupils of Thomas Carlyle.

[3] William Henry Lytton Earle Bulwer (1801–1872), the distinguished diplomatist, created Lord Dalling and Bulwer 1871 ; elder brother of the first Lord Lytton.

accepted his offer of reconciliation—for really to do that would be tantamount to making alliance with fraud, treachery, falsehood, the meanest and most malignant species of intrigue : in fact, with vileness and profligacy of the most barefaced character—but whether I should have resented the liberty he took. I felt no anger ; but really it was a gross impertinence. Talked with Talfourd, who was tipsy, which perhaps accounts for and excuses his indefensible account of the trial of the Griswold cause and the blame he threw upon Smith for his honest and zealous endeavour to gain the cause for the officer. Talfourd *quite forgot* himself. At chambers I ruminated much on the strange occurrence of the evening and thought of writing a note to Kemble on the freedom he had used. I wrote and thought, thought and wrote, and went very late to bed.

Elstree, July 18th.—I wish I were anything rather than an actor— except a critic ; let me be unhappy rather than vile! If I meant by this that men who *usually criticize* are vile I should convict myself of equal folly and injustice. It is the assumption of the high duties of criticism (demanding genius and enthusiasm tempered by the most exact judgment and refined taste) by mere dealers in words, with no pretensions to integrity of purpose or the advancement of literature, that disgusts and depresses me. The sight of the *Quarterly Review*— the arena of Croker, Lockhart, Harness, Hall, etc.—which H. Smith has sent me, induced a train of thought upon the (so-called) criticism of the country. Generally speaking it takes its tone from faction. The most profound ignorance is no obstruction to the most dogmatic assertions—these are made, of course, on points that few persons are interested in contradicting, or in seeing contradicted, therefore they remain as texts for the declaimers from the particular *Review* to preach from. It is really my opinion that in the classification of minds such a one as Lockhart's—hireling, defamer, corrupt (not by direct means of pecuniary bribe, but by party and power), malignant trader in sentences pointed to stab, and draw by slow droppings the life-blood of a man's heart—is of the base the basest.

July 19th.—Sometimes the poignancy of my reflections on the little I have done and the little I now can do is quite distressing. My only hope is to make the minds of my blessed children rich in those good qualities of which I lament the deficiency. Was much struck with the prayer of Plato, quoted in the notes to Milton. Delighted with the morning thanksgiving and prayer of Adam and Eve, which is quite touching in its fervour and beauty. Went to afternoon church.

Read the last book of the *Excursion*. It is difficult for me to express the grateful and reverential feelings with which I think of its author. Milton elevates, thrills, awes, and delights me—but Wordsworth, " alluring to higher worlds " by their types on earth, kindles anew my expiring fervour, strengthens my hope, and reconciles me to myself. He comforts me; he makes me anxious to be virtuous, and strengthens my resolution to try to be so.

July 20th.—Made very indifferent progress with my professional study—the ease and dignified familiarity, the apparent levity of manner, with the deep purpose that lies beneath, which should be marked distinctly in the representation of Hamlet—are so difficult of execution that I almost *despair* of moderately satisfying myself. I cannot congratulate myself on having reduced the difficulty by my efforts to-day.

July 22nd.—Laboured not successfully at Hamlet. I would gladly have discontinued my task, but my little ones pull at my coat—God bless them!—and I cannot bear to add to my causes of self-reproach. Worked fairly for at least two hours.

July 24th.—Among the advertisements I observe Mathews's pictures, etc., are announced to be sold. I shall buy my own picture, which ought not to be put up to auction. Perhaps my ideas of delicacy and the dues of courtesy between men in the society of gentlemen are too rigid and punctilious; it might have been better for myself—in the very dependent calling from which my means are derived—if I had been more frequently disposed to let things take their course. Among all the men whom through my life I have known how very few high-minded men I can reckon! It is a sad and humiliating truth.

Dublin, August 8th.—Went to theatre, and acted Werner with considerable care, and I think with much earnestness and sometimes with reality; occasionally I sank into my old muscular efforts, and was cut out of the most striking opportunities for effect in the play by that very imperfect actor, Mr. Pritchard. I was very angry, but did not allow my displeasure to interfere with the performance. I thought that in a general point of view I acted *well*. I wished to ask Miss Huddart whether I betrayed any deficiency of energy, and sent up to request she would speak with me for a few minutes. She came down, and assured me that she thought I acted *well;* as I was at tea she stayed and drank tea. She spoke about Mr. Calcraft and his *liaison* with Miss H——n, observing upon the injury it had done her. She also, as every one else seems to have done, had heard of Knowles's intrigue with Miss Elphinstone, whom he brought from America. This is

242

CHARLES MATTHEWS

From an engraving

unfortunate, for his singleness and purity of heart—or the character he had for such a rare property—was one of his great holds on the public. May I be wise! Amen!

August 10th.—Went to the theatre, and acted Macbeth in parts very well, but it was an *unequal* performance—part of the murder scene, part of the banquet and the greater part of the fifth act were in my best manner; but still it wants study, polish and perfect collectedness. The "to-morrow" was better than I ever gave it. I was quite exhausted. Miss Huddart called in and sat late. This is dangerous and ill-advised. A woman's company is always soothing, but it is a perilous indulgence.

August 11th.—To my surprise Jerdan came into my room with a Colonel Dick, of New Orleans, who brought me a letter of introduction from Forster, which informed me that Wallace had fought a duel with Mackintosh [1]—a step I can but too readily believe he took to relieve the irritation and pain of mind he must lately have endured. At dinner the conversation led to the alleged cause of Lord Byron's parting with Lady Byron, and some observations were made which occasioned me disagreeable sensations; being evidently perceived, it made me quite embarrassed, and I did not in consequence recover the tone of my mind all day, uncomfortable as to the impression my want of self-possession might have caused, for which there was no actual reason. In the same way I always became embarrassed and confused before I had children, when the want of them was alluded to. I am very weak in this respect.

August 13th.—Jerdan called, and sat some time; agreed to go with Birch and self to Wicklow on Sunday; mentioned the scandal of Lady Mulgrave having broken open the desk of her lord, and sent Mrs. Norton's letters to Mr. Norton! *There!* Went to the theatre, and acted Hamlet to an audience extremely difficult to provoke to applause. I thought that I must have lacked spirit and earnestness in the first act, at which I was vexed, and took all the pains I could with the remainder of the play, but I acted under a sense of effort and a supposition of deficient sympathy in the auditors. The best passages in my mind were the affected madness with Ophelia, and the closet scene. I must not give it up. I must also study my appearance as well as my acting in it.

August 15th.—W. Birch came to breakfast, and accompanied me to Dr. Lardner's, where some friends called for him in a car, and I

[1] Not Sir James Mackintosh who died in 1832.

243

accepted their offer of a seat, W. Birch making his own way. I would
not have wished it so, but there was no remedy. The lady with whom
I sat was very agreeable; we arrived at the Pigeon House and received
much attention from some artillery officers who knew Lardner by
reputation, at least apparently. Sir J. Franklin,[1] who *looks* his
adventures and sufferings, was on the parapet where we stood; Sir
E. Blakeney [2] and others on the pier; the light was sufficiently subdued to give the colours of the hills in full beauty, and yet clear enough
to mark with the nicest precision the outline of the hills, the horizon,
the vessels, etc. The various exercises of small and great guns, mortars
and Congreve rockets were gone through by the artillery on the sands,
who performed their evolutions in the most interesting manner. I
returned with the same party, and entering with Dr. Lardner the
private garden gate of the College, was introduced to Dr. Sandys, and
got the benefit of a clothes-brush at Lardner's room. At the theatre
I found the stage still occupied by the trash of Mr. Power [3]—a person
whose unblushing defiance of truth, whose ignorance, impertinence
and mountebank effrontery make him as *disgusting* as it is possible
for any creature with the common claims of humanity to be. Rehearsed
Oakley. Afterwards Miss Huddart came to inquire about my mode
of going to the Lodge to-night, on Miss Tree's account. I instantly
offered her a seat in my carriage, observing that I did not volunteer it,
as I was uncertain how far it might be acceptable, but that I had purposed doing so at night. She accepted it. Colonel D'Aguilar called,
and in a short but interesting conversation gave me a sketch of his
life, counselled me not to let Edward purchase an "unattached," and
left me with warm professions of friendship. Tried to read Oakley.
Acted it indifferently. *I was not prepared.* Tom Moore came in very
late, and was greatly cheered; the gods would not be satisfied till
he addressed them, which he did in a very short speech. Jerdan came
into my room, and I at his request introduced him to Calcraft.
Dressed and called in carriage for Miss E. Tree; took her and her
mother to the Vice-Regal Lodge. The Lord Lieutenant [4] received us;

---

[1] Sir John Franklin (1786–1847), the celebrated Arctic explorer; he had already headed
three expeditions, involving great hardships and privations.

[2] Sir Edward Blakeney (1778–1868), a distinguished Peninsular officer, eventually
governor of Chelsea Hospital and a field-marshal.

[3] Tyrone Power (1797–1841), an Irish comedian of some note; was lost in the *President*
on a return voyage from the United States.

[4] The second Earl of Mulgrave, afterwards first Marquis of Normanby (1794–1863). He
succeeded the Earl of Haddington on the fall of Sir Robert Peel's Government. Held
various offices under Whig Administrations at home and abroad.

244

supper had been served; I sat by Mrs. Williams, opposite Major
Forster; party of from twenty-four to thirty. T. Moore, Wilkie,
Lady Campbell,[1] (Lord E. Fitzgerald's daughter) were there, and
Mrs. Forster, a piquante woman whom I had met at D'Aguilar's.
Moore sang charmingly. I heard that Mrs. Butler [2] had returned to
this country!!! Am not quite at ease in these parties.

August 16th.—To Christ Church, where I was taken to the organ
gallery—a most unenviable post of distinction—and was gratified with
the Te Deum, Jubilate and anthem (Haydn).

August 17th.—Went to the theatre, where I tried all I could and
all in vain to act Virginius well to the Lord Lieutenant, who commanded
the play. The house was very brilliant, and I did all I could, which
produced little effect. Lord Mulgrave was the great actor of the night.

August 18th.—Lardner called; was to dine with Lady Cloncurry.
This was the result of his handing her to the platform at his lecture
—upon which she said to Birch: " She supposed she must ask him *to
dinner!* " *This is the world.* Rested myself, being very tired. Went
to the theatre, and acted in a very middling manner William Tell to
a very middling house for my own Benefit—it was a bad and *angry*
performance; I was very cross and petulant. Most luckily I was not
called for, which I had much feared. Calcraft informed me that Mr.
Power, who had given him to understand that he was to dine to-day
with the Lord Lieutenant, dined with Sheridan and Captain Williams
in Sheridan's room. Lofty, Brazen, Bobabil and Bessus would be
ingredients only in Mr. Power's character!

Elstree, August 22nd.—Read and slept on until nearing Brickhill,
when my attention was attracted and distracted from my book by a
very pretty *demoiselle*, who was very communicative on all points:
giving me her name, occupation, residence, etc. It would be much
better that I should endeavour to turn my time to my mind's profit
as I might do, instead of trifling it away in idle and not altogether
harmless frivolity. Arrived at home to find all my dear family well,
for which I truly thank God.

August 23rd.—Letters from Forster, informing me that Mathews's
pictures had been bought by Mr. Durrant for the Garrick Club. In
the evening began Wordsworth's last volume of poetry, which, as far
as I have read, offers nothing comparable to his former works; if his
reputation were built upon what I have read it would scarcely rise
above a very low level indeed.

---

[1] Her mother was the mysterious "Pamela."   [2] Fanny Kemble.

To London, August 29th.—Dined, and read that unprincipled newspaper the *Times*—a disgrace to the moral feeling and the intelligence of the age! Saw Stanfield and Durrant. Mr. C. Kemble walked in and walked out again. Looked at some of the pictures of Mathews's collection purchased by the Garrick Club. Wrote a note to H. Smith. Received a volume of poems (qu.) from Mr. Wade.[1] Returned home by Bryant; read Wordsworth; read *some* good lines, but am sorry to say that the idea of *twaddle* obtrudes itself in working through some of the poems.

Elstree, August 31st.—Made out the draught of my engagement with Mr. Bunn upon the terms agreed on between us, and the list of plays accompanying it, in order that I might not be taken by surprise. Read some short poems—*Voluntaries of Evening*—by Wordsworth, which are *not* of a high order; they are often obscure, pointless and often prosaic; there are good lines in them, but that is their chief praise; they smack of senility. Mrs. Hemans's sonnet on her last Sabbath day is worth all of them.

September 2nd.—Finished the sixth book of Milton, and went over the third act of *Macbeth*. My object is to increase the power and vigour of my performance, and to subdue all tendency to exaggeration of gesture, expression and deportment, to make more simple, more chaste and yet more forcible and real the passions and characters I have to portray. After dinner indulged in rioting and disciplining in sport my children; for thus I make them companions to myself, and teach them to "know as a friend," while I can gently check any disposition to wrong which may appear in them. Then sat down to read over attentively, and endeavour to reduce into an acting form and dimensions, Talfourd's sweet tragic poem of *Ion*, which I accomplished, though it occupied more time than I anticipated. I expect to find him refractory on some points—and where some of the most poetical passages are omitted, it is difficult to persuade an author that the effect of the whole is improved; but imagery and sentiment will not supply the place of action. Forster—it occurs now to me —objects to the player's art, because it can employ its powers as successfully on mean, as on sublime, writing—it is not so to the ear and eye of taste; but were it so, in what does it suffer by comparison with music, the noblest strains of which are often wasted on the poorest language—or with painting, which gains a price as well for a *pissevache* as a Salvator Mundi! Read on in Words-

---

[1] Thomas Wade (1805-1875), poet and journalist; edited *Bell's Weekly Messenger*.

worth's volume, wherein I find nothing to reward my time and attention.

September 4th.—Read in Milton the expedition of the Messiah into Chaos to create the world. It moves one's wonder and excites a smile to hear that Wordsworth [1] can think himself fit to be named with Milton—with Milton ! ! !—to whose sublime conceptions we stretch our thoughts, and whose melodious lines we chime over in our musings like favourite tunes. I read some trash of Cibber's, and some passages of the *Careless Husband*, in which I could not discover the merit that extorts praise from Pope. Reduced still further and, I think, to the last point the tragedy of *Ion*, and marked it with ink for reference and use. Read Madame de Staël's preface to *L'Allemagne*. Could any one call a man of such little actions as Napoleon was guilty of a *great* man? Psha! Looked through a very stupid play of Goldoni's—*La Dama Prudente*—horribly dull.

September 6th.—Read the *Examiner* with much anxiety to know the fate of the Corporation Bill; it is yielded by the House of Commons. How difficult it is to subdue the impatience which would work itself into vehement expression on the monstrous spectacle which European governments generally present, viz. the many oppressed, defrauded and brutalized by the few! How long is the general ignorance of man to make him the slave of these stupid aristocrats and these priests, whose lives are a blasphemy against the pure religion of Christ, and a profanation of the worship of the Eternal and Universal God! Went to afternoon service with Letitia; thought how very little the sermon—and sermons in general—are adapted to influence men's minds, and what an instrument of good the pulpit might be made if the true worship of God, in the knowledge of His attributes and His creation, and the adoration of Him through the wonder and delight such a knowledge would induce, were industriously inculcated, instead of the unmeaning stuff which the priests call *doctrine*. Was again in the garden with the children. Finished the *Examiner*, reading the extracts from a poem called *Paracelsus* [2]—of great merit. Read prayers to the

---

Wordsworth's high opinion of his own poetry was notorious, and aroused a good deal of ridicule even among his admirers. Lamb's jest on the subject is well known.

[2] Browning's well-known poem. In her article on Macready, Lady Pollock describes his amazement at her admission that she had not read *Paracelsus:* " He lifted his eyebrows ; he muttered expressions of wonder ; he once or twice said, 'Oh, good God !' He took a turn or two up and down the room, and then said, ' I really am quite at a loss ; I cannot understand it.' I pleaded the claims of the babies, they left me little time, etc. To which he replied : ' Hand over the babies to the nurse, and read *Paracelsus*.' "—(*Macready as I knew Him,* by Juliet Lady Pollock).

family. Why, if religious observances be unimportant, should the attention to them give me, who disapprove of the unapostolic, unsatisfying mode in which they are ministered, such soothing and complacent feelings?

September 7th.—Again took up the volume of Wordsworth, with which I cannot deny I am wearied; it is to me sometimes poor, even to drivelling; lines and passages flash out from its dulness, but not in sufficient brilliancy or number to enliven the heavy labour of working through the book. His politics are in direct contradiction to the general sentiments which he would have supposed to be his principles, and manifest an arrogance and selfishness (pensioned, or beplaced as he is) that is scarcely less than disgusting. Read several of Shakspeare's sonnets, which, quaint and quibbling as most of them are, are far more interesting than Wordsworth's last. Began reading and thinking on Othello, which I fear I shall not realize in representation according to my conception.

September 8th.—Had just sat down to dinner when a loud knock came, and, in vain denying ourselves, we heard Talfourd and Forster give their names. We asked them to dine as we were dining; and adding a little to our table, we soon replaced ourselves, though with the loss of dear Nina and Willie, and dined. In the evening we discussed the whole, and read the greater part, of *Ion.* Talfourd was amusing in resisting several of the proposed cuttings as the best in the play, and that it would be better not to act the play, but he took it all in good part. His account of Wordsworth's silence about his play *disgusted* me. They left me a little after ten.

September 9th.—Practised part of Othello, to which I do not find I yet give that real pathos and terrible fury which belongs to the character. Read over attentively the whole of Melantius.[1] I do not much fancy it.

To London, September 10th.—Calling on Forster I saw a Mr. Mahoney,[2] who writes in Fraser under the name of "Father Prout"; he was, I thought, almost churlish in his manners. Dined with Forster at the club; spoke to Captain Williams about my picture, which I might as well have let alone—perhaps better, but they have used it very scurvily. Saw Beazley, Jerdan, Douglas, Blood; went to the Hay-

[1] In the *Bridal.*

[2] Francis Silvester Mahoney (1804–1866), the brilliant contributor to *Fraser's Magazine.* One of his most ingenious *tours-de-force* was a French version of C. Wolfe's *Burial of Sir John Moore*, which purported to have been written in the previous century to commemorate the death of a French general in some Indian campaign.

market; saw Beazley's five-act piece (it is called a comedy) of *Hints to Husbands*. It really has no claim to criticism—dull and commonplace sentiment, impossible situations, no character, most laboured yet most trashy language, and without exception very indifferent acting. Is this—Mr. Farren's and Mr. Wade's acting—like nature? It was very wretched, and the audience particularly vulgar.

To Knaresborough, September 13th.—Travelled to Knaresborough, and conversed a good deal with a man, rather agreeable and well informed. He had been at the (Leeds) festival, which he spoke of as quite a failure. The Duchess of Kent and Princess Victoria were the *attraction* at the concert room, where, *as in the Minster—in the house of God*—these servile idolaters of wealth and an empty name actually cheered and applauded two human beings! A clever monarch—but where is there such a monster in nature?—might soon enslave this country! " We must look *within* for that which makes us slaves! " Truly said by Talfourd.

September 15th.—Read the paper upon the consequence of the Repeal of the Corn Laws—it certainly contains some strong arguments and, I think, generally speaking, the reasoning is fair, but why does the writer keep out of sight those causes in the expense of the Government that aggravate the pain of the burden to those who labour under it, if they do not add very much to the load? Why have we such an expensive establishment? Why are our chief magistrate's bastards to be pensioned and his widow portioned in that disgustingly profligate manner? Why is not Ireland pacified, the Church reduced, the army withdrawn and disbanded? Why are our Ministers to be found in the means of giving expensive dinners? What stuff! Would Andrew Marvel have thought such banquets necessary to the conduct of state affairs, if he had been a Minister? The instruments of government are overpaid; its creatures and pensioned vermin ought to be made to disgorge what they have obtained. Look at the virtues and merits of our court and say, should the people be taxed for such *worse than nothings* in the great world of intellect and virtue?

Elstree, September 18th.—Laboured to get through the volume of Wordsworth, and made some way, but wearied with the cumbrous verbiage and disgusted with the fulsome adulation that disgrace it. It is a volume which I think Wordsworth ought to be ashamed of.

September 20th.—O'Hanlon's servant arrived, announcing the intended arrival of his master, who very soon after appeared and dined here. Our conversation in the evening was varied and interesting. He told me of his offer to give up his situation on the ejection of the Melbourne Ministry and of the former's confidence in his " discretion " as to what should be withheld from the Peel party; of his offer to Peel to relinquish his office, and of Peel's Surface-like mode of address to him; of his application for the place of Deputy Remembrancer, etc., and of the kindly expressions of the Cabinet to him; of Sheil's and O'Connell's opposition to him, which seems to me very little, especially when exerted for an insignificant person like Mr. Horsley. He seemed to think there was no doubt of Mrs. —— being Lord Melbourne's mistress. We talked of my own prospects and situation, and he frankly spoke of my *personal* unpopularity—which he attributed to various causes. I must endeavour to diminish this prejudice against me, but it is too late to do much. Was very late. Read a little of Horace in bed.

London, September 21st.—Bunn came, and the business of my plays and engagement was discussed. He said, ' The *Bridal* was a pet of mine.' I told him, ' No; that I wished to make it a means of remuneration without loading the theatre with additional salary, and I only regarded it as additional to my income.' *Ion*, he agreed, should be read by me to himself and others, and that he would then come to a judgment on its performance, without at present pledging himself to act it. *Bertulphe* he had decided on not hearing read, and I agreed to write to the author and gain his consent to give it to him. Miss Huddart he declined for the present *season*, but, as I believe, on Calcraft's representation that her terms were £10 to £12. If this be so, shame upon Calcraft! He said Mrs. Yates [1] would do one part in the *Bridal*, Ellen Tree the other—Ellen Tree also Lady Macbeth. We read over the engagement, making the time of the *Bridal* Christmas instead of the Spring, signed and interchanged it, I speaking about room and flesh-stockings. On consideration gave him *The Provost of Bruges*, reading him one passage in it.

September 22nd.—A very delightful walk down to the reservoir with my children. Returning met a poor Dutchman and his little daughter, just going to take their scanty breakfast on the roadside. Spoke to the man, and could understand little beyond " nix monnay." Gave his little child a trifle, whose little face sparkled with pleasure as she first kissed it, then came and took my hand to shake, then Nina's and then Willie's. The spontaneous and graceful manner in

---

[1] Elizabeth Yates (1799–1860), wife of Frederick Henry Yates (see note, p. 75); mostly impersonated Shakspeare's heroines in the earlier period of her career. In later years associated with the Adelphi and the Lyceum theatres. Edmund Yates, the journalist, was her son.

which her gratitude spoke was very touching, and put our own
peasantry, in the quality of warmth of heart, in no very flattering
point of contrast.

September 23rd.—Walked in the garden; after which read *Marino
Faliero*, proposed to be acted by Bunn, and *again* came to the conclusion that abounding, as it does, in beautiful poetry and noble
sentiment, it drags along from want of action and interest. Read
the *Foscari*, which seems to me capable of being made much more
dramatic—but still it is not enough.

September 25th.—Letter from Mr. Bunn, assenting to my arrangement of the *Provost of Bruges*, but reserving to himself the power of
making any alterations in my dispositions! I was at first indignant
with his stupid conceit, but soon composed myself to laugh at it and
reflect on my earlier and more imprudent days when I should have made
hostility more bitter by resenting his impertinence.

September 29th.—I returned to Macbeth. It is strange that I do
not feel myself at all *satisfied* with myself : *I cannot reach in execution
the standard of my own conception.* I cannot do it; and I am about to
enter on the season which will decide my fortune, with the drawback of
the consciousness of not being able to realize my own imaginations.

September 30th (Drury Lane).—Left my dear home to begin this
eventful season, in entering upon which I earnestly ask God's blessing
upon my efforts, and that I may receive and deserve success by my
care and industry; or, if it be the Almighty's will that I should be
rebuked by ill-fortune, I humbly and heartily pray to Him for strength
and wisdom to bear it well, and to turn it to good. Went to Haymarket and saw a few scenes of the *Steward*, in which I thought Mr.
Strickland quite as good as Mr. Farren, who very much oversteps the
modesty of nature. Read through Macbeth.

October 1st.—Went to the theatre, played ill (Macbeth), I must
presume, because ineffectively; and yet I never tried so much to play
well, and never, never was it of so much importance to me to play
well. The audience called for me—a kindness on their part—and I went on,
but when Talfourd, Forster, and Wallace came to my room, not one
had a word of comfort or congratulation. What have I omitted to
make this evening successful? I do not know, but the bitterness of my
feelings is such, with the anticipation of the newspapers to-morrow,
that if I had not ties which bind me down to this profession (and I
could curse the hour that it was suggested to me), I would eat a crust,
or eat nothing, rather than belong to it. I scarcely recollect when

my feelings have been so wrought up to a state of agonizing bitterness as to-night; I feel almost desperate.

October 2nd.—I cannot remember—it may be because the exact recollections of our sufferings cannot be preserved amid the multitude of feelings that sweep over them—but I cannot call to mind more than one evening of my whole life which brought to me more acute distress than yesterday's. The stake of my future life was upon it, for speedy profit or, perhaps, poverty, and it is lost! I cannot charge myself with neglect; I really applied to my task, and bent my mind down to it; my mistake was in not demanding an opening character, and making that one in which I could feel myself independent of the humour of the audience (which I do not accuse) or of the strangeness of the theatre. I could not touch any refreshment; I threw myself on the sofa, and lay there in a state of mind that an enemy would have pitied. In a reckless, hopeless fever of thought I went to bed, and dropped asleep with my candle on my pillow; I awoke to see the danger, which was really very great. I slept again for a short time, and awoke to pass most of the remainder of the night in an agony of despondent fretfulness and sad anticipations. Arose very little better; my bath composed my spirits a little, and the *Times* newspaper, which, though not highly laudatory, was not written in an unkind spirit, gave me back some portion of my wonted tranquillity. The other papers were very cold; I sent them with a letter to my dear Catherine.

October 3rd.—Passed an indifferent night, though better than the preceding, but my mind was still in a very depressed condition, although I made efforts to reason myself into serenity. Looked at my accounts, and thought of my resources in the event of "this blow" proving fatal to my prospects. Went to rehearsal, where I felt uneasy, and not collected on the stage during the rehearsal of *As You Like It;* I returned to chambers, and went back to finish the play. Dined and saw the papers at the Garrick Club, where I saw Fladgate, Bartley and Dunn. Read over the part of Jaques until the time of going to the theatre arrived. Acted—I know not how—so occupied was I with the care of my voice, and the performance, and withal so nervous was I that I cannot guess at the real effect—whether good or ill—that I produced. Came home in a light cab, and reached Elm Place—my blessed home—about half-past eleven. There was all the misery to talk over—and though I was happier, I could not be happy in seeing the dejection of my wife, and my sister's tears. Looked at my blessed children, and drew comfort and encouragement from their dear sight."

252

Elstree, October 4th.—Again passed a very wakeful night, though in my own dear, dear home; my thoughts and forebodings will not yield to any power of reasoning or consolation. I fancy that the deficiency of my performance was a want of spirit, animation and earnestness; and it is a cruel reflection to think on the mischief I have done myself. Heard Catherine read part of the *Examiner* critique, which was most kind—perhaps too kind, but my spirits remain the same. Glanced over the newspaper; saw my blessed children and gave them books, etc. Walked for some time round the garden with Catherine, receiving much benefit from the cool fresh air, and talking over my plans, in case this untoward event should bear with it all the disaster I seem in my concern to apprehend. But for my children—my blessed children—I should be quite indifferent to it. Wrote accounts, arrears, etc. Practised and read Macbeth, and thought I discovered the cause of my failure. Will try to play better—but I cannot recover the false step I have made.

London, October 5th.—I called on Wallace, and was *comforted* in learning that I had acted Jaques very well. Came to chambers in cab, and found a very civil note from Mr. Chester, and one, with his everlastingly unburied play, from Mr. Heraud. *Literary Gazette* dismisses me with kind civility. I am satisfied and thankful. Forster called, to whom I gave orders for to-night and Wednesday. Put by my clothes, etc. Read two scenes of Hamlet. Called at theatre and saw Bunn, who asked me about Morton's play, which I declined—spoke to him about orders. Note from Haynes Bayly [1] about his right of admission; and newspaper from Dyer. Dined and saw newspapers at Garrick Club—another lie of that *scoundrel, Hook*, in the *John Bull*—the *disgusting villain!* Went to theatre, and in acting Macbeth felt that I carried my audience along with me. I was earnest, majestic, and impassioned. The applause was enthusiastic, and I was obliged to go on at the close of the play. I redeemed myself, and most grateful do I feel in saying "Thank God." Talfourd came into my room, and said he had "never seen me finer, if indeed I had ever played it so well." Wallace asked 'Why the d—l didn't I play it so on Thursday?' Tried on dress for Hamlet.

October 7th.—Went to rehearsal, and was agitated by wrathful and indignant feelings at the impertinence of Mr. Farren and Mrs. Faucit—who honoured me by a *cut*. It occurred to me that it was in consequence of Mrs. Faucit being cast a bad part in the new tragedy,

---

[1] Thomas Haynes Bayly (1797–1839), verse-writer, novelist and playwright. Author of " She wore a Wreath of Roses."

253

with which I had nothing to do. I reasoned myself into calmness, but it disturbed my early rehearsal; though in other respects it was of service, as it induced me to speak the satirical speeches with a point and truth which showed me the way to make them effective! After dining, lay down to sleep and think over Hamlet as much as I could. My mind fluctuated much between apprehension, hope, and resolution to do all I could. I sometimes thought I would suppose it a first night, and labour as for life. Acted Hamlet, to judge by the continued interest and the uniform success of all the striking passages, better than I ever played it before. Forster and Wallace came into my room; the former thought it, as a whole, the best he had ever seen; Wallace told me afterwards that he would have been "satisfied with less effect." Farren came in—in consequence of my having (in order to remove the supposed impression of my interference with the cast of the new play) spoken to Mrs. Faucit in the morning and, with great civility to her, noticed the "impertinence" of Mr. Farren. He came in to explain the reasons of his behaviour, which resolved themselves into *imagined* slights, and so we "shook hands and parted." 'Tis the best way to part with all mankind.

October 8th.—Catherine arrived with dear Nina before I went to rehearsal, and I was soon obliged to leave them. Went to the theatre, where I rehearsed Hotspur well, settled my dress (such as it was to be!) and sent over to the Garrick Club to see what the Press said of me last night. It is not unreasonable to ask, *what should I expect from the Press?* The *Times* was, of course, silent because I acted well, the *Herald* the same. The *Chronicle* had a *twaddling* article, which *meant nothing*, and the *Post* was indiscriminately and boldly abusive! I certainly felt disgust and indignation, but I had the consciousness of having *really deserved well* to fall back upon, and I did not suffer it long to disturb me. Mr. Cooper said he had not seen the play of *Hamlet* "*go off* in such a way for years"—it was expected in the theatre that it would have been underlined for repetition. Coming from rehearsal I met Forster—to whom I told the news of the Press—his observation was that it was of no consequence; it *is* of consequence—the consequence of *doubling* and of *aggravating* my labour and diminishing my reward. I had spoken to Bunn about releasing me from Saturday, and after a long endeavour he would not. Acted Hotspur very ill—was wearied and over-borne by work and excitement. Talfourd and Forster came round. Forster left us, and we went together to sup at the Garrick Club, where Forster was supping with young Kean, who very distantly returned my salute. I left late and Talfourd walked home with me.

October 10*th.*—Went to theatre, received the *Court Journal*, with a very kind and pleasing note from Mr. Blanchard. These are the few recompensing events which soothe the mind amidst the bitterness of its sufferings from the persecution of malignant ignorance. Acted Leontes—not to my own satisfaction. I was not clear in the words, and abroad in my performance. How manifestly is this, which is so sneered at by the ignorant, proved to be an art by those who really cultivate it! Forster came round to ask me if I shook hands with the players in Hamlet, which I did, and which, it seems, he has accused me of not doing. I was amused.

October 12*th.*—Went to Garrick Club, dined and saw papers. The *Post* has changed its tone to the *highest pitch of panegyric!* The *Herald* is also eulogistic. Went to the theatre, and acted Macbeth before Her Majesty [1] and a full house. The audience did not come solely and purposely to see *Macbeth,* and the labour to keep their attention fixed was extreme. Wallace came round and said I acted very well; I tried to do so, but am not confident of my success. Talfourd and Forster came to my room. Bunn told me he must do *Othello* on Thursday. I said "*I* could not." He "must." I "would not." He sent me up a note to know which I would do, Othello or Iago, on Thursday. I returned for answer, Iago, and would not do Othello at all. He then sent Cooper to me, to whom I said the same, and in answer to his inquiry said, "I would not do Othello under a week's notice." He left me without fixing anything. I was very much fatigued. Talfourd suggested the propriety of ascertaining the intentions of the management, and I waited for Cooper; while speaking to him Bunn came up, and wished me to go into the room and talk it over. He was as civil as a dog, the dragooning attempt had failed; and after some conversation *Othello* was fixed for Wednesday week, and *The Provoked Husband* for Thursday next.

October 13*th.*—Opened newspapers; the *Post* was the only one that had a lengthened criticism, and stated that my performance of Macbeth had " created quite a sensation."

October 14*th.*—Went to the Garrick Club; met Forster there and Meadows; saw Mr. C. Kean, who made a very formal bow to me. This young man appears very conceited, and surely not amiable in any part of his conduct that has come under my cognizance.

[1] Queen Adelaide.

He *owes* me civility. Read the newspapers, which do not seem to promise much success to the adapted play of last night—*Old Mortality.* Went to Lewis's,[1] the artist, where I was introduced to him and saw some very clever water-colour copies of Murillo, Velasquez, Veronese, etc., Spanish costumes, views of the Alhambra, and a series of subjects from the Bull Fight. Was much gratified. Returning to Garrick Club, Forster insisted on giving me the views of the Alhambra, which he is to have. I resisted strongly, but vainly.

October 15th.—After rehearsal went to Garrick Club, where Captain Williams, Fladgate and Mr. T. Hook were in the room—the latter saluted me, and advanced with one finger ; I met him with one finger and he perceived that I was not disposed to acknowledge his title to be impertinent, for he soon after took Captain Williams upstairs. He is an object of disgust—morally and physically—a puffed-out mountebank. Went to theatre, and acted Lord Townley in a very mediocre manner, occasionally with spirit, but with an utter absence of finish and high deportment. Spoke to Cooper on hearing of its intended repetition on Saturday, and told him that I could not do Othello on Wednesday if my time were thus taken from me.

October 16th.—Note from Forster for orders, enclosing the *Morning Herald's* criticism on my Lord Townley, which *very justly* objected to my want of ease and formality. I cannot contradict or question the fairness of the remark. Was introduced by Bunn to Mr. Joseph Parkes,[2] whom I had long wished to know. Went to theatre and acted Hamlet, not as I did the last time—I felt then the inspiration of the part ; to-night I felt as if I had a load upon my shoulders. The actors said I played well. The audience called for me and made me go forward. Wallace, Forster, and H. Smith, who came into my room, all thought I played well—but I did not. I was not satisfied with myself—there was effort, and very little free flow of passion. I *fear* the papers may notice me to-morrow ! Mr. Bunn came into my room, and spoke to me about *Othello* for Wednesday. I refused ; he wished to see me in his room, and there I was witness to a great deal of gross and blackguard conversation ; was very quiet, and left without any settlement.

October 17th.—A note was brought me from Mr. L——, formerly

---

[1] John Frederick Lewis (1805–1876), the well-known R.A.

[2] Joseph Parkes (1796–1865), solicitor and politician ; prominent as an agitator for reform, to carry which, after the rejection of the Bill he had made preparations to resort, if necessary, to an armed revolt.

Ensign 30th Regiment, who dined at the Mess at Gosport; his wife was the bearer. It was a solicitation for *charity*. His wife and his letter described him as having sold his wardrobe to that extent that he had not the means of appearing, that she was a chorus singer at the Opera House, and he was soliciting Colonel Rowan [1] for employment in the police! I recollect him a handsome, *foolish*, extravagant young man at table at Gosport, drinking champagne to excess. How many of the same regiment have been reduced to a similar condition. This does not say much for the beneficial tendency of our military establishment. Dined and saw newspapers at the Garrick Club—none of them notice me. Blanchard accosted me at the door, and talked some time with me; he was pleased with the note I sent him; I feel very grateful to him. In the Club saw Planché, who related to me the circumstance of a very beautiful girl being enwrapt and violently agitated with the play last night, so as to attract observation. It is pleasing to hear this. Saw Knowles, wild as the wind.

October 18*th.*—Was very much fatigued and annoyed by yielding up my mind to a train of imaginations, depressing and sicklying over my mind to a very painful degree—dreams of ill, of annoyance and strife that made me ashamed of my own absurdity, when I awoke myself from them.

October 19*th.*—Knowles called, and descanted on the merits of Miss Elphinstone; [2] asked me for orders, seemed nettled at Talfourd's classing him with the other authors in his preface, and yielded praise with manifest reluctance and coldness to *Ion*. *This is not just, nor generous*, nor grateful, for Talfourd has written most and best in his praise of any critic. Acted Macbeth, I think, well; perhaps not so careful in the preservation of my deportment as I should have been, but with more *abandon* than heretofore.

October 20*th.*—Forster called; we talked about the knavery of Mr. C. Kemble, and many other things; he walked with me to the Garrick Club, where I dined and saw newspapers. After sitting some time in the library, I came down and talked for a few minutes with Price, Fladgate and Theodore Hook! The papers were all favourable to Covent Garden, the company, and Mr. C. Kemble in Hamlet. So will they not be to me!!—*mais, Monsieur !*

---

[1] Colonel, afterwards Sir Charles Rowan, K.C.B. (1762-1852); served in the Peninsula and at Waterloo. The first holder of the Chief Commissionership of Police after the establishment of the new force by Peel when Home Secretary.

[2] An actress of no note, with whom Knowles had formed a *liaison*.

October 21st.—Went to the theatre, and felt very nervous and unsettled; reasoned with myself, and partially recovered my self-possession; but, in truth, was hurried out in the part of Othello, and was not perfectly possessed of it. The criticism I passed on Malibran's Fidelio will exactly suit my own Othello—it was "elaborate, but not abandoned." In the early scenes I was abroad, making effort, but not feeling my audience; in the jealous scenes I had attention, and certainly had no reason to be discontented by the degree of intelligence, skill, or effort shown by Iago; [1] but the audience seemed to wait for Kean's points, and this rather threw me off my balance. In the soliloquy after Iago's exit I in some degree asserted myself, and though not up to my own expectations in the "Farewell," etc., yet, in the grand burst, I carried the house with me. From that point I should say the performance averaged good, but was not in any, except that one outbreak, great. *The newspapers will, of course, annoy me. They will!* Dow and Forster came into my room—rather satisfied; Wallace, on whom I can better depend, not so much so. *He is my barometer.* I was obliged to go on before the audience, which, as Mr. Vandenhoff was also called for, I had rather not have done.

October 22nd.—After a restless night (which indisposition of body as well as an uncomfortable state of mind tended to make long and unrefreshing) I rose with very uneasy anticipations of the newspapers' report of my Othello. I came at last to the resolution not to see them. Wrote a note to Wallace, excusing myself from sending the orders for to-night. Forster sent me the notice of the *Times,* which, for the *Times,* was highly favourable. It set my mind at peace instantly—as much from the value it set on Mr. Vandenhoff's performance, as for the praise it gave to mine. This man has intrigued and caballed much with country newspapers, and through his instrumentality I have been systematically abused at Liverpool, Edinburgh, etc. He has puffed himself and stuffed some few of his listeners with the notion that I had usurped his place. He had the opportunity of showing his talent last night; he did show it—a poorer, more unmeaning, slouching, ungainly, mindless, unimaginative performance I have never witnessed in any person making pretensions to high rank. He is a man of a very poor, very little, and very vulgar mind. Called on Forster, saw the *Post,* badly written, but highly encomiastic. Truly grateful am I for the impression which my performance seems

[1] Vandenhoff was Iago, Cooper was Cassio, and Harley, Roderigo; Mrs. Yates was the Desdemona, and Miss E. Tree the Emilia (*note by Sir F. Pollock*).

to have made. Went to rehearse the Queen's and Polonius' scenes;
thence to Garrick Club, where I saw a very ridiculous article trying
to make out C. Kemble's Macbeth (a notorious failure) [1] superior to
my own; it is merely proving, if anything be proved, that both are
execrable. Saw Captain Williams, Mrs. W——, etc. Coming to
chambers, wrote to Catherine, enclosing the *Times* criticism. William
Birch called. Read Hamlet, though much oppressed. Recovered my
spirits in going to the theatre, and resolved to do my best in Hamlet,
which I played really well—the play-scene and closet and death better,
I think, than I have yet done. Forster came round and spoke of Mr.
Jones and C. Kemble in Hamlet. I requested him not to speak
harshly of the former, knowing he would not of the latter. He walked
home with me. My cold very bad. Cooper came to ask me when I
should be ready with the new play. I answered I did not know until
I had read and considered it. I fancy they have arrested Bunn, as he
never shows himself *to me!*

October 23rd.—Felt so unwell that I could not come to any resolution as to acting or being excused; tried to nurse myself, and hoped
each hour would find me better, but no; at twelve I sent for Forster,
who thought I ought not to risk Othello if I did not feel equal to it.
This decided me, and I wished to write a note, but he seemed anxious
to bear the communication, and I did not refuse him. He returned at
two, to say that Bunn was a most atrocious beast, and that he had
behaved most cavalierly to him. This he might have expected on such
a message, if he had known the man; but Cooper was to call presently.
Cooper did call, and after much conversation they both agreed that
it would be better I should make the effort at all risks, as Bunn might
seek to do me some mischief. Cooper offered to make an apology for
me, which I declined—I did not fully coincide with their reasonings,
but felt myself so much better that I yielded. A letter from Powell
& Son with the agreement for the purchase of the Granby [2] for £4900.
I hope it is for the best, though it is a great sacrifice. Dow called
and stayed a short time. Sent to inquire after Mrs. Talfourd, who
I was glad to learn was doing well. Received a very kind and enthusiastic note from Mr. Dyer.[3] Answered it very hastily. Went to
theatre and had a short conversation on very good terms with Bunn.
Acted Othello. I am puzzled to say how, for both Dow and Forster,

---

[1] C. Kemble, though excelling in comedy, was not successful as a tragedian.
[2] The Harrogate hotel in which he had invested.
[3] Presumably George Dyer (1755–1841); poet and essayist, a friend of Charles Lamb.

who came into my room afterwards, seemed to think me not so good as on Wednesday night, and in many particulars I thought myself better. The reception which the audience gave me was very marked to-night, and in the presence of Mr. Vandenhoff must and did show him that they considered we stood at a wide distance. He was visibly agitated with—must I not say from this man's previous low and illiberal behaviour—envy? My thanks to God are due and fervently offered.

October 27th.—Still sensations of cold and lassitude upon me; read in the *Times* a notice on Mr. C. Kemble's Macbeth, which was enough to make a whole man sick. This very performance Talfourd last night came away from in disgust, and Hayward, who does not know much on the subject, observed : " This does not seem very good, what do you think of it ? " But of what use is art, or labour to acquire it, or cultivation of mind to elevate it, when our public will crowd at half-price to see an impudent mountebank, and a ranting, mindless, periwig-pated fellow "tearing a passion to tatters "; they make no choice between the filthy garbage and the celestial bed, except as to the price !

October 28th.—Lay down to think over Othello ; was particularly desirous of acting it well, on account of its own importance, and because I wished Catherine to be pleased with it. Went to theatre, where I strove to act with all the spirit and energy that I could command. Found the audience one which, in their anxiety to prevent interruption, suppressed much of the applause, which rather chilled and perplexed me ; still I strove and I think succeeded in performing the *whole character* better—more grandly, deeply, and nobly—than I have yet done.

Elstree, October 29th.—Lay very late, thinking over the play of last night (Othello), and revolving in my mind the slow and comparatively unprofitable advance of my reputation ; the danger it runs from the appearance of every new aspirant, and the reluctant admissions that are made to it. Walked in the garden, and inhaled, with grateful and tranquil pleasure, the pure air of the country. Began to think of Richard III.

London, October 31st.—Went to Garrick Club, where I saw the papers, and the new magazines, in which was nothing to interest me ; several of the performers were there and I learned that the success of the new Opera had been very great, and that Othello was removed from the play-bills. It is as impolitic to take it down from that night, being put up, as it was to announce it; but this fellow, Bunn, was, is, and will be a beast to the last days of his disgusting existence.

November 2nd.—Went to town, was just in time for the rehearsal of the *Provost of Bruges*, to which I went. My hopes were not raised by the nearer glimpse of it which this first rehearsal gave me. I agreed to take the book home and mark the sides ready for the next rehearsal. Mr. Yates [1] wished to speak to me before I left the theatre; I went to his room after the play was finished. I soon perceived which way the conversation was pointing. It appeared from his showing that Mr. Bunn had no funds to carry on the concern if it failed, and that the proprietors, to meet the effect of the Covent Garden reduced prices, had agreed to let one-third of the rent stand over till Christmas if the actors would do the same with their salaries; and to me, in the first instance, the proposal was made. I mentioned to him Mr. Bunn's behaviour to me in Ireland, and subsequently about my week's salary here, which latter he explained to me was Captain Polhill's debt; but, what I did not then think of, it was *Mr. Bunn's contesting it* that prevented its payment. I would give no answer. He said that I was underpaid in proportion to the other salaries. I said I knew that, but did not murmur at it; I would think of his proposal, and see him on Wednesday. I saw Mr. Bunn about *Ion*, on which I could get no distinct answer except that he '*would do whatever I might say.*' How changed from his late conversation, and yet it *means nothing,* except that it may be evaded.

November 4th.—Went to Garrick Club—saw Jerdan, Forster— congratulated Maclise on being made an *Associate;* [2] saw Fitzgerald's last notice of my Othello in *Morning Post,* very complimentary.

November 5th.—Went to dine with Fitzgerald. Hope, the Cattermoles, and Forster dined there. Hayward, N. P. Willis [3] and bride, and some other unknowns came in the evening. The day was to me cheerful and pleasant, but I was an instance of the bad effect, which Bulwer judiciously observes in *Pelham,* of holding an argument in mixed society. I liked my host and hostess very much, and the guests. I felt much amused, and indeed gratified. Mrs. F—— sang some very sweet and touching songs, the words by her husband, the music by

---

[1] Acting-manager at Drury Lane (*note by Sir F. Pollock*).

[2] Of the Royal Academy; he was elected an Academician five years later.

[3] N. P. Willis would hardly have been flattered at being grouped with "unknowns." He was an obtrusive American, who, thanks to introductions and his own assurance, edged himself into London Society, of which he published his impressions, characterized by inaccuracy and bad taste.

herself. It was strange that as I gazed on her, receiving and imparting pleasure, my imagination presented me her form in death—the hands actively pressing music from the instrument, stark and cold, and the lips rigid and pale, that now poured forth such touching sounds. Hayward introduced me to Willis, with whom I chatted of America. Note from Talfourd, who "assumes that *Ion* is to be acted."

November 20th.—Called on Forster, and stayed some time listening to a tale of wretched abandonment to passion that surprised and depressed me. He told me that he had been on the point of marriage with Miss L——, but that rumours and stories pressed in such number and frightful quality upon him that he was forced to demand explanation from one of the reported narrators or circulators, Mr. A. A. Watts [1]—that his denial was positive and circumstantial, but that it was arranged between themselves and their mutual friends that the marriage should be broken off. A short time after Forster discovered that Miss L—— made an abrupt and passionate declaration of love to Maclise, and on a subsequent occasion repeated it! It has lately come to light that she has been carrying on an intrigue with Dr. Maginn,[2] a person whom I never saw, but whom all accounts unite in describing as a beastly biped; he is married and has four children. Two letters of hers and one of his were found by Mrs. Maginn in his portrait, filled with the most puerile and nauseating terms of endearment and declarations of attachment! I felt quite concerned that a woman of such splendid genius and such agreeable manners should be so depraved in taste and so lost to a sense of what was due to her high reputation. She is fallen! Drove to Drury Lane Theatre, and just reached it before the half-price came in. The house was crowded and I was obliged to go to the third circle for a seat. I was obliged to sit through some scenes of the Opera and witness the *disgusting antics* of Mr. H. Phillips.[3] *The Jewess* is the most gorgeous pageant I have ever seen on an English stage—beyond all reach of comparison. The acting was up to the spectacle mark of old times, when I have seen Terry, Wallack, etc. It did not, I think, go beyond—for instance, I do not think Mr. Vandenhoff in the Jew better than Mr. Wallack in the *Rent Day*, or than Terry the first

---

[1] Alaric Alexander Watts (1797–1864) ; journalist, verse-writer, and essayist.

[2] William Maginn (1793–1842), the well-known journalist ; one of the principal contributors to *Fraser's Magazine*. Supposed to be the original of "Captain Shandon" in Thackeray's *Pendennis*.

[3] See note, p. 135.

night of the *Broken Sword*. He was artificial, coarse, and I should say melodramatic; his best scene was his death, but there was no touch of art to elevate the situation; it wanted *heart, soul,* and *mind.* It was good of *its* kind. Ellen Tree disappointed me. Wrote to Catherine.

November 21st.—Rising, I felt the peculiarity of my situation as regards my profession—quite interdicted from its exercise during the greater part, if not the entire, of the season, and all the hopes of profit from new characters, upon the strength of which I made this engagement, utterly falsified. There seems a destiny which constantly prevents me from reaching that happy point of success which will give recompense to my labour. Like the Hebrew liberator, I see the promised land, but am not permitted to possess it. I do not on that account complain of my fate, or lose my energies in despondency. On the contrary, I resolve that I will not yield to this untoward pressure of circumstances. I will diligently persevere in my work of improvement, and endeavour to turn my leisure to rich account, "waiting the event of time," and thankful for what I enjoy. Went to Garrick Club, where I saw newspapers—the letter of that wretched, impotent apostate, Sir F. Burdett,[1] on that dangerous, licentious, turbulent, ill-conditioned man, O'Connell's expulsion from Brooks' Club. Is this his patriotism, to incense a man who with the fury of the tiger has a mammoth-like power in his own country? It is an insult, not any serious injury. Find that my prediction of young C. Mathews turning player is verified already.

November 25th.—Going out called to inquire of Forster about the orders I had given to Cattermole; he walked with me to the Quadrant, talking of the theatre, and seemingly urging me to take up the gauntlet for *the Art.* Were I independent I would make an effort; as it is, my family bind my hands, and it is happier for me that it is so. The temporary indignation that is excited by successful

---

[1] Sir Francis Burdett (1770-1844), who for the greater part of his life had been or affected to be a democrat, had now executed a complete *volte-face*, which he signalized by entering Parliament in 1837 as an avowed Tory. In his new character he made frequent attacks on his former allies the Whigs, a pastime which on one occasion provoked a crushing retort from Lord John Russell. Commenting on an appeal to patriotism made by Lord John in the course of a speech in the House, Sir Francis declared that there was nothing in politics so contemptible as "the cant of patriotism." "I beg to differ from the honourable baronet," Lord John retorted in his iciest manner, "I can tell him of something even more contemptible, and that is the *re-cant* of patriotism !"—a home-thrust which Burdett was powerless to parry.

scoundrelism urges one to wish and even to move towards defeating it—but *who are your adversaries ! What is your reward ?—I will none of it.* Forster told me of an attack, a personal one as well as professional, made on me in that ribald paper, the *Age;* it is impotent, and such I feel it to be; my answer will be made through the Irish Insolvent Court to the writer, Mr. Bunn. I cannot personally soil myself with either of the filthy persons, Westmacott or Bunn, concerned in it. Called on A. Watts, and found Mrs. W——. He afterwards came in. He is manifestly, I think, a low person. I know not why, but I feel in his manner the absence of anything lofty or generous in his mind. Dined and saw newspapers at Garrick Club; wrote note of invitation to Jerdan. Saw an American paper, in which was an attack on Knowles for his intimacy with Miss Elphinstone; the paper is a puritanical one, but must be, if widely circulated, injurious to him. Saw Fladgate, White, Cattermole, T. Hill, Stanfield, Forster and Dowling, who sat with me for nearly two hours after dinner. Went to the Lyceum theatre; saw in the company present the effect of reduced prices! The performances were middling; not so bad as those of Covent Garden.

November 26th.—Read a review, and some beautiful and touching extracts from a dramatic poem called *Paracelsus* by Robert Browning.[1]

November 27th.—Went from chambers to dine with Rev. William Fox, Bayswater. Met with him Mr. Home, author of *Cosmo*, Miss Flower, who lives in the house with Mr. Fox and a little girl, his daughter. I like Mr. Fox very much; he is an original and profound thinker, and most eloquent and ingenious in supporting the penetrating views he takes. Mr. Robert Browning, the author of *Paracelsus*, came in after dinner; I was very much pleased to meet him. His face is full of intelligence. My time passed most agreeably. Mr. Fox's defence of the suggestion that Lady Macbeth should be a woman of delicate and fragile frame pleased me very much, though he opposed me, and of course triumphantly. I took Mr. Browning on, and requested to be allowed to improve my acquaintance with him. He expressed himself warmly, as gratified by the proposal; wished to send me his book; we exchanged cards and parted.

November 28th.—Proceeded to the Garrick Club, where I saw Meadows, Fladgate, Theodore Hook; read the newspapers; heard the

---

[1] Browning was then only twenty-three. *Paracelsus* was the first work of his that brought him into notice, if not with the general public at all events with the *élite* of the literary world.

lamentations for Hatfield House and the old Dowager of Salisbury.[1] There are poor enough to engross my pity till these dwellers in palaces can learn to feel for the inmates of the hovels round them.

December 3rd.—Wrote a note to Mr. Bunn with notice of the *Bridal*, and a contemptuous allusion to his abuse of me in the *Age*. On reflection, feeling that it was debasing myself to bestow even a word of scorn upon the injuries of such a wretch, and yet not liking to address him in terms of civility without an intimation that I only used the terms of civility conventionally, I thought it better to address the letter to Yates, as I am not to know (indeed I do not) that Mr. Bunn is not still at Brighton.

December 5th.—Called on Archdeacon Pott,[2] saw him, Miss Frye, Miss Caroline Pott, found them all very old, in all other respects the same. Called on Mr. Buller ;[3] saw and sat some time with Mrs. Buller, the Cornelia of the day. Politics was the only subject that passed off our tête-à-tête. Left a card at Horace Twiss's.

Elstree, December 7th.—Read *Paracelsus*, a work of great daring, starred with poetry of thought, feeling and diction, but occasionally obscure ; the writer can scarcely fail to be a leading spirit of his time.

December 8th.—Finished *Paracelsus*. I am obliged to confess that the main design of the poem is not made out with sufficient clearness, and obscurity is a fault in many passages, but there is a most subtle and penetrating search into the feelings and impulses of our nature, some exquisite points of character, the profoundest and the grandest thoughts and most musically uttered. The writer is one whom I think destined for very great things. My children were with me, extracting stories from me and amusing me in return. Looked over *Marino Faliero*, which (I again express my decided conviction) cannot be successful to any good purpose. I want to find something to do— something to mend my fortunes and secure my blessed wife and

---

[1] Widow of the first Marquis of Salisbury ; noteworthy as a leader of society, and Tory *grande dame*. She was burned to death in a fire which originated in her bedroom, and did great damage to Hatfield House.

[2] Joseph Holden Pott (1759-1847), Archdeacon of London, 1813-1842 ; he officiated at Macready's marriage.

[3] The father of Charles Buller and his brother Arthur, who was also regarded as a young man of much promise ; hence Mrs. Buller's appellation of Cornelia. Arthur Buller, however, hardly fulfilled the predictions of his friends, his achievements being limited to a Ceylon judgeship (which procured him a knighthood), and, on his retirement, a seat in Parliament, where he made no mark. He was the father of one of the best-looking and most brilliant athletes of his day, Charles Francis Buller, a school Crichton and regimental idol in the Sixties, the sunset of whose life, however, was in a sad contrast to its dawn.

children in competence when I am gone, and I have nothing more to ask of Providence.

December 14th.—I was amused by the superstition of our servants. The cook observed that she turned the beds every day except Friday, then she only shook them; and Phillips hoped the pig would not be killed on Wednesday, as the fulling of the moon was not good for the bacon.

London, December 16th.—Went to Mr. Buller's—passed an unpleasant day—did not feel myself at home; my spirits were sunk still more by the accident of the coach-window falling out, and my expectation of a summons every moment from the coachman to dispute with me the payment of it. It was a very long time before I recovered my composure and presence of mind, and then I thought the persons not cordial, nor in sympathy with me—rather supercilious and reserved —I was decidedly *unsuccessful.* There were present the three Messrs. Buller, Romilly,[1] Leader, Courtenay,[2] Austin,[3] the most agreeable of the guests, Miss Austin; and in the evening Hayward and a very pretty girl, who sang well. I promised to talk with Mr. C. Buller on the management of the voice; walked home with Hayward, whose scandal and compassion for his friends' follies and vices, and whose incredulity upon the enormities he related, as said of them, amused me very much. Among other lamentations of Hayward was a very particular one on my account, viz. that my friend Greaves was black-balled! What an advantage is such a d——d good-natured friend! I should not have known this but for him!

December 17th.—Went to Garrick Club, where I inquired of Winston if my friend Greaves was black-balled. He told me that to the surprise and regret of almost all present such was the fact, and so unexpected was it that they put the beans into the ballot-box again— each time there was one black ball. It was Colonel Fitzroy Stanhope. I spoke to Durrant—who was very urgent with me to put up Greaves again, but this I declined—and to Fladgate too plainly, and too much at length upon the subject. Had a long conversation afterwards with H. Reynolds on the expediency of having strangers allowed to dine with private parties.

[1] Presumably John Romilly (1802–1874), afterwards successively Sir John and first Lord Romilly ; Master of the Rolls, 1851–1873.

[2] Probably William Reginald Courtenay (1807–1888), afterwards eleventh Earl of Devon and President of the Poor Law Board in Lord Derby's and Disraeli's Administrations 1867–1868.

[3] Either John Austin the jurist (1790–1859), or Charles Austin (1799–1874) the eminent Parliamentary counsel, with whom Disraeli, some years later, had a rancorous encounter, resulting in his (Disraeli's) apologetic appearance before a posse of High Court judges.

December 28th.—Wrote note to Mr. Farren, making an appointment with him for Saturday next, from which I look for no further result than the certification of the inutility of occupying my mind further with abortive schemes of regenerating the stage. To be assured is one step towards effecting something, even if not all we wish. Received letters from Greaves, expressing in the mildest and most gentlemanly strain his regret at the vexation which his rejection from the Garrick Club had occasioned me, but taking his own share of the disappointment (which to him is an inconvenience) most tranquilly and contentedly.

December 31st.—Frederick Reynolds arrived a little after four o'clock. Busied myself with "house affairs." Our other guests were Miss Kenney, Forster, Cattermole, Browning and Mr. Munro. Mr. Browning was very popular with the whole party; his simple and enthusiastic manner engaged attention and won opinions from all present; he looks and speaks more like a youthful poet than any man I ever saw. We poured out a libation as a farewell to the old year and a welcome to the new. The year is gone, and with it much of happiness, of care and fear; I am so much older, and lament to say not much better, not much wiser. Let me offer up prayer to God Almighty, who thus far has protected me and mine, to continue His gracious blessings on the dear heads of my beloved family, and to grant me health and energy to make them worthy disciples of Jesus Christ, and happy denizens of this our mortal state. Amen.

Elstree, January 1st.—Our visitors, except Frederick Reynolds, left us. I wished to detain Mr. Browning, but had no opportunity; spoke to Kenney about withdrawing my name from the Athenæum, which he requested me not to do. We parted in uncertainty on the subject.

January 9th.—Mr. Maton became my companion at Edgware, and transferred my attention from the written page to that of mind in the example he presented me. He was gratifying himself by telling me of his intimacy (?) with Kemble;[1] that he was a great scholar, a fine Grecian ("Upon my soul, a lie!"), replete with anecdote, and a first-rate mimic!!! I listened to all, and much more with great complacency. Called on Maclise, who had sketched in the subject of the picture of Macbeth. I did not like it as a whole; the subject was cut in two; the group of witches was admirably imagined and in itself a picture—the figure of Macbeth was superfluous. He has not poetry enough to grasp at my idea, nor I art enough to be sanguine about his. After much discussion I yielded to his genius, which ought to have its unbridled course. Sat, and to work he went.

London, January 11th.—Sat for nearly two hours to Maclise. I have little doubt but that as far as the mechanical part of the picture is concerned it will be good, but it will not be what I wished it. Called at the Garrick Club, where I saw the newspapers! Fladgate and Price urged me importunately to read the postscript of the *Age;* it was so brutal, so bestial, so vilely blackguard (a calumnious invective against the Americans on the late dreadful accident at New York) that I can only wish Messrs. Westmacott and Bunn would more frequently develop their precise characters by such loathsome manifestations. Inquired of Bartley, etc., about Miss H. Faucit's success; learned that it was good, but not first-rate. Went with Dow to Covent Garden, saw Miss H. Faucit in the *Hunchback*—thought she had force and some intelligence, but no elegance, little real abandonment and little true pathos—occasionally violent, flurried *larmoyante* and almost always *stagey;* Kemble[2] looked like an old and faithful footman—his shoulders bend-

[1] Presumably John Philip Kemble.   [2] Charles Kemble.

ing under long service, nor did his gestures, attitudes or intonations betray the slightest variance with his air and aspect. Mr. Bennett was really offensive; the whole play was bad—*provincial.*

Bristol, January 18th.—Went to rehearsal at eleven o'clock; was kept waiting for some time; found things in a decent state, but the Lady Macbeth bad beyond all former out-doings—detestable! Heard of Mr. Woulds' ill success, and his reflections upon the public from the stage in consequence! Mr. Denvil, who was my Macduff with a pair of well-grown moustaches, told me of his having pitched Mr. Elliot, a pantomimist, from a height of eighteen feet, in which the pitched Elliot gloried to that degree that he even suffered pain from the surmise that some of the audience might suppose it was a *dummy* that was thrown! Now, what is ambition in the pleasure its success conveys? Was the Duke of Wellington more inwardly gratified after a victory than this man would be if three or four rounds of applause were to follow him into the black hole into which Mr. Denvil or any other person might pitch him? *Gloria mundi!* Proceeded to the theatre. The house was very fair, and I tried to act with the millstone of Lady Macbeth round my neck. Oh!—Muses! I acted Macbeth very unequally—some parts I thought I did very well; the scene before the banquet and the melancholy of the fifth act particularly. I should, however, say that it was not sustained.

January 19th.—Acted Hamlet. Oh, how unlike my London performances! The best thing in the play was the grave scene; I played it well, the rest was effort and not good. Still worse, I was morose and ill-tempered. Fie! fie! shall I never outlive my folly and my vice? I fear not.

January 21st.—Rehearsed *Othello.* Mrs. D. Lee, who played Virginia last night, told me "how much I had hurt her"; on asking *where,* she said "her arms." "Why, I do not touch your arms with any degree of force through the play—scarcely touch them at all; do you remember the scene?" "I think in the scene where you rush on." Now here is another instance of the vileness of these people! I never touch her arms through the play with the remotest possibility of hurting her, but I had occasion twice in the course of the play to remind her of the business she forgot—*hinc illæ lacrimæ!* Hence this trumped-up story!

January 22nd.—Heard before I went on the stage that Mr. Denvil had been bled by Dr. Riley in the green-room! And yet for £5 he was able to play Iago! I could not have done this—I could not have played Iago so badly as he did under any circumstances, but, under his peculiar ones, I could not have done it at all. I acted a little of Othello very fairly, but this Mr. Denvil was trying to *get behind* me (for what Heaven only knows!), and very much inconvenienced and embarrassed me.

London, January 27th.—Was awoke by a packet from Dow, containing the letters left at my chambers and a note from him requesting my return in the gig which conveyed them. Went quickly to town, but found no note or letter at my chambers; went on to Dow's, where I learnt that the Covent Garden manager had renewed an engagement with Mr. Kemble,[1] that he had put the hypothetical question to him of performing with me, and that his answer was, he would play nothing but *first !* Here is an old coxcomb, who never yet was permitted, but as a substitute, to appear in first characters, who dared not act them even when manager, and now before his four-shilling audiences is obliged to descend to such things as Charles II and Sir Thomas Clifford, talking about playing *first* business with a first artist! What a wretched old coxcomb!

January 28th.—Mr. Cooper came to say that they had rehearsed the *Bridal* that day, and that Mr. Bunn was ready, in compliance with my agreement, to act it on Tuesday next; that he himself thought it a shocking play; that Mr. Warde, the pure-minded, highly cultivated critic, thought it monstrous; this I endured, and waived, by observing it was nothing to the purpose, the agreement was violated. I then asked who had been cast Aspatia?—Miss Tree. Who, then, is to do Evadne? I declare I pause as I write the name: Mrs. Sloman! To her, whom they would not permit to play the easy part of Emilia at my suggestion, as being so bad, they give a character that only Mrs. Siddons could realize! I said "That is enough; if you were to pay me one or two thousand pounds for it, I would not suffer it to be so acted; but I confine myself to the legal objection, and on the violated contract I demand compensation." Mr. Cooper said: "I am instructed to offer £33 6s. 8d. and to withdraw the play." I observed that the same offer had been made by Mr. Yates, which I had treated with the same indignant contempt. "Well, then," said Mr. Cooper, "I am now desired to ask you upon whose authority you went to Bristol." I now lost all temper. I answered: "Upon my own!" and that the question was a gross impertinence. Mr. Cooper proceeded to state that he thought it was not justifiable on former usage, and I replied it was.

---

[1] Charles Kemble.

Dow entered, and he observed that I was ready to perform, if required, in London, and that my Bristol engagement was made dependent on and subject to that of Drury Lane.   In the course of our conversation he had said that Miss Ellen Tree would have flung the part of Evadne in his face if it had been offered to her.   I observed: "She would not have flung it in mine."—"Oh yes," he said, "she would."   This question I shall ask Miss Tree.   This disgusting and servile booby at length left us—if ever a man answered to the description of the moral being of an individual, as sketched by a poet's pencil, go, Mr. Cooper, into the hide of Austria in the play of *King John*, and find your own fitting in the dulness, conceit, falsehood, treachery and cowardice of the Viscount Limoges.   After dinner I wrote notes—statements—to Mr. Bunn, and one to Mr. Cooper, desiring him to confine himself to the duties of his office; my time was wasted so far as the notes were concerned, but the agitation of the question brought my mind to the discovery of the better course, which was that of remaining tranquil and awaiting the movement of Messrs. Bunn & Co.   I was pleased as I meditated on it, in clearly seeing that it was the proper judgment. Looked over my engagement, by which I think Mr. Bunn has no pretence for touching my salary—*none*.   Wrote to Dow, copying out the necessary clauses and making the letter into a parcel for him.   The difficulty I have had in restraining my temper, and the licence I have permitted it, are the causes of my own disquiet, and of my not having more triumphantly exposed and discomfited this base and bad man's attempts to cheat me; with the recollection of *what I lost by the loss of temper* in combating the fraud of Kemble,[1] I ought to show more conduct.   How bitterly do I quarrel with and reproach myself for my want of self-control and mastery over my passions.   God Almighty assist me in my endeavours to amend.   Amen!

Elstree, January 29th.—The midday post brought a letter from Cooper, wishing to know when I could be ready in the *Provost of Bruges*.   I answered that I had long since applied for subjects of study and had received no answer, that I had laid aside the *Provost of Bruges*, and could not immediately state when I should be ready, in two or three days I might be able to do so.   I added that, having found that my last week's salary had not been paid, I desired it might be immediately.   After dinner Dow arrived, having come through one continued storm of sleet and rain and snow from London; he came to

---

[1] This grievance against Kemble, which rankled so sorely, arose during Macready's engagement at Covent Garden Theatre in 1822, when under Kemble's management.

inform me that he had no doubt whatever upon the agreement, but that to confirm his own opinion he had gone down to Westminster and submitted it to Talfourd, who quite concurred with him that Mr. Bunn was not justified upon that agreement in refusing to pay any part of my year's salary. Dow is certainly one of those men who would go through fire and water to serve me; he has made his way through the latter almost this evening, and is certainly entitled to my grateful remembrance.

January 30th.—Received a call for the rehearsal of the *Provost of Bruges* on Monday next. Resolved not to attend the rehearsal unless my salary was duly paid. Read over the part of Bertulphe, of which I do not entertain very sanguine hopes, it is too sketchy and skeleton like; there is a want of substance and strength in the thoughts, which are thin and poor; its situation is all its actual power. If it be successful it will owe much to the acting.

January 31st.—Found no announcement beyond Tuesday in the newspaper, which offered little beyond a very fulsome and false notice of Kemble in Jaffier—to any person of the least taste or discrimination, a thoroughly offensive performance.

London, February 1st.—On my arrival at chambers I found a note from Cooper informing me that ' I had violated my engagement in going to Bristol, and, in consequence, Mr. Bunn had stopped a week and a half of my salary; but that if I chose to give my best services to the theatre in a more harmonious way than of late, Mr. Bunn would be very happy to remit the stoppage.' To which I immediately answered—receiving a note from good old Dow, with a play-bill containing an announcement of myself for Othello and Werner, that instantly decided me—that ' my engagement, in the opinion of an eminent special pleader and a leading barrister, did not allow of Mr. Bunn's deduction; that if he did not intimate to me that my demands were paid, I should at once close the correspondence; that I should wait in town till three o'clock.' Forster sent in some notes, wishing to see me, and, calling on him, I saw Browning; sat with them for some time, when Dow, to whom I had sent Healey with the intimation of my arrival, came in. We did not stay long, and, adjourning to my chambers, I told him what I had done, and of my resolution to quit the theatre if not paid. He agreed in the propriety of the step and would have gone further, but as I told him, in Bacon's words, " A man who has a wife and children, has given hostages to fortune." Forster was talking much of Browning, who is his present *all-in-all*.

WILLIAM CHARLES MACREADY

(1835)

From the painting by Daniel Maclise, R.A., in the collection of Major-General C. F. N. Macready, C.B.

Mr. Cooper called. He said it seemed the dispute was only about terms of speech; that he had signified Mr. Bunn's willingness to pay the money due; and that he supposed, of course, I should give him my best services. I distinctly stated that it was merely a question of whether my salary, according to my engagement, was or was not paid, without any other consideration; if paid I should go to the theatre, if not, I should end my engagement. He complained of being obliged to do " Mr. Bunn's dirty work "—which I thought to myself he might very well avoid. The beginning, as the end, of our conversation was this, that I would not answer his note, but *stood upon my legal claim*, which he promised should be answered, and I told him I should go to rehearsal to-morrow.

February 3rd.—Rehearsed the women's scenes of *Othello*; in suggesting two or three things to Miss E. Tree, she begged me not to demur at giving her any information; but my disgust at witnessing the impertinent forwardness of Mr. Vandenhoff tutoring persons capable of teaching him made me tender of hazarding my own opinions. I did not feel *at home*, but felt resolved to do my best. Mr. C. Buller called and sat for some time; we talked of the theatre and the House of Commons. I promised to give him my best assistance in mastering a weakness in his voice; I like him very much. Lay down in bed, and thought to the best of my power on my night's character. I began Othello with resolution, which was confirmed by the kind reception of the audience; but I found myself a little disconcerted by the strangeness of the theatre during the apology to the Senate, in which my back is turned to the audience. I recovered myself, and threw myself more into the character than I think I had previously done. I was called for by the audience, but this, if a compliment, was certainly much reduced in value by Mr. Vandenhoff receiving the same for playing Iago like a great, creeping, cunning cat. Grimalkin would be a better name for his part than the "honest fellow," the "bold Iago." Mr. Westmacott was in the green-room, and I was indiscreet enough (having drunk some wine) to show my contempt for him in a manner not to be mistaken; he half bowed to me, and I turned my back upon him with the word "beast" quite loud enough for him to hear. This, *though provoked*, had been better omitted. What can I do against a repetition of his insults? Forster, Browning and a M. Fontenai came into my room; the two last seemed much delighted.

February 4th.—I looked in the newspapers to see if any notice was taken of last night—being the first representation of the drama for three months, but the only criticism was of a piece at the Adelphi! This is not the way to draw attention or rekindle an interest for the regular drama. Went to the rehearsal of *Provost of Bruges*. Heard of the insulting behaviour of some friend of Mr. Bunn's to Miss Healey, for which he was, *maugre* Mr. Cooper's reluctance, turned out of the green-room. Saw and talked with Planché.

February 6th.—I called at the Garrick Club and looked at the newspapers. Saw a notice put up by the Committee respecting the invitation of strangers which I think, without exception, the most impertinent and insulting that ever was put up by a few individuals in dictation to a body of (implied) gentlemen. Not an idle day, but in it I have given way to angry thoughts upon a very trifling subject, viz. the act of the Garrick Club Committee, which I believe to be aimed at myself, with others. But if so, why should I vex myself about the proceedings of the members of that body, whose utmost spite only leaves me where I am? Let it pass.

February 7th.—Dow called and informed me of the wretch Westmacott's abuse of me in the *Age*: "that an automaton might be made to play Othello as well; that it was very cold, that the new play would probably fail, and that Virginius was melodrama, etc., also that Mr. Vandenhoff's Iago was the best since Cooke!" I had at least the sense to feel no anger at all this nonsense.

February 9th.—Went to rehearsal of *Provost of Bruges*, which was long and heavy. Of all the thick-headed men that ever were placed in so responsible a situation none was ever less qualified than Mr. Cooper for acting-manager. The lowest performers despise him for his incapacity and his want of manner. Read over the part of Bertulphe, and then went, as a brief relaxation, to dine at the Garrick Club, posting my letters on the way. Hayward asked me to his table, and I dined there, listening to his lamentations on the peccadilloes of his friends, and much amused with them. Went over the part of Bertulphe, trying some parts, but feeling the scandalous conduct of Mr. Bunn in allowing so few rehearsals to a play which may be perhaps lost by his behaviour. I am quite uncertain of the play, and am certain of my own very crude and unpractised conception of my own character.

February 10th.—Went to rehearsal (*Provost of Bruges*), sparing myself as much as I could. In the wardrobe was told that Mr. Bunn would not find me pantaloons, and I was resolved to purchase none; was very angry and therefore very blamable. Received a note from

Sally Booth,[1] requesting orders; but seeing Bunn in the theatre I could not permit myself to ask for any. Wrote a note to Sally Booth and to Pemberton excusing myself from giving the admissions requested. Lay down after looking out what was needed for the evening, and thought carefully over the latter scenes of the play. Went to the theatre very tranquil in spirits, but was slightly disconcerted by the very culpable negligence of my dresser. Resolved to take no wine before I went on and to trust to my spirits to bear me up until fatigue came on. Misjudged in doing so; my nervousness, from want of due preparation, was so great as to mar my efforts in the first scene, which, in spite of my best attempts at self-possession, was hurried and characterless. Gulped down a draught of wine, and, growing more steady from scene to scene, increased in power and effect; but it was a hasty, unprepared performance, the power of which was mainly derived from the moment's inspiration. The applause was enthusiastic, and I was obliged, after long delay, to go before the audience. Dow, Cattermole, Forster, Browning and Talfourd came into my room and expressed themselves greatly pleased with my performance, but did not highly estimate the play. As the others left me, I very thoughtlessly asked Talfourd if he would sup at the Garrick Club. I had already taken too much wine, and, as usual, one fault is the parent of another. Forster was seated in the coffee-room, and pressed us, somewhat loth, to his table. I talked very loud, very freely, and in both respects very foolishly of the conduct of the Committee, who so shamefully, in my opinion, mal-administered the affairs of the Club; but I am not sufficiently independent in circumstances to run the hazard of making enemies, and, even were I more so than I am, what benefit do I reap by exciting hostility? I recalled two or three times to-night in the play the claims of my children on my exertions as a stimulant to me; I should also think of them as a check to my intemperance of disposition and great imprudence. Dowling, Raymond, Browne, Colonel Stanhope [2]—at whom I spoke, *very, very* foolishly, were there. Drank beyond reason and went to chambers at a very late hour.

February 11th.—A violent headache and enfeebled, nauseated stomach kept me, *malgré moi*, in bed. Forster called with Mr. Macrone for the MS. of the *Provost of Bruges;* he, Mr. Macrone, had agreed to publish it on the terms of half the profits, the right of disposing of the copyright remaining with the author, and a certain number of

---

[1] Sarah Booth (1793-1857); played at Surrey and Covent Garden theatres.
[2] The alleged "black-baller" of Macready's candidate, Greaves.

copies being stipulated for. A note of grateful thanks from Mr. Lovell; [1] a note left by Greaves; one from Power; card from Bourne. Forster brought me the notices of the newspapers, which were all highly commendatory; the writer of the *Times* is, I think, acquainted with Mr. Bunn. Note from Mr. Bunn—an evidence that the man cannot speak or *write his own language*. It is, apparently, an attempt to re-establish a communication with me, and to worm out of me the name of the author.

February 12th.—Went to the theatre, where I saw Mr. Cooper, Miss E. Tree, and delivered the thanks of the author to them. Saw Mr. Bunn, who wished me to read *Basil* [2] and *Marino Faliero* and decide between them. He observed that the success of these pieces depended much on the *nomenclature* of the authors. This is a specimen of Mr. Bunn's language—or rather misuse of it.

February 13th.—Kenney resisted my earnest request that he would take my name off the Athenæum list, observing that it would seem (though in fact not so) presumptuous in me to have *expected* an extraordinary election. I agreed with him, and allowed my name to remain, but I do not think I will allow it to go to the ballot. Bartley continued his walk with me to Westminster, where he left me, and I called on the Bullers. Sat some time with them, and appointed Wednesday morning for Mr. C. Buller to call. Read what I could of Bertulphe, but, having acted it without due preparation, I shall never make it worth anything as a piece of art. I acted it but passably.

February 15th.—A note from Forster enclosing the *Spectator's* criticism on myself in Bertulphe, which says, "Perhaps it is my greatest" character. I should say *among my least*—my real opinion. Read the newspaper; am very anxious to play well to-night. Went to bed a little before two o'clock—anxious to keep my mind upon Othello; thought and read the part. Went to the theatre; but previously saw a notice of Mr. C. Kean's "great" success at Bath, and at the theatre received a letter from Clarke, putting an end to the Manchester engagement. These were circumstances, with the absence and drunkenness of my dresser, not likely to improve my spirits; but I do not wish to excuse myself. Othello I acted wretchedly; I could not abandon myself. I could have rushed out of the theatre. With all the desire to make my profession a means of benefit to my children,

---

[1] Author of the *Provost of Bruges*.

[2] By Joanna Baillie (1762–1851), the well-known authoress; her first play, *De Montfort*, had the distinction of being produced by J. P. Kemble and Mrs. Siddons in 1800.

I am perpetually *tortured* by my inability to realize my intentions. Wallace, Forster and Mr. C. Hall [1] came into my room, and Dow, with a familiarity *on the stage* that very much annoyed me. Forster walked to chambers and took tea with me, reading to me passages from a poem by Browning.

February 16*th.*—Forster and Browning called, and talked over the plot of a tragedy which Browning had begun to think of : the subject, Narses. He said that I had *bit* him by my performance of Othello, and I told him I hoped I should make the blood come. It would indeed be some recompense for the miseries, the humiliations, the heart-sickening disgusts which I have endured in my profession if, by its exercise, I had awakened a spirit of poetry whose influence would elevate, ennoble, and adorn our degraded drama. May it be! Acted Bertulphe better than the two preceding nights. Looked through the leaves of the play in a book wet from the press. The author has said all in his power to express his gratitude to me. I did more for Mr. Procter and nearly as much for Miss Mitford. The first requited me by slight and avoidance; the latter by libel and serious injury.

February 17*th.*—Dear Edward born.[2] I return my devout and humble but fervent thanks from my heart of heart to my Merciful God for the happy birth of a son, and for the comfortable state of his blessed and beloved mother. I pray the continual blessing of the Almighty God upon his head, and that he may in health of mind and body grow up to His honour, and in an undeviating course of virtue; on his dear mother I invoke all the best blessings and mercies of Almighty God, and upon the heads of my darling children I supplicate the constant manifestation of His grace and mercy. Amen! Amen! Amen! Read Joanna Baillie's play of *Basil*, which I think can scarcely be made pathetic enough for representation; there is a stiffness in her style, a want of appropriateness and peculiarity of expression distinguishing each person, that I cannot overcome in reading her plays : it is a sort of brocaded style, a thick kind of silk, that has no fall or play—it is not the flexibility of nature.

February 19*th.*—Mr. C. Buller called and sat for about an hour

[1] Samuel Carter Hall (1800–1889); well known as an author and journalist; began his career as literary secretary to Ugo Foscolo, and by reporting in the House of Lords.

[2] Edward Nevil Bourne Macready; educated at Westminster, Sherborne, and Addiscombe. Joined the Indian Army, but soon resigned his commission and became a "rolling stone," finally trying the stage but with little success. Of a bright, attractive disposition he lacked "ballast," and became a source of much trouble and disappointment to his father in after years.

and a half, talking and reading. I hope I shall be able to improve him in his mode of speaking.

February 20th.—Forster called at my chambers and took tea. I remonstrated with him again on his intention to cut up the *Provost*. Note from Bunn, stating his inability to continue the performance of the *Provost* if the terms were not moderated. Note to Cooper, and enclosed Bunn's letter to Mr. Lovell.

February 22nd.—Mr. Norton was my coach-companion, who amused me with stories of the Rev. Mr. C——, rector of S——, which not only proved him to be what Mr. Norton stated—"devoid of all moral perceptions," but a very great scoundrel—*i. e.* a liar for the very basest purposes. I was shocked to hear of his rapacious seizure of the money found by his coachman, who is now suing him for the same. These are the ministers of Christ's Gospel!!! Read the *Times;* Disraeli's farrago under the signature of Runnymede.[1] I acted but indifferently, and was made, unwillingly, worse by the wretched acting of Cooper and others about me. A woman seems nightly very intent on attracting my notice.

February 23rd.—C. Buller called, very much beyond his time, and excused himself by stating that he had been detained in cramming O'Connell for a speech on the Orange Society question. He stayed with me above an hour and a half, during which I gave him what ought to prove valuable instruction. Appointed to dine with and accompany him to the House on Thursday. Called on Bulwer, whom I found in very handsome chambers in the Albany, dressed, or rather *déshabillé*, in the most lamentable style of foppery—a hookah in his mouth, his hair, whiskers, tuft, etc., all grievously cared for. I felt deep regret to see a man of such noble and profound thought yield for a moment to pettiness so unworthy of him. His manner was frank, manly and cordial in the extreme—so contradictory of his appearance.[2] He told me, after talking about the *Provost of Bruges* and recalling our conversation in Dublin, that he had written a play; that he did not know whether I might think the part intended for me worthy of my powers, for that inevitably the weight of the action fell upon the woman; that the subject was La Vallière. He handed me a paper in which I read

---

[1] Disraeli's *Runnymede Letters;* ambitious but not very successful ventures in satire by which he sought to make himself conspicuous as a political *litterateur.*

[2] Bulwer's *déshabillé* was also ridiculed by Thackeray, who disliked him only less than he did Disraeli. He satirized both mercilessly ; Bulwer does not appear to have retaliated, but Disraeli repaid *Codlingsby* with the accumulated venom of nearly forty years in his last novel, *Endymion,* where Thackeray figures repellently as St. Barbe.

that it was dedicated to myself. It almost affected me to tears. I could not read it. He wished me to read the play, give my opinion, and that he would make any alterations I might suggest. I appointed to see him to-morrow. Acted Bertulphe pretty well, though much disconcerted by the din of carpenters. Talfourd came into my room; told me of Sheil's reason for voting in favour of Buckingham's [1] compensation "to prevent him, as being an M.P., from going about the country to lecture at so much per head, and children at half-price. Talfourd, concurring in the propriety of the reason, voted for him also. Found at my chambers Bulwer's play. Read it. What talent he possesses! I must read it again.

February 24th.—Received a letter from Mr. Lovell, offering to have his play acted for nothing rather than let it be stopped, which from the appearance of the play-bills seems intended. Letter from Mr. Woulds, wishing me to go to Bath the week of the 7th March! Wrote a note of excuse to Bulwer, deferring my visit till to-morrow. Forster called; told me of his father's expected death. He did not seem much distressed. Read, or rather looked over, the newspaper. Wrote to Mr. Woulds, assenting to his proposal; to Mr. Lovell, sending him the books which Mr. Macrone had brought me. Saw Bunn and spoke to him about Mr. Lovell's desire that the play should be acted gratuitously rather than withdrawn; also spoke to him, without mentioning the author's name, of Bulwer's play, and asked him what remuneration he would offer. Would he give £100—3rd, 6th, 9th, 16th and 25th nights? He said "Yes." Read very attentively over the play of *La Vallière*, and made my notes upon what I thought it needed.

February 25th.—Mr. Lovell called and gave me a presentation copy; expressed himself satisfied with all I had done. Forster called and I entreated him not to notice the *Provost of Bruges* on Sunday; it would be dealing a death-blow upon it. He seemed to yield to my solicitations. Sent the MS. of *La Vallière* to Bulwer with a message that I would call almost immediately. Received a parcel—another play—from Mr. Wightwick of Plymouth.[2] I could have dispensed with it, but he cherishes kindly feelings towards me and is entitled to my best offices. Called on Bulwer (shopping on the way) and found

---

[1] James Silk Buckingham (1786–1855); M.P. and public lecturer. He had been expelled from India some years before for attacking the Tory Government of the day, and it was, probably, in respect of this incident that he had claimed and received compensation.

[2] An accomplished architect, who became one of Macready's most intimate friends.

him less carefully set up than on my former visit.   We talked over the
play, and I mentioned my objections, at the same time suggesting
some remedies.   He yielded to all readily except the fifth act; upon
that he seemed inclined to do battle, but at length I understood him
to yield.   We talked over terms.   He was not satisfied with Bunn's
proposal, but added to that £200 down, and to be paid through the
two following seasons £5 per night, after which the copyright to revert
to him.   This is rather a hard bargain; I do not think Bunn will
concede so much.   He wished me to write my remarks and send them
to him, for which purpose he would return me the MS.   Took a cab
to Buller's; he had not come in, so that I might have spared my haste.
Looked at the paper.   Dined with Mrs. Buller and the two young men.
Went to the House of Commons; sat under the gallery.   Heard Lord
Francis Egerton [1] talking as loudly as he could for nearly half-an-hour,
and now and then caught the word " paper," about the manufacture
of which he was speaking to himself.   Some words passed also on the
subject of railways.   Mr. Lennard moved for a return of the corporal
punishments in the Army since 1830.   Captain Ferguson, O'Connell,
Major Beauclerk, Hume, Colonel Thompson, General Parry, very badly,
and Wakley [2] best of all, spoke for it.   Two very great blockheads,
General Sharpe and Colonel Sibthorp [3] against it, and for the continuance of flogging!   C. Buller made his motion for a Committee to
inquire into Election Committees, in a speech which he began admirably,
but, having got the ear of the House, he relaxed his care and energy
and nearly lost it.   He became indistinct and flippant, wanted arrangement, and the recapitulation of cases (the evidence of the necessity of
alteration in the law) should have been well prepared—rapidly, clearly
and succinctly, though forcibly, passed in review—and a greater solidity
of manner generally preserved, which would have made his playful

[1] Lord Francis Egerton (1800–1857) afterwards first Earl of Ellesmere; author and
politician; one of the most enlightened members of the Whig party, also an accomplished
litterateur and art patron.   Fanny Kemble, of whose acting he had a high opinion, owed
much to his generous encouragement both professionally and socially.

[2] Thomas Wakley (1795–1862) M.P. for Finsbury; founder of the *Lancet;* coroner for
West Middlesex from 1839 till his death.   He was concerned in an action against a Fire
Insurance Company which was the occasion of a pungent witticism of Sheil.   This company
had refused to pay under the policy, considering the circumstances of the fire suspicious.
Shortly afterwards an M.P. commenting on Wakley's maiden speech in the House added:
" He certainly won't set the Thames on fire."   " No," rejoined Sheil, " not unless he has
insured it! "

[3] Colonel Charles de Laet Waldo Sibthorp (1783–1855); well-known as the ultra-Tory
M.P. for Lincoln.   He was a violent opposer of every innovation, and regarded all foreigners
as scoundrels, characteristics which procured for him the constant attentions of Mr. Punch.

observations tell with more effect. The speech should have been *modelled*, and it would have been much more successful than it was, with all the success it actually obtained. With a little care he will speak very well indeed. Saw, but not to speak with them, Sheil and H. Twiss in the House. C. Wynne,[1] who spoke loud and long, with not one word distinguishable, tired me out, and I came away with Arthur Buller. Looked over Mr. Tyrone (!) Power's book (!) on America. I cannot pass any criticism upon it. He has the impudence to put Latin words in it (for his knowledge of Latin, consult Mr. Bunn on his pronunciation of the words *vivâ voce*), and prints for " de mortuis nil nisi bonum," " nisi just*em*." Shook hands with Cattermole in the square, who introduced me to Mr. Stone.[2]

To Elstree, February 26th.—Read in the *Times* the report of last night's debate, and of the failure of Miss Baillie's play of *Separation;* " Unfortunate Miss Baillie ! " [3] Sent for a play-bill, and found that Mr. Bunn had announced four nights without the *Provost;* his intention is manifest, for, however bad it may be, it must be better than the *Provoked Husband* for Tuesday next.

February 27th.—Read the two last acts of *Ion*, which, if I had personal advantages, I am confident I could make effective in performance. Read some scenes of *Othello*. Continued and finished *La Vallière*, which perplexes me to decide on in reference to its effect in representation ; its story runs so smoothly on in the reading that, though I have misgivings of some scenes, I have at the same time doubts of my own judgment. Made out the sketch of my notes to send to Bulwer. Forster and Browning called in. My nerves and spirits were quite quelled by them all, and I was rejoiced in seeing them leave me—excepting Browning, whose gentle manners always make his presence acceptable. I acted Othello—I scarcely know in what way —not to please myself ; the truth is, I have lost the tone, the pitch of voice, the directness of the part, and I strive in vain to recall it ; perhaps, and as I believe, because I do not *strive enough—Aide-toi, et le ciel t'aidera.* I was better in the latter part of the play. Was called for by the audience and obliged to go forward ; so was Mr. Vandenhoff !

---

[1] Charles Watkin Williams Wynne (1775-1850) a Tory politician whose peculiar utterance earned for him the nickname of the " Squeaker." He is frequently mentioned in the Duke of Buckingham's Diaries.

[2] Frank Stone (1800-1859) the popular artist ; A.R.A. 1851. He was on intimate terms with Dickens and his circle.

[3] A quotation from a notorious ballad dealing with the murder of a lady of that name.

March 1st.—To my surprise, Sheil called.   He told me, among other things, that *C. Kean had talent.*   I would trust his judgment where I would question that of another.   St. Aubyn had said he did not like him, but in reply to my queries had admitted enough to prove that he *had* talent.   There is nothing for it but to endeavour to accelerate my own improvement.   He has the *great* advantage of youth—and a good name.   I must depend upon myself—and God. Sheil told me of the resolution of himself, Woulfe, French, Ball and another member to go to Lord John Russell, and ask him for something for Wallace—observing that he dare not refuse five members. Read review of *Provost of Bruges* in *Monthly Repository*.   Read Macbeth.   Mr. Lovell called and took his books; I counselled him to draw on Bunn for his money, and told him of the cause of the withdrawal of the *Provost of Bruges*—the dresses having been cut up for *Chevy Chase!*   Sent him *Monthly Repository*.   Acted Macbeth very unequally; latter part of first act—second act—part of third act— part of fourth—first and last scenes of fifth act—well; the rest badly. I cannot act Macbeth without *being Macbeth*, which I must have time to prepare my mind for.   I cannot work myself into such a tempest of ever-waking thought.   Wallace came to my room.   I was much tired.   Mr. Willmott told me that the reason of Mr. Ward's nervousness—oh! how nervous he is!—was that he drank nearly a bottle of gin every night!!   Spoke to Bunn about *La Vallière;* he would say nothing, *until he knew the author.*   A man came into the room with a "Hurrah!"   I took him for a vulgar auctioneer, or one of the blackguard hangers-on of Bunn.   Bunn, however, introduced him to me as *Lord Allen!* [1]   Found at chambers a very long note from Bulwer on *La Vallière.*

March 2nd.—Sent the note written last night to C. Buller, and used the intermediate minutes of breakfast to write notes to A. Watts and to Power.   As I was going out, Buller, to my surprise, came in. I expressed my regret that he had not received my note, but he quite understood it, and went with me to rehearsal.   He was amused at the confusion, and remained while Virginius was proceeded with in a true Drury Lane style.   He observed to me that he did not like Macbeth so well as Hamlet, and that he thought I exhibited too much terror after the murder.   I am not quite satisfied on the subject of

---

[1] Joshua William, first Viscount Allen (1781–1845); known as "King" Allen.   Formerly in the Guards; distinguished himself as a subaltern at Talavera; one of the "bow-window" *coterie* at White's, and noted for his not too amiable eccentricities.

282

this criticism, as he only entered the theatre *at that scene*. Therefore he wanted the *preparation* for it; but very likely I exaggerated—about which I will inquire. Called on Bulwer, and evidently came on him by surprise; he could not well avoid seeing me; indeed he did not demur, though evidently a little discomposed. He was in complete *déshabillé*—a white nightcap on his head, looking like a head of Gay or some poet of that time—it was a picture: his busts, papers, etc., around him, and the unornamented man of genius undandified. I told him of Bunn's desire to know the author's name before he committed himself, and that I could not counsel it, as I knew Mr. B——to be *utterly faithless and treacherous*. He at last commissioned me to give his name to Mr. Bunn, but would not consent to his seeing the play to judge of it; the price down was for *his name*. We talked over the objections to his play, and I think he inclined at last to my view.

March 4th.—Buller called, and sat about an hour and a half. I think I did him some good. Wrote a note to Bulwer, returning his MSS., with which I had been very much pleased. Went on to Garrick Club. The only newspaper that mentioned the name of the play last night was the *Post*. Saw Taylor, Villiers, who spoke *out* about Bulwer's play! Taylor informed me that Mrs. Mathews [1] had sent in her claim to be placed upon the Covent Garden Fund!!! Alas! what changes in life! God grant that I may never apprehend such a disastrous reverse to my beloved ones! Amen!

March 5th.—Went to the theatre; saw Bunn, delivered Bulwer's proposal of his play without being looked at. Bunn refused, but said he would write to Bulwer. Spoke about Lovell's money, which he said could not be paid immediately, but should be very soon. A woman called for relief, "because she was of the same name." I paid a shilling for the unlucky accident. Just as I was going into my bedroom, half-past ten, Dow called, bringing with him his friend, Mr. Berry. I told him at once that I could not ask him to stay, that I was very ill and tired and going immediately to bed; on which he seemed to me in a sort of dudgeon—offended and affecting indifference—asked after the family and went away, either in a kind of ill-humour or so sullenly that it looked like it. If a man has so little tact as to think the health, comfort, and convenience of his friends are to stand as naught against his demands for recreation and amusement, and that

---

[1] The widow of Charles Mathews the elder, who had recently died.

a denial of this claim is to be resented by ill-humour, it little matters whether you part with him to-day or to-morrow, for he is too *unsafe* to hold, however worthy a man he may be.

To Bath, March 6th.—An outside passenger was driven in by the rain, and soon began reading the *Age* newspaper. Upon his offering it to me, I was tempted by the heading of a paragraph to look over it, which I did very rapidly, for who could read such stuff? I glanced at the births and deaths, and startled by the name of Green Jeston, read the death of "Lettice, wife of the Rev. R. Green Jeston,[1] aged 34." I was shocked and grieved—the being whom I remembered in her first blush of beauty, whom I had loved, and who had loved me; who, I believe, through her life retained a deep feeling of attachment to me—whom I would have married, had our stars, adverse as they were, permitted. She is gone! How many, many recollections are associated with her; all that I had of independent youth flew by under the perplexing, tantalizing struggle with the affection I bore her. Here it was I first knew her—the beautiful, the radiant girl! All her little foibles are forgotten, and I can only now think of her as dear Letty: she is gone before me, and in her early doom, snatched from her husband and children, gives birth to gloomy apprehensions for my own fate, or still dearer to me, that of my beloved wife and children. May the Almighty God watch over them and guard them! Amen! I thought much upon my poor friend—so young, so beautiful, and once so loved—may I not now almost say, and still so loved—for it is only my love of her that I retain to remember? (*In the stage-coach.*) Captain Bourchier, as I soon learned his name to be, talked much; among other subjects mentioned young Kean's success at Bath, told me that he knew him, and that his dresses cost him £300 per annum, that he was very pleasant and related many amusing stories about the theatre. One of Macready, who is a good actor, but he can never play without applause. He went on one night to play and no notice was taken of him, on which he said to the manager, "I cannot get on, if they do not applaud me." Upon which the manager went round and told the audience that Mr. Macready could not act if they did not applaud him. When Macready reappeared, the applause was so incessant as to disconcert him, and he observed, "Why, now I cannot act, there is so much applause." I told him I rather discredited the story. "In short," I observed, "perhaps I ought to apologize to you

---

[1] A schoolfellow of Macready at Rugby.

for allowing you to tell it without first giving you my name—my name is Macready." He was very much confused, and I as courteous in apologizing as I could be.

March 7th.—Tried to act Werner well, and think I did go through much of it very naturally—perhaps not with all that free and spontaneous energy which I intended, but in an artist-like and impressive manner. From the second act to the end of the play, I was literally in torture; the pain of my arm was so extreme that I was frequently obliged to hold it with my right hand. These are the peculiar hardships of this art, that with a demand of every faculty of mind and body unimpaired and free, we are obliged to conquer even agony sometimes, and superinduce a feeling in direct contrast with the anguish that may be preying upon us. " Vaunting cloud, but racked with deep despair," is often an appropriate picture of an actor's condition.

March 8th.—Went to the theatre in a tolerable state of feeling : not much pain, but as the play, *Virginius*, proceeded, the torturing achings of my arm returned, and the very bad manner in which the piece was acted distressed me mentally almost as much as I was suffering bodily. The Icilius (a Mr. Savile) was either half-stupidly drunk, or is, as is very probable, a born ass. Virginia would have made an excellent representation of Appius' cook, as far as appearance went, added to which she seemed to think that she was playing Virginius, not Virginia, and fortified herself for some extraordinary efforts by a stimulant which was too easily detected on a near approach to her. The whole business was most slovenly—and last year this play was actually a *pattern* of correctness. Therefore last year there was a loss on the theatre, and now there is a considerable profit. So much for the judgment and taste of a Bath public. Pshaw! It is all quackery.

March 10th.—Felt better, but not entirely free from painful sensations in my head. Received a letter from Bulwer, apprising me of the expected termination of negotiation with Mr. Bunn on the subject of his play, and wishing me to impress on Mr. Bunn that the communication was confidential—also desiring to be informed of the extent of my engagement with Bunn, and whether I should be at liberty to enter into any other with Mr. Osbaldiston; further inquiring as to the possibility of Morris's acceptance of the play. Wrote to Bulwer in reply, and to Bunn, urging the necessity of silence on the negotiation. Went to rehearsal and felt extremely ill, and—I believe—looked very ill. The play was in a very bad state. There is no management, no superintendence, no intelligence, and (qu. *therefore?*) the concern succeeds! It is hard to be forced to acknowledge this. Returning from rehearsal, at my lodgings I felt surprisingly better. Laid out my dress, and dined very heartily. Had received in the morning a very kind note from St. Aubyn, which I answered. Made a parcel of books of *Werner* and *Provost of Bruges*, which I sent to Exeter. Wrote a very kind note to Bellamy, regretting that I had not seen him on my last and present visit; I did not choose to lose a friend for such a worthless "snipe" as Mr. Woulds! Went to the theatre, and before I had put on my dress for Bertulphe, the pain in my arm and shoulder, in all its depressing, irritating power came on, and distressed me through the whole evening. Taking my bodily infirmity into consideration—for my arm was so weak I could not hold the Earl, in endeavouring to seize him—I did not act badly. I was called for by the audience rather vociferously, as it seemed, at the end of the play, and I fear I did not behave with all my better judgment. I peremptorily and not very courteously refused to go on. Mr. Woulds was obliged to make the best excuse he could—he might with truth have said I was very ill, but he chose to say that I "declined appearing." Why did I not go forward? *Temper*, I believe, was the real cause. I was angry with Mr. Woulds's treacherous decoy of me into an engagement the week before the Dramatic Fête, and I felt something like impatience—perhaps disgust—at the neglect of the public, who had crowded to see Mr. Kean in such characters as Rolla, King John, Sardanapalus—*which it is certain he could not play*—and who deserted me altogether. I more than fear that I was wrong—indeed, the very admission of anger condemns me. ı was to blame.

March 11th.—Read the newspapers, containing the debates on the Municipal Corporation Bill. We have no right to refuse faith to the asserted convictions of our opponents in argument, but it is difficult to yield belief to the sincerity of the doctrines broached by Sir R. Peel—still more to those of Stanley—and most to those of the apostate radical Graham.[1] Why did not, as O'Connell properly inquires, Sir

---

[1] Sir James Robert George Graham, Bart. (1792-1861); a member of Lord Grey's Cabinet, but resigned with Stanley in 1834; joined Peel's Government in 1841 as Home Secretary. Served in the Coalition Cabinet, and afterwards in that of Lord Palmerston. He incurred great unpopularity by opening the letters of foreign refugees when Home Secretary under Peel, and never succeeded in living it down. As a statesman he was too "crotchety" to command a reputation equal to his abilities.

R. Peel discover before the necessity for sweeping away these institutions, whose corruption now calls for their annihilation? It does not look like honesty.

March 12th.—Rose, not so well as I had hoped. While dressing received letters from my beloved wife, from dear Letitia, and Mr. Bartley, communicating to me Mr. Bunn's intimation to the Drury Lane Company, through Mr. Cooper, of his inability to carry on the theatre beyond Lent, unless the company consented to a reduction of their salaries! I am not included in this precious business by the terms of my engagement. It is right that I should well ponder the issues, before I decide to become a party to any movement. Once I stood forward for the art; and the actors, Mr. Bartley at their head, basely deserted me.

Bristol, March 14th.—Went to the theatre. There was a good house; good old Bristol! I acted Bertulphe particularly well to an audience who came to be delighted. Was loudly called for by the audience, and long and loudly cheered when I went forward. I told them how happy I was to receive their applause, and hoped next season to have another new play to submit to their judgment.

Exeter, March 16th.—Acted Othello as well as the wretched Iago and Desdemona and Emilia would permit me, and better than the miserable account of empty boxes could have expected. Bulwer seems keen after money. He does not let the grass grow under his feet.

March 17th.—Acted Werner tolerably well; wanted a *sustained reality*—which I want, and *must acquire*, in Othello. It is to be done, and if I had gained it, I should have been a very superior artist—but oh! how hard to gain what seems easier the more difficult it is! Mr. Hay told me that Mr. Kean is a palpable, and *avowed* copy of the father, and often for effect at the expense of reason. If this be the case, he will reach no high mark.

March 18th.—Was late in coming downstairs, and did not feel quite well. C. Buller called in whilst I was at breakfast, and sat with me nearly an hour. Went to rehearsal, and soon made an end of it by going through my own scenes consecutively. Sent to my lodgings for any letters, hoping to receive an affirmative answer from Plymouth. There were none, but a card from Captain Bourchier, my *compagnon de voyage*. I had built upon the hope of a favourable answer from Plymouth, the intention of making all I could of next week at Bath, Exeter and even Bristol. But without Plymouth it all falls to the ground, and I must go home. Went to the theatre, where I had the satisfaction to have a very numerous audience. As I dare not strip my rheumatic arm, I was obliged to act Virginius in my shirt sleeves. What would a French critic have said or done? The extreme careless-ness of the actors very much distressed and disabled me. It was inexcusable; I tried to overcome it, but I could not lose myself, so perpetually was I recalled to the painful reality of the unfit state of things about me. Between the third and fourth acts the manager came into my room to apologize for a delay of some minutes, while Mr. H. Hughes stripped the toga and decemviral insignia from Appius Claudius, a Mr. Bartlett, and invested himself with them to finish the character, Mr. Bartlett having been so excessively drunk as to tumble from the *sella curulis* in the Forum. Oh, Rome! If the man had been acting Cato, it might have been taken for a point of character. This is the profession which the vulgar envy, and the proud seem justified in despising! I come from each night's performance wearied and incapacitated in body, and sunk and languid in mind; compelled to be a party to the blunders, the ignorance, and wanton buffoonery which, as to-night, degrade the poor art I am labouring in, and from which I draw an income that scarcely promises me, with a moderate scale of expenditure, a comfortable provision for my old age and a bequest for my children. Oh, ye wretches, that in your coward shelter insidiously murder and pillage—for your slanders (Messrs. Theodore Hook, Har-ness, Thompson, etc.) have stung my heart and have reduced my income—I would I could acquire your obtuseness and callousness. I would almost take your blackguardism and rascality with it!

March 19th.—A letter from Mr. Mude informed me that my terms at Plymouth were acceded to, which, much as I long to return home, I was very much pleased to learn. Seeing that there was a prospect of making something out of the week, I wrote to Mr. Woulds, offering to play at Bath on Saturday. I would not, on ordinary occasions, for trifling gains harass myself, but here is a prospect of adding to my invested money, and such an occasion is not idly to be neglected. Wrote to Mr. Mude. Buller called and sat for about an hour; he was very agreeable, seems very candid, and has, I think, a quick insight into character. Wrote me some franks.[1] At the theatre the manager came in, with an elongated visage, to say that "the rascal" of a

---

[1] Charles Buller was then M.P. for Liskeard, and the privilege of parliamentary franking was still in existence (*note by Sir F. Pollock*).

WILLIAM CHARLES MACREADY

AS OTHELLO

From an engraving of the painting by Tracey

prompter had sent him a note that moment to the effect that he had "never been so insulted as he was that morning, and that he should in consequence not come to the theatre this evening." (This prompter had given away the prompt-book during rehearsal, for which the rehearsal was, of course, obliged to wait, and he was censured for doing so—this is the head and front of the offending against this vagabond.) These are players. Some willing hearts set to work to "double, double toil and trouble," and doubled accordingly their own parts with his. I sent my dresser, also a sort of actor, for my bag, and to call about a warm bath. I waited his return until it became necessary to think of time ; I proceeded to do all I could—at last my mind misgave me that the arch rebel had perhaps "drawn after him" some of Hay's power. I sent for my clothes, which were brought by a strange messenger, and the fatal truth came out that the dresser could not get by a public-house, had been sucked in by the maelstrom, and sunk its victim. I had recommended Mr. Hay to send after the other vagabond, but his answer was, "God bless you, sir! he's dead drunk by this time, that's it! He has written this letter *on the beer*—he's pot-valiant. He'll never be found to-night." Well, with the abdication of one and the desertion of the other we got through very tolerably ; though never did the assumer of royalty justify the act of regicide more truly than the Earl of Flanders this evening.

To Plymouth, March 20th.—Buller parted from me at my lodgings. I fear his health is not good. He seems very amiable. I like him more the more I see him. He is frank and sensible.

March 23rd.—My endeavour to act Werner well was completely frustrated. The whole play was acted very indifferently ; Josephine was dressed like a flower-girl for a fancy ball ; Idenstein, Fritz, Stralaheim all bad—Gaber not good—but Ulric was beyond all power of description—winking with his eyes, then starting, and looking very fine, mysterious and assassin-like—then as flippant as a man-milliner. He quite *paralyzed* me. I contended with this oppressive incubus, and made some effect, but the heart was absent.

March 24th.—Arriving at Exeter, went to rehearsal, where I went rapidly through it. Saw there an Edinburgh newspaper, containing an account of the extraordinary success of young Kean—"the houses literally crammed every night." *Can this be bad ?* Tried to act well to a very good house ; was disconcerted at first by fancying that some persons in the stage box were uncivil, when I found they were warmly admiring. Still more thrown off my balance by a letter from Mr.

Cooper, giving me notice of *Richard III* for Easter Monday. Oh, Mr. Bunn—I was distressed at first, and, as usual, angry, but soon reasoned myself into complacency, or at least resolution not to let it be any advantage to the man who thinks to annoy me and perhaps to make me relinquish my engagement—but it is a night's uncomfortable feeling and then an end! It cannot kill my reputation, for my reputation does not rest upon the past; I will, however, do my best with it. Acted as well as I could to a very prepossessed audience, who would make me go forward at the end, which, after much delay, I did.

March 25th.—In the *Examiner* newspaper I see a paragraph stating that the King has appointed "Alfred Bunn, Esq., one of his honourable gentlemen-at-arms!" [1] *Is* character of any value in this world, when a miscreant like this can *dare* to let his name be seen beyond the eyes of his dirty associates? "Oh, thou world! thou art indeed a melancholy jest."

Elstree, March 29th.—Answered, by acceptance, the invitation of the Literary Fund Committee to be steward at their festival.

April 4th.—Letter from Talfourd, proposing to be here on Friday. Read over *Ion*, in order to get a general idea of its arrangement.

April 8th.—A letter from Talfourd mentioned the time of his arrival, and enclosed Mr. Vandenhoff's refusal to act Adrastus. I did not expect the man to do it from any feeling to me, since he would pay a premium to have my throat cut, and he has no sense of delicacy, but to the character of Talfourd and to the merit of his play, some consideration was due. He excused himself on the plea of his daughter's *début*, which takes place on Monday next—a *fortnight* before the representation of *Ion!* He is, as I have ever observed him, *a nasty fellow!* On Talfourd's arrival about three o'clock we went over the play, he not offering an objection to all my omissions. After dinner we settled the terms of the announcement; Letitia returned from town. Talfourd and myself went together in his carriage to town. On our way, in speaking of the heartburnings and littlenesses practised in the theatrical profession, and observing that, though lawyers said that in their vocation they were exposed to equal annoyances, yet there was the restraint which the character of gentlemen

---

[1] The qualifications for the corps must have differed widely from those of the present day! That Bunn, the insolvent theatrical speculator, should be considered eligible for the Royal Bodyguard, while an actor of Macready's distinguished abilities and high character found himself debarred from so much as attending a levee represents an almost incredible anomaly even for the *régime* of William IV.

laid on them, Talfourd surprised me by replying that he did not think there were any unworthy feelings displayed from rivalry or envy at the Bar. I did not acquiesce in his opinion, but it served to convince me of the happier life they lead who do not stop in their life's journey to remove every impediment from their path and kick every bramble out of their way—how much more easily and more readily the traveller, who steps over the dirt, goes out of the way of obstinate hindrances, and leaves the thorns through which he picks his path, attains the goal of his desires! Talfourd's easiness of disposition, his general indulgence for others' faults, and good-natured aversion to dispute, has proved, in the happiness that has resulted from such amiability, the best wisdom.

London, April 9th.—Called on Miss Tree. To my distress and consternation, she was not at home, nor expected to return until May. Reflected on my situation and thought the matter hopeless without Miss Tree. Pondered on my situation, and called on Talfourd; proved to him the impossibility of acting the play of *Ion* without Miss Tree, but luckily thought of writing to her, to ask her to assist me on a more distant day—if Bunn, as I doubted not, would consent to its postponement. We walked together to Drury Lane theatre, and I went in to see Mr. Bunn. I proposed the delay, to which he assented, and I left him to carry the news to Talfourd at the Garrick Club. Saw there Harley, Meadows, Bartley, Fladgate, H. Reynolds and Price, who asked if I thought of America this year. I said "No; I should not go for a year or two." Repeated to Talfourd what had occurred with Bunn; he wrote me a frank for Miss Tree, and I, going to my chambers, wrote to her, asking her if she could assist me. Mrs. Bradshawe, a pretty little woman, whom I found to be the daughter of Dodd, an old usher at Westminster, sat for two hours, asking and repeating her request that I would procure her a situation in some theatre. Harding sent a note to ask for money, with which I was not quite pleased. Went out, *walked,* to Nelson Square (!) to dine with Dow: was introduced to Miss Andrew—a nice piece of flesh enough, *rien autre.* Dow makes an *ass* of himself by what I suppose he calls "courting," but what I denominate *playing the fool!* He is most absurd.

Elstree, April 10th.—The *Iron Chest* [1] seemed to me an alternative, if *Ion* be out of the question, for my Benefit, should I feel myself capable of studying the character in time, which is doubtful.

---

[1] By George Colman the younger.

April 11th.—Read over the part of Sir Edward Mortimer, to see if I could adopt it for my benefit. Found I could not do justice to myself in it.

London, April 14th.—Rehearsed Lady Macbeth's scenes with Mrs. Sharpe, and to my great surprise—and certainly to my amusement, as I reflected on *the man*, his *personal hatred* of me, and his vanity and pride—Mr. Vandenhoff wished to speak to me in Mr. Cooper's room, and dinned me with the account of his own compromise with Mr. Bunn for a reduced salary on condition of his daughter's appearance—of her success—and his ill-treatment of her. This to *me* showed his own weakness more than anything he could have done. Mr. Kenneth called from Mr. Osbaldiston, to learn whether I would make an engagement at Covent Garden; after much disjointed chat, I said that I had no wish to go to that theatre, but that for money I would, viz., for £20 per night for twenty nights. He is not likely to give it, and nothing but the want of money could induce me to ask it. Took all the pains I could with Macbeth, but had not made due preparation; acted pretty well, but did not finish off some of my effects so well as I should have done with a little more preparation. The audience persisted in calling for me, and cheered me most enthusiastically. Talfourd came in from the House, where he had been speaking on flogging in the Army. He said that he was nervous and rapid, but listened to with great indulgence. Showed him a letter from Ellen Tree which I had just received, in which she mentioned her intention of being in town 22nd May, and her willingness to study Clemanthe for me. Neither Cooper nor Bunn was in the theatre, so that nothing could be settled.

April 15th.—Sent to Talfourd for franks, examined my accounts, and calculated my means. Enclosed a note in a parcel, containing a book of *Ion*, which I had marked, for Ellen Tree, to Clarke at Liverpool. Wrote to Ellen Tree in answer to hers received last night. Called at the theatre to speak about my night, and my dress for King John. Speaking to Mr. Cooper, I saw in the play-bill that I was announced for to-morrow night in *William Tell* as the after-piece. I directly told Mr. Cooper that I would not do it; that it was utterly unjustifiable. He said it was, but I had better write a letter, disclaiming Mr. Bunn's right, and do it on that occasion. I refused. He then said, "What shall I do?" wanting me to play *King Henry IV* (second part) as an after-piece on his night. He talked like a fool, as he is, about my unkindness in not doing it for him, but I cut the conversation as short as I could. Palmer had left the wardrobe and I went on, calling at the Garrick Club, where I read the list of the celebrators of Shakspeare's birthday. Saw the papers—*Times*, of course, did not mention my name—the other papers, as coldly as they could. Looked at Heraud's review of Knowles, in which he makes out Knowles to be the comic writer, adding that the tragic has not yet appeared, but is coming, and that *he* can *see* him. Called on Bulwer; thought I passed Fitzgerald—turned and looked in his face, could not swear to him, but thought it him. If I were sure, his cut should be a deep one. Forster came in and walked to chambers with me. A boy stopped and told me he had left a note for me at my chambers. At my request he returned with me. It was from Cooper, intimating Bunn's intention to keep up the announcement of *William Tell*. I wrote to repeat my refusal and quoted his own assertion of the *unjustifiability* of the action. He wrote again a *dirty* attempt to qualify his free declaration, and I answered refusing to admit any departure from facts, telling him that I would put him into a witness-box upon the words; was much divided and sometimes agitated by varying reflections and resolutions. God help me! The world uses me worse than I use it!

April 16th.—Passed a most miserably uncomfortable night, tormented and kept awake by the headache, and worried by the thoughts of this base scoundrel's attempts to injure me. Did not, for once, find the *consilium* which the night has often before given me. Thought on Forster coming here last night, as if for mere curiosity. I hope it was not so. Rose, after revolving all modes of meeting and treating this business, with the purpose of endeavouring to obtain an engagement that there should be no recurrence of this half-price work, and so far to concede. Sent a note to Dow, after having seen the announcement in the bills, requesting him to call here, and a note to Cooper to the same effect. Dow called and we talked over the affair; he was very averse to my appearing in *William Tell* this evening, but, like myself, had a dread of giving offence to the public. Whilst he went on an embassy to Cooper to state my consent to perform the part this night, provided an engagement was given that nothing of the sort should recur during my engagement, and, in the event of Mr. Bunn refusing to give such pledge, that I should hold Cooper personally responsible for anything he might say derogatory to my interests this evening (all of which he did in a very direct and spirited manner), I wrote out a copy of a handbill, to be delivered at the doors of the theatre, giving notice of my non-appearance. Dow returned with a letter from Cooper, which was a silly answer to that sent by me last night, in which I spoke of the " atrocious villainy " of Mr. Bunn. Dow observed that he grew manifestly more civil after the intimation of his probable " personal responsibility." I observed to Dow that I did not like the idea of issuing a handbill, and that I should prefer playing the game of this scoundrel Bunn, and *giving up my engagement*. He was satisfied that in so doing I should be liable to an action for damages. It was then agreed finally between us that I should stand on the guarantee (having been required to appear in two plays as after-pieces) and, if it were refused, that I should not act. On his departure another note arrived from Mr. Cooper, inquiring if he were at liberty to communicate to Mr. Bunn the notes with " atrocious villainy " and " falsehood "—which last expression I do not recollect. I told him to use his discretion, that I did not care, but wanted an answer to my friend's communication. I thought he wished to shift the personal responsibility and secure himself behind a *mêlée* with myself and Bunn. I was in considerable anxiety to know whether Mr. Bunn would come over here for a scene and endeavour to make a *bullying row*, for which I quite prepared myself; but the time passed and no one came from him. Forster called and told me of the indignant feeling that had been displayed by several upon the indignity offered me; added that Vandenhoff had seceded, and soon left us. He must have seen that I was nervous and *distrait*. Dow called and reported his second interview with Cooper, in which he had made certain what before he had said conjecturally. *He did well.* When he had left me, a strange gentleman (anonymous) called about a play he had written. I received him very courteously, and promised all in my power. A note came in a yielding tone, but declining to give the undertaking against recurrence of the matter, and I wrote shortly back that on no other condition would I consent to appear. Very low-spirited, and oppressed with a sense of degradation and the indignity put upon me. Spoke to Meadows, Brindal, Jones, etc., upon it, very quietly. Lardner called and went behind the scenes with me. Spoke to Mr. Cooper about my Benefit night, to which I required an answer, and asked him if he was authorized to send the note he did? He said " No, for Mr. Bunn was not in the theatre, but that subsequently he, Bunn, had sanctioned it." This I believe to be an equivocation. He dared not have given the guarantee in Mr. Bunn's name unless Bunn had left him a discretionary power to that effect. There seemed to

294

be a very general feeling of disgust at Mr. Bunn's behaviour among the people connected with the theatres. Had not been able to read *William Tell,* but took all the pains in my power with its performance, and rendered it very effective, particularly when the lateness of the hour is taken into account. The audience did not move till the very last, and, after going to my room, I was obliged to return at the call of the remaining audience, who would not depart, and who cheered me most enthusiastically. Talfourd and Forster had come into my room, and stayed with me whilst I undressed. Forster walked to chambers, took tea with me and heard the correspondence between Cooper and myself, which seemed to give him great amusement. So ended a day, and thus was passed over a threatening danger, which might have had an evil influence, with a different issue, on my whole future life. As it is, the events of to-day are more likely to make friends for me than enemies. Humbly and gratefully do I lift up my heart in gratitude to Almighty God for my escape from disasters that seemed to beset me. May I be more circumspect in future, and may my actions be more prosperous. The thought of my children several times to-day served to retard and to impel me, as I grew into passion or sank into despondency. May God Almighty bless them and give us life and means to make them all we wish! Amen!

April 18th.—A note from Mr. Cooper with Mr. Bunn's assent to the proposal of Tuesday, May 24th, for my Benefit; wrote to Talfourd acquainting him with the news, requiring a frank for Miss Ellen Tree, and asking him (for Catherine and self) to be godfather to our little Edward. Wrote to Mr. Cooper, sending him the prompt-book of *Ion* and the cast of the characters as I should advise; at the same time, to save any pain to his feelings, I wrote a note to Mr. Brindal asking him, as an indulgence to myself, to play the part of Crythes, which I had assigned to him. Received a note from Talfourd, very heartily acquiescing in my request. Wrote a letter to Ellen Tree, apprising her of the night fixed for the performance of *Ion,* and thanking her. Returning to dinner, wrote notes to Farren, Harley, and Bartley, requiring them to meet here on Wednesday, to consider our condition, and its chances and means of amendment.

April 19th.—Spent the time of my toilet labour in vain and angry reflections on the impertinence of the self-elected Committee of the Garrick Club. I am certainly impatient of the coxcombry of such *things* as Messrs. Hayward, Theodore Hook, Williams, and the etcs.

295

that make up that very despicable body. But at last I inquired of
myself why I could not be happy without the Garrick Club, and if so,
why I should concern myself with its pitiful intrigues or its profligate
and trifling frequenters. I wondered at my own littleness in wasting
mind upon such trash. It is not my wish to be proud. I would live
a life of love with all mankind, and redeem the sins of my life by
benevolence of thought and deed. Why, then, have I so few companions? Why am I so much a stranger to society as I have become?
Is it a want of that suppleness which makes an empty, and dull, and
dishonoured man like C. Kemble acceptable—or of the effrontery of
Mr. Power, which "will not be denied"? How much I wish I could
see and know myself! Went to rehearsal, when I arranged my dress,
there being nothing in the theatre that could be worn. Notes of orders
and promise of attendance to-morrow from Farren and from Kenneth,
conveying to me Mr. Osbaldiston's refusal to accede to the terms I
had mentioned. I feel no regret at it; for it is money purchased at a
heavy cost of feeling to go into that theatre. Acted King John in a
way that assured me that I could play it excellently; it seemed to
make an impression on the house, but I had not made it sure, finished,
and perfectly individualized. Some fools set up a monstrous hubbub
at the passage of defiance to the Pope, and Mr. Charles Dance told
me afterwards in the green-room that the Catholics would "cut our
throats." Is it a sin—or ought it not to be—to have the faculty of
reason and the power of cultivating it by examination, and yet remain
so low in the intellectual scale? Mrs. Sharpe was very ineffective in
the effective part of Constance. What a character! But it is because
every line is so effective that common minds cannot rise from one level,
and have not the skill by contrast and variety to give relish and effect
without great effort.

April 20th.—Looked at the *Times*, which, as usual, took no notice
of me, and the *Morning Post*, which made but slight mention of me,
devoting much space to Mrs. Sharpe's Constance and to Grisi's Norma.
Mr. Bartley came to his appointment, and we fell into a general conversation upon the condition of the theatres, and the means of restoring
the art to a better state. He spoke of my situation as at the very
head of my profession, and his readiness to go onward in any path
that I might point out as likely to lead to success; he also corrected
the statement of his letter to me in Bath about the advance of money,
saying that he would not render himself liable to unknown responsibilities, but that as far as one, two, three, or even more hundred

296

J. P. HARLEY

From an engraving

pounds would go, he would not hesitate. I told him that was all I could expect, and all that I myself intended to venture ; that I believed I was a poorer man than any of the parties summoned, with heavier claims upon me ; and that nothing could induce me to incur an uncertain responsibility.   Messrs. Harley and Farren came, and I told them that I had summoned them to learn their opinion and dispositions in the acknowledged depressed and oppressed state of an art, as to making some effort towards its re-establishment.   It was difficult to confine Messrs. Harley and Farren to the question ; they would ramble to their individual wrongs and insults. I brought them back, and requested their separate declarations of their resolutions to co-operate or no.   I addressed myself first to Bartley as the eldest present.   He, with every appearance of frankness, gave his entire assent to any plan that wore a face of likelihood for the drama's regeneration, and that as far as £500 would go, he would venture.   I replied, " That was all any one could ask."   Harley seemed disposed to go further, but rested upon a similar declaration, giving in his hearty adhesion.   Farren began with an assertion of his resolution always to *act for himself*, and digressed into complaints of the treatment he had received from the ladies and gentlemen of the company in a vote of censure passed on him. I used the most conciliatory language I could, and represented Bartley and Harley (who acquiesced in the explanation) as having been misled into concurrence by the false statement of Mr. Cooper, that *I had subscribed to the plan of a general reduction of the company's salaries.* They both expressed their regret at having been led into error by the deception practised on them, and I observed to Farren that he must now be satisfied with the *amende* offered him.   He was still rambling and desultory, and I was obliged, as courteously as I could, to *pin him to the point.*   He then at last gave his full consent to go the full length that the others had agreed to, and, unless our union were previously dissolved by mutual consent, to hold himself bound to its resolutions if acted upon unanimously ; but that if nothing effectual were accomplished by the end of July, he, as the rest of us, should then be free to pursue his own separate interest.   This point settled, I asked if any one had any plan to propose ?   Bartley had ; namely, to call a meeting and try and prevail on 300 persons to lend £100 each towards the purchase or erection of a theatre for the drama, without interest or free admission, but with the security of the building for the repayment of their principal.   This I immediately objected to as visionary and impracticable.   I then alluded to the expostulation to

297

the Committee of Drury Lane, which I had thought of, upon letting their theatre to such a bankrupt profligate as Mr. Bunn, and entreating them to protect the actors from his fraudulent tyranny by excepting him from any interference with the theatre in their next lease—or at least requiring them, if they were so indifferent to the trust they held, in the Patent for the actor's security, not to oppose their endeavour to gain their livelihood by employing their industry in some other place. This was partially approved, and Bartley suggested a memorial for a *licence;* I doubted its success, if presented to the King, who gives a licence to Mr. Braham, a rich man in active employ, for vaudevilles, etc., but would refuse *us* because we *need the profits of our calling,* and act the works of Shakspeare! I put the question, if it were not better to try the old Bill of Bulwer in the House of Commons. After some discussion, we agreed to meet at one o'clock on Monday, and consider on the subject of a memorial to the Lord Chamberlain or to the King, exposing our grievances, and supported by the names and recommendations of all the literary and influential men we could procure to sign it. It was also agreed that, previous to its presentation, we should, as I counselled, meet the D.L. Committee and confer with them on an offer started by Bartley, namely, to risk with them the chances of full or partial rent and salaries. On this we parted.

April 24th.—In reflecting on my recent communications with Mr. Cooper, I felt prompted by the indignant feelings which his dirty behaviour excited not to avoid the opportunity of expressing them ; but on considering *what benefit I should draw* from making an *insult* more palpable to his obtuse understanding, what credit I could gain by merely proving a truism in his abject and base character, I saw at once the uselessness of departing from the golden rule I had laid down for myself—*never to quarrel with any one,* and resolved not to annoy him further. I was very glad to find, on turning to the correspondence upon the part of Ctesiphon, that though to a more sensible and honourable man the sneering tone of my replies would have been most provoking, yet not one word was said that was not evoked by the stupid manifest falsehood of this paltry booby. I thank God most heartily for the ability to look the world in the face and say *I owe no man in it one farthing;* the discharge of Beetham's account makes the little I possess my own. May I prosper in my desire and endeavour to increase it for the sake of the blessed beings dependent on me. Amen! Read King Henry, and heard Nina and Willie part of their

298

lessons for the sake of showing to dear Catherine some useful pre-cautions to be taken in their instruction.

London, April 25th.—Came to town by Billings's coach with Jerdan and Mr. and Mrs. Power. At my chambers I found two notes from Mr. Cooper, one " not understanding " my disbelief of his assertion—the other copying a note from Mr. Bunn, *acting the manager* and braggadocio, to Mr. Cooper. The only tangible matter in it was his *exoneration* of Mr. Cooper from playing Ctesiphon for my Benefit ("which of the two to choose? "); he also commissioned Mr. Cooper to *ascertain* whether I would relinquish his *pledge*—to the effect of my not acting in after-pieces—as in the event of my refusal he should play me on Malibran's off-nights through my range of characters at half-price! The miserable scoundrel—what can his insane and stupid spite hurt me? A note from Forster—invitation to dinner from the Literary Fund—and a letter with overture from Clarke. On my way to the theatre saw myself announced for Richard III Friday next. Here was the climax of this dirty reptile's spite; I laughed out in the street at it. It actually amused me. At the theatre I told Mr. Cooper, as the explanation he desired, that he had told the Company "I had given my assent to a reduction of salary," when I had not. He said he had not said so. Immediately afterwards three actors in the green-room declared *that he had*. He is utterly unworthy of belief; he is a wretched creature, quite fit for Mr. Bunn's dirty work. I told him I was quite satisfied with Mr. Bunn's exoneration of him and his refusal. I now understood it perfectly—that I had no reason to return to his inquiry, except that I should hold to my engagement.

April 26th.—At Garrick Club, where I dined and saw the papers. Met Thackeray,[1] who has spent all his fortune and is now about to settle at Paris, I believe, as an artist.

April 27th.—Going out met Dow, and we set out, he intending to accompany me to the theatre; as we passed along, he stopped to read the play-bill, and exclaimed, " What's that?—' The three first acts of *Richard III.*' " So it was announced in the play-bill. He observed, "You will not do it? " and recommended me to go and declare before a witness to Mr. Cooper that I would go on and ask the audience whether they would have the play in its mutilated state or complete. I parted with him at the stage door, and taking the

---

[1] Thackeray had been appointed special correspondent of the *Constitutional*, a newly established paper, which had only a brief existence. His marriage took place in this year (1836). He returned to London in 1837.

prompter into Mr. Cooper's room, I said as much, not at all angrily, but rather amused. Mr. Cooper said he would communicate the message to Mr. Bunn. He then said that he would do the part of Ctesiphon (!) if I would send the book, as he did not wish any ill-blood to exist between us. I answered that I should mention it to Serjeant Talfourd, who would express himself as he felt on the occasion; but that he was not justified in refusing the part, as I had been *compelled* to decline playing Henry IV for him, but did so in the kindest and most friendly manner. What a fool a man is to do wrong ! He must either show himself a very bad man by persisting in his fault, or a very weak one often in retracting. Dined at the Garrick Club, where I saw newspapers and looked over *Sketches by Boz.* Saw Duruset, Durrant and Winston, who were surprised at the " three acts." Lay down in bed for an hour and a half. Acted Macbeth very fairly; I had to goad my mind into the character, for my thoughts wandered to the feverish state of things about me. Mrs. Bartley was the Lady Macbeth; she should take some of the blame for my occasional inefficiency; she was so bad, so monotonous, so devoid of all thought or feeling of character, so artificial, and yet, as it were, elaborating nothing. There was no misconception, because there was no conception, no attempt at assumption; it was Mrs. Bartley. I gave Mr. Warde a hard knock on the head inadvertently, or rather through his own awkwardness, for which I was sorry, but had I laid it open he could not have displayed more agony. I was called for and obliged to go forward and was very warmly received. Talfourd came to my room. I told him of Cooper's assent, and he informed me of Serle's reluctant declining. Cooper came in, and Talfourd thanked him *very earnestly, which I would not have done*, but Talfourd is a prosperous man and I am not. Therefore he perhaps is right and I am wrong. *I don't know.* Cooper had a letter from Bunn, which, as I had told him at the beginning of the play that I would act the three acts of *Richard III* without comment, I would not hear, as I could receive no insult from Mr. Bunn. Spoke to Templeton—all dissatisfied.

April 28th.—Went to the theatre and rehearsed in the saloon " *the three first acts of ' King Richard III.' '* " Every actor expressing his indignation at the proceeding. Went to the Garrick Club, where the subject was opened, and Planché made himself very conspicuous as the advocate of Mr. Bunn, and by his despair of any attempt to overturn the system of abuse now existing. Collier [1] was there, with whom

[1] See note, p. 67.

I talked also. I should, if alone, have touched him on his criticisms; but if I could I would prefer *buying* his praise, though I think him a fool. Spoke with Harley and Meadows. Wrote a sort of protest on *the three acts* to Cooper, but on consideration felt that the thing was not worth it. Had met Mr. Jones (Richard), who was beginning to condole with me on the rascality of Bunn and the annoyance to which I was exposed. I made light of it. Tried in chambers to read —in vain; tried to compose myself by sleep, till I was depressed and unable to think on my character for to-morrow night; I tried and could not. Wrote a letter, a short one, to Edward. Took tea, did what I could to compose and soothe my spirits—it would not be; my inability to prepare myself in the part of Richard—which I have not acted for more than four years—by to-morrow night, quite weighed me down; I tried the part; the consciousness of not having time to duly consider and practise it quite rendered unavailing all attempts. Passion and angry thoughts, angry to a degree of savageness and desperation, agitated me long and painfully. What can recompense me for being subject to the spite of such a reptile as this Bunn? If I were prepared in the character, I should laugh; I am tormented by painful doubts and misgivings. Sometimes I think of resigning my engagement, which is at least £250. I cannot do it; let what may happen I must trust in God, for God knows I have very few friends here. I am very unhappy.

April 29th.—Rose with uneasy thoughts and in a very disturbed state of mind, which I reasoned into more placidity as I proceeded with my toilet, but I had difficulty in controlling my mind, labouring under the alternate sensations of exasperation and depression. Wrote to Dow that I had settled on doing the three acts to-night, although it was against my engagement. Called on Forster on my way to rehearsal, who told me of Kemble's expression of his indignation at Mr. Bunn's behaviour. At rehearsal I spoke to Cooper on the stage, to the effect that it was not worth my while to record any protest, but that I would not do such a thing again as act in a mutilated play, my engagement not warranting the fact. Went to Garrick Club; saw Bartley and Meadows; dined and looked at papers. Spoke to Winston about the patents and licences under which the theatres are now conducted. He promised to send me copies, etc. Charles Kemble and Power were in the coffee-room, and speaking of this scandalous and insulting proceeding. On coming to chambers I wrote a letter to Lovell on the subject of Bunn's debt to him, but thinking that it might

seem an underhand revenge, I threw the letter in the fire.   My spirits
were so very much depressed, so overweighed by the situation in
which I was placed, that I lay down to compose myself, and thought
over the part of Richard as well as I could.   Went to the theatre;
was tetchy and unhappy, but pushed through the part in a sort of
desperate way as well I could.   It is not easy to describe the state of
pent-up feeling of anger, shame, and desperate passion that I endured.
As I came off the stage, ending the third act of *Richard*, in passing
by Bunn's door I opened it, and unfortunately he was there.   I could
not contain myself; I exclaimed : " You damned scoundrel !   How dare
you use me in this manner ? "   And going up to him as he sat on the
other side of the table, I struck him as he rose a backhanded slap across
the face.   I did not hear what he said, but I dug my fist into him as
effectively as I could; he caught hold of me, and got at one time the
little finger of my left hand in his mouth, and bit it.   I exclaimed :
" You rascal !   Would you bite ? "   He shouted out : " Murder !
Murder ! " and, after some little time, several persons came into the
room.   I was then upon the sofa, the struggle having brought us right
round the table.   Willmott, the prompter, said to me : " Sir, you had
better go to your room, you had better go to your room."   I got up
accordingly, and walked away, whilst he, I believe—for I did not distinctly hear him—was speaking in abuse of me.[1]   Dow came into my

---

[1] In his book *The Stage both Before and Behind the Curtain* (1840) Mr. Bunn gives
the following version of the affair : " On Friday the 29th April, I was sitting at my desk, a
few minutes before nine o'clock, and, by the light of a lamp so shaded as to reflect on the
table but obscure the room generally, I was examining bills and documents previous to their
payment on the following morning, when without the slightest note of preparation my door
was opened, and after an ejaculation of, ' There, you villain, take that—and that,' I was
knocked down, one of my eyes completely closed up, the ankle of my left leg which I am
in the habit of passing round the leg of the chair when writing violently sprained, my person
plentifully soiled with blood, lamp-oil and ink, the table upset and Richard III holding
me down.   On my naturally inquiring if he meant to murder me, and he replying in the
affirmative, I made a struggle for it, threw him off and got up on my one leg, holding him
fast by the collar, and finally succeeded in getting him down on the sofa, where, mutilated
as I was, I would have made him remember *me*, but for the interposition of the people who
had soon filled the room.   Had I had the remotest idea of the visit, I should not only have
been prepared, but not very particularly alarmed for the result, because—

> ' I was most ready to return a blow,
> And would not brook at all this sort of thing
> In my hot youth when George the Third was king.'

But this was nothing more nor less than stabbing a man in the dark.   If the provocation had
been never so great, nothing could justify such a mode of resenting it.   But I maintain there
was no provocation given—certainly none was intended. "

302

room, then Forster and young Longman. Wallace soon after, evidently deeply grieved at the occurrence. They talked and I dressed, and we left the theatre together. Wallace and Forster, on Dow leaving us, went home with me and, taking tea, discussed the probable consequences of this most indiscreet, most imprudent, most blameable action. Forster was strongly for attempting to throw Mr. Bunn overboard, on the score of character; but Wallace manifestly felt, as I felt, that I had descended to his level by raising my hand against him, and that I was personally responsible for so doing. I feel that I am; and, serious and painful as it is, I will do my duty. As I read the above lines I am still more struck with my own intemperate and unfortunate rashness. I would have gone through my engagement in forbearance and peace, still enduring wrong on wrong, as for six years I have been doing, but my passions mastered me and I sought to wreak them. No one can more severely condemn my precipitation than myself. No enemy can censure me more harshly, no friend lament more deeply my forgetfulness of all I ought to have thought upon. My character will suffer for descending so low, and the newspapers will make themselves profit of my folly. Words cannot express the contrition I feel, the shame I endure. In my own village I shall not know what I am thought of; my own family know what I have suffered, and will pity me; but I have committed a great error. God Almighty forgive me my forgetfulness of the principles I have laid down for myself, and grant that I may not suffer as I deserve from the reflections which I dread my friends will pass upon me.

April 30th.—Read for about an hour in bed last night, and though at first restless and dreaming of being in the custody of an officer, my sleep was sweet and refreshing. In opening Johnson's *Lives* in bed I began upon the narration of Savage's unfortunate rencontre with Sinclair; the idea of murder presented itself so painfully and strongly to my mind that I turned directly for relief to another subject. My thoughts have been scorpions to me; the estimation I have lost in society, the uncertainty and shame with which, if I am again invited by those who respected me, I shall meet their looks, is a punishment which has anguish in it. All I can do, as I have reduced myself to a level with this reptile, is to allow him the whole advantage of it, and accept any message for a meeting that he may choose to send me. It is some expiation, perhaps; at all events I feel it due to my character and to my children's respect for me. Who will say this alternative is not a most painful one? I acknowledge it, but I will go through with

303

it. If my boys live (as with God's blessing I trust they will) to read this record of their father's ill-governed mind, I hope they will take warning by his weakness and intemperance, and *keep their passions under due restraint*—the first means of happiness, the best worldly effect of wisdom. May God Almighty bless them, and direct them so that they may acquire a perfect self-control! Henry Smith called; it was evident the disastrous report of last night had brought him. I asked him if there was anything in the paper? He said: "Yes"; that he was surprised at the paragraph in the *Morning Chronicle*, and had come to ask if anything could be done. Wallace, Forster, and afterwards Dow, came and consulted on what was best to be done; looked at the *Morning Chronicle*, and Wallace declining to be a party to any draught of a counter-statement, the others adjourned to Forster's chambers and soon after returned, having come to the conclusion that it was better to let the thing pass. Wallace thought differently, and so did I, agreeing that it would be better a proper statement should appear in preference to an improper one. Forster, therefore, was to call on Collier, etc.; Harley, Farren and Bartley called, first speaking on this unhappy occurrence, and then passing on to the business of our meeting. When we came to enter our resolutions on paper Farren *backed out*, and much conversation ensued. At last we adjourned to give Farren time to consider and consult his brother George (!) on the expediency of his joining the union. Sent a note to C. Jones for my salary. The words "no answer" was returned. Sent to Dunn saying, if not paid I should proceed against Mr. Bunn for this amount. Mathews called to see me. Wallace, Dow and Forster called again. Sent note to Mr. Williams for his book. Felt ashamed to walk through the streets, and took a coach; ashamed even to meet the look of the people in the street. Dined with Power. Letters from Dunn, saying that Mr. Bunn was ill at Brompton, and from Mr. Fox, kindly offering to do anything to set the matter right with the public. Drove home in Dow's cab. Told dearest Catherine and Letty of the unfortunate rashness I had been guilty of. They were deeply distressed.

May 1st.—Called on Wallace, whose opinions of the necessity of going out if called were now unequivocally declared, and in which I, as before, most unreservedly concurred. Forster called, and gave me some account of the newspapers, bringing with him the *Observer* and *Examiner*, which had plain statements of my degrading act of intemperance. My shame has been endured with agony of heart, and wept with bitter tears. The fair fame of a life has been sullied by a moment's want of self-command. I cannot shelter myself from the glaring fact. But what have my sufferings not been? I can never, never, during my life, forgive myself. Forster informed me that Stephen Price [1] had been stating at the Garrick Club that he had cautioned this reptile, ' that if he persisted in goading me with the annoyances he was practising against me, that I should lose my self-restraint and inflict severe retribution upon him.' He knew me, it appears, far better than I knew myself. Wrote to H. Smith, who most kindly had called twice upon me. Talfourd, to whom I had sent a note, inquiring his dinner-hour, which Mrs. T—— answered, called and talked on the lamented occurrence. He told me of the newspapers, which he had looked at. Wrote an answer to Mr. Fox's kind note. Sent a note to Catherine, enclosing the *Observer* and *Examiner*, by Billings's coach. Went to dine with Talfourd. Saw on the placard of the *Age:* "Great Fight. B—nn and M——y." It makes me sick to think of it. Felt occasionally uncomfortable at Talfourd's, but on the whole was more comfortable than I had anticipated. Met the Bullers; I thought C. Buller rather cold, and that he was desirous of avoiding a more intimate acquaintance—I have brought all such aversions on myself. I have no right to fortify myself in my pride against the feeling of regret at these consequences of my folly. Met Kenyon,[2] whom I liked, Chisholm, young Ramohun Roy, and many other agreeable men. I was much relieved by the conversation. Returning to chambers, tried to write, but was overcome by sleep.

May 2nd.—My thoughts were little less distressing to me than on the preceding days; my character as a gentleman is "fallen from its high estate," and I can no longer fall back upon the untainted reputation which hitherto has supported me. Wallace and Forster called and returned to the painful subject. There was nothing in the *Times* or *Herald* or *Chronicle*, which I thought most kind. Dow called, and suggested an *objection* to my right of demand for salary upon the plea that my assault on this brute vitiated the engagement. I hope it is not founded in that infernal *law*. Harley called, and after a great deal of rigmarole and wordy conversation I discovered that

---

[1] An American speculator in theatres; he had been lessee of Drury Lane some years before.

[2] John Kenyon (1784-1856); *littérateur* and philanthropist, best known as an intimate friend of the Brownings.

he wanted the pretence of Farren's secession from the combination of actors to serve as a plea for his own. Oh! "what these actors are!" He expressed his distrust of Bartley as well as of Farren. I stated that I would *prove* them to-morrow, and if they fell back I could not help it. Notes from Mr. Williams, a stranger, and from Y. X. S——, both writing on the subject of this villain Bunn. Mr. Pritchard, C.G.T. also left his card. Mr. Lovell called and mentioned his proceeding against B——, which I advised him not to urge on for some days. Wrote a short letter to dear Catherine. On my way to the Garrick Club saw a face in a carriage I thought I knew, and immediately, as I passed, Malibran put her head out of the window and waved her hand to me. She seemed bridally attired. How different her lot from mine! She with fame, affluence, idolatry on every side; I, poor, struggling to maintain a doubtful reputation, which my own rashness endangers, and looking, as my greatest good, to an independence which may be just large enough to educate my children liberally and raise them above want; even this is now very doubtful. What would there be in this world for me to live upon it, if I had not my wife and children? God *help me!* Amen! Jerdan came to my dinner table at the Garrick Club. I spoke to no one, until each accosted me. Lord William Lennox [1] was the only acquaintance there that did not, and I sat next to him, my back turned to him. His is a notice I can lose without loss of honour. Saw the papers. Talked with Stephen Price, J. Smith, Blood, Willett, Douglas, etc., who were all very civil to me. Dow called to report to me his conversation upon his apprehension of the *objection* with Talfourd, who also had his doubts. Returning to chambers, had a letter from dear Catherine, which I answered.

May 3rd.—Messrs. Harley and Bartley called, and we waited upwards of an hour for Farren, during which time Mr. Bartley informed me that they had found a boy, a nephew of Algar's, to come forward to say that he was at Bunn's door when I approached it, that I pushed him aside, entered, and that he saw me strike him, then ran

---

[1] Lord William Pitt Lennox (1799–1881); a younger son of the fourth Duke of Richmond who, as Colonel Lennox, fought the famous duel with the Duke of York in 1789, and gave the ball at Brussels before the battle of Waterloo. Lord William, after serving in the Blues, and sitting for a couple of years in the House of Commons, became a club lounger and dabbler in literature, contributing to the magazines, and, later on, publishing more than one set of reminiscences. He was a good deal addicted to theatrical society, and as a "man about town" would no doubt have found Manager Bunn—rollicking, convivial, and always ready to give him the run of his theatres—a more congenial associate than the austere and not too sociable Macready.

to the prompter Willmott, and said : " Mr. Macready and Mr. Bunn
are fighting." Mr. Willmott then declares that he came into the
room, and saw me upon the sofa, holding Mr. Bunn's hair in my two
hands, Mr. Bunn over me and striking me ; that he swung Mr. Bunn
round to the other side, and desired me to go to my room. As
gross a perjury as ever the mouth of a villain uttered—so help me
God ! So may my soul know peace here and hereafter ! Talfourd
called. I thought he seemed as much disconcerted at *Ion* being withdrawn as at my suffering. He recommended a note to Cooper to
extort, if possible, a notice of dismissal. I wrote it and he approved
it. A note arrived from Mr. Farren, excusing his absence, and on
several selfish, silly, and contemptible grounds receding from the
union he had entered into. The two other worthies, Messrs. Bartley
and Harley, took the walk after him.

May 4th.—I looked in at the Temple to see Talfourd. He told
me he was going to Lady Lansdowne's to-morrow evening. This was
a little piece of innocent vanity, and quite excusable, but rather
amusing. How are our fortunes changed from our respective conditions upon our early acquaintance ! How more than ever at this
present moment ! Several times to-day I have wished to be rid of
existence. *I am very unhappy.*

May 5th.—Slept better than I have done for some nights, but the
weight upon my spirits is not to be dispelled. I have made my own
unhappiness, and in one little moment have rendered years as nothing.
There are not many persons who suffer keener stings of self-reproach
than I do ; I am indeed *most unhappy.* Talfourd called, having reconsidered the subject of the advertisement of the Benefit, to dissuade me
from it, but rather wishing me to wait. Dear Catherine arrived with
Willie and baby ; it was a *comfort* to see them—to look on what I
love and *feel them near me.* Dear Catherine had brought a letter
from Kenneth with an offer of £200 for twelve nights from Mr.
Osbaldiston, and an invitation from Calcraft. I wrote to Kenneth
wishing to see him. Kenneth called ; we talked on the matter, and
he took down my modification of Mr. Osbaldiston's offer. I observed
that I did not wish to trade upon, or raise my terms on, this unfortunate occurrence ; but that I could not, under the circumstances of the
season, take less than had been offered to other actors ; that I did not
wish him to say £240 for twelve nights, but would he say £200 for
ten nights, or £120 for six ? For *Ion* I also stipulated. At my
chambers I found Dow, who went upstairs with me. A letter was

lying on the table for me, the hand strange to me. On opening the envelope I found a letter from the wretched villain who has caused me all this suffering—to the effect that he considered my engagement, etc., "*cancelled and determined*" by my "*attempt to assassinate*" him on Friday evening and that he had given orders to the door-keepers, etc., not to admit me "on any pretence whatever." It was a great relief to me to receive this letter—and I was as much, if not more, gratified by his accusation of my "*attempt to assassinate*" than by the release I have obtained from the perplexing dilemma in which his silence left me. I trust it is for good; I hope it is, and humbly, devoutly and penitently do I pray God it will be. Amen! What may be the further result of this most miserable forgetfulness of decency, pride, and station on my part I cannot tell, but if it were for ourselves to judge of the proportioning punishment to crime I should be disposed to say my sufferings have exceeded my offence. I know, however, that it is not so—that the great law of morality fits the torture to the crime, and I, at the age I have reached—— My God! My God! can I ever be forgiven? Can I ever think without *sickening shame* of my *insane conduct?* Forgive me, oh my God! And you, my blessed and beloved children, pity while you condemn this intemperate ebullition of your unhappy parent, who has so deeply sunk his own reputation and thereby prejudiced your interests. Had I learned, what I have tried to teach myself, that first and best lesson of *self-control*, I never should have tarnished my character and have poisoned with the remembrance of this shocking folly every feeling of my future life. There have been moments when I have felt it not worth retaining, and when, I fear—but I must not look back upon my madness. To Almighty God I lift up my prayer in penitence and shame—imploring His forgiveness, and His grace to regulate my evil passions for the time to come. Amen! Amen! Amen!

May 6th.—In reflecting on the letter received from Mr. Bunn last night, it occurred to me that the occasion should not be lost of fixing the question as to the honourable feeling which has actuated me. I wrote to Wallace, wishing his presence and advice, and wrote out the substance of what I thought ought to be returned to Mr. Bunn; I also sent to Kenneth, requesting him to see me. A note from Mr. Conquest of the Garrick theatre, Whitechapel (!), offering me an engagement for six nights—to divide the house, ensuring me £100. A very kind letter, and one that would comfort me, if anything could, from Colonel Birch; an offer from Clarke of £165 for ten nights at

Liverpool, etc. Answered Mr. Conquest, civilly declining his offer.
Wrote to Dow wishing to see him before I sent to Cooper for my
book. Mr. Kenneth called, and I assented to £200 for ten nights,
giving in two nights and to take my Benefit on the same terms Mr.
C. Kemble had his. He left me to see Mr. Osbaldiston. Shall I
ever know peace of heart again? The very thought of meeting such
men as Young,[1] so prudent, so discreet, and therefore so respected,
of knowing that high-minded men like Colonel D'Aguilar read in the
newspapers my wretched self-degradation, tortures and agonizes me.
I close my eyes with the hated idea, and it awakens me with the earliest
morning. I know what misery is, that misery which cannot be escaped :
it is " myself " that am the " Hell " that is consuming me. Kenneth
returned with the terms of Mr. Osbaldiston, which I accepted, viz. £200
for ten nights, and a Benefit divided, after £20, beginning Wednesday, May 11th, and ending Saturday, June 11th. I gave my promise
to act two nights in addition gratuitously. Kenneth then went for
Mr. Osbaldiston, and, returning with him, we interchanged agreements,
which I pray God may prosper. *C. Buller has not called upon me*—
our acquaintance is therefore at an end. I am sorry, but it does not
seem, from this evidence, of great value. Wrote to Talfourd for books
and frank. Sent notes to Drury Lane for my books and clothes.
Robert brought me his account, which I paid, and made him a present.
Forster and Dow called—determined on dining and going down to
Elstree. Walked with Dow to his chambers and on to his house;
dined and came in his cab home. Found all well, thank God! No
subject of conversation but this *hateful* yet *inevitable one*, except when
Dow breathed out his own lamentations on the excessive amount of his
upholsterer's bill. This was misery to him, and how light and endur-
able it seems to me. Looked at my darling children as they slept.
God Almighty bless them and may they never know the restless anguish
of my mind. Amen!

May 7th.—Walked out to call on Henry Smith; in the Covent
Garden play-bills my name was blazing in large red letters at the head
of the announcement. May it be prosperous! Went to the Garrick
Club. On my way met Bartley, Meadows, and Power; they spoke of
the affair, stating that Bunn had given confused accounts, and that
he admitted his inability to recollect distinctly the occurrence—that
one statement was I had knocked the table over, and that Stephen
Price had observed upon that, that a person *could not overturn that*

---

[1] The actor Charles Mayne Young (see note, p. 34).

table; but if I did, who had reinstated it with its etcs. when the people entered? Power addressed me in reply to a question I put, whether I should be attacked on my appearance, and they all assented to his assertion that there would be no opposition; I do not feel confident of that. White came up and returned with me to the Club. Saw Price and T. Hill at the Club; G. Robins. Kemble came in as I was going out. I told the waiter to ask him to step into the strangers' room, which he did. I said that it had gratified me much to hear of the liberal way in which he had spoken of me before and subsequently to this unfortunate affair; that I had commissioned my friend Talfourd to say as much to him, but, seing him there, I chose to anticipate his intention and to express myself the sense I entertained of his liberal manner of mentioning my name, having so long been in a state of hostility with him. He replied that he had never cherished any hostile feeling towards me, and that his language had always been in the same tone; that every one must feel indignant at the infamous conduct of this Bunn towards me, and that he had ever entertained the best feelings for me. I drew off my glove, and said that I had much pleasure in acknowledging the liberality of his conduct. He shook hands very cordially, saying that it had been always a matter of regret to him that our acquaintance had been interrupted, and I replied that I regretted this reconcilement had been forced from me by the generous and liberal behaviour which he had shown, and had not rather proceeded spontaneously from me. We then talked a little of the circumstance, he observing that he was glad Bunn had not challenged me, as my name would be so much more mixed up with him; and I added, that I was not quite sure how far it would have been better or not, as I had made arrangements for receiving his message, to which he observed: "If you were challenged of course you must go out; every man must go out, when challenged." We parted in the hall; my feelings were excited and won over on this occasion; but I cannot help pausing to remark how very much I yield to impulse, instead of guiding my course through life on a stern, undeviating principle of justice. I call charity only justice. I fear I am often weak on this account, and seem vacillating where I ought to be unmoving. I certainly feel no ill-will to Kemble; on the contrary, feel kindly disposed to him on account of his language, etc., at this juncture, which, it is manifest, he wished me to be acquainted with. But Kemble has not redeemed those errors in his character which leave him open to overwhelming censure. Should I then have obeyed a kindly and

310

sort of grateful feeling, or have weighed in my judgment the value, motive, and sincerity of his conduct? *I am not quite clear.*[1] Sent the books of *Ion* with a note to Mr. Osbaldiston; sent a letter which I had written to Ellen Tree, and returned home by Billings reading *Ion* on the way. Found my children all well, thank God!

London, May 9th.—Came to town by Billings's, reading *Ion* by the way; alighted at Cambridge Terrace, and called on Wallace, who told me that the Sunday papers had not extended their comments on this wretched affair, which I was glad to hear. I submitted to him the address I thought of delivering on Wednesday, which he considered as too lofty, and as attacking Mr. Bunn. Knowing that I am not a proper and dispassionate judge of my own condition, I so far yielded to his observations as to leave the paper with him, which he is to return with his own views of the style of defence. Called at Covent Garden theatre. Saw Mr. Osbaldiston. Settled the night of *Ion*: 26th instant. Spoke about orders, dressing-room, etc., in all of which Mr. O—— seemed desirous of accommodating me. Was introduced to Mr. Fitzball [2] (!), the Victor Hugo, as he terms himself, of England—the " Victor No-go " in Mr. Keeley's nomenclature. Dined at the Garrick Club, where I am regarded with an " eye askance " by the *roué* set, the Lennox, Stanhope, and black-leg party; this will not kill me. Saw Dowling; [3] Meadows; Villiers, who spoke to me of D'Aguilar and Bulwer; Stanfield; and Simpson, who renewed the expression of his wish to paint my picture. Read a very amusing article on Sir A. Agnew [4] in *Fraser's Magazine*. Forster gave me an account of some opinions, which, I think, were *Power's* (with whom he spent yesterday),

---

[1] *August 8th.*—I now am—that I was, as I too requently am, *precipitate*, and acted on impulse in a matter that should have been duly deliberated on.

[2] Edward Fitzball (1792–1873) originally a printer's apprentice ; wrote several dramas, some moderately successful ; also various romances, lyrics, and librettos. His *Reminiscences* appeared in 1859.

[3] Probably Serjeant Dowling, mentioned by Serjeant Ballantine in his *Experiences* as a frequenter of the Club. To judge by an anecdote in the *Experiences*, he was of a type that was turned to good account by Dickens. As a junior, he had been engaged in a case where his opportunities of distinction were confined to the asking of a single question, namely the address of a witness. This not very striking achievement was recorded in one of the succeeding Sunday's newspapers with which he was connected in the following terms : " Here Mr. Dowling rose, and with a most impressive tone and manner asked the witness where he lived."

[4] Sir Andrew Agnew, Bart. (1793–1849), a Scotch Sabbatarian, who led an abortive agitation for a *Lord's Day Protection* Act.

upon my taking an engagement from Bunn *at all*. *What could I do?* At chambers read over my address and read *Macbeth*. Wrote a note to Catherine; not happy, not comfortable.

May 10th.—Went to rehearsal, calling on Forster by the way, who related to me and showed me a statement in the *Chronicle* of the occurrence that Jerdan had cut to pieces (as he had said at Elstree he would do) Maclise's portrait of Sir J. Soane,[1] who has been absurdly and tetchily desirous of destroying that too faithful record of his personal appearance. At Garrick Club saw the papers; and from thence went to take a warm bath, in hopes of reducing my rheumatism. My spirits continued very low, though I am quite resolved not to let these vile rascals nor my own imprudence defeat my purpose of labouring for my children. *Tu ne cede malis* is my motto, and may God speed me and prosper me in overcoming them! Amen! Amen! Amen! An oration from Mr. George Jones—I have no time for nonsense now. Every interval of my day was given to the words I have to utter to-morrow, which I cannot get the complete command of. Sent notes to Palmer and Davis about Ion's dress. Sent my thanks, etc., to Covent Garden theatre. Notes, very kind and comforting ones, from dear Catherine and Fanny Twiss, both of which I briefly answered.

May 11th.—*My prayers have been heard!* My heart lifts up itself in humble but fervent gratitude to God Almighty for His constant goodness to one so unworthy of it. Blessed and praised be His name, and may I by my future life show my gratitude in acts of virtue and a continued course of piety and benevolence! Amen! Amen! Amen! Arose nervous and uneasy; sent a note to Wallace, requesting him to send round to me at the theatre this evening, if it should not seem necessary to speak. A short but most kind letter from Ellen Tree; it quite affected me. A clerk brought a note from G. Barker, as I was going out, informing me that Evans had inquired of him if he was not my solicitor, as he wished to serve a process on me, he (B——) offering him friendly assistance towards settling the matter, which he thought should not come before the public. I answered it, that I had placed myself in my counsel's hands, who had disposed of me, thanking him kindly for his offer. He was so indifferent in my affairs before that, although I felt disposed to call back my note and take his offer,

---

[1] Sir John Soane (1753–1837); R.A., son of a mason; his real name was Swan; an eminent architect and donor to the nation of the museum bearing his name in Lincoln's Inn Fields.

I am not, on reflection, sorry that I did not.   Went to rehearsal, then
to Garrick Club, where I saw and talked with C. Dance and Power.
Dance walked with me to chambers.   Called on Forster, who reported
some impertinences of Messrs. Poole and Dunn, which annoyed me.
It is difficult, in such a nervous state as I have been in, to discipline
one's mind, or listen to one's judgment.   Sent a note to Talfourd for
the introduction to Messrs. White and Whitmore,[1] which he sent
in the course of the afternoon.   Dow called and rather cheered me by
the view he took of my case; I lay down, and tried to *lay my nerves
down*, as it were, in a state of perfect passiveness; but I was very
nervous—*nervous*—could not think of the play—now and then went
over the address, but was uncertain of it.   Went to the theatre and,
in dressing, still felt my nerves were untrue to me; looked over the
early part of the play, and just before I went on I screwed up myself
to care for nothing, and went boldly and resolutely forward.   On my
entrance in *Macbeth* the pit—indeed, the house—rose, and waved hats
and handkerchiefs, cheering in the most fervent and enthusiastic manner.
It lasted so long that it rather overcame me; but I entered on my own
task determined to do my best, and, I think, I never acted Macbeth
more really or altogether better.   The applause was tumultuous at the
fall of the curtain, and the person who went on was driven back with
cries of "No," and I went before them.   When silence was gained, I
spoke an address as follows : " Ladies and Gentlemen,—Under ordinary
circumstances I should receive the manifestation of your kindness with
silent acknowledgment; but I cannot disguise from myself the fact
that the circumstances which have led to my engagement at this
theatre, after an absence of many years, are uppermost in your minds.
Into those circumstances I will not enter further than by two
general observations : first, that I was subjected in cold blood, from
motives which I will not characterize, to a series of studied and annoying and mortifying provocations, personal and professional.   The
second, that, suffering under these accumulated provocations, I was
betrayed, in a moment of unguarded passion, into an intemperate and
imprudent act, for which I feel, and shall never cease to feel, the
deepest and most poignant self-reproach and regret.   It is to you,
ladies and gentlemen, and to myself, that I owe this declaration, and
I make it with unaffected sincerity.   To liberal and generous minds,
I think, I need say no more.   I cannot resist thanking you."
This seemed to affect many and engage the sympathies of all.

[1] A firm of solicitors, whom Macready thenceforward frequently consulted.

Talfourd, Dow, Smith, Forster, Wallace, Maclise and the editors of
the *Post* and *Herald*, who wished a report of the speech, came into
my room, but I was too nervous to have pleasure from their presence.
All were delighted, and I felt greatly relieved and truly grateful. Mr.
Fitzball came in with offers of accommodation, attentions, etc.
Wallace walked part of the way with me to chambers, and when there
Bourne came in from the Westminster dinner. He sat whilst I wrote
out a copy of my address, and then most kindly took it to the *Morning
Post* office. Mason had left a note inviting me to dine with him next
week. A *dear* letter from Catherine—God bless her! The messenger
from the *Post*, called but the note had been taken by Bourne. Wrote
a line to dear Catherine. Thank God! Thank God! Thank
God!

May 13th.—Passed on to the Garrick Club, where I saw the evening papers of yesterday, which were all kind, and the *Times* of this
day. It is difficult to speak or think with temper of such a nasty fellow
as the conductor of this paper; it is a waste of honest indignation to
lose words or thought on anything so profligate and flagitious. It
copied my address, and added the falsest and most offensive comments
it could apply. I could eat little dinner after reading it. G. Dance
came up and spoke to me about it, the purposed dinner to Mr. Bunn (!)
observing how ill Mr. Westmacott was used. In talking of the
matter I observed that it was impossible for me to send a message
to Mr. Bunn, let him behave as he would have done. After leaving
him and reaching Lincoln's Inn Fields, I recollected what I had said
and, apprehensive of a misconstruction on the part of Dance, posted
back to set him right on the point, and stating that I had taken
immediate measures to give him a meeting. He said he was aware of
that; but I was glad I had taken the precaution. O'Hanlon sent a
kind, congratulatory note for orders, which I sent him. Chilton
called, which I thought kind. He told me that I could not set off my
loss against Bunn, but that I must proceed by a cross-action, on which
I resolved, if attacked. Wrote a note of thanks to Mr. Black,[1]
Morning Chronicle, for his kind attention. Sent a note to Wallace,
wishing to see him to-night about the *Times*. Lay down in a most
unhappy state of mind. Went to the theatre and acted Virginius in
a splendid manner, quite bearing the house along with me. My reception was most enthusiastic on my entrance, and when I appeared at last

---

[1] John Black (1783-1855); for over a quarter of a century editor of the *Morning
Chronicle*.

in obedience to the call of the audience. Thought of going to the Club, but feeling myself in a very irritable and excited state, deemed it prudent not to do so. Went to chambers in a wretched, wretched state of mind; thought of the villain who had in so cowardly and infamous a manner attacked me in the *Times*. Felt that life was not worth holding on such terms, and, but for those dear ones who make it a duty to me, think I should either lay it down or put it to the hazard in punishing the scoundrels who are thus torturing me. These are neither religious nor philosophic thoughts, but I feel myself merely a weak, frail creature, the sport of passion, and *in consequence* a very wretched being.

May 14th.—I allowed my candle to burn till some time after one, and again awoke in twilight at about three—lying in a very restless state both as to mind and body. *I am not what I have been! Ichabod! Ichabod!* It was a night of misery. The shoemaker Davies called about some sandals. I do not like the man; he is *inaccurate*. Wrote notes to Bulwer in reply to his—to C. Buller, with invitation for himself and brother, which I do not expect him to accept, and do not care that he should—to White, to Ransom's, enclosing cheque for £54 10s. 6d.—to Robertson for salary. Palmer called, and I settled with him about the first dress for *Ion*. A poor man called to ask for a subscription. I am in no state of mind to shut my heart or purse to the necessitous. Called at the offices of Messrs. White and Whitmore. Found there that the process had been served by Evans, Bunn's attorney, and that they, W—— and W——, had entered an appearance for me, so the battle is begun. May God Almighty be my aid and defence through it! Amen! Mr. Whitmore promised to send Mr. Gray to me, and I returned to chambers. Wrote notes of thanks, etc., to H. Smith and to Mason, naming Thursday to dine with him next week. Forster called, and in referring to the blackguard behaviour of the *Times*, I could not speak. I covered my face with my grasping hands, and was obliged to go into the next room, where some cold water, etc., restored me to a composed appearance, and I returned with an appearance of cheerfulness. Wrote to Calcraft, inquiring of him what would be his evidence on the *Bridal*. Mr. Gray called, and we talked over the matter of the cross-action, which he thought should be proceeded on immediately, I, of course, concurring; he seemed to think I might go for the whole of my engagement, and it seems to me only fair; but who can divine the scope of law? He took my engagement with him, and I appointed to call on him at a quarter past nine on Monday next. Sent the advertisement of *Ion* to the newspapers. Came home by Bryant, whom I very nearly lost by being late. Read the kind, the very kind, notices in the *Court Journal* and the *Literary Gazette*. Had gone several miles before I could sufficiently withdraw my mind from this *hateful subject* to attend to anything; at length began to *try* to read *Ion*. Oh, what a state am I in to read! Found all my dear ones well at home. This is some comfort indeed.

Elstree, May 15th.—But one subject seems to fill my mind; sorrow and shame alternately depress and agitate my heart. When I think of those who might have been disposed to esteem me and whose esteem I coveted, I sink at once into despondency; when the thought of any proud and fastidious person occurs to me, I feel that I have no longer the power to repel his insolence with a lofty and unaltered brow. I feel my degradation. I did not think I could have borne so much. There was no change in the subject of my ruminations till I came downstairs. Looked at the newspaper, which gave a very judicious and brief comment upon the extracted account of the *Morning Post*. Rehearsed *Stranger*. Talfourd and White came. Talfourd read *Ion* in the green-room, and was evidently happy in his employment. Who would not be? Should have acted the *Stranger* well, but was quite *bouleversé* by the *drunken* or *insane fustian* efforts of Mr. Barnett [1] in Steinfax. He was really disgusting. I was called for by the audience, but would not go on without Miss H. Faucit, whom I led forward. Went afterwards to Mrs. Baker's, where I saw Palmer, Mrs. Jameson, Mrs. Marcet [2] (not introduced), Talfourd and White, with whom I adjourned to Garrick Club—where was Mr. Poole, to whom and to Mr. Planché, the sticklers for Mr. Bunn, I was very distant. On reflection I was wrong—it was *undignified*.

May 19th.—Rehearsed *Ion*, which seems to me to *come out* in the acting—we shall see. Spoke about my name being put in the bills by Mr. Osbaldiston after Mr. Kemble's. This is to me of no importance, but I have no right to be placed out of my own rank before the public. They, as a body, know nothing of the art and only take their opinions from what they are told, therefore I have no right to let them be told what is not true and against my interest. A note from Heraud for tickets, which I answered, addressing him, "My dear sir." When

---

[1] Presumably Morris Barnett (1800–1856); dramatist and comedian.

[2] Mrs. Jane Marcet, *née* Haldimand (1769–1858); of Swiss origin; the well-known author of "popular science" text-books.

my note had gone I perceived his style to me was " My dear Macready." I therefore wrote another note to despatch in the morning, that he may not think me repulsive or proud.

May 20th.—Went to rehearsal, where I took all the pains I could. A note of invitation from O'Hanlon, which I answered, and wrote to Walker, expressing my inability to visit him. Wrote also a letter of thanks to Miss Huddart. Henry Earle called as I was dining, and he lunched with me. He told me that none who knew me would think worse of me for the late occurrence. It may be so, but it is their indulgence that leads them to such lenient judgment. I have forgotten the dues of a gentleman; it cannot be cloaked or denied. It is very true that I am not sought for by persons of rank, as they are termed, by persons of distinction, but heretofore I could repel this indifference with indifference. I feel my title to rank with any man as a gentleman unquestionable; how can I now answer the objections that may be made against me? Why are we sent into this world?—to undergo a torture which makes the fabled physical endurances of Hell an enviable alternative. If I were alone, I could bear my disgust with the world to solitude, and die and rot in peace in some lonely corner—but I am chained to bear the consciousness of the *curse* that is upon me, with witnesses of my misery. I lay down and slept long and deeply from very weariness. Acted Hamlet as well as I could under a most excruciating attack of rheumatism and much fatigue. I think I did much of the part well, though not so well as when last I played at Drury Lane: I was called for and made my obeisances. Knowles, Forster, and Talfourd afterwards came into my room. Talfourd talked much of his play; my cause seems quite an unimportant matter; he is right to revel in his happiness : he *deserves it*, he has earned it, and it is fit he should enjoy it. But the contrast of our several conditions now, and sixteen years ago, is most humiliating to me. I seemed then to have fortune and honour before me, and he was a clever, industrious young lawyer. *I am now a wretch!* He is all he can wish to be— courted and caressed by the wise, the illustrious, and the titled many! But he *well merits all—all.*

May 21st.—A note from Bulwer told me that his play was rejected at Covent Garden.

May 23rd.—Went to the theatre. The audience were so noisy that some scenes—the dagger soliloquy, that with the murderers and Lady Macbeth—could not be heard; but where I could be heard I did not act badly, and the house was very warm in its testimonies of approbation. I was called for, and obliged to appear at the end of the play. Browning, Talfourd, and Forster came into my room and stayed some time. I recollect the disgust with which I heard of a Mr. A——, a singer, fighting with a Mr. B——, thinking to myself how impossible it was that I could descend to lift my hand against any one. Is it, then, to be wondered at that I feel my degradation as I do?

May 26th.—Rehearsed *Ion* with much care. Went to the theatre and acted the character as well as I have ever played any previous one, with more of inspiration, more complete abandonment, more infusion of myself into another being, than I have been able to attain in my performances for some time, particularly in the devotion of Ion to the destruction of Adrastus, the parting with Clemanthe, and the last scene. But—as if events arise and are forgotten without leaving the benefit of experience in their passage—I lost my temper again to-night: a particular scene for a particular picturesque effect had been decided on in the morning, and when I came to look at its disposition, I found another, to which I had objected in the morning, substituted for it. I was foolish enough to be *very angry*, very much agitated, and yet all passed off, and I might have been so much better by the government of my temper, which *effected nothing but my own exposure*. Oh! how bitter—how very bitter is the reflection that follows these unwise, unworthy transports of passion! Was called for very enthusiastically by the audience, and cheered on my appearance most heartily. I said: ' It would be affectation to conceal the peculiar pleasure in receiving their congratulatory compliment on this occasion. It was indeed most gratifying to me; and only checked by the painful consideration that this might be perhaps the last new play I ever might have the honour of producing before them. (Loud cries of ' No! No! ') However that might be, the grateful recollection of their kindness would never leave me.' Miss Ellen Tree, I heard, was afterwards called forward. Talfourd came into my room and heartily shook hands with me and thanked me. He said something about Mr. Wallack wishing him to go on the stage, as they were calling, but it would not be right. I said: "On no account in the world." He shortly left me, and, as I heard, was made to go forward to the front of his box, and receive the enthusiastic tribute of the house's grateful delight. How happy he must have been! Smith, Dow, Browning, Forster, Richardson, etc., I cannot remember all, came into my room. I dressed, having sent to Catherine to request her not to wait for me, but to go at once to Talfourd's, and, taking Knowles in the carriage, went there. I felt

T. N. TALFOURD

From an engraving

tranquilly happy. Happy in the splendid assemblage that had graced the occasion, happy in the triumphant issue of this doubtful experiment, and happy in the sensation of relief that attended the consciousness of its being achieved. I was also happy in having been an agent in the pleasing work of making others happy. At Talfourd's I met Wordsworth, who pinned me; Walter Savage Landor, to whom I was introduced, and whom I very much liked; Stanfield, Browning, Price, Miss Mitford—I cannot remember all. Forster came to me after supper, which was served in a very elegant style, and insisted that it was expected in the room that I should propose Talfourd's health, whose birthday it was. After some contest, and on the understanding that no further speeches should be made, and briefly alluding to the day being the birthday of the poet, as well as to the beautiful play that night presented, I proposed Talfourd's health. He returned thanks and afterwards proposed my health with much of eulogy, to which I replied as I best could. Subsequently, Mrs. Talfourd's health was proposed by Douglas, and was very pleasantly and humorously acknowledged by Talfourd, who in a very lively vein ascribed to her the influence which had given birth to much that had been honoured with the praise of the company—that, in fact, the whole merit of the production was hers, etc. It became then a succession of personal toasts, Miss E. Tree, Miss Mitford, Mr. Stanfield, Mr. Price, Mr. Poole,[1] who made a most egregious ass of himself; Browning, and who else I do not know. I was very happily placed between Wordsworth and Landor, with Browning opposite, and Mrs. Talfourd next but one —Talfourd within two. I talked much with my two illustrious neighbours. Wordsworth seemed pleased when I pointed out the passage in *Ion*, of a "devious fancy," etc., as having been suggested by the lines *he* had once quoted to me from a MS. tragedy of his; he smiled and said, "Yes, I noticed them," and then he went on—

> "Action is transitory—a step—a blow,
> The motion of a muscle—this way or that—
> 'Tis done ; and in the after vacancy
> We wonder at ourselves like men betrayed."

Landor, in talking of dramatic composition, said he had not the constructive faculty, that he could only set persons talking, all the rest was chance. He promised to send me his play of *Count Julian*, and expressed himself desirous of improving his acquaintance with me. I

[1] See note, p. 224.

spoke to Miss Mitford, observing in badinage that the present occasion should stimulate her to write a play; she quickly said, " Will you act it ? " I was silent. Catherine, who sat near her and Harness, told me that he said: " Aye, hold him to that." When I heard that *that* was Harness, the man who, I believe, has inflicted such a deep and assassin-like wound upon me, through *Blackwood's Magazine*, I could not repress the expression of indignant contempt which found its way to my face, and over-gloomed the happy feeling that had before been there. Moroseness—unchecked will—when am I to learn and practise a sensible, restrained and philosophic bearing? We went home together; Catherine, Letitia, Miss Haworth, and myself in the carriage, talking of nothing but the evening's events—this happy evening. We reached home about two, and went to bed with the birds singing their morning song in our tired ears. Thank God!

Elstree, May 27th.—Rose, quite worn out—with a feeling of weariness and incapacity to employ myself that was almost distressing. I did write two notes—one to Mr. Notter, about a fan of Miss Haworth's, and another to Mr. Farren on the subject of Miss Faucit's Benefit. Miss Haworth remained with us through the day; like ourselves, I suppose the excitement of yesterday left her indisposed to do more than talk over and ruminate upon its occurrences and sensations. I lay upon the grass or strolled about the garden all the morning; in the afternoon, walked down to the reservoir with Nina and Willie, taking the dogs with us. It was a quiet, happy, idle, languid day, but such an one as yesterday is an event in a life, and requires an interval of rest to sober oneself back to one's ordinary state. In the evening I walked home with Miss Haworth—a beautiful moonlight. Oh, what a world is this, where only love and benevolent feelings have existence! And how shocking—how wretched and disgusting the converse!

London, May 28th.—On my way to London vainly strove to occupy my thoughts with the character of Cassius; deep and heavy sleep came on me—the effects of the past excitement and fatigue soon weighed me down. Found at my chambers notes and cards of congratulation on the success of *Ion;* sent a card with message to Messrs. White and Whitmore. Called on Forster, who gave me the criticism of the newspapers for Catherine, of which that of the *Times* was the warmest, though all were enthusiastic. The *Chronicle* was most niggardly. Went to the theatre to rehearse *Cassius*, and found the call-man had made a mistake of two hours in my call. Saw Knowles, who was

320

vehement in his praise. A note from Arthur Buller; fervent in his congratulations, and confessing his surprise at the result. At the Garrick Club, where I dined, I saw the other papers—an equal tone held throughout. Saw Bentley, Meadows, Dow, Fladgate, etc. Forster called in for a short time. I acted the *Stranger* but indifferently—still was called for by the audience, and led on Miss H. Faucit, who was not.

May 30th.—Felt rather more refreshed than I had yet done since Thursday, but was overcome by sleep through the greater part of my journey to town by Billings, and discomfited in my efforts to read Cassius. Arriving at chambers I found a note from Browning. What can I say upon it? It was a tribute which remunerated me from the annoyances and cares of years: it was one of the very highest, may I not say the highest, honour I have through life received. Received in bed a note from Forster requesting me to call or to receive him, as *Landor* was with him and desirous of seeing me. I could not get up and dress myself, and thus lost the pleasure of again seeing Landor. Went to the theatre; the audience were rather noisy through the early scenes, but I was not disposed to yield to them. I do not think that my reception was quite so long as Kemble's, or I did not use sufficient generalship with it; but I acted Cassius in my very best style, and made the audience feel it. I was good; I was the character; I felt it. The audience were rapid and vehement in their applause; I was first and most loudly called for at the end of the play. Knowles got through Brutus far better than I anticipated; he came into my room, and said that I was wonderful. I was certainly pleased with my own performance this evening; it was fresh, characteristic, and majestic. Talfourd came into my room and, among other things, reported the enthusiastic praise of Lady Blessington and D'Orsay of my performance of *Ion*. The praises of Knowles, the barrister, pleased me still more. He told Talfourd he had laughed at the idea of my performing *Ion;* that he hated me ten years since; and that he could not have believed that such an improvement could have taken place in any one. To Forster also he observed how I must have studied. Went to Garrick Club, where Barham and Lincoln Stanhope came directly to chat with me. Supped with Talfourd, and an *Ion* supper for Friday next was settled. Received a very nice note from Lane. I feel truly grateful for the improved condition of my reputation. May I by my future conduct sustain and merit it! Oh, God, in whom I hope and trust, direct and support me!

May 31st.—Looked at the newspapers which, as for a Benefit, do

not notice my performance last night.   Received a note from Mr.
Lovell, informing me of the settlement of his dues by Mr. Bunn.
Mr. Holt called, but I obtained little or no information from him.
He promised to look for the account of Mr. Bunn's trial v. West-
macott, in which he got one shilling damages.   Went to rehearse
Clemanthe's scenes of *Ion*, and passed on to the Garrick Club, where
I looked at the other newspapers; they contained nothing.   Met
Winston on my return, who told me that it had been given out that
I had engaged for Covent Garden next season.   Mr. Fitzball came
up, and walked with me to Great Queen Street.   Asking my terms, I
said I should not take less than £40 per week, on my late Drury Lane
articles—and I would not say that I would take that.   Called on
Forster for a few minutes.   Wrote out the heads of my case for
Messrs. White and Whitmore; wrote to Browning, sending the note
to Forster.   George Macready called with his diploma as surgeon,
which he obtained last night.   I am very grateful to God Almighty
for having given me the power of saving this young man from an
idle, dissolute and ignorant life as a subordinate player, and of placing
him in a creditable sphere of life.   I was truly grateful in thinking
of it; gave him a sovereign to amuse himself.[1]   Called on Messrs. W——
and W——, gave them my case, and talked with them; it seems settled
to let judgment go by default.   Left a card at Mr. Norton's.   Called
on Miss Ellen Tree, and sat with her a short time.   Dined at the
Garrick Club and saw the magazines.   The *Metropolitan* has a friendly
notice of me; read part of Forster's review of *Paracelsus*, which is
very good.

   June 1st.—Rehearsed *Ion*, and have all the feeling of *second* night
about me, and the uncomfortable addition of a strange actress, Miss
H. Faucit, whom I do not like; she wants heart.[2]   Farren spoke to
me about his engagement for next season at this theatre.   Looked in
for a few minutes to the Garrick Club.   Saw Fladgate, Dance, etc.
Coming to dine at chambers, wrote to Mrs. Robertson, to Dow, to
H. Smith, to Blanchard, and to Catherine.   After dinner lay down
and slept long and heavily, but forced myself to look over the play
before I rose.   This lawsuit hangs heavy and wearingly upon my
mind—my thoughts are prevented and dogged by the alternate con-

----

[1] Macready had been most helpful and generous to this young man, a half-brother by
his father's second marriage, and was not too well requited.

[2] Though a true friend of Miss Faucit, Macready never ranked her as a first-rate actress;
with considerable abilities and attractiveness, in his opinion she lacked genius and magnetic
quality.

jectures and misgivings about this odious business. Went to the
theatre. The house was remarkably well filled, but I had all the
languor and inertness and *absence* of a *second night* upon me. I
strove against it, but ineffectually. I acted *Ion* but indifferently. I
was called for by the audience, and made my acknowledgments.
Browning, Forster, Wallace came into my room. I went with Forster
into Mrs. Talfourd's private box. They are much displeased with
Miss Mitford,[1] who seems to be showing herself *well up*. She was bad
from the beginning. How strange with so much talent!

June 2nd.—My mind was restless and uneasy. How can I expect
to find ease under this liability, to which *my madness* has exposed
me; I can call it, can regard it as nothing else. Looked at the newspapers. Prepared my letters, etc., for my solicitors. Gray called,
and appointed a meeting at two in Talfourd's chambers. Continued
my employment with the letters, when C. Buller surprised me with a
call. He sat some time. A letter from Birmingham—a note from
Smith and one from Dow, accepting invitation for Sunday. Forster
called. Went with me to the Temple, where I met Talfourd, Whitmore, and Gray. The chances, etc., of the different measures were
discussed. Talfourd said that Lord Denman[2] had said the damages
ought to be a farthing; but my nature is not sanguine. It was all but
concluded on to let judgment go by default. I cannot, of course, be
a judge in such a case.[3] Went to Covent Garden about Talfourd's
private box. Lovell called and told me that Mr. Hugh Evans, the
solicitor against me, had said that it was believed I had instigated
him, Lovell, to this proceeding. I was very angry about it. Lost
my evening in angry efforts to write a cool note to the blackguard
solicitor, Mr. Evans. Sick with anger and disgust.

June 3rd.—Wrote a note with orders to Wallace, and one to
Catherine. Read over *Ion*, and then proceeded to sort the letters
necessary for the case of Mr. Bunn, and to make fair copies of my

---

[1] Miss Mitford was then staying with Talfourd. Macready was prejudiced against her
on account of some difference between them as to a play of hers which he accepted and
afterwards required to be altered, without, it seems, allowing her sufficient time. He was
consequently attacked by an anonymous contributor to *Blackwood's Magazine,* who he
always believed was Harness.

[2] The Lord Chief Justice.

[3] The assessment in damages in Bunn *v.* Macready took place before Mr. Under-Sheriff
Burchell and a Jury, at the Sheriff's Court, Red Lion Square, on June 29, 1836. Mr.
Thesiger (afterwards Lord Chelmsford) and Mr. Ogle were counsel for the plaintiff;
Serjeant Talfourd and Mr. Whitmore for the defendant. No evidence was given for the
defendant. The damages were assessed at £150 (*note by Sir F. Pollock*).

rough ones. Wrote a letter for Mrs. Robertson, and then, going out, called at Covent Garden, where I saw Mr. Fitzball; spoke about Talfourd's box, which he promised to take care of. He also spoke to me again from Mr. Osbaldiston, on the subject of an engagement for next year, offering me from him, first, £35 per week, and then £40 per week, and half a clear Benefit, with six weeks' vacation. I said I would think about it. Went on to the Garrick Club, where I saw Dance, Raymond, etc., and Mr. Otway's [1] posting bill: "Wanted an independent Member of Parliament to present a petition for a licence to act the regular drama." Received a note from Blanchard, and a letter from an anonymous friend, remonstrating with me upon my supposed intention of retirement from the stage. Wrote notes of invitation to the Foxes and Adamses. Lay down and slept long and heavily—my cold pressing much upon me. Acted Ion pretty well, but occasionally annoyed by my colleagues. It was an unequal performance. I was called for at the end. Wallace came into my room. I went to supper at the Garrick Club, where Douglas (in the chair), R. Price (vice), Planché, Dance, Jerdan, Forster, Palmer, Lucena, Barham, Dowling, and others, whom I ought not to have forgotten, received Talfourd and self at supper. It was a pleasant evening. Talfourd replied to the encomiums passed on him with great animation, alluding to his early love for the drama, his interest for Miss Mitford, and his friendship for me, whom he eulogized very warmly. I acknowledged the compliment paid afterwards to myself without embarrassment, and alluded to the pure and benevolent spirit that gave life to Talfourd's work, and to the faith I had in the truth that breathed throughout it. Talfourd was obliged to go down to the House, a message having come that O'Connell had just finished, and that Peel was on his legs—the amendment of Stanley on the Irish tithes. I begged to propose the healths of Jerdan and Forster, as uniform and earnest supporters of the cause of the drama. I alluded in my speech to the want of fidelity to the cause of the art in the actors themselves. Broke up about two o'clock. Jerdan made a good speech, if at all to be questioned, only for his too much kindness to me.

Elstree, June 4th.—A letter from Knowles declining for himself and family an invitation for to-morrow; every ceremony of this kind has been repeated sufficiently often, and we are now free from any further necessity of the kind. Henry Smith arrived in the afternoon with the *Morning Chronicle*. I read the debate with avidity, and was

[1] Probably Cæsar Otway (1780-1842); an Irish man of letters.

particularly disgusted with the discord-breeding speech of Whittle Harvey.[1] "I do not like thee, Dr. Fell."

June 6th.—Mr. Gray called to inquire how far the necessity of prompt payment upon the assessment of damages, in the event of letting judgment go by default, would inconvenience me in a pecuniary point of view, as that was a matter to be considered in arriving at a conclusion upon their proceedings. I told him if the expense was not likely to exceed £1000 the blow might as well, or better, fall at once, as hang over my head. Talfourd wrote to me, wishing to see me on a very particular subject. I surmised it to be the same as Mr. Gray's communication, and sent to say that Mr. Gray would see him.

June 7th.—Mr. Fox, Miss Flower, and Mrs. Adams arrived; we spent the day very agreeably—talking over the best course for Mrs. Adams to adopt in following the theatrical profession; advised her as I thought best for her. In the drawing-room Mrs. Adams acted several scenes—*Lord Ullin's Daughter; the Cid*—of Mrs. Hemans—*My boy Tammie;* and the mad scene of Ophelia, in which, particularly the three first, she displayed more poetical conception, more imagination, and more genius than Malibran, Grisi and Pasta combined could have done. She is a wonderful woman.[2] They left us at ten o'clock. There was a fracas in the kitchen—the footman and housemaid fighting.

June 8th.—Before setting out to come to town by Billings, I had the disagreeable and painful task to perform of discharging Connor for his behaviour last night. This is the world! I am obliged to punish a fellow creature for the same vice—intemperance of conduct—in which I stand condemned. There is the aggravation of my servant's case, that he raised his hand against a woman—an unpardonable offence. Tried to think of *Ion* as I journeyed along, but was overpowered by sleep the greater part of the way. Purchased rouge, and on reaching chambers sent cheque for five guineas to Literary Fund. Mr. Corkran [3] called about his play, and I was glad to find him so

---

[1] See note, p. 223.

[2] This is surprisingly high praise of a lady who apparently gave no subsequent evidence of the qualities Macready attributed to her. She was probably Sarah Flower Adams (1805–1848), a minor poetess, best known as the writer of the hymn *Nearer to Thee*.

[3] J. Frazer Corkran; the *Daily News* correspondent in Paris, where he was well known in literary circles. His daughter, Miss Alice Corkran, is a charming story-writer and accomplished journalist. Thackeray, who knew Corkran well in his Paris days, once said of him: "Corkran is so good a man that when he goes to Heaven the angels will turn out and present arms."

satisfied with the little pains I had taken. Called on Forster, whom I found full of Eton and aristocracy. Dined and looked at papers at the Garrick Club, where I saw Bartley, etc. Returning by Covent Garden, looked in, and found a very kind letter from Mr. Hill of Wisbech. In Mr. Osbaldiston's room saw Farren, who, in a full and fresh burst of friendliness, wished me to act for Miss H. Faucit's Benefit, from which I escaped by my absence from London. Mr. Osbaldiston talked with me about my engagement, and agreed to give me £40 per week and half a clear Benefit for twenty-two weeks. We are to sign, etc., on Saturday. At the theatre found a note from A. Buller, accepting Saturday's invitation. Acted *Ion*, in my own opinion, better than I have done since the first night; the house was good, and the audience entered into my performance. I was called for, and very fervently cheered on going forward. Saw Polhill, and met Knowles, who had left Literary Fund in dudgeon, because his toast the Drama was not given while the Duke of Somerset was in the chair. Knowles and Talfourd were to have acknowledged the toast, but Knowles would not receive it from the deputy, Emerson Tennent, and left with the Duke. When our natures come to be sifted there is a greater quantity of real pride found in the hearts of those who have been esteemed most lowly than in the individuals who have been pointed at in life for their overweening opinion of themselves. Went up to Mrs. Talfourd's box, and talked a short time with her. Coming to chambers found a note from Lardner, who really *bores* me, about Jenny Vertpré—appointing a call before eleven to-morrow ! ! A letter from dear Edward (with a few affectionate lines from Catherine), enclosing me the papers, statements, etc., of the quarrel and duel between Sir J. Wilson and the Chief Justice of Ceylon, in which Edward was " second " to Sir John. I felt *extremely pleased* (but I begin to doubt the policy of his behaviour) with his conduct to Sir W. Horton,[1] whom he seems to have *walked over* in a very dignified and soldier-like manner. He, Sir W. Horton, as Governor and President of the Council, was bound in the first place to have prevented the Chief Justice from giving the cause of offence, and secondly to have forbidden what he authorized : the publication of the offensive matter. As a man and a gentleman and a soldier Edward did himself

---

[1] Sir Robert John Wilmot Horton (1784–1841); M.P. and Tory Under-Secretary for War and Colonies for some years. Governor of Ceylon from 1831 to 1837. Represented Mrs. Leigh at the burning of Byron's Memoirs. His wife was the subject of Byron's famous lines : " She walks in beauty like the night."

honour. A man of the world would perhaps take exception to his style of conduct. *But he did well.*

London, June 9th.—Felt tired and loth to rise. Wrote a note to White about the Saturday's Club Dinner and paid Freeman. Lardner called to carry us to Jenny Vertpré, and Forster looked in while he was here. The conversation was on general subjects. Went with Lardner to call on Jenny Vertpré in Albemarle Street. I found her a very piquante, engaging little creature, but I think profoundly deep. She wished me to act a scene of *Virginius* on the occasion of her Benefit ; luckily, though I should have been very happy to have served her, I shall be engaged in the country when her night takes place. I promised to send her a private box for *Ion* on Saturday. I called on T. Cooke (seeing Bartley and Sir G. Smart [1] on my way) to ask him if the new Opera was at all delayed by Mr. Bunn's illness. He said in the most unequivocal manner that it was not—that it could not have been produced previous to the 27th May under any circumstances.

June 10th.—Send to purchase books of *Ion*, and was very much pleased with the grateful and touching *Notice* which Talfourd has substituted for the Dedication to Dr. Valpy,[2] in the published edition. Lay down, much fatigued—so much so that I could not read. It is evident, I cannot—to do myself justice—play on consecutive nights ; I am beaten down. Acted Ion pretty well ; not as on Wednesday night. The house was great, which some persons, as well as Knowles, may attribute to *his* name ; but it was the play, with an added motive for selecting this night. I was called for, and went forward at the end—very warmly received. It seems they now regret not having extended my engagement ; I am disposed to do so, but if anything insolent or unpleasant should be said by that base wretch's counsel on the trial, I should not like to be playing here underneath the pain it would give me.

June 11th.—Mr. Gray called, and talked over the matter of my lawsuits with the scoundrel Bunn—about which I am altogether in the dark. I have not even the power of a guess at the result, but my apprehensions picture something bad. A moment's indiscretion must be paid for by perhaps the labour of a year, whilst this fellow's villainy actually makes a premium for itself by the extent of his knavery —*it is too bad!* Note of invitation to Mrs. Buller, which I answered ;

---

[1] Sir George Smart (1776–1867), the well-known composer and conductor.

[2] Talfourd's Head Master at Reading School (see note, p. 227), who had died since the dedication of *Ion*.

and, having written to Catherine and packed up my sword-box, I went to the theatre, where I saw Mr. Osbaldiston, who would most gladly engage me for a succession of nights to continue the run of *Ion*. I acted Ion fairly—pretty well, and was loudly called for, and enthusiastically received by the audience.

June 12th.—Forster called and remained some time, whilst I continued my employment, talking about all sorts of things. He seems to think that Talfourd is quite in earnest about getting up *Ion* as "private theatricals," and acting Ion himself. He alluded to it at supper last night, but I humoured what I supposed the joke. It begins to look serious, for private actors are very awful personages. Since the wild and unwise, ungentlemanly burst of passion into which I suffered myself to be betrayed by my impatience of a base and bad man's conduct—knowing well how base and bad that man is—my mind has had scarcely one minute of repose, my body has been in almost equally constant exercise. I now look back, in a moment's pause of rest, and with astonishment, contrition, and deep gratitude thank Almighty God that the consequence and punishment of my offence— my offence against every dictate of prudence, every principle of gentlemanly demeanour, every precept by which I sought to guide my conduct—has been so lenient. Such an act under slightly modified circumstances, and against any other person *might have been my ruin!!!* May it act as a warning to me! But my life seems to be passed in forming schemes and making resolutions of conduct, only to break through them.

June 14th.—I looked into some papers, and saw that Mr. Morris was said to have obtained Talfourd's permission to perform *Ion* with Ellen Tree as Ion. Here was another instance of my exacting temper. I felt *displeased.* My interest was menaced, and I only looked at my own supposed degree of damage. In strict justice, I do think that having arranged the play (which Talfourd would not have done suc- cessfully—see *his* version) and put it upon the stage, it is scarcely fair, before the attraction is decided as past, to turn over my labours to any other persons. But it is not *worth* caring for, even if Talfourd *has* given permission, which is not certain, though far from improbable. On reflection I almost wished it might be so, for the conversation upon the play would be maintained, and I cannot think it *possible* that the experiment can succeed. But here is another instance of my selfish temper—why could I not regard it, as I should have done, with indifference? Went to the theatre, and acted Virginius passably to

ELLEN TREE

(MRS. CHARLES KEAN)

From an engraving by J. Brown after a miniature

a very good house. Dentatus had to play a fop in the farce, and he anticipated it in the tragedy, making the Roman Achilles a coxcomb.

June 15th.—Went to rehearsal, where I found Mrs. Robertson, my Lady Macbeth—very old, poor woman, not very perfect, and cutting out the passage " I have given suck," etc., as too *horrible!* I am now *prepared* for this evening, and do not think that I shall lose my temper, though it will be tried—but I think I shall only laugh in my sleeve. Called on Mrs. Hill, who showed me some very beautiful drawings illustrating the *Giaour* and *Last Days of Pompeii*— by Miss Margaret Gillies,[1] the young lady I met and liked so much on Monday evening. Went to the theatre, and met the several checks to the abandonment of myself to Macbeth with tolerable evenness. Lady Macbeth acted, and hauled and patted me, and I endured most heroically—most philosophically. It was a trial. I got angry at the last at an occurrence that was stupidly gratuitous. The thought of darling Catherine when a girl, as her face looked at me in this very play, arose and pleased my fancy for a short time. Mrs. Hill sent to invite me to supper; I could not go. I find it quite true, as Forster says, that the performance of a character is my day. I can do nothing else of any moment when I have an important part to act. I cannot do it.

Lincoln, June 18th.—It seems difficult to assent to the fact that twenty-one years have passed away since the battle of Waterloo was fought, my greatest interest in which event is derived from the remembrance of Edward's presence there, and the anxiety it occasioned me. Looked over the newspaper, and was caught by the utter recklessness of the *Times* in throwing away all considerations for persons or past transactions when interfering with the cause it champions. It is barely decent in its mention of Moore,[2] who was until lately one of its powerful contributors. Made up some very heavy arrears of record, which occupied me long. Sauntered out to discover the theatre and see the cathedral; found the first very soon, and was directed to the cathedral, the towers of which rose directly before me. How much pleasure do objects of art afford, particularly when rich in associations as these monastic temples are, whether general as to the usages of

---

[1] Margaret Gillies (1803–1887); a well-known exhibitor at the Old Water Colour Society, of which she was an associate for thirty-five years.

[2] Thomas Moore the poet, who had been a frequent contributor to the *Times*, mainly of rhymed satires against the Tory party, also, in earlier days, against the Prince Regent.

past times, or preserving any individual recollections! The front of this beautiful pile held me in delight for some time, and the very observation of its imperfectness is an amusement to the mind. Acted Virginius, not as well as I could have wished; the house was very fair; but two or three accidents interfered with me. How little does an audience guess upon what filmy threads an actor's effects depend!

Birmingham, June 19th.—My first journey through this place, when a boy, to return to my mother and father for my first holidays from Rugby—when I arrived to kiss the cold brow and marble lips of that ever beloved and respected, that blessed mother—these, with many other less touching memories, were fresh upon my mind. At Meriden similar recollections of time, passed there with *her*, awoke vividly to my thoughts.

June 24th.—Received a letter from Messrs. White and Whitmore, informing me that the inquiry as to damages is postponed to Tuesday next, in consequence of the lateness of Lord Melbourne's trial. Went to rehearsal—a very tedious and fatiguing one. Received the newspaper, with the account of the trial—Norton *v.* Melbourne.[1] Went to the theatre, where I was cut up by the actors "root and branch" —scattered "horse, foot and dragoons"; the stuff they talked! The hash of nonsense, the mysterious, the inscrutable jumble of words they all by turns dealt in would have persuaded old Doily that they were acting the play in the Argive dialect of the early Greeks. Was stoutly called for, and said a few cheerful words to the audience.

June 27th.—Went to the theatre, and laboured under the great disadvantage of a *wretchedly* cast play: the Virginia, Icilius, Lucius, Numitorius were too bad for the smallest theatre. I really contended with the depressing effect of such disenchanting persons, and in the latter part of the play acted with some correctness and reality. But —what must I say—what language is strong enough to give the full

---

[1] An action for *crim. con.* brought by the Hon. G. C. Norton against Lord Melbourne, who was Prime Minister at the time. The Attorney-General, Sir John Campbell (afterwards Lord Campbell), appeared for Lord Melbourne, and Sir William Follett for Mr. Norton. The jury found a verdict for Lord Melbourne against whom the evidence was ludicrously trivial. In fact it suggested the evidence introduced by Dickens in the immortal trial of Bardell *v.* Pickwick. The Melbourne case created an immense sensation at the time, such an action against a first Minister of the Crown being unprecedented, though, curiously enough, nearly thirty years afterwards Lord Melbourne's brother-in-law, Lord Palmerston, then also Prime Minister, was cited as a co-respondent in the Divorce Court. The case, however, did not reach a hearing, being dropped at a preliminary stage.

measure of condemnation that my passionate and intemperate and undignifed deportment calls down upon me? *What will become of me* if I permit the continuance of this *odious*—this *degrading*—this *spiteful* and *little* conduct? I am really *ashamed*—deeply ashamed of my phrenetic temper. It is no excuse to say I am provoked. I am angry when the effect of the provocation is past and determined. *I am worse than I ever was!* Oh, God!—oh, God! who hearest the anguish and shame of heart it costs me, let me implore Thy Divine Grace and assistance to aid me in over-mastering and expelling from my nature this detestable and disgusting vice! Amen!

June 28th.—On this day is the *pecuniary* penalty of my foolish and vile fault determined. To add to the sums of which this pitiful and wretched scoundrel has already robbed me cannot be felt otherwise than as galling, and as a hardship; but I have erred, and ought to bow to the punishment which I prepare for, not as the infliction of men, but as a chastisement from Providence, whose justice I acknowledge, and whose bounty I am most grateful for. But this hasty—this precipitate temper must be subdued, if I hope for peace in my remaining years, or look for the esteem and respect of my fellow-creatures. It seems—and I hope it is so, for then I may look forward to a successful effort to conquer myself—that my temper has become worse since this harassing and fretting business has weighed upon and galled it; but of late I have been so irritable that I am shocked as I look back upon my imperious and impatient bearing. God of mercy, forgive and succour me! Amen!

June 29th.—Prepared my mind by meditation and prayer to receive with resignation and contentment the news of my folly's punishment; went into my sitting-room armed with patience and secure of submitting with serenity of mind to the blow. Found only a letter from dear Catherine, with one from Calcraft. The slackening of the nerves from their braced-up state quite threw me into low spirits. *Cependant!* Read the newspaper, and felt a momentary swell of passion at reading the paragraph of an "entertainment to be given to Mr. Bunn for his splendid management, and for the late outrage committed on him." A little reflection convinced me that the compliment of one knave to another—for example, Lord —— to Mr. Bunn—does not reduce the quantity of baseness in their character, nor does it at all affect that of an honest, upright man. Let them celebrate their orgies and drink themselves into imaginary respectability; the next morning will find them as actual scoundrels as they ever were. Endeavoured to

331

look at Werner, but was overcome by sleep. Went to the theatre, where, in acting Werner, I was murdered. I tried to keep my temper, to be cool, and to act, but I was beaten down. The audience called for me, and I made my parting salaam. Phipson came into my room, and told me that no notice of the trial had yet appeared! He expressed himself most cordially, and has indeed shown me the *greatest attention*, which I cannot forget.

Elstree, June 30th.—Was called earlier than I had ordered, and rose without considering the time that was before me. Paid my bill, which was a very exorbitant one, satisfied the servants, and passing through the market-place, which is very fine, went to the Nelson Hotel, from whence I set out at seven o'clock. At Brickhill Major Smith left us; an outside passenger had come in, and the guard lent him a *Morning Chronicle* of this day—which, as I caught a glimpse of the words Bunn v. Macready, I begged him to let me see for one instant. I looked for the damages, which I saw were £150. I felt relieved and satisfied as far as the pecuniary consideration went; but when he had read through the paper he handed it to me. I found the statement of Mr. Thesiger [1]—the plaintiff's counsel—to be a gross and scandalous misrepresentation from beginning to end: direct falsehood, most groundless inferences, and the basest imputations on my character. My agitation was so far suppressed as not to be visible to my fellow-passenger, but the wolf was tearing at my heart. My mind was away while he was speaking to me. I was suffering an inward torture, which only persons of acute sensibility can conceive or sympathize with. I could not confront the passengers who stayed at Redbourn to dinner, but walked on with my *compagnon de voyage*. Reached home by a little after six, and found my dear family quite well. I thank God for His mercy to me in regard to these precious

---

[1] Frederick Thesiger (1794-1878); afterwards Lord Chelmsford, and twice Lord Chancellor of England. When appearing for Bunn he was already in large practice on the Home Circuit. To those who recollect the distinguished-looking, urbane nobleman of later years Macready's allegations must be difficult of acceptance; but it is quite possible that Thesiger did not mince his words in dealing with what was, after all, on Macready's own admission, a most unjustifiable assault. Bunn's attorney had no doubt not erred on the side of moderation in his instructions, and if Thesiger improved a little on his brief, it must be borne in mind that the very fact of Macready having suffered judgment to go by default (the case was simply one for the assessment of damages in the Sheriff's Court) rendered him especially vulnerable to attack. On the whole he got off very lightly, and probably no one except himself gave another thought to Thesiger's fulminations when once the case had been disposed of. With Macready, however, they continued to rankle till the end of his life.

creatures, who are the bonds that hold me on to life! Dow and his wife arrived in their cab about eight o'clock—not expecting to find me, but with the purpose of reporting to dear Catherine the proceedings at the trial. They did not leave us till after ten. I expressed to Dow my indignation at the base and scandalous conduct of the hired calumniator, Thesiger; he tried to palliate it, but ineffectually.

London, July 1st.—Went up to town to consult Wallace on the stigma which this paid libeller had fixed upon me; he seemed backward to make a question of the insult, but on my repeating the language contained in the *Morning Chronicle*, he thought it right that we should see Talfourd on the matter previous to any step being taken. We got into a coach, which broke down in Oxford Street, and in another we pursued our course to my chambers. I stepped in to Forster, who told me that Evans, the plaintiff's solicitor, when Mr. Thesiger in the court said that I had "attempted to tear out the tongue" of that wretch, came up to him and requested him, if *this was spoken of among his friends, to say that no such expression was in the Counsel's brief.* I mentioned this to Wallace. We went on to Talfourd's chambers, and learned that he was in Guildhall, whither we followed him. He was speaking in the Common Pleas when we arrived. Retiring to the Guildhall Coffee House I wrote a note, wishing to see him, and gave it to one of the attendants in the court. Talfourd soon after came out and took us upstairs into the counsel's room. I there stated to him the indignity which had been cast upon me and my intention of requiring a disavowal or retractation of his slander. Talfourd seemed extremely distressed, and endeavoured, *more suorum*, to explain it as being without meaning—as merely professional licence, etc., and intimating that the consequences of a message to Thesiger would be very injurious to me, inasmuch as he would appeal to the Bar, who would be sure to maintain him in his right of resistance to such a demand, and that he would refuse to meet me and probably move the Court of King's Bench against me in a criminal information. For all this I cared little; I could scarcely suffer more than I did from the ignominy he had cast upon me. Wallace spoke out upon the licence assumed by counsel in venting their scurrility, and said that it ought to be checked. We left Talfourd and conferred, as we drove along to my chambers; thence to Ransom's, where I lodged £210, having purchased a *Morning Chronicle* on the way. We agreed that it would be better I should return home to-night, and be in town betimes in the morning to write a letter to

333

this foul-mouthed slanderer, which Wallace should take. I bought
Willie a ship, long promised, and having written a note of excuse for
to-day and invitation for the morrow to H. Glassford Bell, who was
in town from Scotland and had invited himself down to-day, I
sauntered along, waiting for the coach. As I got into it I was hailed
from the top, where to my surprise I saw Bell. I got on the roof with
him and we went home together. He asked me about the cause of
my annoyance, and I told him. He combated my purpose of calling
on Thesiger for retractation on the same grounds with Talfourd.

July 2nd.—Went with Bell to town in chaise, and called on
Wallace—parting with Bell at the door. I found Wallace shaken in
his previous opinions; he acknowledged himself perplexed and uncertain how to proceed. He represented the "awkward and dangerous
observations to which I might be liable in calling out a man who, I
must be presumed to know, would not go out with me." This was
very startling and not easy to be got over. I asked him if he had
spoken to Lardner on it; he said he had, and that Lardner was quite
agitated and distressed about it as fraught with so much injury to
me. Lardner, on Wallace's invitation, came up, and the matter was
thoroughly discussed. It was agreed between them that it was impossible I could call the man out. What then remained *but to endure?*
It was suggested that I should write to Talfourd for a written statement of his opinion, as delivered yesterday on the subject; then, that
three persons of acknowledged respectability should record their
opinions that I could not proceed hostilely against Thesiger—and at
last it was left with nothing done! My lesson is patience. I am to
read the mendacious assertions of a fee'd scoundrel—that my assault
on a worthless villain, which was rash and incautious even to a pitch
of madness, was "*unmanly, dastardly and cowardly.*" I am to know
that this salaried liar has gone beyond the instructions of his brief in
his defamation of me, and that he has charged me with falsehood from
the stage of Covent Garden without the power of contradicting or
refuting of his calumnies. *Is this justice?*—or what is life worth where
character is made the essential of happiness, where it is placed at the
mercy of a licensed trader in falsehood, and where hypocrisy and baseness enjoy all the good derived from it, whilst honesty of purpose and
purity of intention are held up by misrepresentation to public odium?
It is *frightful!* Went to chambers. Wrote to Dow and to Bell upon
the relinquishment of my purpose. Sent for *Morning Herald* of
Thursday. Very unhappy and depressed in spirits. Went to Garrick

Club, where I saw Reynolds, Planché, Hook, Kemble and Winston.
Looked at magazines. Saw Rafaelle's drawings. No heart to enjoy
them, my mind was sick with its depression. Forster overtook me as
I returned to chambers, talked much. I walked in the garden after
dinner, but my spirits were wretchedly low—sunk beyond the power
of revival. I am indeed, with almost all in life that should make a
man happy, very, very wretched. The poison of a villain's slander has
been thrown into the cup which I am forced to drink, and I find I
have not that religious or philosophic resignation which can find comfort and repose in bowing to the punishment inflicted, and in submitting to the execution of that will which is all-wise, and if we could
but know it, all-benevolent. May God assist me, for my tortured
spirit needs some consoling and sustaining power, which it cannot find
here. Amen!

Elstree, July 3rd.—Rose late, and with a disinclination to exertion
of any kind, arising chiefly, if not entirely, from the dejected state
of mind in which I still remained. I looked at the newspaper and
sauntered through the garden—listlessly—and with the miserable consciousness of having around me everything to enjoy though deprived
of the power of enjoyment by a base-minded brawler who had stung
me with his envenomed words into torture. Languid, indifferent to
everything that looked full of beauty around me, thoroughly unhappy,
and incapable of applying myself to any occupation. I had intended
going to church, but I shrank from the meeting persons who might
have read Mr. Thesiger's speech. How very wrong! A duty, in the
cultivation of a religious and grateful feeling and in the example
offered to others, I neglected for my vain concern for *man's* opinion
and observation. Let me never again thus shrink from an imperious
duty—rendered more necessary by such circumstances, my own offences,
as now weigh upon me.

After dinner I played with my darling children; my spirits rallied
a little. As we were sitting down to tea a ring of the bell and the
sound of carriage wheels made us conclude that Dow had descended
on us. It was Talfourd, Mrs. Talfourd and three of the children. It
was quite a surprise. They took tea. Mrs. Talfourd, etc., went into
the garden, whilst Talfourd, who was greatly pleased and relieved by the
dismissal of my thought of calling on Thesiger, discussed with me
the points of the trial—told me of the *Age* threatening an indictment
—(posh!)—and of Morris's offer of £300 for the exclusive right of
acting *Ion*, which Talfourd had declined, and which I advised him to

335

take for the permission to act it, omitting the word "exclusive." Talfourd again expressed his opinion of the unfair and ungentlemanly tone adopted by Thesiger, wondering at his want of taste and proper feeling, and intimating his readiness to *write* to me the declaration of his conviction that I could not notice what fell from Thesiger. They left us about ten. We sat up late, talking over the trial. I went to bed as depressed and low in heart as I had risen.

July 4th.—My spirits were still very, very low; the obloquy which this vile hireling has thrown upon me clings like a poisoned garment to my flesh, and as I write each emotion wounds and tortures me. After breakfast put my papers in order; my spirits seemed rather to sink still lower, beyond the power of rallying them. Mr. Greaves arrived. His conversation upon the late trial and the verdict was very cheering to me, not alone as regards the public opinion upon the transaction, but also upon the impression conveyed by Mr. Thesiger's speech, which was felt to be an ungentlemanly *distortion and misstatement of facts.* After dinner we walked down to the reservoir, taking the dogs with us. The evening was beautiful. To-day is the anniversary of the American Declaration of Independence. I, as one of the great family of mankind that have profited by that event, thank God for it; how much has the great cause of liberty and improvement been advanced by it!

July 5th.—The post brought a very kind note from Bell, expressive of his satisfaction at my silence upon the slanders cast upon me, and repeating the assurance that that man's, Thesiger's, calumny in no way touched my character as a gentleman.

July 7th.—I turned back to the sad and undignified action, which has cost me so many days of keen and, indeed, agonized suffering. I find a record of imprudence, want of self-government, moroseness, precipitation, imperiousness, and tetchiness that grieves and shames me. The fact of my ill-temper cannot be concealed, nor extenuated when admitted. I am wholly unjustified—religion, philosophy, policy, all cry out against me. I feel weary of self-complaint from the little benefit I have derived from it; if I wish or expect to pass through the remainder of my life with respectability and honour, I must overcome it. I will try to do so, and I implore the blessing of God upon my efforts.

July 8th.—A note from Talfourd, with the information that he had concluded with Morris an agreement allowing him to perform *Ion* at the Haymarket theatre, and wishing the loan of my book, as marked for representation. This naturally caused me to think much upon the effects and motives of the proceeding. I had much rather it had not taken place, and something like dissatisfaction arose in my mind on perceiving the credit I had gained partially endangered by the possible success of a performer inferior in rank. A little consideration, however, made me see that selfishness was the mainspring of my reasonings, and that I thought chiefly of my interests and fame, as Talfourd, very justifiably, did of his. I cannot hope the experiment to succeed, and I trust it will not, as it cannot harm Talfourd by failure, and in its triumph may take much from me. Such is an actor's reputation! Walked in the garden, enjoying the freshness of the air and perfume of the flowers. Answered Talfourd, and sent him by Drinkwater the book requested, giving him the use of it till Tuesday or Wednesday. Heard dear Willie read, and took some pains with him. Went to look at the progress of the haymakers, and lay among the hay, looking with delight and gratitude on the two dear children, Nina and Willie, who were playing among it.

July 9th.—Heard with much satisfaction of the failure of Malibran's renowned engagement. It is most unjust that a foreigner should be brought into a national theatre to receive enormous terms at the expense of the actors of the establishment.

July 13th.—Was suffering from pain of heart and depression in ruminating on the feeble defence set up by Talfourd to the charges brought against me. It was so manifestly a got-up case that the least energy in following up a penetrating consideration of the subject might have exposed the whole *composition.* The charges and insinuations, never attempted to be proved, were, it might be supposed, suggestive of the falsehood of the rest; but not having chosen to make himself acquainted thoroughly with the real facts of the case, he proceeded as if apprehensive of their truth, and as if fearful of grappling with the question. It was the juryman who, by his cross-examination, convicted the boy of falsehood. Why did not Talfourd pursue the ridiculous assertion about tearing out his tongue to its exposure, and overwhelm the falsehood of the other counsel? Also about the hair torn from that fellow's head, as asserted by the surgeon—why did he not make him state the particulars. Could he have distinguished such a thing unless some of the scalp had been injured also? It was a got-up case, and endeavoured to be fitted in its parts—and might have been safely torn to pieces. Where were the bruises of his body, which was " *kicked* and *jumped upon* " ? Talfourd suffered this Mr. Thesiger

337

to designate my conduct as " cowardly, unmanly and dastardly "—to make assertions without the least attempt to prove them—to challenge scrutiny of Mr. Bunn's character as " honourable and eminent " and something else—and never took advantage of these opportunities. He eulogized me, when it would have been a greater advantage to have been silent upon a life, which, as to its public conduct, he might have pointed out as blameless. Oh! but it makes my heart sick to look back on such a defender—such a friend—not for his will but for his ability. He did what he could, he *declaimed*, but he had not the *moral* courage to vindicate and defend me.[1]

London, July 14th.—Called on Wallace, and talked with him about Talfourd's defence, which he thought, as he had anticipated—and as I had feared—was unequal to the case entrusted to him. His business was to disprove by cross-examination the statements of the false witnesses against me, and to expose the baseness of the assertions and insinuations of Mr. Thesiger, which he had failed, or not attempted, to prove. *But he passed them all by;* he declaimed upon my character and ventured a *hint* at the badness of Mr. Bunn's. Was this what the case required? My character did not need his eulogy—it was defamed, and called for his scrutiny; he could not, or dared not make it. He seems hung like a clog by destiny around my fortunes! It is not his *fault*—it is his inefficiency, his want of moral courage, of sternness of purpose, of resolved will! God help me! Amen! Wallace urged me to *forget* all about it! The very injunction proves the difficulty in the necessity; it is not *to be forgotten!* At Covent Garden theatre met Mr. Osbaldiston, and, after urging him to engage Mr. Vandenhoff and Miss E. Tree, read my article of agreement to him, to which he assented, and also to my claim of flesh-coloured stockings and to the announcement of my name as first. We talked long, and I was to send him the dates of Lent and Easter.

July 16th.—Called on White and Whitmore, who were out, and returned to chambers to expect Mr. Gray. He called, and we talked over a little of the trial. He said the feeling of indignation was general in the court at that gowned libeller's assertion of charges

---

[1] Talfourd, of course, had a lamentably weak case, which it must be admitted he did not contrive to improve by a turgid overstrained speech of the Buzfuz type. The truth is that in his heart he knew that Macready had put himself hopelessly in the wrong, and the utmost he could do was to endeavour to mitigate the gravity of this particular lapse by enlarging on the normally irreproachable conduct of his client. A good deal of allowance must be made for Macready, but he was undoubtedly unjust to Talfourd, who had a very difficult task in representing a self-confessed delinquent.

which he never attempted to prove. Is this the act of an honest man—of a gentleman? I gave Mr. Gray a cheque for £200 to meet the verdict and costs, with which my impatience of a villain's acts of treachery and robbery has been visited. The punishment of my offence has been in my own heart! The world is no longer what it was to me—and with my feelings I cannot think it has been much.

Elstree, July 17th.—This week sees me £200 minus in my small possessions through my own indiscretion.[1] This sum is lost to my children, and I am loaded with the painful and oppressive remembrance of having exposed myself to the censure of every one who may choose to raise his voice against me.

July 19th.—Considered seriously the expediency, the propriety, of giving up my house, and reducing my whole establishment; it presses strongly upon me, but I will not be rash. God grant that I may be wise and just in my resolve. My blessed children, it is for you that I think, and that I will with a cheerful heart resign the luxuries and comforts of my present abode.

July 20th.—The whole of this day, the morning, afternoon, and evening, was passed in examining my accounts, calculating and discussing the subject of my last night's thought. I retired to rest still undecided, unable to ascertain precisely the amount of difference between a town and country residence.

July 21st.—At last came to the decision that the small difference between town and country would not overweigh the advantages of remaining here, which we accordingly resolved on doing.

July 26th.—Talked with H. Smith of my situation. He counselled the abandonment of the action against Bunn. I believe he is right, for I fear that indignation—or more plainly speaking, passion—actuates me more than the belief that it is necessary to my character to expose the fraud he has practised on me. It is hard that such a wretch should be permitted to go on with impunity; but *I cannot be right to lend an ear to passion—the worst of counsellors.* H. Smith also recommended me to come to town, but on searching my own mind I fear I could not overcome, *here*, my tendency to expense. Went to dine with Forster; met Browning and Ainsworth;[2] passed a pleasant afternoon, and invited Ainsworth for Sunday.

[1] As will be remembered Macready was at one time quite prepared for a verdict of £1000 against him.

[2] William Harrison Ainsworth (1805-1882) ; author of *Rookwood, Jack Sheppard, Old St. Paul's*, and other popular novels.

August 1st.—Came up to town by Billings's, in company with Mr. and Miss Lane, Browning, Forster, and Mr. Ainsworth. Parted with my guests apparently well pleased with their excursion. On my way read very nearly the whole of Bulwer's play of *Cromwell;* [1] though containing some passages happy in thought and strong in expression, I do not think, either in respect to character, arrangement, or poetical beauty, that this play will quite reach the level of his existing reputation.

London, August 3rd.—Called on Forster to inquire the success of *Ion;* heard but an indifferent report of Miss Tree and Mr. Vandenhoff, not sufficiently good to induce me to remain in town to see them. Forster told me that Browning had fixed on Strafford for the subject of a tragedy; he could not have hit upon one that I could have more readily concurred in.

Elstree, August 5th.—Finished the perusal of *Nina Sforza,* a play of very great merit with which I was very much pleased, though it cannot be successful in representation. Read Heraud's other play of the *Death of Nero;* an impossible subject, not treated in a manner to give hope of its success. Made up very long arrears of record.

August 7th.—Accompanied our guests with Catherine to Harrow Weald to show the splendid view to be seen there. Fonblanque went to town to dine—as I afterwards understood—with Lord Lansdowne.[2] We had music in the evening, more than I almost wished; my spirit became low and languid under it, and a feeling of disappointment, arising perhaps from my own vanity, depressed me.

London, August 8th.—Went to the Haymarket to *Ion;* it was tiresome and sleepy to a degree; over at ten o'clock. Miss Tree's performance of Ion is a very pretty effort, and a very creditable woman's effort, but it is no more like a young man than a coat and waistcoat are. Vandenhoff was frequently very false and very tiresome; some things he did very well. The play was very drowsy, very unreal.

August 9th.—Called on Wallace and Lardner. Coming up—I

---

[1] Apparently it never saw the footlights.

[2] The third Marquis (1780–1863), who, as Lord Henry Petty, had been Chancellor of the Exchequer in the *All the Talents* Administration, with Charles Fox, at the Foreign Office, as his colleague. He was more prominent as the Mæcenas of the Whig party than as a politician though he held office in Canning's Administration, and sat in most of the Whig cabinets down to the time of his death. He was almost the last of the nineteenth-century *grand seigneurs,* a princely host and an enlightened patron of art and letters. Tom Moore's Diaries give charming glimpses of him both at Bowood and at Lansdowne House.

think—Hanover Street I saw that dirty wretch Bunn arm-in-arm with Calcraft! I looked forth at them both, with a smile of contempt at that reptile, but the one *dared not* and the other *would not* look across the narrow street, in which they *must have seen me.* It would be exacting, indeed, in me, if I could expect men should relinquish intimacies or friendships on my account—but here is quite a different case. Mr. Calcraft told me yesterday that Mr. Bunn was a coward; he has before told me that he would be hanged, and then changed his opinion on the conviction that he was too great a coward to peril his life in any way; he was privy to his rascality in cheating me in Dublin; he was privy to his cheating his friend, young Kean; Mr. Bunn charged him with a dishonourable mode of getting the Dublin theatre into his own hands—and I see this person, whom I have essentially served, who holds a commission in the King's service,[1] walking arm-in-arm and manifestly on terms of intimacy with a man whom he proclaims one of the greatest rascals living and an irredeemable coward! Can I entertain respect for the character of Mr. Calcraft? My suspicions—my strong suspicions of his mind and heart are confirmed.

August 27th.—Went to the theatre and rehearsed *Ion*, which I no longer feel pleasure in performing. I feel, I fancy, rather *dégoûté* with Talfourd's " delight " at seeing Miss Tree's appearance in the part; if it is the author's feeling that it is the nasty sort of epicene animal which a woman so dressed up renders it, I am very loth to appear in it, and to this notion the author seems to lend his opinion.

August 28th.—Endeavoured to come to some decision with regard to the plot of Bulwer's play, but find it more difficult than I had supposed; on one point I am clear, that to make a play of Cromwell, he must begin *de novo* and be content to lose all he has already done; patchwork never is of value. Began to read, with the hope of finding it adaptable, *Marino Faliero.*

September 2nd.—At theatre; on going to see a gentleman who was inquiring for me, I met again " Tom Steele " [2]—poor fellow. What a warm-hearted creature! How exactly made to be the dupe of cold-blooded designers, the victim of his own guilelessness! He was quite running over with affection and enthusiasm. I was amused by his

---

[1] Calcraft was originally in the Army, but must have retired when taking up the stage as a calling (see note, p. 14).

[2] Thomas Steele (1783–1848); a prominent follower of O'Connell whom he supported at the famous Clare election in 1828. He was tried together with O'Connell for sedition and remained his firm adherent, supporting him against the " Young Irelanders "; after O'Connell's death he attempted suicide.

instructing me in the means by which he acquired that "clear judgment" which he "used so powerfully during the period of his agitation"—he had "given up agitation now these three years." He sat in admiration of the rehearsal of Hamlet, which I conducted with much temper. He talked of my foolish attack on Bunn, which he thought a matter to rejoice in, but which I never can think otherwise of than as I have done, and do.

September 4th.—Began the day with needful attention to my clothes, which occupied me some time; looked over and cast up my accounts, and began the draught of a letter to Bulwer upon his play of *Cromwell*. This same play has cost me much time and pains. I am not sure whether I ought to have undertaken it, but he has been kind in his expressions to me, and that has been my inducement. Called on Miss Huddart, who talked much about herself, Mr. Calcraft and Mr. C. Kean. I find her opinion of the talents of the last-named person very much raised. It is strange that a person should possess the mental qualifications of an actor whose life is passed in trifling and amusement! If it really be good—of a high order—I shall think of art infinitely more lowly than I have yet done.

September 12th.—Deferred, from *mauvaise honte*, repugnance, and a bad hat, my necessary calls. Returning to lodgings, slept, and read three Odes of Horace, which had a good effect upon my mind. Read over the part of Bertulphe. Ate an *exceedingly moderate* dinner—*one mutton chop—rien autre.* Went to the theatre, prepared for a bad house, but thought it an occasion for expressing myself in the study of my art, and in the better art of keeping my temper. Cannot say that I was very successful in either experiment. Acted Bertulphe very badly; strove, but vainly, to act well; couldn't infuse reality into my performance. I never felt more strongly the *invita Minerva*. Fortunately, made no exhibitions of ill-humour, though frequently feeling, and subduing, the rising of petulance and anger. The house was *very bad*. I am teaching myself philosophy, but I could wish to learn it with less anxiety for my dear family. Made up my mind that it was of no consequence at all what Kemble did at Covent Garden; it is *impossible* he could persuade the people that he is an actor—"let him do his spite!"

Elstree, September 22nd.—Wrote a letter, which I copied, to Miss Ellen Tree, expressing my desire to offer her a mark of regard, and suggesting a farewell Benefit as the most serviceable mode of doing so, mentioning Mr. Osbaldiston's assent to the proposal of having it at

Covent Garden theatre, and offering to do anything myself upon the occasion—to study Adrastus for her, if she would wish to have *Ion* for her play. I was glad when I had done it, as a kind thing to her, and an evidence to Talfourd and his friends that I had no unworthy feeling in respect to this play's subsequent performance.

Shrewsbury, September 27th.—Went to rehearsal. It was my wish to be courteous and good-natured, but my tolerating spirit was tried by the sullen demeanour of more than one person. It is not fair to compare the disadvantages of this art, or profession, or whatever name may be accorded to it, with those of the other callings which require *education*. In the others men must be educated as gentlemen. What are players? The refuse of trades, discarded servants; in short, idle persons from every low stage of society. It is some excuse—it really *is*—that my lot has cast me among such persons. Went in a heavy rain to the theatre, to play Virginius. The drudgery of my employment was painfully present to my mind. There is little or nothing to disguise the bare meanness of my occupation from me. Crowded theatres, enthusiastic audiences, the adulatory attentions and caressings of the distinguished and influential might, if I had enjoyed them, hide my actual condition from myself, but with an intellect and taste to detect and grieve beneath the vile trade of "making myself a motley to the view," I have all its labour of study and practise with the full sense of its degradation, and a very, very moderate success attending it. I continue it in the hope of making by my gains my blessed children's lot more happy. Oh, God, grant it, and then I shall not have toiled and borne these frettings of the heart in vain. I strove to act well—was frequently thwarted and sometimes annoyed by the imperfectness, inattention, and wilful neglect—or rather the *refusal* to do their rehearsed parts—of the performers. With several successful efforts to restrain my temper, it once or twice escaped my power of repression, and gave me additional pain and dissatisfaction. In thinking over Miss E. Tree's letter, I do not feel that it is quite responsive to the act of kindness shown to her. I may be mistaken, but the tone of the epistle is rather cold and, I think, *lofty*. I hope I misconceive it. Returning to my inn—in discontent and repining at the fate which exposes me to these unhappy transports of temper, while I wish and strive to check them—I asked for the newspaper. I had read three pages of it, and one or two columns of the fourth—it was the *Standard* —when my eyes struck upon the words: "*Malibran is no more !*" The loudest clap of thunder in the calmest sunshine could not have given me a greater start. I felt as if my mind was stunned; it was a shock that left me no power to think for some little time. I read on, when recovered from the horror and surprise of the news, and was quite restored by the stuff—the *newspaper sentiment* and string of falsehoods that went to disfigure the melancholy and affecting truth of one—in youth, so rich in talent, once so lovely, with so much to enchant and fascinate, and so much to blame and regret—suddenly taken from a world so full of delight to her, and to which she was so frequently a minister of delight. I once could have loved her, and she has since said that she loved—" was in love with "—me. Had I known it for certain, I might have been more miserable than I am. Latterly she had decreased in my regard, and in my esteem she had no place. This world is a sad loss to her, and she to it. Poor Malibran![1]

September 28th.—Went over with care the dagger soliloquy of Macbeth, which I think I can improve, and I feel I must (as this is the only profession by which I have a chance of earning my own independence and my children's education) give my mind diligently to it. Went to rehearsal. How exceedingly distasteful to me is the character of William Tell! I cannot throw myself into it now. While finishing my letter to dear Catherine, I had the comfort of receiving one from her. Looked again at the account of Malibran, the thought of whom kept me wakeful through the greater part of last night. I was cold, and in my inability to sleep could retain no other thought but of her and her untimely fate. Acted William Tell to an indifferent house but indifferently. How much I wish that all tyrants were like the Gesler of this evening, and then mankind would rise *en masse* and smother them. I never saw his fellow—Termagaunt and Herod were fools and innocents to him—and he enjoyed it. I envied him the relish he had for his own grimacings and intonations. Happy being! In thinking upon the very little I do in life beyond attending to my profession, and to that I cannot give much attention out of the theatre, I was surprised to find that, in these country engagements where I have usually a daily rehearsal, the time that is consumed in the theatre, rehearsing and

---

[1] She died at Manchester on September 23, at the age of twenty-eight. Her last appearance was on the 14th. She had been ailing for some days, but was determined not to disappoint the public. In repeating the duet of " Vanne se alberghi in petto " in Mercandante's *Andronico*, it was manifest that she was making a painful effort, and on leaving the stage she was seized with the illness that proved fatal a few days later. Of fragile and delicate physique she for a long time seriously overtaxed her strength. In fact, in the words of Lablache: "Son esprit était trop fort pour son petit corps."

acting, is very rarely, if ever, less than eight hours! This does not leave much time or spirits for other labours.

September 29th.—My spirits were rather low, as I went to rehearsal, determined to make the utmost of it as a study. I *did* try, but—*try !* With all the discouragement this wretched art labours under, and the *utter neglect* that I have to deplore, I wonder how I can rally my resolution to persevere as I do—but these efforts at animation are like a dying candle's flashes! Called on H. Bloxam; saw his wife and children—not *very* interesting—everyday sort of persons. I was forcibly struck with his picture, taken when a boy by Harlow [1] and touched by Lawrence; it gave back the *very child* I recollect so well— the lovely boy—and opposite to it was an accurate resemblance of him as he is, bald-headed, long-faced and spectacled; it made me feel the utter worthlessness and insecurity of beauty—and yet how irresistible it is! He walked with me by the Castle to the inn. Read after dinner a chapter in Montesquieu on the reign of Justinian. Looked over also the *Standards* of yesterday and to-day. Buckland's [2] treatise has, it appears, given birth to much controversy, and the *Standard* has devoted a leading article to the defence of the Mosaic account of the Creation; or, as it piously observes, gives a " word for his *Master.*" Now really this is too bad!—it is enough to drive men, by the attempt to stultify them with such blasphemy, from the Church of England, if it were less exceptionable than it is. But *why* should men be at such pains to defend the *ipse dixit* statement of Moses? If it be strictly true, of what consequence is the interference of man in the question?—it is before mankind, as are many other accounts of the Creation as widely believed. Why, then, is not man to exercise his unbiassed reason— *the reason God has given him to use*—upon this and other questions, which, as those of morality, for example, materially affect his salvation? The Moslem, Hindoo, Japanese, Pagan, Christian, all term each other infidels! Need he, who feels he possesses the truth, or is near the truth, disturb himself with the obstinacy or pitiable blindness of his less fortunate fellow-creatures? The Christian is expressly forbidden to do so, but his religion, which from its blessed Author was a religion of charity and love, is now a base and bloody trade, extorting money

[1] George Henry Harlow (1787–1819); a gifted pupil of Lawrence, who painted various theatrical celebrities. He is, however, probably best known by his drawing of Byron, whose intimate friends considered it the most lifelike of the many portraits taken of the poet.

[2] William Buckland (1784–1856); geologist and Dean of Westminster from 1845 to 1856; he was the father of " Frank " Buckland, the well-known naturalist.

by artifice and violence, and caring little or nothing for the immortal objects which ought to be its care. I believe I am a Christian—so distinguished from that Moloch-and-Mammon-worship, the Church of England. . . . I acted Macbeth very unequally. I strove, but sometimes through my own fault, and others through the inattention of these cloggers, I was far beneath myself. Banquo, who had no ring, *pretended* to pull one off his finger and give it me, but I would not take it! I was not so cross as I have often been with less provocation. The very niggardly scale on which this theatre is conducted subjects one to great inconvenience; no attendant, one towel to last the whole week, no fire, and other deficiencies make it a hard task to go through a heavy night's performance. I did not put on my second dress from the ill-humour in which I was.

Worcester, October 1st.—A Mr. Brough saluted me from the coach that met us, and came down to speak to me—for the *sake of speaking* to me. One of his fellow-passengers, who had learned from him who I was, accosted me (!)—told me I was anxiously looked for at Worcester. I bowed. He went up to his coach and, I suppose, told some one inside that I was on this coach. I heard the vulgar fellow say: " Ask him how Mr. Bunn is? " On which this person again approached the box where I sat, and said: " Pray, how is Mr. Bunn? " I suppose I looked rather surprised, but said nothing. The man laughed very loudly, and seemed to think it a very witty thing. I do not know whether he was intoxicated or no. Coming out of Kidderminster, I think, I met Turner, an old Rugbeian, in his carriage. On approaching Worcester, having gone over my part of Ion by the way, I had my old battle to fight with the *mauvaise honte* that always harasses me in entering a town where I have to play, but wet and soiled, and outside—oh, *quelle horreur !* I managed very well to reach the theatre, having left my luggage with the book-keeper, an old actor (" See, actors, what things ye are! "), where I shaved and got tea, and acted Ion very fairly to a crowded house, for which unexpected good fortune I feel most grateful. I received a letter from Mr. Osbaldiston, wanting the book of Werner to rehearse with!—and very plainly showing me that Mr. Pritchard is to be the Ulric of my first night. Mr. Osbaldiston is a very ignorant and incapable man, but that is not within my province to notice. *Il faut cultiver notre jardin !*

Elstree, October 2nd.—Anticipated the call of the servant, and was down to breakfast, and took my departure by the six o'clock coach; found Mr. Anfossi, the double-bass player, my companion; we talked

over music meetings; Malibran, her predecessors in opera; Tramez-
zani, who went mad from his failure in Paris—something for very
harsh critics to pause upon; and Ambrogetti, who has become a
Trappist! I slept occasionally, and went over to myself the character
of Werner, endeavouring to guard against monotony and tameness,
and above all to set myself above impatience and ill-temper.

London, October 3rd.—Forster called in, and to my great astonishment told me the play of the evening was *Macbeth* ! I felt that anger
or irritation would only make that an evil which was *mal à propos*, and
that the best must be done that could be with the circumstances as
they stood. I was very quiet and self-possessed. Oh! *the advantage
of being so !* Several notes were lying on the table, but I had not the
time to open them. Went to Covent Garden, and observed to Mr.
Wallack that I had only just learned that *Macbeth* was to be acted,
that I was quite unprepared, and that it would be out of the question
to attempt it without a rehearsal. In consequence, *Macbeth* was
rehearsed in lieu of *Werner*. I tried to keep myself in a state of self-
possession, and to look at what I had to do. Returning to chambers,
I laid out my Macbeth's dress, read the notes from H. Smith, Ransom's,
enclosing stock receipts; Archdeacon Robinson wishing to see me;
Mr. Phail, with a tragedy and farce; Mr. Whitehead, wishing me to
play his Cavalier. I could only read them. Tried to keep my mind
on the task before me; dined, and went to bed. Rose and went to the
theatre, having just received a note from Lardner relating to Wallace,
who now is comfortable, but for whom, I perceive, he entertains strong
apprehensions. Was very warmly received by the audience, and acted
Macbeth—I think—in many parts as well as I could. If I had had the
advantage of a little time, I fancy I could have smoothed several things
which I fear were harsh. The enthusiasm of the audience seemed raised
very high at last, and I was very loudly called for, and when I went
before the curtain, most cordially greeted. I felt very thankful for the
kindness shown to me, and my heart turned upwards to my God, as
the fountain of all the good that flows to me. May He enable me to
be worthy of it! Amen! Fitzgerald, Forster, Cattermole, and
Browning came into my room. They were glad to see me.

October 4th.—At the theatre, whither I went to rehearse *King
John* and *Werner*, was much amused by Kemble, when I met him, not
offering to shake hands with me, and it occurred to me that the
reception of the play last night might have cooled his cordiality. *I
believe it to be so.* Spoke to Mr. Osbaldiston about Miss Tree's

Benefit. Called on her after rehearsal and sat some time with her; she seemed very grateful for my disposition to serve her. Went to the Garrick Club and saw the newspapers—*Post*, *Chronicle* and *Standard*, brief but very warm in their report of last night. At chambers found the *True Sun* sent to me—very laudatory. Wallace had called and left a note for orders. A note from a Mr. Percy for a few shillings! Forster had called at the theatre and requested me to go to dine with him, Fitzgerald, and Cattermole; and in the morning I had received my book of *Ion* and a very kind note from Wightwick of Plymouth. Sent the two papers I had received to Elstree. Called on Forster, who went with me to call on Cattermole, with whom we found Fitzgerald; all went to dine at the *Café de l'Europe;* spoke to them about Miss E. Tree; all agreed to become Committee. Fitzgerald left us; we took tea at Cattermole's. Forster told me of a tragedy which Browning had completed in ten days (!) on the subject of Strafford. I cannot put faith in its dramatic qualities—the thing seems, not to say incredible, but almost impossible. *I cannot place reliance on the world.*

October 5th.—Acted Werner, *as well as I could under the circumstances.* I rehearsed it more powerfully and naturally than I had ever done, and hoped to make it a splendid impersonation—to be *le personnage;* but Mr. H. Wallack was prompted through the whole of Ulric and otherwise distressed me, and Mr. G. Bennett was as sensational as the gasping out the text could make him.

October 6th.—Forster called. I looked in the newspaper—*Times* —for the chance of some notice of Werner, but of course there was none. Tried to read King John, but, if one has not made oneself master of a character before the day of performance, it is not then to be done; all is chance, and raw, and wild—not artist-like. Acted King John in a style very much beneath myself—no identity, no absorbing feeling of character; the house was great, and at the close (my dying scene was the best) there were calls for Kemble and myself; we went on together. I do not fancy these duets.

October 10th.—Called on Forster, at whose chambers I saw Browning, who had not yet finished his play, which I think a circumstance to rejoice at. An application for relief from Mr. Y——, an indifferent actor and not a good man. He strove to run his sword into my father on the stage at Manchester, and when my father asked him why he was so violent, he said: "Because you struck me, sir!" which, in the character of Cassio, my father had to do. I gave him what I ought not to have given him. Went to theatre. Acted Macbeth as badly as

348

I acted well on Monday last. The gallery was noisy, but that is no excuse for me; I could not feel myself in the part. I was labouring to play Macbeth; on Monday last I *was* Macbeth. Mr. Pritchard came into my room to try over the fight and asked me not to "strike so hard." I observed to him that he struck much harder than I did, to which he replied: "Yes, but I am obliged to do it"!!! I said I could not act gently on purpose, and that it was a mere accident that he was struck; he was disposed to be very absurd, and said that I had "damned him" on the previous night. This I declare to be a shameful *falsehood*. I never uttered a word to him. He made me extremely angry and threw me into great agitation, just as I was going on the stage. I was *very much to blame—very much indeed*—for losing my presence of mind, and especially to such a fool, for he is really no better. Oh, God! Oh, God! *Shall I never learn to act with wisdom?*

October 13th.—Acted Ion very much beneath my summer representations; and yet I strove to act well; but I have lost the freshness, the *directness*, the energy of heart and mind with which I broke out in Macbeth. I cannot account for it. I am all effort now, not artist-like at all. I was called for at the end of the play, but the applause was not—at least it did not *look*—so cordial and general as on my previous nights. Dow walked to chambers with me; we talked about *the trial*—Mr. Thesiger—the scoundrel—Talfourd and the wretch Bunn. He attempted to defend that hired calumniator Thesiger, but admitted that Talfourd had not satisfied him in his exposition of that wretch's villainy.

October 14th.—Went to Adam Street, to the Garrick Club, to Covent Garden theatre, inquiring for the address of Mr. Forrest; called at Mr. Hughes's for it, and found him there. Liked him much— a noble appearance, and a manly, mild, and interesting demeanour.[1] I welcomed him—wished him success, and invited him to my house. He mentioned to me his purpose of leaving the stage, and devoting himself to politics—if he should become President! On going to the Club, I met Mr. Bartley, who told me that Mr. Forrest would do, that his play was good, and he himself likely to hit. This I could *sincerely wish*, while it did no injury to myself; but my home is so dear to me that charity must satisfy itself there before it can range abroad.

Elstree, October 15th.—Rose late, and canvassed with my counsel

---

[1] This favourable impression of Forrest, the American actor, is especially interesting in connection with the fierce enmity, nearly culminating in a tragedy, which afterwards sprang up between him and Macready.

of the Home Department the best mode of arrangement in inviting Mr. Forrest to our home.   Wrote a note of invitation to him.

London, October 17th.—Dow called, and brought me the news of the Drury Lane representation, viz. that Mr. Forrest had quite succeeded, and that the play had been as completely damned.   His opinion was that he was a very good actor, but he did not think him a great one.   I cannot of course have, as yet, any opinion; but this I know, that when I saw him nine years ago, he had everything within himself to make a very great actor.

October 18th.—Woke late and much fatigued.   Wilkin called about greatcoat.   Looked at the *Times* for the account of Mr. Forrest, whom they pronounced to be " more spirited than any tragic actor now on the stage."   It is not surprising; the only wonder is how I have retained any spirit at all, that I have not long since—— My heart is chafed, bruised, and almost crushed; yet I must bear; it is the lesson of my life, which I must early teach to those beloved children. At Garrick Club saw newspapers, high in praise of Forrest, which the persons there were not.   Wrote a note to Forrest; enclosed with a note George's letters to him in Bulwer's frank.   Lay down—*quite tired.* Dow called about nothing.   Acted Ion, judging from the little applause, *very feebly*, and yet I strove to be in earnest and energetic.   Miss —— would make me think, if I were a young man, that she had designs upon me—but I suppose it is all the truth of acting.

October 19th.—Called on Forster, and learned there that my misgivings about Talfourd's coldness were not ill-founded; he has taken some caprice into his head and is weak enough to indulge it.   I am sorry, very sorry for this; but it is most unjust, for I have ever acted honestly, zealously, and with pure disinterestedness in my whole course of friendship with him.   He has *twice* sought my intimacy, and I suppose will twice relinquish.   This is not well—but here is the *rise* of pride!   Very, very unworthy.

October 20th.—Wrote to Forster urging him to deal liberally and kindly by Forrest in his notice.[1]   Began to read *Othello*, which occupied me the whole evening.   Debated upon the propriety of writing a note to Talfourd, but am so entirely at a loss to guess at the cause of his conduct that I really know not how.

October 21st.—Battle of Trafalgar.   On my way to rehearsal

---

[1] This is an important entry inasmuch as Forrest afterwards alleged that Macready had taken an exactly opposite course, thus furnishing him (Forrest) with a just ground for retaliation.

called on Forster, who would have stimulated me to repel with indifference Talfourd's conduct. Such is not my nature. Went to rehearsal, where I was depressed by finding myself not possessed with the character of Othello, and annoyed by the carelessness of the people about the arrangement of the last scene. Oh, what a change has taken place in this theatre! I remember it offering accommodation to the actor in every particular, and now it is a dirty desert except before the curtain, which perhaps may be looked on as a reproof to my complaint. Lay down and looked over Othello, about which I was exceedingly nervous. Forster called for an order. Suffered very much from want of self-possession—in truth from want of time to have prepared myself. Very fortunately there was a riot from the exceeding crowd in the theatre, which made, I fancy, other persons as nervous as myself, and I was pleased and encouraged on hearing the other actors in the play receive as little applause as myself—if indeed they did not meet with less. But in the third act of *Othello* I rose into energy, though wanting finish, and produced a great deal of applause; in fact, I felt myself lauded, but I was very much distressed. I held the audience through the play, and was called for at the end; when I went on, I was very enthusiastically received.

Elstree, October 22nd.—It was a great relief—a great gratification to me to read in the *Times* a very laudatory notice of my Othello. I read two acts and the preface of *La Vallière* and enjoyed my walk in a sweet, sunshiny morning to my dear home, where, thank God, I found all well.

London, October 24th.—My spirits were very low, and I had begun the page on which I am now writing, when old Dow—staunch old Dow —came in; shortly after him, Forster. They gave me an account of Mr. Forrest's performance of Othello. It would be stupid and shallow hypocrisy to say that I was indifferent to the result—careless whether he is likely to be esteemed less or more than myself; it is of great importance to me to retain my superiority, and my wishes for his success follow the desire I have to be considered above him! Is this illiberal? I hope not. Their accounts of his performance have certainly reduced very much my opinion of his mind, which from the particulars they related cannot be of the highest order. Forster says that he will be greatly praised in the papers, but both agree that he will not attract.

October 25th.—Looked at the newspapers with great anxiety for the account of Mr. Forrest's Othello. The *Times* had a most insidious article—a *Times* article!—upon which, if charged, it would disclaim all intention of comparison, but intended to convey the idea of superiority in Mr. Forrest, still unable to use strong terms of praise—to apologize for and offer excuses and reasons for *much* which it admitted to be feeble and ineffective. The *Herald* and *Post* were both qualified; felt the performance not to have been a thoroughly successful one. Letitia arrived. I wrote a note, with order, to Colonel Birch and to Sir J. Marshall. Forster called, angry about the newspapers to Mr. Forrest. Wrote an invitation to Dowling. Lay down, my spirits depressed by the unfair tone of the newspapers, and read over Othello. At the theatre there was a violent disturbance from the overcrowded state of the pit; the audience demanded that the money should be returned, the play could not be heard. Charles Kemble went forward, addressed the audience, spoke to Mr. Wallack—but by merely temporizing he effected nothing. The first scene ended in dumb show. Mr. H. Wallack went forward in the next scene, but his speech was shuffling, evasive—anything but an answer to the downright demand of " Return the money! " The audience would not allow the play to proceed and, at last, after speaking to Mr. Vandenhoff, I went forward. I said that ' under the circumstances of peculiar inconvenience from which so many seemed to be suffering, I scarcely knew what to say, and that if I should say anything that might appear to give offence either to them or the management, I hoped I should stand excused; but as the only means of remedying the present inconvenience and relieving both those who were desirous of going and those who wished to remain, if the ladies or gentlemen who could not obtain room would require their money from the door-keeper, and tell him to charge it to my account, I should be most happy to be responsible for it.' The whole house cheered very enthusiastically, and like the sea under the word of Neptune, the waves were instantly stilled. Kemble said afterwards, " If he had thought of it, he should have said the same, but it never entered his head." *Voilà Kemble!* I was shaken out of my identity by the disturbance, but I *did my best*—not very good, though Forster, who came into my room, very kindly thought it was. Was called for at the end, and went forward. Forster walked to chambers with me.

October 27th.—I sent in to Forster, and heard further from him of the *set* that is making against me to elevate Mr. Forrest. This is ungenerous, but as I did not wish to be an ungenerous rival to him, I again requested Forster not to write in harshness or hostility upon his performance. He was very peremptory and distinct in his expressed

352

CHARLES KEMBLE

From an engraving

resolution to keep his own course. At Garrick Club I saw the papers—the *Morning Herald* also of yesterday, of which the Editor ought to be *ashamed*. It was an effort to abuse and depreciate me, but in the most positive manifestation of his own *ignorance* the writer seemed as if he could not or dared not—I do not know what he means. The play-bills of Drury Lane pronounce Mr. Forrest the "most extraordinary actor of the day." He has never been cheated by, nor punished the writer—it is therefore true! Saw Kemble, Fladgate, and Price,[1] who came to me with a list of names for a complimentary dinner to Mr. Forrest, asking me to put my name to it. I had no alternative, but it is very indelicate, to say the very least, that an American should thus make himself a party in such a business.

October 28th.—Mr. G. Dance told me that C. Kemble had been appointed, without solicitation, to the office of Licenser *vice* George Colman,[2] who died the day before yesterday. How poorly he has shrunk out of existence—a man of some talent, much humour and little principle. Fortune seems to shower her benefits on those who certainly from their talents and virtues can make little claim to them. For character, look at C. Kemble—what he really *is* and what he *passes for*! I feel discontented (am I envious?) at seeing place and wealth conferred so unmeritedly; but thus it almost always has been, and I suppose ever will be. They called me to go on the stage, but I heard one or two voices roaring out "Vandenhoff," and I declined the honour. I do not know if they had him on. Talfourd came into my room and seemed very glad to see me. Dow walked home with me and sat very late. I expressed to him strongly how very much annoyed and distressed I felt at Forster's expressed resolution to write a severe article on Mr. Forrest; he being known to be a friend of mine, my situation was particularly painful.

October 29th.—Read Forster's criticism on Mr. Forrest, which gave me very great pain. I thought it ill-natured and not just—omitting all mention of his merit, with the enumeration of his faults. I would have done much to have prevented it. Forster came, and I expressed candidly my dissatisfaction to him.[3]

October 30th.—Browning arrived, told me of a most exaggerated

---

[1] Stephen Price, manager of the Park Theatre, New York.

[2] George Colman the younger (1762-1836); dramatist and theatrical manager. He fulfilled his duties as licenser with scrupulousness and judgment.

[3] This article was the origin of Forrest's animus against Macready; it was evidently one of Forster's "slashers," and though honestly intended in Macready's interest had the most disastrous consequences.

353

notice of Mr. Forrest's Othello in the *Athenæum*—"Decius (Mr. C. Dance) was once my friend;" he is now the close ally of Mr. Price, and thus we obtain just and correct criticism. Whilst I was dressing, Messrs. Forrest, S. Price and Jones arrived. We talked in the drawing-room with Browning and Dow, till the arrival of Talfourd and Mr. T. R. Price and White. Introduced all to Forrest. Asked him to take Mrs. Macready down. Spent an agreeable and cheerful afternoon. My American friends did not return to the drawing-room. I was very much relieved from any feeling of regret I may have felt in learning from Talfourd that he thought Forster's article in the *Examiner* borne out in its fidelity by the evidence it gave; he thought it well done. Dow and Browning left us early—then the Talfourd party.

London, October 31st.—Forster and Browning called. Browning, who said his play of *Strafford* was finished, soon left. Forster told me that Bulwer would call at one o'clock. He did, and we discussed the alterations I had suggested, to which he assented. I advised him to see Mr. Osbaldiston, and we agreed that the play should be read on Wednesday. Called at Covent Garden theatre, but Mr. Osbaldiston was not to be found. Went to Garrick Club, where I dined and saw newspapers—and puffings of Mr. Forrest in all directions: "Macready's opinion of Mr. Forrest: 'Sir, there has been nothing like him since Kemble!'" Fact! *Globe.* This is rather too bad. My spirits were low. Every one around me seems helped on by fortune; I have the dogged course of labour to pursue with all its uncertainties. Acted King John tolerably well—the second scene with Hubert better than before by *taking time* between the periods of passion.

November 1st.—I think I acted Othello well with considerable spirit, and more *pause* than I generally allow myself, which is an undoubted improvement. Dow and his friend came into my room—I wish he would not bring his *friends* to me!—Forster, and afterwards Wallace; Wallace thought I acted pretty well, but not *so well as he had* seen me. I think that this must have referred to a want of finish in deportment and *aplomb*, which I have not had in the character at Covent Garden, from want of notice to prepare myself. Forster was in my chambers when I reached them. He wished to tell me of an intrigue that is on foot to secure Knowles's new play to Drury Lane and Mr. Forrest; he suspects that Mr. S. Price is concerned in the purchase or traffic, whatever it may be. Mr. S. Knowles requested the loan of £50 from me a few days since. I think he might have paid back the kindness I showed him by giving me at least the refusal of his play, as he said to Forster he would do. But I have only known Mr. Knowles, to know him as a man utterly forgetful of the deepest obligations; if I live, I shall see severer retribution than I wish to do. Forster told me of Browning's play which he praised most highly; but I fear he has such an interest in the individual characters, the biographies of whom he has written, that he is misled as to its dramatic power; character to him having the interest of action. *Nous verrons !* Heaven speed it! Amen!

November 2nd.—Read Bulwer's play of the *Duchess of La Vallière* in Mr. Osbaldiston's room. The actors and actresses were, or seemed to be, very much pleased with the play, but I cannot put much confidence in them. Going out of Covent Garden theatre I met Mr. Sheridan Knowles at the door; he did not seem, because he endeavoured to seem, at ease in meeting me. He asked, I think, what news? I told him none, but that his play had been sent to Drury Lane. "Yes," he said; ' that it was entirely a woman's play, and he could not trust it to Miss Faucit—that I should not have done the man's part in it.' "Then," I observed, "it is as well you have not given me the pain of refusing it." I asked him what woman they had at Drury Lane. He said that they were expecting some one. I answered, "Yes, Miss Phillips." I then called Mr. Pritchard, spoke to him a word or two on *La Vallière*, and left Mr. Knowles rather coolly. Dined at the Garrick Club, where I also received with marked coolness the advances of Mr. Bartley. Of what use is it to keep a smiling face? They cut your throat or heart while they smile on you—Mr. Meadows, Price, W. Jones (!), Fladgate. Called on Forster; Mr. Mahoney (Father Prout) called in. Wrote notes to Dow and to Catherine, and read over part of Ion, which I acted very well; the audience were quite tumultuous in their call for me, but I was undressed. Dow came into my room. Spoke to Mr. H. Wallack about the National Theatre, New York, and told him I should be happy to receive communications from them and send them any books, etc. I spoke a long time with Mr. Osbaldiston, suggesting the expediency of making an offer to Miss Phillips—either by that means to secure her services or to raise her terms at the other theatre. Osbaldiston agreed to do so.

November 3rd.—Called on Miss Martineau,[1] who told me of many friends she had seen in the United States, and of her intended book upon the country. I was surprised and sorry to hear her say of

---

[1] Harriet Martineau (1802–1876), the well-known writer, then just returned from a two years' visit to America.

355

Webster [1] that his private character was bad. Alas! Alas! She liked Clay the best of the American statesmen. She is a very zealous abolitionist, but, I think, has got some illusive notions on the actual state of opinion on that perplexing question. She talks more than she did—should I say *too much?*—and it fatigues one to hold her trumpet long. She spoke in the warmest terms of Mrs. Butler; her qualities of head and heart. Forster and Browning called, and settled next Wednesday sennight for the reading of the *Earl of Strafford.* A note from Dowling. Dined with Forster at the Garrick Club, where I saw the papers, in which was a quiz upon the Drury Lane players giving a box to Mr. Forrest in token of their appreciation of his "private worth." "Price the clown had thrown thirty-one somersaults successively, for which the company had given him a box in testimony of their admiration of his talent as a somersault thrower and his worth as a man, but they had known him a week!" James Smith, Poole, Price, Fitzroy Stanhope, etc., dined there and left soon. Murphy and Raymond came in, and I was indiscreet enough—mad enough—to let my "dear judgment out," and lose my temper in speaking of the Drury Lane proprietors, and Mr. Bunn. Mr. Raymond was first speaking of his cleverness, and then appeared to doubt the correctness of the general persuasion that he was a scoundrel. I very foolishly spoke very vehemently upon the subject. *"Oh! fool! fool! fool!"*

November 4th.—Acted Othello—not perhaps quite equally—but, taking one part with another, very fairly. Is Miss —— disposed to coquette with me? I cannot quite understand her. Called for and very enthusiastically received by the audience. Talfourd, Forster, and Dow came into my room. Forster, who did not like Mr. Forrest's Lear so well as his Othello, left soon. Talfourd spoke in the highest strain of the last night's *Ion*, which he saw, and was prevented from coming round by Mr. H. Wallack's declaration that I had left the theatre. I spoke to him about my action against Bunn; he coincided with my views, and counselled the letting it rest, and if *they* moved in it, to pay the dues upon it—my own purpose. Dow walked home with me, and we took oysters and porter in the alley leading to Holborn.

November 7th.—Drove dear Catherine to town in Dow's cab, but the difficulty of getting his horse (old Bob) along made it a very uncomfortable journey. I took a coach in Great Portland Street—leaving the horse and cab, which I could not pretend to get through the streets. I was much wearied with whipping and with nervousness.

---

[1] The United States President.

Forster called; was very much annoyed and distressed by the abusive article in yesterday's *Age*. I told him I had at first thought he ought to chastise the reptile, Westmacott, but on reflection was decidedly averse to any notice being taken of anything so utterly contemptible. He told me that he had consulted Fitzgerald and Fonblanque; the first recommended a severe horsewhipping without a word; the latter stated his general principle, viz. that if a man was worth horsewhipping, he was worth calling out—which horsewhipping might lead to, and that therefore, if Forster took any notice of it, he ought to give it the option of a gentleman's conduct. I strongly dissuaded him from doing anything, but he could only listen to his passion, and judgment had no chance. Lay down after writing him a short note, urging his forbearance, and tried to think of Othello. Met H. Smith on the stairs, who walked with me to the theatre. Acted Othello, not exactly well, but again derived great benefit from *taking time* between my sentences. O'Hanlon's suggestion about greater slowness was not lost to me. Called for by the audience and went on—was well received.

November 8th.—Sent to Forster, whom I wished again to see—to reason with against proceeding in *re* Westmacott. Forster called, and gave me to understand that the matter was to be referred to Henry Berkeley,[1] on whose opinion he was to act. This is all wrong in my mind. He should either not act at all, but pass with indifference and contempt the expressions and insults (if the vituperation of a villain can be called an insult) of so vile a wretch, which I think most decidedly he ought to do; or, without consulting any one, if he has any unknown personal motive for resolving to stop any future impertinence, he should go at once, and inflict a most memorable chastisement upon him. He is in a fret, and not in a passion. I fear he will not come well out of it; and, as I really regard him very much, I wish he would be more temperate and more decided.

November 9th.—Sent in to inquire after Forster, heard that he had gone to Brighton and would be home at night. I imagine it is in pursuit of Mr. Westmacott. I can only add, "Nobly, ye gods! oh, nobly!" I hope he will not discredit himself. Went to the theatre in low spirits. Could not force my spirit into the shape and body of Ion, which I acted but feebly—ineffectively. Talfourd and his son Frank, and Dow, came into my room. Dow and myself went to an oyster shop, and then tried to make Forster hear, but we could not get in.

---

[1] A well-known "man about town," belonging to the somewhat militant family of that name.

November 10th.—Sent in to Forster, heard that he was returned and lying down; in my anxiety to know what he had done, went in and spoke to him. He said he would call on me in half-an-hour. Sent orders to Wallace. Bourne called and Forster, whom I saw and talked with in my bedroom. He told me he had been down to Brighton to see Mr. C. Kean, in consequence of a report, widely circulated, and communicated to him by Mr. S. Price, that " Mr. C. Kean had said Forster had declared in his hearing that no man should succeed as a first actor while Macready was on the stage." This having been said to Mr. Cooper, Forster called on Mr. Cooper, who confirmed the statement. He obtained a statement from Mr. Kean, which I could not well understand, but it seemed to me that he merely stood upon what he had said to Mr. Cooper, viz. *that he had understood Mr. Forster to use words to that effect three years ago;* and adding that, whether he considered it a compliment or no he could not tell, but that he was kept from town by his dread of the *Examiner.* I told Forster I thought that, having moved so much in the business, he ought *to do* something and do it determinedly and completely in regard to Mr. Westmacott; he left me to *consult* Fonblanque. . . . Forster called, and the upshot of all is that he put the declaration of Mr. Kean in Mr. S. Price's hands at Fonblanque's suggestion, and at the " earnest entreaty " of both Fonblanque and Price he had decided on *taking no further notice of Westmacott.* Acted much of King John—all but the scene of accusation against Hubert—very well indeed; was called for but did not go forward. Mr. W. Jones was behind the scenes, and I was talking to him. I asked him to step into my room after the play; inquired of him when Forrest's engagement was likely to close, as I should like to pay some professional compliment to him. He said it was uncertain, it might end in a week or go on for months. He added that Mr. Forrest was very much gratified by the attention I had paid him. I told him I wished him to be pleased with his visit, and, while speaking on the subject, in strict confidence, wished to observe that the articles which were so severe in the *Examiner,* having been written by Mr. Forster, who was a particular friend of mine, I begged to assure him that, knowing Mr. Forster's opinion of Mr. Forrest to be less flattering than that of other persons and other newspapers, I had used all my influence with him—by word of mouth, by writing, and by the mediation of friends, to induce him to abandon his intention of expressing an unfavourable opinion; that he had yielded partially in his first review, but had peremptorily and repeatedly refused to suppress or qualify his opinion on the subsequent performances. Jones said that it had been said the articles were *through me,* but that neither he nor Mr. Forrest had ever given attention to the insinuations and assertions of the base persons who are to be found about a theatre. I observed to him, that to contradict any such persons would be quite beneath me ; that if my character were vulnerable to the attacks of such persons as Mr. Westmacott, etc., it really was not worth the care necessary for its preservation. He told me that Talfourd had sent him, Mr. Forrest, his play of *Ion* with a very kind note, which he had pointed to in refutation of *my* interference to his prejudice, and that Forrest was more gratified by my calling on him, etc., than by anything he had met with here.[1]

November 12th.—Acted Othello very fairly. Called for by the audience and was very warmly received. Talfourd, Forster and Dow came into my room. Talfourd said he had seen the two first acts of Mr. Forrest's Lear ; that he played the first act very well, but the second not so well. Forster quite agreed with him. Dow was enchanted with the last act of Browning's *Earl of Strafford.*

November 14th.—Acted Brutus in *Julius Cæsar* very, very feebly— crudely—badly—I was not prepared for it and *ought not* to have yielded to the desire of the stupid and ignorant manager. I am punished for my folly by a *complete failure.* Such a thing I have not known these many days. The Senate scene, altered at my instigation, was very good. The play altogether was bad.

Elstree, November 15th.—Lane called with the drawings of Miss E. Tree and myself, C. Kemble, Mr. and Mrs. Bartley and Mr. Farren. " An I be not ashamed of my company," etc. My experience of the professors of my art confirms me in my opinion of their vileness, their utter unworthiness. Yesterday some of them went to the church, St. Martin's, where Bannister [2] was buried privately, to pay respect. I would, if I could, have a police officer stationed in the church where I may be buried, to take out these vile intruders on the sorrows and rites of affection and respect. Out upon them ! *Odi et arceo !*

November 16th.—Looked at as much as I could of Othello. Took all the pains I could with it, and acted it very well. I improve nightly, I think, in the character—from taking time ; I acted it *well.* The audience called for me, and received me most enthusiastically. Talfourd

---

[1] Forrest gave a very different account in after years.

[2] John Bannister (1760–1836) ; the original Don Whiskerandos in the *Critic ;* a useful all-round comedian. He retired from the stage in 1815.

and White came into my room, and afterwards Dow, who also told me of the cordial tone of the newspapers on Brutus. Talfourd and White talked much of Forrest. Talfourd showed me a letter he had received from Forrest in acknowledgment of his own note with his book of *Ion;* he showed it me—in his own words, ' that I might see by the answer the sort of note he had written to Forrest.' This is poor work; why should I object to any fair demonstration of respect to Mr. Forrest's good qualities as a man, or his talents as an artist? I do not—but Talfourd is a weak, an inconsistent, not a sterling man. I do not like *the mode* of showing me the letter.[1] Talfourd wished me to dine with him on Sunday. I could not. Endeavoured to see Mr. Osbaldiston, or Mr. Wallack, about Bulwer's play. *Could not.* Went to the oyster shop on my way to chambers; called on Forster, found Cattermole there, talked over an edition of Shakspeare—to be illustrated by him. Forster talked of a critical work on my performances after I had left the stage. I was pleased to hear him speak of it.

November 18th.—Rose late—I do not know why; read the newspaper, in which I was pleased to see that the attempt of Bunn to get a new trial *v.* Vandenhoff was defeated; it is now established by law that a manager *cannot* be guilty of the infamous injustice this wretch was guilty of last season driving away Miss Tree, Messrs. Harley, Yarnold, at his will against their express engagements. Forster called, but had no conclusive information to give me respecting Bulwer's play. I fear it; I see clearly that Forster has apprehensions about it as a reading play, which I had not; and I have my misgivings, from the mode in which it will be acted, of its success in representation.

November 19th.—Browning came with Dow to bring me his tragedy of *Strafford;* the fourth act was incomplete. I requested him to write in the plot of what was deficient. Dow drove me to the Garrick Club, while Browning wrote out the story of the omitted parts. I found remaining of the party of eighteen who sat down to the dinner given to Mr. Forrest—himself, Talfourd (in the Chair), Mr. Blood opposite, S. Price, C. Kemble, W. Jones, Zachary (!), Dance, Murphy, Raymond and three others unknown. I greeted Forrest, and told him I was anxious to be among his hosts; Talfourd mentioned that my health had been drunk very cordially, but repeated it in my presence. I was drunk to, and briefly stated that "the attention was unex-

---

[1] Talfourd was evidently aware of Macready's extreme susceptibility on matters affecting his professional position, and not unnaturally wished to protect himself against any ground for grievance or complaint.

pected; that I came to pay, not to receive, a compliment; and could assure my highly-talented friend that no one extended the hand of welcome to him more fervently or sincerely than myself, in doing which I only endeavoured to repay a small part of the debt of gratitude which had been heaped on me by the kindness of his countrymen,' etc. C. Kemble wished that we should take wine together, which we did. Browning and Dow soon summoned me, and I received the MS., started in a cab to Kilburn, where I found a chaise, *vice* fly, waiting for me. I bought a couple of cigars and smoked to Edgware. Got comfortably to Elstree and found, thank God, all in tolerable health.

Elstree, November 20th.—Applied myself to the perusal of Browning's MS. of *Strafford*. I was greatly pleased with it, read portions of it to Catherine and Letitia. My little remainder of the day was spent with my darling children—playing with and telling them stories.

London, November 21st.—Browning called in some anxiety to have my opinion of his play. I told it frankly, and he was very much pleased, agreeing in my objections, and promising to do everything needful to the play's amendment. He sat very long. Read some part of Brutus—acted the part—partially well—not altogether. Dow came into my room, having previously seen Mr. Booth's [1] appearance in Gloucester; he thought it very bad. Went with Dow to an oyster shop, and thence we adjourned to my chambers, where I gave him tea. Letters from Mr. Freeman about his trash, which he calls a tragedy of *Amasis;* from Mr. Lazarus—I wish he were in Abraham's bosom.

November 22nd.—Forster called—about nothing. I spoke to him of the importance of his new undertaking, and that he should not trifle with it. I fear he gives too much to indulgence to carve out a great reputation—"to scorn delights and live laborious days" is no more his motto than that of many others; and yet it is the only one under which to be *secure of advancing*. Forster called with Browning's MS. Mr. Booth, I perceive, has made a signal failure last night. Talfourd came in; Forster, Dow. I thought Forster in rather a splenetic mood. There is a want of manly consistency in Talfourd's character which is not pleasing to his intimate acquaintance. *I* do not admire it. Forster was annoyed with his praise of Mr. Forrest. The conversation turned on Miss Mitford, who, it seems, has been making application to Mr. Forrest to act *Rienzi*—a new play of hers to be written. I made some observations on Miss M—— not very com-

---

[1] Junius Brutus Booth (1795–1852); tragedian. He played chiefly in America. He had failed as Richard III at Covent Garden some years previously.

plimentary, which Talfourd did not seem to like, I thought. I cannot understand this sort of capricious siding with a person whom he has proved so base and worthless.   When I compare the demeanour of Talfourd now, and his frank, unembarrassed heartiness, speaking out in looks, words, and actions, a year ago, I am reluctantly obliged to let go the half-belief, half-hope, to which I clung, that no change had taken place.   I must say I now feel it too true.   It is a painful admission, but one I am forced upon.   In my own conduct I can find no grounds for this falling off; he is not a high-minded man; he is, and ever has been, compromising, in some cases to a degree of servility— I may almost say meanness.   This has seemed to me arising from, and in some degree explained, if not excused, by his timidity of disposition. It is very painful to me to entertain such opinions, but I believe the " cooling " of this " hot friend " began in the ardour and successful issue of my exertions for his play, and settled in his own weak and timorous advocacy of my cause.   He is not what he has been, when he had a play in prospect of performance, which performance could only have been effected by myself, and was undertaken *solely because I believed it would make him happy.*   I have nothing in his case with which I can accuse myself.[1]

Elstree, November 23rd.—Began *very attentively* to read over the tragedy of *Strafford*, in which I find more grounds for exception than I had anticipated.   I had been too much carried away by the truth of character to observe the meanness of plot, and occasional obscurity. Went into the garden to induce my children to exercise; set them at play and returned to my work on *Strafford*.

London, November 24th.—Browning called, and I told him that I could not look at his play again until Bulwer's was produced, in which he acquiesced.   Dow called when I was trying to snatch a few minutes' sleep; he told me that the *Age* abused me in Brutus for having a " *pug nose* and *massive* face."   I *laughed sincerely.*   Acted Brutus very well, better on the whole than I think I had done before.   Talfourd came into my room, and gave me the book (bound) of *Ion* for Birth.   I was much pleased with it.   He told me that he had had a letter from Miss Mitford, informing him that she had written to Mr. Forrest, and that

---

[1] Macready's attitude to Talfourd was at this time largely dominated by his resentment at the proceedings in the Bunn case, in which he considered that Talfourd ought to have taken a much stronger line as his advocate.   Brooding over this grievance, he allowed himself to conjure up suspicions, which, in view of Talfourd's acknowledged character, had little justification.   The incident illustrates the desirability of trusting your fortunes in a Court of Law to any one but your " own familiar friend."

her father had settled with him that he was to play Otto after Christmas, and that, her novel being postponed, she was to finish her play immediately. I have no faith in her power of writing a play, and to that opinion Talfourd subscribed to-night—concurring in all I thought of her falsehood and baseness! He asked me to dine on Saturday when Lane dines with him—to which I assented.

November 26th.—Went to Talfourd's. Met Kenyon, whom I much like, White, Lane, and some agreeable men. Found on my return to chambers a note from a Mr. Milford, asking my autograph. Talfourd had mentioned his intention of making a book of the autographs of the distinguished persons from whom he had received letters on his *Ion*—a most interesting collection, and what a treasure to the child who inherits it.

Elstree, November 27th.—Dr. Elliotson arrived.[1] Saw and prescribed for Letitia; he took tea with us. I liked him very much. He talked of Dr. Gregory,[2] the homœopathic system, of which he expressed the absurdity, and other subjects very agreeably. I gave him a cheque for twelve guineas, which I hope was right, thanked him, and he left us greatly relieved by his visit.

London, November 29th.—Dow and Forster came into my room from Drury Lane, where they had been attending the representation of Knowles's new play, the *Wrecker's Daughter*. They both agreed in the opinion that it was not good, indifferently acted, and melodramatic in its plot and construction; that it would not be greatly attractive. When Knowles parted with his purity of mind, he threw away the great power of simplicity and truth that made him so strong. Delilah has shorn the head of Samson!

November 30th.—Went to rehearsal. Bulwer came with Forster; went over part of the play. Is the frank—the volunteered expression of admiration and partiality of the part of Miss —— simplicity, deceit, coquetry, or passion? I really do not know, but suspect that neither the first nor last have much to do with it. Mr. Farren has, in my mind, seriously injured this play by his intrusion of himself into the part of Lauzun. He does not understand it. He is a very, *very ignorant* man. Sent coat of arms to Johnson and Allen, coachmakers.

---

[1] John Elliotson (1791-1868); an eminent London physician; professor of medicine in the University of London, a post which he was compelled to relinquish owing to his practice of mesmerism. He was consulted by, and intimate with many distinguished literary men of the day, among them Thackeray, who dedicated to him one of his novels.

[2] Probably George Gregory (1790-1853); F.R.S., F.R.C.P., author of *Elements of the Theory and Practice of Physic.*

I already repent the order for the carriage, and wish my money in my pocket and the horse in Yorkshire. Acted King John tolerably well, but was much less applauded than either Miss Faucit or Kemble. I do not think that the *low prices* raise the judgment of the audience, for they hail rant and roar with an ardent spirit of reciprocity.

December 1st.—Saw the papers and was amused to read the *Times'* criticism on Mr. Forrest's Macbeth—as "inferior to his former efforts —in the last act tame and not sufficiently studied—deficient in that robust power, which is the main characteristic and essential quality of his acting "—his "variations of tone not in accordance with the text "; but "it is *questionable* if his second act could be surpassed by any actor now on the stage—on the whole, considering the state of the stage, the performance is entitled to considerable praise." Has Forster said worse than this? He has spoken truth honestly and not like a craven parasite, as the writer of this recanting article is. *It is too bad.* Went to the Garrick Club; took up *Post,* saw that it was a flaming panegyric upon Macbeth, about which even the play-bills are cold, and laid it down again. Saw a notice of myself in Brutus in the *Athenæum*—trash! Saw Mr. H. Harris, now an old man—twenty years ago in all the lustihood of youth and vigour—careworn and fast falling to a wreck! Oh, my God!—what is this life?—what is my life?—days worn out without the least improvement of mind, without any enjoyment, merely to get the means of living! Good fortune seems to help the base and profligate.

December 2nd.—Acted Othello with earnestness and spirit, but occasionally weak as to physical power; very much applauded, and in possession of the audience; heard that Mrs. Butler [1] was in the theatre before the fifth act, and from a feeling of pique which I cannot alto- gether account for, except that I thought her an impostor in the art, took particular pains with the last scene, and played it very powerfully; was much applauded, and heard a call begun for *me* as I left the stage. The prompter came to my room for me, but when I reached the stage I heard that Mr. Kemble (!) had gone on; this was too good, so I observed that they would no doubt be quiet, and returned. This was either a most extraordinary freak in the audience, or a most consum- mate piece of jesuitical impertinence in him—to make something of himself before his daughter. I was not very pleased, but showed no feeling about it.

December 5th.—Acted Brutus fairly; was much struck by a person

[1] Fanny Kemble.

whom I thought to be Mrs. Butler—leaning forward with looks of extreme—intense fondness on C. Kemble, when he stood in his military dress in the last act of the play.   Lane [1] was behind the scenes, making a sketch of C. Kemble (*pourquoi ?*).   Talfourd came into my room, and after dressing went with me to the Garrick Club, where we discussed a supper and Mr. Forrest's merits with Poole, Douglas, White, etc.

December 6th.—Miss Huddart, to my great surprise, called, and sat an unreasonably long time, informing me of the performers of Drury Lane having been recommended to make an " offer " of their salaries till Christmas to Mr. Bunn; also mentioning the utter failure of Mr. Forrest in Macbeth, and Mr. Abbott's regret at having been led into such a mistake as to think him a man of genius.

December 7th.—Went to rehearsal of *La Vallière*.   Mrs. Glover observed to me, hoping I should not be offended at the observation, that she had never seen such an improvement in any person as in myself lately.   I told her I was extremely gratified to hear her say so, since every art needed study and was progressive in its course towards perfection.   Rehearsed Bragelone. [2]   I cannot make out Miss ——.

December 8th.—A note from Miss Huddart, informing me of the submission to Mr. Bunn's or Mr. Dunn's proposal of yielding, in addition to the salary of the past week, half their salaries till Christmas; the beast is made for the burthen—the player is fashioned to paltry oppression.   Called at the Garrick Club, where I saw Mr. Meadows, Planché, and C. Dance, who were speaking of the exaction made upon the Drury Lane Company.   Dow called, and half-amused, half-displeased me by his folly, and utter want of judgment, in railing at Mr. C. Kemble for advertising singly in the newspapers his Benefit, and not in *all at once*, by which accident he, Dow, not seeing the announcement until three days after the first advertisement, was too late to get places.   No name was bad enough for Kemble.   I endeavoured to convince him of his absurdity, but when he inclines to stupidity and folly of this kind, he knows no mean; he is donkey from ears to hoofs. Acted Macbeth to an indifferent house in a very earnest and grand manner.   I think I was very good; called for by the audience, but declined going on.

December 9th.—Went much fatigued to an early rehearsal of *La Vallière*, of which I begin to entertain strong and painful apprehen-

---

[1] John Bryant Lane (1788–1868) ; portrait painter.
[2] Macready's part in Bulwer's play, *La Vallière*.

sions. Mr. Farren does not convey to me the least tinge of resemblance to the character of Lauzun. Webster [1] seems very unmeaning and inefficient in Montespan; Vandenhoff not very impassioned in the King, Miss Pelham awfully bad in Madame Montespan, and Miss Faucit frequently feeble and monotonous in La Vallière. I do not feel that I can do anything worthy of myself in the part, but I will do my utmost. Bulwer and Count D'Orsay [2] were at rehearsal. The necessity of deferring the play until after Christmas was suggested, and upon reflection espoused by Bulwer. Dined at that vulgar place, the Garrick Club, where the principal conversation is eating, drinking, or the American Presidency! It is really a disgusting place. Mr. Price in reference to his *falsehood* of Wednesday, admitted that Mr. G. Raymond had been misinformed. Saw newspapers, in one of which, the *Morning Chronicle*, was a letter containing unqualified abuse of me in Othello—praising Messrs. Kemble, Young and Pope (!) in the part, depreciating Kean, and extolling C. Kemble as a " Cassio and a man " beyond all Cassios and all men. I strongly suspect this attack to be the production of an ignorant coxcomb who writes the notices in *Cumberland's Theatre* and signs himself D—— G——. Read some amusing papers of Theodore Hook's in the *New Monthly*. Coming to my chambers lost more than an hour in disgust and ill-humour at the liability to insult and injury under which my calling lays me. What have we in this unhappy art to compensate for what we endure—the mischievous puncture of such a rude goad as this wretch's abuse gives more pain than Bulwer's or D'Orsay's eulogy can give pleasure. Bulwer and Forster called to consult with me on Osbaldiston's proposed postponement of *La Vallière* to Christmas week. I concurred. Wrote a note to O'Hanlon about the *Morning Chronicle* attack.

December 10th.—Acted Brutus particularly well. Lady Blessington and Count D'Orsay [2] were there, and I took pains. I felt the part; I think I may say " *J'étois le personnage.*" Forster came into my room and told me they were delighted.

December 13th.—Called on Forster, and proposed to him to write

---

[1] Benjamin Nottingham Webster (1797–1882); afterwards the popular manager of the Haymarket and Adelphi theatres; from 1829 he took rank as a leading London comedian.

[2] Count D'Orsay (1801–1852) was then at the height of his vogue as an "exquisite." Macready, who soon afterwards became acquainted with the Count and Lady Blessington, appears to have entertained an unqualified regard for him, in spite of shortcomings which he would have severely denounced in members of his own fraternity. D'Orsay, in fact, stripped of his social glamour was anything but an estimable character, and it is surprising to find so austere a moralist as Macready a frequent visitor of the tarnished D'Orsay-Blessington establishment.

a courteous valedictory notice of Mr. Forrest, disclaiming personal feelings and paying a tribute to his private character. Forster very decidedly refused—upon the belief or suspicion that Mr. Forrest had looked, if not with a gratified, at least an indifferent eye upon the attacks that had been made upon me.

December 15th.—Acted Brutus moderately. Was weak enough to retort on Mr. Vandenhoff the tricks to which he has nightly resorted in Othello, and latterly in Cassius, to deprive my effects of their applause. He wanted the hint and I gave him a strong one; he is a most unfair actor—a regular Jesuit—he was very angry, but dared not show it beyond his discontented look. C. Kemble seems very gloomy or glum.

London, December 20th.—Browning called and left with me the omitted scenes in his play. I called on Forster, who reported to me of Mr. Forrest's Virginius last night that it was the worst of his performances—he almost seems now in each new character to fit to himself the line: "But worse remains behind." Lay down on the sofa and read part of Brutus. Acted the character *well*—with energy, dignity, and freshness. I was anxious to do so, and I felt my own superiority. Mr. Vandenhoff again resorted to his dirty tricks of endeavouring to impede my effects, and take the applause from them, but I left him to the enjoyment of his unavailing efforts, and made my character stand conspicuously foremost in his despite. At the end of the play Mr. Kemble lingered in a ridiculous manner about the scenes, so that I was forced to pass by him. I heard some noise afterwards and sent to see if the audience were not applauding on the occasion of Mr. Kemble "going forward." The prompter came to say that the audience were calling for me, Mr. Kemble having gone on; I merely observed that I should not go. I cannot believe that the sense of the audience (if sense were indeed among them) could be in favour of paying a compliment to the worst among the leading actors of the play, and for such a miserable performance as is the Mark Antony of Mr. C. Kemble, and that at the expense of those who stood before him. If they did it was very insulting, whether through ignorance or prejudice. Mrs. Butler and Miss Kemble [1] were behind the scenes, but I did not look at them. I thought the latter, whom I saw before I knew who she was, a very pretty girl. Dow came into my room, and corroborated the account of Forster regarding Mr. Forrest's Virginius.

---

[1] Adelaide Kemble (1814–1879); afterwards Mrs. Sartoris, singer and authoress; daughter of Charles Kemble and sister of Mrs. Butler.

He spoke of it as a failure, unredeemed and even offensive; doubting if he would return to London. Read over the omitted scene in Browning's play of *Strafford*, which still is not up to the high-water mark. I have performed for the last time with Mr. C. Kemble—my professional account is closed with him, and I part with him without regret or esteem. As an artist, I think him by comparison *good* in second and third-rate characters; *excellent* in parts of them, as in the drunkenness of Cassio, but complete in scarcely any, great in none, and very bad in those of a *higher class*. There is no *character*, no assumption in anything he does—the only difference between the serious scenes of Cassio and Mark Antony are, with him, a Roman-looking dress in this and in the other doublet and hose.

December 24th.—The coldness of the morning contested with my good resolutions the hour of quitting my bed, but I was not late. After breakfast I lost some time in calculating and reflecting on my means, and my chance of increasing them. Last night Mr. C. Kemble left the stage with an income of, at least I should suppose, £1200.[1] Seven years ago—or indeed five years ago, this man, after having enjoyed an excellent income all his married life, was *worse than nothing !* With a moderate degree of talent, without learning, without one amiable or estimable trait of character, he makes us wonder at his good fortune, and would create discontent and doubt in the minds of those who believed the recompenses of Providence to be distributed in this world. It has been his luck—and luck, as the sun shines, smiles indiscriminately.

December 30th.—In the course of the morning Bulwer came to the theatre, and I mentioned to him the omissions I had suggested and left for his approval—in all of which he acquiesced. Acted Ion with considerable care, and with considerable effect; was in some sort interrupted by the noise of the galleries. Talfourd came into my room and was as usual *delighted* with the performance; he wished us to dine, if in town, *en famille* on Sunday—and on going away hoped I would "promote the repetition of *Ion.*"

---

[1] This was derived from the place given to him by Government—£500 per annum—and the interest of the money made by Fanny Kemble in the States.

1837

January 2nd.—Acted Lord Hastings very, very ill indeed, in the worst possible taste and style. I really am ashamed to think of it; the audience applauded, but I deserve some reprobation. I have no right to trifle with any, the least important, character; whatever is good enough to play is good enough to play well, and I could have acted this character very well if I had prepared myself as I should have done. Without study I can do nothing. I am worse than a common nightly drudge.

January 3rd.—Before I rose thought over some scenes of Brage- lone; saw Mr. Brewster and arranged my coiffure with him. Griffiths called also about my dress. Went to theatre, found they had begun before the appointed time. Rehearsed Bragelone; suggested some improvements in the arrangements of the last scene. Tried on and settled my dress. Bulwer and Forster were there; Bulwer liked what I did, but authors are no judges of the performance of their own plays. The rehearsal was not over till past four o'clock. Read the *Times*, which highly-principled paper is the advocate of Mr. Bunn. Wrote to Kenny, requesting him to withdraw my name from the candidates' list at the Athenæum Club.

January 4th.—Sent to inquire after Mrs. Fitzgerald—to Brewster and to Thresher's. Sent also my note to Kenny, requesting him to withdraw my name from the Athenæum books. I feel relieved in having done so, as there would be little convenience, great expense, and no compliment in my election, and my rejection, independently of the mortification it would cause me, might be used by my enemies to my disadvantage. Received, in a note from Forster, an invitation to supper from Lady Blessington. Acted Bragelone well, with earnest- ness and freshness; some passages were deficient in polish. Being called for, I did not choose to go on without Miss Faucit, whom I led forward. The applause was fervent, but there had been considerable impatience manifested through the play, which did not end until eleven o'clock. I fear it will not have any considerable success. Dow, Fitzgerald, Browning, Talfourd and his son Frank, C. Buller, came into my room; they all seemed to think much of my performance, but otherwise thought the play much under-acted. It was *shamefully performed*. Bulwer came in when they had gone, and in the most energetic and ardent manner thanked me for my performance, and for making him cut out the first scene of the fifth act, which I had done. Mr. Standish took Forster and myself to Lady Blessington's; Count D'Orsay and herself received me most warmly. We had too rich a supper; our talk was all on the play. Bulwer did not seem happy—his mind was " away! away! " Byng and Chorley [1] were there. Bulwer drove me home, all his talk was *La Vallière*.

January 5th.—Sent for the newspapers; they were all in a faint tone, except the *Times*, which was maliciously abusive. A very kind note of thanks for my performance from Fred. Reynolds. Forster called, and accompanied me to the theatre, where the process of cutting was in act. Bulwer was there; Forster proposed his own rearrangement, which was acceded to. Mr. Farren came to explain to me that " merely to oblige the theatre, Mr. Bulwer, etc., he had undertaken Lauzun, which was not in his line "; this part, and only this the man insisted on doing, and certainly was one of the causes of the play's ill-success. Received a play (oh!) and a note, full of admiration, from a Mrs. Warton. No wonder that a player is vain, the praise he gets is so immediately to his face. R. Price and Talfourd came. Very absurdly lost a guinea in a wager with Dow about the *Times* criticism—a just punishment, but one I cannot with propriety afford.

January 6th.—Bulwer and Forster called about my note, and after talking on the proposed omission of the third act, on which I did not feel competent to speak decisively, they left me to urge it on Mr. Osbaldiston. I agreed that it was a desperate experiment, but perhaps worth making. Acted pretty well. I thought Miss Faucit was inclined to play some tricks to mar my effects, but it did not much disconcert me. I was called for, and went on; as far as I could judge, the play seemed to run on very smoothly, but I heard that there was disapprobation expressed at the short third act—not ten minutes long! Bulwer, full of delight at my performance, came into my room with Forster. They have concocted some plan for a new scene for me—

---

[1] Henry Fothergill Chorley (1808-1872); a well-known musical critic, for many years on the staff of the *Athenæum*.

to which I decidedly objected; indeed, as far as I can judge, it would destroy the character.

January 7th.—A note from Bulwer came couched in the strongest terms, asking as "a personal favour" that I would act the scene he had written and sent me. I did not stay to read the scene, but wrote back by his servant to say that I could not resist the impulse of striving to show my appreciation of the honour he had done me, and that I would do it. Forster called, and I explained to him wherein I thought it hazardous and impolitic, but he seemed to regard it as another desperate stroke to retrieve the cast-down nature of Bulwer's fame. I felt it so, and did not repent having assented. Note from Count D'Orsay—as if to urge me to do it, I could only send a verbal answer. My domestic affairs occupied me much; I left directions for Richard and went to the theatre. Bulwer again expressed himself most deeply obliged to me; he and Forster came into my room.

Elstree, January 8th.—Read over—both to correct and to study— the introduced scene of Bragelone. *There is nothing in it,* and no play can derive strength from a scene which is not missed when omitted, and which does not contain some new and striking effect with regard to the character. I think this has no power, and is merely to make time!—the worst motive for a scene.

January 9th.—Heard the children go through part of their lessons, and was delighted with their progress. Received a letter from Bulwer with some brief alterations. I hope he does not flatter himself with too sanguine hope, but under any result I must admire the indomitable resolution that struggles to the last against defeat; it deserves to triumph. Returned to the new scene and went over the whole part of Bragelone—*who is now the play.*

London, January 10th.—Forster called, and I inquired of him how far I was right in the alterations I had made in the scene. He smiled at me, which decided me in retaining the original of Bulwer—which was very feeble. Went to theatre, anxious to make an effort with Bragelone, but did not act the part to satisfy myself, being disconcerted by the inaudibility of Miss Faucit, who was ill, and the nervousness I endured about the new scene. Was called for by the audience, and went forward. Bulwer came into my room, and was in very good spirits. I did not myself *feel* the play to go so well as he, Messrs. Osbaldiston and Wallack seemed to think it had done; and I fear the report of it will not be very cordial. Bulwer took Forster and myself in his cab to the Albion, Aldersgate Street, where the Garrick Club gave their complimentary dinner to C. Kemble. I went into the room, and after looking at the several tables for some one whom I knew, sat on a vacant chair at the bottom of the L. Table—near Mr. Blood and Captain Williams. I was beckoned soon to the cross-table and taken there by Captain Williams and placed between Sir G. Warrender and Standish. Sir G. Warrender introduced me to the Chairman, Lord Francis Egerton. Mr. Knowles returned thanks for the dramatic authors in a very rambling drunken speech—it was nothing, and a little worse. Captain W—— had come to me twice or three times, to ask me to return thanks when "The stage and its professors" was drunk. I declined, but saw at last that I had no power of retreat. The toast was given by Mr. S. Price, in rather a confused manner, and his want of self-possession restored my confidence. I replied, first, to him—in reference to his allusion to the American stage—expressing the cordial feeling that all actors felt towards that country who had visited it, and of my own particular attachment to it; that the toast which had been given, in referring to what we possessed, made us more strongly feel what we had to deplore; that the sentiment of regret was universal among the members of the profession at the loss of our guest, and that none was more sorry to lose his companionship than myself, when I reflected how, in "many a well-fought field, we had kept together in our chivalry"; that I was only expressing the general feeling of the professors of the art in congratulating him upon and lamenting his retirement, and that I only uttered their wishes in my desire for every joy, every good, that the remainder of his life could give him. This was very well received, and as good a complimentary effusion as I could hope to make, where my heart was not interested and my esteem was not conciliated. Supped on oysters, as I came home with Forster. I forgot to notice Mr. Yates's speech, which was in the worst style and taste of the worst green-room.

January 11*th.*—A note from Bulwer with the altered passage of the introduced scene; informing me also that Mr. Farren had written to him to be removed from the part of Lauzun; really the ignorant effrontery of this empty coxcomb is most offensive.

January 12*th.*—Forster called and told me that Osbaldiston had written to Bulwer on the ill-success of the play, wishing to modify the terms agreed on—the shabby fellow! Bulwer behaved like himself —like a gentleman—in a high-minded and proper manner.

January 16*th.*—Lay down and tried to think of Hamlet. Acted the character pretty well; the effect of the influenza in the house obliged me to pitch my voice (for the sake of overmastering the coughs) in an unusually high key, which in some measure, I think, interfered with the nicety of many touches, but there was a good deal of earnestness in the performance. The play was disgracefully—*disgustingly* acted—Mrs. W. West, Mr. Thompson, Mr. G. Bennett are really unfit persons to place in important characters on such a stage! This does not justify my.*loss of temper*, which I have again to bewail and condemn; but, indeed, the conduct of the stage is most disgraceful. I was called for after the performance, and very warmly received.

January 17th.—After dinner read over the part of Bragelone. Bulwer has, I fear, added very little to the general effect of the play by the insertion of the new scene, and in my particular case he has done actual mischief. If he has not diminished the interest by lessening the probability (which, I think, he has) in the too sudden change of Bragelone from the warrior to the monk—yet he has so flurried me, so thrown me off my centre by the want of due preparation and proper harmonizing of the scene with the rest of the character, and so distresses me nightly by the hurry and fret into which I am thrown by the very brief allowance of time for my metamorphosis, that I am confident he would have acted more judiciously in leaving the play as it stood on the third night—or of restoring some other person's scene. Acted Bragelone as well as I could, but not well. I am *spoiled* in it by Bulwer's injudicious amendments. There was disapprobation at the end of the play. Bulwer looked into my room for a minute in the middle of the play.

January 18th.—Forster inquired of me if I were willing to undertake an edition of Shakspeare. I said that I should like the task, and had thought of it, but that I could not venture on the attempt whilst occupied with my profession. He said Moxon [1] was the person who wished it, and that he would speak of it as a thing for my hours of retirement. Met Miss Stephens,[2] Miss Johnson, her niece and her brother; Miss Stephens!—" the cynosure of neighbouring eyes! " We talked very cordially, she asking me why I did not sometimes call as I passed, and observing that she had never been so happy as when

[1] Edward Moxon (1801-1858); one of the most enlightened and discriminating publishers of the nineteenth century; also a graceful verse-writer. Published for Landor and Wordsworth; also for Tennyson, Browning. Barry Cornwall, Patmore, and other Victorian poets. He married Lamb's adopted daughter, Emma Isola (see note, p. 92).

[2] Catherine Stephens (1794-1882); the celebrated ballad-singer, also a considerable actress; retired from the stage in 1835, and married the fifth Earl of Essex in 1838.

she was on the stage. Ah, me! how much I wish I had her means of being free from it. Very much fatigued, went to the theatre; took pains and, though a little put out by Miss Faucit's inopportune coughs, acted well.

January 19th.—Mrs. Fitzwaylett called. In answer to my inquiries she told me she had ten shillings per week—six children and a sick husband; that Lady Byron,[1] who had found her in such a state of destitution at Ramsgate, had written to Mrs. H. Siddons about her, but had given *no other assistance of any kind whatsoever.* Is this a specimen of *evangelical* charity? I told her I would do what I could, giving her ten shillings.

January 23rd.—Forster called—among other things mentioned that Trelawney[2] had said Mrs. Butler was so delighted with the performance of Bragelone on Friday that she had requested her father to introduce me to her, which he had promised to do. In what way I cannot exactly foresee. Browning, with all his kind heart, called and sat a few minutes.

Manchester, February 6th.—Clarke talked much of Mr. C. Kean, giving his opinion that he would not succeed in London, that he did not *improve;* it is natural to ask how should he. He observed that he was *arrogant* and extravagant—lived at hotels and squandered his money. This young man ought to have started into wisdom from the sight and consequence of his father's follies and vices, but it is not improbable that he has been spoiled. It is very hard (qu. is it possible?) for a person on the stage to preserve a well-regulated mind. Called on Mrs. Clarke, who is in the same house with me. She gave me an account of Mr. C. Mathews, not much dissimilar to that I had just heard of Mr. C. Kean. Bitter and galling hours of wounded pride and repentant self-accusations seem to be laid up for those young men. Read a few pages of Goldoni. Slept a little and looked over part of Macbeth. Acted the part with energy and discrimination—the audience seemed to be riveted by the performance; they were loud in their calls for a re-appearance, and very enthusiastic in their reception

---

[1] The widow of the poet; her charity as a rule was not of the open-handed order, one of the many characteristics in which she presented a marked contrast to her much-maligned husband. The more that is known of Lady Byron the less cause is there for surprise that her marriage resulted as it did. Not content with helping to wreck Byron's life, she spared no pains to brand his memory with infamy after he had been nearly half a century in the grave; but time, however tardily, has now done justice to them both.

[2] Presumably Edward John Trelawney (1792–1881), well known as the friend of Byron and Shelley.

of me, when I went on the stage. I was exceedingly distressed by extreme weakness, and my cough. I endeavoured to get through the play without the assistance of wine, but was compelled to have recourse to a small quantity. Was very, very much fatigued, and I thought to myself—surely this is earning bread by the brow's sweat.

February 10th.—Going to the theatre in the rain, I expected but an indifferent house; was most agreeably surprised when I went on the stage to see a very well-filled theatre; was very anxious to act well, and did as well as the drawbacks of the inefficient representatives of the other characters would let me. I was gratified to see the play of *Ion* go so well. I was called for and very warmly received at the end of the play. The actors here, who are very bad, and very conceited, wish to show me their low estimation of me by an absence of all courtesy. They are welcome to do so. Condy came into my room, to express his surprise and pleasure at the effect of the play. Miss Faucit asked me to write in her album, which I did—some lines from Metastasio. The house was excellent, thank God!

February 25th.—At my lodgings read with great interest the conclusion of the debate on the Irish Municipal Bill, with Sheil's splendid speech. Let those who think little of the advantages of labour look at the result of that man's application. Like Demosthenes, he was hissed at the Catholic Association when in its infant state, and is now the most eloquent man in the Imperial Parliament.[1] On one occasion that he was hissed, he extorted the applause of his assailants by observing to them : " You may hiss, but you cannot sting ! "

February 26th.—Colonel D'Aguilar seemed to think that Lord Mulgrave was much more a man of pleasure than of business. He is a man of some talent, but I begin to suspect it is not of great depth or extent.[2]

[1] Lord Chief Justice Bushe thus described Sheil's oratory : "His mind is one of the richest in poetry and eloquence I ever knew. For the purpose of producing an effect upon a popular audience in Ireland I consider him as standing in the very first rank. He seems to me to have high powers for didactic poetry. The rich poetical invectives with which his speeches abound, if versified, would be fine satirical poems." In 1837 Sheil probably deserved Macready's description, though in Stanley, Macaulay and Whittle Harvey (see note, p. 223) with, in the Upper House, Grey, Lyndhurst and Brougham, he had by no means inconsiderable competitors.

[2] Macready's judgment of Lord Mulgrave (afterwards Lord Normanby) was on the whole correct. He was no statesman, in the higher sense of the term, and far from successful as a diplomatist. Having held various Cabinet offices, besides serving as Irish viceroy and ambassador at Paris, he ended his public career in the second-rate position of Minister at Florence, where his diplomatic achievements were less notable than his wife's entertainments. She had a pretty wit, and one of her *mots* is still quoted in Florence with lively

375

March 1st.—Calcraft called, under the annoyance of having been refused a "command" by Lord Mulgrave. For a professed patron of the art, who, as such, is President of the Garrick Club, and besides takes pleasure in private theatricals, to refuse his patronage to a leading artist, and that upon the request of a person like Calcraft, who explained to him the necessity of the case, and its importance to him —especially as he "dragooned" him (to quote Calcraft's expression) into the Italian's engagement, which has cost C—— above £700—to refuse his name under such circumstances was neither good-natured nor liberal. I think it directly the reverse. Calcraft asked me if I had received an invitation from the Castle, and expressed his surprise that I had not. I do not expect one, nor do I wish one. If I were in fashion I should be sought. These things do not reach me.

March 2nd.—Spoke with Calcraft about the future plays, and he, of course, recurred to the ill-natured refusal of Lord Mulgrave. I am not sorry to see these traits, which at once display a man's character. Mulgrave is good-tempered, but particularly selfish and very vain, which renders any services he may confer on others indulgences of his own self-love, and not benevolences; he is a man of the world, in its most sordid acceptation, and a man likely to be very popular with those who see little of him—his manners are most agreeable.

March 3rd.—From time to time—and sometimes for hours together—my heart has been racked with the torture I have endured in recalling the calumnious misstatements, the slanderous misrepresentations, and base insinuations of that unprincipled man, Thesiger, in his charges against me in the trial; my determination to retaliate upon him a *palpable disgrace*, though sometimes it has relaxed before the arguments of religion and reason, has always been resumed and has become fixed in my mind. I now see that if I longer allow such thoughts and feelings place, I must abandon the hope and intention of purifying my mind—I cannot *make a bargain* (for such would be the gross and impious fact) for the indulgence of a particular sin with God—or my conscience—for it is the same thing. It cost me some very severe struggles to resolve to submit to the opprobrium cast upon me, and *leave to time* to give that contradiction to my calumniator, which he ought to receive, and to repose upon the clearness of my own conscience. But I have done it—I have relinquished my inten-

appreciation. The Brownings with their child were then resident there, and on one occasion when Lady Normanby only expected Browning, he appeared accompanied by his wife and son. " Not one incomprehensible but three incomprehensibles! " she murmured protestingly to a friend, as she advanced to greet the trio.

tions. I have expelled all passionate feeling on the subject. I have resolved never again to permit the idea to remain in my thoughts—I thank God. I am already much happier for it. Prayed to God to confirm me in my good resolves, and rose with a lighter heart than I have felt these many days. Went to dine at Colonel D'Aguilar's; met Major Hankey, the principal amateur performer here, Sir Charles and Lady Morgan and her niece, Miss Clarke, Miss Hopkins, and Frank Sheridan. The conversation was lively and diversified. Colonel D'Aguilar mentioned an anecdote of Sir Sidney Smith,[1] in instance of his great but harmless egotism. Having minutely narrated the circumstances of his escape from the Temple, and upon Colonel D'Aguilar's expression of his gratification at the great interest of the relation, he significantly put the question: "Did you ever hear me tell it in French?" "No," replied D'Aguilar. "Then I'll tell it you;" which he did, fact for fact, only varying the language.

March 4th.—Read the newspaper, and was pleased to see that bad man, that priest of Moloch and of Mammon—not of Jesus Christ— the Bishop of Exeter,[2] so held up to the just indignation of the House and the country by Lord Plunkett.[3]

March 6th.—Calcraft mentioned to me a fact that brings out Mr. Sheridan Knowles's character more strongly, as it relates to another than myself. After civilities and avoiding the question whilst here, of payment for his plays, he sent him (C——) an attorney's letter in London and would have arrested him for £53—charging five guineas per night for the *Wife*, which never brought *expenses*—had not his solicitor had more consideration and mercy than himself. This is Mr. Sheridan Knowles. Shame on him!

March 7th.—Saw W——, the publisher, at the theatre. Calcraft told me that this man, who has just been declared insolvent, has a

---

[1] Sir William Sidney Smith (1764–1840), the well-known admiral whose egotism was scarcely less conspicuous than his gallantry. He was an intimate friend of Queen Caroline, when Princess of Wales, an association which at one time threatened to involve him in serious consequences.

[2] Henry Phillpotts (1778–1869); for nearly forty years Bishop of Exeter, in which diocese his disciplinary methods earned him considerable unpopularity. Earlier in his career he took an active part in political literature, vigorously championing Lord Liverpool's Government; and it was Copley's unacknowledged piracy from one of his pamphlets that provoked Canning's felicitous quotation: "Dear Tom, this brown jug that now foams with mild ale, out of which I now drink to sweet Nan of the Vale was once *Toby Philpot*"—a sally that left Copley, for once in his life, completely discomfited.

[1] William Conyngham Plunket (1764–1854); the distinguished orator and advocate, at that time Lord Chancellor of Ireland.

house in Bagot Street, which with its furniture is worth at least £3000—that he says he has completely settled with his creditors, which means that he has obtained the power to pay them five shillings in the pound in two years, *which he will never do*, and that in the meantime he retains this house, etc., by means of some fraudulent assignment, while God knows how his creditors may be pinched for means. The robberies I have endured and by which I have been *impoverished* in this way, make me feel indignant at the use, or rather profanation of the term *honesty* and *honour* in society. *Who is honest ?* I know very, very, very few, for whose honesty or honour I would vouch. Lay down to rest, and think of Othello. Thought also of making some arrangement with Calcraft about cancelling next week—*where is the money to pay me ? It is very hard—very hard on me—that the harvest of my year* is thus lost to me; but I must try to make the best of what is bad, and "not for that, bate I one jot of heart or hope." Acted Othello in my very best manner, and quite carried away the audience and the actors. There was a long call for me at the close of the play, but I declined going forward.

March 8th.—Calcraft showed me a list of the receipts, which have averaged £37 something per night—my terms being £29 per night; this is frightful—though Mrs. Jordan took £50 per night from my father for a fortnight, never playing once to that sum, and Kean arrested him in a most wanton and expensive manner for the residue of a sum left unpaid on an engagement in which he received for three nights £150—when the *total receipts* did not amount to £130 ! !—and this man was called generous. So is Mr. Sheridan Knowles ! Where is truth to be found? Offered to give up £82—with the next week's engagement, which Calcraft was too happy to accept. He wished to try the Tuesday night, but that was left dependent on circumstances. I strongly urged him to go to the levee, but he would not; he is wrong. I am indifferent to Lord Mulgrave, but he should be ready to seize opportunity. Sir —— called, and after sitting some time asked me if I could promote his views in bringing on the stage the woman who lives with him ! ! She had made an essay (and, from his account, manifestly a failure) at Edinburgh. I showed him as much, and he said he would abandon the idea.

March 9th.—Called on Calcraft. He spoke again about Lord Mulgrave's pointed neglect of me, at which I laughed a good deal, and requested him not, as he talked of doing, to speak about it. There is nothing to speak about. Lord Mulgrave has not invited me—he

JAMES SHERIDAN KNOWLES

From an engraving by Finden of a drawing by T. Wageman

has invited others whom he thinks more worthy, or agreeable—what then? Was very anxious to act well, but *could* not—the fault, I suppose, was in myself, but surely it was aggravated by the *offensiveness* of the persons set about me, Mr. Cathcart, Miss Rankley—act Ion with such utterly disagreeable people, I could not. It was a bad performance. Read the newspaper—another three acts of *Strafford*— clever, but——.

March 11th.—Employed half-an-hour, that was otherwise un-occupied, in packing; and then went to a rehearsal of the play and farce for the evening. I found it impossible to be myself in juxta-position with this Miss Rankley; such an antidote to sympathetic emotions I never met before. Agreed with Calcraft on the mode of settling the amount due; having remitted £82 and lost by illness £58, and having received £20, there is due £420. He engages to give me £120 cash, and bills within two months for the remaining £300, "which," he says, "shall be paid," and that he will not behave as Mr. Bunn did to me. I have lost my faith in men, except those whom I *know*, and therefore when these bills are paid I shall be glad to bear testimony to Mr. Calcraft's punctuality. I have behaved to him, I conceive, in a kind and considerate manner—as I ought to *any man;* I hope I have acted rightly. Mrs. Calcraft came into the room, but with so cold and distant an air that an observer would have suspected I had been subtracting £82 from her husband's effects, instead of resigning so much! Read over Bragelone. Acted it— tolerably well—not—not *myself* in *Bragelone*—but tolerably well and in some parts very effective. There was disapprobation at the end— the *result is no catastrophe.* Bulwer has made a great mistake in that particular. But certainly Miss R—— was the d——! Acted the tragedy scene of Puff in the *Critic* very well for the last time that I ever will appear in that part—it is *infra dig.* During this engagement I have never once been before the curtain at the end of the play; this is curious, taken in connection with its general ill-success.

To Liverpool, March 12th.—Colonel D'Aguilar called and ex-pressed himself delighted with Bulwer's play, and charged me to tell Bulwer as much. Calcraft adverted to the Lord Lieutenant's passing me over without any notice or invitation, which I did not wish him to do. D'Aguilar said that he was talking a long time with him a few days before about me, and that he had said he "must have me to dinner." So that it is perhaps a mere matter of indifference and not of purposed slight on his part—*c'est égal*. It does not touch me. Calcraft observed that I had not dined with him during my stay. I recalled to him that he had been twice in London for long periods and had never come to our house, and that I kept away from his designedly. He seemed rather relieved in thinking that was the sole cause. I did not choose to tell him—it was not my business—that I had met him arm-in-arm with Mr. Bunn shortly after he had been struck by me.

Elstree, March 18th.—Received a note from Forster, appointing Monday for the visit of himself and Browning about *Strafford*. I answered him, assenting to his proposal. Walked out with the children through Aldenham Park and the wood. Read before dinner a few pages of *Paracelsus*, which raises my wonder the more I read it. Sat with the children, narrating stories to them. Looked over two plays, *Petronius* and *Bertrand*, which it was not possible to read, hardly as I tried. They are utter trash, and it is really trying to one's patience to lose so much time over such worthless, hopeless stuff; I cannot longer afford the time. Read some scenes in *Strafford*, which restore one to the world of sense and feeling once again.

March 19th.—Read *Strafford* in the evening, which I fear is too historical; it is the policy of the man, and its consequence upon him, not the heart, temper, feelings, that work on this policy, which Browning has portrayed—and how admirably.

March 20th.—Forster and Browning arrived—cheerful evening— though more of the conversation turned on Dow than I could have wished. Browning related an amusing story of his application to him for an epitaph on his father—to which, when Browning had promised it, he added his mother, her sister, and an infant two years old; and subsequently, on receiving the report of the marble-mason of Barnsley, wished two more lines to be added to the complete epitaph as the stone would hold two more! Forster read the counsel's speech in the *Pickwick Papers*.

March 21st.—Browning came with me into the study, and with much interruption over the discussion of points and passages, we read through his tragedy of *Strafford;* I must confess my disappointment at the management of the story—I doubt its interest. Walked out with Browning round the reservoir. After dinner Browning and myself resumed our conversation about *Strafford*, and I resolved—seeing no other course—to read it again to-night—after tea I did so, but I am by no means sanguine, I lament to say, on its success.

March 22nd.—Resumed with Browning the conversation of last night on *Strafford;* showed the necessity—as far as Mr. Osbaldiston was concerned—of his direct declaration, yes or no, as to his ability to give the finished play on Saturday. After some deliberation he decided in the negative, and preferred withholding the play till my Benefit. He seemed to think much of the objections and suggestions I had offered. He left us. Looked over the play of the *Death of Socrates* by a person signing himself "Nemo." If he is not deranged, he is the most enormous ass I have yet encountered. Would any one believe that a person could introduce Socrates—addressing Plato—

"I will instruct you—come along, my beauty!"

And his disciples thus—

"Come along, my sheeps-trotters!"

Another specimen of this mad piece of nonsense is the entrance of Marsyas, the Satyr, running—

> *Marsyas:* "I see them a-galloping!
> I see them a-galloping!
> I see them a-galloping
> And all within the air!
> And Calliope a-walloping
> And Calliope a-walloping
> And Calliope a-walloping
> The sides of the mare!"

In another play the same author makes one of his characters say, "Let those who need eggs, lay them!" This heap of nonsense is called *Fadeorowna.* Looked over some *Pickwick Papers* as a digestive after an early dinner.

March 23rd.—Wrote to Forster, on his intended removal to the Albany, which I am certain will bring down upon him all the fatal consequences of extravagance and rashness. I sincerely regard him, and hope he will consent to be persuaded. Sat with my children, and heard their prayers. Wrote to Browning on a thought that had struck me for the last scene of his tragedy.

March 25th.—On coming downstairs I gave my attention to the remainder of the heap of MS. that awaited my examination. Looked over *Pandolfo* — trash! *Corsair* — do. *Robert the Bruce* — id. *Recluse*—better. *Lass of Hawthorndene*—ohlie Hieland—trash. *Marriage à-la-mode—trash.* Read over *verbatim* Mr. Solly's play, *Gonzaga di Capponi*—in which there is some talent—and by that cleared off my debt of MSS.

March 28th.—Called on Forster, who talked about Browning's play—read in his chambers the account of the murder of Hannah Brown by Greenacre.[1] How much worse is man than the brute, when he descends to crime. The beast injures, only to gratify his pinched appetite, or upon the necessity of self-defence. Man is wanton in his cruelty, and the slave of no impulse—he reasons as he destroys. Each new occurrence of this sort only makes more difficult of solution the enigma of our being. *Othello.* Sent private box, with a hasty note, to Miss Martineau. A youth called to know if I taught elocution, and on my information he went off very abruptly. Dow called and did not remain very long. Used the little time left me by these ill-timed visitors in reading part of Othello—for which I was totally unprepared. Went to the theatre and resolved to do my best; my reception encouraged me, and I made the best I could of my raw and uncertain notion. I spoke the address to the Senate particularly well; thought of an improvement in its conclusion, and also another in cashiering Cassio. I made the best effort in my power under the circumstances, but it was a crude, unpolished performance; the audience persisted in calling for me, and I went on at last. Captain Polhill came into my room and delayed me very long, talking of his alteration of Œdipus, to the amusement of Forster, Browning, and Dow, who were in the room. O'Hanlon also called. Browning and Forster walked to chambers with me, and we sat discussing the plot of *Strafford* until two o'clock.

March 29th.—Browning called and brought me the play of *Strafford;* he looked very unwell, jaded and thought-sick. Forster called while he was here. Browning left me the MS. I began the perusal of *Strafford*, but was interrupted by the visit of Mr. Solly, who detained me some time in conversation about his play; he left me very gratefully. Went through the alterations of *Strafford*, and proceeded to the theatre, where I saw Mr. Osbaldiston—spoke with him on *Strafford*, appointed eleven to-morrow to read it to him, and mentioned the private box I had last night. Forster had talked to me about the subscription of Kemble's plate, and urged the policy— " to still the murmuring lips of discontent "—of compromising with my conscience and putting my name to the list; it *sickens* me to do it, but my dear children make me more dependent on opinion than I would be without these dear little hostages. I inquired for the

---

[1] James Greenacre (1785–1837); he murdered Hannah Brown, who was about to become his fifth wife, under circumstances which secured to him perpetuation at Madame Tussaud's.

treasurer to pay in my money—the least sum I could with propriety give. Wrote to Browning, at Forster's request, mentioning my opinion of the play. Read over attentively, noting down my objections, the play of *Strafford;* it consumed much time.

March 30th.—I went to the theatre soon afterwards and read to Mr. Osbaldiston the play of *Strafford;* he caught at it with avidity, agreed to produce it without delay on his part, and to give the author £12 per night for twenty-five nights, and £10 per night for ten nights beyond. He also promised to offer Mr. Elton an engagement to strengthen the play. Browning and Forster came in; I had the pleasure of narrating what had passed between Mr. Osbaldiston and myself, and of making Browning very happy; I went over the memoranda I had made of corrigenda in his MS.; the suggestion of the children's voices being heard in the pause following the announcement of Strafford's death he was quite *enraptured* with; he took the book and promised to work hard. Forster is trying to induce the Longmans to publish it; I doubt his success. Browning asked me if I would allow him to dedicate the play to me. I told him, of course, how much I should value such an honour, which I had not anticipated or looked for.

March 31st.—Called at the theatre and proceeded to the box office, paid in (more reluctantly, I think, than I ever paid money in my life) a cheque for £2 2s. to the subscription for plate to Mr. C. Kemble. This is the consequence of my own inexperience and indiscretion. Had I, by a proper care of my money, and a watchful attention to my temper, secured my independence and incurred no suspicion or blame from those who dislike or envy me—I might have followed the dictates of my own conscience and have refused this compromise of principle, which it is, and of which I actually feel ashamed. A man—really of *no* consideration in his art—a mere actor, *and not a very good one*, of *second and third rate parts*—a dishonest, deceitful, selfish, base-minded, *degraded* man!!! and to avoid the chance of any addition to my enemies (Mr. Harness, for example!!!) I am forced to assist in a compliment to this paltry fellow. It really disgusts and makes me ashamed of myself. It is too bad. Utterly ignorant of the learned languages and with merely a smattering of some living ones, he calls himself a scholar!—beaten by Mr. Harris and most contemptuously insulted by myself, he proclaims himself a man of honour! Guilty of a fraud and a falsehood to conceal it during his management, he asserts himself a gentleman! This perhaps he has a right himself

383

to do, but what is to be said of those who support him in these claims? Honour and worth have no business in this world, or in that part of it which believes and calls itself the *whole*. I am sick of it. Heard that Forrest had quarrelled with the wretch Bunn, and raised his hand over his head to strike him. Looked over King Richard and Othello. Acted Othello—in parts—a few parts—extremely well, but very, very unequally. Mr. Vandenhoff was disposed to play a dirty trick, but was *frightened* from proceeding with it by my look and gesture. Another of them!!

Elstree, April 2nd.—Read over King Richard, in which character I do not feel confidence of success. I know, I think, how it should be acted, but I am not sufficiently at home in the execution. Nothing but great presence of mind can sustain me. And I pray to God that I may be true to myself, and support my reputation by the effort. Amen!

London, April 3rd.—Looked and thought over my character. I *dared* not send the order I had written, with a note, to H. Smith, nor a private box to Miss Martineau, so uncertain did I feel of myself. I became more self-possessed when I rose, and much more collected and resolved to do my best when I was preparing for the play at the theatre. By the time the play began I felt secure that I would not discredit myself. I acted King Richard III with much energy, and seemed to carry my audience with me; the house was not good—it might be called middling, but the audience appeared to have been brought solely by the play—indeed, there was nothing else. I was called for, and obliged to go on afterwards. Browning, Forster, Dow, Wallace (with Bryden) came into my room. Browning and Forster accompanied me to my chambers, drank a bottle of champagne which I found for them, and read the two last acts of *Strafford*, discussing the alterations in it. Browning left them with me, and took notes of what was yet to do. They left me a little after three, and I got to bed about four!! Forster informed me that Lords F. Egerton, W. Lennox, and Allen had been drawn out of the Committee of the Garrick Club, and that Talfourd, Stanfield and myself had been elected in their places—Mr. S. Price opposing Stanfield and self with a list— " Zachary, Bredel, Bartley "—which was scouted.

April 4th.—Looked in the *Times* for the chance of some notice of my performance of King Richard, but I might have reposed on my experience; there was nothing. Browning called in with alterations, etc.; sat and talked whilst I dined. A young gentleman came in, who spoke with a foreign accent, and, on speaking to him in French, he replied in the same language, telling me he was a Greek—that he was an enthusiastic lover of the drama, and such an admirer of mine that he called to request my autograph in his album. I introduced Browning to him as a great tragic poet, and he added his name. The youth told us that he was setting off for Athens directly. He was an interesting, lively person. Forster called; they sat late, talking much about Dow's extraordinary request to attend the reading of the new tragedy, which they resolved he should not do. Read a little of *Ion* after they left me, but I was too much fatigued to do any good. Acted Ion very, very languidly and ineffectively. Read over three copied acts of *Strafford*.

April 5th.—After thinking in bed of the want of connection in the scenes of Browning's play, and also thinking on the necessity of continuing my study of my art—going over the fourth act scene of King John—I rose and sent for Forster; explained to him the dangerous state of the play, and the importance it was of to remedy this defect. We sat down to work—he first mentioning an attack on him in the *Times*, through a piece of trash by that very wretched creature, Mr. Poole, and also showing me a notice of my Richard in the *True Sun*. We went over the play of *Strafford*, altered, omitted, and made up one new scene; we were occupied from eleven till four o'clock; the day entirely surrendered to it. Went to the theatre to procure the two last acts of the play. Warren called; I did not let him in, and could not recollect his name—was obliged to say "Madame" in speaking of his wife. Sent a note to Catherine. Began Forster's life of *Strafford*. Acted King John very well—to a most wretched house, but I felt the advantage of taking pains. I must study more. Forster and Dow called with the MS. of *Strafford*. Read and marked to read, etc., the four acts they left us.

April 7th.—Mr. Pritchard came to me with a statement about Mr. Webster threatening to assault him, and a parcel of nonsense about publishing, from which I endeavoured to dissuade him. Forster and Browning both came to my room—Browning with some of the passages to be supplied—very feebly written. Forster and he had rather a warm altercation—Browning, as I understood him, asserting that no change had been made in the conduct of the play since its first draught, which was not, in my mind, correct.

April 8th.—Browning called, whom I accompanied to the theatre. Read over *Strafford* to the persons in the green-room, but did not produce the impression I had hoped—it dragged its slow length along. Read *Strafford* to Catherine and Letitia, and I lament to say they were oppressed by a want of action and lightness; *I fear it will not do.*

Elstree, April 9th.—Dined with Fred. Reynolds, arriving about an hour after the hour he had named. Met the two Bulwers, Henry [1] and Edward, General Palmer [2]—a Dundas—and Bernal [3]; spent *rather* an agreeable day. Bulwer took me to chambers in his cab, mentioning his conviction that he could write a play with the experience he had gained.

London, April 11th.—The first intelligence of this day was enough in itself to make it an unfortunate one. A letter from Mr. Calcraft, asking me to renew his first bill due on Friday next. In truth, I expect that I shall lose all this money due to me from Mr. Calcraft, as I have done with Mr. Bunn. It is very hard, and I do not think it strictly honest to make an engagement which he would have enforced to the uttermost farthing against me, unless he had the means of strictly observing his part of it. I am much distressed and not a little disgusted. Forster came to breakfast; after which we read through the play of *Strafford*. Forster evidently felt all the objections that I had stated—was obliged to acknowledge the feebleness and heaviness of the play.

April 12th.—Forster called; I gave him the MS. of *Strafford*, which I had cut, and went to the rehearsal of *Julius Cæsar*. Knowles accosted me as if he had been my best friend and in the habit of doing me all manner of kind offices. I have done my last to him; he is utterly worthless—and yet what a man! I looked at him with admiration and pity this morning, as I thought on his powers and his misuse of them. Spoke to Osbaldiston about *Strafford*, and, having been anxious to find some of the actors restive about their parts, to

---

[1] The diplomatist, afterwards Lord Dalling.

[2] Charles Palmer (1777–1851); major-general, and proprietor of the Bath theatre. Formerly in the 10th Hussars. Gronow tells a curious story about a speculation of his in some vineyards, the claret from which (a lighter wine than that then in vogue) he introduced to the Prince Regent, who though himself favourably impressed, was malevolently prejudiced against it by Lord Yarmouth (afterwards the "Steyne" and "Monmouth" Lord Hertford). Palmer in consequence expended large sums in endeavouring to improve his vines, but without success, and became thereby involved in heavy losses which permanently impoverished him.

[3] Either Ralph Bernal, M.P. for Rochester, and Chairman of Committees (well known as an art connoisseur), or his son, Ralph Bernal Osborne (then about twenty-nine), the caustic politician of a later period.

furnish Browning with a decent excuse to withdraw the play, was disappointed at their general acquiescence. Forster called, and went twice over the play of *Strafford*—approving of all the omissions and expressing himself much raised in hope by the alterations. He thought my view of the work quite a clear one, and in the most earnest spirit of devotion set off to find and communicate with Browning on the subject—a fearful rencontre. Talfourd, Browning, Forster, Dow and Mr. George Stephens [1] came into my room; at his own request I introduced the latter to Talfourd. Called at Forster's chambers, whence Browning and he came to mine. There were mutual complaints—much temper—sullenness, I should say, on the part of Forster, who was very much out of humour with Browning, who said and did all that man could do to expiate any offence he might have given. Forster (who has behaved most nobly all through the matter of this play—no expression of praise is too high) showed an absence of sense and generosity in his behaviour which I grieved to see. There was a *scene*. Browning afterwards told me how much injury he did himself in society by this temper, corroborating what Talfourd had just before said of my poor friend Forster's *unpopularity*. I was truly sorry to hear from Browning much that rendered his unpopularity scarcely doubtful. Browning assented to all the proposed alterations, and expressed his wish, that *coûte que coûte*, the hazard should be made, and the play proceeded with. Bulwer would scarcely have done this, and in playing the great game he has before him he should regard this as a trivial offence, and so dismiss it. He left me at a late hour.

April 14th.—Calling at Forster's, met Browning, who came upstairs and who produced some scraps of paper with hints and unconnected lines—the full amount of his labour upon the alterations agreed on. It was too bad to trifle in this way, but it was useless to complain; he had wasted his time in striving to improve the fourth act scene, which was ejected from his play as impracticable for any good result. We went all over the play *again* (!) very carefully, and he resolved to bring the amendments suggested by eleven o'clock this evening. Met Browning at the gate of my chambers; he came upstairs and, after some subjects of general interest, proceeded to that of his tragedy. He had done nothing to it; had been oppressed and incapable of carrying his intentions into action. He *wished to withdraw it*. I

[1] George Stephens (1800-1851); a fertile dramatist of that day, whose plays were only moderately successful.

cautioned him against any precipitate step—warned him of the consequences, and at last got him to offer to go and bring Forster, whom I wished to be a party to all this business. He came with Browning, and we turned over all the pros and cons—for acting or not acting the play. They both decided on its performance, Browning to have more time than he had asked for the completion of his alterations. It was fixed to be done. Heaven speed us all! I thank God I felt quite satisfied with my conduct throughout this delicate affair of Browning.

April 15th.—Went to Covent Garden theatre, where I spoke to the copyist about *Strafford*. We were obliged to make arrangements —very tardy in their effects—subservient to the parsimonious regulations of Mr. Osbaldiston. Went to dine at the Garrick Club, saw two or three persons with whom I have a slight acquaintance, but not to speak to them. Was disgusted by a most filthy and offensive speech made by a man whose name I do not know whilst I was dining; it *is a horrid club!* In low spirits I dressed and went to Miss Martineau's party, where I knew—was acquainted with *no one;* was introduced to a Mrs. Gaskell,[1] and a Mrs. Reade—a very pretty Boston girl—*U.S.*— and to Hallam. Rogers, Mrs. Butler, and Harness were there, and many *distingués* whom I did not know. Harness came into the study, where I was, and retreated as if he had trod upon a serpent; it was curious; if that man has not wronged me, his bearing and behaviour are inexplicable. I was not comfortable; I came away in an unsatisfactory state of mind, and sat for a long while brooding on my own uncomfortable feelings. I am quite a *stranger in society!* I fear I must be a disagreeable companion, or my acquaintance would be more sought. I feel as if people left me with the notion that there is nothing in me; *there is not much;* there is certainly a want of the necessary power to express those thoughts which pass through my mind, so as to impress my listeners with a favourable opinion of my understanding; and what there is, is scarcely communicable. My mind is chiefly employed in self-discipline and weak endeavours to make itself better.

April 18th.—In thinking this morning upon my own advancement in public opinion, and its many disadvantages and impediments, the truth passed convincingly on my mind, that no labour is thrown away; PATIENCE—that great virtue, that true philosophy, that alleviation of all toil and care—and industry are sure of their reward: it is the

[1] Probably Elizabeth Cleghorn Gaskell (1810–1865); the distinguished novelist.

388

impatience of obscurity, the immature anxiety for reward and distinction in such men as Disraeli, junior,[1] that makes empirics.

April 20th.—After dinner read over *Strafford*, which I strongly fear *will fail*—it is *not good*.

April 21st.—Miss Faucit said to me that her part in Browning's play was very bad, and that she did not know if she should do it. She wanted me to ask her to do it. But I would not, for I wish she would refuse it, that even at this late point of time the play might be withdrawn—*it will do no one good.* Forster and Talfourd came into my room. Mr. Fitzball also asked me if I would play Iago to Mr. Forrest in *Othello*, to which I gave an unqualified refusal. "Would I refuse to play with him?"—to which I answered, "*By no means,* but *I must play my own parts.*"

April 22nd.—Browning came to breakfast, very pale, and apparently suffering from over-excitement. I think it is unfortunate that without due consideration and time for arranging and digesting his thoughts on a work so difficult as a tragedy, he should have committed himself to the production of one. I should be too glad of any accident that would impede its representation, and give me a *fair* occasion for withdrawing it; but this I cannot now do without incurring the suspicion of selfishness and of injustice to him, and therefore, though I feel convinced that the performance of this play on my Benefit night will cause much dissatisfaction—will in some measure compromise my judgment, and injure my future benefits—yet still, *coûte que coûte,* Browning shall not have the power of saying that I have acted otherwise than as a true friend to his feelings.

Elstree, April 23rd.—Took up the part of *Strafford*, at which I continued, having looked over the newspaper at breakfast, during the entire morning to dinner-time. The more I consider the play the lower my hopes smile upon it; I expect it will be damned—grievously hissed at the end—from the unintelligibility of the motives, the want of action, and consequently of interest. Looked at Browning's alterations of the last scene of *Strafford*—found them quite bad—mere feeble rant—neither power, nor nature, nor healthful fancy—very unworthy of Browning. I felt certainly convinced that the play must be utterly condemned.

[1] Disraeli had already made a reputation as a novelist, and in July of this year (1837) he first entered Parliament as M.P. for Maidstone ; in December he delivered the memorable maiden speech which many believed would extinguish him as a politician. His methods in pushing his fortunes were at this time not over-fastidious, and Macready was not singular in regarding him as an aspiring adventurer with a genius for self-advertisement.

London, April 26th.—Thought in my bed some time on *Strafford* —how I could make the most of every line. I am deeply anxious, though despairing, for Browning's sake, and shall not lose effect from not labouring for it. Told Forster my conviction about the fate of the play, which I look upon, despite all that can be done, as inevitable. Forster related to me the substance of Browning's preface and dedication,[1] which appear very good.

April 27th.—Went to the rehearsal of *Strafford* (after a hasty breakfast and a glance at the newspaper), with which I took much pains and the general effect of which I improved considerably. Called on Forster with Browning. Browning amused me much by his confidence in the success of the play; he looked at the acting and movement of a subject in which he had a deep interest—ensure that same *interest* in the audience, and I will ensure its success—but the question is : will the audience be kindled to such an interest? I grieve to think that my experience will not allow me to say yes. Gave the evening to the perusal and study of *Strafford*.

April 28th.—Thought over some scenes of *Strafford* before I rose, and went out very soon to the rehearsal of it. There is no chance in my opinion for the play but in the acting, which by possibility might carry it to the end without disapprobation; but that the curtain can fall without considerable opposition, I cannot venture to anticipate under the most advantageous circumstances. In all the historical plays of Shakspeare, the great poet has only introduced such events as act on the individuals concerned, and of which they are themselves a part; the persons are all in direct relation to each other, and the facts are present to the audience. But in Browning's play we have a long scene of passion—upon what? A plan destroyed, by whom or for what we know not, and a parliament dissolved, which merely seems to inconvenience *Strafford* in his arrangements. There is a sad want of judgment and tact in the whole composition. Would it were over! It must fail—and it grieves me to think that *I am so placed*. Browning will efface its memory by the production of *Sordello;* but it will strike me hard, I fear. God grant that it may not be a heavy blow. Called at the box-office for a private box for Miss Martineau. Forster introduced me to young Mr. Longman there, who consulted with me

[1] The dedication, dated April 23, 1837, runs as follows in Browning's *Collected Poems*—

"DEDICATED, IN ALL AFFECTIONATE ADMIRATION,

TO

WILLIAM C. MACREADY."

ROBERT BROWNING

From an engraving by G. Cooke of a painting by Field Talfourd

upon the publication, and yielded to my reasons for delaying it until Monday afternoon. Sent Miss Martineau her box with a note. The friend of the young man, who, I find, was dissuaded by me from his foolish desire of going on the stage, called for some tickets. I did not like to give them; they seemed to me the *price* of an act of duty. I sent him to the box-office. Forster called here idly. I thought over Browning's play when he had gone; I am confirmed in my opinion of its ill-success. Mr. Knowles came into my room to ask me to play St. Pierre in his play of the *Wife* for his Benefit!!!—a piece of effrontery, which is *really disgusting*. A man steeped in ingratitude for *ill*-requited kindnesses to have the *impudence* to ask such a favour of me! I *refused* him. Talfourd came into my room for a few minutes; I went into Mrs. Talfourd's box to speak to her. I thought her not quite so free as usual, and having the appearance of tending towards—*assumption*. Perhaps if I were elevated in life I should be the same—and yet I know no person to whom I have felt kindness that I have since disregarded because I had grown richer or more valued.

April 29th.—Brewster called with my wig for Strafford. Went to the theatre and rehearsed *Strafford*, which I am disposed to think might *pass muster*—not more—if it were equally and respectably acted, but Mr. Dale in the King must ensure its utter failure. Browning was incensed at Mr. Dale's unhappy attempts—*it is too bad*. A year ago I was hurried into the intemperate and frenzied act of striking that most unworthy and disgusting wretch, Mr. Bunn. My sufferings from compunction have been very great, not perhaps more than my folly has deserved; but I pray to God that I may never again so far forget what is due to His laws, to myself, and to society.

Elstree, April 30th.—Called on Forster, who gave me a ludicrous account of the silliness of Dow about this play of *Strafford*, which he thinks so *very fine*, and that it is to be so greatly successful. Again I repeat my conviction that it *must fail*—if, by some happy chance, not at once to-morrow, yet still at best it will only stagger out a lingering existence of a few nights and then die out—and for ever. It is dedicated to me most kindly by Browning. Dow still clings to the chance of my presence at his party—which I have never intended. Read over *Strafford*—which I pray God may far exceed my hopes of its success, and send Browning and myself home in happiness to-morrow night.

London, May 1st.—Called at the box-office about the boxes and places for which I had been applied to. Rehearsed *Strafford*. Was gratified with the extreme delight Browning testified at the rehearsal of my part, which he said was to him a full recompense for having written the play, inasmuch as he had seen his utmost hopes of character perfectly embodied. He was quite in raptures, I warning him that I did not anticipate success. Parted with Browning with wishes of good fortune to him. Read Strafford in bed, and acted it as well as I could under the nervous sensations that I experienced. Edward and Henry Bulwer, Fitzgerald, Talfourd, Forster, Dow, Browning (who brought his father to shake hands with me), and Jerdan came into my room. Went back to chambers, whence I proceeded with Catherine to Elstree. Arrived there about half-past one.

May 2nd.—Looked at newspapers, which I was gratified to find lenient and even kind to Browning. On myself—the " brutal and ruffianly " journal observed that I " acquitted myself exceedingly well." Sent a note to Mason, accepting his invitation to dinner. Called on Forster—with whom I found Browning. I told him the play was a grand escape, and that he ought to regard it only as such, a mere step to that fame which his talents must procure him.

May 4th.—Looked at newspapers ; read a criticism on *Strafford* in the *Morning Herald*—it extolled the play as the " best that had been produced for many years," and abused me for " pantings—a-a-s, etc." which the writer supposed " it was too late to cure." This attempt to fasten upon my acting a general censure for a vice that was only detectable in one unstudied character is made by Mr. Conan, who has quarrelled with Forster.

May 7th.—Looked at the *Examiner*, and thought that Forster had given a very kind and judicious criticism on *Strafford*. Wilkin arrived on business ; I endeavoured to induce him to vote for Leader against that very unworthy—that false and vain man—Burdett. He would only engage not to vote for Burdett—another proof of the necessity for the ballot. A letter from Ransom acknowledging £118 7s. 3d., the proceeds of my Benefit. Answered the invitation, or rather solicitation, of the Covent Garden Theatre Fund Committee—a set of persons who *beg* for their own annuities and ask the persons to whom they apply to *condescend* to answer them ! Is it to be wondered at if players are despised ?

London, May 9th.—Called on Forster, who informed me how much he had been hurt by Browning's expressions of discontent at his criticism, which I myself think only too indulgent for such a play as

392

Strafford. After all that has been done for Browning with the painful apprehension of failure before us, it is not pleasing to read in his note, "Let . . . write any future tragedies"! Now, really, this is too bad— without *great assistance* his tragedy could never have been put in a condition to be proposed for representation—without great assistance it never could have been put upon the stage—nor without great assistance could it ever have been carried through its "perilous" experiment.[1] It is very unreasonable and indeed *ungrateful* in him to write thus.

May 12th.—Note from Bulwer inviting me to dine on Sunday week. Called on Forster. Acted Ion but in a middling style. Mr. Dale, as Adrastus, was indeed too bad. Talfourd came into my room—I invited him to dine at Edward's christening on the 24th, and we settled finally for the 25th. The indifference with which the audience received the substitution of Mr. Dale for Mr. Vandenhoff this evening ought to impress on my mind the conviction of how little importance our art is to the community—how easily the best specimens (not meaning Mr. Vandenhoff to be included among them) can be dispensed with—and of what consequence to us it is rightly to appreciate our value.

May 13th.—Mr. Gass, junior,[2] called with specimen of silver plate —I chose a salver value £50 for Talfourd. Went to the rehearsal of scenes of *King Henry VIII;* thence to the Garrick Club, where I saw the newspapers and attended the Committee, where was debated the mode of meeting the attack intended to be made upon us by a set of resolutions proposed by Mr. S. Price and his clique. Hayward was there and asked me if my Benefit was not next Saturday. This was either affectation or only strange ignorance of what was proceeding; if the first, my good-humour made it recoil on himself. At chambers saw the *Literary Gazette* on Miss Martineau; Jerdan is not a man of sufficient intelligence, extent of view, probity or philanthropy enough to estimate such a work—his notice is in my mind a disgrace to himself. He does not understand, nor can he feel the truth contained in the book. Went in the evening to Miss Martineau's; knew no one, but passed a cheerful evening.

May 15th.—I endeavoured to act Cardinal Wolsey well, but the clamours of the gallery were so great in the last scene that I could not

---

[1] Whatever the literary merit of *Strafford*, it is quite certain that Macready did not exaggerate its shortcomings as an acting play ; and, considering how little Browning was known at that time, to produce it at all needed no ordinary amount of enterprise and courage.

[2] Still an honoured house among West End jewellers, being one of the very few firms of that day still carrying on business under the same name.

play them down. Forster, Browning, Dow, Cattermole—whom I engaged to go to the Club on Saturday—and Fitzgerald came into my room. I went with Forster in a cab to Fonblanque's. On our way he acquainted me with the particulars of a row—which Fitzgerald [1] had spoken of—that he (Fitzgerald) had had with a hackney coachman, in which he had given and received a severe beating, and finally had to pay £80 for the rascal's insolence and his own want of self-command. At Fonblanque's, whom I invited to Elstree, I saw Begrez, who is *passé*; Lady Stepney, who is a very dull and empty person—a mindless beauty, striving to keep up an appearance over her years, that grow too fast upon her; Doctor Lardner, who had brought his sister, a kind act, but I question its discretion; she could not have been comfortable; he must have been and was very much the contrary; she is strange to society and never likely to become familiarized with its usages; Bulwer, D'Orsay, and Miss Roberts with her embroidered shawl. Went home in carriage with Catherine.

May 18th.—Acted Posthumus in a most discreditable manner, undigested, unstudied. Oh, it was most culpable to hazard so my reputation! I was ashamed of myself; I trust I shall never so commit myself again. The audience applauded, but they knew not what they did; they called for me with Miss Faucit. I refused to go on, until I found it necessary to go in order to hand on the lady. They then called for Mr. Elton, who had been *very bad* in the play—and he went on. They called for Thompson, who did not. Browning—who walked home with me and again evinced an irritable impatience about the reproduction of *Strafford*—Dow, and Talfourd came into my room. Talfourd had come from the House, where he had been making a speech on his Copyright Bill; his manner seems to me changed or changing. I thought he displayed much affectation, and I am really not disposed to look for failings in him. I am *very* glad I have prepared this present for him.

May 19th.—Acted Wolsey, at which I had not one moment to look, but in a mediocre style, and what I might have done was impaired, if not destroyed, by the shamefully imperfect and inaccurate manner in which the play was done—it was worse than in a country theatre.

May 20th.—Went to the rehearsal of *Winter's Tale*; in the interval of the third and fifth acts went to the Garrick Club and dined, looking at the papers. Saw Fladgate, Williams, etc. At the con-

---

[1] Not the poet.

clusion of the rehearsal returned to the Garrick Club, where I met the Committee; was introduced to Mr. Barney—very quiet man—congratulated Mr. Broadwood on his election for Bridgwater—which I wish he had lost. The General Meeting of the Club took place, at which a cat's-paw of Mr. Price's moved some resolutions reflecting on the Committee. Mr. Barham [1] put the question on its actual merits, and threw the Committee upon the judgment of the members, who were very numerous. Mr. C. Dance disclaimed all personal feeling or objection individually to the Committee, but wished a more democratic delegation. Mr. Price, the *doli fabricator Epeus*, merely objected to the indifferent accommodation of the coffee-room; he afterwards recommended the mover to withdraw his motion, which the meeting would not allow. He (Mr. Price) was white with rage or shame, and the Duke of Beaufort, who was in the chair, took the sense of the meeting; the Committee urged a division, and the malcontents were left with seventeen—chiefly Mr. Price's clique—to seventy-four. A more pitiful figure (undeserving, however, of pity) than Mr. Price made I have rarely seen. Mr. Planché was importantly absurd. Planché and Jerdan accepted my invitation on the spot. Acted Brutus tolerably well, Mr. Vandenhoff being the Cassius of the evening, *vice* Mr. Ward announced, but arrested. Webster [2] told me he had taken the Haymarket, and proposed an engagement to me, settling to call on me in the morning. Went to Warren's, [3] where I found Catherine, Mr. and Mrs. Austin, Sir Howard and Lady Elphinstone, [4] Major Anstruther, Etty, [5] with whom I was delighted to renew my acquaintance.

May 21st.—Arose with a very severe headache, and was obliged to bear up against it during a long breakfast, and much longer story which Warren inflicted upon me of his early fortunes. He is the son of a dissenting clergyman in Manchester, a schismatic from his sect; was intended to study physic, left it in disgust—refused to qualify himself as a dissenting preacher, gained credit at the University of Edinburgh, and was turned out of doors by his father; wrote to his uncle, whom he had never seen, for assistance to follow the law; to his surprise, the answer gave him liberty to draw for £300; he came to London, struggled, and at last married his present wife, then a widow, with a good fortune. Mr. Webster and I talked over the engagement

---

[1] The author of the *Ingoldsby Legends*.
[2] Benjamin Nottingham Webster (1797–1882); the well-known actor and play adaptor.
[3] Samuel Warren.
[4] Sir Howard Elphinstone, Bart. (1773–1846); a distinguished Engineer officer.
[5] William Etty (1787–1849); the well-known R.A.

he had spoken of last night. I dissuaded him from it in the strongest manner, fearing its success, and more than half wishing not to go. I asked high terms, which he tried in vain to make me moderate. Went to dine with Bulwer, with whom I met Fonblanque, Auldjo, Count D'Orsay, Fred Reynolds, Mill and Trelawney, and some other persons. It was a very pleasant day. His house is fitted up in the best taste, and he is well learned in the *savoir vivre*. From thence I went to Mrs. Leicester Stanhope's, where I saw a crowd, and remained but a short time.

May 22nd.—Called on Forster, who gave me a letter from Browning, at which I was surprised and annoyed; as if I had done nothing for him—having worn down my spirits and strength as I have done—he now asks me to study a speech at the end of the second act, and an entire scene which I am to restore in the fourth act. Such a selfish, absurd, and useless imposition to lay on me could scarcely have entered into any one's imagination. I was at first disgusted by the sickly and fretful over-estimate of his work and was angry; but reflected that he did not know what he required me to do, and had forgotten what I have done; "so let him pass, a blessing on his head!" I shall not do it.

May 23rd.—Webster came into my room, and, after a long conversation upon the bargain, it was concluded. For two months at the Haymarket theatre, £20 per night, at three nights per week, the first fortnight; to return £10 per night the third week if the *Bridal* be produced, for which I am to receive £12 per night additional; during its run to throw in an additional night per week, or, if it fails, to be liable to be called on for a fourth night, extra work at £10 per night. Acted Posthumus.

Elstree, May 24th.—Note of excuse from Mr. Forrest, to whom I have now shown every courtesy, and who must admit, "if he have any justice," my conduct most attentive to him; from Stanfield, excusing himself, to my sorrow, on the score of illness. The salver for Talfourd arrived, which I thought very handsome. Took a cab, and in it wedged out our way through the crowds of Piccadilly and Regent Street, gaping at the illuminations of a set of fools and slaves who, in their own "weakness, gasping for the shows of outward strength," build up an earthen idol whose weight may one day crush them.

May 25th.—Talfourd, Mrs. Talfourd, Price, White arrived. As the Talfourds were leaving us I placed the salver and its case in the carriage, and then went up to the drawing-room, where I gave the key

BENJAMIN WEBSTER

From an engraving by W. J. Pound of a photograph by Mayall

to Talfourd, telling him it belonged to a case which I had put in the carriage, and in which he would find a small remembrance that I hoped he would keep for my sake.

London, May 26th.—Arriving, I found a note from a Mrs. Matthew Linwood, whose name I knew in Birmingham as a boy, but who, a brewer's daughter, would have looked down on me; she now applies to me to give an opinion upon her son's qualifications for the stage. Was exceedingly fatigued; looked at newspaper. Lay down after dinner, and could 'do nothing but sleep. Acted Pierre with as much spirit as I could, but I require a complete reconsideration of the character. Heard the prompter go and summon Miss Faucit to appear, having been called. He afterwards came to me, and after him Mr. Webster, to say that I was required, but I thought it no compliment if the audience had summoned me *after* the other performers; and if they had required me first, it was only right the persons guilty of the impertinence of placing me in such a position should be responsible for it. A most gratifying note of acknowledgment from Talfourd, making me very happy in the reflection of having done rightly and kindly by him.

Elstree, May 28th.—Left dear home in the carriage a little after six, and reached Lady Blessington's about a quarter before eight. Found there Fonblanque, Bulwer, Trelawney, Procter, Auldjo, Forster, Lord Canterbury,[1] Fred Reynolds, and Mr. and Mrs. Fairlie, Kenney, a young Manners-Sutton, Count D'Orsay and some unknown. I passed an agreeable day, had a long and interesting conversation in the drawing-room (what an elegant and splendid room it is!) with D'Orsay on pictures. He has great taste and the proper accompaniment of fine taste, if indeed it be not its primary element, great enthusiasm. Lardner was there in the evening, but I merely shook hands with him; spoke to Fonblanque about coming down to Elstree next week, to which he most pleasantly and cheerfully agreed. Walked home with Forster and Trelawney.

London, May 30th.—Was a little displeased to see Mr. Liston's and Madame Pasta's names put in the playbill as superior persons, and felt disposed to make Mr. Rodwell pay for the impertinence, but with Lord Falkland I say, " Peace ! Peace ! " Called on Miss Huddart,

---

[1] Charles Manners-Sutton, first Viscount Canterbury (1780–1845); G.C.B.; Speaker of the House of Commons from 1817 to 1835, when he was defeated by Abercromby in a contest for the Chair, and was created Viscount Canterbury. His wife was a sister of Lady Blessington.

whom I found much less tractable than I had expected. I would not advise or persuade her, but endeavoured to make her distinguish between the fallacy of certain opinions which led to nothing, and facts which were frequent with substantial advantages. I lost time, which I needed much; but at last she agreed to take £9 per week, if Mr. Webster would give it.

Elstree, May 31st.—Miss ——, in her nightly flirtation, told me that she thought of going to the Haymarket, and chiefly because I was to be there. *Nous verrons !*

June 2nd.—I should almost say, *virtue is impossible in a theatre— the mind cannot remain pure,* unless some strong attachment absorbs the heart on the first lighting up of passionate emotion. It cannot be the same in other stations—at least, nowhere is there so much to be said in palliation of frailty as on the stage, and THEREFORE it should be shunned as infection or as death—*for purity cannot live there.*

June 3rd.—A person, calling himself Mr. Monteagle, of good property, wished to know what I should require for instructing him so completely as to bring him not exactly up to my own degree of talent, but very near it. I told him I would pay very willingly to be taught, if any one could teach. I civilly dismissed him, after enduring the bore for some time. Acted Othello pretty well—unequally, but some parts, in the third act particularly, forcibly. Was called for at the end of the play and well received. Thus ended my Covent Garden engagement, which, thank God, has been profitable and agreeable to me. God be praised. Mr. C. Mathews had the cool impudence to ask me to play Joseph Surface for his Benefit! The self-satisfied assurance of this young man really surprised me. Spoke to Webster about Miss Faucit.

Elstree, June 5th.—Found at chambers a note from George Barker, inviting me to subscribe to a monument to Dr. Wooll at Rugby, which, it now appears, is stopped for want of funds, and therefore I am honoured by a notice of the measure. There is no use in being offended; I shall think on what I ought to do, and do it. Called on Miss Martineau—on the arrival of the carriage drove her home, talking the whole way. After dinner heard the dear children's prayers, and, with the exception of one walk round the garden, talked away the whole evening. The only subject on which I did not cordially agree with this fine-minded woman, and on which I do not clearly understand her, is her advocacy of the restoration of the rights of women. I do not see what she would have in point of political power, nor for what.

She told some things of Calhoun, the Senator for South Carolina, that quite surprised me; and gave me information upon Lord Durham's character [1] which raises him greatly in my estimation.

June 6th.—After breakfast, when I asked Miss Martineau if she would like to see Ascot races, and on her expressing her desire to do so, decided on going there; took up Hamlet, and studied part of the second act. Received a letter from dear Letty, written apparently in very good spirits. Drove out through Aldenham to Watford, and thence to the tunnel of the railway, returning through Bushey, with Miss Martineau and Catherine. The weather was beautiful, and Miss Martineau's conversation most agreeable; it was a very delightful drive. Listened to Miss Martineau's narration of the proceedings of the Abolitionists at Boston, and their persecutions; Miss Martineau's share in them, as far as any public act went, was the acceptance of an invitation to be present at a meeting of the Society, and, being there, *in obedience* to a question, which might be regarded as a challenge or test of her sincerity, her declaration before about 130 ladies of her adherence to anti-slavery principles.

London, June 15th.—Went to the Haymarket, and read the *Bridal* in the green-room, which seemed to interest the actors much.

June 16th.—Sent to the theatre about the rehearsal, and after looking at the newspaper to ascertain the state of the King's health [2]— what an absurdity that the natural ailment of an old and ungifted man should cause so much perplexity and annoyance!—went to the Haymarket and rehearsed, with some care, Othello. Acted Othello in some respects very well, but want much attention to it still. Mr. Elton is not good, and is unfair. I was called for, and after long delay went forward. Forster came into my room with a gentleman, whom he introduced as Dickens, alias Boz—I was glad to see him. [3]

[1] Miss Martineau had a very high opinion of Lord Durham, both in his political and private capacity, which was not generally shared at that time. In her *Autobiography* she pays him a feeling and eloquent tribute, laying the responsibility for his early death on Brougham, whom she charges with the grossest treachery to his friend and former colleague. Of this, unfortunately, Brougham in other instances had shown himself to be fully capable; but according to the verdict of history Durham was hardly deserving of Miss Martineau's glowing eulogium. He was an able man with some generous impulses, but inordinately ambitious, and a headstrong and far from tractable colleague.

[2] William IV was then dying, but Macready was too rigorous a democrat to feel much sympathy with Royal sufferers.

[3] Thus began a friendship of the happiest and most genial description that was only terminated by Dickens's death, thirty-three years afterwards. Dickens was then not more than twenty-five, and had not yet published any of his novels, though the *Sketches by Boz* had brought him a good deal of reputation as a magazine contributor.

June 17th.—Called on Mr. Robertson and spoke with him about his note to me on the subject of entering into the management of Covent Garden theatre; premising that I would not venture any part of my little property, nor make any venture beyond that of my own talent. He was to lay Mr. Osbaldiston's refusal to continue in the management before the proprietors, to sound them upon the re-opening of the theatre, and give me notice of their views.

June 18th.—Dined with Talfourd, where I met Hayter [1] (Chancery Bar), Dickens (Boz), Procter, Price, Forster. Lane and another came in the evening. Procter *sounded* me on a new play, but I did not encourage him.

June 19th.—Went to rehearsal, having previously looked at the newspaper for the King's health. Went to theatre; when half dressed a person passed my door saying the King "was off." Upon inquiry I heard that notices of the event—his death—had been fixed up at the offices of the *Courier* and *Observer*, and it was said that it had been up at the Mansion House more than two hours since. The state of suspense in which I was kept to the very moment of the beginning of the play so agitated me that when I went on the stage I was weaker than I often am when I finish a character. I laboured through Richard, but it was labour, and most ineffectual. I was very bad, very bad.

June 20th.—Breakfasted at the Garrick Club, where I heard of the King's death—a subject that the newspapers will moralize and sentimentalize upon, until one becomes ashamed of one's species—the ruthless, heartless, shameless *sicarii* of the *Times* canting about "the affectionate adieux" and "death-bed *counsels*" of the poor old King to his successor, *if* she had been permitted to see him. What a wearying riddle is this world! Nothing seems vile to the vile majority of its inhabitants but poverty. There *must be* a better, since this is so hard to endure. Went to the Garrick Club and read a most unmanly and Billingsgate attack of the *Times* on the Duchess of Kent. [2] Bartley walked out with me, and we talked long on the subject of Covent Garden theatre; he seemed to expect that he was to be a "brother of the war," but I discountenanced that idea. He thought it best *last year* that I should stand *alone*—I think so *now*.

June 22nd.—Overtook an omnibus on my way to the theatre, in which I found Lane, who showed me a drawing he had made (which he

---

[1] Sir William Goodenough Hayter (1792–1878); Q.C. 1839; afterwards Chief Whip of the Liberal party.

[2] The Duchess of Kent had not been on good terms with the King, and was considered in many quarters to have given herself undue prominence as mother of the future Queen.

acknowledged to be too handsome) of the young Queen for a medal—the gold medals to be £10 10s., the silver £1 10s., the copper 10s. Does it not sicken a rational mind to see the great gifts of reason enslaved and debased to such senseless folly as that *men* should set up these golden calves to worship, of their own fabrication, and then bow down before them, instead of keeping their eyes fixed on the mighty God who made them, and all His mighty works that He created with them and for them? The crowd of fools that herded together yesterday to sweat for hours under a burning sun, choking the streets, and lining the house-tops and the windows upon the occasion of the proclamation of Queen Victoria, shows how distant is the hope of the people in this country living for themselves and seeking the *real truth* in the knowledge and machinery of Government!

June 23rd.—Called on Forster, with whom I found Browning; we talked of the abuse of human reason in the worship offered to a *creature* (for what *is* it but worship, and what other God, or kind of God do these people bow down and pray to, etc.) whom we choose to call king or queen, instead of the adoration of mind and heart poured forth in thought and deed by the effort to approach nearer to His perfection—to *Him*, the Almighty, the All-wise, All-good!

June 24th.—The anniversary of my marriage—a day which recalls to my heart its duty of gratitude to Almighty God for the manifold blessings He has bestowed upon me through my dear and blessed wife, upon whose dear head, as upon my precious children's, I implore, in all humility and earnestness of heart, the continuance of His divine protection and mercy, now and for evermore.

June 26th.—Acted Melantius in the *Bridal*, which I had altered with some scenes by Knowles, from Beaumont and Fletcher's *Maid's Tragedy*. The play went with considerable applause. I did not please myself in the acting of Melantius, which was a crude, unfinished performance. Being called for, I led on Miss Huddart. Wallace and Bryden, Browning, Forster, and Dickens came into my room.

June 27th.—Called at Forster's, where a note had been left, which I got at 61, Lincoln's Inn Fields, and on its direction proceeded to Dickens's in Doughty Street. Another note directed me, under the guidance of his brother, to Cold-Bath Fields, where I found Dickens, Forster, Cattermole and Brown, the Pickwick artist. I went through this sad scene of punishment and shame, and my heart sank in its hope for the elevation of my kind. From this place we proceeded to Newgate, over which we went, and in the second room into which we were shown I saw a man reading; he turned as we entered—it was

Wainewright [1]—with large, heavy moustaches—the wretched man over-laid with crime. Several in solitary cells under sentence, and one to be hanged for rape. He seemed the most cheerful of them all; but in all the pride of our nature seemed eradicated or trodden down—it was a most depressing sight. We proceeded to Dickens's to dinner, where Harley, Mr. Hogarth,[2] and a Mr. Banks (who had married Maclise's sister) joined us. Our evening was very cheerful, and we laughed much at Mr. Harley's theatrical efforts to entertain.

June 28th.—At Forster's chambers I met Browning—prevented what seemed to be ripening into a quarrel between them; told them of Miss H.'s match, and was sorry to find my worst fears confirmed by Forster. He wished me to "stop the marriage." I explained to him that I could not, on his vague abuse, interfere between two persons so engaged, and that he was speaking without judgment. Browning walked with me to H. Smith's, complaining by the way of Forster's unreasonable expectations; that he (B——) should shake off acquaintances with whom he (F——) had quarrelled. This seemed absurd, and I so expressed myself, though one of these persons I believe to be a very poor and little-minded person. Forster, walking towards home with me, complained much and censured severely Browning's behaviour. Note from Ransom's; played with the children. Wrote to Maclise, Mrs. and Miss Martineau, L. Twanley.

June 29th.—Called on Forster, who mentioned some things about Browning that gave me concern.

July 11th.—Wrote to Miss Faucit,[3] offering her £15 per week. Went to dine with Mrs. Buller, where I met C. Buller. Thackeray came in the evening, Dickens, John Mill,[4] Martineau, Hawes,[5] Stanley, Miss Martineau, Miss Austin. Walked with Dickens to Garrick Club, where we met Forster. Took a cab home.

July 14th.—Received an answer from Miss Faucit.[6] Spoke to

---

[1] Thomas Griffiths Wainewright (1794–1852); art-critic, forger, and suspected poisoner. He was at one time acquainted with Charles Lamb, and other well-known literary men of the day.

[2] George Hogarth (1783–1870), musical critic; father-in-law of Charles Dickens.

[3] Macready was negotiating for a lease of Covent Garden theatre, with a view to management and provisionally forming the company.

[4] John Stuart Mill (1806–1873); the distinguished philosopher.

[5] Probably Sir Benjamin Hawes (1797–1862), a Whig politician; at that time M.P. for Lambeth.

[6] Miss Faucit's letter was as follows :—

> "36, *Hunter Street,*
> "*Liverpool.*

"MY DEAR MR. MACREADY,

"I have just received your letter, and let me say how proud and happy I should

Farren about Miss Faucit. Fladgate, T. Hill, and some others spoke to me about "having taken Covent Garden theatre." I told them I had not taken it.

July 18th.—Called at the Garrick Club, and looked at newspapers; went on to the Haymarket theatre, where I saw Webster, and learned from him that it was true Mr. Phelps [1] was to have a trial there, whom I thought of engaging if he should prove good.

July 19th.—Acted Melantius not well. The occupation of my mind in other matters is already beginning to display its effect on my acting, and I must be most careful to guard against its encroachment on my labours for improvement; I was not good to-night. Spoke to Mrs. Humby,[2] and secured her for £6 10s. per week.

July 23rd.—Rose rather early and considerably tired, to go post to Penn, where Liston lives. On my way I arranged in my own mind the business of *Hamlet*, scenery, etc. Arriving at Penn, I drove up to Liston's house, and found that he had gone to church; I was glad of the opportunity, and, going in, was shown into a pew. The service was most respectably performed, the church very clean and neat, and the sermon, according to the opinions of the preacher, in a very becoming tone. I was pleased and interested, and happy in the opportunity of imploring the Divine blessing upon the enterprise I

---

feel in being under the management of one for whom I entertain such warm feelings of respect and regard.

"I am very sorry I am not at liberty to answer your letter as I could wish, but I am almost a novice in my profession and should be fearful of doing wrong and incurring the censure of my friends were I to give an assent to what you propose without first consulting them; indeed, as Mr. Farren arranged my engagement with Mr. Osbaldiston, and as I had no hand at all in it, I *could* not relinquish any part of that which is entirely at my mother's disposal, without *his consent.* I must therefore, if you please, refer you to Mr. Farren for an answer to your letter. I shall write home by this post, and state every particular of what you have so kindly explained to me, and what they consider *best,* and decide upon (which I *think* will be as I *wish*), I feel it my duty to abide by.

"With many thanks for your kind inquiries after myself and sister, who I grieve to say is still very ill indeed,

"Believe me, my dear Sir,
"Yours most sincerely,
"Helen Faucit.

"Wednesday evening,
   "*July* 12*th.*"

[1] Samuel Phelps (1804–1878); the eminent Shakspearian actor; his first London appearance was as Shylock at the Haymarket in 1837. He produced Shakspeare's plays at Sadlers Wells theatre with marked success from 1844 to 1862.

[2] Anne Humby, *née* Ayre, an excellent light comedy actress; she first appeared in 1817, and died in 1849. Her charms were celebrated in a couplet more ingenious than conventional which has not yet wholly passed out of circulation.

have in hand. After service I looked about the churchyard for Liston, whom I had observed very gravely attending to his duty in church, and when I approached him his surprise was extreme. I walked home with him, and saw Mrs. L—— and another lady; talked for some time, lunched, and walked out with Liston to look at Taylor's house, and see something of the country, which is pretty, but not comparable to the neighbourhood of Elstree. We talked of many things, chiefly theatricals, and I asked him to come to Covent Garden. He said that he never intended to act again. I did not urge him, but as we talked on, I told him we should not differ on terms, and that I should be happy to see him and would make him as comfortable as I could. I got a frequent repetition of the promise from him that, if he acted anywhere, it should be with me, and I thought I perceived a disposition in him to yield, which I thought it better not to press. Met Taylors, declined their invitations to dinner, and left them on Liston's premises. Returned to *Hamlet.* Reached home by half-past five.

July 24th.—Went into the theatre to take possession of it, invoking the blessing of Almighty God upon my undertaking. Talked with Marshall, who seemed to enter into all my plans respecting scenery, etc.

July 25th.—Mr. Buckstone called.[1] I received him very courteously, but was by no means captivated by his manners, or sentiments. I thought him a coxcomb.

July 27th.—Answered Messrs. Bennett, Montague, and Tilbury. Received a letter, in very kind strain, from Calcraft, lamenting my undertaking; his lamentation was a prophecy. Called on Wallace to ask his opinion of memorializing the Queen for her special patronage, and the liberty to assume the title of Her Majesty's Company of Performers. He thought, if obtained, it would be of great service, and assented to the proposal to get an introduction to Lord Durham, and ask his interest. I called on Miss Kelly, who wished me to hear some pupils of hers. Went on, in my day's cab, to Covent Garden theatre, saw Mr. Bartley, and received many letters.

July 29th.—Dickens and Forster called, and I walked out with them, Dickens speaking to me of the comedy he was desirous of attempting.

August 12th.—Proceeding to Covent Garden theatre; listened to a long account of Mr. Bartley's about Lord Hertford[2] and the sub-

---

[1] John Baldwin Buckstone (1802–1879); the well-known actor-manager; he was principally identified with the Haymarket theatre, which was under his management from 1853 to 1876..

[2] The original of Thackeray's Lord Steyne and Disraeli's Lord Monmouth.

committee and Mr. Bunn, which very little affected me, except to confirm me in my contempt for such disgusting blots on humanity as these things called *Lords* generally are; here is a man uttering a parcel of the greatest folly and falsehood that was ever heard, vouching for the character of a notorious scoundrel, whose life has been a series of failures and unsuccessful knaveries, for the purpose, as it is supposed, of quartering some prostitute upon his Drury Lane salary list! Mr. Farren called, and detained me about two and a half hours. I was wrong, perhaps, not to sign the shameful article he imposes on me at once, since it must be signed, but I vainly and therefore injudiciously —indeed absurdly—thought that reason might have some weight with a fool. I could not move him, and once I thought him on the point of starting off; but the conversation ended in his agreeing to send the article as mutually agreed on to myself and to Miss H. Faucit for signature.[1]

Southampton, August 14th.—Saw the play of the *Iron Chest;* what a thing it is. I was disgusted with the patches of sentiment

---

[1] The agreement as signed by W. Farren on Miss Faucit's behalf was as follows :—

" It is hereby agreed between William Macready, Esq., Lessee of Covent Garden theatre and Miss Helen Faucit of No. 30, Brompton Square, that the said Helen Faucit shall be engaged to perform in Covent Garden as the principal Tragic Actress from the commencement of the season 1837 to the final close thereof, 1838.

" That Miss Faucit shall receive a salary of Fifteen Pounds per week for every six nights of Theatrical performances at the said Theatre to be paid on the Saturday of each week during the period of the above specified season.

" That in every Tragedy or serious play performed during such season at Covent Garden theatre Miss Faucit shall have the choice of the principal character with the privilege of refusing any and every one which she may deem detrimental to her interest to perform; all dresses proper for the characters Miss Helen Faucit may act to be found by the Management.

" It is also agreed between the named parties that Miss Helen Faucit shall have a Benefit at Covent Garden theatre on paying the usual charges in case she should deem it to her advantage to take one.

" That if orders be written by the Management, Miss Helen Faucit shall be entitled to write admissions for two persons to the Boxes and two to the Gallery on every night the Theatre may be open, save on such nights devoted to Benefits.

" That Miss Helen Faucit shall retain every and all characters which she had already acted in Tragedy and Comedy at Covent Garden theatre with the exception of Queen Catherine in *Henry VIII.*

" That Miss Faucit shall be subject to the Rules and Regulations of the Theatre, as far as they extend to this engagement.

" It is also agreed between the within named parties that if either break this engagement the damages for such breach of engagement shall be estimated at Two Hundred Pounds.
                                                            " WILLIAM FARREN.

" Witness,
    " GEO. BARTLEY.
      " 16th August, 1837."

and claptraps upon national privileges, humanity, and all the other virtues in which G. Colman was so rich—on paper. Mr. Phelps in Sir Edward Mortimer displayed intelligence, occasionally great energy, some imagination—not much; want of finish, of experience, of logic in the working out the character—(to lay violent hands on the term) —of *depth* in all the great parts. His best scene decidedly was his death, but even there was a want of method. His level speaking is often very pleasing—always sensible, I expected from his opening more than he achieved. There was no *absorbing* feeling *through* the great scenes, no evidence of the " slow fire " " wearing his vitals "; this was particularly manifest in the last act, where he was direct and straight-forward even to commonplaceness. I think he will improve, and run both Warde and Elton hard, and very likely do much more. I left my note for him. He called at the Dolphin, and I offered him either the salary he might take from Mr. Webster, or to give him now a salary, if he would name one, that I could meet. He preferred waiting for Mr. Webster, and we interchanged agreements to that effect. I liked his tone and manner.

To London, August 15th.—Rose early; in leaving Southampton old Mr. Maxfield, the former manager of Southampton theatre, got into the coach to go to Winchester to see a cricket match; it was pleasing to see so hale, active, and cheerful an old man of seventy-five years of age. He mentioned what very much disgusted me with that old wretch, the Duchess of St. Albans [1]—that, though an old theatrical acquaintance, she would only communicate with him from one room to another by an intermediate messenger.

To Elstree, August 16th.—Took Bartley in carriage to Hyde Park. Called on Lord Conyngham [2] at Dudley House; saw some good pictures. Lord C—— received me very courteously and entered (or seemed to do so) into my views, promised to present my memorial to the Queen, and to say all he could for it. I left him much pleased. Returned to Covent Garden theatre. Occupied the whole morning. Wrote to Phillips. Signed articles with Diddear, Miss P. Horton,[3] Wilson, Mrs. East. Wrote to Mr. Pritchard. Dickens called with Mr. Hullah,[4] who has a comic opera nearly ready. I do not think his

[1] Harriet Mellon.

[2] The second Marquis, then Lord Chamberlain.

[3] Priscilla Horton (1818–1895); afterwards Mrs. German Reed, then a young actress of much attractiveness, also a charming singer.

[4] John Pyke Hullah (1812–1895); the well-known musical composer and teacher. His *Village Coquettes*, for which Dickens wrote the words, was produced in the preceding year.

manners argue much genius—if the contrary, it can only be musical genius.

London, August 19th.—Wrote my memorial to the Queen, requesting her to let me call the Covent Garden players, "Her Majesty's Company of Performers." Inclosed it in a note to the Lord Chamberlain and sent it.

Elstree, August 23rd.—Bartley came; he brought me letters, news, and a message from the Lord Chamberlain. In answer to my memorial the Queen had expressed herself much interested in Covent Garden; stated that she had great respect for Mr. Macready and admiration for his talent, that the precise object of his request required consideration, but if it should be deemed impracticable to concede, that she trusted other means might be found of rendering assistance to his undertaking. Talked over various matters, and decided on several. After dinner arranged the first fortnight's business, and cast the plays.

To London, August 26th.—Left my dear, my blessed home, its quiet, and its joys, to enter on a task for which nature and taste have disqualified me. I seemed to catch hope from what looked to me like omens of good yesterday, but to-day, when I make trial of the disposition and intellects of those around me I sicken into despondency even before I begin my course. I lift up my heart to God for my children and myself, for I am not a match for the baseness and treachery of those with whom I must deal.

September 1st.—Miss Huddart told me that Messrs. C. Kean, Bunn and Hughes were seen very familiarly arm-in-arm together in the street—this is Mr. C. Kean, who set up for a preux chevalier! Acted Werner very unequally; could have played it better than I ever in my life did; and did perform some parts in a perfect style, but was cut up by the dreadful inaccuracy of the actors in others.

September 3rd.—Thought over and calculated on paper my chances, and find on the present prices, and with the advantage I give the proprietors in my name, that the bargain with them is *very* hard and *heavy* on me; but I have no complaint or discontent with them; they did for the best for themselves; I ought not to have been led away so inconsiderately. Read over *King Richard III.* Read in Homer.

Birmingham, September 10th.—Went down to the railway; Bartley waited to see me off. I felt much excited—wonder and delight filled my heart at enjoying this triumph of human intellect over the obstacles of matter and of time. I could not satisfy the fulness of

407

my feelings but in saying my prayers. It is much to see and to enjoy. We want no aristocracy for such works as these.

September 11th.—Went to rehearsal—half amused, half disgusted with the mad conceit of the premier tragedian of this company. Heard much gossip of the profligacy of players. It does me good to listen to these stories, for the deformity of the lives of such men as Messrs. —— is quite frightful enough to drive one into the arms of virtue. Rather unwell, and a little disconcerted by the conceit and presumption of the actors here.

September 12th.—When it (the rehearsal) was over, I talked with Miss Faucit about her engagement—told her how Mr. Farren had behaved in altering the agreements and what they were. Demonstrated to her the impracticability of such an engagement, and the danger it contained to herself in the case of the hostility of authors—the necessity of keeping her out of business, etc.—that in the worst result to me if the experiment were unsuccessful it would be of no consequence; if it were triumphant the penalty would be of little consideration. She was seriously affected by this representation, and wished to think that Mr. Farren did not *mean* all in what he did, but promised when she was of age—after October 11th—to strike out of my article the obnoxious clause and sign her name to it. I told her that it did her great honour, and that it bound me more than all the parchments in the world to be her friend, and to do my utmost to promote her welfare—*which I will do.* I was very much pleased with her. Acted Othello indifferently. I was made nervous at the outset and, though I laboured, I could not hide the labour—it was a bad performance. The great error of my performance of Othello was in the heavy, stately tone in which I pitched the part, instead of the free, bold, cheerful, chivalrous bearing of the warrior, the happy lover, and the high-born man.

September 13th.—Went to rehearsal; talked with Clarke about Messrs. Phelps and C. Kean, from whom he does not expect much. Made calculations, which were more cheering than they have been. Lay down on the sofa. Not at all well. Cold and disordered system. Letter from Lord Dudley Stuart,[1] requesting me to act on Monday, 25th inst., for the destitute Poles. This I cannot do. Went to

[1] Lord Dudley Coutts Stuart (1803–1854); a younger son of the first Marquis of Bute, and grandson on his mother's side of Thomas Coutts the banker. His whole-hearted efforts in the cause of Poland only ceased with his life, which he devoted to it. He died when visiting Stockholm, where he was endeavouring to enlist the sympathy and aid of the Swedish King.

theatre. Began with a feeling of inability to strive with my own depression and the languor of the audience. In some degree over-mastered it as I proceeded, and finished the play—in a sort of doubtful manner—really not knowing what effect I had produced. Mr. Pritchard came into my room, and afterwards Clarke. Both told me it had made a very strong impression, the latter saying that it would be repeated on Monday. I cannot understand this audience. The labour is *great* to act to them.

September 14th.—Rose in very good time, and wrote an answer to Lord Dudley Stuart's application, excusing myself from playing at the Haymarket, and enclosing a cheque for £5. Was very anxious to act Hamlet well; really tried to do my duty; began well, spoke the first speech to the Queen *excellently* well—as I proceeded, I fancied I had reason to complain of the coldness of the audience, and the neglect of the actors—perhaps my own inefficiency was the real cause of blame, and yet I did some things certainly very well; the soliloquies, the play, with the players, part of the closet, etc., but the audience were by no means enthusiastic. I suppose the fault was in myself.

September 15th.—Acted Melantius—partially well, certainly not to my own satisfaction throughout. The audience were unusually sympathetic, and the play was said to have gone well. After the terrible moral of the play, in which she had just been acting for the first time, Miss —— preferred coming to my room—rather than receive me in hers, because she knew in hers some one would be present. It seems a weakness in her, an *unconsciousness of wrong*—yet what does she propose to herself? Is it that she does not know, or does not set the due estimation on the worth of character? Does she think? or does she *only feel*—and *obey* a *feeling?* What a world this is! And how little of it beyond its thin surface do those in it know of it!

September 16th.—The uncomfortable position in which I am placed with this girl disturbed me, but I came to the resolution of not allowing myself to suffer from my own vanity or weakness. I really like her much as a friend, and I will be a friend to her. Gave Miss —— the part of Clothilde in the *Novice.* She told me that she had not been to see her sister, and that she had expected me to call in the afternoon! She had no grounds for doing so. Looked over the play of *Wives as They Were.*

Semptember 17th.—Lardner detailed the history of Babbage's quarrel with Government about his calculating machine. It seems Government assisted him with funds to the amount of £15,000 to

£16,000 for the construction of the first, which he relinquished, and for a second, an improvement on the first, which he discontinued, because Government had not given him the distinction and reward to which he thought himself entitled. Government said, " Finish the work, and then——" but he said to his friends that he ought not to be kept waiting till he was old, but should be remunerated now! He has subsequently discovered a still further improvement, and leaves the second (No. 2) machine to Government—desiring to make a fresh bargain with them for No. 3. Professor Airey [1] says the thing is a humbug; other scientific men say directly the contrary.

September 18th.—Went to call on Miss ——, who, I hope, would not have returned from Wavertree, but she was at home. I received the book of *Foscari* from her, and she decided on the character of Mariana in preference to that of Isabella, *Measure for Measure*. She told me that she had made up her mind not to be disappointed in travelling to town with me, so that I had no alternative—not that I had even expected she would change her mind. I cannot affect or doubt as to her affection for me. She must either love me, or be one of the most extraordinary and senseless deceivers that ever existed. I would to God it were not so, or that I could believe it not so.

September 19th.—Miss —— did not like to say she would act Hester in *To Marry*, and feared she had incurred blame by taking Miss Dorrillon, from which I relieved her at once. I sent in a note afterwards, requiring a *Yes* or *No* answer to the part of the *Novice*. She wrote back very affectionately and promptly " Yes." Finished copying the address. A little of Hamlet.

September 20th.—Acted Ion very languidly indeed; occupation through the day is scarcely compatible with a really successful performance. The nerves and spirits cannot keep their tone. How strange are the thoughts that pass through one's brain, when acting without being *possessed* by *the character*. I was *looking at* the Adrastus, and thinking to myself was it *the proper business* of a human being, with the " god-like qualities " peculiar to him, to expend his life in repeating parts of plays, and trying to represent human passions. How I *felt* the low condition of a player! And when we know *what these players are*, oh God! Worked at Talfourd's address. Miss —— declined Hester in *To Marry or Not*, also refused to act Emma in *William Tell* for me.

[1] George Biddell Airey (1801–1892); F.R.S., K.C.B.; Astronomer-Royal from 1856 to 1881.

September 22nd.—Letter from Bartley; the defection of Warde, and the envious malice of that reptile —— leaves us in a very serious dilemma, but I feel strong in myself, and my hope and reliance is on the goodness of God to protect me. And yet, as I write this, am I not conscious of thoughts in my heart which are evil? Oh, man! man! Let me hope that I shall root them out.

September 24th.—Forster and Talfourd came in, and they were all against me on the subject of the *pit tickets,* but I heard *no reasons* against it, and would not yield, till Talfourd suggested the possibility of a *row* on the first night. This decided me, and I resolved to leave the question for the first two or three weeks, and endeavour to bring it on afterwards. The address, prices, etc., Waldron, many matters were discussed and settled. Robertson told me that Sir H. Wheatley had, on the part of the Queen, expressed a wish that the price of her box should be reduced from £400 to £350. If this be Royal Patronage, commend me to popular favour! Patronage to a declining art!

September 26th.—Forster called to inquire if I would advance Knowles money on the new tragedy he was going to write. I said, "Let me know his subject and his confidence in the treatment, and then the matter will wear a face of business."

September 27th.—Going out, called at the *Morning Herald, Morning Post, Chronicle, Spectator, Globe, Sun, True Sun, Courier, Athenæum.* Saw editors of the *Post* and *Courier,* and explaining to them my motives in taking the theatre, hoped that the undertaking would have the support of the papers; they were most courteous.

September 28th.—After dinner went to look at my blessed children, as they slept, blessed them, and in the hope which my heart in silence lifted up to God that He would bless them, and me for them, I went out to the theatre. Still upon the address. Was very much pleased with the appearance of the theatre—it looked very elegant; spoke on several points and gave directions. Conferred with Knowles and Forster on the terms for his plays; Knowles agreed *upon those terms* to give me the *refusal of all his plays.* This in the presence of *Bartley, Robertson and Forster.* It was a clear understanding.

September 29th.—Called on H. Smith on my way to Mr. Delane [1] of the *Times,* who in Mr. Barnes's absence had answered my note to him. Called at the *Times* office—that mighty cauldron or vomitory

---

[1] Father of John Thadeus Delane (1817–1879), the famous editor of the *Times* from 1841 to 1877.

of ill—and good! Was directed to Mr. Delane's house; saw him; my pride had been hurt by Mr. Barnes not answering my letter, but I determined to act for *the cause*, not for myself. Found Mr. Delane very civil, and, mentioning the object of my call, settling matters of advertisements, and giving unlimited leave of orders, I left him, satisfied in having called.

September 30th.—When I am actor I must forget that I am manager. Covent Garden theatre opens. Before coming down I prayed from my heart to Almighty God, imploring His mercy upon me in the effort, which this day begins, and in what so much of good or evil to my beloved family is involved. When I was going into the coach it was like the setting out upon a long journey (may it be a pleasant one!). I kissed my dear children, and bade adieu to my home with a heart full to overflowing. Repeated the address on my way, and entered the theatre with an invocation of God's blessing on me. Rehearsed the play,[1] and attended to the various claims on my notice; received many letters of acknowledgment for the freedom of the theatre. Took every occasion of repeating the address. Bartley and Robertson came into my room with a slip from one of the newspapers of an address to the public by that reptile, Mr. Bunn; it was meant as an answer or comment upon mine. I thought it inconsiderate in Bartley to pester me with such a thing at such a time, and gave as little attention to it as I could; it simply left the notion with me of being an ebullition of temper from *such* a person! I thought little of it. It consumed some time to arrange my dresses, etc., and when this was done I lay down in bed. Repeatedly went over my address, and also read over the first scene of Leontes. Dressed and, being called to the address, went and found the overture only just begun. Much agitated, the thought of the Rubicon-like plunge I was about to make and my home came upon me and affected me for a moment. When I went on the stage the enthusiasm of the audience was very great; I began my address with tolerable composure, but in the last part of it I stopped— it was a pause of about half a minute—but, in agony of feeling, longer than time can measure; I recovered myself, and tripped slightly again before the conclusion of the address. Mr. Vining came to speak to

---

[1] Covent Garden opened under Macready's management with *A Winter's Tale* and *A Roland for an Oliver*. Boxes, 5*s*., second price, 2*s*. 6*d*. ; pit, 2*s*. 6*d*., second price, 1*s*. 6*d*. ; lower gallery, 1*s*. 6*d*., second price, 1*s*. ; upper gallery, 1*s*., second price, 6*d*. Second price at the end of the third act of plays, and the second of operas. Stage director, Mr. Willmott; musical director, Mr. G. H. Rodwell; acting manager, Mr. Bartley (*note by Sir F. Pollock*).

me as I was going on the stage, but I put him away. Acted Leontes
artist-like but not, until the last act, very effectively. Was called on
to give out, which I did. Fitzgerald, Forster, Procter, Talfourd,
Kenny came into my room; Talfourd made no secret of his authorship
now—how very weak he is on these points of vanity! I thought it
for his interest not to avow it, but he left me a discretionary power
to publish it or no, as I might deem best from the tone of the papers
respecting it. Forster brought D'Orsay to see me, with that old
débauché, Lord Allen. Bartley and Robertson also came in. Sat up
late, and when I went to bed slept very little.

October 2nd.—Rose in good time and tried to keep my thoughts
on *Hamlet*. Went in coach to the theatre, and arriving there spoke
about the bad delivery of the bills. Robertson sank my spirits very
low by an account of the *Times'* report of our opening, which he
represented as altogether blame. I went through the rehearsal of the
play—taking pains with it, and attending to other business as it fell
out. Among other letters was one—I should say ruffianly, if intended,
as I suspected, to convey a personal menace—from that wretched
profligate, Mr. ——. Other letters. I dined, and lay down in bed.
Very, very much dejected. Felt myself quite unequal to perform.
As the time drew near I rallied, dressed. Mr. Brewster failed in his
appointment; I would not let it annoy me, but went on, determined
to do my best. I acted the greater part of *Hamlet* in my best manner;
and the play was put beautifully on the stage. The audience noticed
with applause several of the improvements.

October 5th.—Called on Mr. Dilke;[1] saw Mr. D——, junior,[2]
talked with him upon the " splenetic or unscientific " invective of the
Athenæum critic upon the *Bridal*. He assured me that there was no
hostility to myself, but quite a contrary sentiment on the part of the
critic; I liked his frank manner. We agreed that the *Athenæum*
orders should pass, and our advertisements be inserted gratuitously. I
left him seemingly well pleased. Sent freedom of theatre to Rogers—
with note. Lay down, very much tired, for about three quarters of
an hour. A bad headache. Acted Leontes—feebly, but with care;
spoke to Miss Huddart about her acting, on which subject I feel apprehension and concern. Was called for feebly—gave out the play.

[1] Charles Wentworth Dilke (1789-1864); editor and critic ; was long connected with the
Athenæum.
[2] Charles Wentworth Dilke, jun. (1820-1869); son of the above. Created a baronet ;
father of the late Sir C. W. Dilke, Bart., the Liberal statesman.

413

The house was very respectable—most satisfactory. Saw a little of the farce, which was well acted.

October 6th.—Thought on the business of the theatre as I awoke and dressed. Went to the theatre, where I arrived at a little before ten, applied to business, reading, and answering letters. Rehearsed the *Bridal*, and took much pains with Mr. Anderson. The Messrs. Dilke called, and went over the affair of the *Athenæum* criticism, speaking with great candour and good-nature, endeavouring to palliate the false statement of the *Bridal's* "want of attraction," and coming to a very amicable, agreeable arrangement, as settled yesterday, respecting the interchange of orders for advertisements. Parted very good friends. Mr. Fisher called and told me he had bailed Mr. Warde, who he hoped would be *out* to-morrow, and that the money required would be—the round sum—£100. Superintended the rehearsal of two acts of the *Novice*, which occupied me till past four, took all pains with it. Had promised Miss Taylor a new wig, and sent for Brewster to measure her for it, which he did. Received a note from Faraday [1] abjuring his claim to knighthood, thanking me for the card of admission, but returning it on account of the "Sir"; answered him and sent him a corrected card. Sent note and cards of admission to Milman,[2] his wife, and friend.[3] Wrote notes to Messrs. Willmott and Meadows with additions of one pound per week each to their salaries. Acknowledged Murray's present of Lord Byron's works.

October 7th.—Arose reluctantly, feeling indisposed from the very indifferent night I had had. Went to the theatre—and applied myself to business. Bartley came to speak about Warde, whose solicitors had gone out of town, and in their place a friend and relation appeared whom I did not know how to trust. Sent Bartley with cheque to settle the various matters. Miss Huddart, who had asked to see me, now told me that Mr. Abbot (a . . . attorney!) had, on hearing of Warde's approaching release, said, "I think I'll let him play on Monday night"—adding that he had a writ against him. I sent for Bartley, and it became a question whether the money should be risked or no; the question to me was whether the money should be risked, or

---

[1] Michael Faraday (1791–1867); the celebrated scientist. He died without having even received the offer of a knighthood, much to the discredit of the various Governments of his time.

[2] Henry Hart Milman (1791–1866); afterwards the well-known Dean of St. Paul's. His drama *Fazio* (produced in 1815) had, with other dramatic pieces, already gained him considerable reputation.

[3] Under Macready's managements free admissions were sent by him to persons distinguished in science, art, and literature (*note by Sir F. Pollock*).

414

the season. I did not long hesitate, and gave the word for his release, and despatched Bartley; the matter superintended by one of White and Whitmore's clerks occupied the whole day, and I had several communications on it. Meantime rehearsed the *Bridal*. Felt much obliged to Miss Huddart for her kindness and friendship. Lay down, not well. Various notes—one from Meadows, another from Willmott, expressive of their gratitude for my addition to their salaries. Acted Melantius pretty well. Kenny was in my room, whilst dressing, and he told me that Planché "had been inveighing most warmly against his erasion from the Free List, saying that he had written one act of a play for the theatre, which had been submitted to me and Mr. Bartley—a falsehood. Called on after the play, and gave out the three next nights. Mr. Anderson was also called forward, of which I was very glad. Kenny, Talfourd, Wallace, Forster and Robertson came into my room. Warde also, who expressed himself very grateful for his liberation, and for the *manner* in which it was done.

October 8th.—Rose at a late hour after a sleepless night, but before I got up read over a one-act piece by Haynes Bayley, a very milk-and-water production. Read over a notice in the *Atlas*, which seemed reluctant to be kind and yet unwilling to compromise its character. I did not like it, but got one or two hints from it; *fas est et ab hoste doceri.* Wrote note to Talfourd, excusing myself from dinner. Wallace called. I proposed to him the publication in pamphlet of Forster's notice in this day's *Examiner*. After some consideration he assented to the idea.

October 9th.—Among notes received one, very kindly written, from Rogers.[1] Lay down, and glad to do so, in bed. My mind a good deal excited, but I acted Hamlet pretty well. My self-possession returns to me in a surprising way. Kenny, H. Smith, Wallace, and Forster came into my room. I spoke to the latter about the article in the *Examiner* being reprinted in a pamphlet form. The house falling off in the half-price, decided, with my council, on putting up *Othello* for next Monday.

October 10th.—Rose, after a night of very little sleep, in which I thought of Othello, at an early hour, and reached the theatre by nine o'clock; found no carpenter, in fact, no workmen there! Received a very civil acknowledgment of his card from Milman. Wrote eight notes or letters, and then gave myself entirely to the rehearsal of the

[1] The veteran "banker-poet" (1763-1855). His poem, the *Pleasures of Memory*, was published the year before Macready was born.

play of the *Novice;* [1] took great pains in endeavouring to infuse a spirit into the actors engaged in it. Settled the cast of *Othello* with Mr. Bartley for the Duke, as an example to the other actors, and to show the public that there would be no impediments to the best possible disposition of the characters in a play. Looked over papers and dined at the Garrick Club, saw only disagreeable and most vulgar persons there. Forster had taken a note home for me to say I should not dine there. Miss —— had begun to talk to me in a way that inclines me to waver in my opinion of her constancy or sincerity. We shall see! Attended a night rehearsal of the *Novice*, in which all did their best. Forster was there. Came home and cut the play of the *Novice*.

October 11th.—Rose much fatigued. Went to the theatre. Letters from a French pantomimist, wishing to represent animals and a fly! Attended the rehearsal of the *Novice*. Spoke to Sloman about his men; not satisfied with the state of the accounts, nor with the vigilance of Robertson. The play of the *Novice*, which if acted well in the part of Carolstadt would have been most effective, was marred and almost ruined by the inefficiency of Mr. Vining. It escaped, but will do no good. Forster, Talfourd, Wallace, etc., came into my room. The house was wretched.

October 12th.—Rose rather tired, and went to the theatre as soon as I could. Summoned a rehearsal of the *Novice*. Wrote answers to Mr. Horne and a person who wrote very kindly to wish me success. Sent a note to Miss Faucit to come to rehearsal or send her part. Searched for plays and afterpieces. At twelve o'clock went out to call on Liston at Brompton; saw and sat with him some time. He said he should never act again, and I certainly think he never will. He seems to be breaking up. I left him with an expression that he had *carte-blanche* from me. Returning to the theatre, took the book of the *Novice*, and went over the play with the actors, cutting their parts and arranging all for a rehearsal to-morrow. I lay down about half-past three, and rested most comfortably till half-past five, thinking over some part of Melantius, which I acted very fairly. Was called for, and very enthusiastically received by the audience. Talfourd, Forster, and Bartley came into my room.

October 13th.—Went to the theatre, and sent for Robertson to speak about the accounts. Mentioned the fact of the bills I had twice before spoken of being continued despite of my complaints. Sent for Mr. Harris—he began again to talk; I checked him, and told him it was

---

[1] A translation, attributed to W. Dimond.

merely a question of business; he was inclined to be impertinent, as often idle persons are to hide their own faults. My dresser thought he could undertake the office of regulating the coals and candles for twelve shillings, which saves me at once eighteen shillings per week. Went over Bradwell's account with Willmott and Robertson; the latter is *not* the *man* for such a duty in such a time; he is one of those on "Lethe's Wharf." A letter from Mr. Phillips to Bartley, refusing to act Rashley in to-morrow night's bill, threw us into embarrassment. This fellow, who never attracts individually one sixpence, will now receive a week's salary—£35—for playing in one farce—and perhaps not that. Miss Shirreff was affecting nerves and hysterics, and to pacify her I was obliged to change *Artaxerxes*, announced for Tuesday. So much for these knavish singers. Went over the *Novice* in the saloon. Messrs. Paine, of the *Morning Gazette*, called for advertisements and orders. Bagnall called for an engagement; I heard him speak and dismissed him civilly. Wrote several notes. Spoke with Head about Othello's dresses. Coming home, tried to read an adaptation of *Volpone*, but fell asleep, overpowered with fatigue of mind and body. Went to theatre after dinner with Catherine and Letitia. Saw the *Novice*, which is destroyed by the stupid, unmeaning and tedious recitation of Mr. Vining. Spoke to Miss Faucit about her illness.

October 14th.—Very tired when I arose. Went to the theatre, and found that the play of *Othello* was in course of rehearsal—attended to it. Transacted business of various sorts; wrote answers to letters. Talked over several matters with Kenney. A note from Mr. Phillips—inquired why *he did not act to-night*. The cool effrontery of this man, who picks my pockets in this manner, is too bad. Mr. Webster called to speak, as he said, about Mr. Phelps, who, it appears, has received £10 per week from him (Mr. W——), and given in a protest against the same being a precedent for his engagement with me. Wallace, Forster, Talfourd came into my room. The latter told me of some abuse of himself and Forster in the *Age*, which was unimportant except as its matter testified that there are some treacherous persons about the theatre.

October 15th.—Rose with feelings of heavy weariness, and, coming downstairs, gave my first attention to my domestic accounts. Then looked at the theatrical business of the week. It is, I think, this week which will show me the degree of hope that a reasoning man may entertain of the final issue of my enterprise. The impossibility of

417

revoking the step I have made enforces the propriety of putting a resolute and cheerful face upon the matter; and though I go forward with very little hope, yet still I do not bate much of heart in urging my purpose forward. There is at present a loss upon the concern, and this is beginning early, but the statements laid before me could not be accurate; and though I do not think that Robertson has wilfully deceived me, yet certainly things are not as he represented them to be. Let me, however, strenuously persist in the fulfilment of my duty, and put my trust in Almighty God to protect me from all evil consequences, and to guard and bless my beloved family. Wrote notes to Bartley and to the *Sunday Times* on their very shameful abuse of Talfourd upon a misconception. Kenney called, and sat longer than I wished, as did also Wallace. When they left me, I turned to the reading of *Othello*, upon which I continued, rather drowsily, till dinner-time. After dinner, looked over the newspaper, and was shocked by the *worship* which the base wretches of this world are transferring from their God to a girl of eighteen, whom they choose to call a Queen! They haunt her path, and receive (and to the equal shame of the other party, are given) *tickets* to have entrance to the chapel on Sunday where she is supposed to pray. Mighty Heaven! how long is folly and impiety like this to be triumphant on earth? Read *Othello* the remainder of the evening. Read prayers to the family.

October 16*th.*—Attended to what business I could; just before I lay down, Mr. Anderson came to inform me that he had received from an agent of Drury Lane an offer, which I afterwards heard was ' double his present salary, to act what he pleased, and to play a new part in a play which the author would only consent to his performing.' Mr. Bunn is certainly an honest man, and his friends are honest men. Lay down, and tried to think over Othello. Very much dissatisfied with my own performance of the part of Othello, very much indeed. I can scarcely tell why I was so heavy and cold, except that the fatigues of management are beginning to tell upon my acting. The Council of Forty was a scene of beautiful effect, one of the most real things I ever saw. Talfourd and Browning came into my room; the former asked me if I had seen the *Age*. Mr. Phelps called, but I did not see him.

October 17*th.*—Went to the theatre, where I immediately began on business; read my letters, etc., and went upon the stage to look at the condition of the new melodrame; did not think it good, and was not satisfied with the acting; it will not serve us. Signed the articles of Messrs. Bennett, Leffler, and Anderson. Faraday called and sat a short time. I was quite glad to see him. Dined at the Garrick Club; looked at the papers, not one of which noticed the *mise en scène* of *Othello !* So much for the assistance of the Press! Spoke to Miss Faucit about Virginia; she promised to do her best. Looked over Serle's melodrame. The house was wretched.

October 18th.—Went to theatre. Miss Huddart, in talking to me, showed *temper*, which I did not like to see. Miss Faucit assented to Virginia, saying that her mother was very much against it, etc. Forster, Talfourd, Dickens, Kenney, Bartley, Robertson and Willmott came into my room.

October 19th.—Saw Bartley and asked him his opinion of our prospect; he said that he began to be afraid of it.

October 20th.—Braced up my nerves, and strengthened my mind to look cheerfully in the face of the fate that is before me. The question of *interest* has now ceased *entirely;* it is now a point of character—upon that I am resolved to stand, and be consistent not only with my conduct, but with my thoughts. The hope of elevating my art is now lost to me, but I will do my utmost to protect those who have confided in my fortune, and devote myself to that—I hope— honourable effort. It is that thought and resolution that keep a smile upon my face, when sorrow and foreboding look with gloomy pity on me from almost every eye. I will be true to them and to myself. May God assist me! Amen! Went to theatre, leaving poor Letty with the tears in her eyes; it seems she is fretting for me, but that, though kind, is unwise.

October 21st.—Went to theatre. Rehearsed *Werner*, and gave Robertson a cheque for £300 to meet the week's deficiencies. Saw Elton and talked with him on business. Bartley brought me some casts for this and next week, which I looked at, but felt some effort must be made. I spoke with Marshall, who has quite betrayed his trust, and deceived me. Mr. Rooke, the composer, came into my room, and insisted that his opera could not be done for three weeks. We had a long altercation; the singers were sent for; they behaved very well—*for singers !*—and were ready to make an effort to produce it to the day announced, but it appeared at last that Mr. Rooke had not the music ready to give to the band!!! And for this the theatre loses another week! Looked over *Werner*—my spirits, body, and mind exhausted. Anxious to play well, I took great pains, and very success- fully. I touched off the character very happily, and quite satisfied

419

myself. I was called for and very enthusiastically received. Talfourd, Forster, and Wallace came into my room.

October 22nd.—Came down at eleven o'clock to meet Robertson, and settle my amount of loss, and give him in the full amount of what I could still permit him to count upon. My banker's account stands—

	£	s.	d.	£	s.	d.
Paid in .				3682	1	1
Drawn .				2734	9	4
Balance at Ransom's .				947	11	9
Already paid on account of Covent Garden	623	14	0			
Making myself liable for the remainder of £1,000 .	376	6	0			
My salary to be returned .	90	0	0			
				466	6	0
Leaving in at Ransom's an available surplus of .				£481	5	9

October 23rd.—Called on Stanfield, taking Letitia and Catherine with me on their way to Shoolbred's. Asked Stanfield to paint me a diorama for the pantomime. He almost promised, and in the kindest manner. He is a fine creature. Went to theatre, where of course business awaited me. Signed engagement with Mr. Howe.[1] Business with Robertson and Bartley, who went down on a message to the Vice-Chamberlain's Office, and brought word that the Queen would come to the theatre in November. Agreed with Mr. Phelps. Cut part of the *Royal Oak*,[2] which I think will make a decent after-piece. Lay down, very much tired; fear my health is beginning to shake. Acted *fairly* to a very *un*applauding audience. Forster and Kenney came into my room. I gave Kenney the *Royal Oak* to finish. Sat up late. The papers are almost all unfriendly to me. So much more probable is it that my cause is good, and that I am honourable.

October 24th.—C. Buller called, and stayed with me some time. He mentioned his disappointment in my Othello not being more tender, a criticism that I will not forget.

October 25th.—Called on Stanfield, whom I found what he is said to be, and must be thought to be, the very spirit of kindly feeling. He assented to my request and promised to make all arrangements

[1] Henry Howe (1812-1896); originally Henry Howe Hutchinson, the well-known Haymarket actor. His first appearance in London was in 1834, and he was a member of Sir H. Irving's American Company at the time of his death, sixty-two years later.

[2] By W. Dimond.

with me. I told him I could not thank him, both for the act itself, and its moral influence on the undertaking I have in hand.

October 26th.—Went to the theatre, and applied to business. Looked over the accounts of last week. Colonel D'Aguilar called, who seemed—and I know is—most anxious for my success. My success is not to lose my principal. Beyond that hope, all seems visionary. A kind note from T. Moore. Went over business of the pantomime with Young. Rehearsed *Pierre*. Miss Faucit wished to alter her engagement, but I did not think it necessary, choosing rather to rely on her word than on any obtained advantage. Confidence is generally, where there is any feeling, the strongest bond.

October 27th.—As I begin to note briefly the events of this day, I must observe that it is the most disastrous one that has yet occurred under my management. I have been tried severely. I went to the theatre, where I learnt that Mr. Rooke's opera was not *in the theatre*, nor could be on the day it was announced to be acted! The effect on my head was such that it ached all day after. I rehearsed *Pierre*. Attended as well as I could, which was scarcely at all, to business. This news had *struck me down*. My income is destroyed—my mind tortured. I sat down for a few minutes *overwhelmed*. I saw Mr. Haines, who shuffled and could say nothing. I would not see Mr. Rooke, or I should have told him my opinion of him. I sent Mr. Bartley, etc., to him. He and Willmott, after a long absence, returned to say that "perhaps the music would be in the orchestra on Saturday, November 11th!!!" I did not know what to do or say. I lay down for three quarters of an hour, and prayed to God to tranquillize and strengthen my mind. I acted indifferently; was called for—on account of Mr. Phelps, I suppose. Kenney, Wallace, Jerdan, Bartley, and Robertson came into my room. Passed a wretched night.

October 28th.—Went to theatre. Acted Werner to a *wretched, wretched* house as well as I could, but not well. I spoke with Miss Faucit after the play, asked her to play the part in the new drama to *oblige me*, to which she kindly assented, but told me that she suffered much at home for it. When Robertson heard of her acquiescence, he observed that "there was nothing like a little rational conversation," to which I assented. She is a kind, good-hearted girl.

November 1st.—Browning came into my room, Robertson, etc. As this day closes I begin to have doubts of my ability to rally. I fear "it is a hopeless struggle."

November 2nd.—Uneasy and unhappy thoughts. I begin to

despair, but I hope I shall not despond. The hopelessness of the struggle, unaided by the Press, and thwarted by the knavery of one and the indolence of another, begins to weigh upon me. Still, I bate nothing of resolution; I will do all I *ought to do*. I only fear I have already done much more than I should have done. God help me! I murmur at His dispensations sometimes, but I hope and pray He will forgive my ungrateful forgetfulness of His many mercies. Amen! Rehearsed, with much care, *Virginius*. At half-past four tried to snatch a little sleep in my chair. Acted Virginius pretty well considering that I had no time to read it; was called on, and very warmly received by the audience. Forster came into my room. I **got** angry about the Press, which I never ought to do.

November 3rd.—Thought over part of Macbeth before I rose; went to the theatre. Superintended the rehearsal of three acts of *Macbeth*, which was not satisfactorily proceeding. Sat down to my letters and wrote ten, dining on my daily chop. *What am I doing all this for? What is to be my recompense?* Indifference, pity, and, from some very few, respect; I should have thought of this before. I bear up well against the load that is thrown on me, but I cannot long up-bear it.

November 4th.—Went to the theatre. Saw the *Parole of Honour*,[1] which was more than once in jeopardy from bad acting, but was eventually very well received. Thank God! Met the Committee of the Jewish Charity, and discussed with them the subject of letting the theatre. Forster and Wallace were in Catherine's box, Talfourd came behind; Forster told me of the abuse of the newspapers, and that the *Times* had a paragraph directing public attention to the fact that at the Olympic old pieces were produced with the most rigid attention to costume, etc., "which was done at no other theatre."

November 5th.—Much tired in mind and body, I lay late in bed revolving Macbeth, and my own unthankful labours. Why have I done this? What have been my motives? I hoped for good, but certainly I have been either precipitate or far too confiding. I was in low spirits, and a word of praise in the newspapers made me weak and nervous. A Monsieur Lasnes sent up his name—he was the person who first gave me instruction in Italian; he had been in the French Army and served under Napoleon. He was then a handsome, interesting young man; he looked now a sort of person that one would expect to see in the farce of *Victorine*, and smelt strong of drams. He asked me for Wallace's address, and for pecuniary relief. I gave him five

[1] By T. S. Serle.

422

shillings. Read prayers to the family. Read over Macbeth, which I pray to God I may perform successfully. Amen!

November 6th.—Went to rehearsal of *Macbeth*, which kept me fully employed with looking after dresses, scenery, etc., till half-past three o'clock. I had not even time to open the notes on my table, but went to bed for a short hour. Felt rather nervous and wearied, but tried my best to act Macbeth well, and did much of it very well— particularly the scene before the banquet. The whole play was very beautifully put upon the stage, and the audience seemed to appreciate it. I was called for, and very enthusiastically received. I heard of the complete failure of the *mélange* called *Caractacus* at Drury Lane theatre, and took hope and heart from the issues of both experiments. I had drunk much wine, and was very vehement, swearing rather loudly (unwise, ungentlemanly and dangerous passion!) at Mr. Phelps in the fight. Forster, Browning, Bulwer, Wallace and H. Reynolds came into my room. All was congratulation and earnest hope. I went to bed very late, but *could not* sleep all night.

November 7th.—Arose wearied and with headache; went to theatre, when much of the morning was talked away; my spirits and body were equally wearied. Had a long conversation with Mr. Phelps, to whom I sent in order to excuse myself for my last night's violence. He did not take offence at it. *I was very much to blame.* Serle brought more of *Joan of Arc*, which I do not so well like. Found so wretched a house that my spirits sunk again. I fear it is a hopeless cause, or that I have been most unfortunate in my time of taking up its defence.

November 8th.—My spirits were very low, and I could draw no hope from any view of the prospect before me; I resolved, however, to meet its consequences firmly; but I want recruiting, my mind and body are fatigued. Acted Virginius languidly—could not rouse myself. Was called for and went forward. Morton wanted me to defer the opera. I told him I would close the theatre if it was not done; he acquiesced in its performance. Saw Jerdan and Mercer, of the *Globe*. Told them how much I had been disappointed and hurt by the conduct of the Press.

November 9th.—Walked half-way to the theatre, and found a general desertion. Spoke with Marshall and Head and read over the MS. scenes which Serle brought me, with which I was pleased. Went to the Garrick Club, where I looked at the papers, and saw Messrs. Price, Fladgate, Power, to whom I spoke about our engagement, and several others. Came home, Forster called, and took his wine with us. He

423

accompanied me to the theatre, where, to my surprise, I found a very good house.   A note from Miss Faucit, requesting me to release her from the farce on Monday night, with which I complied.

November 10th.—Bartley came to tell me that the Queen had sent to command me Friday night.   I acted Hamlet pretty well.   After the play Sir Harford J. Brydges came round to introduce himself to me; told me that he had known many great men, but never known a greater than myself! *Dii immortales !* What greatness! Mr. Vining sent back the part of Gower in *King Henry V*, which made me very angry. Mr. Hullah insisted on having his name as composer put in the bills; but, after a conversation with me, wished it withdrawn.   Thought of substituting *Marino Faliero* for *The Two Foscari.*

November 11th.—Went to the theatre at night with Catherine to see the new opera of *Barbers of Balsora*, which was so inefficiently acted that I could not sit to see it.   Went to Drury Lane theatre, where I saw the last act of *Caractacus*—such trash; such an exhibition is a disgrace to an English public; its sufferance and stupidity is disgusting. The opera was but moderately successful.   Went with Talfourd and Forster to sup at the Piazza.   Talfourd recounted to me the plot of his new tragedy; parted from Talfourd in the New Road at about one o'clock.

November 12th.—Resolved on advertising no change of price on the occasion of the Queen's visit.   Rose very late, at four o'clock in the afternoon.   Bartley called to inform me of a communication from the Lord Chamberlain's Office, signifying the Queen's command that *Werner* and the *Irish Ambassador* (with Mr. Power from the Adelphi theatre) should be acted on Friday night.   After dinner attended to my accounts.   Wrote to Mr. Martin, Vice-Chamberlain, to Lord Conyngham and to Stanfield.   Marked Serle's *Joan.*   Read prayers to the family.   Began arrangement of *Marino Faliero.*

November 13th.—Went to theatre, and superintended the rehearsal of the new farce of *The Original.*   Received a note from Mr. Martin, the Vice-Chamberlain, which I answered in the strongest terms, putting before him, and whomsoever it might reach, the injury and injustice done to me by foisting Mr. Power upon me.   He shortly afterwards called, and, in discussing the subject, admitted the prejudicial effect that such a partial proceeding would have upon my arrangements.   Forster gave me the papers of the *Age;* and Catherine suggested the retaining Serjeant Wilde,[1] which I will do.

---

[1] Thomas Wilde (1782-1855); afterwards Lord Truro.   Originally an attorney; one of

November 14th.—Thought over, and did what I could to imprint the *character* of King Henry V on my mind—taken thus by surprise as I am with it. Called on Stanfield, and settled with him for the painting of the diorama. Went to the theatre, where I rehearsed *King Henry V.* Saw on the Drury Lane playbills a gross allusion to myself for announcing *Joan of Arc*, which excited a great deal of laughter through the theatre. Transacted business with many persons —occupied the whole morning. Received a note from Mr. Martin that the performances would be, for the command, *Werner* and *Roland for an Oliver*—was much gratified to learn that I was freed from this *embarras.* Sent the two copies of the *Age* newspaper to White and Whitmore for counsel's opinion as to libel. Read *King Henry V.* Acted the part as well as I could; not well, for I was not prepared; and I will do this no more. Heard from Lord Conyngham that he had no hand in recommending Mr. Power, and that it was not easy to alter the first proposal. Understood that there was to be a second attack in the Drury Lane bills to-morrow. Let them be so!

November 15th.—Sent for Jones—Edward's tailor—to measure me for a Court suit—a livery of servility. Came home to dinner. Returned to theatre; answered a very nice note from Dickens. Wrote notes and cards of invitation for Friday. Home—very tired and sleepy. A most delightful letter from Bulwer.

November 16th.—Mr. Martin, Vice-Chamberlain, called to say that the farce commanded was the first act of *Fra Diavolo*, and that " all was right " about the matter lately agitated.

November 17th.—My morning was engrossed by the needful care and arrangements for the evening, preparing for the Queen's reception, the reception of our own visitors, etc., my dresses for the night, etc. Received a multitude of notes, application for admission behind the scenes, which I was obliged to answer as I could. Among the rest, Lord Augustus FitzClarence [1] wrote to request admission. I sent him a card, having understood that he was not the *roué* who frequented Drury Lane. Martin, the Vice-Chamberlain, was most careful in scrutinizing all particulars as to the Queen's box, rooms, etc. I was quite worn out and lay down, desiring no more notes to be given me till the next morning. I could not help thinking, as I sat dressed for Werner, waiting for my call and listening to the acclamations of the

---

the counsel for Queen Caroline at her trial. Afterwards successively Solicitor-General, Attorney-General, Lord Chief Justice of the Common Pleas, and Lord Chancellor.

[1] One of the natural sons of William IV by Mrs. Jordan.

audience on the Queen's arrival, of the folly and impiety of thus pampering and spoiling the mind of one human being, and in the same act debasing those of millions. There was a great tumult arising from the overcrowded state of the pit, a great number were lifted over the boxes in a fainting and exhausted state. Mr. Bartley had leave from the Queen to address the audience, which he did, tendering the price of admission to those who, not having room, might wish to return. When order was restored, the play proceeded. I acted, not to please myself; I could not recover my self-possession. The Queen sent to say she expected to see me as she retired. I dressed myself in full dress and went with Bartley to wait on her as she retired. Thanked Lord Conyngham for his kind attention to my request about Mr. Power. The ladies-in-waiting and the officers, etc., passed through the room, and at length the Queen—a very pretty little girl—came. Lord Conyngham told her who I was. She smiled and bowed, and said : " I am very much obliged to you." Pointed me out to the Duchess of Kent, and bowed repeatedly to me. I went home with Miss Martineau and Catherine, very, very tired.

November 18*th.*—Very late up—much tired—went to the theatre ; on my way continued my curtailment of *Marino Faliero.* Mr. Fisher, Mr. Warde's solicitor, called to announce the fact that the money paid for him was quite gone—that he had not kept to his engagements of paying the small instalments agreed upon, and in consequence could not now appear—could not indeed perform on Monday next. There was no hope. Sent for Mr. Vining, who very meritoriously consented, without murmur, to take the part of Malcolm. Employed myself on arrangements—search for plays—occupied till nearly five; then went to the Garrick Club, where I saw Barham, Murphy, G. Dance, Jerdan. Jerdan and I walked together to the Prince of Wales's tavern, where a party were assembled to dine with Dickens, on the completion of his Pickwick volume. We were detained long for dinner, but the day was interesting. Ainsworth, Forster, Lever, Talfourd, etc., were there. Talfourd proposed Dickens's health in a very good speech, and Dickens replied—under strong emotion—most admirably. Left them directly that ceremony was over. At the theatre saw Mr. Ranger and endeavoured to open a negotiation with him. Miss Faucit wrote to ask me to change the *Parole of Honour* from Wednesday—after the *Bridal*—to Tuesday. I reasoned with her, and she was nearly overcome by my persuasion, but at length I conceded the point.

November 19*th.*—Went to Talfourd's—met Dickens, Forster, Ainsworth, Keating, Hill, etc. Passed rather a heavy day. Gave my opinion injudiciously upon some actors—C. Kemble, etc. Forster informed me that Thackeray had inquired of him to-day the reason why Mr. Price so violently and constantly spoke against me! Told Dickens of darling Nina, when she was told that the Queen had spoken to me on Friday night, having asked me if I told her "to be kind to the poor." The dear child! Just reached home as Letitia was reading prayers to the servants.

November 20*th.*—Went to theatre for the rehearsal of *Macbeth.* Notes and letters. Sloman told me that Mr. Stanfield had heard I was going to close, and wished him, if he had not begun the diorama, not to do so. Stanfield called, as he said, to speak to me, and I told him what I had heard. He admitted it, but was glad to hear it was false. We sent for Bradwell, and Stanfield arranged with him about the engagement of an assistant. Mr. Phelps refused the part of Exeter— is afraid to play the first and averse to take the second characters. I told Bartley to tell him I should shut the theatre if he did not play it.

November 21*st.*—Employed through the day in cutting *Coriolanus.* Sent a note to Miss Faucit. Thinking of *Wonder* and other plays. Miss F—— came to my room and spoke with me about it. She seemed very happy, and was to return after the farce. In the meantime spoke with Miss Taylor about Flora in the *Wonder*, thinking to flatter her into acquiescence. It really annoyed me that Miss Taylor refused to accommodate me, and, with the return of the house, I scarcely see what is to be done. I will do all I can, and then—God help me! Amen! Resolved on some plays for the ensuing week.

November 22*nd.*—At the theatre I found another amusing paragraph in the Drury Lane bills, noticing "the disgraceful scenes that occurred elsewhere." The ludicrous abuse of this wretched ass quite entertains me—it assisted my spirits.

November 24*th.*—Acted Werner pretty well. Note, enclosing a squib—the notice of a publication, the Life of "J. Forster, the butcher-boy," [1] etc., a piece of ribaldry of Mr. Bunn's or Westmacott's—was directed to "Mr. Macready," another to "George Bartley, Esq."! Advised Forster as to his conduct with regard to the dirty fellows he has to deal with him. Lord Augustus FitzClarence thanked me again for my civility to him.

November 25*th.*—Was going to dine at the Garrick Club, but

[1] In reference to what was generally believed to have been Forster's parentage.

reflecting that I might take cold or get into heat with some of the low and vulgar frequenters of the place, I ordered my chop, etc., in my room; attended to business with Head, Griffiths, etc. Received a note from Mrs. Norton.

November 27th.—Found another more abusive article in yesterday's *Age*, which I sent to White and Whitmore. Talfourd and Forster came into my room. We spoke of the *Age*, and Talfourd seemed to imply that it was very uncertain whether I could obtain redress, but that he (who had merely been insulted) would proceed criminally against the editor, and punish him. I was much excited, and had drunk some wine, and was a good deal irritated by these heartless and selfish observations, and I broke out into vehement declamation against the fraud of law terming itself a means of justice. I was quite carried away by my indignant feelings.

November 28th.—The play had scarcely begun when Robertson rushed down to tell me that some persons in Mr. Almond's box were making a disturbance, and had been twice called to by the pit. I hastened up to the box, and entering it said: "I understand this box is taken by a person of the name of Almond; the conduct of the persons here has twice attracted the notice of the audience. I beg you to understand that if any similar outrage occurs I shall hold Mr. Almond responsible. My name is Mr. Macready." *Joan of Arc* succeeded entirely. Passed a disturbed night.

November 30th.—The new opera was rehearsed, with which I was very much dissatisfied. The composer is a man of genius, obstinate on his own theories, and the writer is a conceited fool. Mr. Moore, nephew of Moore in Bond Street, and another person whose name I did not catch, called to make inquiry or ask explanation of the circumstances about the private box on Tuesday. The gentlemen said that the ladies had stated Mr. Macready to have behaved in a very ungentlemanly manner. I observed: "You say that ladies said so, and therefore I can only answer they labour under a complete mistake; if you tell me any gentleman says so I will give the assertion the flattest, most direct and grossest contradiction. I was informed by Mr. Robertson, etc. I went into the box and said exactly the words repeated Tuesday, November 28th. If this is ungentlemanly I cannot deny it, but I must learn the language of a gentleman if it be so. Had I acted as I could have done, I might have ordered the police officer on the stairs to have turned them out." They stated that Robertson had said 'Mr. Almond was a blackguard.' I said I did

428

not know that, but that I was sure he said so under strong irritation, and would be willing to admit as much, which he did.   One of them observed that if I had not supposed the party actuated by malicious feelings towards the interests of the theatre, I probably would have dealt more ceremoniously with them; I said no doubt I should have done so.   This seemed quite to satisfy them, and they left us well-pleased.   Captain Polhill gave me positive information that Bunn was the writer of the libels in the *Age*.

December 2nd.—Went to theatre, where I sat for some time revolving the hopeless condition of the concern.   I strove to calm my spirits, and devise the best means of meeting and winding up the losses that appear hanging over me.   I could not rally, my heart had quite sank within me.

December 5th.—Dined with Forster, with whom I met Procter. Went to Drury Lane, where I understood the Queen came.   Went over to Covent Garden, where I was rejoiced to see a very respectable house.

December 6th.—Mr. Martin called to announce the Queen's intention of coming to-morrow night, and went with me to look at her box.

December 7th.—Whitmore called about the *Age* prosecution.   He told me that the presumption was Mr. Westmacott would do battle; also mentioned that from a false registry the proprietors of the *Age* were liable to penalties of £50 for every publication under such registration.   Whitmore decided on issuing the writ to-morrow either against Bunn or Westmacott as it might seem best.   Mr. Haynes, editor of the *Morning Herald*, called and I had a long explanation with him; he admitted that the article of which I complained was unjustifiable, but suggested the policy of avoiding any further notice of it, to which I acceded, and he promised that he would do his utmost to alter the tone of the criticisms for the future.   Went to the theatre.   The Queen had just arrived.

December 8th.—Rose later than I should have done.   Looked over the debate, and was amused with the farcical failure of B. Disraeli.[1] A note from Lane, wishing me to act *Adrastus*.   Continued the arrangement of *Marino Faliero*.   Went to look at Drury Lane—a better house than I could have wished to have seen.   Read Miss Mitford's play of *Otto of Wittelsbach*, which is too gloomy and heavy to be worth acting.

[1] This was Disraeli's memorable maiden speech; though it was generally considered a fiasco, Sheil perceived beneath its extravagance and absurdities qualities that indicated oratorical capacity.

December 9th.—Again later in rising, which is attributable to the late *gossip* of the previous nights. Looked over the debates in the newspapers. Went to the theatre; at the box-office saw Robertson and Bartley, who both had very long faces, and seemed intent on some prophetic moans; but I only put on a more cheerful face when Robertson told me, despite the receipt of the week which has not been bad, that he must draw upon me; here I accuse him for not correctly representing the probable expenses. I do feel that I have been decoyed into this business, but I will bear myself well through it. Suggested to Messrs. Young, Bradwell, and Willmott the expediency of having the interior of Guildhall, and changing it to the view of Ludgate Hill illuminated. My object is to meet the Drury Lane effort, and in a different way. I think it is well conceived. Went to hear the pantomime read. Robertson came to my room. Power called and brought his piece of *Quentin Durward*, taking away with him Kenney's comedy. He spoke very confidently of the final success of my management, but then he has an interest in its success. Forster took with him Miss Mitford's play of *Otto*. Mr. Ebers called, wishing me to admit parties of eight into the private boxes charged £1 11*s.* 6*d.*—which I positively refused to do. I am resolved to stand or fall upon the principle with which I have set out. Forster having told me that Bulwer's dinner was put off, I resolved on devoting the evening to *Marino Faliero*, to which I therefore applied myself, and with occasional interruptions finally arranged.

December 10th.—Again late in bed. Looked at the newspapers. When I came down I read Mr. Lover's farce, which seems to me very indifferent. Devoted the whole of the rest of the day to the reading over and further compression of *Marino Faliero*, of which I now begin to entertain great fears. Sat with my children after dinner. Read over *Marino Faliero* to Letitia and part to Catherine, but it did not seem to interest them much. Read prayers to the family.

December 12th.—Looked at the play of the *Tempest*, with a view to its adaptation. Went to the theatre, was kept talking on business the whole morning. Mr. Hughes, the author of *John of Albi*, brought me a letter from Sheil to request my attention to him; he read me part of a poem on the stage, which I could have spared. Spoke to Mr. Thomas and Rodwell about the choruses of last night, and Mr. Leffler, who sang so badly. Sent for Mr. Leffler and spoke to him. Sent to Mr. Rooke and asked him to teach Mr. Leffler the music of *Amélie*, which he promised to do. Stanfield wished his diorama to be moved earlier in the pantomime—a palaver about that! Wrote many notes. Read over the greater part of Mr. Power's *Quentin Durward*. Very much dissatisfied with the return of the house, which looked nearly as good as last night. Miss Martineau was in our box. Note from Dickens with his volume of *Pickwick*.

December 13th.—Went to the theatre. Met Messrs. Bartley and Robertson in my room; was displeased with the former for a note he had written to Mr. Holt about his piece. Not very well pleased with the latter about the house last night. He is scarcely ever at his post—never watching the proceedings of the doorkeepers, which I take it to be his business to do; was dissatisfied with the return, and not assured by the account he gave me. He is a very inefficient officer. Wrote to Bowes about the *Domino Noir*, and to Dickens, thanking him for his present of the *Pickwick Papers*. Power called; spoke to him about his piece. Spoke with Stanfield about his diorama, and satisfied him on the subject of its place in the pantomime. Went over the play of the *Tempest*. Jerdan called in and spoke about the progress we were making in public opinion.

December 14th.—At the theatre, attended to business; watched part of the pantomime, and made some little alterations in the dialogue. Received the estimate of the gas alteration, which, though very expensive, I ordered, in justice, as I thought, to Stanfield and the work he is engaged on for me. Saw Stanfield, and told him I would have it, and accordingly ordered it. Received a letter from Calcraft by a Mr. Wakemore, heard that his (C.'s) houses were *crowded!* Thought he might have paid me my money due. Saw Sir G. Smart [1] about the concert, at which Phillips is engaged, and Wilson and Miss Shirreff have engaged themselves to sing on Wednesday next; he kindly undertook to do his utmost to make an arrangement that should not stop our opera. Cast several plays; Miss Faucit called in—looked not well, and seemed not well. Forster came in, and told me that Mr. Evans, Mr. Bunn's solicitor, had commenced an action against the *Examiner* for libel. I did not see his object in telling me this. I did not like his manner, it was not manly, nor direct. I believe he has in some way, not yet declared, committed himself. He *said* he called to put me on my guard against Friswell, Polhill's solicitor, and said something which I did not thoroughly understand, about his having promised Molloy, Westmacott's solicitor, not to attack Mr. Bunn personally, if the *Age* attacks on Talfourd were discontinued.

[1] Sir George Thomas Smart (1776–1867); the eminent musical director and composer.

I do not understand this. *There is more under it.* Called on Whitmore; saw him and Friswell's evidence; he said all was right. Altered some of the pantomime dialogue.

December 15th.—Went to the theatre, where I wrote a note to White and Whitmore, pointing out what I thought was evidence of Mr. Bunn's inculpation with the two first libels of the *Age*. Proceeded to the Garrick Club, to search the *Morning Herald* for the paragraph, but could not find it. Asked Winston to send me up the files of the *Age;* Winston told me that they talked in the Club of a report, which these wretches had set about, of a prosecution against Talfourd, Forster, Polhill and myself ! ! !—for a conspiracy to put down the *Age!* I clearly see that they are desperate. Returned to the theatre, where I saw Sir George and Lady Smart. Sir George had settled the matter of Toulmin's concert for me, and our opera continues unimpeded. Forster and Dickens called, and confirmed what I had heard of Talfourd's egregious folly and weakness regarding the *Age* newspaper.

December 16th.—Went to the theatre, where I attended to business, looking out for plays, etc., after Christmas. Had the account from Robertson, which I looked over, and found myself about £2200 to make up, to bring in even balance; profit therefore is beyond all hope !

December 17th.—Rose late; looked at the newspapers, and afterwards gave my attention for some time to my accounts. More comfortable in the returning health of my darling Nina. These dear children are the solace of my fretted and repining spirit. God bless them ! Wallace said that Forster was harsh and unjust on Forrest last year. I was very sorry to hear this, of which I could not judge—never having seen him; but Forster has not a *cool* judgment, and is certainly, though an ardent, yet a dangerous friend and ally. Read over *Macbeth,* in which I find myself much abroad. The cares of management are distracting me from ruminating upon my art. My spirits very low, and my mind occupied with pondering on the sacrifice I have made, and the false step I have taken in embarking my property on this desperate enterprise. Am I not punished enough? Read prayers to the family. God help me !

December 18th.—Mr. Martin, the Vice-Chamberlain, called to report to me the Queen's intention of visiting the theatre this evening. Sent for Bartley, Bradwell, etc., and gave directions for her reception. Sent letters to the papers informing them of the circumstance. Lay down on bed, and tried to think of *Macbeth,* but it would not rest in my mind. Received letters—one from White and Whitmore with

Richards's opinion on the case *v.* Bunn and Westmacott, in which he seems averse to proceeding with the action. Acted Macbeth tolerably well, particularly the latter part of the play. Was called for, but her Majesty took precedence, and I hid my diminished head. Forster and Wallace came into my room.

December 19th.—Awoke at five o'clock much disturbed by the thought which crossed me, that possibly the subject of the pantomime might be considered indelicate from the indecent character of the farce acted at Drury Lane and the Haymarket last night; lay thinking upon it, until at a late hour I fell asleep. Rose late, and looked at the papers; the *Times* gave us no notice, the *Herald* a very cold one coupled with a very impertinent one on the Drury Lane performance. Are not these newspaper reporters wretches? Is it easy to imagine men made up of viler materials? Answered a note from Lane; went to theatre. Expressed my apprehensions about the possible attempt to fix the character of indecency on our story, and recommended a slight alteration in its conduct, to which they agreed, Mr. Young asking me to do it for him. Gave Mr. Bartley directions. Bartley told me that Lord Conyngham had sent to say that the Queen was very much pleased with the last evening's entertainment.

December 20th.—Note from Bulwer, informing me of his having begun a play and of his confidence in its success. Wrote notes. Came home in very low spirits; found my darling children ill, and my beloved Willie labouring under a nervous disorder, the effect of the shock he received in his dream a few nights since, which quite strikes his spirits. He makes me very unhappy, the blessed fellow! Reluctant to go to work—spirits low—the elasticity of my mind impaired.

December 21st.—Asked Stanfield what I was to give him for his labour, name and talent. I could not induce him to name his price. Superintended the rehearsal of the opening of the pantomime, and attended to various matters appertaining to it.

December 22nd.—Heard a rumour that Mr. C. Kean was not about to complete his engagement with Drury Lane in consequence of his approaching marriage with Miss Burdett; [1] the news appeared strange and too good to be true. Spoke to Stanfield, who was much gratified with what I had said of him and his kindness to me in the playbill. Received the *True Sun* of this evening, in which there was a leading article relating to myself, that from the warmth of its eulogy and its enthusiasm quite affected me.

---

[1] An absurd *canard*, if the allusion is to Miss Burdett-Coutts.

433

December 23rd.—Went to the theatre for an early rehearsal of the pantomime. Letters, notes and business. There was a paragraph in the Drury Lane playbill of the very lowest order, reflecting upon that which was inserted in yesterday's Covent Garden bill respecting Stanfield. Robertson drew on me for another £100. I am now at the verge of my managerial fate; whether I am to sink disastrously, or to spring aloft to better fortune is on the event of little more than one hour. God will ordain my course for the best. Would I could prevent my ignorant heart from fretting and murmuring at the adverse circumstances that seem to gather round me! I trust I shall bear myself through the worst of them in a manly and dignified manner. Forster called in at the theatre. My spirits are *very low*—very much depressed indeed.

December 24th.—Saw the newspapers, and in them some attacks upon me—one most impudent one in the *Satirist*, which irritated me, as did a passage by that foolish man Collier—to whom I wrote a very civil request that he would say what he had written. Mr. Lover called—not a very love-able person, a man to ask to parties for amusement's sake, but nothing more. Mr. W. Kennedy called, and made a visitation. After he had left me I read part of his tragedy, the *Siege of Antwerp*—it is clever, but not, I think, sufficiently so for representation. Went about seven o'clock to the theatre, where I remained during the working of Stanfield's diorama, and Bradwell's last scene until a quarter past two o'clock. My expectations were greatly raised as to the effect of Bradwell's scene, in which I was *totally disappointed*, when it was all put together. It was quite a failure. Went home, walking part of the way with Bartley in very low spirits.

December 25th.—Haunted by the thought of the pantomime, which disturbed the little time allowed me for sleep. Went to the theatre to mention a plan for extricating us from the dilemma of the last scene and found Bradwell busy, and confiding in the measures then in progress. Spoke with Stanfield and Marshall. Saw Robertson and Bartley, told them of my intention to resign if we approached the sum total I had agreed to stake. Spoke to Wallace upon the *Satirist* libel and the *Figaro*. He recommended the terms of a letter to the *Satirist*, which I took down.

December 26th.—Dearest Nina's birthday. Went to the theatre, where all was in a state of anxious preparation for "the great work," the pantomime. Rehearsed Lord Hastings; watched the rehearsal of the pantomime,[1] which I could not leave, for had I gone to my own room I could not have given my attention to my own character, my thoughts would have been with the success of the pantomime. Rehearsing on the stage, which was not over till ten minutes past five. Dickens, Cattermole, and Forster sat it through. They all mentioned their intention of quitting the Garrick Club. Forster wished all to go *in a body*, which I protested against, as indicating a spirit not exactly according with the feelings of a gentleman. Sent a letter written by Robertson to the editor of the *Satirist*, whose orders, with those of the *News* and *Figaro*, I struck off the Free List. Acted Lord Hastings pretty well, taking the circumstances into consideration. Saw Kemble and Jerdan on the stage to-night. The pantomime succeeded completely, for which I feel most gratified.

December 27th.—Saw the newspapers, which were, I thought, reluctant admissions of success at Covent Garden. Have I not cause to loathe the name of a newspaper? Sent invitations to Talfourd, Dickens, and Forster, and asked Stanfield to dine with me to-morrow.

December 28th.—Saw Forster and told him of Fitzgerald's dining with us. Forster asked me if he ought to stay away, and I said I thought not. He agreed to come. Received *Le Domino Noir*. Received a note and play of the *Fraudulent Marriage* from Bulwer. Returned home to a party—Wallace, the Talfourds, Miss Ely, Dickens!—Fitzgeralds, Forster, Cattermole, Stanfield. Asked Fitzgerald to allow me to say to Forster that "he regretted the occurrence"; after some demur he consented. I said this to Forster, who did not receive it as he should have done. All the party went to the theatre. Read Bulwer's play.

December 29th.—Acted Werner very indifferently. I am falling off in my art through my attention to the management. I must reform it altogether.

December 30th.—O'Hanlon called before I went out, and talked among other things of my proceedings against that wretched piece of villainy, Mr. Bunn. I sicken at the man's name. He regretted the

---

[1] *Harlequin and Peeping Tom of Coventry.* It was illustrated by a moving diorama, painted by Stanfield, of scenes from the north of Italy, the Alps, Germany, and France, including the Col du Bon Homme by moonlight, and concluding with the British Channel. In the playbills Macready expressed his obligations to Stanfield, stating that "at a sacrifice, and in a manner the most liberal and kind, he had for a short period laid aside his easel to present the manager with his last work, in a department of art so conspicuously advanced by him, as a mark of the interest he feels in the success of the cause which this theatre labours to support" (*note by Sir F. Pollock*).

prosecution. I do also, under the feeling that law is so far removed from justice. Mr. Pope called; looked at the newspapers. Catherine went in a carriage for Kenney, and brought him here; had a long conversation with him upon *Le Domino Noir*—which I gave him to read, and on which we are to speak to-morrow. Went in Catherine's carriage to the theatre. Attended to business, found a letter from Bowes. Spoke with Robertson and Bartley on business. Mr. Roberts sent me a letter of expostulation about the part of Paris, which was taken from him unwittingly. I sent to him, and spoke to him very kindly about it. Miss Huddart called. I told her her name was altered in the announcements to Warner,[1] and gave her the part of Regan—which she kindly undertook to do. Miss Faucit called, who, I think, is very ill; gave her a box; she seemed disposed to quarrel with Cordelia! This is too bad. Went to the Garrick Club, where I was much concerned to see Thomas Campbell black-balled![2] It was indeed an indignity for such a club to black-ball such a man! Talked with some of the members about enlarging or altering the dining-room to avoid the impertinences of Messrs. P——, etc. Read Bulwer's play—first to myself and afterwards to Catherine and Letitia. They had discovered the author! Note from Bulwer.

December 31st.—The last day of this eventful year has arrived, and in the hasty glance I am able to cast back upon it I see, with occasional starts of industry and effort, much waste of time—much abuse of opportunity—much idle, vain and dissipated conduct. Since my entrance on this unhappy speculation of management, my mind has, if not retrograded, certainly stood still. My care of my blessed children has been surrendered to others. I cannot but regret this and much more—such as the sort of conflict into which I am thrown with that degraded and vile character, whom I loathe to name—as a serious cause of deep regret. I pray God to shield and protect me through the remaining portion of my trying task! Amen! Looked over the newspapers. Forster called. As I went out to call on Bulwer I set him (F——) down in Oxford Street. Talked with Bulwer about his play; he has not settled his fifth act, and I cannot help him. A Dr. Quin,[3] a homœopathic, called and inquired into his state.

[1] Her married name.

[2] He was, nevertheless, decreed worthy of Westminster Abbey; but he had certain idiosyncrasies which would probably have rendered him unpalatable at the Garrick.

[3] Frederick Hervey Foster Quin (1799–1878); M.D., Edinburgh. At one time physician to Prince Leopold afterwards first King of the Belgians; began to practise in London in 1831; regarded in many quarters as a quack; a *persona grata* at Gore House; in later life had many distinguished patients, among them Disraeli; a diner-out and *raconteur*.

1838

London, January 2nd.—Read over part of *King Lear*, and then went to the theatre, where I found a letter from Miss Faucit, returning the part of Cordelia. Mrs. Clifford wished to speak to me, and I found her object was to procure an engagement for her daughter; I seized the opportunity and engaged her. Spoke with Bartley, and wrote to Miss Faucit, sending back the part of Cordelia with a very kind note of remonstrance. Called at the Garrick Club, where I saw Kemble, Fladgate, and Poole, who spoke to me upon the black-balling of Campbell.

January 3rd.—Heard at the box-office that Mr. C. Kean had called there to ask Notter how he did!—to complain that he had lost his voice —through nervousness! and asked Notter if *we did not wish him at the Devil!* The conceit and effrontery of this puppy is really disgusting. Went to the Garrick Club to look at the magazines. Met Mr. C. Dance, and returned his salute very coldly. I do not justify quarrelling with any one, but this man I have been friends with, have conciliated him by all gentlemanly attentions, he has called me his friend, and he has done his utmost to injure me. I cannot keep a semblance of regard for such a person. Received note from Collier with a dramatic piece by Lord F. Egerton, which will not do. Collier excused himself from dining on Saturday; Rooke accepted. Went to theatre. Note from Bulwer, stipulating for a frank opinion, and professing himself ready to begin another play, if I disapproved of this. Note from Miss Faucit, very ungraciously consenting to act Cordelia.

January 4th.—Went to the theatre, where I went on a first rehearsal of *King Lear*. My opinion of the introduction of the Fool is that, like many such terrible contrasts in poetry and painting, in acting representation it will fail of effect; it will either weary and annoy or distract the spectator. I have no hope of it, and think that at the last we shall be obliged to dispense with it. Settled the scenery, which will be very striking. Received the last act of Bulwer's play with a note from him. Read it, and have my apprehensions about it; he writes too hastily, he does not do himself justice. Note from Bartley with account of

437

house, and information that Polhill had challenged all the sub-committee of Drury Lane theatre, all of whom had refused to go out; that Westmacott was to leave the *Age* on Sunday, and that Bunn was to receive £760 for his two shares on Tuesday!! What a mass of filth!

January 5th.—Robertson paid me back a cheque for £965 10*s.*—the money I had advanced. God grant I may be able to keep it! Amen! Attended to business. Speaking to Willmott and Bartley about the part of the Fool in *Lear*, and mentioning my apprehensions that, with Meadows, we should be obliged to omit the part, I described the sort of fragile, hectic, beautiful-faced, half-idiot-looking boy that he should be, and stated my belief that it never could be acted. Bartley observed that a woman should play it. I caught at the idea, and instantly exclaimed: "Miss P. Horton is the very person." I was delighted at the thought. Received notes from Stanfield, declining to name any sum in compensation for his labour. Bulwer called and talked with me about the play. I went over the last act with him. He told me of the works upon his hands; his industry is astonishing! Consulted Robertson and Bartley about Stanfield; mentioned my purpose of sending him £250 and a present of plate, value £50. Robertson thought it liberal; Bartley thought it only what was requisite. Bartley is liberal with others' money, and I was annoyed to think that I might be supposed to undervalue Stanfield's kindness.

January 6th.—Spoke to Miss Faucit, who seems to have taken up a very discontented tone.

January 7th.—Began to read with much attention the play Bulwer had left me yesterday. Talfourd came in, and, after some conversation upon the action against Bunn (which I feel disposed to relinquish from disgust at the mixture of his filthy name with mine), Talfourd took me into the dining-room and told me he had finished his play, and asked me if I would come and dine with him and hear it read this afternoon. I declined it, as I could not judge of it from his reading. He told me that he was quite disappointed in it. Wallace mentioned to me a letter he had written to Lardner in a most gentlemanly tone, expressing his deep concern at having written that harsh article against Bulwer, which was shown to Bulwer. How much more noble is atonement than obstinacy! How positively beautiful it is! Talfourd called again to say that in his ride he had reconsidered his tragedy, and did not feel the despondency about it he had before expressed. I told him I did not pay any regard to what he had said on such a subject. Finished

438

the perusal of Bulwer's play, which I think, considering the time in which it has been planned and written, is really wonderful.

January 8th.—Waited with some impatience until eleven o'clock for the arrival of Bartley and Robertson from Drury Lane; they came with Forster, and gave an account of the reception and performance of Mr. C. Kean. In going over the different points, each one enumerated confirmed me in the opinion I had long since taken up on very good grounds, that this young man has been trading in the part of Hamlet upon my conception and performance. Willmott exclaimed as they detailed the various passages: "Every point is Mr. Macready's." They spoke of it as a dull affair. The papers will, of course, laud it beyond all measure. We must trust in the strength of truth, and the God of truth.

January 9th.—Thought upon King Lear in bed; on coming down, read two of the newspapers upon the début of Mr. C. Kean. They were evidently disposed to give all the praise they could, but in spite of their partiality they could not raise the tone of their commendation sufficiently high to give me any cause of apprehension on the success of our theatre. I hope I do not deceive myself. Went to the theatre; wrote a letter to Stanfield, enclosing a cheque for £300.

January 10th.—Received a paper of the *Figaro* in London, containing a page and a quarter of the most violent abuse and strangest inventions of falsehood about myself. I laughed at it, and enclosed it without notice or comment to Mr. Beckett, St. James's theatre. Called at the Garrick Club to look at some costumes for *Lear;* saw Thackeray, who promised to send me a book on the subject. Coming home read Talfourd's tragedy of the *Athenian Captive.* This was a great disappointment to me; no one could believe it to be by the author of *Ion;* it has nothing of it but its faults of style exaggerated. How am I to tell Talfourd this, I scarcely know. I fear the effect of such a communication, but I will do "all in honour." A letter from Stanfield refusing to accept the £300 I sent him, returning me the cheque I had sent him, and asking for £150. This is one of the few noble instances of disinterested friendly conduct I have met with in my life. God bless him.

January 11th.—Talfourd called to know the fate of his tragedy. I could not deal otherwise than honestly and kindly by him. I told him he should dictate as to its performance; that if he wished it, I would act it, but as a friend I advised him on every account not to do so. It was painful—he was evidently much disappointed. I said I would read

439

it again, and talk with him upon it. I think *he will have it done*—and if he does, it will be a serious calamity to him. I feel sure of it.

January 12th.—Read part of Talfourd's tragedy. Saw some salvers, and chose one for Stanfield. Rested. Acted Werner middlingly. Called for, and very kindly received. Received in a note a slip of paper—to be printed, I suppose, in some Sunday paper—abusing Forster and essaying to turn me into ridicule. A passage from a letter of mine to Mr. C. Kean was referred to.

January 13th.—Looked at the newspapers. Read in the *Literary Gazette* a notice of Mr. C. Kean's performance. It was in a kind tone of praise, seemingly anxious to do him justice. I should think it did so. Came home. Catherine showed me the criticism on Mr. C. Kean in the *Examiner*, which Mr. Forster had carried up here. I was astonished—dejected—and sickened with disgust at the recreant contradiction of his own strongly expressed opinions in my room on Monday night before Bartley, Robertson, etc. This is the man, who to my earnest entreaty last season refused to compromise his character for integrity upon the merits of Mr. Forrest, a stranger and a visitor!— and this is my friend!—and so is Talfourd! Friends!!! Such men have neither the heart, the courage, nor the honesty to be friends. They do not know what the noble and romantic bond means.

January 14th.—Before I had dressed I received a note from Forster, evidently intended to sound my state of feeling upon his criticism, under which I had been suffering much. I answered it as coolly as I could, expressing my surprise and disappointment. Read over the newspaper, and was just about to begin my accounts when Forster called. He said that he could not remain at home, he was so distressed by my note, and he came here to explain it, and to prove to me that it was not likely to be as injurious as I supposed. He was evidently deeply pained and affected by the circumstance, and my displeasure vanished at once. We all talked it over, but his very anxiety to persuade me of its harmlessness only fortified my conviction of its power of mischief. We shall see. I was too hasty in my angry feeling towards him, for I must think his regard for me deep and sincere. Read an act of Talfourd's play, which is *not* good.

January 15th.—Newspapers. The *Times* as usual puffs Drury Lane! Read the two acts of Talfourd's tragedy, which on reconsideration I think positively bad. Went to the theatre, where I attended to business; was detained long by Mr. Gye,[1] who wanted to argue with

---

[1] Frederick Gye the elder (1781–1869); originally a fishmonger; won £30,000 in a

me that I ought to retain his light through the run of the pantomime, which he charged at £1 10s. per night, with no stipulation or statement as to the expense.

January 18th.—Received a querulous note from Talfourd, who seems annoyed at my opinion upon his play, which he says, having been written for the most disinterested purpose of serving the cause I uphold, he cannot consent to let his labour perish, and insists on its performance! How different from Bulwer, who, without giving his name, writes a play for the same ostensible purpose, and desires me not to act it unless I feel confident of its success! Talfourd has relieved me from all thought of obligation by the evidence he has given of seeking to gratify his own vanity *at the expense* of the cause he affects to wish to serve! Thus we deceive ourselves!

January 19th.—Collier called, and I mentioned to him Stanfield's noble conduct, etc. He told me that he had said to a friend of Mr. Kean that his—Mr. K.'s—performance of Hamlet was not half so good as my own, and that the Messieurs of the Garrick Club ascribed Forster's criticism to the effects of influence upon him and of fear! So much for temporizing! Talfourd came into my room, and kept me late; he said he did not mean his note to impugn my motives. Told me of the surprising efforts that had been made by the friends of Mr. C. Kean in Scotland, etc., to induce people—*viz.* from the House of Commons and the Courts of Law—to go to see him!

January 20th.—At home; received a note and the salver, properly inscribed, from Gass. Stanfield, Kenney, Wallace, Cattermole, Forster, Browning, and Robertson dined with us; we spent a cheerful afternoon. Before we went upstairs I expressed to Stanfield how deeply I was indebted for the noble act of friendship he had shown me, and that I had a slight tribute to offer him, on which the record of my gratitude was engraved, though not so deeply as on the more perishable substance of my heart. I gave him the salver, which was admired, and the inscription, as altered by Wallace, was read.

To CHARLES STANFIELD, ESQ., R.A.

In remembrance of the kindness and zeal with which he brought the magic of his pencil and the celebrity of his name to the aid of a discouraged and declining sister art, this humble tribute is presented by his grateful friend,

WILLIAM CHARLES MACREADY.

January 20th, 1838.

---

lottery and embarked on various speculative enterprises, including Vauxhall Gardens; was M.P. for Chippenham from 1826 to 1831.

Stanfield, dear fellow, was quite overcome, but seemed very happy. I was happy in seeing one making him so.

January 23rd.—Received a note from Mr. Capel, the clergyman of Watford, who wanted "to have permission to come behind the scenes in the evening "—a modest request for a clergyman.

January 24th.—Received the account of house, which was, considering all things, not to be complained of ; but with it heard that the Drury Lane house was *very good*. This is news that really disturbs my patience—giving up, as I do, my talent (such as it is), my experience, my mind to the advancement of the interests of this art ; and here is a person quacked into celebrity without one original thought, without anything to constitute superiority, made an attraction ! It is too disgusting.

January 31st.—Saw Fitzgerald in Catherine's box, who told me of an interview with Mr. C. Kean, that I should have thought incredible if not borne out by facts. This young man's egotism and coxcombry amount almost to insanity.

February 1st.—Lady Charlotte Bacon,[1] Lord Oxford's daughter, called, wishing to go on the stage ; she read before me. I dissuaded her from the attempt. She gave me part of her history.

February 2nd.—Miss Martineau called, and sat a short time. Dr. Elliotson called, thought me much better. Wrote to Thomas Moore with cards of admission. Read over *King Lear*. Went to the theatre and acted King Lear pretty well ; was called for, and very enthusiastically received.

February 3rd.—Wrote a long letter to Bartley about Mr. Wilson's refractory declaration respecting his part in the *Domino;* these opera people are enough to turn one sick, and what are they worth, at their very best ? Received a letter from Bulwer with the title of *The Adventurer*,[2] but when I saw it written down I would not consent to it. Received a note from Bartley, from which I learn that he has not attended to my instructions sent this morning ; that Mrs. Glover sent an apology for her non-appearance this evening (the ——— !) ; and that Mr. Anderson was very well received in Felix, which will make him untractable, to a certainty ! A note—rather an impertinent one— from Mr. Manvers about the mistake as to his part in the *Domino*. I wish they were all tied in a sack together ! They worry my heart out.

February 4th.—Read over, in the course of day, Bulwer's play ;

---

[1] Lord Byron's " Ianthe."
[2] Afterwards named *The Lady of Lyons* (*note by Sir F. Pollock*).

a conversation with Forster on its degree of power, and more particularly of the quantity given to the character of Melnotte induced me to give it a more scrutinizing examination. To my surprise and regret, I find that it tapers off after the third act, and that the female character has the strength of the two last acts—*tant pis!* Read prayers to the family.

February 5th.—Acted Macbeth with a care and an energy that I have not done these many nights; and in the intervals of the scenes my heart was almost breaking, to think of the time, toil, and money that I have so heedlessly thrown away on so ungrateful a cause. An empiric like this Mr. C. Kean is paid £40 per night, and followed by crowds; an ignorant and infamous wretch like that disgusting beast is sustained in his system of open pillage on the actors, while all my labours, enterprise, and talent, such as it is, would only lead me and my children to beggary, if my fate now depended on the integrity and intelligence of the newspapers or the taste of the public. There was a report that the Queen was at Drury Lane to-night—another cause of thankfulness. Was asked for and very enthusiastically received. Forster and Robertson brought reports from Drury Lane—the first that C. Kean's Richard was a failure, the last different.

February 6th.—Heard the accounts in the newspapers of Mr. C. Kean's performance, which record it as a triumph; and, coupled with the Queen's presence, will no doubt make it fashionable for many nights to come. It is not possible for me to receive with placidity a blow like this, which, giving power to empiricism and ignorant puffery, prostrates all my hopes of making a permanent asylum in Covent Garden theatre for the drama. The hope is gone, and I have to toil on with the conviction of the uselessness of my efforts. This indignation I suffer from is great, and I could curse the fate that threw me into a sphere of life with violent passions, where these passions are so *cruelly* acted on!

February 9th.—Acted King Lear pretty well; took pains, but was not equal to myself on Wednesday. Bulwer came into my room at the end of the second act. I sent him round to a private box and he returned to me at the end of the play. Expressed himself in very warm terms upon what he styled my " gigantic " performance, talked about the play, with the arrangements for which he seemed well satisfied. In speaking of the Ballot question, he said he would never support Ministers again if they did not leave it an open question. Was called for, and very cordially received by the audience.

February 15th.—Went to an early rehearsal of the new play.

443

Message from the Vice-Chamberlain to say that the Queen was not coming, which I hailed as excellent news. Acted Claude Melnotte in Bulwer's play pretty well; the audience felt it very much, and were carried away by it; the play in the acting was completely successful. Was called for, and leading on Miss Faucit, was well received; gave out the play. Forster, Kenney, Bartley, etc., came into my room.

February 17*th.*—Forster called, spoke against the base conduct of the *Morning Post*, and mentioned his conviction that the play was Bulwer's! I evaded him as well as I could. Read over part of the play, being anxious to play well, as I knew Bulwer would be there. Acted pretty well; was called for, led on Miss Faucit, and was very cordially received. Spoke to Miss Faucit about standing behind me, etc. Bulwer came into my room, and expressed himself much pleased; offered to give his name, whenever I might wish it. Was disappointed in not finding the character of Melnotte more prominent.

February 18*th.*—Saw the newspapers, which I only glanced over— political as well as theatrical matter. I do not feel that our play will be attractive; fearing that it cannot overcome the insidious imputation of disaffection which was inserted in the *Times* newspaper. The indignation and vindictive emotions which those despicable assassins of men's reputations excite in me would alone resolve me to relinquish the management of the theatre, had I no other motives, but in my distressed and disquieted mind I have more than enough to compel me. Bulwer called, and, giving me full power to act on my own judgment, seemed not to wish his name to be published until further experiment of the play's success had been made—until Thursday. I resolved to wait the whole week.

February 21*st.*—Bulwer called; I was preparing to go on the stage, and mentioned his uncertainty about the policy of publishing his name. I told him of the improvement in the prospect of the house, and we agreed that we would wait and see the progress of the night. I acted well. Bulwer came into my room. My dresser was there. I affected surprise at his appearance, and talked of the play for a few minutes, then *in French* told him I had given up the idea of publishing his name to-night, and requested him to wait and observe what I would do. He said: "Then I shall see you again," and went away. I was loudly called for, and said: "Ladies and Gentlemen,—After the very kind reception with which you have honoured this play, I hope I may be permitted to say a few words in regard to some objections which have been urged, and from opinions I am disposed to respect, upon passages

444

that are said to be political. I beg to assure you that, upon the strictest investigation, there are no political allusions that do not grow out of the piece, and are necessarily conducive to the working of the story. Had it been otherwise I am certain the author, whom I have the honour to know, would never have descended to such means to entrap your applause; the licenser would not have permitted it, nor, I believe, will you think that I should have had the bad taste to encourage it. If I may associate such a name with an existing author's, our divine Shakspeare is liable to similar imputations, and I trust I shall receive credit for the assertion of the principle upon which I conduct this theatre—that art and literature have no politics." Saw Bulwer, who left with me *carte-blanche* as to the time and mode of announcing his name.[1]

February 24th.—Saw an attack in the *Times* newspaper on Bulwer and the play, arising from the publication of his name; it was vulgar, virulent, and impotent from its display of malice—such an article as I would *wish* my enemy to write against me.

February 27th.—Forster came into my room, and told me of some very paltry meanness on the part of Talfourd about Bulwer's play, which, he said, perfectly *disgusted* him. What he told me of Mr. and Mrs. Talfourd quite roused my indignation, and, what was worse, made me lose my temper—an unpardonable folly!

March 1st.—A violent love-letter from some person who had seen me in Melnotte. Heard that the Queen had gone again to Drury Lane this evening—that it had been announced in the evening papers. Her patronage of the effort I am making to uphold the drama—to preserve decency behind the curtain—is quite intelligible.

March 3rd.—Acted Claude Melnotte very well. The Queen came in just after the beginning of the last act; was loudly called for and very warmly received. Lord Conyngham wished to see myself or some one. Sent Bartley to him. It was to say that the Queen would come to see the whole play on Tuesday, and wished Bulwer to know it.

March 6th.—Acted Claude Melnotte very well. The Queen came to see the play—no notice was taken of her. Received books of the play, which is dedicated to Talfourd. This is heaping coals of fire on his head with a vengeance! Was called for by the audience, and well received. Forster came into my room.

---

[1] The name of Edward Lytton Bulwer was first announced as that of the author of *The Lady of Lyons* in the Covent Garden playbill of Saturday, February 24, 1838 (*note by Sir F. Pollock.*)

March 8th.—Acted Claude Melnotte middlingly ; was called for by the audience, and well received.   Miss Faucit wished to speak a few words to me—they were, to ask me if she had not " better leave out the line between my two long speeches."   Bulwer came into my room and seemed very much delighted with the success of his play.   He told me of a message he had received from the Queen, full of courteous expressions to him about the play, and wishing him to communicate to me how very much she was delighted with my acting the comedy, the third act, and ,the fifth.   He added that she did not like Miss Faucit.[1]   It was curious to see a man of Bulwer's great mind evidently

---

[1] In later years, after her marriage with Mr., eventually Sir, Theodore Martin, Miss Faucit became a *persona grata* with Queen Victoria, as is shown by the following letter written to Macready not long before his death—

" 31, ONSLOW SQUARE,
" *March 2nd, /*70.

" Will you accept, my very dear friend, my heartiest greetings on your Birthday, with my best wishes that it may find you in better health than when I last heard of you.

" I fear this trying winter has been hard for you to bear—all have suffered more or less— but now we may believe the worst is over and may we all revive and take good heart, and look up hopefully once more !   I have been more delicate than usual—only getting rid of one cold to fall into another.   This has brought me into such low health that neuralgia has seized hold of me, and for the last week I have been writhing in its grasp.   However, all will be well soon, no doubt, and we must leave this exhausting London air as early as possible in the season.

" The Queen honoured us again this winter with an invitation to Osborne for five days. The first time I saw Her Majesty the morning after our arrival, she asked most kindly after your health and said with what great regret she had heard of the loss you had sustained and with what pathetic and tender interest it was all entwined.   H.M. has the most winning way with her !   All who converse with her are soon made her captives.   I am sure this arises from the kindness of her heart.   This makes her remember everything that is kind and gracious and is a right queenly part of her character.   We dined twice at the Queen's own table, where since the Prince's death only a very small number meet daily by H.M.'s special invitation.   I think I told you before that I had often been asked to read to the Queen in the evenings when she retires to her own private drawing-room with only the Princess.   On this occasion I read twice.   On the first evening *Dora* and some of Tennyson's short poems—on the second *Lady Geraldine's Courtship*.   I read usually what I like, but consult with the Princess as to the authors and poets the Queen likes best.   H.M. admires Mrs. Browning immensely.   I had her own private copy to select and read from and found it marked admiringly from beginning to end.   But, oddly, she does not care for Mr. Browning—says she cannot understand him.   I wish the Queen had time to read for herself *The Ring and the Book.*   How she would change her opinion !   What a grand poem it is ! The drawing of even that one character alone—the fine, dear old Pope—would make it immortal.

" Do you remember *who* first put Tennyson into my hand ?   Your remarks upon *Dora* and other of your favourites still remain, and I never read the poems but out of this your gift copy.   This was only one act of your kindness.   I have many others to remind me, if I ever wished to forget, how good you were in putting things before me to help to work upwards !

HELEN FAUCIT

AS PAULINE IN "THE LADY OF LYONS"

From a lithograph by R. J. Lane, R.A.

so much delighted by the praise and compliments of a little girl—because a Queen!

March 12th.—The house was very indifferent; this was a blow. The reputation of this theatre for producing Shaksperian plays ought to have commanded more attention. I give up all hope! Lay down to rest. Acted parts of Coriolanus well; parts not to satisfy myself. Jerdan, Dickens, Bulwer, Blanchard, Forster, came into my room.

March 13th.—Read the newspapers, and in them, excepting always the eloquent writer in the *Morning Chronicle,* found additional cause to regret that I had devoted myself to the ungrateful task of striving to win the opinions of such profligate, ignorant, and bad men. The labour of the two or three past weeks was dismissed by the *Times* in about six lines of the coldest, faintest kind of admission.

March 20th.—Saw the *Times* newspaper, which couples the *Coriolanus* with the *Magic Flute* (!) as to the skill, learning, and taste of its production—pronouncing the acting merely "passable." My spirits were affected by this infamous attempt to injure and depreciate me. A note from that ass, Captain Polhill, about the *entrée* of the stage, which I answered. Acted Claude Melnotte in a middling style; was called for and well received.

March 21st.—Went to the theatre, reading the *Foscari* upon my way. Arrived there, I had to *encounter* Mrs. Glover, who came in the highest tone of offended dignity to complain of the treatment she had received, in my neither having called on her nor sent the money. The fact was, I informed myself of her health through the messages taken by Partridge, and did not think it right to pay her salary, as she had met with her accident in seeking to deceive and defraud me in asking leave to go to Brighton to see her son, when, as it afterwards appeared, she went to Coventry to play. She wished to have her engagement returned to her. I told her I would give the matter consideration, but could not answer her immediately. Next was introduced Mr. Wilson, who persisted in refusing to act in *Amélie*

"I must not weary you longer with all this egotistic talk—especially on a day when you will have so many friends claiming your attention.

"Will you tell dear Mrs. Macready that at her convenience I would ask an account of your health. That it may be a good one I earnestly desire.

"Mr. Martin unites in all kindest wishes and regards and desiring to be remembered to Mrs. Macready.

"I am always, dear Mr. Macready,
"Your very affectionate friend,
"HELEN FAUCIT MARTIN."

447

if at all reduced. I spoke to him with great temper and good-nature, but also with firmness as to my intentions. He, after a long discussion, yielded the point, and all was settled. Read—or tried to read—*The Athenian Captive*, but was obliged to give the two last acts to Serle, who finished it. The opinion was evidently against it. Miss Faucit came to refuse her part. I recommended her, against her will, to write me a note of expostulation, and consent to act the part; which letter I would send to Talfourd.

March 22nd.—Received a letter from Bulwer returning me the cheque for £210, a letter which is a recompense for much ill-requited labour and unpitied suffering; it is an honour to him, and a subject of pride to myself. Acted Claude Melnotte very well—though the audience were cold; was called for, and very warmly received.

March 23rd.—Looked at the newspapers, in which I read an advertisement for a dinner to Mr. C. Kean, to present him with a piece of plate, Lord Morpeth in the chair! This is to take place in the saloon of Drury Lane theatre (a fitting place for such an exhibition) on the 30th inst. How long is the intelligence of this country to be insulted by his quackeries? I was not angry, but really the stolidity of the many, and the knavery of the few, make it difficult to keep one's patience.

March 25th.—Looked at the *Examiner*. The other papers that I heard of only irritated, sickened, and disgusted me, showing me what are the judges to whom I have to appeal, and making me impatient of my own quixotism, that has led me into the sacrifice I have made; it will soon, however, be over, and let the work of gulling and gullibility go on. I am sick—sick of it all. Forster called and, staying dinner, read a very interesting letter from Savage Landor.

March 27th.—A pretty girl, with a strong lisp, came to present herself as a would-be Thespian. I thought she had mistaken her vocation and seemed much better adapted for a Cyprian. I did not, however, tell her so. Acted Claude Melnotte pretty well; was called for and warmly received by the audience. Some person, a lady, I fancy, sent me a laurel chaplet; I do not see the exact meaning of the anonymous affair. Wallace came into my room, and told me that he had seen Mr. C. Kean in Hamlet, and Sir Giles Overreach, and in the last act of *King Richard*—that " he had nothing in him," that " he could not stand." This is an authority more convincing than any I have yet heard. Faraday sent me a note with his pamphlet on electricity.

March 30th.—Received a letter from Talfourd, enclosing a note from Miss Faucit. Jerdan called in answer to my note of yesterday; I told him the object of my note that I thought Bulwer's behaviour should be known, and that he might be happy in the opportunity of giving publicity to it.

March 31st.—Read in the *Literary Gazette* Jerdan's report of Bulwer's noble conduct to me; in the *Morning Herald* the report of the dinner to Mr. C. Kean and the plate presented to him; at which ceremony the credit of having restored the national drama was given by Lord Clanricarde [1] and the *Morning Herald* to Mr. C. Kean; and the wretched creature, Mr. Bunn, took his revenge for the chastisement he received by asserting that the reason he had hitherto not laid out money on Shakspeare was because till now he had not been able to find an artist capable of acting his characters. It is well that such a wretch should talk thus; truth even in degree would misbecome him.

April 1st.—Looked at the newspapers; was disgusted (what wonder at a newspaper?) with the writer in *John Bull*, who seems now *trimming* to Mr. C. Kean, whom he has tried to stamp with the impress of mediocrity; he also writes ignorantly on the subject of Rome in two instances—one the site of the temples, the other the habits of the slaves. Wallace called; told us that in consequence of a reflection cast upon him and his work on the History of England, he had sent a retorting letter to Lord Mahon,[2] who had (as he wished) sent a message to him by a Mr. Ashley; that S. French, M.P., was his (W.'s) friend, and that after some negotiation, it was agreed that the letters on both sides should be withdrawn, Lord Mahon undertaking in writing to give a satisfactory explanation and retraction in the House of Commons.

April 5th.—At home heard of the death of poor Miss Stackpoole, who taught dear Nina music. I had known her slightly in affluence, but did not know the degree of poverty to which she had been reduced. My heart bled to hear of what she had endured. And to see the success of cant and roguery in this world. My God! My God!

---

[1] The first Marquis, so created owing to the influence of Canning, whose only daughter he married. He held office under Lord Palmerston, but the revelations of a *cause célèbre* in which he was indirectly concerned terminated his political career.

[2] Philip Henry Stanhope (1805–1875); afterwards fifth Earl Stanhope, the well-known historian. The incident is noteworthy as being one of the few instances in which an adverse criticism gave rise to an interchange of hostile messages. Lord Mahon, one of the mildest and most amiable of men, was the last person willingly to give offence; but in those days affairs of honour were still settled in the field, and Wallace's " retorting letter " was doubtless of a nature that could not be passed over.

April 6th.—Rose, rather tired, after a bad night. My night was disturbed by angry and passionate thoughts. How strongly returned upon me the line I had been repeating—"Fellest foes, whose passions and whose plots have broke their sleep to take the one the other." My ill-conditioned nature, my ill-disciplined mind is a constant cause of self-infliction. God send that I may so instruct my blessed children as to save them the loss of quiet and of time that my evil propensities induce! Amen!

April 7th.—Acted Foscari very well. Was very warmly received on my appearance; was called for at the end of the tragedy and received by the whole house standing up and waving handkerchiefs with great enthusiasm. Dickens, Forster, Procter, Browning, Talfourd, etc., came into my room. Jerdan came also into my room and talked with me about the Garrick Club, which he wished me not to leave. The operetta of *Windsor Castle* was in active process of damnation as I left the theatre. Note from Mrs. C. Buller, wishing me to go to her on Wednesday.

April 14th.—Thackeray came to the evening rehearsal and told me that he had written the criticism on Macbeth in the *Times*, but that much of it had been cut out [1]—that in what he wrote of Bulwer every word of praise was omitted. How sick I am of that scoundrel paper! Attended the night rehearsal, which reduced me to despair; it will be almost a miracle if the piece goes through. The painter has behaved in a very scandalous manner. At the last moment half-past twelve—when all was over—settled on an alteration of the last scene. Left the theatre at one.

April 16th.—Went to the theatre, where I was engaged incessantly the whole day with the superintendence of the Easter piece. The labour was oppressive. Here am I sacrificing myself, and still I must ask, for what—for whom? At a quarter past four I lay down to rest until five o'clock. Notes from various persons. Acted Macbeth in an odious style; was called for and well received by the audience. Spoke to Miss Taylor about her name being in the Haymarket bills. She said she thought she had been very ill-used. I told her that I heard her say so without any self-reproach. The afterpiece,[2] to which

---

[1] Thackeray had a similar experience with an article contributed by him to the *Edinburgh Review*, and protested against the curtailment in a humorous letter, which appears in *The Correspondence* of Macvey Napier, at that time editor of the *Review*.

[2] *Sindbad, the Sailor ; or, the Valley of Diamonds.* The pieces performed in this week were : *Macbeth, The Lady of Lyons, The Two Foscari, Coriolanus, The Hypocrite, High Life Below Stairs,* and the opera of *Amélie ;* and this is a fair sample of the variety of per-

I carefully attended, was not over until nearly half-past twelve; reached home at one.

April 17th.—H. Smith called, and told me, among other things, that he had received a note from Mrs. Leigh,[1] which he showed me. In it she said "that she had not been able to go, and only could afford to send two to bring her the news of Foscari's success." Sent for Mrs. Humby (whom Mr. Webster announced in his bills to play this evening) and desired her to give Mr. Webster notice that he was not authorized to put her name in the bills without permission from Covent Garden. She assented most cheerfully, and asked me to write her a copy of the note. Looked over *Morning Chronicle.* Read over Claude Melnotte. Acted the part very well; was called for by the audience and very warmly received.

April 18th.—Spoke with Willmott and Marshall about the alteration of *Sindbad;* directions were given about it. Talking with Serle, we entered into a discussion of the practicability of carrying on the theatre next year; Bartley and Robertson came in and participated in the conversation. Much as I lament to see the work I have done fall uselessly into nothing, I do not feel that I can with propriety continue in the direction of the theatre. Read as hard as I could the part of Foscari. Acted it indifferently, for want of preparation; was called for and well received by the audience. Miss Faucit came to my room to speak to me about her Benefit.

April 19th.—Went to the theatre; made arrangements for closing the house on the 16th of May—which I shall do unless some unlooked-for turn of fortune should warrant me in keeping it open longer.

April 20th.—Gave the evening to the study of Thoas,[2] a bitter drug. Account from the theatre most wretched, £55. So that this at least tells us the value of *Coriolanus,* and even the *Foscari.*

April 21st.—Saw the papers, and went to the theatre, where I was startled at learning that there was only just enough cash to meet the day's demands; and this included the remainder of my Benefit. The prospect is fearful. I sent for Willmott, and immediately made arrangements to dismiss *Sindbad* from the bills, and reduce every expense. Went to the Garrick Club, where I saw White, Collier, etc. In the Committee I put in a white ball to Lord de Tabley,

---

formances given under Macready's management, himself playing in four of them (*note by Sir F. Pollock*).

[1] Byron's sister, Augusta.
[2] In Talfourd's *Athenian Captive* (*note by Sir F. Pollock*).

but did not ballot for the friends of Messrs. Oyle, Evans, and Bacon. They were elected, and I requested Winston to take my name off the books, ' knowing nothing of the two latter persons, except that they were the intimate associates of the greatest scoundrel and blackguard I know (Mr. Bunn), I did not choose to meet the society of their recommendation; that if hereafter the Club should undergo re-organization I should be very happy to return to it.' Stanfield motioned me to return; this was strange, as he was most resolute to leave the Club!— but men are very uncertain. On consideration I regret I did not leave the Club without any notice of these people. Walked home and in the evening learned second act of Thoas. Oh, what a life!

April 22nd.—Looked at the newspapers before I went to work. Very uncomfortable in my mind from apprehension of the evil consequences of my precipitate—at least ill-considered—splenetic and ill-tempered—(I do not well know how to characterize it)—ill-judged proceeding yesterday at the Garrick Club. I felt that it merited a return of punishment upon me, and was consequently very uneasy. I thought if I escaped trouble and annoyance upon it, that I would be more circumspect in future. Gave the whole day to learning the words of Thoas, which I find a more difficult task than any of the same kind I have ever in my life had to encounter; laboured at it, but it escaped me, after I had gained the power of repeating it. It is so overloaded, and so roundabout the subject. Beazley called from the Committee of the Garrick Club to say how very sorry they all were at my resignation, which they would not accept; that they hoped I would not persist in my intention, and that it was their wish that things should be comfortable, etc., all in a very kind and complimentary strain. I explained to him my motives of action, and that I did not wish either to injure the Club, nor the feelings of those to be elected, but that I did not like the society of Mr. Bunn's friends' friends, etc. As, however, they complimented me by asking me to return, I could in courtesy do no less.[1] Forster called again from Talfourd, to ask if he might invite his friends to supper. I was obliged to say *Yes*. Reflecting afterwards upon the *consequences of failure* to him, I resolved to do my best in *arranging the play* without consulting him. Forster came again and brought me *carte blanche*. I set to work and worked away.

[1] Macready adds in a footnote: " Forster was very much annoyed at my assent to the request of the Committee of the Garrick Club to return—and yet would have continued a member of the whole year, although anxious to induce me to leave it ! "

452

April 23rd.—Rose early, and applied to the study of Thoas. Received a note of kind expostulation from Jerdan about the affair of the Garrick Club—which I received as it was intended, and answered in the same tone.   Wrote a note to Forster, requesting him to call at the theatre about the cutting of Talfourd's play.   Went to the theatre, where I rehearsed *The Athenian Captive.*   Forster and Dickens called at the theatre, and I submitted to them the proposed omission of two scenes.

April 24th.—Heard to my great disgust from Forster that Mr. Webster is actually a member of the Garrick Club ! ! !   This puts the seal upon the door.   I will not have anything more to do with it.[1]

April 26th.—Rehearsed *The Athenian Captive,* in which I find no effect for my character.   Arranged business with Head, Marshall, etc. Talfourd called.   I told him that my part had no effect in it, that the play lay upon Mrs. Warner and Mr. Anderson.   Willmott called with a note from Mr. Warner informing Bartley of Mrs. Warner's sudden indisposition (her labour having come unexpectedly upon her).   Mrs. Clifford had Volumnia sent to her and we talked over the business of the ensuing week, deciding on closing the theatre Saturday night. Forster came *in great fuss* about the postponement of *The Athenian Captive,* and busying himself very much, set off to find Talfourd and apprise him of the disappointment.   Acted Coriolanus pretty well. Talfourd, Dickens, and Forster came and debated on what was to be done.   Talfourd who had come from Lord Lansdowne's dinner party, went up with Forster, etc., to see Miss H. Faucit and ask her to act the part.   She entertained the subject, but could give no answer till the morrow.

April 27th.—Sent Partridge up to Miss Faucit for her answer. She very soon afterwards arrived, and agreed to play Ismene in *The Athenian Captive,* but just before her entrance a note came from Mrs. Talfourd, written in a less courteous strain than I would write to any servant, or poor trades-person—it is an outrage on good breeding and decency which I never would have permitted a wife or sister of mine to have been guilty of—it was *shocking.*   I sent it to Forster, from whom I had just received a note of inquiry, and detained Miss Faucit, that I might tell her what she was to do.   Mrs. Talfourd's note was to the effect of declining Miss Faucit's performance of Ismene, which Talfourd had last night requested her to perform !   I had sent Bartley in quest of Talfourd to Westminster Hall, to learn

---

[1] Macready had for some time been on bad terms with Webster, against whose character there was nothing to disqualify him for membership of the Club.

from *him* distinctly whether the play was or was not to be acted. Bartley had been calling on Mrs. Talfourd, and described her in a state of excitement little short of frenzy. I fear he has done no good, if he has not done actual mischief. Forster and Dickens came, the former loudly indignant at Talfourd's weakness, and at being made, as he termed it, such an ass of by Talfourd. They sat long waiting for Bartley's return, who came unsuccessfully back, and whom I again despatched to Talfourd's chambers. Dickens told me one thing that pained me much—for human nature, as well as for the individual. I had mentioned to him Mrs. Talfourd's visit here (after her *very cold* reception at her own house of Catherine and Letitia) and her extravagant tone of cordiality. He said : "Yes, I saw her after, and she told me she was ' quite *fatigued* with *over-acting*.' " This is about as bad an instance of duplicity and bad feeling as I ever heard of in friendly social intercourse. Bartley at length arrived with Talfourd— and a more melancholy, pitiable sight I think I never saw than the poor dejected fellow. I truly pitied him. He was depressed almost to tears ; I got Willmott out of the room, as I thought he might wish to say something and I did not desire W—— to witness the pain he endured. He said very little—endeavoured to get from me an expression of a wish that the play should be done. I said, as I had from the first said, that "I would not utter one word." I mentioned having received a note from Mrs. Talfourd, which too manifestly was the result of feeling and temper—that as written by a lady I could not comment upon it further than to say : "It was unmerited, that I had not deserved it—it was an injustice." I added that had I the same occasion twenty or twenty thousand times, I should in all I had said or done, do and say exactly what I had done—that I had acted by Talfourd as I should have done by my own brother ; that it was at an end, etc. We shook hands, and they left me to my labours.

April 28th.—Rehearsed the play of *Romeo and Juliet*, with my part of Friar Lawrence. Settled with Marshall the scenery for *Ion* and *Romeo and Juliet*, and with Head the dresses for the latter.

April 29th.—I told Kenney that I had cast his piece of *Love Extempore*, and was satisfied that Harley would do the part in it well. Forster called, and showed me a note from Talfourd, in which I must say he manifested an *abject spirit*, observing, that "if Bartley were to call at his house, whilst he were at home, Mrs. Talfourd might perhaps be worked upon to consent to its performance." The tone of the note was most unmanly and most pitiable. Forster told me much about

Mr. Bartley that leads me to believe he has been most impertinently communicative, if not treacherous. Much of Mrs. Talfourd's silly intemperance of conduct has been evidently fomented by the busy interference of this faithless servant. Read over the acts of *King Lear*. Went to dine with Dickens, at whose house I met Procter, Ainsworth, Bell of the *True Sun*, and Forster. An agreeable day.

April 30th.—Went to the theatre, where I attended to the various matters requiring inspection, etc., in the painting-room and wardrobe. Rehearsed the play of *Romeo and Juliet* with much attention. Received two books of *The Athenian Captive* from Talfourd with his "regards, thanks, and regrets." Read over Friar Lawrence. Acted it. I find the playing a part of this sort, with no direct character to sustain, no effort to make, no power of perceiving an impression made, to be a very disagreeable and unprofitable task. Having required many of the actors to do what they conceived beneath them, perhaps it was only a just sacrifice to their opinions to concede so far—but it is for the first and last time.

May 2nd.—Bartley called in, and told me that the Edinburgh papers had turned round upon Mr. C. Kean. I lay down on bed to rest, and read Lear. Acted the part—not to my own satisfaction, but apparently to the content of the audience. Liston was in the greenroom, and rather drunk. I saw him for a few minutes. Was called for by the audience and very kindly received. Bulwer came into my room to inquire after the circumstances of Talfourd's tragedy.

May 3rd.—Robertson and Bartley came into my room; the receipt was so bad that I was obliged to decide on closing the house on Thursday.

May 4th.—Lay down to rest and read *Ion*, which I did diligently. Acted Ion tamely—indifferently. Forster and Knowles came in. Mr. Serjeant Talfourd had taken a private box and paid for it! This is the climax of their disgusting behaviour—having the freedom of the theatre and the privilege of sending, when they pleased, for a private box. *Talfourd* was in the box with the rest, which was most miserable of all—the poor, pitiful creature!—and this is a man!—a high literary character, a philanthropist and a legislator—mighty God! how is one to judge of men? He has done me, for vain and selfish purposes, the greatest possible injury, and he adds insult to his offensive behaviour. (*Written upon partial information.*—*Saturday.*)

May 5th.—Found that I had prematurely condemned Talfourd for the insult which I believed him to have offered me last night in taking

455

and paying for a private box.   The box—with another—had been taken for *The Athenian Captive*, and, on its withdrawal, transferred to the night of *Ion*.   This shows the impropriety of forming a judgment without due inquiry.   I have wronged Talfourd by the accusation I yesterday made against him.   I am very sorry for it—have been very wrong.   Acted Jacques pretty well, not so well as I could and ought to have done.   Was called for but did not go on.   Saw the farce of *High Life Below Stairs*, with which I was much amused.

May 7th.—Received a letter from Walker—at Eton—about his farce of the *Veiled Portrait*.   The unblushing selfishness of this man is almost vexatious; I was so indignant with him that I wrote a very angry answer, but afterwards thought it was not worth my while to be angry " with such a snipe," and that I would treat him as he deserved by not replying to him until it suited my convenience.   I had *promised* him, when I endeavoured to get the piece acted for him, that his name should not be known, and he now writes to hope it is not.   If he does not understand the confidence which should subsist between gentlemen, I will teach him.   Forster gave the title of *Woman's Wit; or, Love's Disguises*, to Knowles's play.

May 8th.—Read the papers.   Went to the theatre, where I was first in the house (alas! for duty paid for).   Superintended and directed the new farce of the *Veiled Portrait*; afterwards read Kenney's farce of *Love Extempore*, which went off rather heavily.   Dickens called with his wife and Forster, and asked me to dine *en famille*, to which I agreed.   Dined with Dickens.   Forster after dinner accompanied me to the Haymarket, where I saw an act and a half of a most wretchedly acted play, *The Wife;* it was *offensive*.   Passed on to Madame Vestris's theatre, where I saw a stupid piece well done.

May 9th.—Acted Melnotte pretty well.   Was called for with Miss Faucit, for whose Benefit it was acted, and well received.   Arranged conclusively the characters of *Woman's Wit*, and sent them out.   Saw Dickens, Blanchard and Cruikshank,[1] the caricaturist, who seemed set in for a *booze* in Forster's study.   I am much more comfortable with a cool head and quiet thoughts.

May 12th.—Went to Hamley's toy-shop, where I bought some toys and waited for Bryant's coach.   On my journey to Elstree read the

---

[1] George Cruikshank (1792–1878); the well-known caricaturist.   If Macready's supposition was correct, Cruikshank greatly changed his habits in later years, when he became a ervent advocate of temperance.   His chief work, *The Worship of Bacchus* (1862), is a Hogarthian exposition of the evils resulting from alcohol.

Literary Gazette, and some scenes of Knowles's play. My home, my children, and the quiet of the country, how sweet and precious everything seems about me.

London, May 14th.—Took leave of my dear, dear home, Nina and Willie running up to the village with me, and came to town—to the theatre. Went over the part of Wolsey. Acted it very indifferently. This sacrifice of my time and thought to the interest of others begins to tell upon me in my inability to do justice to myself in my art.

May 17th.—Looked at the newspapers, in which I only saw fresh evidences of the baseness of the wretches who are quartered upon them to impede the progress of knowledge, and, like the monks of old, perpetuate for their own livelihood the ignorance of their fellow-creatures. My soul sickens at them, and at the gross selfishness of this disgusting world—disgusting as to the moral constitution of it. Went to the theatre, and rehearsed Knowles's play, of which I have little hope. Miss Faucit came to pester me about a room to herself, to be free from the annoyance of Miss Taylor's noise! Miss Taylor to receive hints about her part. Forster came round and I told him I thought Miss Taylor and Miss Faucit should change parts, leaving them to settle it if they could.

May 19th.—Rehearsed *Woman's Wit*. Knowles and Forster were present at the early part of the rehearsal. Knowles was very much struck with the beauty of the scene for the opening of the play; he observed to me: " My dear Mac, for all the plays I have ever written, there has never been done so much as is given in this one scene." He went on to say, he would " set to work on *Procida* without delay for me," etc. Read over Melnotte, being anxious to play it well on the last night. Did act it very well, and was very enthusiastically received when called on. Went to Fonblanque's with Forster. Saw Hayward, F. Reynolds, Savage, Dr. Quin, D'Orsay, Savage Landor,[1] Bulwer, Lord Nugent,[2] etc. Went home with Forster, who got tea for me.

May 21st.—Gave up the entire morning to the rehearsal of Knowles's play. He and Forster were both on the stage the whole morning. Knowles was very much struck with the mode of putting

[1] Walter Savage Landor (1775–1864) ; the distinguished author ; he had returned from Italy in 1835, and in 1838 took up his residence at Bath, where he remained for twenty years, during which period he figured prominently in the literary world, both as a brilliant writer and a pugnacious disputant.

[2] George Nugent Grenville (1788–1850) ; younger son of the first Marquis of Buckingham. Succeeded to his mother's Irish barony of Nugent in 1813. Ridiculed by Canning, and reviewed by Macaulay.

the play upon the stage, drilling the actors, and teaching them their business; I was glad he was present that he might know, in any event, his trust had not been misplaced. He told me the proprietors, if they knew their interests, ought to give me £4000 per annum to conduct their theatre—about the amount that I shall give to them!

May 23rd.—From six o'clock to eight I was boring at the concluding speech of the play, having closed my eyes with it last night, and could not get it into my head. Saw the papers, and went to rehearsal. Rehearsed the play of *Woman's Wit,* and attended to all the various matters connected with it; scenes, dresses, etc. Read over my own part, and laboured at the concluding speech, writing it out repeatedly from memory, but unavailingly, to make a secure lodgment with it. Acted Walsingham [1] in a very crude, nervous, unsatisfactory manner. Avoided a call by going before the curtain to give out the play; there was very great enthusiasm. Led on Knowles in obedience to the call of the audience. Bulwer, Lardner, Beazley, Forster, and Dickens came into the green-room. Much offended with Miss Faucit, refusing to go on, led by Mr. Anderson, taking Miss Taylor's hand from him, and forcing her on. These are players!

May 24th.—Went over the part of Walsingham in bed. Read the newspapers, all of which, except the *Times,* gave liberal notices of last night. Went to the theatre, where I spoke to Miss Taylor about the affront offered to Mr. Anderson, in which she had no participation. Attended to part of the cutting of the play. Spoke to Miss Faucit on her behaviour to Mr. Anderson. She was at last penetrated by my rebuke, and promised to apologize to him. She behaved very well.

May 25th.—Knowles came into my room. I told him to go to the Literary Fund dinner to-morrow. He borrowed two sovereigns of me for a person who, he said, actually wanted food. I ought to have *given* him some assistance—it was a great neglect; I was acting, and forgot my duty.

May 26th.—Wrote to Bulwer, saying I should be glad to see him if he were strolling near; I wish to ask him if I can be of any use to him in improving his elocution.

May 28th.—My spirits were very low. I believe they were not raised by reading the account of the Literary Fund dinner. I feel my folly in supposing that a man has any chance who wages war with charlatanry and blackguardism. It is a hopeless struggle. My spirits were broken down. My mind has had its share of care and grief.

[1] Macready's part in *Woman's Wit.*

458

Dozed away the afternoon, vainly endeavouring to read. Acted very drowsily indeed. I feel wretched to a pitch of impatience that is most painful.

May 29th.—Had a long conversation with Bartley and Robertson on the conduct of next season; they, but more particularly Bartley, seemed to be very anxious that I should be continued, with safety to myself, in the management. Bartley mentioned that the actors were to meet on Thursday, and that Serle had a plan to propose, but that this plan included an operatic company. I am nearly certain Serle's plan must be of a republican character, with which I said I would have nothing to do; as a director I must be a *despot*, or *serve*. Dined with Forster and Dickens. Forster told me of Talfourd's *little* conduct— eulogizing Mr. C. Kean's great talents and no word to bestow on Knowles in his play, nor on me except as to my sacrifices and getting up of plays! Dickens and Forster were disgusted with him. Wrote to Babbage for a voucher for Herschel's [1] dinner. Acted Walsingham middlingly.

May 30th.—Finished the number of *Nickleby* in bed; talked with Forster on the subject of next season's management, upon which he is as usual very sanguine. Miss Faucit came, on my invitation, into my room. I wished to speak with her, but our conference was very short, as she was rather sullen and reserved. Bulwer came in. I told him that Forster had mentioned to me how anxious he was to endeavour to improve his elocution, and that if *I* could be of any assistance to him in that respect, I should be most happy. He seemed very much obliged and pleased, and though doubtful of a good result, would be happy to receive my assistance. [2]

May 31st.—After the interlude [3] was over, Warde, Harley, Meadows, and Stanfield came into my room to ask me to step into the green-room, where I found my company assembled. They all stood up as I entered, and I bowed to them, and Bartley addressed me in their names, deputed by them. I cannot remember his speech, but it was very well arranged and delivered, to the effect that they, "the company, had been deeply penetrated by the part I had taken in standing forward to champion the cause of the fallen drama, and been sensibly

---

[1] Sir John Frederick William Herschel (1792–1871); the famous astronomer; he was created a baronet in 1838.

[2] Sir E. Bulwer Lytton's delivery was defective to the last, but in spite of it he made a reputation as a Parliamentary speaker, attaining, during his second period in the House of Commons, a position only just short of the first rank.

[3] The performances of this evening were: *Woman's Wit*, *The Original*, and *High Life Below Stairs* (*note by Sir F. Pollock*).

alive to the labours I had encountered, and the sacrifices I had made
for the drama's sake; that they wished me to be apprised of their high
appreciation of my noble conduct, of my uniform deportment towards
them, and of the various acts that together had brought back to them
a season equal in its effects to them to the best days of the drama
within the memory of the oldest actor; that they were well aware I
should be most pleased with any testimonial of their regard in proportion to its unostentatiousness, and therefore they had selected the
simplest offering as a mere tablet, on which to inscribe their names and
record their gratitude to me; that though it possessed little value
beyond that, yet that perhaps on some occasion it might find a place
upon my sideboard, and that Mrs. Macready, and perhaps my children,
might derive some little pleasure from the sight of it." The salver
was produced and the inscription read. He was affected as he closed
his speech, which I can only very imperfectly recollect. I am nearly
as much at a loss to recollect the particulars of my reply; he said something about "the motives" of my undertaking—I forget in what
manner. As nearly as I can remember, I said: "Ladies and Gentlemen,—I am utterly at a loss to reply to what has been so kindly communicated to me from you by our common friend, Mr. Bartley. I
really do not know how to thank you. I am wholly unused to address
extemporaneously any body of persons, and not always exact in the
expression of my ideas in ordinary conversation. I thank you most
truly. I can say little more than this, but whilst I assure you that I
feel most gratefully your kindness in this instance, I must also be permitted to say that I regret it; I regret that, in your wish to testify your
estimation of my conduct, you should have altered the high position
on which we stood relatively to each other—it would have been far more
gratifying to me to have received the record of your kind appreciation
on even perishable paper (which, however, never could have perished
while I or any dear to me could have preserved it) and have held faith
in the sincerity of its declaration. But as it is I can only again thank
you, and assure you how truly I value this testimony of your regard.
I truly and gratefully thank you. Mr. Bartley has alluded to the
' motives ' which induced me to embark on this speculation or experiment. I may observe that less disinterested motives have been attributed to me by some persons who have been remarked in society for a
most ungenerous hostility to our cause, and who, perhaps, are scarcely
worthy of notice. These persons have laid down their opinion that I
took the theatre ' only to fill my own pockets.' I am sure you give

460

me credit—indeed,, you have proved so—for motives not altogether mercenary and selfish. And, in contradiction of these persons' assertion, I need but refer to your several engagements and to my contract with the proprietors, by which I might long since have closed the theatre when all hope of reimbursing myself had departed, and when I could only continue the season by a continuance of loss. As a further evidence that my motives were not exclusively selfish, I had pledged myself, before the opening of the theatre, to Mr. Robertson and Mr. Bartley (and I am glad of the opportunity of mentioning it) to pay to the full the salaries of those performers who consented to their reduction, and who consented to share with me in part the risk I was venturing upon. I pledged myself, as those gentlemen know, to pay the full amount at which these salaries were previously rated before I touched one shilling of the profits, if any had arisen upon the season. I may also refer to the principles on which the theatre has been conducted, to show that my motives were not altogether mercenary. They were in fact not so. Among my motives the primary one was the wish to elevate my art, and to establish an asylum for it and my brothers and sisters professing it, where they might be secure of equitable treatment, of friendly consideration, and most of all, of that respect which man should show to man or, which is most important, which man should show to woman. I cannot be so presumptuous as to suppose that I have been able to give universal satisfaction; in a large establishment like this the interests of individuals must often be merged in that of the community, but I may ask credit for intention. I have endeavoured to be just, and though perhaps sometimes I may have been betrayed into a manifestation of infirmity of temper, I have at least striven to make kindness go hand in hand with justice. Once more I must thank you; but let me indulge in one more observation, which is, that in no theatrical season I remember has there ever been less discord between a company and its manager, a circumstance of which we may all be justly proud, and in the honour of which we generally participate. In again repeating my thanks to you I may mention that, in a letter addressed to me on business at the beginning of the season by a gentleman I believe now present, the writer told me that I was regarded— yes, he intimated widely—as the actors' friend; it was the most gratifying character that could be applied to me. Let me believe that the testimonial now before me may be considered by me as an attestation of your assent to the justice of the term, and let me entreat of you that my name may never be dissociated from the appellation. Thank you once more, truly and cordially ! '' I shook hands with those near me and left the room. Stanfield, Knowles, Forster, Bartley, etc., came into my room; I was pleased to hear that Mrs. H. Phillips's and Power's, etc., names were inscribed on the salver.

Elstree, June 2nd.—Walked in the garden—a day of complete relaxation and indulgence spent with my dear children. Entered some arrears of record, and walked, played and talked away the day. Enjoyed the beauty of the country and the fineness of the day. Amused the children with the ascent of a balloon and descent of parachute. Talked away the evening.

June 5th.—Read the essay on '' Envy '' in Bacon—endeavouring to examine myself by it. Heard a strange story (an incredible one, I should say) of a present having been sent from that wretched fellow at Drury Lane to the Queen. Talked away my time, all upon the subject of next year's management. Willmott told me of the extravagant expectations of the actors, who expected to share with me in the chance of their salaries, and also to divide any surplus ! I see the impracticability of the attempt to raise them from the condition of serfs; they have not the nobleness to be really free; they will not even with example make a sacrifice to be so. Found Fox at Forster's; he stayed very late. Knowles proposed, as a means of continuing in the management, twenty of the aristocracy taking private boxes. Fox suggested fifty persons advancing each £50, and said he would start it.

June 6th.—Looked at the newspapers and set myself to copy out the two speeches on the occasion of the salver on Thursday night last for Mr. Fox, who called in before I had finished my task. When I had done, I handed them over to Forster, who said he would copy them for insertion in the *Morning Chronicle.* Had a long conversation with Robertson about Fox's plan of raising fifty £50 loans, on which he said he was confident the proprietors would do everything requisite.

June 7th.—Read the newspapers, and was much pleased with the insertion of the account of the actors' tribute to me. Harley wished to speak with me, to say that if it would be of use, or were needed, he would be most happy to put down a sum of money to assist the continuance of my management. I thanked him and expressed myself pleased with his offer, but could not accept it.

June 9th.—Read some pages of Schlegel on Calderon's writings, with which I was very much pleased, and which made me immediately renew the desire, if not adopt the resolution, to learn Spanish. Read the newspapers. It is curious to see how very few of them—only two—

have copied the account of the tribute paid to me by the Covent Garden actors; had it been Mr. Kean, or Mr. Bunn, or any blackguard, how would the columns have blackened with it!! Bartley came in, introducing Vandenhoff, arrived from America, looking very well, and speaking of his *great* success in a tone and manner that convinced me it was *small*. I was very civil to him. Heard news of the American theatres. Messrs. White and Whitmore's clerk, Mr. Green, called, and spoke to me on Mr. Webster's defence; he has let judgment go by default, retaining Mr. Thesiger. I hope that gentleman may again abuse me.

June 11th.—Miss H. Faucit came in, and I had a long conversation with her on the subject of her next year's engagement, she saying that her friends would expect her to receive a higher salary; I observing that I would not conduct the theatre to give it, and warning her to be liberal and just in her engagements.

June 12th.—I had reflected on Forster's recommendation to me to subscribe to the memorial to be erected in commemoration of the Duke of Wellington's military achievements, and remarked to him (though at first, in my general estimation of the Duke's character as a strictly honest and straightforward man, I had signified my intention to subscribe) that I thought it would be inconsistent with my principles to do so; if justice to the full—even to overflowing—had not been rendered him, I would gladly add my mite of tributary gratitude and respect, but he has been certainly remunerated to the height of his great deservings, whilst many greater minds—and far more benevolent and beneficial to mankind in their labours for them—have been disregarded, or meanly requited. Politicians—and their instruments, soldiers—are enriched, ennobled, and, as far as brass and marble will endure, immortalized; but science, art, and literature, the elevating and purifying elements in which man's spirit should cleanse and regenerate itself, are inconsiderable subjects for the great traders in place and pension to sometimes amuse themselves withal! Where are your statues, Shakspeare, Milton, Bacon, Locke, Newton, Watt, Sir John Eliot, Hampden, Burns, Wordsworth, Fielding, Harvey, and the many benefactors and blessers of your kind? Antiquity has left us the features of its philosophers and poets in far greater proportion to their actual number than it has of its statesmen and warriors, who were often really *patriots* and not mere traffickers for place. I do not think I ought to give what I owe more justly to others.

June 14th.—Leigh Hunt called on Forster; I saw him, and talked with him about his play, assuring him that I would give my whole attention to it, and do all in my power for it. I was quite moved in speaking to him. It is curious to mark the revolutions in human affairs. I remember when Leigh Hunt, as the editor of the *Examiner*, seemed to hold my destinies in his grasp; as the person on whom, in respect to this play, he now depends, I appear to have his in my keeping. Mr. Webster sent up his card and came in. He proposed an engagement—asked me if I would take £20 per night. I said, No; that I did not wish to act, and would take nothing under £25 per night for four nights per week for five weeks. He said, "Well, Mr. Macready, I will give it," and named the time—the middle of July. He then detained me till past five o'clock, disclaiming any malice towards me, making very lame excuses, and saying he did not remember that I had made him a present of £50 when leaving the theatre. I told him I would not act Shakspeare's tragedies at the Haymarket, to which he agreed—Knowles's play was the object. Put him on the free list. Forster called to tell me of Knowles's distress and to ask if I would give him a Benefit, dividing after £105. I said *No*; but I would divide with him after £60.

June 15th.—Reflected much on the circumstances of ——. It is scarcely to be wondered at that she should be keenly alive to the influences of passion—but it is not right. A sterner rule of conduct must be adopted if I wish to be happy and at peace with myself. Read the newspapers, and saw Knowles, who came with a letter from Lord John Russell, implying the Queen's intention of visiting the theatre after the Coronation. I went with K—— to the theatre, and spoke to Robertson about the extension of the season to meet the possible command.

Elstree, June 17th.—Sat down to read Leigh Hunt's play, which I did, not without difficulty; the unhappy construction so deprives it of interest that I cannot entertain a hope for it, which on every account gives me great concern. Went again into the garden, delighting in the sight of my children at play; passed a luxurious, idle evening; all tranquil, sweet, and happy about me.

London, June 18th.—Saw Knowles, who gave me an account of Lord Morpeth's [1] Blackwall dinner, at which Knowles had told him in his speech that he was "the first of his order from whom he had ever received the courtesy of hospitality." Sent Knowles to Lord Conyngham to ascertain if there is to be a command. Read the newspapers,

---

[1] George William Frederick Howard (1802–1864), Viscount Morpeth, afterwards seventh Earl of Carlisle; at that time Irish Secretary; subsequently twice Lord-Lieutenant of Ireland. Well known as a philanthropic statesman; he had also considerable literary attainments.

in which was a most *disgusting* account of the duel between Lord Castlereagh and Monsieur de Melci,[1] eulogizing the behaviour of this profligate puppy, who deserved a severe horse-whipping—at least whose conduct should have been held up to public reprobation instead of approval. What a world!

June 19th.—Forster, Fox, H. Smith, and Wallace came into my room. The three former went with me to Forster's rooms to sup, and hear Hunt's play; but we supped and talked, not very harmoniously, on the subject of the plan for opening the theatre next season. Forster quite lost his temper.

June 20th.—Received a note from Talfourd, expressive of his gratification at my invitation, but declining on the plea of a journey to Bexley. It is a satisfaction to me that I have done what I feel to have been generous; it is not always that we can see the advantage of being above false pride and standing upon our supposed dignity. A long discussion with Forster upon Leigh Hunt's play; he is very uncomfortably placed respecting it, and would have me in the imbroglio, but I cannot lend myself to it. I give my sincere advice, and if it is not taken, I will entertain no compromise.

June 21st.—Dickens came in. Miss Faucit had written me a note, assenting to the salary, but desiring the right to refuse parts, and wishing for a dressing-room to herself. She came to my room, and, after trying if she would give up the point, I told her she might as well have done so, for I should not be manager. She was much concerned. Kenney was there early in the evening, and repeated the information I had received from a note of Robertson, that I was elected a member of the Athenæum.

June 22nd.—Notification of my election from the Athenæum Club.

June 23rd.—Looked at the papers, which now more than ever disgust one with the perpetual *stuff* of the Coronation, and those to be concerned in it. The *Morning Post* mentioned—as a marvel— that the Duke of Nemours "*was exposed to a raging sea for nearly twelve hours, and we understand was sea-sick nearly the whole voyage!*" Mighty Heaven!—would it not be better that such trash as the Duke of Nemours, and all the fools and sycophants that make up their mob of idolaters were buried fathoms below the surface, rather than that the reason *which God has given man* should be prostituted and abased to such vile purpose as communicating or reading such disgusting absurdity? *Can England ever be intellectually and morally*

[1] The duel was caused by Lord Castlereagh's too ardent attentions to Grisi, M. de Melci's wife. He fired in the air, but was wounded in the wrist.

free? I think—never. Drury Lane with its advertisements in the papers has closed—only opening for the Coronation night! Thus ends for the present season the impudence, falsehood, knavery, and swagger of that disgusting scoundrel.

Elstree, June 24th.—Our wedding day. To Almighty God I lift up my heart in earnest thankfulness, and deep but I hope humble joy, blessing his Holy Name, as the Giver and Author of the countless blessings and vast sum of good I have received in the dear woman whose life has been, and I fervently implore of God long may be, partnered with mine. Went to afternoon church. Mr. and Mrs. Dickens, and Forster arrived. Amused ourselves with sending up balloons before and after dinner. Mr. and Mrs. Haynes Bayley arrived just as dinner was announced. A cheerful day. My blessings on it—on dearest Catherine and my blessed children. Amen!

London, June 26th.—Blanchard told me that at the theatre on Friday night Mr. C. Kean, with two companions, by his indecent behaviour—sneering and observing upon the performance of the *Lady of Lyons*—attracted the attention and frequent notice of those around him; that no language of his could convey at all an adequate idea of the insolent and offensive conduct of this vulgar-minded and conceited young man. There is no genius in such a nature. He asked my autograph for a young friend. Forster called, as also Cattermole. I did not feel much inclined to go to see the Coronation, though if I could have done so without much trouble I would. Webster called and expressed the great pleasure he should have, in case of my relinquishment of Covent Garden, to make my engagement last to the end of his season with Knowles's and Bulwer's plays. Robertson came and we talked about the lease of the theatre. He took a plan I had written down; but I sent to him afterwards desiring him not to show it to the proprietors until I had reconsidered it, and also to send me the account book, that I might look it well over. Acted Claude Melnotte—indifferently, so wearied that I dropped asleep under my hairdresser; was called for, and went forward with Miss Faucit.

Elstree, June 27th.—Cattermole arrived (to my surprise) with Mr. Froude.[1] They dined with us, and I passed a most agreeable evening, being very much pleased with the intelligence and bonhomie of our new guest. . . . Is the pleasure of this air—these fields—the presence of my dear wife, the society of my friends, and this sight of my blessed children to be relinquished for the puppet-show of a *Coronation?*

June 28th.—In speaking with Catherine about a future lease of

---

[1] John Froude, a brother of the eminent historian.

466

Covent Garden theatre, she very strongly opposed it. Wrote to Robertson a final offer to the proprietors.

London, June 30th.—Robertson brought me word that the proprietors agreed to the proposal I had given in, but wished something definite about surplus. I told him I would say nothing; that I did not intend to make a gift to them, but if the surplus should reach to a high sum, say £7000, I should consider it only fair that they, as having participated in the risk, should be considered in the remuneration; that I should send them £1000 on such account.

July 2nd.—Webster called, and seemed greatly disappointed at my continuance at Covent Garden theatre. He, however, expressed the most friendly intentions, and promised to call on Wednesday, and let me know if he could spare me Mrs. Clifford on our opening.

July 4th.—Settled to close the theatre on Friday next. Miss Faucit signed a fresh engagement. An anonymous letter charging Mr. Kean with indecent noise.

July 5th.—Acted Claude Melnotte very well, was called for and led on Miss Faucit. Many bouquets were thrown on the stage. Bulwer, Talfourd, Forster, G. Bucknill came into my room. I got away as fast as I could, and came home in the carriage. The last night of my performance this season at Covent Garden.[1]

July 6th.—Went into the box to hear Bartley deliver the closing speech; he had said to me a little before that it had occurred to him the audience might call for me; I said if they did I would instantly run out of the theatre, so that he might with perfect safety say I was not in it. The audience did call from the time the curtain fell, but not strongly enough, till Bartley appeared, when their vociferation a good deal disconcerted him, and a momentary darkening of the lights, which made the audience laugh, did not tend to restore his self-possession. The cheering was so loud and long on his announcement of my continuance in the lessee-ship that I thought it time to decamp, and went out of the theatre. I saw Serle afterwards, who said that the address had been most fervently received, and that the audience were still calling uproariously for me. I sent for Catherine, who came down to the carriage, and taking Kenney on the dickey, to set him down at the Regent's Park, we started for Elstree. Kenney told me that the attempt had been made to bring Mr. C. Kean into the Athenæum, but that it had failed.

July 7th.—Took leave of my blessed family, and came to town. Entering Oxford Street, saw a man, seemingly of a baker's trade,

---

[1] The performances were *Woman's Wit* and *Fra Diavolo* (*note by Sir F. Pollock*).

rush at a chimney-sweeper and strike at him first with a basket and then with his fists, which brought on a contest. I saw before me in positive colours and in form my own *mad* folly in resenting the insult of such a black and filthy wretch as that Mr. Bunn—exposing myself to the comments of the lookers-on, and sure to bring away some of the dirt from such a filthy subject. It actually made me feel *sick at the stomach*. I made an internal vow never again, if it were possible, never again to give way to the sin, the madness of passion.

July 31st.—Called on Mr. Anderson at the Fleet Prison—passing through the galleries and seeing the persons confined there; was struck with the inutility of such a punishment! Saw Anderson, who seemed surprised to see me; gave him a cheque for £20; wished to know if I could do anything further for him or his wife—near her confinement; expected that he would discharge all his *real* debts on his release, and parted very kindly from him. Dined at Mrs. Haworth's, met Mr. Lewis and family and Mr. Leach; *forgot myself* in finding fault with the profession of a barrister—otherwise an agreeable day with Tories.

August 2nd.—Acted Mr. Oakley very well.[1] Miss —— was behind the scenes. A painful example of the pernicious consequence of a young girl following this calling. She was a pretty engaging girl two or three years ago; now her appearance only suggests the idea of a second or third class girl of the town!

August 3rd.—My mind was occupied for some time in endeavouring to compute my pecuniary loss by management. I find I managed to lose, as I first thought, judging from actual decrease of capital, and absence of profit by my labour, £2500, or, measuring my receipt by the previous year, £1800. It is a painful subject for rumination, but repining never amended misfortune. Was much pleased to mark the deep interest which a lady in the stage-box took in the last scene between Lord and Lady Townley. These are the sort of auditors that lend a temporary fascination to the exercise of our art.

August 4th.—Felt at the rehearsal that my part *must fail* of effect, and in consequence became very low-spirited and uncomfortable; but I must use the interval as I best can, and trust in the Provident Care that has hitherto befriended me. Lay down on bed, reading over and attentively considering the part of Thoas, resolving to throw as much energy as I could into it, and consoling myself with the thought that one indifferent performance could not ruin me—*a very bad reflection to resort to.* Energy and confidence in one's own resolution to do our

---

[1] Macready was now acting for a short period at the Haymarket theatre.

best, with faith in Providence, is the best tone of mind in such emergencies. Acted Thoas with vigour and effect; quite bore the play on my own strength. Was called for by the audience; went on leading Mrs. Warner, and was very cordially received. Talfourd came into my room in a state of high excitement and delight; was lavish in his acknowledgments and surprised, as he expressed himself, at the effect I had produced. Dickens, Browning, Forster, Horne [1] came into my room.

August 8th.—Serle called and told me that he had arranged with Webster that his play of *The Spanish Maid* should be the first novelty of the next Haymarket season. He also told me that he had spoken to Oxenford, who was busy with a farce for Covent Garden theatre, who had told him, when he consulted him on what was the course to pursue about the *Times*, that he himself had been spoken to for writing too liberally about myself. This, with Thackeray's statement, is surely a conclusive proof, if any were wanting to the evidence the paper itself affords, that a shameful system of injury is practised against me by that paper. Talfourd came into my room; talked of "his friend, C. Kean" (!), and told me of Lord Brougham's insane conduct—that he had become of late extremely obscene in his conversation, which he never used to be; that the other night at the Duke of Sutherland's he said: "Look at those men. Did you ever see such a Ministry? There is Lord Melbourne always ——; Lord John Russell ——; and —— his secretary constantly ——" What a state of mind! Are his talents worth this condition of heart and morals? Note from Dr. Elliotson, inviting me to an exhibition of animal magnetism.

London, August 9th.—Went to lodging, and thence to Haymarket, where I took pains with Thoas, and acted it better than I had done since the first night. Talfourd came into my room and afterwards Hayward, who wished me to see Lady Harriet D'Orsay [2] and Mrs. Norton to their carriage. I dressed and went to their box; sat through some of the *Artist's Wife*, a disagreeable piece, and handed them down to their carriage. Went with Talfourd to Hayward's chambers. Mrs. Norton and Lady H. D'Orsay were there. C. Sheridan, Blood, and afterwards Colonel Lincoln Stanhope joined the party. Blood's singing was delightful, Lady H. D'Orsay—beautiful. Stayed to a

[1] Richard Hengist Horne (1803-1884); best known as the author of *Orion*, an epic poem, published at a farthing. An intimate friend of Mrs. Barrett Browning.

[2] Lord Blessington's daughter by his first marriage. Her father arranged her marriage with D'Orsay, which turned out very unhappily. After separating from him she contracted a *liaison* with the Duc d'Orleans (Louis Philippe's heir), and eventually married the Hon. Spencer Cowper, a son of Lady Palmerston by her first marriage. It was said that Spencer Cowper won her from D'Orsay as a stake at *ecarté*.

very late hour. Enjoyed the freshness of the night walking home with Blood and Lincoln Stanhope.

August 22nd.—Continued my work on the book of the *Tempest.* Agreed to take 13, Cumberland Terrace, from 15th September to March 24th at £7 10s. per week.

September 13th.—After dinner read Mrs. Hemans's *Crusaders,* which leads me to think that if I had known her in life, and she had consulted me instead of that thick-headed man, C. Kemble, or that puppy, Mr. Harness, she would have written a successful tragedy. This is vain, but I feel confident of it. She only wanted the occasional hint of some person acquainted with stage effect in composition. Looked over Shakspeare's plays of *King Richard II* and *King Richard III.* Astonished at the base venality of the disgusting newspaper writers—the wretches—who dare to laud the fustian of Cibber, and tried to keep the many in ignorance by praising his trash called *Richard III.*

London, September 17th.—Went to Covent Garden, where I immediately entered on the business that was waiting for me. Letters from Bulwer about subject; Horne, about an annuity to be subscribed for Leigh Hunt, to which my name was given for £5; from Wade about his play, etc. Much business was before me, and occupied me variously through the day; the price of work was settled; the ladies' rooms appointed and settled; the private boxes, lobbies, and whole part of the theatre inspected, and finally settled as to its cleaning, etc. The expenses of the men's wardrobe reduced, and alteration made as to the lighting; to reduce still more the expenses, question about the laundry work—still, still imposition! Scene-room, wardrobe, carpenter's room; business with all; cast pieces and made out the bill for first night.

September 24th.—Began the day with packing up things for the theatre; looked over my children's sums, and read in *Hamlet.* Went to Covent Garden theatre where I attended the rehearsal of *High Life,* and the play of *Coriolanus.* Arranged and read my letters, giving several to Serle and Robertson to answer, answering others myself. Spoke with Marshall on business, and was fully occupied each moment of the day. Thought of what I would say if I were to be called on. Began to unpack my portmanteau and to arrange my wardrobe, etc., in my room. Dressed myself and prepared for the play. After " God save the Queen " there was a general call for myself. I went down from the box, and returned flurried, prepared to go on; the reception of the audience was most enthusiastic. I said that I was at a loss to thank them for the compliment. I hoped my exertions would prove the estimation I set upon their kind opinion, that professions were of little avail, and therefore I would only assure them that unremitting zeal, good intentions, and good faith should be my rules of conduct in the establishment. I was to play Coriolanus, which is certainly beautiful. Bulwer came and sat it out with me; he talked of a subject on which he is thinking. A fine house.[1]

---

[1] Notice had been given of the re-opening of the theatre by the following announcement :—

THEATRE ROYAL COVENT GARDEN.

MR. MACREADY begs most respectfully to announce that this
Theatre will be re-opened

on Monday, September 24th, 1838.

In entering upon this second, and to him most serious, experiment, he will only say the same views with which he undertook the conduct of this establishment last season will be followed up, and his more specific pledges will continue to be strictly fulfilled.

No exertion will be spared in presenting the National Drama, whether as a branch or literature or as a department of art, with every advantage.

The revival of the standard plays of Shakspeare in the genuine text of the Poet will be persevered in with increased activity, and without regard to expense in attaining the utmost fidelity of historic illustration.

New pieces will be brought out in quick succession, with the same attention to decoration, especially pieces of such a character as to depend mainly upon extrinsic attractions; and the system of abstaining from all exaggerated and delusive announcements in the playbills will be rigidly adhered to.

THE COMPANY OF THE SEASON CONSISTS OF
MESSRS.

ANDERSON,	FRASER,	ROBERTS,
AYLIFFE,	HARLEY,	SERLE,
BARTLEY,	HOWE,	STRICKLAND,
G. BENNETT,	LEFFLER,	C. J. SMITH,
BEDFORD,	LEE,	TILBURY,
BURNETT,	MACREADY,	VANDENHOFF,
BENDER,	MEADOWS,	F. VINING,
COLLETT,	T. MATHEWS,	WARDE,
DIDDEAR,	PHELPS,	WALDRON,
ELTON,	W. H. PAYNE,	YARNOLD, Etc.

MESDAMES

W. CLIFFORD,	GARRICK,	SERLE,
CHARLES,	P. HORTON,	TAYLOR,
EAST,	HUMBY,	VANDENHOFF,
HELEN FAUCIT,	E. PHILLIPS,	WARNER,
FAIRBROTHER,	RAINFORTH,	WORTLEY, Etc.
GRIFFITHS,		

Acting Manager, MR. SERLE.   *Musical Director,* MR. T. COOKE.
Stage Director, MR. WILLMOTT.

(*Note by Sir F. Pollock*

471

September 25th.—Read the new drama to the performers, but was disappointed in the impression I hope to produce. Bulwer called whilst I was reading it. I told him I did not think it *possible* to make the *Murder of Clytemnestra* palatable to an English audience. He seemed stiff and not pleased at my want of enthusiasm. Read the papers; *heard* that the *Times* was as disgusting in its insidious treatment of me and my exertions as ever.

September 26th.—Spoke to Miss Faucit about her boy's dress for Imogen, and suggested to her, on the supposition that her legs were rather thin, the use of a pair of fleeced stockings " such as Malibran used to wear." I managed this " delicate negotiation " as dexterously as I could, and reconciled her easily to the experiment; went out and purchased a pair for her, which were sent home at three o'clock, with a pair of my own, and I gave them to her. Surprised at the return of the house, which far exceeded my expectations.

October 1st.—Rose early, and, after looking over my dear children's lessons, turned over the leaves of *Hamlet*, about which I felt very doubtful and uneasy. Bade good-bye to my children and Catherine with depression—that was a misgiving. Went to the theatre, where I was annoyed by finding my orders and intentions completely frustrated through the indolence and ignorance of the persons employed; the closet scene, which I had intended to be a beautiful effect, was necessarily left in its original state. Rehearsed the play very feebly and unsatisfactorily; in one or two places I proved to myself that I could act the character well if I could only throw myself heartily and naturally into it. Looked at my letters. Lay down on my bed, which I was obliged to make up with cloaks, etc. Rose almost hopeless, nerved myself as I dressed, and acted Hamlet perhaps altogether as well as I have ever done; was very cordially received, and called on afterwards with much enthusiasm.

October 8th.—Went to Covent Garden theatre; attended to business in the painting-room and stage, etc. Superintended the rehearsal of the three last acts of the *Tempest*. Head came to me to go over again the dresses I had arranged on Saturday. Lay down, slept, and thought of *Hamlet;* acted Hamlet in parts tolerably well. His advice to the players I never gave so well; was called for, and well received by the audience. Settled again the clothes for the *Tempest* with Head.

October 13th.—Went to Covent Garden theatre. Attended to the business of the day. Rehearsed the play and made some valuable

472

alterations. Read Prospero as well as I could; acted it as well as I could—but how could I act it well with the excitement and load of such a production on my mind? Was greatly received. Called for after the play, and received again with enthusiasm. Dickens and Forster went to our box. Spoke to Miss P. Horton on her performance; thanked her and kissed her. Gave largess to the carpenters.[1]

October 14th.—Could not recover myself from the excitement of last night. The scenes of the storm, the flights of Ariel, and the enthusiasm of the house were constantly recurring to me.

October 15th.—Went to the theatre, where I saw the newspapers, renewed the excitement that I thought had subsided. I tried to tranquillize myself, but vainly. This is not a life to live for one who wishes to improve himself by living—it is a tempest itself.

October 16th.—Acted Prospero very roughly—was called for, and led on Miss P. Horton. Spoke to Willmott about inaccuracies; to Mr. W—— about his probable arrest, of which I had been apprised by Notter. Would not permit the sheriff's officer to enter the theatre, nor would I consent to Mr. W.'s request to let him through the private boxes.

October 22nd.—Bartley brought the news of the failure of the "horse and beast" piece at Drury Lane. I do *feel thankful* for this defeat of a bad man's attempt to debase still lower the art and artists he has so long and brutally oppressed. Serle came into my room; told me that Mr. G. Smith—in the *John Bull*—had violently abused the *Tempest!!!*

October 24th.—Letter from Bulwer informing me that he had made out the rough sketch of a play, an historical comedy, on the subject of Richelieu. I answered him, delighted at the news.

October 25th.—For the last two days, having been excited by the base unmanly conduct of the papers, the *Times, Post,* and *Herald,* who have been lauding the trash of Ducrow and Van Amburgh[1] and depreciating the business of Covent Garden theatre, I have suffered from internal throes of passion and indignation until life has felt painful to me. In my prayers I have failed to tranquillize myself; my suffer-

---

[1] The cast of the principal characters in the *Tempest*, as brought out by Macready, was: Alonzo, Mr. Warde; Sebastian, Mr. Diddear; Prospero, Mr. Macready; Antonio, Mr. Phelps; Ferdinand, Mr. Anderson; Caliban, Mr. G. Bennett; Trinculo, Mr. Harley; Stephano, Mr. Bartley; Miranda, Miss Helen Faucit; Ariel, Miss P. Horton; Iris, Mrs. Serle; Juno, Miss Rainforth. The music was selected from the works of Purcell, Linley, and Dr. Arne (*note by Sir F. Pollock*).

[2] Ducrow the equestrian, and Van Amburgh the lion-tamer.

ings have been most acute; these circumstances revive all I have endured from that mercenary villain, Thesiger, and the vindictive sensations I undergo are terrible; I lift my heart to God—but in vain. I must hope for repose and comfort, or I shall sink under the torture of mind I undergo.

October 31st.—Looked over the new romance. Acted Melnotte tolerably well. Miss Faucit talked about *declining* her character in *Ruthven.* I did not yield in any way to her. *Nous verrons!* Mr. Howe—whose salary I raised last week 10s.—writes to say he expected more, viz. £1 10s. He was very civil, but he overrates himself. Well called for, and well received by the audience.

November 1st.—Miss Faucit returned me her part in the new tragedy with a note, which made me very angry. I began a note to her under much irritation, but had just sense enough to resolve to defer it till to-morrow. *Never do anything in passion. In nocte consilium.*

November 2nd.—Went to Covent Garden theatre and attended the whole morning to the rehearsal of the new opera; spoke with Mr. Hullah about his usurpation of the office of director; told him that there was an express understanding with Mr. Kenney that the departments of the theatre should not be interfered with. He was very restive, but I could not give up my point, and requested him not to interfere further with the orchestra. He said that Mr. Kenney had an understanding with him that he was to preside—and Mr. Kenney stated the direct contrary. Wrote to Miss Faucit, sending back the part of Lady Catherine to her. Brydone called, and I signed the weekly bills. Spent the evening with my children. Sat up until half-past one o'clock, cutting and arranging the tragedy of *Ruthven.*

November 3rd.—Miss Faucit again wrote to me, again returning the part in Haynes's tragedy. I sent for her and spoke to her between the first and third acts. She remained obstinate. Acted Prospero pretty well, was called for by the audience and well received. Went into the box to see the new opera; received a note from Miss Faucit consenting to act the part. Went down and spoke to her. Was made very angry by some enemies in the theatre endeavouring to excite opposition towards the conclusion of the opera.

November 4th.—Read over and cut the melodrame—*lose hope in everything!* Looked over and further cut the tragedy, which will be a very dull affair. Read prayers to the family. Wrote a copy of letter to return the letter of that offensive fool, Mr. Pritchard, who now

474

tells me that he was insulted last 13th of November by me! I told him then I wished him to go, but he chose to remain—to take my money—to profit by his engagement—to pass me every day without decent courtesy—and *now* he lets me know that his feelings were insulted!

November 5th.—Looked at the papers which (the *Chronicle*, with all the rest) were most shamefully and profligately abusive of our opera of Saturday. I quite lost my spirits in considering the disgusting venality and shameless betrayal of their duty on the part of the Press —the wretches!—the lowest race that disgrace humanity! Acted Macbeth pretty well; was called for and well received. Looked at some of the scenes of this play. The putting of this tragedy on the stage is perfectly beautiful, it is what every one should go to see— they will never see it again.

November 8th.—Forster came into my room and proposed on the part of Dickens the dramatization of *Oliver Twist*, with Dickens's name. Nothing can be kinder than this generous intention of Dickens, but I fear it is not acceptable.

November 9th.—Looked at the newspapers, and read over the part of Ruthven, which I fear I cannot make sufficiently effective. Uneasy about it, and the difficulty in which the want of strong novelty places us. Forster sent me the volumes of *Oliver Twist*, which I looked carefully through, sending the first to Serle with a note. The dear children went to the Lord Mayor's show. The skimming over *Oliver Twist* occupied me more than the whole day.

November 10th.—Forster and Dickens called; and I told them of the utter impracticability of *Oliver Twist* for any dramatic purpose. Had a long consultation about the expediency of choosing *Rizzio* or *Marino Faliero*. Could not decide.

November 11th.—Forster called, and presented me with his book of Cromwell—Vol. I. From some questions I asked, I feel assured that he has divulged everything he knows about Bulwer's play. He is very indiscreet. Read the death of Rizzio to Catherine and Letty; the effect was heaviness and tediousness. Wightwick, Browning, and G. Bucknill dined with us.

November 12th.—Looked at the newspaper, and went to the theatre, where the rehearsal of the *Royal Oak* was going on. I could not attend to it, being occupied with the discussion and consideration of what was to be done in the case of the play of the death of Rizzio. Serle took it to read, and I wrote to Haynes, appointing him to call

475

and talk of it to-morrow. Serle gave his opinion that it could not succeed, and that the author ought to re-write it. Lay down, wearied, and slept; could not think. After, Bulwer called, and promised to send his play of *Richelieu* up to Cumberland Terrace. Acted Macbeth but indifferently, not altogether well; was called for by the audience and well received; but must be careful. Found Bulwer's play at home; sat up till half-past two to read it.

November 13th.—Awoke wearied and brain-tired. Wrote a note to Bulwer. Went to Covent Garden theatre and superintended the rehearsal of the *Royal Oak*. Haynes called. I gave him my opinion and he assented to it—to withdraw the play and re-write it. Jerrold [1] sent two acts of his play. Bulwer called and I thought seemed disappointed that I did not show more enthusiasm about his play.

November 14th.—Read the two acts of Jerrold's play, with which I was much pleased. Went to Covent Garden theatre, and attended to the rehearsal of the *Royal Oak*; gave much attention to it. Spoke with Serle about Jerrold, and gave him an order for £50 upon his play. Forster showed me a note of Bulwer's, enclosing a letter to him from Mr. C. Kean in a most sycophantic strain, asking him " to write him a play, in consequence of his success in the country in *Claude Melnotte* after going twice to see me play it! Saw the *Royal Oak*, which the clique, who attend all our new afterpieces, hissed; it is too bad.

November 15th.—Read greater part of Bulwer's play of *Richelieu*, which, though excellent in parts, is deficient in the important point of continuity of interest. I should also say that the character is not *servatus ad imum*. At home read some scenes in the latter part of *Richelieu*, which are not effective. I fear the play will not do—cannot be made effective.

November 17th.—Looked at the newspaper. Read a very strongly put charge of gross inhumanity against Sir H. Halford [2] leaving his friend to die in the road and going on to his own dinner! He *is* a

---

[1] Douglas William Jerrold (1803–1857); the well-known wit and dramatist. His *Black-eyed Susan*, produced in 1829, at once made his reputation as a playwright.

[2] Sir Henry Halford, Bart. (1766–1844); the fashionable physician of that day, who, it was said, owed more to his manners than to his knowledge of medicine. He was much in the confidence of George IV, and numbered among his many distinguished patients the Duke of Wellington, for whom, on the strength of his use of Latin in prescriptions, he was invited to compose the Duke's inaugural speech as Chancellor of the University of Oxford! So the Duke informed Thomas Raikes; presumably at the time (1834) his Grace was still on bad terms with his elder brother, Lord Wellesley, who, as one of the most elegant Latinists of the century, was his obvious resource on such an occasion.

heartless man.   At Rugby, on a visit to Dr. Wooll, he went to see a dying boy at the school, and only took £20 for it!—*jam satis!*   Called on Bulwer, and talked over the play of *Richelieu*.   He combated my objections, and acceded to them, as his judgment swayed him; but when I developed the object of the whole plan of alterations he was in ecstasies.   I never saw him so excited, several times exclaiming he was " enchanted " with the plan, and observed, in high spirits, " What a fellow you are! "   He was indeed delightful.   I left him the play, and he promised to let me have it in a week!   He is a wonderful man.   Left him to go to the theatre, where I caught the new piece [1] in rehearsal, which I did not much like.   Mr. Scharf [2] called, to whom I gave the freedom of the theatre, to encourage him as an artist.

November 18th.—Sir E. Bulwer called, and showed me two scenes, good ones, that he had already written.   Settled the plot of the remainder.   Forster called.   Read part of *Cinq Mars*.   Considered *William Tell*.   Read prayers to the family.   Heard of the continued abuse in *John Bull*; angry at first, but soon learned to disregard it.

November 20th.—Read *Cinq Mars* in bed.   Letters from Mrs. Jameson warmly complimenting me on my revival of the *Tempest*. Acted Prospero coldly; called for by the audience and well received. Saw Morton's farce, which I thought very poor, and that it would have failed had it been produced after the *Tempest*.   Forster wished me to ask Bulwer to dine on Sunday and read his play to him.   George Meredith [3] in his letter tells me that I am considered a " great man." If I am, I do not feel the difference!

November 21st.—Finished the novel of *Cinq Mars*, much of which I thought very clever—very graphic—sometimes profound—the characters well sustained, and the situations deeply interesting—sometimes overstrained, and persons like Milton, Corneille, etc., uselessly paraded before us.   Sent back *Cinq Mars*, with a note of invitation to Bulwer.   Read a short account of Richelieu in Disraeli.   Bulwer called, bringing with him the completed *Richelieu*.   Seemed glad to come here on Sunday.   Arrived at home, read through Bulwer's play

---

[1] A farce, called *Chaos is Come Again, or the Race Ball* (*note by Sir F. Pollock*).

[2] Mr. George Scharf, whose early production, under the modest title of *Recollections of the Scenic Effects of Covent Garden Theatre* during the season 1838-9, gives an admirable notion of the scenery and stage grouping of the plays produced under Macready's management at Covent Garden theatre (*note by Sir F. Pollock*).

[3] Not the author of that name.

of *Richelieu*. I begin to be deadened to the interest of its story; it seems to be occasionally lengthy. I fear it has not the clinging interest of his present successful play, but hope and trust are good supporters.

November 22nd.—Thought over *Richelieu*—do not yet see my way into it. Marked the first act for cutting, snatched a hasty dinner, and went to the theatre. Saw Serle on his business of *William Tell;* sent a note to Mrs. Talfourd, with a private box for Friday night. Rooke called with the libretto of his opera. Robertson read and marked the second act of *Richelieu.* Very much fatigued. Note of thanks from Chantrey. Brydone on business. Slept for about a quarter of an hour. Acted Prospero feebly. Called for and well received by the audience.

November 23rd.—Thought over *Richelieu* before I rose. Read and marked the third act. Went to theatre, reading *Richelieu* by the way. Received notes from Dr. Elliotson inviting me to an exhibition of phenomena in animal magnetism on Sunday next; he is infatuated on this subject. Answered Bulwer's note. Read the remainder of the libretto of Mr. Haynes for Rooke's opera, which I think the greatest mass of unintelligible trash that ever perplexed a moderate intellect— perfectly detestable.

November 25th.—Began the reading and punctuating and cutting of the play of *Richelieu*, which lasted through the whole day until dinner-time. Was obliged to write a note to Dr. Elliotson—excusing myself from attending the exhibition of mesmerism. Sir Edward Bulwer and Forster came to dinner; after which I read the play of *Richelieu* to them and Catherine and Letitia; its effect was not what I had hoped, and in the fifth act Forster was asleep. This evidently hurt Bulwer, and we talked long after it. Forster, when Bulwer had gone, sat long talking over it, and admitted (what he never would have done but for this accident) that the interest of the play was not sufficient. I deeply feel the disappointment on Bulwer's account, to whom I am *so much indebted.*

November 26th.—Forster came into my room, and went to our box, where Catherine gave me a letter from Bulwer; chagrined, and evidently *angry* with Forster. It gave me great pain. Forster was importunate on its purport, which I was obliged to tell him I could not (according to Bulwer's expressed wish) communicate. He has warmth of feeling (Forster), but not much judgment, and wants the fine tact of good breeding. I went home very ill, and hastened to bed.

478

Liston had called on me in the morning—old and rickety—to ask for a " friend's " name to be added to his wife's on the free list.

November 27th.—Wrote to Bulwer in answer to his note, expressing to him how foremost in my consideration was his reputation ; that his play would have been valuable from any other person, but that it would not serve his interest, whether in reference to his literary fame, his station, or his political position. Acted Prospero rather better than I have lately done, but was not called on. Bulwer came into my room, and in a very warm manner expressed himself most gratified with my note, and much obliged. He sat and talked about *Richelieu,* and left me the note (a very valuable one) that he had written to me.

November 28th.—Went to theatre, where I was informed that Messrs. Warde and Waldron had refused their parts in *William Tell.* Took summary proceedings with Mr. Waldron, and sent for Mr. Warde, who *would not be found.* Rehearsal of *William Tell;* spoke to Read about dresses, to Young about the pantomime, several scenes of which I read, disapproving of some reflecting on the Queen's partiality to foreigners and Lord Melbourne's stay at Windsor.

November 29th.—Forster called, and showed me a very kind letter from Bulwer to him ; asked my advice as to his proper course of conduct with Thackeray, who he said had disclaimed acts of treachery, of which he, Forster, was well assured (on confidential statements) he had been guilty. I told him his only course was to be passive. He then talked about " the world's opinion," and I observed to him that there was no such thing as " the world." " The world," of which we all talked, consisted of the two or three friends or listeners who would in the course of conversation entertain our story ; and it was by this foolish word, " the world," that we constantly argued ourselves into foolish actions. He took my advice. Spoke to Mr. Warde about his refusal to act Gessler ; explained to him his own value and my estimation of him ; he consented to do it. Acted Prospero tolerably well ; was called for and well received.

November 30th.—Acted Werner, not by any means to my own satisfaction. The incessant occupation of my mind in the management does not allow me to do justice to my acting. I was extremely displeased with myself, although the general opinion would have induced me to think differently ; but I know when I act with truth, energy and finish. Was called for, and very warmly received.

December 1st.—Looked at my letters after dining, and then began

479

to read, for a few minutes only, an opera which Fonblanque, who had called in the course of the morning, and whom I was delighted to see, had left with me. Acted Prospero very fairly, was called for and warmly received.

December 2nd.—Finished reading the opera, begun in bed last night, which Fonblanque left with me; it is the best libretto in point of plot and words of the songs that I have yet received. Bulwer called and discussed at great length the plot of *Richelieu* and also read me the plot of a new comedy.

December 3rd.—Went to the theatre; looking at the play as I drove along. Gave the whole day to the rehearsal of *William Tell*, which cost me much time and toil. There is no one that I can trust —no one to whom I can devolve the care of a scene. I am alone, and cannot bear up against the pressure. Nothing but the conviction of it being my last season could sustain me in it. Lay down a little before five o'clock. Acted William Tell indifferently—not by any means so well as I rehearsed it; I was *very* nervous and dispossessed. Was called for by the audience, and very enthusiastically received.

December 5th.—Dickens brought me his farce, which he read to me. The dialogue is very good, full of point, but I am not sure about the meagreness of the plot. He reads as well as an experienced actor would—he is a surprising man.

December 6th.—Gave the whole morning to compressing and correcting the pantomime. Wrote to the editor of the *Weekly Dispatch*, striking that paper off the free list. Letter from Hon. R. Grimston [1] about a reading in Shakspeare.

December 7th.—Read the paper. Knowles called, ostensibly to ask for *two* private boxes, but, as I think, to ascertain what money was likely to come. He said he would make no charge, but as the play of *William Tell* did not belong to Covent Garden I might pay him for it *by the night.* *N.B.*—He had given me a promise several years ago to *give me* the gratuitous right of performing this play ! ! ! I would not take it on this footing, but gave him £20 for the work he had done—which was *very little!* A very grossly insulting letter from the

---

[1] The Hon. Robert Grimston (1816–1894); the well-known sportsman. He and the Hon. Frederick Ponsonby (afterwards sixth Earl of Bessborough) were for many years familiar figures in the Harrow cricket-field, where they coached successive " elevens " of their old school with a thoroughness rivalling that of the best professional. " Bob " Grimston was as much at home across country as he was on the cricket-ground, while as the able chairman of more than one important telegraph company, he acquired a high reputation in the business world.

editor of the *Weekly Dispatch*—which, in my first impulse, I re-enclosed in its own *turned* over; but hesitated, under the supposition that it might seem too haughty, and wrote a gentlemanly letter of retort, quietly repeating that falsehood had been my provocation and that the subsequent reply to me was impertinent. Brydone suggested the return of the letter, as I had at first intended, and I, concurring with him, re-enclosed it in its own cover, and sent it back to the editor.

December 8th.—Looked at the paper, and read a very pretty sonnet on the *Tempest* and its revival in the *Literary Gazette*. Mr. Willmott told me that Mr. Williams, the editor of the *Dispatch*, had published my letter and the one he sent me (which I returned to him) in the paper—the wretched blackguard! He had not said that I had returned it! Miss Faucit asked me to write my name on a print of Virginius, which I did. Note from Bulwer with his play, which I read; it is greatly improved, but still not quite to the point of success.

December 9th.—Rose very late after reading the newspaper, in which Forster had written no notice of *William Tell*—an omission which I felt as a disservice. He told me of an insidious article in *John Bull*. Bulwer called and I agreed to ask some person to hear the play read on Sunday next.

December 10th,—Wrote notes of invitation to Browning, Fox, Rintoul, Wallace, H. Smith, Blanchard, asking them to dine and hear Bulwer's play on Sunday. Dickens, Forster, Serle, Willmott, etc., came into my room. Dickens agreed to read his farce to-morrow.

December 11th.—Dickens came with Forster and read his farce. There was manifest disappointment; it went flatly, a few ready laughs, but generally an even smile, broken in upon by the horse-laugh of Forster, the most *indiscreet* friend that ever allied himself to any person. He has goaded Dickens to write this farce, and now (without testing its chances of success) would *drive* it upon the stage. Defend me from my friends! It was agreed that it should be put into rehearsal, and, when nearly ready, should be seen and judged of by Dickens! I cannot sufficiently condemn the officious folly of this marplot, Forster, who embroils his friends in difficulties and distress in this most determined manner. It is quite too bad.

December 12th.—A long discussion on Dickens's farce; called in for their opinion Messrs. Bartley and Harley. The result was that Forster decided on withdrawing the farce.

December 13th.—Wrote to Bulwer, and to Dickens, about his

farce, explaining to him my motives for wishing to withdraw it, and my great obligation to him. He returned me an answer which is an honour to him. How truly delightful it is to meet with high-minded and warm-hearted men. Dickens and Bulwer have been certainly to me noble specimens of human nature, and show out strongly the pitiful contrast that a man like Talfourd offers. Answered Mr. Warren, sending him the freedom of the theatre. Wrote to Mrs. Buller about her piece; to Hayward about his note, sending him the freedom.

December 16th.—Attended to my accounts, and then gave the whole morning to the conclusion of the marking of *Richelieu*. Henry Smith and Serle called first, then Browning, Fox, Blanchard, and Lane to hear the reading of the play. I told them that no one must speak during the process, gave pencils and paper to each, with which they were severally to write down their opinions. The play was listened to with the deepest interest, and the opinions, all of which were favourable, were given in. I then spoke to them individually and endeavoured to gain their precise opinions more in detail. Mrs. Serle, Miss P. Horton, Mr. and Mrs. P. Cooke, Mr. Vining, and Mr. Sloman came afterwards to dinner; spent a cheerful evening; music afterwards. Wrote an account of the result to Bulwer.

December 19th.—Received a letter and MS. of a play from Mrs. Butler,[1] of Philadelphia, brought by Mr. Power.

December 20th.—Went to Covent Garden theatre; on my way continued the perusal of Mrs. Butler's play, which is a work of uncommon power. At the theatre gave my attention to the rehearsal of the pantomime. Business with Serle, Willmott, etc. Read the newspapers. Saw that the printer of the *Times* was found guilty of libel on Sir J. Conroy;[2] will be imprisoned for the villainy of some wretched coward who skulks behind his incognito. Finished the reading of Mrs. Butler's play, which is one of the most powerful of the modern plays I have seen—most painful, almost shocking, but full of power, poetry, and pathos. She is one of the most remarkable women of the present day.

December 21st.—A son born.[3] A note from Jerdan asking me

---

[1] Fanny Kemble.

[2] Sir John Conroy was a prominent member of the Duchess of Kent's household, and an article in the *Times* had imputed to him not only mismanagement of her affairs, but the application of her moneys for his own purposes. Conroy in consequence took proceedings against the printer of the *Times* for libel, which resulted in a verdict of guilty, and a sentence of one month's imprisonment together with a fine of £200.

[3] Henry Frederick Bulwer, died August 12, 1857.

482

to withhold the cheque for £70, upon the faith of which he had borrowed that sum from me. The fact cannot be disguised; he is a man who has no conscience in obtaining the means of other men. The money is gone! Wrote notes to Ransom's, to withhold Jerdan's cheque. It is useless to make strife with a man who has it in his power to cheat you, and is determined to do so. One's mind must be made up. He has sold me, as others have done! Wrote to a person of the name of Rahles, who very kindly sent me a rich velvet cap in testimony of the pleasure he had received from my performances.

December 22nd.—Letter from Jerdan. More frivolous excuses. He has robbed me, and there is an end.

December 24th.—Went to Covent Garden theatre, where I found Forster, Dickens, and Browning, who, with Fonblanque, came to see what I would gladly have been excused from, the rehearsal of the pantomime. I remained attending to it from eleven o'clock, the hour of my arrival, to twenty minutes past eight. Towards the close it appeared in a state so utterly desperate, that I had the carpenters, etc., into my room to give me information respecting my contemplated alteration of the playbill. I found that much of the confusion arose from the stupidity of the men—always excepting Marshall's shameful inefficiency and still more shameful vanity and presumption in undertaking what he could not hope to effect. Discovering the cause of their difficulty, I made arrangements for easing them, and so far relieved the pantomime from so much cause of fear; but there is not in its execution, whatever may be its fortune, justice done to the lavish expenditure which has been made for it. If successful, I shall owe most to the exertions of Bradwell; if unfortunate, its ruin rests with Mr. Marshall. I have very, very little hope and great fear; indeed, I am bracing my mind up to the event. God befriend me in all my doings! Amen! A letter from Bulwer—the noble-hearted fellow!—wishing to try the play before the green-room. I wrote assenting.

December 25th.—My dear children's voices greeted me with the wish of a merry Christmas and a happy New Year. Mr. Pope called whilst I was in dear Catherine's room, who with her blessed babe is, thank God, going on extremely well. Was reluctant to go out, but thought it my business to be seen by the workmen in the theatre, and therefore went there, taking dearest Willie with me, and leaving him in the coach outside at the box-office, whilst I went into the theatre to observe the progress the men had made. Was much cheered by the tone of all, and the appearance of diligence among them.

December 26th.—Went to Covent Garden theatre, and rehearsed Hastings; then giving my attention to the pantomime until twenty minutes past five o'clock. Acted Lord Hastings indifferently—my mind was on the pantomime.[1] From the utter absence of arrangement on the part of Mr. Marshall, his clumsy attempt at contrivance, and the deficiency of his work, the pantomime completely failed. What will be the result I cannot guess—it will go near to ruin me. It is a terrible blow.

December 27th.—After a bad night I awoke to think of the desperate state of our affairs, and looked with a very complacent face upon the gloomy prospect before me. Poor Letitia was sadly broken down by it. Went to Covent Garden theatre; on my way looked through the often-searched Shakspeare for some play. Thought of *King Henry V,* with the choruses to be spoken by Vandenhoff. Attended to the pantomime, which I cut, and set the performers and the carpenters about. Serle, when I suggested *Henry,* observed that the choruses would admit of illustration, a hint which I instantly caught at, and determined upon doing it. Attended to the performance of the pantomime, which went off very smoothly. Afterwards arranged business for rehearsing it. Received notes from H. Smith and Winston, wishing me to withdraw my resignation at the Garrick Club. Attended to the performance of the pantomime, which, thank God, went off very smoothly. Afterwards arranged business for rehearsing it. Wrote notes to Serle and Winston, persisting in my withdrawal.

December 29th.—Miss H. Faucit came into my room, during the play, to ask for a box for Monday. I spoke to Miss P. Horton about her insubordinate language. She was much distressed about it.

December 30th.—Forster sent the papers to Letitia, by which it seems our pantomime stands fair for attraction. L.D. Forster and Talfourd called. Spoke about Mrs. Butler's play, which Forster thought I was called upon to act. After dinner continued the attentive perusal of *King Henry V.* Talked with Letitia over *King Henry,* explaining to her how I would produce it. Resolved to defer it to Easter, and make it the last Shakspearian revival of my management. Wrote to Mr. Powell, thanking him for his dedication of an edition of Shakspeare's plays to me.

December 31st.—Forster called to ask me for private boxes; told me he believed that he should continue in the Garrick Club! Now he

---

[1] The title was *Harlequin and Fair Rosamond; or, Old Dame Nature and the Fairy Art* (*note by Sir F. Pollock*).

has *laboured* to induce me to retire from it, and I have no doubt has instigated Dickens to leave it; his words had no weight with me, but he gives me a very low opinion of his "gentlemanly" feelings to endeavour thus to make cat's paws of his friends to satisfy his own vindictive feelings. Cut the first act of the new drama. Looked at newspapers. Mrs. Warner rode rather restive about the part of Mrs. Placid. I was not altogether pleased with her. Bulwer called and talked long about *Richelieu*, which he is to send me to-morrow night. Cast up my accounts for the year—at the end of which I prostrate my heart in humble gratitude before the throne of mercy, the seat of His Divine Power, to whom I owe all the blessings I enjoy, and from whom alone is happiness and peace. Blessed be His Name!

London, January 1st.—Knowles came in, and wished to *back out* from the undertaking he gave me the other day; he is a b—g—d in heart—a mean, blood-sucking, loud-tongued, vulgar-minded man; an unjust man. Read the papers. Reduced the drama of *Siege of Alençon* to two acts. Wrote notes to Cattermole, Harness, Warde. Read part of Mrs. Butler's play. Acted Prospero tolerably. Called for by the audience and well received. Miss H. Faucit came into my room about her dress. Mr. Duncan, Warde's friend, called and talked over his affairs. I recommended, as his only chance, the Insolvent Act. Sent him £5, as Mr. Duncan said he was starving. Received a letter and the MS. of *Richelieu* from Bulwer.

January 2nd.—Wrote a note to Bulwer, sending him Mrs. Butler's MS. Went to Covent Garden theatre, where I found notes from Mr. Warde, thanking me for my kindness, and stating his intention of taking again the benefit of the Insolvent Act! We were young men together at the head of the theatre in Bath! Forster and Dr. Quin came into my room; afterwards poor Blanchard, in dreadfully low spirits; it now appears that poor L. E. L., the gifted creature, perished by her own hand! [1] What is genius? Cattermole came and sat some time with me. Appointed an amanuensis to come and copy Bulwer's play to-morrow.

January 3rd.—The copyist, whom I had appointed, was disposed in the drawing-room, where I saw him, and found that in two hours he had not written twenty lines. Talfourd came in, and gave me another copy of *Ion* and *Athenian Captive*, with the sonnet on Nina's birth altered, and one to Dickens on *Oliver Twist*. Spoke again to Robertson about the Gloucester box, which the proprietors hold from me, and nightly use. Last night, in addition to this, Captain Forbes

---

[1] She had married George Maclean, Governor of Cape Coast Castle, and accompanied him to the colony, where her death took place in October of the previous year, only a few months after her marriage. Macready suggests that she committed suicide, but the circumstances, when fully known, seemed rather to indicate that she died from an accidental overdose of prussic acid, taken medicinally.

me to remain. Declined. Left my coach at Newman Street, and met there the writer of the letters—a fine-looking young woman, of modest deportment. I inquired of her, as we walked, her object in writing to me, and wishing to see me. She begged my pardon, and I learned that she had been living at Sir ——'s. She asked if I was married. I told her I was, which seemed a bitter shock to her. I told her I was many years older than herself, and spoke to her with kindness. She made me uneasy from the deep and—as it seemed to me—*desperate* melancholy of her expression. I told her to let me know if I could do anything to serve her, and I would do it. I parted from her by Westminster Hall. I felt quite uneasy and dejected at what seemed to me her unhappiness. She had evidently encouraged the hope of *marrying* the ideal that had filled her mind from the representation of Claude Melnotte. Poor girl! I was quite depressed. How much are we the victims of an inevitable destiny! Read two acts of Jerrold's play, which is too didactic.

January 9th.—Read the remaining three acts of Jerrold's play, which I was concerned to find a very heavy and, in my opinion, a hopeless affair; but alterations may give it a better chance. I was in very low spirits, and could not disguise the dejection into which the thought of that poor girl whom I saw last night sunk me. How hard seems to me the lot of the uneducated, with all the passions and feelings of those who are instructed to control and subdue them, yet subject to merely equal, or perhaps not so severe, penalties for indulging them! A strange world! Went to Covent Garden theatre, where I attended to business. Mr. Jerrold called, and in the presence of Serle I gave him my opinion on his play, of its want of action and purpose. He assented to much that I urged, and Serle agreed to read the play and give his digested opinion. Brydone afterwards came and showed me the account. The pantomime has cost £1500!!!—just £1000 more than it should have cost, and more than it appears to have cost. Began to punctuate *Richelieu*, which we had decided to produce without further delay. Acted Claude Melnotte pretty well; was called for and well received. Note from Harness, about Mrs. Butler's play.

January 10th.—Went to Covent Garden theatre, where I found several letters, one from a Mr. Winfield, in great anger about not having his money returned last night. How very foolish does passion make men look!—the folly of our lives is for the most part *passion*. An angry man is almost sure to expose himself. Answered very civilly Mr. Winfield's note, telling him to call for his money.

489

January 11th.—Looked at the newspaper.   Went to Covent Garden theatre, superintended the rehearsal of the new drama, which I saw there was an absolute necessity for altering still further, and took the MS. for that purpose.   Serle and Willmott came to speak on business; looked at the dresses for the *Invincibles*, and was sorry to note the prudery of Miss Horton and Miss Taylor.   Revised the third act of *Richelieu* and gave it to Wilson.   Brydone brought me the bills, which I signed.   Acted Werner very unsatisfactorily.   I am really deteriorating from the surrendering my time and thought to the management. It distresses me to think of it.   Was called for and well received by the audience.   Mr. Thompson was brought in by Harley to speak to me about some banners for the new drama.   Serle gave me the first act of his melodrame.   Heaven grant its success!   A note from a Mr. Glenny, editor and proprietor of the *Court Gazette*, very abruptly and, I think, rudely questioning me upon the admission granted to his paper.   Found a note from Bulwer at home.   Answered Mr. Glenny's note.

January 12th.—Went to theatre.   Spoke to Miss P. Horton on her unreasonable objection to the dress of the character in the *Invincibles:* to Mrs. Warner, suggesting to her the part of François in *Richelieu*. It seems, however, I had some years ago recommended her, as a woman, not to wear male attire at all, and she has scrupulously adhered to my advice, and now resolutely acted on it.   I did not press the point, for I respected her grounds of objection.   A note from Miss Horton, resisting, most prudishly, the dress already spoken of; annoyed by it. Bulwer called, and we talked over the play.

January 13th.—Read the newspaper; noted an excellent extract from Bulwer's works on good sense.   I have received *great benefit* from his observations; far more than from anything that Talfourd can write, and yet how the latter decries him!—it is envy.   Noted also an observation on the licence of that foul-mouthed man, Thesiger, in dragging forth some circumstance of H. Berkeley's private life.   I shall remember it to use it.   Read over and proceeded to alter the new drama, which is weak and has no strong points.

January 14th.—Looked at the newspaper, in which were some really *brutal aristocratic* charges of brutality on the Irish people by those wretched things of Lords—or *roués*, ——!   Is it not a disgrace to human reason that such wretches as these, the —— and such a herd of worthless reptiles in human form should be allowed to legislate for men!   It sickens one of the world.

490

DOUGLAS JERROLD

From an engraving

January 15th.—Harness called to tell me the strong opinions of Mr. Milman and Miss Martineau against Mrs. Butler's play, that he had written to her informing her of them, and leaving it to her to decide. I told him I could not abide by *her* decision, of which I felt already sure; that I must have an *appui* in the opinion of her friends to fall back upon, if roughly taxed for producing such an immoral play; that I could not compromise the character to which I had been endeavouring to raise the theatre.

January 16th.—Willmott told me of Miss Taylor's continued opposition to her dress in the *Invincibles,* which I stated (as it was universally allowed to be most delicate) she must wear or resign the part. Acted Claude Melnotte pretty well; was called for and well received. Letter from Mary ——; poor girl, she must suffer very much. I feel for her. She is evidently possessed with a deep and absorbing passion, and has right notions. I feel (what I have in reality endured) for her when she speaks of her agony as she will see the curtain fall and shut me for ever from her sight. Poor, poor girl! All were talking about her Majesty's second visit to the Haymarket theatre to-night, and her neglect of Covent Garden. I receive it, whether a token of dislike to our establishment or no, with perfect good-humour; the sovereignty of the people is the only true rule. Let her, while she can patronize the morality of Drury Lane and the fine taste of the Haymarket, leave Shakspeare and Covent Garden to the " low " rabble. . . . The Queen did not go to the Haymarket.

January 17th.—Went to Covent Garden theatre; found a card of Lord Alfred Paget, and on it that " the Queen comes early to-morrow night." Acted Prospero rather better than usual. I took pains with it chiefly because Miss Martineau was in the theatre. Received a note from her.

January 18th.—Looked in the newspaper, in which I was glad to see that O'Connell had denounced that wretched creature's (Lord Oxmantown's) speech [1] as it deserved. Note from Knowles—a very rude one, I thought; he is a vulgar person, anything but a gentleman in mind, heart, or manners. I sent him a private box without any other answer. Rooke called to speak about his opera—" I fear thee, ancient Mariner ! " Lunn brought to me at home specimens of

---

[1] The speech was made at a meeting of the King's County magistrates, a few days after the murder of Lord Norbury, in denouncing which Lord Oxmantown made an excursion into politics which appears to have incensed O'Connell and elicited a rebuke from the Lord-Lieutenant.

bouquet-holders, from which I chose one for the Queen's box.   Revised two acts of *Richelieu.*

January 19th.—Forster called.   Fox called, and told me that East-hope of the *Morning Chronicle* had given way to the importunities of Mr. Bunn's friends, and that hereafter the notices of Drury Lane theatre were to be—not written by Mr. Fox! The last of the daily papers that made any pretensions to honesty of opinion. Robertson came in, and told me that the *proprietors were going to advertise the theatre to be let.* I told him it would ruin the season, and very soon close it. He justified the proprietors, which he always does, and certainly ought not to be in a double office. He cannot serve *two masters.* I told him that I would not depend on my own opinion, I felt so strongly on the matter, but that I would ask others.

January 20th.—Endeavoured to prepare a counter-advertisement to neutralize the mischievous intention of the proprietors' announcement of the theatre to let. Could not easily satisfy myself, being anxious to avoid all appearance of inculpating those *honourable* persons (!) the proprietors. Forster called in, talked of the business, and made some good exceptions to the heads I had written down. He stayed dinner. Received from Forster a copy of the resolutions passed by the meeting of friends who subscribed the £1000 for Covent Garden theatre. Most kind and flattering to me. Leader, M.P., in the chair —Gaskell, M.P., mover—Osborne seconder.

January 21st.—Went to Covent Garden theatre; spoke with Robertson in a very long conversation. I told him that I was quite indifferent now to the insertion of the advertisement, which the proprietors were welcome, as far as I was concerned, to publish. He declared that the proprietors had no feeling of hostility towards me whatever, that they had most at heart the welfare of the performers, etc., and much which the conduct of the preceding Saturday did not seem to bear out. He, however, positively withdrew the advertisement, which I told him I was *fully prepared* to meet.

January 23rd.—Note from the Vice-Chamberlain informing me of the Queen's intention to command next week, and wishing a list of plays. Received a number of sketches by young Scharf, with a letter, wishing to dedicate the work to me. Went into the painting-room, and spoke with Marshall. Acted Claude Melnotte pretty well. Found Forster at home, and a note from Mr. Hall, wishing to dedicate a volume of his *Book of Gems* to me. Dickens sent me his *Oliver Twist.*

January 24th.—Heard that the Queen was going to pay a third visit to Drury Lane theatre to see the lions, and after the performance to go on the stage![1]

January 25th.—Read in the *Morning Post* the account of the Queen's third visit to Drury Lane theatre to see the beasts, and of her going upon the stage after the pantomime to see them fed. Mr. Martin, the Vice-Chamberlain, called, wishing to know if we could send him word of the *length* of each that I could offer. He did not *exactly* know the night she would come (I believe he was enjoined *not* to communicate what he *did* know), and thought the *Lady of Lyons* would be the play.

January 26th.—Mr. Martin, the Vice-Chamberlain, arrived to inform me of the night on which the Queen would command (which they knew two days ago!) and of the plays she had selected : *Lady of Lyons* and *Rob Roy*. Received a note from Dickens, wishing me to look in upon the Shakspeare Club in the course of the evening. Went to the Shakspeare Club, where I had to return thanks, greatly to my annoyance.

January 31st.—Found my desk covered with notes and letters ; one from Count D'Orsay, most kindly suggesting to me the avoidance of several defects complained of by the Queen at Drury Lane. I answered it, and asked him to obtain for me some information respecting *Richelieu* from Count de Vigny, the author of *Cinq Mars*.

February 1st.—Looked at the paper, and went to Covent Garden theatre, where I was occupied with business, fuss, etc., the *whole day*— the preparations for the evening, the refreshments, the Queen's box, etc.; all little affairs, very teasing, very fatiguing ; seeing persons applying for cards ; notes from the Vice-Chamberlain, etc. A very kind note from Count D'Orsay, enclosing one, most kind and complimentary, from the Comte de Vigny :

"J'ai tardé à te répondre, cher ami, dans l'espoir de pouvoir déranger mes affaires de manière à me rendre à ton invitation, mais je ne le pourrai pas, je le vois aujourd'hui. Il me faut aller dans le Berkshire, et je ne sais pas quel jour je reviendrai ; mais il sera dans peu de temps. En revenant, je t'écrirai sur le champ, et je prendrai un matin ou une heure pour causer avec le grand tragédien, que j'ai admiré et applaudi (sans qu'il s'en soit douté) dans presque tous les grands rôles, et dernièrement dans la *Tempête*. Il sera bien beau dans *Richelieu*, et j'aurai beaucoup à lui dire de cet homme, dont j'ai été *l'ennemi intime* pendant tout le terme que j'ai écrit *Cinq Mars*. Quand on attend une réponse à ma porte, je

---

[1] Macready seems to have forgotten that the Queen was still in her teens, and more likely to appreciate Van Amburgh and his lions than the "legitimate drama," to which, moreover, she had given by no means illiberal patronage.

suis au supplice. J'avais bien des choses à te dire de mon amitié, mais j'irai achever ma phrase en t'embrassant,

"A toi mille fois,

"ALFRED DE VIGNY."

Acted Claude Melnotte very fairly. Her Majesty did not arrive until twenty-five minutes past seven. My reception was most enthusiastic, and the play, *Lady of Lyons*, was very warmly received. I had undressed, and was preparing to put on my court suit, when an equerry came from her Majesty to desire me to go on, as the audience were calling for me. I did not know what to do—told him, and showed him that I was quite undressed, but that I would do whatever her Majesty desired. He left me, and I thought it better to put on my dress again, which I did, and receiving a second message from her Majesty, went on as Melnotte before the audience, and met with a most enthusiastic reception, her Majesty and the Lord Chamberlain joining in the applause. Dressed in full court dress, went up to see Miss Martineau, and then into Marianne Skerrett's box. She was delighted to see me, and introduced me to her two friends, colleagues in office! The *coulisses* were crowded. I saw, just to grasp hands as I passed, Fladgate, R. Price, Warren, Harris, Browning, Forster, Mr. and Mrs. T. Chitty, C. Barker—an old schoolfellow, to whom I had given a card in the morning—Fitzgerald, Troughton, etc. Went into the anteroom when her Majesty came out. Lord Conyngham called me to her, and she condescended to say "I have been very much pleased." I bowed, and lighted her down. Glad to conclude a day that has been very wearying to me. All went off very satisfactorily.

February 2nd.—Saw the newspapers. The *Morning Post* reported the proceedings of the night in a fair spirit. The *Morning Herald* and the *Times* merely mentioned what related to the Queen—these honest persons. Saw the *Court Journal*, which contains a wretched piece of trash, justifying the Queen's patronage of Mr. Van Amburgh!

February 3rd.—Answered D'Orsay's letter, and copied Comte de Vigny's note to him.

February 4th.—Received a note from Marianne, giving me a long account of the Queen, Baroness Lehzen,[1] and the Duchess of Kent.

February 5th.—Very kind note from D'Orsay, enclosing one from Byng, Comptroller of the Household, expressing the satisfaction which was given by Covent Garden theatre at the command. Miss Taylor

---

[1] Formerly the Queen's governess. She had great influence over the Queen, which was much resented in certain quarters.

494

refused to wear the dress in the *Invincibles,* and I accordingly was obliged to take her out of the part. Note from the Queen's equerry informing me of her intention to visit the theatre this evening. Looked at the papers—*Times* and *Herald*—both of which noticed in terms of high commendation Mr. Van Amburgh's beasts; of course were silent on Covent Garden. Acted Prospero partially well—not entirely. The Queen came but was not recognized. Attended to business.

February 6th.—Acted Claude Melnotte tolerably well in parts. Was called for, and in leading on Miss Faucit was offended with her ill-humour, evidently arising from not having been called upon the Queen's visit. Was well received. Sir E. Bulwer came into my room and sat some time. Forster came in.

February 8th.—Barham called to thank me for his card of *entrée* on Friday last; told me he feared the Garrick Club would not stand. Received a note of invitation for Saturday from D'Orsay to meet De Vigny. Went home; spent an evening with my children, romping and playing. They were very happy.

February 9th.—Answered two girls, who wrote, wishing to come on the stage. I thought it much better not to see them. What business have I with them? Note from Brockedon enclosing one, attesting the spread of my reputation to Germany. Wrote to a petitioner in great distress, sending him £1. Heard from Mr. Burnett that the Anti-Corn Law Committee had decided on holding their meeting at Covent Garden, although Drury Lane was offered for £50 less!

February 11th.—Bulwer, Tennyson D'Eyncourt, and Forster came into my room and sat some time. Note from D'Orsay. Found a note informing me that he had a play from *B. Disraeli !!!*

February 12th.—Serle, Robertson, and Brydone came into my room; the latter told me that the Queen was at Drury Lane; that the *claqueurs* tried to get up a call to bring the performers on, and that the Queen came forward in her box and responded to it!

February 13th.—Read the newspaper, or rather that portion of it which gave the debate on national education, in which I entirely sympathized with the feelings and opinions uttered by Mr. Wyse. All that these wretched Lords John and Francis, Stanleys, Ashleys, Peels, etc., think of is the question of *place;* the welfare of millions, their intellectual progress, the cultivation of their reason is to depend on the question. Is this earth still to be the mere material for these wretched knaves' ingenuity to work power and name out of? Or is there—can there be a hell of adequate punishment for such cold-blooded perverters

495

of benevolent and gracious purposes? I am sick at heart with them all. Called on Mrs. Jameson. She wished to read a play with me— made an appointment for to-morrow.

February 14th.—Received a note from the equerry-in-waiting to intimate her Majesty's intention of coming to the theatre this evening. Mrs. Jameson called, and read the greater part of her MS.—a translation from a German play by the Princess Amelia of Saxony. There was much to praise in it. Acted Claude Melnotte rather wearily. Mrs. Jameson's visit had knocked me up. Was called for, and well received by the audience. The Queen and Duchess of Kent were at the theatre to see the farce.

February 16th.—Went to Lady Blessington's with Forster, who had called in the course of the day. Met there Count de Vigny, with whom I had a most interesting conversation on *Richelieu.* I made an appointment with him to see him on *mardi prochain.* Met also, with D'Orsay, Bulwer, Charles Buller, Lord Durham, who was very cordial and courteous to me, Captain Marryat, who wished to be re-introduced to me, Hall, Standish, Chorley, Greville, who wished to be introduced to me also, Dr. Quin, etc. Passed a very agreeable two hours. Mr. Greville told a story of Le Kain in *Mithridate.* When some one on the stage observed, "Il changera son visage," one in the *parterre* exclaimed, "Laissez-le faire."

February 18th.—Letter from the equerry-in-waiting, apprising me of the Queen's intended visit to Covent Garden this evening. Read over *King Lear.* Went to Covent Garden theatre. Acted King Lear well. The Queen was present, and I pointed at her the beautiful lines : "Poor naked wretches! " Was called for, and well received.

February 19th.—Received Jerdan's dishonoured note, or draught on Longmans for his debt to me of £70. Oh, Jerdan! Jerdan! Attended to business with Marshall, who engaged to have the scenery of the new play finished on Monday ; with Bradwell about the armour for play ; with Serle on various matters. Robertson informed me that there was every chance of the ejection of that scoundrel, Mr. Bunn, from Drury Lane theatre. If such an end be accomplished I shall think my pains and sacrifices amply recompensed in the wide benefit conferred on all engaged in this profession. Went over his part of Mauprat with Mr. Anderson ; afterwards the part of François with Mr. Howe ; settled dresses with Head, and talked on business with Brydone.

February 20th.—Read the newspaper, which, with the debate on Villiers's motion for hearing evidence on the Corn Law question, and

496

some sparring about Mr. Turton [1] in the House of Lords occupied me long. Gave my attention to the consideration of the character of Richelieu, which Bulwer has made particularly difficult by its inconsistency; he has made him resort to low jest, which outrages one's notions of the ideal of Cardinal Richelieu, with all his vanity, and suppleness, and craft.

February 21st.—Walked out, and called on Comte de Vigny; sat with him very long, and was amply repaid for the time I gave. He related to me a variety of anecdotes illustrative of the characters of Louis XIII, Richelieu, of *Cinq Mars*, etc. He is an enthusiast, particularly for dramatic literature. He made a literal translation of *Othello*, and produced it at the *Théâtre Français*. He spoke with fervour of my performances, and was much dissatisfied with our custom of allowing women to frequent our pit, because the sympathy was checked by their intervention. He spoke like a poet, and with all the power and characteristic effect of a superior actor. I was very much pleased with him. A MS. tragedy and note from B. Disraeli.

February 22nd.—Read the paper, and gave my attention to the inquiry as to the possibility of reconciling the character which Bulwer has drawn under the name of Cardinal Richelieu with the original, from which it so entirely differs. Was not much cheered by the result of my investigation and experiment. Mr. Elton called by appointment, and I spoke to him about the manner in which he had rehearsed the part of Louis XIII. He talked in his old strain of disappointment, etc., although he came from playing in the *Love Chase* at the Haymarket to act Edgar, Beauseant, etc., at Covent Garden. He is bent on his ruin, I am confident. I read him various extracts from *Anquetil* and *Cinq Mars*, to show him the weak and nervous character of Louis, of which he knew nothing, nor would he have known anything. He went away seemingly more at ease about his part than he came. A letter from Wightwick (who had heard that I was coming to Plymouth) informing me that Mr. C. Kean had been playing to houses of £140 and £150 each—more than the theatre will hold!—and entreating me not to come, as I should be mortified by the contrast. It was kind in him, but I had no thought of going, as I told him in my answer. Resumed *Richelieu*, which I must *fabricate*. Attended to it in the evening.

February 23rd.—Found at the theatre a letter about a play from

---

[1] One of Lord Durham's secretaries in Canada; though an able man, his antecedents were somewhat questionable, and his appointment was severely criticized.

Mr. James,[1] the novelist. Rehearsed the play of *Richelieu*, with which I had some trouble. Miss Faucit spoke to me about her dress. Note from the equerry-in-waiting, announcing the Queen's intention of coming. The Queen came and went directly the play was over. I was called for, and well received. C. Buller came into my room, and stayed talking some time.

February 24th.—Went through with some attention, though I *could not* read word for word, the tragedy of Mr. G. Stephens.[2] Serle has given a very complimentary opinion upon it. This gentleman, in my mind, with very superior abilities, has a warp in his mind or taste, which nullifies his best efforts. Answered Mr. Phelps's application very courteously, sending him an order for £50. Wrote to Count de Vigny with the card of the Kent box. Mr. and Mrs. Dickens, Forster and O'Hanlon called.

February 25th.—Acted King Lear, not to my own satisfaction, though I was called for, and very warmly received by the audience. Bulwer and Forster came into my room, and afterwards the Comte de Vigny, who expressed himself much pleased with the play. Bulwer spoke to me about Richelieu, and satisfied me on the justice of his draught of the character from the evidence that history has given us. *Allons donc à la gloire!* Coming home found letters (as he had forewarned me) and more MS. from Bulwer.

February 27th.—Read the paper, in which was a very sensible article on the canting restriction put upon the Lent nights of performance. Misconceived the substance of a note from that ludicrously wretched fellow, Mr. E. Reade, author of *The Deluge*, etc. He had endeavoured to *bribe* me, by a promise of dedicating his miserable play to me, to act it. There were two previous dedications *erased* in the MS. to make way for me—one to Sir, something, Charles Reade, his cousin; the other to J. S. Knowles. He had also published his intention of dedication. He, now that I *again* refuse to act it, writes to intimate his intention of publishing it "and dedicating it accordingly"! For this relief much thanks! Note from Bulwer, which I answered. Note from Forster, which I also answered. Bulwer has asked Lady Blessington and D'Orsay to go to the rehearsal—an indiscreet step—to me an unpleasant one. Continued my work on

[1] George Payne Rainsford James (1799-1860); the well-known novelist and historian. He had written a novel on the subject of Richelieu some years previously.

[2] George Stephens (1800-1851); a dramatist of no particular note. His best-known work was a tragedy entitled *Martinuzzi*, produced by Phelps at the English Opera House in 1841.

Richelieu. Received a note from Comte de Vigny. Gave the evening to *Richelieu.* Wrote another note to Bulwer.

February 28th.—Went to Covent Garden theatre. Received two MSS.—one from a person signing Septimus, another from Mr. Mayhew, with a recommendatory letter from Mr. G. Smith, the gentleman who has been doing us all the injury in his power in *John Bull!* Rehearsed the play of *Richelieu,* which occupied the whole morning till past four o'clock. Forster was present for most of the time. Bulwer called to seek him after he had gone. A letter from Knowles inquiring " when the play of *Woman's Wit* would be done " ! A play that was only sustained by the proprietors foregoing rent and I salary ! ! Miss Faucit wished to speak to me—to ask for leave of absence to-morrow, which I could not grant.

March 1st.—Looked at the paper, in which was the debate upon theatrical entertainments on the Wednesdays and Fridays in Lent. I am quite indifferent to the question, which does not now affect myself; but could any man, with a desire to distinguish religion from hypocrisy and cant, read the speeches of Lord John Russell and Lord Teignmouth, and that recreant caitiff, Sir James Graham, without feelings of indignation and disgust. Such seemed to have been the general feelings of the House of Commons; and these are our legislators—our rulers ! ! ! God help us !

March 2nd.—Went to Covent Garden theatre, where I rehearsed *Richelieu;* was much annoyed by Mr. ——'s absence, who is confined by gout—induced by a system of nightly intoxication. He is too bad —a wretched man, on whom there is no dependence. Paid constant attention to the progress of the play, and thought it wore an improved appearance. Miss Faucit dined with me at half-past four. Mr. J. Vining called at the theatre in the course of the morning to inquire if I intended to act on *Wednesday,*[1] as they would do so at Drury Lane, and if I did the same that Madame Vestris would. I said certainly not; that while the law existed, though I condemned, I thought it more graceful to obey than to infringe it.

March 3rd.—Looked at the newspaper, in which was an excellent review of Sydney Smith's letter; a clergyman ! ! Mr. and Mrs. Dickens, Mr. and Mrs. T. Cooke, Forster, Ainsworth, Cattermole, Maclise, G. Bucknill came to dine with us.

---

[1] At this time there were no theatrical performances on Wednesdays and Fridays in Lent at the London theatres under the Lord Chamberlain's jurisdiction (*note by Sir F. Pollock*).

March 5th.—Went with much care through the rehearsal of *Richelieu*. By an accident of the printers Mrs. Warner's name was inserted in the bills for Catherine in the farce instead of Miss Faucit's; notice was sent to her, and she came in very ill temper to speak about it. I accosted her very kindly, and she attacked me, asserting that the measure had been adopted "for the mere accommodation of Miss Faucit." This was too bad from a person under such obligations as Mrs. Warner is to me. It is indeed *most ungrateful*. She wished to speak to me again, and I went to hear what she had to say, expecting to find her anxious to express her regret for her previous intemperance, but she only aggravated what had passed before. Bulwer came in and saw the last three acts rehearsed, with which he seemed very well satisfied.

March 6th.—Rehearsed *Richelieu*. Mr. Bainbridge, of the Lord Chamberlain's office, called to say the Queen was coming to-morrow night, and wished to have a book of the play. I wrote to Forster about it; received his answer, to which I returned a reply, and dismissed Mr. Bainbridge with the assurance that a copy would be sent to Lord Conyngham in the course of the evening. Tried on my dress with Head. Went home about six o'clock. Read through the part of Richelieu. God grant a triumph! Amen!

March 7th.—Colonel Cavendish and his two sons called; his business was to tell me that the Queen would come this evening. Lay down after dinner to compose my shaken nerves. Bulwer called, and *disturbed* me—to give me a book for the Queen. At the same time a letter was delivered to me; when Bulwer had left me I opened the letter. It was from Colonel Cavendish to inform me that the Queen would *not* come this evening. Acted Cardinal Richelieu [1] very nervously; lost my self-possession, and was obliged to use too much effort; it did not satisfy me at all, there were no artist-like touches through the play. How can a person get up such a play and do justice at the same time to such a character? It is not possible. Was called for and very enthusiastically received; gave out the play for every night. Jerdan, Smith, Brydone, D'Orsay, Bulwer and Forster came into my room. The success of the play seemed to be unequivocal. What will the papers say?

March 8th.—Saw the papers. The *Morning Chronicle* was as usual

---

[1] The principal parts in *Richelieu* were cast as follows: Louis XIII, Mr. Elton; Gaston, Mr. Diddear; Richelieu, Mr. Macready; Baradas, Mr. Warde; Mauprat, Mr. Anderson; De Beringhen, Mr. Vining; Father Joseph, Mr. Phelps; Huguet, Mr. George Bennett; François, Mr. Howe; Julie de Mortemar, Miss Helen Faucit; Marion de Lorme Miss Charles (*note by Sir F. Pollock*).

most kind and eulogistic ; the *Times*, although trying to damn with faint praise, admitting much more than I expected, and enough to give to its readers, who know its baseness, the assurance of success. Went to the theatre, where I cut the play with the performers, and expressed myself much obliged by their zeal and industry. When we had separated, Bulwer came and altered all that we had arranged— annoying and disconcerting me very much. I struggled for the omission of several passages, but he was triumphant, and therefore no longer *so docile* as I had heretofore found him.

March 9th.—Met Mrs. Warner, who looked very differently at me, poor foolish woman. Spoke with great kindness to Miss Rainforth about her neglect of the opportunity afforded her, ascribing it to the attention a gentleman in the theatre was showing her, cautioning her against the danger of trifling with the part in the new opera. She seemed very grateful, and promised to give her mind to her study. Colonel Cavendish brought me word that the Queen, prevented by the weather on Thursday night, would come this evening.

March 10th.—Bulwer called and remained for about two hours making alterations. Forster called with the various newspapers. Forster related Bulwer's domestic imbroglio.[1] Read passages from a play of Landor's *Giovanna of Naples*—of great beauty.

March 11th.—Note from Comte de Vigny. Attended the rehearsal for the cutting of the play. Acted the part of Richelieu very indifferently ; was quite out of temper with myself and everybody else. Was called for and well received—much better than I deserved. Business with Bulwer, making further alterations.

March 12th.—Saw the paper, in which Lord John Russell, upon the debate on Duncombe's motion, drew a comparison between the conduct pursued at Covent Garden and Drury Lane to my advantage —it is, however, a poor compliment to be mentioned in company with that wretched dastard, Mr. Bunn. Looked again at the play. Acted Cardinal Richelieu well ; was called for and very enthusiastically greeted. Forster, Brydone, Serle, Robertson, etc., came into my room.

March 13th.—Two long notes from Bulwer [2]—with more last

---

[1] Bulwer's differences with his wife, which led to separation and soon became public property.

[2] One of these is given below :

" MY DEAR MACREADY,

"I saw a good deal of the play last night, which went off better than on Monday. The restitution of the second scene, Act III, was quite right. I wish time could allow a little

words—and a lengthy criticism on some points of my performance, in which he wishes me to substitute coarse and vulgar attempt at low farcical point in one instance, and melodramatic rant in another for the more delicate shadings of character that I endeavour to give. I have long had surmises about Bulwer's taste from several things in the comedy of *La Vallière*—in the original of *The Lady of Lyons* and in the original copy of this play. I am *sure* that his taste is not to be

of the comic part, Act II. It is missed, and has been complained of to me in *many* quarters. But, perhaps, at all events it is too late to re-alter, even if time could be spared.

"I wish to say I was much more struck by your acting in the three last acts to-night than even heretofore, and so, I think, was the House generally. Forgive me if I say that the *more* you come out from subdued dryness into power (which you did to-night) the more brilliant your success will be, and the more you will realize the Cardinal—" *colère* et *orgueilleux* dont chaque pensée avait tout le *chaleur* d'une passion." De Vigny was wrong in thinking him so *sec*; there was plenty of animal spirits in him. In the grave part of your performance I see only one sentence in which I could wish another conception. It is the end of the act—where you say 'away with him.' Now you speak 'away with him ' with contemptuous sport like a man brushing away a trifle ! The audiences, however, are prepared for something much more vehement—and the thought of your conception is almost too subtle for the gigantic audiences you have—but I think it would be more like the Cardinal, who is accustomed to come and feast over the execution of his foes, to throw more of the deadly force of malignant and exulting vindictiveness into the words—something more to correspond with his laugh in baffling the murderers at the castle. I would have him release the devil of his rage upon his victim. I would make him follow with eyes that threaten savage victory the retreating form of Baradas—in fact, here I would have the effect that of power, the closing power of the speech. In the comic part (you must pardon my presumption in this) I must still fancy that greater breadth of humour—more of what the French call *malice*—would illustrate the character more vividly, and be infinitely more effective. I fancy the Cardinal with a CHUCKLE—'le rire presque gai, mais toujours insultant '—which is ascribed to him. Thus in 'Colonel and Nobleman, my bashful Huguet, that can never be ' —if it could be said with a more jovial laugh, and then with a pointed slyness (no pause, but fronting the audience) and almost a wink of the eye to Joseph, 'We'll promise,' etc.—this, I think, would be more effective. So after he has told Huguet he may be noble, why not let him exchange a broad humorous glance with Joseph, whom he passes at the moment, as much as to say, 'There now, isn't that cleverly done ?' In 'Joseph, Bishop Joseph,' I think it will be much more effective if you don't repeat *Joseph* twice—but make the point more sudden and hearty, 'Ah Joseph—Bishop Joseph,' and absolutely touch his ribs with the forefinger ; there should, I am sure, be no pause and no reiteration between Joseph and Bishop Joseph. Now I have said eno' to make you think me the most presuming dog you have ever seen thrusting his paw into other people's paniers ! But, mon cher, you have been as frank with me—so tit for tat.

"May I further beg you to IMPLORE Miss Faucit to say, ' I love AND I am a woman ' ; and with as much majestic swelling as she can ; to-night she says ' I love *but* I am a woman,' which is nonsense, and she whined it into the bargain.

"Think as leniently as you can of my suggestions.

"Yrs. ever,

"E. L. B.

"H. of C.

" *Tuesday night.*"

502

depended on. Saw the *Times*, in which was a letter from that contemptible wretch, Mr. Bunn. His anger and indiscretion look as if he were near the end. God grant it! Amen! Difficulty in answering Bulwer's notes without giving offence—at last dismissed his worrying prosings with brief generalities.

March 14th.—Received a note from Bulwer proposing another subject for a play this season, if I wished it. What an indefatigable man. Read over *Richelieu*. Acted the part very fairly; was called for and well received. The Queen was in the theatre. De Vigny came round after the play and expressed himself delighted. He said he would write to me from Paris, and would come over to see Shakspeare's plays acted; he could not dine with me, as he was leaving town.

March 18th.—Bulwer looked in; asked me if I would come and dine to meet Lady Holland. Sat to Miss Gillies for the portrait. Forster came in.

March 21st.—Webster called, and expressed his anxiety to give me £100 per week—£25 per night for four nights a week, for his whole season, to the 15th of January. I promised him that I would sign with him directly the proprietors of Covent Garden theatre declined my offer.

March 23rd.—Called on Dickens, and spoke to him about Haynes Bayley; he gave me £5. He is a noble fellow; he promised to go to the Literary Fund about the £50. Robertson came into my room, and I explained to him the nature of the offer which I intended to make to the proprietors. He seemed to think it not unlikely to be entertained by them. Serle behaved very nobly, when the engagement at the Haymarket as affecting his play was brought forward; he said in greater matters smaller should give way, and his play should not be an obstacle to an arrangement. Miss Faucit came for my signature to two prints of Virginius.

March 24th.—Sheil and his son Richard, whom I last saw in petticoats, now a young man, called. Horne with his horrid moustaches and a curious cape of a " cloak around him " called. Sheil promised to urge Leigh Hunt's claim for a pension.

March 25th.—Mr. and Mrs. Procter, Mr. and Mrs. Stanfield, Mr. and Mrs. Dickens, Mrs. Reid, Dowling, Price, Martin, Etty, Forster, Rooke, Stone, dined with us; a cheerful day.

March 26th.—Went to Covent Garden theatre, reading by the way Disraeli's play. Coming home, I finished the perusal of Disraeli's play, which will never come to any good. It is taken from an old

Spanish ballad on the Count Alarcos, and the Infanta Solisa, etc. Mr. and Mrs. Blanchard, Mr. and Mrs. Lough, Mr. and Mrs. H. Smith, Messrs. E. Webbe, Z. Troughton, Mr. and Miss Pope, Mr. Harley, came to dine.

March 27th.—Read the newspaper; was disgusted with the tone of the American Press anticipating a war with England. War! war! That men, the creatures of a God of wisdom and of love, should rush forward in savage delight to mangle and slay each other! Oh, God! oh, God! when will Thy blessed gift of reason be universal in its use among men? Mr. and Miss Rolls, Mr. and Mrs. Fonblanque, Miss Martineau, Mr. Carlyle, Dr. Elliotson, Charles and Arthur Buller, Browning, Darwin, Miss P. Horton, and Mr. Brockedon dined with us; an agreeable day.

March 28th.—Forster called at the theatre, and told me that Bulwer had nearly finished his play, which is most powerful. Returning from the theatre, read two more acts of Mr. James's milk-and-water play. Mr. and Mrs. Horace Twiss, Mrs. Kitchener, Fanny and Amelia Twiss, Barham, Fladgate, Munro, Walker, Cattermole, Maclise dined with us.

March 29th.—Mr. and Mrs. Kenney, Mr. and Mrs. Serle, Mr. and Mrs. T. Cooke, Forster, Wallace, Vining, Anderson, Jerdan came to dinner.

March 30th.—After looking over the newspapers, gave my attention to the consideration of what I ought to say, and how I should say it, at the dinner to be given to me to-day by the Shakspeare Club. My whole morning I was fretting and endeavouring to string together in my mind some connected chain of ideas to serve me for a speech or speeches this evening. Went to dine at the Shakspeare Club. Dickens was in the Chair, Jerdan and Blanchard, the two Vice-Presidents, Procter, Stanfield, Leigh Hunt, Maclise, Cattermole, Jerrold, Thackeray, Lover, Charles Landseer, T. Landseer, Dow, Stone, Forster, King, T. Hill, Bell, Harley invited, and about twenty more sat down to dinner. The day passed off most agreeably; the dinner was very handsome, songs well selected. One song immediately after the health of my dear wife and family, "Was She not passing fair?" was very sweet, as also the "Love and Glory." The most hearty sympathy I almost ever witnessed was unbroken through the evening. I was obliged to remain until the business of the day was done, and was astonished to learn from the waiter that it was a quarter past twelve. I set Mr. Harley down, and on coming home, racked with headache

CHARLES DICKENS

(1839)

From an engraving by Finden of the painting by Daniel Maclise, R.A.

from the heat of the room, reported all to Catherine and Letty, whilst I had the power of remembering. Dickens's speech in proposing my health was most earnest, eloquent, and touching. It took a review of my enterprise at Covent Garden, and summed up with an eulogy on myself that quite overpowered me. In reply I said, "That in expressing the peculiar gratification of such a compliment from a society met to do honour to Shakspeare, I disclaimed all credit beyond what was due for faithful service to him, transferring from the priest to the object of their adoration the honour they offered. I had no claim for originating or creating; I had merely removed and restored; was only the purifier of the temple, had only restored to its sublime simplicity the text of Shakspeare. I said that I must ever deeply feel the obligations they had conferred on me; that it added to the pleasure I felt, to know that among those willing to contribute their sympathy to the occasion, I might reckon my excellent and amiable friend, our absent President, whose genius as poet and as critic had shed such additional lustre on the glories of our dramatic literature; to see presiding on this day my highly gifted friend Mr. Dickens; and to number amongst my distinguished hosts the poet, whose youthful muse, when just 'waving her joyous song,' stooped from the nobler flight she was pursuing to bestow a wreath upon my then unnoted efforts—the poet whose beautiful dramatic scenes, then just given to the world, induced us to believe that the sweet and brilliant spirit of Fletcher, which we had thought long dead, had only been sleeping. With so much to enhance the pleasure they conferred upon me, I could not adequately convey the expression of my feelings, but I requested them to believe that I thanked them, as I felt, most fervently and most deeply, and that I never could forget their kindness," etc. I sat down amid loud applause, and then prepared to enjoy what was left of the day. Dickens spoke on each occasion remarkably well; dear Stanfield said his little with his usual modesty. Mr. Bell made a very good speech, kindly adverting to me. Leigh Hunt was called up, being an honorary member and guest of the day, and in a rambling, conversational style talked of what Shakspeare would think if he could walk into the room and ask on what man's account all this festivity and sympathy was raised, and how surprised and pleased he would be to learn that it was himself. Jerdan spoke very well; Doo the engraver; Forster; Stanfield gave Mrs. Macready and her family, and I answered by wishing that I had the readiness of one of them who would be delighted to be there (a little girl) and to make a speech on the occasion. I rose to propose

Dickens's health, and spoke my sincere opinion of him as the highest eulogy, by alluding to the verisimilitude of his characters. I said that I should not be surprised at receiving the offer of an engagement from Crummles for the next vacation. All went off in the happiest spirit. Procter—*mirabile dictu!*—so yielded to the spirit of enjoyment that he fell at last into a profound sleep of nearly two hours; we parted, in the best of spirits, at past one o'clock.

March 31st.—Forster called, and spoke very warmly of the success of yesterday's fête—that the delight was universal through the party. I am pleased to hear it. Finished the perusal of Mr. James's play, and came to an opinion that will shock his anticipations. Wrote a very courteous note to J. Disraeli [1] on his play, and to Mr. G. B. James on his; it is not so easy to write a play as a novel.

April 3rd.—Went to Covent Garden theatre; on my way looked at *Marino Faliero*, with a view to its production for my Benefit.

April 6th.—Received a note from Miss M. Gillies, with the miniature of Richelieu, which she asked me to present to Catherine. Webster called, talked over with him the terms of engagement; he yielded everything to me that I required, and I signed an agreement with him to the 15th January next. Forster called and heard the news, which seemed to stagger him. When he had had time to think over it, he thought it for the best. Went with Forster to Covent Garden theatre. Robertson had been inquiring for me. When he came in, he had nothing to say—looked very gloomy and seemed to understand that the business of my separation from the theatre was finally settled. Decided on announcing my retirement. Drew up the advertisement. [2]

April 7th.—Called on Stanfield, and told him the state of affairs at Covent Garden theatre—that I should get out *King Henry V* and wish to have his aid. He most readily—heart and hand—went with my views, blaming extremely the stupidity of the proprietors. Took Willie with me, and called on Messrs. Chalon to see their pictures; met Mr. Ward there; went on and called on Sir D. Wilkie; saw his sister and himself; the picture of the "Highland Cotter's Grave," "The Discovery of Tippo Sahib's Body," etc. Met Dickens and his wife there.

---

[1] If the initial of the Christian name was accurately given by Macready, the author of the play must have been James, not Benjamin Disraeli.

[2] Negotiations for a prolongation of Macready's tenancy had been broken off.

April 8th.—Willmott came in, spoke of the grief and gloom that had been spread over the theatre. Robertson came; informed me that Mr. C. Kean was engaged by Mr. Webster. I was not disposed to believe it. Serle and Brydone were in my room; nothing but lamentation and despondency on the subject of my retirement. Harley came in, and was quite affected in speaking about it. Elton called to ask me to be a Trustee to the General Theatrical Fund; also inquired if I should object to Mr. Farren as a colleague. I said certainly I should. He then spoke of Bulwer and Talfourd. Haynes called, in a state of weak despair. I cheered him as well as I could and recommended him to get the programme of *Rizzio* ready for me. Webster called. I questioned him about Mr. C. Kean; he admitted it; I thought it very disingenuous in him and was not pleased. I recommended—*if* he could with prudence and safety to his financial arrangements and *if* he wished to make his theatre a miniature Covent Garden, that he should strengthen his company by engaging Mr. Anderson, Willmott, and Mrs. Warner. He said he certainly would, though the recommendation did not seem very palatable to him.

April 9th.—*In nocte consilium.* It should be a rule for every man to forbear a judgment upon his own affairs or condition, until the passion and excitement attendant upon any circumstance acting on them shall have passed away. My *greatest enemy*—the *stumbling-block of my life*—has been *passion*, and its consequent evil, *precipitation*. If I could have deferred acting or speaking (and speech is action—"words are things ") until I had deliberated, how much of pain, how much of misrepresentation I should have escaped! In this recent affair of retiring from Covent Garden theatre I now see, that though my retirement is injurious to the interests of dramatic taste, and will jeopardize the comfort of certain individuals, yet it is a thing with which the public will no further concern itself than by a casual expression of regret or indifference. We hold our own conduct and actions so close to our own eyes that they seem to fill all space of sight —the world looks at them in their proper distance, and sees their infinite littleness. I ought to remember my poor father's " world " —which he conceived in his affairs. It consisted of two or three miserable dependents! I must go quietly on, conduct myself evenly and modestly, and be contented with what God gives me. But this impatience of opposition is one of the ills, induced or aggravated by a course of *Management*. Let me then be thankful that I am again restored to the healthier state of meditative tranquillity and peace of mind! God bless my dearest family and grant that I may make them good and happy. Willmott came into my room to tell me that a notice had been put up in the Hall, requiring "the performers to meet the proprietors in the Saloon at three o'clock.—Signed H. Robertson." I was shocked at this gross impertinence of my servant, Mr. Robertson and the vulgar outrage on my rights by the proprietors. Passing by the green-room I saw the same notice on the glass. I pulled it down and threw it into the fire. As the play proceeded I saw more clearly the very low conduct of these men, and my equanimity returned—particularly on reading and repeating some of the beautiful maxims of Prospero. There is some *virtue* in poetry; it has often helped my mind in its struggles. Acted fairly Prospero; was called for by the audience, and well received. (Miss P. Horton and Miss Faucit came to speak to me. I desired them both to go to the Actors' Meeting.) Talfourd thought that they might just as well have called the "Meeting" in my private room, or even in my "drawing-room at Cumberland Terrace." Talfourd thought it a most happy thing that I was released from the management, which was actually consuming life, health, and all delight.

April 10*th*.—Dickens called, and told me that the Shakespeare Club had an objection to Mr. Fox as a member, and that he certainly would be black-balled, except through the effect of my proposal of him; he wished the ballot therefore to be deferred, to which I very regretfully assented. Brydone called. Webster came and spoke to me about his engagements. A little after five Willmott came from the meeting of actors and proprietors, and told me that Serle had been behaving in the noblest manner, and had defended me from the attacks made upon me by Messrs. Lowndes, Forbes, and attested by Mr. *Robertson*, who *read all the letters* that I had written in confidence to him!!! Serle came in and gave me an account of the rascally proceeding of these men, and the dastardly behaviour of the players. Of all the base occurrences that have come to fret my life, this has been among the most disgusting. I was dreadfully excited, my head aching with its throbbing. Sent for Mr. Robertson; he came the very picture of the *most abject guilt* that I ever in my life saw. I very quietly upbraided him with his perfidy, and desired him to make up his accounts and pay my balance into Ransom's. He said that he could not do that without speaking to the proprietors. So that it appears these wretched scoundrels have kept me on for two years in the delusion that I have been the lessee of the theatre upon a mutual pledge of honour which they

508

have utterly disregarded and held as nothing. Acted well; called for and well received.

April 11th.—Looked at the paper. Went to the theatre. The business of the negotiation occupied the whole day—it was to get the theatre exclusively into my hands—to get rid of Mr. Robertson. Letters passed; I am now in such a state of excitement that I cannot write down the circumstances. This is the worst kind of torture, this *St. Vitus's dance of the mind*—it is *horrible.* Dreadfully excited! God help me!

April 12th.—Went down to Covent Garden theatre—Willmott and Serle—debated over the state of things; Willmott read the papers which Mr. Robertson had sent as the basis of the agreement, and we found that, according to them, I was manacled in every way as, literally, the *servant*—instead of the tenant—of the proprietors. They went away, saying it was useless to contend with these papers; I was in the toils, and I must be patient. Mr. Harley called, and with *much weeping* offered to be security for the payments of my offered £2000, as lessee of Covent Garden theatre. I thanked him, but told him I was engaged elsewhere. Lay down in bed and tried to sleep; could neither eat dinner nor drink wine; ate nothing the *whole day;* was surprised to find myself so strong upon two cups of tea. Acted Claude Melnotte very fairly, but was much excited by seeing Captain Forbes [1] with a large party behind the scenes, and occupy the Kent box! Felt disposed to insult him; thank God, I did not!

April 13th.—Willmott and Brydone returned from their appointment with Messrs. Robertson and Bartley, Mr. Bartley who, on the two previous evenings, had distinctly remarked that I was the uncontrolled, undisputed " lessee, or—for he wished to quibble on that word —director, or conductor or tenant "—" aye, that was the word, tenant "—had, as he expressed it, " slept upon it, and this morning found out that he had recollected wrongly before, and that Mr. Robertson was the person who was to have the whole custody of the monies, etc.!!! Mr. Bartley was a traitor from the beginning, and, as Swift says of Walpole, only acts according to his nature. It therefore now appears that I am the *foreman of this concern upon a salary from the proprietors.* The effect of the communication was very distressing to me. I resolved at first to withdraw my name from the bills, and let the theatre close itself. I could not bear the thought of keeping the piece of plate which the actors had given me, after their late behaviour

---

[1] One of the proprietors.

to me. I showed my Diary to Serle, Willmott, and Brydone, and they felt that it was evidence. Brydone began with some of his prudential suggestions, which excited me to such a pitch of impetuosity that poor Brydone was quite overcome. I explained to him afterwards that it was not *ad hominem*, but *ad rem* that my impatience went. Resolved at once to summon the performers, and state the facts before them. They were in considerable numbers in the green-room when I entered with the proprietors' letter and this book. I began my address to them by informing them what I feared from a recent circumstance would seem strange to some of them—that it was possible a man might have high aspirations and be actuated by nobler motives than the merely getting money. I asserted the intentions with which I had entered on the theatre, and went through the history of my being ensnared into this shameful toil; of my conversations, etc., with that wretched Robertson; of Mr. Bartley's *treacherous* memory; of my proposal for a future lease, and the full account of my conduct and motives since I had entered on the theatre; my principal object having been, not *wishing* to ruin or injure myself, *their* advancement and comfort. I stigmatized as it deserved the shameful falsehood and dishonourable conduct of the proprietors; I concluded by stating the position in which I stood—having been for two years juggled into the belief that I was the lessee, and finding myself only the salaried foreman of the theatre. But, without any conditions, as our connection was soon to end, I would under all the indignities I endured, for their sakes, carry on the theatre to the end. There was great emotion, indignation, and much applause in various parts of my long speech—for it lasted more than an hour and a quarter. Mrs. Warner came into my room, quite overcome, and unable to speak for her tears; I kissed her, and understood perfectly what she could not give utterance to. The assembled actors, etc., sent a message to me by Serle and Willmott, expressive of their *unqualified* admiration, gratitude and sympathy, and thanking me in the strongest terms that they could find for my care of them. They also sent a resolution, which a committee was to meet and prepare for signature on Monday. I was greatly relieved by this *discharge* of my irritation and indignation, and felt quite comfortable; it was a sedative to me. Acted Richelieu as well as I could. Poor Miss Faucit was very ill— fainted away, and Miss P. Horton read the remainder of her part. Saw her after the play; she was much better. Talfourd came into my room, Forster and Dickens also.

    April 14th.—Dined with Mrs. Rolls; met an agreeable party. Sir

W. and Lady Herries, Mr. Powell, Mr. and Mrs. Bohn, and Elliotson ;
Etty, Miss Rolls, etc.

April 15*th*.—Looked at the paper, and was glad to find that there
was no notice from those base persons, the proprietors. Went to
Covent Garden theatre. The deputation of the company came into
my room—Messrs. Harley, Vandenhoff, Anderson, Elton, and Phelps—
to present me with the resolutions of the Covent Garden company, and
expressing their desire to *publish* them, if I would permit it, and that
they would receive my answer to-morrow. I replied in a few words,
expressive of my satisfaction that the understanding which should
subsist between myself and the *company* had been re-established, and
thanking them, etc. When they had left me, I found the resolution
altered and *emasculated* from that of Saturday ; in fact, I set no value
on it ; a mere string of empty praises from men, whose praise has no
charm for me, and an omission of the important passage of the first
copy, attributing their acquittal of the proprietors to the *misstatements*
made by those persons. I was shocked and pained to see the hopeless
feebleness and servile character of these men. Serle came in, and
expressed a cordial sympathy with me on the subject, adding his conviction that they never *could be depended upon ;* that they were, and
ever would be, slaves.

April 16*th*.—Went to Covent Garden theatre. I sent for Mr.
Elton, and told him that I supposed it was unnecessary to see the whole
deputation of performers, but that I might communicate to him for
the body that I had read the *resolution* and wished it not to be printed.
He was very much confused, and evidently distressed. He said he
feared that it was not altogether satisfactory to me. I told him that
it was useless to enter upon any question upon the subject, that I had
said all that was necessary last night, and that I had only to-day to
return an answer to the question of publication. He left me very
uncomfortably. Mr. Fox wondered at my coldness, but when I narrated
to him the facts as they had occurred, he said that I was perfectly
right. Acted King Lear *very well*—as well, if not better than I had
ever done. Was called for by the audience, and went on, leaning
upon Miss P. Horton ; was very greatly received. Note of invitation
to dinner from old Lady Cork [1] for Friday next. Dickens and Forster
came into my room.

---

[1] Mary, Countess of Cork and Orrery (1746–1840), *née* the Hon. Mary Monckton ; the
aristocratic " blue stocking " ; for over seventy years she had mingled in the most brilliant
circles of the eighteenth and nineteenth centuries, and could claim to have entertained nearly

April 28th.—Woke early, and fell into reflections, painful at first from the indignation and disgust which must arise in thinking upon baseness and evil; but I have thought myself into a happier state of mind by considering the *actual* amount of injury which these base and bad men have the power of doing me. If I do not injure myself, if I only preserve my temper, and let the facts between us speak, I must remain with a great increase of reputation, and they, when their conduct is known, must be condemned; they may rob me of my claims for surplus, but what is £350 to the peaceful possession of the honour that must attach to me for what I have done, and striven to do! I feel myself *above them.*

April 30th.—Went to Elstree in the carriage with Catherine and Willie; enjoyed to a degree I cannot describe the air, the freedom, the sight of the country, and the old familiar objects of my passage to and from Elstree; it was luxury, quiet, ease, content; it was happiness. I could only liken my sensations to those of a person first tasting the fresh and genial air from the long confinement of a sick room, or the captivity in a prison. It was delightful. Surprised to find Elstree, that used to look so pretty, now appear close, flat, shabby! Thus we judge of all things in this world—ah, how unwisely!—by comparison; the glory in the grass, the splendour in the flower, the delicious breath of heaven, and its gorgeous vision of cloud, and star, and sun, are everywhere the same.

---

every literary and political celebrity during that period. In her youth she had been flattered by Johnson and painted by Reynolds. There are many anecdotes of her eccentricities, which included in her old age an inability to appreciate the distinction between "meum and tuum."